RAOUL WALLENBERG IN B

To Suzy ½ PETER,

THANK YOU FOR YOUR
INTEREST IN THIS SUBJECT,
AND THIS MAN...

Paul Levy

RAOUL WALLENBERG IN BUDAPEST
Myth, History and Holocaust

PAUL A. LEVINE

VALLENTINE MITCHELL
LONDON • PORTLAND, OR

First published in 2010 by Vallentine Mitchell

Middlesex House,
29/45 High Street, Edgware,
Middlesex HAB 7UU, UK

920 NE 58th Avenue, Suite 300
Portland, Oregon,
97213-3786 USA

www.vmbooks.com

British Library Cataloguing in Publication Data

Levine, Paul A. (Paul Ansel)
Raoul Wallenberg in Budapest : myth, history and Holocaust.
1. Wallenberg, Raoul, 1912-1947. 2. Holocaust, Jewish
(1939-1945)—Hungary. 3. World War, 1939-1945—Jews—
Rescue—Hungary. 4. Diplomats—Sweden—Biography.
5. Holocaust, Jewish (1939-1945)—Hungary—
Historiography.
I. Title
940.5'318'092-dc22

ISBN 978 0 85303 727 9 (cloth)
ISBN 978 0 85303 728 6 (paper)

Library of Congress Cataloging-in-Publication Data

Printed in Great Britain by the MPG Books Group, Bodmin and King's Lynn

To Melissa Rachael

Contents

List of Plates   viii

Acknowledgements   xi

List of Abbreviations   xiv

Dramatis Personae   xv

Introduction: Framing the Issues   1

1. Myth, History and the Historian's Social Responsibility   19

2. A Life before Budapest: Wallenberg's Background,
   Personality and Motives   35

3. March 1944: The Holocaust in Hungary, An Overview   72

4. April–May: Swedish Diplomacy in Budapest
   Prior to Wallenberg's Arrival   101

5. June: Myth and Fact: Understanding Wallenberg's
   Recruitment and Mission   132

6. July: Wallenberg Arrives in Budapest   164

7. Summer 1944: Per Anger, Archbishop Erling Eidem
   and the 'Everyday' Politics of Genocide   191

8. August: Valdemar Langlet and Carl Ivan Danielsson,
   the Forgotten Swedes   212

9. September: The Calm before the Storm   250

10. October: Raoul Wallenberg Enters History   290

11. November–December: Death, Despair and Heroism   318

12. January 1945: The End of Diplomacy and Freedom   361

Epilogue: 17 January 1945: Wallenberg Leaves History   372
   and Enters Myth

Bibliography   376

Index   386

Plates

1. Central Budapest in 1944.
2. Budapest 'central ghetto'.
3. The route of the winter 'death marches' from Budapest to Hegyeshalom, November–December 1944.
4. Wallenberg, aged 3-4, with his highly influential paternal grandfather, Gustaf Oscar Wallenberg. (Courtesy of The Jewish Museum, Stockholm and Karl Gabor.)
5. Wallenberg in his early teens. (Courtesy of The Jewish Museum, Stockholm and Karl Gabor.)
6. Wallenberg (to left), aged 23, with two Swedish friends in Cape Town, South Africa, during his business apprenticeship there. (Courtesy of The Jewish Museum, Stockholm and Karl Gabor.)
7. Edmund Veesenmayer, German Plenipotentiary in Hungary, leaving the Royal Palace after providing Regent Horthy with his 'letter of appointment', immediately after the March 1944 occupation. (Yad Vashem, Jerusalem.)
8. Veesenmayer was also an SS *Brigadeführer*. (Bundesarchiv Bild, Koblenz, Germany.)
9. A page from Wallenberg's diplomatic passport, stamped by UD, and issued a week before his departure to Budapest. (Courtesy of The Jewish Museum, Stockholm and Karl Gabor.)
10. Another page from the passport. (Courtesy of The Jewish Museum, Stockholm and Karl Gabor.)
11. Wallenberg's appointment's diary. (Courtesy of The Jewish Museum, Stockholm and Karl Gabor.)
12. Wallenberg's telephone diary. (Courtesy of The Jewish Museum, Stockholm and Karl Gabor.)
13. Wallenberg's Hungarian driver's license. (Courtesy of The Jewish Museum, Stockholm and Karl Gabor.)
14. A 'typical' Swedish 'Schutzpass'. (Courtesy of The Jewish Museum, Stockholm and Karl Gabor.)
15. Wallenberg at his desk, in conversation with some of his closest aides. (T. Verés Collection, Courtesy of USHMM Photo Archives).
16. Wallenberg standing at his desk. (T. Verés Collection, Courtesy of USHMM Photo Archives.)

17. The Swedish Legation on Gellért Hill, with a municipal policeman guarding the main gate. (T. Verés Collection, Courtesy of USHMM Photo Archives.)

18. This political cartoon was published in the Budapest newspaper *Pesti Posta* on 10 September, and sent to Stockholm. (Riksarkivet, Stockholm.)

19. A Swiss 'collective' passport which nonetheless indicates the name of one individual. (Author's photograph, taken at the Glass House Museum, Budapest.)

20. The 'Glass House' factory in the heart of Pest used by Swiss diplomats and Zionist activists in their assistance activities. (Author's photograph, taken at the Glass House Museum, Budapest.)

21. A Swiss 'Schutzpass', issued for an individual and his wife, and signed by Karl Lutz. (Author's photograph, taken at the Glass House Museum, Budapest.)

22. Karl Lutz, Swiss diplomat and colleague of Wallenberg. (Author's photograph, taken at the Glass House Museum, Budapest.)

23. Ferenc Szálasi, head of the *Nyilas* Party and Hungary's self-styled 'Führer', on what is believed to be 16 October, entering the Royal Palace for his installation as prime minister. (Courtesy of USHMM Photo Archives.)

24. Szálasi greeting a German soldier on the same day. (Courtesy of USHMM Photo Archives.)

25. Budapest Jews at an assembly point, probably in late November or early December in preparation for a 'death march' towards the Austrian border. (T. Verés Collection, Courtesy of USHMM Photo Archives.)

26. Another photograph from that same occasion. (T. Verés Collection, Courtesy of USHMM Photo Archives.)

27. Another 'secret' photograph taken by T. Verés, this time male Jews being marched out of Budapest on a 'death march'. (T. Verés Collection, Courtesy of USHMM Photo Archives.)

28. Jews assembled on a city street, guarded by *Nyilas* militia, most likely in preparation for a 'death march'. (Yad Vashem, Jerusalem.)

29. *Nyilas* militiamen guarding the Swedish Legation on Gellért Hill'. (Courtesy of USHMM Photo Archives.)

30. A photograph taken in Buda in early 1945 by Karl Lutz showing the extent of the destruction in Budapest. (Yad Vashem, Jerusalem.)

31. A block of flats that in 1944 was in the centre of the

'International ghetto'. In these buildings, dozens of Jews were forced to exist in a single room. (Author's photograph.)

32. A corner of a block that in 1944 was in the centre of the 'international ghetto'. (Author's photograph.)

33. The wall-mounted memorial to Wallenberg on Wallenberg utca in what was the 'international ghetto'. (Author's photograph.)

34. The Swedish Legation on Minerva utca, on Buda's Gellért Hill, today. (Author's photograph.)

35. The memorial plaque mounted on the wall of the (former) Swedish Legation. (Author's photograph.)

36. The building on Benczúr utca in Pest where it is believed Wallenberg spent his last night as a free man. (Author's photograph.)

37. 'The Snake Killer, or Wallenberg Memorial Statue'. (Author's photograph.)

Acknowledgements

Gustave Flaubert once wrote. 'Our ignorance of history makes us slander our own times'. Through the study and teaching of history, I seek to honour the time that I live, not to slander it.

This book has taken some time to write and has been difficult to complete, and I hope that it will be of interest to scholar and citizen alike. I have been studying Raoul Wallenberg, his work and the many myths which surround him, for over twenty years. My study of Swedish diplomacy in wartime Budapest began in 1989 when I was asked to be research assistant for an oral history project about Wallenberg. These many years on, it is my hope that this book succeeds in presenting him as an extraordinary man, yet a real human being and not an otherworldly 'saint of rescue'. I hope also that this analysis of his moment in history does justice to his memory.

There are of course many to thank as it is completed.

I particularly want to thank my students over the years who have challenged and inspired me to think more precisely about so many important aspects of studying and teaching the history and memory of the Holocaust. My colleagues at Uppsala University's Programme for Holocaust and Genocide Studies have commented helpfully on several draft chapters presented at research seminars.

The map of Budapest in 1944 and the 'central' ghetto are adaptations of a map produced some years ago by the Jewish Agency in Budapest. László Csösz of Hungary's Holocaust Memorial Center graciously provided permission to use it. He also put me into contact with Bela Nagy, who drafted the map of the 'death marches'. In Stockholm, 'Herr Director' Magnus Wigg has, with great generosity, shared his artistic skills in adapting these maps for this book.

My esteemed colleague Stéphane Bruchfeld has been, over the years, a source of much knowledge, wisdom and support, and I thank him with gratitude. Professor Emeritus Harald Runblom has graciously read the manuscript, saving me from numerous errors. Profound thanks to him also for his support and encouragement while we, starting in 1998, built the Programme for Holocaust and Genocide Studies.

My former student and current colleague Ursula Mindler, MA, of the Centre for Jewish Studies at Karl-Franzens Universität, Graz, has translated with precision and patience the German documents cited in the second half of this study. My thanks to her are limitless. In Budapest, my friend Andrea Szónyi translated portions of Maria Ember's book on Wallenberg, as well as several important Hungarian documents.

My editor at Vallentine Mitchell, Heather Marchant, has provided invaluable guidance as the manuscript evolved into a book.

Ambassador Jan Lundvik is one of the few officials at Sweden's Foreign Ministry who have over the decades genuinely engaged in trying to understand Wallenberg's significance, and contributed to the search to discern his fate. I thank him for numerous helpful conversations in the last few years. Other friends and colleagues too numerous to name, in Sweden, England, Israel and the United States, have also contributed in myriad ways to this book.

No single person is capable of comprehending the tragic enormity and continuing impact of the Holocaust. It is therefore with gratitude that I acknowledge the incalculable contributions to my understanding of the event obtained from the work of hundreds of scholars from many nations. This book would be unthinkable without this international league of deeply insightful Holocaust historians.

On a more personal note, I wish to express my gratitude to Professor Omer Bartov for his continuing support and inspiring scholarship since I had the good luck to meet him at Rutgers University in 1992. Thanks also to Professor Yehuda Bauer for many invaluable conversations since I first met him in 1989, and of course for his decades of invaluable scholarship.

While this study was being crafted, two pioneers of Holocaust and Genocide studies tragically left us. Professor Eric Markusen influenced my thinking about how these two fields of history and memory are intellectually and morally necessary for each other. Professor Stephen Feinstein became a good friend over the years, and was reading some of the manuscript when he so suddenly and tragically passed away. Both are sorely missed.

Arnold (Raff) Raphael's distinguished house in Somerset was a frequent refuge in which to think and write, and I thank him most sincerely for the very many occasions when I enjoyed his and his family's classic English hospitality.

Many thanks are due also to my great good friend, Professor Lance Bennett. His encouragement to keep at it, expressed during countless entertaining conversations about wine, whisky, basketball and much else, were invaluable. His and Sabine Lang's annual summer hospitality in Berlin are deeply appreciated.

My parents, Seymour and Josephine Levine, both passed away while this book was in preparation, and it saddens me greatly that they did not live to see its completion.

My children have always wondered what 'the book' actually meant, and they have exercised indefatigable patience with me. They have grown as it has, and it gives me great joy to express my boundless love for Johanna, Viktoria and Max for their unqualified love and support.

This book is dedicated to Melissa Rachel Raphael. She completed her latest book as I wrote across the desk from her. She, like so many others, was intrigued and inspired by Wallenberg many years ago. She read much of the manuscript with her unerring eye for proper English grammar and wondrous vocabulary. Without her love, support and practical help, this long-delayed study would never have been completed.

All mistakes that remain are, of course, my sole responsibility.

Paul A. Levine
Uppsala and Cheltenham

Abbreviations

AusAmt	Auswärtiges Amt (Nazi Germany's Foreign Office)
ICRC	International Committee of the Red Cross
JDC	Joint Distribution Committee
KEOKH	Hungary's National Central Authority for Control of Foreigners
NA	National Archives (Washington, DC)
Nyilas	Arrow Cross (Hungarian Nazi Party and Government)
OSS	Office of Strategic Services
SRK	Svenska röda korset (Swedish Red Cross)
UD	Utrikesdepartementet (Sweden's Foreign Ministry)
WRB	War Refugee Board

Dramatis Personae

Anger, Per

Chargé d'affaires at Sweden's Budapest Legation, and a central figure in shaping and carrying out rescue policies and activities.

Arnóthy-Jungerth, Mihály

Hungarian Deputy Foreign Minister for most of 1944.

Assarsson, Vilhelm

Interim *Kabinettssekretarare* (Permanent Under-Secretary) of UD at the time of Wallenberg's appointment.

Baky, László

Hungarian State Secretary between March and July 1944, and a central figure in the destruction of Hungarian Jewry.

Becher, Kurt

SS Lieutenant Colonel (*Obersturmbann-führer*), SS *Reichsführer* Heinrich Himmler's personal conomic representative in Budapest in 1944, sent there to plunder Hungary's economy.

Berg, Lars

Junior Swedish diplomat at Budapest Legation, August 1944–February 1945.

Billitz, Vilmos

Budapest businessman, friend of Kurt Becher, and a Wallenberg contact.

Boheman, Erik

Kabinettssekretarare (Permanent Under Secretary) of UD during most of the Second World War.

Born, Fredrich

Swiss businessman and head of ICRC delegation in Budapest in second half of 1944.

Böhm, Vilmos

Prominent Hungarian émigré, resident in Stockholm and involved in Wallenberg's recruitment.

Danielsson, Carl Ivan

Sweden's Minister (ambassador) in Budapest, and a central figure in shaping and carrying out rescue policies and activities.

von Dardel, Maj	Wallenberg's mother.
Ehrenpreis, Marcus	Chief Rabbi of Stockholm's Jewish Community before and during the Second World War.
Eichmann, Adolf	SS Lieutenant Colonel (*Obersturmbann-führer*), played a central role in the destruction of Hungarian Jewry in 1944, and other Jewish populations during the Holocaust.
Eidem, Erling	Archbishop, Head of Sweden's State Lutheran Church 1931–50.
Endre, László	Hungarian State Secretary between March and July 1944, and a central figure in the destruction of Hungarian Jewry.
Engzell, Gösta	*Utrikesråd* (Under-Secretary) and head of UD's Legal Division during the Second World War. He played a critical role in formulating Sweden's rescue and assistance policy for Jews during the Holocaust.
Ferenczy, László	Colonel in Hungary's gendarmerie and a central figure in the destruction of Hungarian Jewry.
Grafström, Sven	High-ranking Swedish diplomat during the Second World War, interim head of UD's Political Division.
Grell, Theodor	German diplomat in Budapest in 1944, responsible for 'Jewish Affairs'.
Gustav V	King of Sweden 1907–50.
Günther, Christian	Swedish Foreign Minister during the Second World War.
Hansson, Per Albin	Swedish Prime Minister during the Second World War.
Horthy, Miklós	Regent of Hungary between 1919 and mid-October 1944.
Johnson, Herschel	United States Minister (ambassador) in Stockholm during the Second World War.
Kemény, Gábor	*Nyilas* Foreign Minister.

Komoly, Ottó	Zionist activist in Budapest and ad hoc official of the ICRC.
Lagergren, Nina (née von Dardel)	Wallenberg's sister.
Langfelder, Vilmós	Wallenberg's last chauffeur. He drove Wallenberg to Debrecen and disappeared with him into the Gulag.
Langlet, Valdemar	Swedish academic resident in Budapest who led SRK's rescue and assistance activities in the city in 1944–45.
Lauer, Koloman	Hungarian-Jewish businessman in Stockholm, and Wallenberg's business partner.
Lutz, Karl	Swiss diplomat for several years in Budapest who came to lead that country's rescue activities in 1944.
Malinovsky, Rodion	Soviet Red Army Marshal whose forces liberated Budapest in 1945, and the Soviet official Wallenberg is thought to have wanted to negotiate with when the Swede was detained.
Mallet, Victor	Great Britain's Minister (ambassador) in Sweden during the Second World War.
Olsen, Iver	American Treasury Department official and diplomat who represented both the WRB and OSS in Stockholm. He was an important contact for Wallenberg.
Pehle, John	Head of the WRB in Washington, DC.
Perlasca, Giorgio	Italian adventurer and 'Spanish' diplomat in Budapest in the second half of 1944.
Petö, László	Mid-level official of Budapest's 'Jewish Council', and perhaps the last non-Russian to see Wallenberg.
von Ribbentrop, Joachim	Nazi German Foreign Minister during the Second World War.
Richert, Arvid	Sweden's Minister (ambassador) in Berlin during the Second World War.

Rotta, Angelo	Papal Nuncio in Budapest and doyen of the city's diplomatic corps.
Schmidhuber, Gerhard	*Wehrmacht* General who acted to halt the planned *Nyilas* attack on Budapest's 'central ghetto' in January 1945.
Szálasy, Ferenc	Head of Hungary's nazi *Nyilas* party, and prime minister between mid-October 1944 and the end of the Second World War.
Szalai, Pál	*Nyilas* functionary who warned German General Schmidhuber of the impending attack on Budapest's 'central ghetto'.
Sztójay, Döme	Pro-Nazi Prime Minister of Hungary between March and August 1944.
Vajna, Gábor	*Nyilas* Interior Minister.
Verés, Thomas	Wallenberg's photographer in Budapest.
Verolino, Gennaro	Nuncio Rotta's assistant, Vatican cleric.
Veesenmayer, Edmund	SS Brigadier General (*Brigadeführer*) and German Plenipotentiary. He led Germany's occupation of Hungary from March 1944.
Wallenberg, Jacob	Prominent Swedish businessman and cousin of Wallenberg.
Wallenberg, Gustaf Oscar	Wallenberg's paternal grandfather.
Wallenberg, Marcus, Jr	Prominent Swedish businessman and cousin of Wallenberg.

Introduction: Framing the Issues

Raoul Wallenberg has no need for us to exaggerate his achievements or give him credit for that done by others.

Jenö Lévai, Hungarian journalist, 1948[1]

There is nothing to be taken from the Holocaust that imbues anyone with hope or any thought of redemption, but the need for heroes is so strong that we'll manufacture them.

Raul Hilberg, Holocaust scholar[2]

RAOUL WALLENBERG IN HISTORICAL CONTEXT

Raoul Wallenberg's story is one of the most widely known of the Holocaust, and one of the few positive memories from those profoundly barbarous years. Worldwide, his name is recognized in a fashion rivalling Spielberg's filmic hero Oskar Schindler, and the Swede's fame seems only to increase.[3] There are dozens of publications and almost a score of documentaries and feature films telling his story. Around the world his name is honoured with honorary citizenships and postal stamps, statuary and city squares, professorships, academic seminars, university institutions and courses, and public schools. Even amateur plays, poems, youth leadership academies and museum exhibitions have been dedicated to the deeds and memory of Raoul Wallenberg.[4] For those Hungarian Jewish survivors assisted or actually saved by him, Wallenberg will always be virtually an angel of salvation sent from heaven. Indeed, his activities and accomplishments are invariably said to represent a redeeming moment of humanity woven into the tapestry of despair which is the Holocaust, and some scholars have argued that Wallenberg was a genuinely 'altruistic personality'. Today, some sixty-five years after his detention by Soviet troops, Raoul Wallenberg continues to be a powerful symbol of ultimate good during an epoch of radical evil. What explains such unprecedented interest in the story of someone who is, after all, a relatively minor figure from Holocaust history?

For literally millions around the globe, Wallenberg is a man of and from history. Many, and not only survivors, consider him a virtual saint who, they have read or been told, 'saved' Hungarian Jewry from the gas chambers of Auschwitz-Birkenau, even though historians know this is empirical nonsense. Interest in Wallenberg's deeds and fate began soon after the war, and was concurrent with his first years of Soviet detention. The early post-war publications of Hungarian journalist and historian Jenö Lévai are still valuable, although they have to be used carefully. For many years, however, it seemed that the only people concerned with Wallenberg's disappearance and unknown fate were his immediate family, who all suffered for decades as they struggled in vain for answers. The Swedish government seemed either to have forgotten about him or to have lost interest, but in 1966 he was recognized as a 'Righteous Gentile' by Israel's Yad Vashem Institute.

Following the invasion of Afghanistan by the Soviet Union, interest in Wallenberg quickly increased.[5] With publications in the first half of the 1980s by journalists such as the BBC's J. Bierman, America's T. Clarke and F. Werbell, E. Lester, K. Marton, and H. Rosenfeld, these mainly hagiographic and often empirically dodgy descriptions of Wallenberg's role in the Holocaust in Budapest played a central role in shaping the public's image of him, and of putting firmly into place some of the key myths about him. Aided by works of pure fiction, poorly-sourced documentaries, TV and feature films, a narrative of almost mythic heroism emerged. Today Wallenberg has achieved the status of an iconic hero, a courageous, swashbuckling 'Scarlet Pimpernel', racing about the streets of Budapest challenging German and Hungarian Nazis to stop their relentless murder and mayhem. The fact that much of this adulation is based on fundamental misunderstandings of the historical realities prevailing in Budapest during the second half of 1944 does little to diminish the aura of admiration and hero worship which envelops the memory of Wallenberg. Long before the term 'memory' became part of the discourse of Holocaust studies, an identifiable, international narrative about him emerged, one which continues to develop. The fact that this narrative sometimes borders on historical nonsense only makes the phenomena of Wallenberg more interesting and, in some ways, even more important as an element of Holocaust history and memory. As will be argued, distortions and myths which surround him detract from, rather than enhance, his true symbolic value and power. It will be argued, instead, that Wallenberg becomes even more important to us as a powerful and necessary moral symbol, the better we understand who he was, how he did what he did, and within what political and genocidal context he acted.

A scion of one of his country's most prominent families, the young businessman who became an ad hoc diplomat is the best-known link between 'neutral' Sweden and Hitler's genocide. Respected journalists, academics, politicians, rabbis and teachers have credited Wallenberg, undoubtedly one of the most famous Swedes of the twentieth century, with 'defeating Eichmann', 'stopping the Holocaust' and 'defying Hitler', with his personal bravery seemingly solely responsible for saving '100,000 Jews'. Called by one prominent Swedish intellectual a 'fighter for human rights [who] was one of the 20th century's true heroes', Wallenberg is often compared with such figures as Gandhi, Martin Luther King, Mother Teresa and Nelson Mandela.[6] He is one of only four foreigners named as an honorary citizen by the Congress of the United States, an honour granted also by Canada and Israel. In this context it is worth noting that such a high honour can be granted only after a complicated and often controversial political decision-making process. Yet such is the power of Wallenberg's symbolism that conventional politics in those countries was trumped.

It is no coincidence that deceased scientist Andrei Sakharov, one of the great champions of the twentieth century's struggle for human rights, said: '[He] is one of those people who make not just all of Sweden but all of humanity proud.' A Soviet dissident who suffered deeply from political oppression, Sakharov stated that 'The fate of Wallenberg torments me, as well as thousands of other people around the world.'[7] Those who reflect on Wallenberg's heroism are particularly pained, as was Sakharov, by knowing that after contributing to the salvation of thousands of innocent people, in early 1945 Wallenberg disappeared into the Soviet Gulag, when only 32 years old. Tragically, he was to never know the life and freedom he enabled others to enjoy, nor would he ever see his beloved mother or family again.

Fascinatingly, his mythical status flourishes because Wallenberg has become, in the modern sense of the concept, a celebrity. One sees this not least in the frequency with which he is mentioned in a wide array of media. Because his 'name recognition factor' is so high, one finds, for instance, commemorative speeches by respected community leaders, or newspaper articles, which contain his name in what seems more an attempt to spice up the presentation than to explain his actual significance. Through the decades, newspapers and journalists have consistently given valuable space and time to stories about him with what seems like illogical frequency. To take but one example, what explains the decision by the hard-bitten editors at *The New York Times*, the world's most influential newspaper, to give scarce editorial space to obscure and unverifiable rumours about Wallenberg's alleged fate, passed to them, in this case, by an elderly Ukrainian infantry veteran who suddenly remembered something about Wallenberg's six months in Budapest.[8] Tourists in Sweden are advised to visit monuments and places dedicated to him, and even prime ministers have written about Wallenberg.[9] It is not a coincidence that Gordon Brown wrote a paean to Wallenberg's courage in his book, published simultaneously with his ascension to the political summit. Nor is it a coincidence that although a trained historian, the British prime minister repeated many of the usual myths and mistakes which have come to dominate Wallenberg's story.[10] The critical observer rightly fears that Wallenberg's name is sometimes, perhaps even too frequently, invoked less to explain his important story than it is in order for an author, politician or clergyman to bask in some reflected glory through proximity to a name considered literally to be magical.

Importantly, his story and legacy are unburdened by the troubling moral ambiguity surrounding the actions and personality of Schindler, the Nazi Party member whose womanizing was legendary, and who chose to help 'his' Jews only after brutally exploiting their slave labour for years. Indeed, it was only this immoral act that enabled Schindler to compile sufficiently large amounts of cash with which to subsequently bribe other German officials for the safety of his charges. Wallenberg's story is not only more morally uplifting than Schindler's, it is in many ways even more dramatic. More actual 'lists' were drawn up by Wallenberg and other Swedish diplomats than by Schindler, under far more dangerous circumstances than those to which Schindler was ever exposed. Though the exact number of Jews saved in Budapest by the Swedes remains uncertain, there is no question that many thousands more lives were assisted or saved by Wallenberg and his Swedish colleagues (as well, of course, as by other neutral diplomats in Budapest) than by Schindler. As noted, Wallenberg was one of the first individuals named as a 'Righteous of the Nations', or 'Righteous Gentile', by Israel's official state commission. Subsequently, other rescuers of Jews during the Holocaust have been named by their own admirers as, for instance, 'the Portuguese', 'Japanese', or 'British' Wallenberg.

There is no question that Wallenberg occupies a special, perhaps even unique, place in the memory of the Holocaust – if not its actual history. It is, therefore, important to ask why, for instance, far-flung civic leaders and private philanthropists have commissioned, approved and paid for statues of and about him in numerous cities around the world. Why has his image taken on some characteristics of an almost totemic iconography?[11] Why, it should be asked, rather than simply and mutely acknowledged, have diverse academic institutions in different nations named programmes, institutions and buildings after him, and why do streets, parks, schools and hospitals around the world bear his name, rather than that of more significant individuals from

Holocaust history, or of some other 'local celebrity' from the city or nation in question? Such namings do not happen either easily or without contention but, again, Wallenberg's symbolism seems to make sure that 'normal' political and commemorative conflicts disappear.[12] Even though his local connection may seem at times rather obscure, teachers instruct their pupils to write plays and poems about him, and even local community 'sewing circles' have gathered in his name and memory.[13] It should be emphasized that such 'celebrity' is even more striking when we realize that many of these people and institutions who have chosen to use Wallenberg's name for important civic functions have, at best, only the vaguest understanding of who he really was or what he really did. Few, if any, have a serious understanding of the complicated but essential political context in which he and the other neutral diplomats in Budapest functioned, in a city swept by genocidal forces. One recently founded group, whose goal is to educate about the Holocaust, is typical of this genre of commemoration. It states that its mission is to 'preserve the example of Raoul Wallenberg with the aim of promoting peace among nations and peoples, as well as developing educational projects based on concepts of solidarity, dialogue, and understanding'.[14] These are, of course, noble goals, but it seems important to answer the question of why the memory of this particular individual is made to shoulder such a utopian task, not least when so many other admirable individuals also saved lives during the Holocaust. Why Wallenberg, and why has this phenomena of history and memory developed as it has?

It is pertinent to point out that even in his own country, where the Wallenberg business and banking empire has in many ways dominated Sweden's economy since the late nineteenth century, the details and essential contexts of his story and its significance are scarcely understood. For decades, Sweden's government and people maintained what can only be described as a tepid interest in his story and fate, discomfited by the legacy of their dubious 'neutrality' during the Second World War, and largely preoccupied with building post-war Europe's most successful welfare state. Though his still unexplained disappearance into Stalin's Gulag was nominally on the nation's diplomatic agenda for almost six decades, recent studies confirm that leading politicians, government officials and even some family members seem to have cared little about his disappearance.[15] Scandalously, they simply failed in their political and moral duty to obtain his early release from Soviet captivity. For there is no question that he was alive during the critical first post-war years.[16]

TO WHOM DOES THIS HISTORY BELONG?

In view of Wallenberg's evolution into such an exceptional, and exceptionally public, symbolic figure, it is necessary to ask: to whom does he really belong? What, or perhaps where, is his rightful place in Holocaust history and memory? The latter is itself a particularly interesting phenomenon because of the special place occupied by the genocide of the Jews in Western civilization today. Because he has evolved into such a powerful and oft-utilized symbol, it is important to ask if this very real man who did so much good has been removed from history and placed within myth. It is helpful to consider, as his dramatic story is described and analysed here, whether Wallenberg ' belongs' to 'the public', and the 'ages', and should remain uncritically appraised, because the pantheon of Holocaust heroes is so sparsely populated? Or does his narrative more properly belong to historical scholarship, his actual place in Holocaust history soberly weighed and evaluated using the methodologies available to the professional historian and university teacher? Such questions derive, in the main, from the fascinating tension that exists (which it does equally for most academic disciplines) between 'town' and 'gown'. This tension is, however, of particular importance in Holocaust studies. As two leading British historians recently observed, 'all history is viewed through prisms imposed after the fact. But this is of particular significance in the study of the Holocaust because of the extreme and emotive nature of the events in question, and where reason is sometimes challenged as a mode of analysis and where popular "ownership" discourages interpretative leadership by the scholarly profession.'[17]

Important political, pedagogic, commemorative implications are evident when studying Wallenberg, and when perusing these questions of 'ownership' and the nexus of tension between scholarship and the public's understanding and use of history. Personal and professional experience has shown that calling into question the many myths which have enveloped Wallenberg's story makes many people uncomfortable, particularly survivors – but equally so, it often seems, his countless admirers, such is his symbolic importance. Nonetheless, it is necessary to ask, as this study does, if our essential understanding of this unquestionably important and morally vital figure is helped by the swirl of inaccurate commemoration and other artistic, sometimes fantastical, representations which dominate the various narratives constructed about him? Or is it hampered, distorting in a morally problematic way his true symbolic value? Is his pedagogic value actually diminished rather than enhanced by the myth-making around him? Turning the question around, as this study does, is his pedagogic and symbolic value actually enhanced when his story and significance are placed into a methodologically sound, carefully analysed context? This issue is of particular importance when considering the role of education in maintaining and defending our liberal democratic values – values which were shaken to their core by the genocide of the Jews. I have long felt it justifiable to ask, even if it discomfits some, if the virtual 'cult of personality' which surrounds this long-disappeared man is salutary, or problematic? Is our democratic society bettered served, I have often wondered, by making Wallenberg a 'Holocaust celebrity' instead of contemplating the actual deeds of a man who, though he grew up in highly privileged circumstances and had a sterling personality, was still fundamentally an 'ordinary man' thrust into an extraordinary situation? In virtually every public manifestation about Wallenberg, one encounters a figure more likened to 'Saint Raoul' than the real man one who, to take but one example of his actual humanity, was at least partially motivated to leave Sweden for Budapest because the spring of 1944 found him rather bored, and anxious about his professional future? In summary we may ask if Wallenberg's undeniably vital symbolism is more valuable to our democratic society if we view him critically and realistically, or are the social benefits of his story more evident if we allow him to remain within the existing framework of myth and misunderstandings?

WHICH IS MORE IMPORTANT – MYTH OR HISTORY?

The framing of these and other related questions can commence with my assertion that what is most widely believed by the general public about Raoul Wallenberg's activities in Budapest, and their essential geopolitical context during the Holocaust, is based more on historical fantasy than demonstrated empirical fact and sustained analysis. This argument, which will be demonstrated empirically throughout this study, will be supported by a short discussion of my use of sources and methods.

Those representations, including the most widely read popular and/or journalistic publications (all of which have a hagiographic nature), which have largely shaped the public's understanding of Wallenberg, make many mistakes. Perhaps most problematically, they create what is essentially a one-dimensional, almost cartoon-like character who is parachuted into a simplistic, easily remedied situation: that is, holocaustal Budapest in the second half of 1944, in the European war's last full year. They remove Wallenberg's genuine diplomatic and humanitarian accomplishments from their actual highly complex and fluid geopolitical circumstances; they fail to understand the background to his mission, and distort and simplify his motives and methods. In sum, the Wallenberg as understood by the majority of admirers is more akin to a Hollywood caricature than to a real man, a businessman and ad hoc diplomat, who chose to help others in Nazi-dominated, mid-1940s Central Europe. Interestingly, and this will be discussed more fully below, those who have created this distorted narrative almost universally have done so with only the best of pedagogic and public intentions. They seek to increase public understanding of Holocaust history and its universe of implications but, this study argues, they have tended to accomplish the opposite.

I argue this because during twenty years of studying the Holocaust, and Wallenberg's role in it, I have encountered, on scores of occasions and in talking with hundreds of individuals interested in Wallenberg, a strikingly similar and rather specific narrative which illuminates many of the myths surrounding Wallenberg.[18] This narrative, based on what those encountered believe are historical facts, is at best highly simplistic, and at worse shows an almost total lack of understanding of the 'hows' and 'whys' which determined the realities of the diplomacy conducted on behalf of Jews in Budapest during the second half of 1944. Crucially, this narrative fails to take into account the decisive political, ideological and physical realities which prevailed in the city before and during Wallenberg's months there. Also important is the fact that, as will be shown, even the majority of professional scholars (of various disciplines) who have commented on Wallenberg and/or Swedish diplomacy in Budapest have made some elemental mistakes in relating important parts of his story.[19] Indeed, one expert historian of the Hungarian Holocaust succumbed to hyperbole about Wallenberg, calling him 'a legend for his activities [in Budapest]'.[20]

There are two basic reasons for these problems. The first is that the 'standard' narrative about Wallenberg has relied far too heavily on oral testimonies of Jewish and other survivors of Budapest. The issue of why these oral testimonies are not as useful as is generally thought will be discussed below. The second reason is that almost all who have written about or represented Wallenberg in their stories have largely, if not wholly, failed to use the contemporary Swedish sources which give, without question, the best picture and understanding of Wallenberg. These are Swedish diplomatic (and other) sources written by Wallenberg himself, his UD (Utrikesdepartementet, the Swedish Foreign Ministry) colleagues – both before and while he was involved – and others in Sweden who knew something of who he was and what he was doing in Budapest. Without these sources, most particularly the Swedish government sources, it is impossible to either narrate or understand Wallenberg's story with any real credibility.

The two existing publications by professional historians who read Swedish also fail to explain Wallenberg and his actions fully. *The Stones Cry Out: Sweden's Response to the Persecution of the Jews, 1933–1945* was published over twenty years ago by historian Steven Koblik. This pioneering work of historiography analysed several aspects of Sweden's response to the Holocaust and, while surveying Swedish diplomacy in Budapest, used some of the same documentation as this volume. However, its treatment of Wallenberg is brief and of necessity incomplete.[21] The second publication is Hungarian-Swedish historian Attila Lajos's doctoral dissertation of 2003, *Hjälten och Offren: Raoul Wallenberg och judarna i Budapest.*[22] Lajos also uses UD documentation and, most usefully, makes use of some relevant Hungarian documents. This study fails, however, to understand events in Budapest within the all-important context of the Holocaust at large or as a product of the dynamics of Nazi and Hungarian policy in the second half of 1944 – neither of which related exclusively to events in Budapest. Most problematically, this methodologically flawed study pursues a thesis about the nature of Wallenberg's character and activities based more on the author's own ideological agenda, and distorts how others perceived Wallenberg after the events in question, rather than during them.

As noted, most representations of Wallenberg to date have relied heavily on the type of source which all historians of the Holocaust and other genocides know is important but often highly problematic. Oral testimony, it may be briefly asserted, can only complement the use of contemporary documentation – it can never replace it. Though some oral testimony will be used in this study, it is limited to a few individuals who were in a position to see and understand some if not all of what Wallenberg was doing. Survivors of the Holocaust – whether saved by Wallenberg or not – deserve, at the very minimum, whatever measure of emotional comfort is provided by reflection upon Wallenberg. Indeed, the hundreds of available oral testimonies about Wallenberg merit their own study, but that endeavour lies largely outside the scope of this single-volume analysis of Holocaust diplomatic history.

All Holocaust scholars are aware of the evidentiary tensions between oral testimony and survivor memoirs, and contemporary sources. Reflecting on this tension, Israeli historian Yosef H. Yerushalmi observed: 'Memory and modern historiography stand, by their very nature, in radically different relations to the past ... The historian does not simply come in to replenish the gaps of memory. He constantly challenges even those memories that have survived intact.'[23] Concerning Wallenberg, there has also been the wholly

understandable, if still mistaken, tendency by journalists and chroniclers to give survivor testimony extra moral weight. Reflecting on similar instances, Lawrence Langer, a leading Holocaust scholar of the
meanings and uses of oral testimony, recently observed: 'Instead of
moralizing the event, we need to accept the sufficiency of reclaiming
it by recognizing the intrinsic value of documenting the historical
record and cherishing the intellectual worth of exploring the sources
that establish it.' He adds: 'There is enduring educational merit to
separating myth from truth.'[24]

This study is founded upon a close, textual analysis of a variety of
contemporary documents such as letters, memoranda, diplomatic
cables, reports and others. Separating itself from existing publications
on Wallenberg, the empirical core of this study will consist of many
documents never used before – documents which illuminate
Wallenberg's situation and activities within the multilateral diplomatic interests and goals which framed his mission. A treasure trove of
documents from Sweden's National Archive forms the empirical foundation of this study, along with other documents from relevant
German, American and Hungarian sources. Another gold mine of
information exists in the dozens of letters written by Wallenberg, as
he matured, to his grandfather, in the 1920s and 1930s. These are
supplemented by some of his correspondence from the 1940s, as well
as his highly detailed diplomatic reports from Budapest. Many of
these documents are cited at length. This documentation is contextualized by some of the vast scholarly literature about the Hungarian
Holocaust. Yet apparently there were, according to one eye-witness,
some important collections of documents destroyed in Budapest
itself.[25] Additionally, scores of documents stored at Sweden's Budapest
Legation were destroyed during the *Nyilas* (Arrow Cross)[26] raid of late
December 1944.[27] This makes it impossible to claim that each and
every document relevant to Wallenberg's story has been available for
analysis.

ARE NUMBERS IMPORTANT FOR HEROES?

To take but one well-known example of 'information' about
Wallenberg which is in fact a myth, we can note how the figure of
'100,000 Jews saved' has become central to the public Wallenberg narrative. This figure has achieved almost totemic status in the mind of the
interested public, and is drawn, most broadly, by combining the
approximate numbers of Jews who found shelter of sorts in the city's
two main concentrations of Jews. The first was the so-called 'international ghetto' located near the Danube. The second was the short-lived

'central ghetto', established by the Hungarian government in the heart of Pest, anchored by the famous Dohany Synagogue. This wildly inflated number can be understood as emblematic of how the failure to understand much of what happened in Budapest has been utilized, almost promiscuously, in the hagiographic literature and public commemorative presentations about Wallenberg. We see in this case a situation in which commentators and commemorators (all of whom, again, have only good intentions) seem determined to impart not a deeper understanding of his deeds and their significance, or to take the time to actually explain why he is important, but rather to impart, even to impose, an almost maudlin, emotive sentimentality and historical inaccuracy. All writers of history, including journalists in a hurry, have an obligation to get their facts right, and to analyse the evidence in a sound and reasonable fashion. This is particularly true for publications advertised as 'true history', or the 'actual story' of one particularly dramatic individual within Holocaust history. Such egregious inaccuracy and promotion of myths would be impermissible when practising their own profession or vocation, but in this episode of Holocaust history (and many others, of course), amateurism and inaccuracy are not only published or publicly articulated, they are promoted – and accepted. As Langer reminds us, there are 'boundaries between Holocaust fact and Holocaust fiction, between history and imagination'.[28]

We see the effect such a number can have when looking at a 'customer review' of one such hagiographic book. In my experience, the reader's gushing review can be understood as quite typical: 'Although this book is based on carefully researched facts, it holds your interest like a spy novel. Schindler saved 1,000. (That's great.) Wallenberg saved 100,000 lives. That's spectacular! Read how he emptied trains headed for death camps, had face to face confrontations with German leaders.'[29] The actual numbers to be associated with Wallenberg are far less. These numbers and their significance will be discussed throughout this study, as well as numerous other myths central to the problematically fictitious narrative about Wallenberg which still prevail.

TO CRITICIZE A HERO

I certainly hold Wallenberg's achievements and character in great admiration but, as a historian, it is self-evident to me that even such an honoured and symbolically important figure must be subjected to critical analysis. There is a professional obligation to appraise and evaluate Wallenberg, just as with all figures from history, Holocaust or otherwise. Yet over the years I have learned that the historian's methodological obligations disturb and discomfit many of Wallenberg's admirers. I have been told many times by members of the public that he is such an important symbol he should be 'left alone', and that even if there is some exaggeration to his 'tale', even this may serve a purpose. What harm is caused, I have been asked, by some 'minor' inaccuracies in the 'master' narrative when compared with the moral potency of Wallenberg's rare and courageous story? Time and again in public forums a sometimes emotional clash has occurred between what I have asserted is the 'hard' and most credible evidence about Wallenberg, and how it must be placed into a plausible context, and memory – whether direct or received – as articulated by someone in the audience. This fascinating and important tension between 'town' and 'gown' is particularly striking in the case of Wallenberg. Because of this, brief consideration must be given to the question of whether the historian has the moral right to challenge such a valuable, and rare, moral symbol.

Intimately related to this issue is another, even broader concern which is central to understanding both methodologies employed by, and the public role of, Holocaust studies today. This concern is what I and others have labelled a problematic 'gap' between the training and methodological precision demanded of the historian in order to reach published conclusions, and society's apparent unwillingness to, in essence, 'learn more' about the Holocaust by grappling with the detail, nuance, ambiguity and complexity underpinning even the event's most well-known episodes. Though scholars frequently request that the public should leave behind some long-held and quite anachronistic 'truths' about the Holocaust, the public seems not to be listening. In the case of Wallenberg, the gap between scholar and society seems at times quite unbridgeable. Yet the effort to span it is necessary, and this re-evaluation of a Holocaust hero should be understood as contributing to the effort to bridge this gap.

The Holocaust is different because it so clearly occupies a special place in today's existing common memory of the last century. Indeed, far different in public fora from most other fundamental 'events' which have shaped our world, rarely does a day go by in which one thing or another related to the Holocaust, Nazism, Hitler, the Second World War, and so on, is not referred to, discussed, debated or commemorated in the media in Europe, the United States, Israel and elsewhere. Those years of tragedy, drama and trauma seem always in focus, and are never far from daily political, cultural and educational concerns. Yet in spite of the Holocaust's ubiquity, the gap between scholarship and public memory seems only to be increasing. From my innumerable discussions with students (of different educational levels, from middle school to university postgraduates, and from numerous countries), talks with community members and leaders, and consumers of media and historical literature, I have come to understand that at the heart of the clash between 'town' and 'gown' is the fascinating paradox that as scholars only begin to understand the Holocaust – utilizing ever growing amounts of data in their analyses – the less this essential advance seems understood by society at large, which holds on to 'truths' about the event, long ago absorbed.

This gap is particularly interesting when realizing the centrality the Holocaust plays in forming contemporary conceptions of 'good' and 'evil'. The Holocaust, and its large and well-known cast of characters, seems at times almost inevitably invoked as a metaphor for both. It is, however, much more complicated than that. Though the gap can be narrowed when employing the often-invoked categories of 'perpetrators, victims and bystanders', categories of historical actors, states and institutions which have long dominated Holocaust studies, even these long-debated categories have become intolerably leaky. More persuasive today is an understanding of the Holocaust which is situated firmly within what Primo Levi influentially called 'the grey zone' – that space where human ambiguity, confusion, brutality, betrayal and incomprehension replace easily gained moral clarity, be it good or evil. This 'grey' makes the event much harder to understand, and makes it much more difficult to fit this or that character into one or another category, but it is a situation which must be acknowledged – even by the interested public, who seem by far to prefer simplicity to complication. One of the most insightful commentators on Holocaust history and memory, Levi understood that when challenged by the memory of genocide, most individuals will seek, almost instinctively, the easy and seductive comforts of simplicity. 'This *desire* is justified', Levi warned, 'but the same does not always apply to simplification itself, which is a working hypothesis, useful as long as it is recognized as such and not mistaken for reality. The greater part of historical and natural phenomena are not simple, or not simple in the way that we would like.'[30] Langer sees in this urge to simplify an almost serial distortion of the event, and rightfully understands it as a serious moral issue which must be confronted: 'It appears that when the Holocaust is the subject, misdirected popular enthusiasms form easily, especially when they deflect us from the task of tackling the authenticity of unbearable truths.'[31] The problem of the public's unwillingness to wrestle with 'unbearable truths' is critical because, as Langer also rightly asserts, the Holocaust remains central both to our everyday lives and as an existential threat to democracy. This is because the event left behind 'a sense of violation so immense and extreme that the imagination has difficulty encompassing it. It threatens our faith in the stability of social and moral institutions and reminds us of eruptions of mass violence in history that were not subject to the restraints of virtue or good will.'[32] Genocidal Hitlerian Nazism was rarely, if ever, 'subject to restraints of virtue or good will', and any publication or pedagogic moment which asserts that it *was* 'subject to restraints' has failed to understand its loathsome essence. Everything and everyone forced to confront it manifested a complicated, multi-varied response which must be understood if anything of value is to be gained from examining its 'unbearable truths'.

In a simplified world, the perpetrators of 'ultimate evil can be stymied by intrepid and dedicated individuals, by 'Righteous Gentiles' who 'stopped the Holocaust', or who 'saved the world by saving one'. But in the actual 'universe' of humanity which was the Holocaust, this was not possible, and it is not correct to assert this today. In the simplistic and hagiographic renderings of Wallenberg which have shaped his public image, we see it often asserted, as we shall see in several examples, that he not only successfully challenged Hungarian Nazis and German authorities in Budapest, Berlin and elsewhere, but even the fundamentals of racist Nazi ideology. Some authors have written that Wallenberg is said to have directly irritated Hitler and blocked Eichmann. However, the only thing which stopped the Holocaust was the total defeat of Hitler's Germany, and though the world of European Jewry was not saved, thankfully some few Jews were.

Representations and commemorations of Wallenberg are noteworthy in this regard. When his name is invoked, it is invariably as part of an effort – pedagogic, literary, artistic or commemorative – to ask the listener or reader to believe that the 'real' story of the Holocaust was not death, destruction, misery, catastrophe and the 'triumph of *evil will*'. Rather, the final scene, lesson or story seems to be the 'triumph of *good intentions*'. This is objectionable for many reasons, not least because it is so untrue. Another seemingly inevitable use of Wallenberg's misunderstood legacy is the overlaying of his story onto a more general context, using it as a bulwark against feelings of distress often suffered by students and citizens who learn about the Holocaust. Indeed, if a sentient person is not distressed during and after any reasonable perusal of Holocaust history, then he or she wasn't paying attention. Nonetheless, it is problematic both pedagogically and morally when distorted and simplified 'positive' stories are used – one might even say abused – as a psychological and emotive 'remedy' against the despair. However understandable this desire for an easing simplicity is, it carries with it an unintended result. 'The current popularity of "forgiveness" and "reconciliation"', Langer writes, 'as fruitful responses to the agents of atrocity only confirms how little we have advanced in our journey to appreciate the nature of the beast.'[33] Langer argues that this is because 'Western civilization lacks a discourse for a culture of atrocity. Against the evidence of contemporary history, it resists such labels for the world we live in.'[34] Though it may be easier to repeat and disseminate a simplistic, short, comforting and easy to understand narrative about Wallenberg, ultimately this does not serve society's health or its potential for progress.

MAKING A HERO MORE HUMAN

At this juncture it seems prudent to state without equivocation that Wallenberg's accomplishments are stirring to this historian's imagination and soul. Wallenberg chose to help when the opportunity came to him. Neither his own life nor the safety of his nation was in any way directly threatened by the ongoing genocide. He could have chosen to stay in Stockholm, 'watching' the genocide, but he did not. Indeed, the sources make clear that, contrary to myth, there is little real evidence that Wallenberg was noticeably interested or concerned by what he knew of Hitler's war against the Jews.[35] Rather, the sources make clear that his primary concerns during the war years were commercial, financial and social. But we also know that when his moment of opportunity came, he grabbed it with energy and a moving spirit of humanitarianism. And that in doing so, he and his colleagues made an enormous difference in the lives of many thousands of innocent people. Nonetheless, even while in Budapest Wallenberg had an eye on post-war business opportunities – and why not? He was, after all, a Wallenberg, and he most certainly neither planned nor imagined that he would never resume his life in Stockholm.

Yet simultaneously it must be acknowledged that what Wallenberg did in Budapest between July 1944 and January 1945 was in no way decisive for what happened there, let alone for the Holocaust at large. Nor can his inspiring story be used as a metaphor either for the Holocaust at large or even for rescue during it. Rescue and resistance during the Holocaust came in many diverse forms and figures. What happened in Budapest was both singular yet similar to other diplomatic circumstances during the Holocaust. As will be demonstrated throughout this study, though Wallenberg the individual may have been sui generis, the diplomatic context in which he operated and the methods he used were not. There was, as we shall see, ample precedent for both.

What, then, are we to make of the fact that this relatively minor figure of Holocaust history has come to occupy, not least since the early 1980s, a space in the collective memory of the Holocaust which is unprecedented, perhaps even unique? It might be more accurate to say that Western society's collective 'memory-work' has *given* him the unique space he occupies today, a space larger that his actual deeds merit when placed into the vast context of Holocaust history and memory. What explains this hold that Wallenberg has on our imagination, and what are the consequences if much of what is said and written about him is simply wrong, or exaggerated, or misinterpreted? What seems certain is that no other figure from the Holocaust has been 'treated' in this way, and this phenomena requires an explanation. What seems equally certain is that a more empirically and analytically credible analysis of Wallenberg's diplomacy will help us to understand both his actual accomplishments and the context in which he worked, and his hold on our imagination.

By asking some relatively new questions about Wallenberg, and answering them with credible and relevant documentation, the groundwork will exist for a more sustainable and credible understanding of this individual and his genuine significance for Holocaust history and memory. While doing this, I also hope to rectify the many myths which distort the prevailing general understanding of him.

It is important to underscore that this study is not an attempt to deny, debunk or diminish Wallenberg's genuine heroism. He was, and is, a hero – but he is a misunderstood hero. Nothing useful is served by any attempt or wish to deny his extraordinary heroism, and to do so would be equally as distorting as are some of the myths which surround him. On the contrary, it is argued that because Wallenberg was a perfectly real man who did historically important things during a critical period in recent European history, scholarly scrutiny of both his actual accomplishments and his symbolic and moral importance will enhance the general understanding of this brave man and, with it, his significance.

Finally, apart from a brief epilogue, what happened to Raoul Wallenberg after 17 January 1945, when he was detained by soldiers of the Soviet Red Army, is not discussed. A full account of why he was never released from Moscow's infamous Lubyanka prison, and most likely died there, remains to be written. That noted, I think it also important to emphasize that Wallenberg remains important for us today not because of how or why he died, but because of what he actually did in Budapest. It is hoped that what follows will convince the reader that Wallenberg deserves to be moved out of myth, and back into history.

NOTES

1. J. Lévai, *Raoul Wallenberg – hjälten i Budapest* (Stockholm: Saxon & Lindströms, 1948), p.8.
2. R. Hilberg, cited in A. Grobman, 'Keeping the Rescuers in Historical Perspective', on the website of the Holocaust Teachers' Resource Center, http://www.holocaust-trc.org/resc_doc.htm.
3. In May 2001, a Google search for 'Raoul Wallenberg' produced 14,800 hits. In May 2005, a Yahoo! search produced 136,000 hits. In September 2006, a Google search produced 665,000 hits, and Yahoo! approximately 371,000 hits in 0.13 seconds. Clearly, by any standard, a remarkable level of interest for an individual from Holocaust history.
4. As research and administrative assistant of Uppsala University's Raoul Wallenberg Project between 1989 and 1992, I quickly understood the depth and intensity in what I came to call the 'world of "Wallenbergania"'– something worthy of its own analysis. The project was the first scholarly oral history research about Wallenberg. This project's rich and largely unused archive of some 170 survivor testimonies is located in Uppsala University Library.
5. At that particular spike in Cold War tensions, it is not hard to find a connection between interest in Wallenberg's fate and often intense criticism of unrelated aspects of Soviet policies and practices.
6. P. Wästberg, 'Wallenberg hedras med nya skulpturer', *Svenska Dagbladet*, 6 May 2001, p.2.
7. A. Sakharov, cited in *I was also looking for Wallenberg*, an exhibition catalogue from the Sakharov Museum and Swedish Institute, published in conjunction with the exhibit 'One Man Can Make a Difference', 5 September 2007, Moscow, Russia, pp.9–10.
8. 'Tale of Swede, Savior of Jews, Adds to Puzzle', article by M. Wines, *The New York Times*, 22 October 2000. Anything published in *The New York Times* will inevitably be reprinted in many other media outlets worldwide.
9. Z. Ross, *Thomas Cook's Guide to Sweden* (Peterborough: T. Cook Publishing, 2008), p.51.
10. G. Brown, *Courage: Eight Portraits* (London: Bloomsbury, 2007).
11. For a catalogue of the public memorials dedicated to him, see www.chgs.umn.edu/visual_Artistic_Resources/Public_Holocaust_Memorials/Raoul_Wallenberg_Memorial.html. See also T. Schult, *A Hero's Many Faces: Raoul Wallenberg in Contemporary Monuments* (London: Palgrave Macmillan, 2009), and T. Cole, *Holocaust City: The Making of a Jewish Ghetto* (New York and London: Routledge, 2003), especially Chapter 9.
12. To give but one examples, we see the fact that even though Wallenberg had demonstrably little, if anything, to do with its history, Rutgers, the State University of New Jersey in the US, devotes resources to maintaining a Raoul Wallenberg Professorship in Human Rights. At Sweden's Lund University there is a Raoul Wallenberg Institute for Human Rights and Humanitarian Law, while Tel Aviv's Bar-Ilan University has established a Raoul Wallenberg Chair for the Study of Human Rights.
13. The descriptive headings of many of the links with information and narratives about Wallenberg are telling. Some examples are: 'Raoul Wallenberg – He more or less shocked the diplomats at the Swedish Legation. His first task was to design a Swedish protective pass', see Jewishvirtuallibrary.org; 'RW, Angel of Mercy ... Russia formally rehabilitated RW', Auschwitz.dk; 'RW – with the support of the World Jewish Congress and the American War Refugee Board ... ', historyplace.com; 'RW and the Rescue of Jews in Budapest ... RW was assigned as first secretary to the Swedish legation', USHMM.org; and finally, 'Knitting Circle RW ... ', Myweb.isbu.ac.uk. A more serious example of the 'memory-work' associated with Wallenberg is the recently established International Raoul Wallenberg Foundation. See their website at www.raoulwallenberg.net. Salient to these examples is that each of them contains, even in these short blurbs, an empirical error. All such users of the 'advantages' of the web presumably mean well, yet these examples point to the problem of historical distortion based on empirical mistakes.
14. See the Raoul Wallenberg International Foundation's website, www.raoulwallenberg.net.
15. The 'Wallenberg Case' is the single largest file created in the long history of Sweden's Utrikesdepartementet. The results of the two Swedish government commissions into the Wallenberg case, 'Swedish–Russian Working Group Report' (2000) and 'Eliasson Commission Report' (2003), will be discussed in the epilogue.
16. A recent investigative article in the *Wall Street Journal* describes the devastating effect that official Sweden's decades-long and callous indifference had on Wallenberg's parents and siblings. See J. Praeger's important article of 28 February 2009.

17. D. Bloxham and T. Kushner, *The Holocaust: Critical Historical Approaches* (Manchester: Manchester University Press, 2005), p.2.
18. The many mythical elements of this hagiographic narrative are detailed in Chapter 2.
19. Tellingly, many of the most common misunderstandings about Wallenberg are also held by otherwise careful scholars of the Holocaust, many of whom I have met over the years at scholarly conferences, seminars, etc. There has often been genuine surprise at my description of things based on Swedish documentation.
20. R. Rozett, 'International Intervention: The Role of Diplomats in Attempts to Rescue Jews in Hungary', in R.L. Braham and S. Miller (eds), *The Nazis' Last Victims: The Holocaust in Hungary* (Detroit, MI: Wayne State University Press, 1998), p.152, n.63.
21. S. Koblik, *The Stones Cry Out: Sweden's Response to the Persecution of the Jews, 1933–1945* (New York: Holocaust Library, 1988).
22. A. Lajos, *Hjälten och offren: Raoul Wallenberg och judarna i Budapest* (Växjö: Svenska Emigrantinstitutets skriftserie, no.15, 2003).
23. Y.H. Yerushalmi, cited in L.L. Langer, *Holocaust Testimonies: The Ruins of Memory* (New Haven, CT, and London: Yale University Press, 1991), p.51.
24. L.L. Langer, *Using and Abusing the Holocaust* (Bloomington and Indianapolis, IN: Indiana University Press, 2006), p.122.
25. See N. Langlet, *Kaos i Budapest: bertättelsen om hur svensken Veldemar Langlet räddade tiotusentals människor undan nazisterna* (Vällingby: Harrier, 1982), p.36.
26. Hungary's brutal, anti-Semitic Nazi party. Throughout the text, the Hungarian term *Nyilas* will be used.
27. This loss, however, is greatly ameliorated because most relevant Swedish documents were either cabled or sent by diplomatic post to Stockholm before being destroyed during that raid.
28. Langer, *Using and Abusing the Holocaust*, p.126.
29. See www.Amazon.co.uk/Raoul-Wallenberg-Sharon-Linnea/dp/customer-reviews/08, 3 April 2008. This is a review of S. Linnea, *Raoul Wallenberg: The Man Who Stopped Death* (Philadelphia, PA: Jewish Publication Society, 1993).
30. P. Levi, *The Drowned and the Saved* (London: Abacus, 1988), p.37. This brilliant memoir is actually a work of philosophy about the Holocaust. It represents the acme of his thinking about his time in Auschwitz and the life of memory afterwards.
31. Langer, *Using and Abusing the Holocaust*, p.xiii.
32. Ibid., p.116.
33. Ibid., p.xv.
34. Ibid., p.119.
35. Wallenberg and his fellow Swedish citizens had access to a surprisingly large amount of accurate information about what we today call the Holocaust.

1

Myth, History and the Historian's Social Responsibility

The messiah came ... He said that he was there to save lives ... This messiah pushed my mother and me into a room along with the others to be saved. The others were taken to Auschwitz. He led us out of the building. For me, for my mother, it was a genuine miracle ... Raoul Wallenberg was not an ordinary human being ... He was a saint; *to me* a messiah. [Emphasis added.]

Agnes Sereni, Holocaust survivor from Budapest[1]

Raoul Wallenberg [was] the hero who had fought, bluffed and outsmarted Eichmann, the Third Reich, the Final Solution, and the Arrow Cross, saving tens of thousands of Jewish lives at great risk to his own.

Alan Levy, journalist and historian[2]

[Wallenberg's] triumph over Nazi genocide reminds us that the courageous and committed individual can prevail against even the cruellest state machine.

John Bierman, journalist and author[3]

THE HOLOCAUST AND MYTH

There seems little doubt that the myths which prevail about Wallenberg came about through an interplay of scholarship and collective memory that took place within the 'gap' discussed in the Introduction. This gap exists between how, on the one side, the public or society at large sees and uses history and how, on the other, history is written and used by professional historians. Its existence arises within the context of the 'clash' which occurs where public memory, and historical inaccuracies and myths believed by the lay public, meet the scientific goals and social role of the historian. This gap is particularly acute, it seems clear, when the results of professional Holocaust historiography clashes with long-held ideas about, or putative understandings of, some of the fundamental issues suffusing Holocaust history. Though these concerns and questions exist for all popular and scholarly history, they come into sharper focus when observing how they relate to the history and memory of Wallenberg.

The growing gap in Holocaust history between 'town' and 'gown' seems particularly odd in the light of, firstly, the tremendous advances made by Holocaust historians in understanding fundamental elements, both large and small, of the event and, secondly, the still-growing public and political interest in the event. The paradox is evident in the fact that as historians have come to understand more, the general public seems to absorb less.

Perhaps another way of articulating the question may be to ask: who should write and interpret Wallenberg's place in Holocaust history and memory, and in social memory more broadly? Who can best mediate the acknowledged moral value of Wallenberg to society at large, in order that society can obtain the greatest effect from it? Is it the journalist, hagiographer, filmmaker, poet or rabbi – or the trained historian? Another way of phrasing the question might be to ask, who owns Holocaust history? Regarding this, British historians T. Kushner and D. Bloxham wrote, 'Issues connected to the "ownership" of historical knowledge are increasingly interesting for a variety of reasons, not least because the individual citizen throughout the Western world seems more interested in history today than has been the case for many decades.'[4] Certainly Holocaust history is more popular today than ever before and, just as with other subjects in history, who 'owns' it is a question of some social significance. A central factor explaining this increased interest is a growing awareness that the abstract phenomena of 'memory' is a matter of considerable importance to the current health and future prospects of our democratic societies. Who shapes and uses history most effectively is of considerable political importance, not least in Europe.

There is broad scholarly agreement that within the daily life of society there exists something which can usefully be labelled as 'public', or 'social' memory: that there are broadly accepted narratives which shape the manner in which the general public understands the past, and faces the future. Studies in the 'memory' of the Holocaust are by now commonplace, and though this sub-field of Holocaust history continues to confront some important methodological challenges, the expanding number of well-argued publications exploring the causes and consequences of collective historical memory have erased any notion that the study of memory is methodologically impossible. As several historians of the Second World War and Holocaust recently observed:

> Since the mid-1980s, Europe and America have witnessed an unprecedented memory boom. At its center stands the production

and consumption of representations of the Holocaust and the
Second World War, and the bitter debate about who was a perpetrator and who a victim, who resisted and who collaborated, who
knew what and when ... Simultaneously, the gradual replacement of
memory by post-memory, of experience by representation, has
opened new debates about the reading of visual evidence, the
memorialisation of victims, and the purpose of historical museums.[5]

As a result of this boom, we realize that human beings living in a
collective – be they families, communities, regions, ethnic groups or,
most saliently, nation states – possess and act upon a storehouse of
common memory. We also know that a mutually acknowledged (if not
always agreed upon) and identifiable historical narrative plays a central
role in the creation of essential identities – individual, collective and
national. Significantly, historical memory has both private (or individual) and collective components, and these constructed identities play
an important role in how both private and civic life functions. Such
constructed historical identities, scholars agree, are shaped by information disseminated by a variety of sources which influence both the
intellect and emotions of those receiving this information. Moreover,
these identities are themselves the result of a process of an almost
inevitably subjective process of selection. Writing about this process,
British historian Simon Mundy concluded:

> Cultural identity is not merely a matter of nationality ... nor even
> of language, background, class, religion or education. It comes
> into being when these external markers are combined with a
> powerful dose of mythology: *the half-felt, half-remembered sto-
> ries which bear little relationship to historical fact or chronology.*
> The mythology is a matter of selection from the past, the mas-
> saging of time and an individual (and sometimes communal) deci-
> sion *about where to place the emphasis.*[6] [Emphasis added.]

Who, then, is – or should be – most responsible for presenting the
public with the chronologies and facts which form the basis for interpretations, which then in turn are elements of identity? Is it the scholar, or the popular writer, filmmaker or influential community figure?

Framing the following discussion about how society uses – and abuses – 'historic memory' is an issue which has been usefully labelled as the
historian's 'social responsibilities'. If progress is to be made in closing
the gap between society's understanding of Wallenberg's deeds and
motives – issues which are inevitably broached when his symbolism is
invoked – then it is necessary to briefly discuss what the historian's
social responsibilities are, where they come from, and how they might

conflict with common or public memory of him. Virtually all previous representations of Wallenberg, in whatever medium, have ignored these issues. This neglect has largely created the contrast between the mythical Wallenberg and the real man who accomplished important things in a very particular set of geopolitical circumstances for six months during the latter stages of the Holocaust.

THE BACKGROUND TO WALLENBERG MYTHOLOGY

For some two decades, I have been giving public lectures about my research on Wallenberg and Swedish diplomacy during the Holocaust. During this time I have encountered – indeed, been confronted with – the mythic Wallenberg instead of a real man who became an ad hoc diplomat and who did some specific things during a specific time. I have argued for the primacy of documents in helping us best to understand him, while many of my listeners and questioners have argued for the primacy of the memories (even decades later) of survivors, or, just as frequently, 'what I saw in the film', or 'what I read in the book'. A truly startling aspect of lecturing publicly about this particular figure from Holocaust history has been a fascinating encounter with the emotions, incorrect facts and often confused thinking about Wallenberg expressed by many who have attended my lectures. The literally thousands of individuals I have met and/or taught – students, teachers, politicians and other citizens alike – articulate with passion their interest, admiration and awe for the man whom they believe they 'understand' – again, because they 'saw the film or read the book'. This passionate reverence is unquestionably fuelled by what is understood as Wallenberg's symbolic importance and moral worth. Time and again these always memorable encounters and discussions have brought home for me that this particular figure is thought about, imagined and largely misunderstood in a variety of fascinating and socially significant ways.[7]

Exploring where and how the Wallenberg story and phenomenon fit into the gap between incorrect collective memory and historical scholarship is of particular interest because it seems quite odd that those who care so much about him seem to care so little about who he *actually* was, and what he *actually* did. Most commonly, people have come to a lecture (or purchased a book or seen a film) because they have heard or read at least something about him as a figure from Holocaust history who has sparked their moral imagination. Unquestionably, his tragic fate in Stalin's Gulag is another central factor in motivating people to learn more about him. And it has been a constant surprise that the why, how and who of the mythic Wallenberg as understood by my audience are so distant from the empirical facts established by research, and also that those interested in him are largely uninterested or unconvinced by the empirical facts.

My writing and lecturing about Wallenberg is based on primary research, reading and analysis. Over the years I have brought to the classroom and lecture hall the essential documents, written or otherwise created by those who were there, and that best describe what happened when and why, to whom and where. For a historian it is self-evident that fundamentally, all history writing and narration must be based upon the contextualized analysis of primary sources, and my pedagogy both about the Holocaust in general and Wallenberg more specifically has been based on a concept I call 'from the archive to the classroom'.[8] Though this is obvious for the professional historian, experience confirms that most people have only a vague conception, or no real idea, that this is how it is done. Not least regarding Holocaust history, the general public clearly believes that the best (and perhaps only 'real' sources) are the testimonies of survivors. Even within the interested public, there seems to exist a widespread belief that history is a more a matter of a good story or dramatic narrative than a nuanced, empirically grounded interpretation. Fascinatingly, the empirical data and specific context(s) of Wallenberg's story as communicated in my lectures invariably have come as a considerable and often even unpleasant surprise to my listeners. Experience shows that even an audience interested in Wallenberg doesn't like having its hero contextualized and analysed.

This is because most of those interested in Wallenberg have read books (or seen films) about him which are based largely if not exclusively on survivor testimonies, which all historians know are extremely problematic sources. Most lay people seem to believe that testimonies are, if not the only way to teach and learn about the genocide, certainly the best possible sources and, indeed, for certain types of Holocaust histories, survivor testimony may be the best source. However, historians know that memories are a highly problematic source, particularly for the political historian of Wallenberg and his six months in Budapest, and it is undoubtedly the case that the prevailing collective memory of Wallenberg has been based almost exclusively upon survivor testimony, with little if any reference to relevant primary source documents. This study will demonstrate the frequent 'conflict' between these types of sources.

COMMON MYTHS ABOUT WALLENBERG

My many encounters with those interested in Wallenberg, combined with the hagiographic literature and film representations (including insufficiently researched documentaries), have enabled me to identify a series of myths about Wallenberg. These myths, which might also be described as distortions, empirical mistakes or simplistic contexts, form the foundation of the general misunderstanding which prevails about Wallenberg's background, character, personal motives for his task, political motives which brought his mission about and, perhaps most importantly, the extraordinarily complicated political–diplomatic context which existed when he arrived in July 1944 in Budapest, and which made up the historical stage upon which his story played out. But perhaps most important in creating the distortions which have long blocked any real understanding of Wallenberg's actual significance is the general failure of those who have written or spoken about, or 'represented', Raoul Wallenberg to understand the background to, and details of, Swedish diplomacy on behalf of some endangered Jews during the Holocaust. This lack of context has allowed literary and rhetorical fantasy about Wallenberg to flourish.

The most common and influential myths which criss-cross and infuse the prevailing and distorted collective memory of Wallenberg are listed below, and are largely if not exclusively the result of the following reasons and factors. They are:

1. A failure to use Swedish diplomatic documents and other contemporaneous Swedish and other nations' documents which best explain and describe his background, motives and mission.
2. A reliance upon the wholly honourable yet often faulty memories of Jewish survivors of Budapest, most of whom had no insight or understanding about what the Swedes, Wallenberg and other neutral diplomats were actually doing and how they were conducting their diplomacy.
3. A failure to absorb the international advances in Holocaust historiography in general and in Hungary in particular.
4. The desire to highlight something positive from Holocaust history at the expense of empirical accuracy.
5. The consequences of an always well intended but uninformed use of an isolated element of Holocaust history in commemorative occasions.
6. An unwillingness on the part of those who have mediated narratives about Wallenberg to employ the basics of historical methodology and source criticism.
7. The wilful and sometimes politically and or financially motivated efforts by some who distort Wallenberg's story.

The myths, mistakes and distortions which follow can be found throughout the books, films, documentaries, plays and speeches about Wallenberg which have appeared since the end of the war; or in what has been related to me by people I have met when speaking about Wallenberg. It seems indubitable that these notions have largely if not completely misshaped the public's general understanding of Wallenberg.[9] The following ideas, erroneous assertions and fantasies are in basic chronological order in relation to his life and story. All of them are either wholly or partially wrong:

1. Wallenberg was a 'black sheep' of the Wallenberg family and business empire, and prior to his time in Budapest, he was virtually disowned by the leaders of the family's business, financial and industrial empire.

2. He had 'Jewish blood' in him, and this factor of 'blood and background' played a major role in his alleged sympathies for Jews threatened by the Nazis, and motivated him to go to Budapest.

3. Prior to 1944 he felt himself in preparation for some great historical deeds, and his business travels before the war and in occupied Europe in 1942 and 1943 were conducted in order to collect information about Nazi anti-Jewish policies in preparation for some future use.

4. He was sent to Budapest by the American government and not Sweden's, even though, according to some accounts, he was a 'cousin' of Sweden's King Gustav V.

5. He was either a War Refugee Board (WRB) or Office of Strategic Services (OSS) agent working for the Americans, and was US President Roosevelt's 'personal representative' in the effort begun in 1944 to halt the continuation of genocide in either Europe at large, or Hungary.[10]

6. He went to Budapest to stop the 'Final Solution' and save all of Hungarian Jewry.

7. Swedish diplomacy on behalf of Jews during the Holocaust commenced with his arrival in Budapest, and he 'invented' the methods used by Swedish and other European diplomats to shield Jews from Nazis.

8. He was responsible for initiating the idea that diplomatic documents in the form of 'protective passports', or *Schutzpässe*, could be used to assist Jews to survive the Nazis.

9. Upon his arrival in Budapest he met Hungarian leader Miklós Horthy, who then ordered the departure of deportation trains from Budapest to Auschwitz-Birkenau to be halted.

10. He inspired and led other neutral diplomats to help Jews using a wholly new form of diplomacy.

11. He was a 'Lone Ranger' working solely on his own and sometimes even against the wishes and directives of his superiors and diplomatic peers.

12. He had a long and dramatic dinner with Adolf Eichmann, during which he intimidated the veteran Nazi, creating doubt in Eichmann's mind about the morality of the task at hand.

13. He personally saved tens of thousands of Jews from the 'death marches' from Budapest towards Austria in November and December 1944.
14. Wallenberg's primary antagonists were Germans stationed in Budapest, including most prominently the aforementioned Eichmann.
15. He spoke Hungarian, enabling him to more effectively challenge *Nyilas* militia from harming Jews.
16. He was most effective in saving Jews through dramatic, personal interventions at assembly points in Budapest and along the 'march' routes.
17. He had a passionate love affair with a beautiful Hungarian countess who happened to be the wife of Hungary's *Nyilas* foreign minister.
18. He was personally responsible for the establishment of the 'international ghetto', and convinced other neutral diplomats such as the Swiss and Vatican to set up their own 'safe houses'.
19. He was personally responsible for halting the assault planned by the *Nyilas* on Budapest's 'central ghetto' in late December 1944. He did this either by threatening an SS general with post-war retribution, or by facing down the *Nyilas* men assembled to conduct the attack. This 'deed' is generally thought to have saved some 70,000 Jews in one stroke.
20. He was detained by the Soviet Red Army and not released, because he had extensive plans for the post-war rehabilitation of Budapest, threatening the Soviet occupation; or because he was a Nazi spy; or because he was an American spy.
21. He was personally responsible for saving 100,000 Jews from death.

In the chapters to follow, all of these fallacies, misconceptions, illogical notions and myths will be subjected to a source-critical review and contextualized analysis, causing them to be either dismissed entirely or largely modified.

CHALLENGING MYTH WITH HISTORY

As we consider the essential clash between how 'town' and 'gown' approach the writing and understanding of history, particularly of such a revered figure as Wallenberg, it seems fair to begin with a key question. Does it matter if Wallenberg never met Regent Horthy or *Obersturmbannführer* Eichmann; that he did not have an affair with a beautiful countess who could then influence her husband – a man who was part of an effort to kill thousands of Jews; that he didn't come up with the idea of using documents to protect Jews; or that he may have actually saved 'only' several hundred, or thousands of people, rather than 100,000? Is it necessary to disabuse either survivors or their descendants of the notion that Raoul Wallenberg was a 'messiah'? Isn't it a better story if he did outsmart and outmanoeuvre Eichmann, the experienced, Jew-killing SS administrator, and his 'allies', the *Nyilas*, on their own home ground? Isn't it important for children to hear the story of how this amateur Swedish diplomat bluffed Germany's machinery of death, and was able to save 100,000 Jews from death, and maybe even more?[11] Is in not a socially valuable morality tale to think of Wallenberg as 'The Man Who Stopped Death', because at least he did something when so many others did nothing?[12] And might it not be correct, as one chronicler has written, that 'Hitler was angry with him' for what he was doing in Budapest?

If one accepts that there is value in establishing historical truths, then it must be acknowledged that it does matter when a respected publisher puts into the public domain erroneous information that readers are predisposed to believe because they respect the source. It matters, for instance, when a respected author said to be an expert on Wallenberg (because of one published book) is given a highly visible platform at a major inter-governmental conference about the Holocaust, sponsored by the Swedish government, and from that platform gives a well-attended talk about Wallenberg which is riddled with errors, exaggerations, and historical distortions.[13] It must also be acknowledged that it is altogether more difficult to understand the Nazi era when a veteran BBC journalist such as John Bierman asserts that one man 'triumphed' over the continent-wide genocide which occurred largely while the man who 'achieved' this 'triumph' was, in fact, in the safety of neutral Stockholm.[14] Though an experienced journalist such as Bierman probably understood that no single individual could or did, 'triumph' over a highly organized and systematically executed genocide which no one person had any power whatsoever to halt – apart, of course, from Hitler himself – that is not what he wrote.

On many occasions, typically at a commemoration ceremony about Wallenberg or the Holocaust at large, I have heard a respected community leader quoting a book he or she has read about Wallenberg, or citing a film or documentary seen, which conveys incorrect information and wholly unsupportable interpretations of what actually took place during six months of the Holocaust's last year. Though rarely acknowledged as such, it is a pedagogical and epistemological problem when, for example, a Holocaust survivor gives testimony in a speech for a university class, saying: 'After Wallenberg personally met Regent Horthy, he then convinced Adolf Eichmann himself to stop deporting

Jews, and thus my family was saved and not deported from Budapest.'
Such impressions and ideas are not easily corrected for an audience of
impressionable listeners, and the pedagogic problem created is considerable.[15] Correcting such mistakes, either verbally or in print, is easy
enough, yet experience confirms that once such historical distortions,
myths and misunderstandings become part of the public's general picture, it is exceedingly difficult to remove them. The public does prefer
a pithy sound bite to an academic publication of several hundred
pages, even if the result is that less rather than more is understood by
the listener or reader about the Nazi genocide.

We may also consider the issue from another angle. In an aspect of
the Wallenberg phenomenon with both positive and negative consequences, an important part of his symbolic importance is built on the
desire, both expressed and implicit, of individuals, associations, institutions and even nations to associate themselves with, and be linked to,
his legend and powerful moral symbolism. This wish for some sort of
link with Wallenberg is in virtually all cases based on positive motives,
and it is strikingly international, articulated by individuals, voluntary
organizations, philanthropic institutions and even national governments. In a different context, this aspect of the Wallenberg phenomenon has been identified by historian Omer Bartov, who argues that
many of the controversies reflected in debates about Holocaust history and memory have common elements, regardless of their national
origins: 'Depending on the specific national context, such debates concern the relationship between history and memory, tensions between
group and national identity, distinctions between complicity and resistance, generational conflicts, and not least, the links between past and
present atrocity.'[16] This last point is particularly relevant when considering issues and myths connected to Wallenberg, because virtually
every manifestation of his memory seeks to make this always emotional link between past and present atrocity.[17] This is because 'memories'
and commemorations of Wallenberg are generally designed to soothe
feelings and to assist individuals to reconstitute their faith about society in the wake of the vast catastrophe that was the Holocaust. That is,
it is always asserted and often the case that thinking about Wallenberg
makes us more optimistic about human nature, even if the speaker
understands precious little about the historic realities which determined how and when Wallenberg was able to help so many.

In brief, is it necessary to revise the commonly held picture and
understanding of Wallenberg? Isn't there a possibility that this present
exercise in standard historiographical revision might deprive society of a
valuable, perhaps even irreplaceable symbol? Do we risk, in the following revision of Wallenberg, 'throwing the baby out with the bathwater'?

To put it another way, it must be asked if this revision of Wallenberg succeeds in turning a 'saint' or 'rescuing messiah' into an ordinary man whose legacy and symbolic value risks being diminished and thus losing something essential? We might also ask if anything is gained by disabusing the general public, for instance, of the notion that Denmark's wartime king rode his horse daily in Copenhagen, bearing proudly the hated yellow Jewish star as a powerful protest against the Nazi occupiers, when this is historical nonsense – apart, of course, from King Christian's daily rides?[18] What is the pedagogic advantage gained in telling a survivor, and his or her family and descendents, that it is highly unlikely that Wallenberg personally pulled them off a deportation train, and that the Swede could not possibly have had anything to do with halting the deportations in early July because he was not yet in the city on the day that the deportations were halted by the Hungarians?

In other words, we must ask if there is not some genuine social value in allowing such inspiring perceptions to remain unchallenged, even if they are not *exactly* the historic truth as determined by historians. Ultimately that question can be answered only by the reader, but when considering this, and before turning to a brief discussion of what has been described as 'the historian's social responsibility' as they themselves conduct their lives as citizens in a democratic society, we should ask: is it, in fact, a benefit to society, and is it genuinely necessary, to correct such well-intended assertions of hope and humanity, even if they are myth passed off as history? Is not there social value in allowing people to feel just a bit better when contemplating the Holocaust?

THE HISTORIAN'S ROLE IN SOCIETY

My interest in exploring the complex nexus between history, myth and memory is motivated by my strong belief (one not always shared by academic colleagues) that if professional historians are to have any social relevance apart from the intrinsic value of their research and publications, then the results of their work must become part of, and influence, the general political and social discourse of our democratic societies. There seems little point in producing scholarship that is read by only a handful of individuals equally interested in the same topic as the author. This leads me to ask: what is the professional historian's social responsibility, and how does he or she balance it with his or her professional obligations, learned during years of training?

One particularly telling incident occurred when one individual reacted in a particular manner to my basic arguments (after reading of them in a non-scholarly format) about the necessity of revising the widely held and distorted understanding of Wallenberg, his work and his significance. This particular individual was someone who cared very much that people in the United States should learn about Wallenberg, and who was active in philanthropic and commemorative work about Wallenberg and the Holocaust. His initial response to my article was to write an aggressive 'letter to the editor' of the cultural magazine in which I had published my short article. He asserted that my position on Wallenberg made me a so-called 'revisionist', or denier of the Holocaust. Informed of this letter, and shocked that someone would seek to damage me by such an accusation, I contacted him. When I asked for an explanation for his sordid accusation, he erupted with fury, shouting into the telephone, 'Don't f—k with the myth!' A mere graduate student at the time, I still managed to answer, 'Well, that's my job!' The conversation did not end on a friendly basis.

When embarking on research about Wallenberg's diplomacy, I would never have suspected that either my basic thesis or the methodology guiding it would create such consternation. I learned that this animus towards basic historiographic methodology being applied to such a revered figure was shared by many others who revere Wallenberg, and who care about the world learning more about the Holocaust. I soon found that revising the accepted picture of him, including the numbers associated with him, was not an exercise welcomed by all. I soon understood that for some very fine people, correcting the prevailing myths was considered to be unworthy of a 'real' Holocaust historian, a Jew, or anyone who cared about our 'children's education'! Because Holocaust history in general and Wallenberg in particular are such emotive subjects, engendering such complex reactions, it was seen as somehow different to other subjects, not subject to the same demands expected of scholarly work within the discipline of history. No clearer point of departure for exploring the nexus where history, myth and the historian's social responsibility meet could be desired. For as the French historian Francois Bédarida writes, 'the historian [is] called upon to disentangle events and to furnish a guiding thread, frequently by blending his role as a critic with a civic and ethical one'.[19]

This tension between 'town' and 'gown' is epitomized by scholarly inquiry into the story of Wallenberg, and is brought into sharp relief when asking, who 'owns' the history of Raoul Wallenberg? Although I had no desire to remove him from the lightly populated pantheon of Holocaust heroes, it became clear that the search for the 'historical Wallenberg' was not always applauded. Frequently, in public situations when I spoke of Wallenberg, my effort to explain the methodological demands placed on the professional historian seemed to fail, with those who cared most for 'Raoul' becoming offended by efforts to critically analyse all aspects of Wallenberg's story as understood by a historian. I was often taken aback by the emotional pressures encountered when attempting to frame queries about Wallenberg within professional guidelines. Frequently it seemed that scholarly inquiry about Wallenberg offended many, and even 'violated' the memory of survivors, their descendents, Wallenberg family members and others who literally revere him as they would a saint or prophet. Time and again I experienced the odd circumstance that even quite evidently honourable people (who again would always claim to support the writing of Holocaust history) were not genuinely interested in learning the truth about this aspect of the Holocaust if it interfered with or contravened what they wished to believe about Raoul Wallenberg. I was surprised to discover that many of those interested in Wallenberg (and other important aspects of Holocaust history) were far more comfortable holding on to cherished myths, rather than appreciating the benefits of new evidence and new perspectives. Indeed, there seems little question that because the gap between scholarly understanding of the Holocaust and the general public is both vast and growing, this problem is by no means confined to inquiry about this singular figure from Holocaust history.

Nonetheless, the professional demands of Holocaust scholarship can only be met when the scholars' responsibilities towards what historians recognize as historical facts and credible contextual analysis are met. This issue is particularly noteworthy with regard to survivor testimony. For many understandable reasons, an aura of sanctity has grown around the memories of Holocaust survivors. For the general public, the recorded or voiced testimony of the survivors' understanding of an event, place or personality is the most authoritative. Primo Levi's emblematic 'grey zone' is not a comfortable one for many lay readers of Holocaust history, nor is it a place where most participants in commemoration ceremonies wish to tread. Be that as it may, as historian Christopher Browning has saliently pointed out, there is a heightened need for Holocaust historians to get things right. As he wrote: 'I would note that there is a need particularly for Holocaust scholars, insofar as possible, to get the facts right, because there are people who do not wish us well. They stand malevolently prepared to exploit our professional mistakes and shortcomings for their own political agenda. [We should] not wish to make their dishonest tasks easier.'[20]

Over time, I learned that a methodologically sound study of Raoul Wallenberg which sought to overturn many of the prevailing myths would raise many hackles. This is because for a historian of the Holocaust, one who is guided by evidence, method and a sense of the historian's social responsibility, there are no saints, and all myths must be subjected to critical inquiry. In a different but not dissimilar context, German historian Konrad Kwiet also incurred the opprobrium of his lay readership when he confronted the obviously (at least for him) false testimony of a survivor of Auschwitz. He knew the man was a survivor of Auschwitz, but he also understood that a particular aspect of this individual's testimony could simply not be true, and that it was based more on remembered or learned myth than on what the experienced historian understood was plausible. Kwiet understood in advance that he was courting the criticism and even hostility of a national establishment which had granted broad approval of both the author and the book's content. He also understood that he was likely to be accused of being an ally of so-called 'deniers' or even of being an anti-Semite, for his source-critical analysis. Nonetheless, this professional scholar did not hesitate to publish his professional judgement of the survivor's claims and memory. Kwiet wrote:

> In my view it is futile to debate [this] story further, even if, as is to be feared, antisemites and revisionists will seize the story and exploit it for their own purposes ... historical myths are known not to disappear easily. [Yet] it is one of the most important tasks of historians to counter with every means at their disposal the creation and dissemination of historical myths. If they do not fulfil this obligation or if their warnings are ignored, the way is paved for the ruthless manipulation and falsification of history.[21]

Addressing this dilemma, Omer Bartov has asked: 'To what extent can we mould public opinion without compromising our professional principles and reputation? And conversely, can we remain entirely aloof from the influence of our environment, its politics, prejudices and seductions?'[22] There can be no question that critical and even discomfiting questions must be posed even about Holocaust heroes such as Wallenberg. Consequently, the following study will both raise questions about Wallenberg and produce evidence about his time in Budapest, and before, that will discomfit some. Though in a different context, Bédarida has written about how such uncomfortable dilemmas can be faced, even for the self-conscious historian of Wallenberg – a historian who seeks neither to violate the genuine sanctity of survivor memory, yet one whose goal is to revise or remove the web of myths which distort the popular understanding of Wallenberg. Bédarida wrote that if the historian is to meet his professional goals

> [he must] be attuned to the world around him, for he treads a narrow path between two contradictory missions ... On the one hand, he must disassociate himself from those myths that exist in the common mind and from the deformations of collective memory so that he can juxtapose them with a demystifying discourse that is

both supported by the evidence and [is] rational. On the other hand, as a person who builds and diffuses knowledge, he must contribute to the shaping of the historical conscience and the memory of his contemporaries. *To put it differently, his being a social actor is inseparable from his being a researcher.*[23] [Emphasis added.]

It is both true and desirable that the historian of Wallenberg 'must be attuned to the world', otherwise he or she risks falling into social irrelevancy, and thus plays no part in 'shaping the historical conscience and memory of his [or her] contemporaries'. If that happens, then one's work as a historian becomes little more than an empty academic exercise, of interest only to one's colleagues. For the self-conscious historian of Wallenberg, it is vital to remain both relevant *and* independent. In order to achieve this, the historian's goal of acting as a responsible citizen can be met, as Bédarida has argued, if it is based on two conditions:

> the responsibility exercised by the historian in his own sphere is based on two conditions. There is first of all independence: be it political or intellectual, social or financial. This is the urgency of liberty. Second, there is the scrupulous and meticulous respect for the canons of the discipline; this is the urgency of truthfulness ... In short, the independence of the historian is a *sine qua non* of his being able to pursue his profession and this freedom must extend to both his ability to communicate and to produce knowledge.[24]

Tragically, the years of horror which constitute the Holocaust were not witness to the advent of a 'messiah' who saved the Jewish people from their powerful, almost omnipotent Nazi persecutors. There were, however, some men and women who, circumstances and motivations permitting, did choose to try to save some lives, and to ameliorate at least some of the mayhem and killing. Raoul Wallenberg was one of them. We shall now turn our attention to the task of examining his background, personal motives and personality. All three of these factors helped to determine why he chose to save some Jews in Budapest in the second half of 1944, and how he had the means to do so.

NOTES

1. A. Sereni, cited in H. Rosenfeld, *Raoul Wallenberg, Angel of Rescue: Heroism and Torment in the Gulag* (Buffalo, NY: Prometheus Press, 1982), p.51.
2. A. Levy, *Nazi Hunter: The Wiesenthal File* (London: Robinson, 2002), p.198.
3. J. Bierman, cited by R. Chesshyre, *Guardian*, 17 January 2006.
4. D. Bloxham and T. Kushner, *The Holocaust: Critical Historical Approaches*, (Manchester and New York: Manchester University Press, 2005), p.2. This exploding interest is made manifest, to take but two examples, in the popularity of 'history channels' on cable TV, and

the growing number of 'popular history' magazines written for a broad public. Filmmakers never tire of history, and particularly the Second World War, as a subject to interpret.

5. O. Bartov, A. Grossman and M. Nolan, *Crimes of War: Guilt and Denial in the Twentieth Century* (New York: New Press, 2002), Introduction, pp.xvii–xviii. The authors could also have included discussions about the 'bystander' and rescuers.

6. S. Mundy, 'State of the Arts: Is Culture a Source of Closer unity or further division among Europeans, *Time*, Special Issue (Winter 1998–1999), p.110.

7. My teaching and lecturing has been conducted primarily throughout Europe (eastern and western), North America and Israel. Thus I am, in the main, describing encounters with people from these quite varied countries, cultures and educational systems.

8. On this, see P.A. Levine, 'From Archive to Classroom: Reflections on Teaching the History of the Holocaust in Different Countries', in M. Goldenberg and R. Millen (eds), *Testimony, Tensions and Tikkun: Teaching the Holocaust in Colleges and Universities* (Seattle, WA, and London: University of Washington Press, 2007).

9. Some of these assertions have been related verbally to the author while lecturing about Wallenberg, hearing assertions and being asked questions in both academic and lay conversations in the United States, Europe and Israel between 1989 and 2008.

10. The WRB is an important but not decisive part of Wallenberg's story. The OSS was the United States spy agency during the Second World War, and the predecessor of the Central Intelligence Agency (CIA).

11. See C.A. Lawton, *The Story of the Holocaust* (New York: Franklin Watts, 1999), p.31, who wrote that Wallenberg may have saved more than 100,000 Jews!

12. S. Linnea, *Raoul Wallenberg: The Man Who Stopped Death* (Philadelphia, PA: Jewish Publication Society, 1993).

13. See the speech given by author Kati Marton at the Stockholm International Forum on 26 January 2000, in *Proceedings: Stockholm International Forum on the Holocaust: A Conference on Education, Remembrance and Research* (Stockholm: Graphium Norstedts, 2000), p.25–8.

14. It is telling that out of Bierman's long career, remembered in the obituary cited, this is what Bierman's fellow journalist chose to highlight.

15. Necessary corrections, which lie at the heart of the academic exercise, cannot for social and moral reasons be made in the presence of such a speaker, nor, for several reasons, even on a later occasion.

16. O. Bartov, 'Reception and Perception: Goldhagen's Holocaust and the World', in G. Eley (ed.), *The 'Goldhagen Effect': History, Memory, Nazism – Facing the German Past* (Ann Arbor, MI: University of Michigan Press, 2000) p.34.

17. One vivid example of this is the speech made by Swedish diplomat Jan Eliasson in 1995 to Sweden's parliament (Riksdag) on the occasion of the fiftieth anniversary of Raoul Wallenberg's disappearance: 'we look around the world today, searching for a Raoul Wallenberg. He would be needed in Pol Pot's Cambodia, in Idi Amin's Uganda, in the civil wars in Angola and Mozambique ... in the genocide of Rwanda and in the nightmare of Bosnia.' Copy provided by Ambassador Eliasson.

18. This 'story' is a tale and simply never happened in a German-occupied country in which neither the Nazis nor any domestic Danish collaborators attempted to impose this vile and otherwise widespread mark of humiliation and persecution.

19. F. Bédarida, 'Historical Practice and Responsibility', in F. Bédarida (ed.), *The Social Responsibility of the Historian* (Providence, RI: Berghahn Books, 1994), p.1.

20. C. Browning, *Nazi Policy, Jewish Workers and German Killers* (Cambridge: Cambridge University Press, 2000), p.33.

21. K. Kwiet, 'Anzac and Auschwitz: The Unbelievable Story of Donald Watt', *Patterns of Prejudice*, 31, 4 (October 1997), p.60.

22. O. Bartov, 'Reception and Perception: Goldhagen's Holocaust and the World', in Eley (ed.), *The 'Goldhagen Effect'*, p.34.

23. Bédarida, *Historical Practice and Responsibility*, p.1.

24. Ibid., pp.2–3.

2

A Life before Budapest: Wallenberg's Background, Personality and Motives

I am returning early [from holiday] to do some reviewing of other subjects before school starts. I think this is a good idea and I don't think my French will suffer ... I heard from Mother that deliberations concerning my education are now underway ... You wrote in your last letter that your intention is that my education be designed to afford me the chance, right from the start, to earn my living in a practical job, so that later ... I can take on whatever I feel most attracted to and best suited for. Everything points to my final career beginning when I'm 30 or older.

Raoul Wallenberg, aged 17, to his grandfather Gustaf, July 1929

My dear boy ... You must not take it as an attempt on my part to pass off the remarkable statesmen that populate [the books I sent you] as some kind of ideal to model yourself on. No, I assure you that I have no such false hopes. I want to shape my dear boy into a useful member of society, someone, first of all, who knows how to stand on his own two feet ... Instead, I would love to train you to take care of yourself and to become an independent man, [so] you will be able to tackle such problems as prove to be compatible with your temperament.

Gustaf Wallenberg to his grandson Raoul, July 1929[1]

THE IMPORTANCE OF BIOGRAPHY

Raoul Wallenberg was not yet 17 years old when he chose to return home early from holiday to study before the new school term began. The letter cited above, along with many others, demonstrates an emotional sophistication and seriousness of purpose which characterized his all too short life. The young Swede was, by any measure, an intelligent, charming, socially sophisticated, strong-willed and capable person. An experienced traveller from an early age – this was made possible by his family's affluence at a time long before the age of mass travel – he closely observed what and whom he encountered. He was gifted at languages and – perhaps most importantly – was aware of who he was, his family's status, and what was expected of him.

Wallenberg was determined to succeed in life, and he was given a formal and practical education which made this likely, if not inevitable. His familial background conferred social status, and much was expected of him. If the boy had any doubts, his grandfather made it clear to him: '[You] belong to a respected family with a name that predisposes people to receive you well, since those who carry it have universally been recognized as a benefit to society.'[2] Knowing what we do about Wallenberg, it is not unreasonable to conclude that long before he went to Budapest, he was destined to make a life that would be interesting, noticeable and perhaps even socially useful. What actually happened in his life was of course unknowable, even if the most widely read hagiography would have us believe that what he did and what happened to him was virtually inevitable.

We have already noted and will further discover that what Wallenberg did and did not do in Budapest was the result both of prevailing circumstances and choices he made. Therefore it would be both folly and a distortion of history to deny that Wallenberg's own personality did not play a decisive role in shaping not only the course of his life, but also of the historic choices he made while in Budapest. Though this is not a biography of Wallenberg, even the political historian must recognize that history is shaped not only by events; it is also shaped by individuals. However influential the 'structural' forces of history may be, they are created by both individuals and groups of people. Historian Fritz Stern has expressed it thus: 'In our times and in [historiography] it has become rare to speak of individual greatness ... But not to recognize true stature in a person is a terrible loss, a needless relinquishing of a historical reality.'[3] As Stern recognized, individual choices play significant roles in determining outcomes, even in the peculiar, even epochal circumstances in which Wallenberg found himself. Put most simply, Wallenberg *did not have to do what he did*, whether in choosing to go to Budapest or in deciding what to do when actually there. The choices he made are evident to history, and they were to a significant, if still not decisive, degree based upon who he was. If we are to understand as fully as possible his contribution to Holocaust history, it is important that we understand something of the man himself.

Moreover, for the purposes of this study, one which explores the myths surrounding him would lack much if Wallenberg's background, personality, and motives were not explored. Therefore it is necessary to examine him in some detail, prior to his departure for Budapest. To ignore his character and background is merely to exacerbate errors of distortion which can be found in non-scholarly literature; and those who have argued that 'the mission created the man', exclusive of his personality, are also incorrect.[4] In this chapter, several key examples of how his personality and motives have been portrayed in the hagiographic literature about him will be surveyed. These few examples must serve to illuminate the manner in which this genre has distorted important aspects of the man and his motives for going to Budapest. It is necessary to point out these mistakes, of which a much longer list could well be compiled, not least because of their implications for any discussion regarding the motives for rescuers of Jews during the Holocaust.

Some years ago, one of the better publications from the genre of journalistic hagiography about Wallenberg wrote: 'the man had met the mission and they were to prove perfectly matched, much more so than [anyone] could have imagined'.[5] Though such a conclusion remains unsuitably simplistic, it contains sufficient explanatory value to be used as a framework for this chapter, the goal of which is to create a more nuanced and fully developed picture of Wallenberg. This will help us to understand better that Wallenberg in Budapest was a real man who accomplished much during an extraordinary time. This, in turn, has significant implications for how society might in the future confront the scourge of genocide, a notion which will be addressed in the book's epilogue.

A RICH HISTORICAL SOURCE

Happily for the historian of Wallenberg, there is a primary source through which a fuller picture of the man who became a rescuer during the Holocaust may be drawn. This source is the lengthy and fascinating exchange of personal correspondence written between 1924 and 1936, between Wallenberg and his paternal grandfather, Gustaf Oscar Wallenberg (hereafter referred to as GOW). Usually, the historian must rely on descriptions of historical figures given long after the fact by others. In this case, we have a virtual gold mine of illuminating correspondence written by the subject himself as he grew into maturity – long before he entered history.

The many letters he exchanged with the formidable GOW[6] were found and compiled by family members some years ago. They were often lengthy, always animated and profoundly intimate – and they are a historian's delight.[7] Written during Wallenberg's most formative years, they offer an unfiltered view into the mind and heart of a privileged boy growing into a worldly young man. They provide the critical reader with genuine insight into Wallenberg's thoughts, feelings, observations, experiences and encounters with people, cultures and situations. His own plans, goals, desires, frustrations and relationships are described in great depth, as well as the expectations placed on him. Though this is by no means a study in psychology, it is safe to conclude that GOW undoubtedly had a profound impact on the adolescent who, as a young man, chose to become a rescuer during the Holocaust, for this correspondence provides significant evidence of an always loving, yet ever more complex, relationship.

The correspondence is supplemented by other equally interesting, if less plentiful, material written by Wallenberg himself. This includes a revealing and lengthy travelogue of his months in pre-Second World War South Africa, and other personal and professional letters (sometimes one and the same) written by Wallenberg between 1936 and 1944 to various individuals, including his powerful older cousins, Jacob and Marcus Jr Wallenberg. The historian is thus provided with the rare chance of observing in great detail the development of a man's personality *before* the mantle of history fell upon him. Further essential material written by Wallenberg while in Budapest comes to us in the form of his detailed diplomatic reports, and letters to the UD, to his business partner Koloman Lauer, and to his mother; we also have letters written to him.[8]

A GRANDFATHER'S INFLUENCE

Raoul Gustaf Wallenberg was born in a Stockholm suburb on 4 August 1912. Though born into one of Sweden's richest, most socially prominent and politically important non-royal families, his life commenced with tragedy. His father, Raoul Sr, contracted cancer while his wife Maj was pregnant, and died before Wallenberg's birth. Though Wallenberg was much loved and supported by his mother and extended family, who did their best to fill that terrible gap in the boy's childhood, there is no question that losing his father was a dreadful blow which greatly affected him.

Gradually, Wallenberg's paternal grandfather, Gustaf Oscar Wallenberg, became the predominant influence in the boy's life, even more so than his beloved mother Maj. *Farfar* (father's father, in Swedish) Gustaf's own attitudes seemed to have played a major role in shaping the boy's attitudes, and his wishes concerning the boy's development – not least his education – were clearly more important than his mother's. Only towards the end of their relationship, when Wallenberg was in his mid-20s, did he begin to question this influence. GOW was an ex-naval officer (a tradition in the family), businessman and veteran Swedish diplomat much experienced in the world, particularly in the Far East, America and post-Ottoman Turkey. With the apparent full agreement of Wallenberg's mother, GOW was determined that the boy should be prepared for life as a Wallenberg. While still a teenager, Wallenberg travelled widely in Europe, with extended visits to France and England – all financed by GOW. Throughout their relationship, the older man supplied the unquestionably intelligent adolescent with a constant stream of detailed advice, consciously shaping his grandson for the worlds of business and diplomacy, which he understood as key elements of social and financial success. The extensive correspondence makes clear that Wallenberg's mother had far less impact on who the boy became.

After graduating from *gymnasium* (Swedish secondary school) and following the completion of a brief, obligatory military service, Wallenberg left Sweden in autumn 1931 to matriculate at the University of Michigan in Ann Arbor. He entered this phase of his life with great enthusiasm, and was enthralled by this new world. His tireless curiosity fed his natural sense of adventure, and he readily absorbed what he understood to be American ideas, methods and attitudes. In the typical fashion seen in his letter-writing, Wallenberg expressed himself clearly, even forcefully, to his grandfather: 'I think what you intended by sending me here was not so much to acquire the skill to build skyscrapers and movie houses as to acquire a desire to build them! In other words, to catch some of the American spirit that lies behind their technological and economic progress.'[9]

Wallenberg's letters during his four years in the United States reveal many of the characteristics and qualities generally associated with him. Though he naturally missed his mother and family (although not excessively so, as the letters make clear), his powers of communication and observation are on full display, as are GOW's characteristics, ideas, prejudices, etc., in his letters. Interestingly, one of GOW's favourite topics was the danger of settling into an easy life in Sweden as a Wallenberg, including the 'dangers' posed by young and 'inappropriate' young women. Shortly before graduating from university and returning to Sweden, GOW wrote to his grandson in May 1934:

> Behind my wish that you stay away as long as possible is, as I am sure you understand, my fear that until you have acquired a sufficiently strong and markedly global (not mundane) perspective you will be unprotected against the frivolity and pleasures to be found at home ... The opportunities accorded you by your global education must not go to waste. They are to be used to make you independent before you assume [your] responsibilities.

Some months later, the elder Wallenberg made the point even more emphatically:

> If [older family members] would like to help you, accept their
> offers most graciously, always by pointing out that your practical
> education is not yet complete and that you will probably not be
> ready for any tasks at home for several years. You must not fail
> under any circumstances to do this, for should it be arranged that
> you find work at home you would become part of a collection of
> clever and select young men all competing for the fleshpots ...
> My advice to you is to stay home for as short a time as possible.[10]

While in America, Wallenberg travelled extensively and recorded
much of what he saw, in sharp and illuminating detail. Several documents and course essays from his studies at Michigan reveal that he did
quite well, not least because his written English was of the highest
quality. One essay written in October 1931 for an English class, interestingly entitled 'What does the Idea "The United States of Europe"
Mean?' received the highest mark (A). It was also graced with the
instructor's comment: 'This is an excellent piece of work.'[11] His ability to learn from the present and plan for the future was consistently on
full display, as he kept a steady eye on his hoped-for future as part of
the Wallenberg business and banking empire. He frequently asked his
grandfather and influential cousins for contacts, letters of introduction, and help in setting up meetings with important Americans and
Swedes far more powerful and influential than the average university
student would meet in a typical course of studies. Reading these letters,
one comes away with the firm conclusion that little if anything was
average about Wallenberg, and it seems clear that he made a strong and
positive impression wherever he went, with those whom he met.

He graduated from the university in spring 1935 with a degree in
architecture, and left the United States infatuated with its people and
spirit. Some weeks before departing, he wrote to GOW that it felt 'very
peculiar to end these pleasant and interesting years of study in
America. I have had a wonderful time and the parting was very sad.'[12]
It was a confident and charming young man who returned briefly to
his home and family in Stockholm, albeit one uncertain about his
future.

Following his own advice, GOW endeavoured to keep his grandson
out of Sweden for as long as possible, and decided that the young graduate would become an apprentice at foreign businesses and banks. As
a result, after only a few weeks back home in Stockholm, Wallenberg
obediently departed for a prearranged, unpaid job with a Swedish firm
in Cape Town, South Africa. As with the sojourn to America, physical
distance between Wallenberg, home and his grandfather led to the creation of a fascinating written record. In it we see the continuing

growth of a young man with many admirable qualities: an intelligent and restless curiosity, energy, charm and emotion. His descriptions are always vivid, often lengthy – he wrote both by hand and with a type-writer – and they offer a genuine window into his heart and soul.

After a mostly uneventful but interesting seven months doing business in South Africa (which was quite exotic to the young Swede), Wallenberg departed for Palestine to another unpaid apprenticeship arranged by GOW, this time at a bank.[13] Although the young man remained obedient to his grandfather's wishes, he began to grow noticeably impatient, even a little resentful. One incident in particular caused tension, creating for perhaps the first time a palpable frustration at his grandfather's dominating influence.

After arriving in Cape Town, which 'turned out to be a disappointment', he found some other Swedes whom he liked (something which irritated his grandfather), and work which proved to be only mildly interesting: 'The social life here is hardly what you would call booming and for my part has been limited to movies and drinking beer or whisky in one of the innumerable old-fashioned bars around the city.'[14] Even before learning of the young man's initial impressions, GOW reminded Wallenberg why he was there, and with whom he should keep company:

> I want you to be better trained in the art of business techniques (a good word), so that you would have an opportunity to learn how to earn money – crass, I know – but you will never achieve a satisfactory kind of self-sufficiency unless you become financially independent. The program in Cape Town, as well as in Haifa, is designed to teach you that art, which dominates developing countries ... It is consistent with what I have often urged you to do during your travels, namely get to know people's frame of mind and way of thinking ...
>
> To sum up: I was very satisfied with your stay in Stockholm. You have given your parents and me great pleasure ... But I want you to start *a course in bookkeeping* immediately ... It would be better to find local friends instead of Swedes.[15]

About two weeks later, Wallenberg wrote a long letter to his grandfather in Istanbul. The following exchange is quoted at some length because it reveals much about how the two men thought about other people, not least the women in their lives:

> I've been rather upset the last few months, including when I was in Stockholm. A girl whom I used to spend all my time with in the United States and whom I liked very much unfortunately fell in

love with me, and I've had a very difficult time of it, when everything I wrote or did only hurt her. I have found it depressing to
be the cause of so much pain. About two weeks ago, I decided to
tell her that we should stop writing, but it was difficult. I think it
was for the best.[16]

Believing that Wallenberg had impregnated his erstwhile girlfriend,
GOW's response was rapid and fierce. It was received in Cape Town
on 11 October:

What you told me in your letter of August 26 about a love affair
in the States has caused me great anxiety. You must let me have
the full details of how this has developed, or I will not be able to
advise you. It is imperative in a matter in which you yourself have
no experience … If you have seduced the girl, then things are
very serious. If you seduced an American girl, then you are
trapped. Then all the castles in the air I have constructed on your
behalf will tumble. If this is indeed the case, your future is very
bleak … you will be forced to make a career in America …

I cannot help but view your case very pessimistically. If it
turns out that my fears are unfounded, you must break off all
correspondence forthwith. If she writes, leave her letters unanswered. It may seem cruel and heartless, but believe me it is an
absolute necessity … Young women use any and all means at
their disposal to get their claws into whatever young man suits
their designs. They want to be taken care of … to acquire social
standing. The male is always driven by sexual urges, girls much
less so … The danger is greatest from that class of girls who
come from humble circumstances. It is far smaller with girls
from our own class.

A young man with your prospects does not have time to tie
himself down until he has time to organize his life and his work.
A young wife wants everything to revolve around her … A young
man absorbed by his sexual urges pays no attention to [impor-
tant] considerations. He wants her body. He wants the pleasure
of the moment and she does nothing but offer it. Those who are
not from his own class are the most skilful and therefore the most
dangerous.

In your case, I assume that the fault is yours. You have not been
careful and prudent enough, and that is what makes the matter so
tragic. But you may not sacrifice your life. You must not deprive
your mother and me what we are expecting of you. You must not
pay attention to this foolish love …

I am so upset and sad at having perhaps lost that which I had made the object of my dreams. Nothing can make me happy except the news that you have managed to extricate yourself completely from this unpleasant affair.[17]

In immediate response that same day, Wallenberg sent an expensive telegram from Cape Town to his anxious grandfather. Cabled in English, it read: 'Please dont [*sic*] worry/no complications/affection her part only/correspondence finished=Raoul.'[18] Three days later, Wallenberg responded more fully to his grandfather's fears. Again, the letter will be cited at length, as it is so revealing. For some reason the most pertinent part, cited below, was penned by Wallenberg in English, even though he had a Swedish typewriter available:[19]

As it appeared you were very worried, I permitted myself to wire you an immediate answer to allay your fears. I do not quite understand what in my letter of the 26th August could have given rise to your anxiety in regard to the American girl.

I was never in love with the girl and have told her so often. On the other hand I liked her very much and we were together, too much perhaps, during the greatest part of my stay in Ann Arbor. I did not know she was in love with me and it did not become apparent until she had been writing me for some time while I was in Sweden. I answered in a manner calculated to tell her in a friendly and mild way that although I respected and admired her, I did not love her. She evidently did not or did not want to understand the nature of my feelings for her and her letters became more and more expressive of her love for me ... On my birthday [4 August] I received a cable asking me if I loved her. I immediately wired back a negative answer, and the day after I wrote a friendly letter telling her goodbye and wishing her the best of luck.

I liked her so much and hated to know that I was the cause of her unhappiness. Unfortunately she was older than I and therefore it will be rather more difficult for her to recuperate.

Your resulting letter which you have written serves as a new proof of your love and care for me. I am so glad that you spoke so clearly and that you immediately offered your help and advice even in the case of the girl being pregnant ... My worry was entirely due to anxiety in regard to the girl and her unhappiness. I only hope that time will cure her wounds.[20]

Those words ended the English portion, whereupon Wallenberg continued in Swedish, transcribing for his grandfather a newspaper article about his architectural proposal for a public swimming pool in

Stockholm! Why he never named the American girl is not known, and this seems uncharacteristically cold on his part. Naturally GOW responded quickly to the telegram: 'My dear boy, I was so pleased to receive your telegram [cited above] ... I have considered the message from every conceivable angle to see if there was anything hidden or omitted, but I have come up with nothing. I found it clear and straight-forward and was reassured. Thank you for sending the wire!'[21]

Though Wallenberg had only begun his time in South Africa, GOW impatiently urged his grandson to begin planning for Palestine. We know from two letters of recommendation written for Wallenberg in South Africa by men he worked for that he distinguished himself in many aspects of business, yet already GOW was thinking ahead.

The elder Wallenberg's choice of Haifa as the next step in the young man's education seems motivated partly by self-interest. He had some ideas about establishing a bank of his own in Istanbul, and envisaged his grandson taking a leading role. Therefore, rather than steering him towards a European bank – which was the practice of other members of the Wallenberg family as they schooled younger generations – he sent his grandson to an 'oriental' land, one not dissimilar in many ways from the Turkey he had long lived in.

In late December 1935, GOW wrote that he expected a quick departure because he was impatient that the young man's tutoring as a banker should begin under his friend Freund, a Dutch Jew: 'As you have noticed, I have hinted at my wish that you come under Freund's guidance as soon as possible. The reason is that I consider that part of your training of primary importance ... Cape Town is secondary. Another reason is that I want to accelerate your education, for I am getting old and I would so very much like you to come to the end of your education.'[22] He also advised his grandson that it would be useful for him to spend time in a non-European land: 'The stay in Palestine will also be good for you from [another] standpoint. When you have the occasion to spend a lot of time among minorities you arrive at the conclusion that their rights are not always well served by the great powers. A great part of politics has always been egoism. The best thing, as I [have] said, is to refrain from taking sides. It has served me well.'[23]

The mid-1930s was, of course, a time of rapidly escalating interna-tional tensions, something the two discussed in their letters. About the time Wallenberg was due to leave South Africa, Mussolini's Italy was close to completing its one-sided victory over Ethiopia. GOW was angry that Sweden's government had condemned the invasion, creat-ing tensions in Swedish–Italian relations. He wrote: 'By taking sides we have lost the Italian market completely ... The Italians were badly treated at Versailles and want to acquire more territory. I find it rather natural from their point of view, but they have proceeded unwisely and collided with the British. That is their business, not ours.'

On his way to Palestine, Wallenberg stopped in Nice to visit his grandparents. There Wallenberg and GOW argued vociferously, apparently because of Wallenberg's growing anxiety about where his grandfather's planning was taking him, and because he remained obliged to follow plans laid out for him without being consulted. Not unnaturally, considering how little time he had spent at home during the previous five years, Wallenberg proposed a detour to Sweden. Some days later, while in Genoa waiting for passage to Palestine, Wallenberg wrote to his grandfather:

> I want to apologize again for losing my temper. I'm far too aware of my debt to you not always to yield to your decisions. But I was sorry that you sought to find ulterior motives in my objections. All I wanted to do was contribute to the planning of my program, to make it broader and more effective ... I have no particular objection to living abroad and no particular urge to go home at this point when I have not earned any money.[24]

Also of interest in this letter is the brief mention of 'negotiations' that Wallenberg was unexpectedly compelled to have with British consular officials in Genoa. Before leaving South Africa, he had failed to obtain a suitable visa for Palestine, which lead to complications in mid-passage. 'I was misinformed ... and failed to get an evidently crucial visa for Palestine while I was in Cape Town ... when it comes to visitors to Palestine the restrictions are apparently much stricter than you would think.' This risked keeping Wallenberg in northern Italy for some time. Yet only four days later he wrote triumphantly to GOW: 'I was lucky with my passport, and after arguing with the British consul for an hour managed to get a tourist visa without a deposition.'[25] Knowing what we do about him today, the reader's attention is caught by the fact that though he had seemingly made a mistake by telling the British authorities in Genoa that he was going to Palestine to work (albeit unpaid), and not strictly as a tourist, he evidently talked his way out of the bureaucratic cul-de-sac.

This was during a period when ever-increasing numbers of German Jews sought to flee Nazi Germany and reach Palestine. As is well known, the British were reluctant to allow them in, not least because of Arab pressure. Wallenberg was demonstrably not a German Jew but a Swede, and – as his grandfather noted during their time together in Stockholm – an increasingly persuasive talker. By his own account, Wallenberg managed to convince the consular official, who perhaps was violating his government's rules, to put a tourist visa into the

Swede's passport. There seems no question that, as when hitchhiking in America, Wallenberg genuinely enjoyed the give and take of negotiations with others, including officialdom, and that he was good at it.

It may be acknowledged here that though the historian is required to maintain a suitable distance from his subject, there is in this case some intellectual difficulty in keeping the man revealed during the mid-1930s within a strict chronological context. We know that these are the words of a man who less than ten years later would, during a time of unprecedented crisis, provide life-giving assistance to thousands of humans. Keeping this in mind, one can only marvel at the prescience of some of what Wallenberg wrote during his short time in Palestine. One particularly poignant example of this can be seen in the following lament:

> What I have seen of banking so far makes it seem like a kind of glorified pawn- shop ... I would guess that once you've mastered this routine, there are few areas in which you have a chance of finding yourself faced with a new situation calling for an extra measure of intelligence or imagination. All the rules have been written, everything has been foreseen ... One thing I do find interesting is the organization of the work itself, the structure of the office, etc.[26]

His interest in organizational questions would serve him well eight years later in Budapest. Yet it must be kept in mind that Wallenberg was not a diplomat in training, nor even less, as the hagiographers would have it, an incipient 'rescuer' in the making. In no way is the interesting young man we see developing denigrated by the assertion that, at least in his correspondence – and it is hard to imagine a more revealing source apart from a personal journal, which he seemed not to have kept – there are few if any signs of a great humanitarian in the making. There are no signals that this individual would risk his life to save strangers. He did, however, have a strong sense of himself, which can be seen when he wrote to GOW, complaining again about his unsuitability to become a banker:

> '[Grandfather] you mustn't lose sight of one thing, and that is that I may not be particularly suited to banking at all ... I don't find myself very bankerish; the director of a bank should be judge-like and calm and cold and cynical besides. Freund and Jacob W. are probably typical, and I feel as different from them as I could be. My temperament is better suited to some positive line of work than to sitting around saying no.[27]

In contrast to the assertions of the hagiographers, even in Palestine

Wallenberg was not an incipient 'angel of rescue', preparing in temporal training for fate to call upon him. Indeed, as we shall see below, evidence of any emotional connection to the Jews he met while in Palestine is completely absent from his Palestine letters, though he did comment positively on the ideals and goals of Zionism. In fact, this surprising *absence* of an emotional or intellectual connection, or interest in Jews, either while in Palestine or Europe, becomes even more evident in correspondence and other material he wrote between 1936 and early 1944. In the only documented reference by Wallenberg to Jews, before arriving in Palestine, he expresses himself quite negatively, making a broad, almost anti-Semitic generalization. After he received information, shortly before departing from South Africa, that his sailing from Italy to Palestine would be on a boat filled with Jews on their way to a Zionist conference, Wallenberg wrote that this made the prospect of that particular journey somewhat unpleasant: 'Knowing what I do about the average South African Jew, I'm quite pessimistic, but it can happen that in spite of this, the trip may turn out to be pleasant.'[28]

Such a comment indicates that Wallenberg was very much a man of his times, when it was common to express oneself negatively about a 'people' with an almost unthinking, but affirming, broad stroke. Such a statement – one unsupported by any real evidence – indicates his acceptance of a 'common' prejudice against Jews. Today such a statement would be considered by some to be racist – in 1936 it was commonplace.

In autumn 1936, when back in Sweden, Wallenberg composed a lengthy travelogue about his months in South Africa. Published in the Swedish travel magazine *Jorden runt: magasin för geografi och resor* [Around the World; A Magazine for Geography and Travel] his article is a well-written, detailed and thoughtful account of the exotic world and people he encountered in South Africa. It provides genuine insights into aspects of Wallenberg's character, insights which are articulated here at greater length than in anything else extant written by Wallenberg himself.[29] As with his personal correspondence, this magazine article demonstrates considerable fluency with language, a sharp eye for observation, and an intellectual precision grounded, not least, in his rapidly obtained knowledge of the area's history. Though the essay is primarily descriptive (it was published with a number of photographs he took himself), the travelogue analyses a phenomenon which interested him more the longer he was there: 'The longer I stayed in Cape Town, the more I became interested in South Africa's big problem, the race question [*rasfrågan*].' Noting that although there were some things which spoke for a sort of equality between races, 'such as one finds in French West Africa', he observed that there were also problems arising if one permitted the mixing of races. Such a stance would give blacks (*negrerna*, in the Swedish of the times) equal standing with whites, which he found problematic. He opined: 'But it is not only happily that one can offer blacks the feeling of equal standing with whites. One must also defend against racial mixing, which would then occur between white and black. To maintain [sufficiently] low levels of racial mixing would be very difficult, as in other countries with many white inhabitants, such as the United States, Australia and South Africa.' After noting that French colonies successfully kept the races apart because few whites were permitted to settle in them, he expressed regret that the situation in South Africa was not satisfactory: 'Because in past years an unfortunately large and little contested contact between the races was permitted to occur here in Cape Province, a mixed race has been created, which constitutes a very significant problem.'[30] In the main, Wallenberg reported things as he saw them, and though the reader should be careful not to expect what is not there, it may at a minimum be concluded that he found the separation of races desirable. He most certainly neither condemned such racist segregation nor found it cause for moral outrage; he described what he understood as 'inequalities' between ethnic groups as he viewed them. Though opinions such as those noted here do not necessarily demonstrate a deep-seated racism within Wallenberg, his unprotesting acceptance that 'miscegenation' was a problem to be avoided does show a man comfortable with some of the more insidious notions and prejudices prevailing amongst most Europeans in the 1930s. It also stands in stark contrast to the unsupported hagiographic assertions that Wallenberg was an altruist 'in training' to rescue, some years later, a threatened minority.

It is interesting to note something else that Wallenberg wrote in his first letter from Haifa. He described in detail the journey across the Mediterranean, including the spectacle of an assembled British naval flotilla in Alexandria.[31] He joyfully evoked the scene as his passenger ship glided past an Italian troop transport approaching the Suez Canal on its way to the conflict in Ethiopia. He wrote: 'Our crew and I and the 2,000 men on the troop carrier waved frenetically at each other, yelling wildly and screaming, "Duce, Duce, Duce". Then we sang the nice new Italian song, "Facetta nera, bella Abessinia" [Black jewel, fair Abysinnia]'.[32]

That same letter contains something even more interesting. His journey to Palestine occurred during the very days when Hitler shocked the world by retaking the Rhineland. That operation, which began on 7 March, was the Führer's first international crisis caused by crossing international borders, and naturally it was a subject of intense conversation on the boat, particularly among the German Jews who had only recently fled Nazi oppression.[33] Wallenberg wrote:

> The atmosphere was especially jolly the evening a rumour went around that the Germans had occupied the Rhineland, that the French had mobilized, and that the British navy had left Alexandria to anchor outside Kiel in protest. The news service on board was poor, as you can see, but that rumour got the Germans on board really going. I was sorry to encounter such widespread pessimism concerning the prospects for Europe's future. This was, for the most part however, concentrated amongst the Jews, but they had in any case their own reasons. [Den var emellertid speciellt koncentrerad till judarna men de hade väl sina skäl.][34]

Wallenberg's few months in Palestine were shaped around his increasingly unsatisfying apprenticeship at Freund's Hollantsche Bank Uni. They were also filled with sights, outings and encounters with different people from different cultures (he observed that his French and German were rapidly coming back to life). He admitted to his grandfather a growing realization that banking was not where his heart lay, and that both emotionally and intellectually he liked less and less of what he saw of that line of work. He grew increasingly anxious about the prospects of becoming a banker:

> The nature of banking, such as I see it manifested in [this] bank, has surprised me in one respect, i.e., in its civil service capacity. I had always thought banks were the apotheosis of 'rugged individualism', a concrete example of the superiority of private enterprise to state ownership. Now I see that though it is privately owned rather than state owned, it is so mechanically managed that it might as well be run by the state.[35]

One event Wallenberg experienced was the Arab Uprising of 1936, which sent political tremors around the world. Naturally Wallenberg found this interesting, yet not particularly frightening. He discussed the disturbances in his letters to GOW, offering this analysis: 'The effects of the disturbances have been disastrous, but I still don't think there is much physical danger. The total number of Jews and Europeans killed is 33. I have a vague feeling that this week and the next will be decisive; we'll be able to form an opinion on whether this will continue or not. I think most of it will be over in three weeks, but others are more pessimistic.'[36] Together they decided that despite the uneasy atmosphere, the apprentice should remain in Palestine.

Something, however, changed Wallenberg's mind, and shortly thereafter we see that it was decided – by whom is uncertain – that the six-month stay would not be extended. At the same time, we see his frustration growing, at being so tightly controlled by his grandfather, however beloved the old man was. Wallenberg sought GOW's blessing to return home sooner rather than later by invoking the 'necessity' of returning to Sweden to fulfil his military obligations. About a month before leaving Haifa, his frustrations and anxieties burst forth:

> In a way, these [last two] letters have made me happier than any others you've written to me. You cannot have helped but notice that my letters this last year have betrayed a certain anxiousness, stemming from the fact that while I thought my present course of study – which is entirely your doing – clever and logically direct-ed toward *the goal you set*, namely a foreign bank, didn't serve the purpose of preparing me to earn an income in the near future.
>
> I was also afraid that your plan was too inflexible. I had a feel-ing that you had made up your mind that I was to stay in Palestine for a couple of years, no matter what I felt about the place. [Now] I detect a willingness to adjust the plan to the circumstances. On those terms, I'm willing to be cooperative and accommodate myself to your wishes more than I had thought lately, because I don't want to hide the fact that during the last few months I began to believe, that in order to make myself heard, I would have to cry 'wolf' more than the wolf actually deserves. [Italics in the original.]

Raoul Wallenberg was a confident young man who for years main-tained an emotionally complicated relationship with the most influen-tial person in his life. He was obviously chafing at his grandfather's dominating influence, and increasingly resented it. Nonetheless, the young man's devotion and gratitude towards his grandfather never left him. The letter cited above was lengthy, reflecting the complexities of their relationship. Its conclusion is telling:

> I can never fail to think about the love and care which grandfa-ther wastes on me (in addition to money), and I see in grandfa-ther's trip home [to Sweden] further evidence of that. If I were a worthy grandson I would naturally thank grandfather by follow-ing [his] directives without question or objection. I am therefore ashamed of the comments and suggestions I occasionally offer, but I don't regret them, since I don't think any good would result if I hid my worries.[37]

Also playing a role in his change of plans was his mother's longing to have her son back home, something she hadn't enjoyed for some five years. The result was that Wallenberg's international banking career came to an abrupt and unplanned end. In August 1936 he left Palestine and returned to Sweden.

Back home in Stockholm, his primary concern was to find a sufficiently interesting job which would support him. This need was rather urgent because his grandfather supported him only while abroad, and he naturally desired neither to be a burden on his parents, nor to live with them. Though he was not in any way threatened financially – he was after all a Wallenberg – his correspondence from the next several years makes clear that though he belonged to that powerful family, suitable employment and proper financial status was not given by powerful family members as a matter of course, and that he would have to search for employment both inside and outside the family empire.[38] It is also clear that his failure over several years to find a satisfying position was connected to the fact that his American degree in architecture found little favour with potential Swedish employers, making it well-nigh impossible to find professional work in Sweden.

Upon returning, Wallenberg did complete his reserve military service obligations, which he was good at and found very interesting. He wrote to GOW: 'My military service wasn't too bad, except for the occasional disagreement with my company head, Capt. Kallner, who bawled me out on several occasions and called me just about every name he could think of. The manoeuvres were fine. We only got a couple of hours sleep at night, but the whole thing was very exciting.'[39] The last letter Wallenberg wrote to his grandfather, whose health failed during the second half of 1936, is dated 19 January 1937. To the end, the two exchanged views on national and world affairs, and the grandson's final words to his grandfather were: 'As far as trade policy is concerned, the talk of the day – i.e. in the newspapers – is the lowering of tariffs among the Nordic countries. Everyone is dazzled by our domestic prosperity, to the point that no one sees the shadows on the trade front. All best wishes from your devoted, Raoul.'[40] The elder Wallenberg died in Sweden, in March 1937, and presumably his grandson saw him during those final weeks. As mentioned, there is no evidence that Wallenberg kept a personal journal, so we don't know how he felt about the passing of his beloved and dominating grandfather. But it is reasonable to speculate that GOW's passing left a gap in Wallenberg's emotional life. It did, however, also give him the freedom to make his own decisions, and to follow his own path into the future.

In this connection we can dispense with one prominent myth about Wallenberg, one which I have been 'assured of' numerous times by members of lecture audiences, particularly in the United States. It is widely believed that Wallenberg was a 'black sheep' of the powerful family, estranged or even isolated from the haute-bourgeois life and financial solidity of the larger family and its lively social world. Most often this has been asserted by my interlocutors as an example of his hardy individualism, a quality borne of difficult family relations. The available documentation, however, leaves no doubt that this was simply not the case. Wallenberg's correspondence throughout his life, and particularly in the late 1930s, is replete with letters both personal and professional to his two older second cousins, the powerful Jacob and Marcus Jr. In them he often used familiar forms of address, which he would not have done were he estranged from them or the family at large. In addition, office records for Jacob and Marcus Jr show that Wallenberg was a regular if not frequent visitor, and his letters are consistently filled with news of family members and gatherings. Indeed, his appointments calendar from 1944 is replete with dates for family meetings.[41]

Of interest, however, is the fact that though it was well within their power to do so, Jacob and Marcus Jr seem to have decided not to give their now 25-year-old second cousin a permanent position which would provide an opportunity to rise into the empire's upper reaches, which he undoubtedly wanted to do. Though during the next several years they and other important members of the family empire engaged him for some temporary assignments, including market research for a coffee company backed by Jacob, there is no doubt that he was frustrated by his situation.[42] Indeed, in spring 1939, Wallenberg wrote to Jacob in a plaintive tone, complaining that not more was being done to find him something suitable. After being put in touch with a family contact whose business was in India, Wallenberg wrote to Jacob, almost three years since returning from Palestine, in some desperation:

> This [situation] is sad, since naturally I would prefer to work in Europe or America rather than in the colonies ... It is rather depressing to walk around waiting like this. I would therefore be grateful to you, if you could tell me whether, as in early February, you advise me to wait for the job [for] which you held out the prospect or if conditions are such that you would rather advise me to try and get a job on my own. In the former case, I wonder if you possibly could offer me anything to do in the meantime.
>
> Once again I take this opportunity to thank you warmly for the kind interest that you have shown in me and for your efforts as regards my future employment. Your affectionate, R. Wallenberg.[43]

Although Jacob was sometimes said to be Wallenberg's role model, this is not the only time that Wallenberg felt compelled to write to his uncle with a somewhat pathetic plea for help in finding a job. The second such instance would come under rather more dramatic circumstances than merely biding his time in Stockholm, waiting for a suitable opportunity.

An earlier temporary assignment came in a personal letter written in late November 1936 by Marcus Wallenberg Sr, the 73-year-old patriarch of the family. The salutation read 'Dear Raoul' (*Käre Raoul*), and it offered him a chance to pursue a new business opportunity in Germany.[44] The formidable banker and industrialist had been informed that a small factory in the town of Neustadt, near Freiburg, produced a superior zip for trousers. He decided that, if profitable, one of the empire's leading companies should buy the 'ingenious' patent and produce them in Sweden. The young erstwhile banker was given the task of determining if the project was worth pursuing. Wallenberg seized the task with great enthusiasm, and days later he was on the road in provincial Germany, heading for the factory.

It is an established fact that throughout the Nazi era, virtually to its blood-soaked end, countless Swedish companies – including central elements of the Wallenberg empire – did business with German companies of various sizes and character. Trade ties which were close and mutually important characterized Swedish–German relations throughout the 1930s and 1940s. Throughout the Nazi era, Swedish businessmen, diplomats, politicians, bureaucrats, athletes and artists were constantly travelling back and forth between the two countries, engaged in 'business as usual'. The start of the war in September 1939 did nothing to change this situation and, for most of the war, Swedish businessmen were active throughout Nazi-occupied Europe. It was therefore perfectly commonplace that 'a Wallenberg', in this case a younger member of the family, would do business in Hitler's Germany, and the task Wallenberg now undertook would not have raised any eyebrows – on either side of this mutually beneficial trade relationship. That the Wallenbergs and Sweden's business establishment continued doing business with Germany long after the mass murder of Jews was well known is an established fact, but discussion of that fact lies outside the framework of this study.[45]

When Wallenberg undertook this new business project in the heart of provincial Germany, he could well have seen the 'typical' anti-Semitic banners or signs which were plentiful in the countryside. Yet almost four years after the Nazi takeover, there is no evidence to support the notion that he was in any way troubled by any qualms for conducting business in Nazi Germany. Nor can there be any doubt that the accelerating persecution of Germany's (and soon Austria's) Jews was unknown to Raoul, Jacob or Marcus Jr, since they were all avid newspaper readers. This particular project began long before the 'crisis year' of 1938, during which the Anschluss in March, the autumn political summits which remapped Central Europe, and November's shocking *Reichskristall-nacht* all occurred. But it did commence a little over a year since the infamous Nuremburg Laws of September 1935 were announced, with Jewish citizens of the Third Reich 'legally' stripped of their German citizenship. Interestingly, Wallenberg also undertook the zipper project soon after his stay in Haifa. Several of the hagiographic publications, and many a commemorative occasion about him, assert that his time there 'convinced' him that he had to do something to help Germany's Jews – or even, in some renderings, all of Europe's Jews. Though the practice of so-called 'Aryanization' of Jewish commercial assets had yet to reach its deplorable height, there is no reason to doubt that the Wallenbergs were by that time acutely aware of many of the details of 'Aryanization'. Whether they were in any way troubled by this policy's violation of the very foundations of capitalism inherent to this 'legalized' robbery is unknown. Countering this, however, is the fact that within the financial and industrial sphere they controlled, the Wallenbergs refused even to consider instituting any notion or aspect of 'Aryanization' as part of their corporate practice. Though German officials and businessmen tried, throughout the late 1930s and early 1940s, to force Swedish companies to adopt their insidious practices, they had limited success.

The Wallenbergs knew what 'Aryanization' was, as well as many other of Germany's anti-Jewish policies, because virtually no public manifestation of Nazi persecution of Jews was unknown in Sweden. This was because the country was particularly well informed of events in their powerful neighbour to the south through newspapers, radio and, of course, the constant traffic of travellers back and forth.[46] Daily newspapers reported regularly on the seemingly endless series of petty persecutions and government-dictated social and economic segregation and humiliation inflicted upon Germany's Jews. Nonetheless, on 12 December 1936, Wallenberg wrote to GOW: 'The start up of the factory [in Sweden] will in part depend on the result of my investigation. The whole thing sounds quite attractive.'[47]

One of the people to whom Wallenberg wrote long and detailed letters was his sister Nina, born nine years after him. One letter, written just two days before *Reichskristallnacht*, is filled with comments comparing the history and social policies of England and Sweden. 'Today I've mailed you a booklet in English about Stockholm's social programs. I myself know nothing about the matter.' This quite interesting if mundane letter concludes with Wallenberg telling his sister, 'I have nothing more to tell you, and therefore send my heartfelt greetings to my dearest sister, from her devoted Raoul.'[48] Though he may not have been interested in Sweden's burgeoning welfare state and systems, he remained deeply worried about his own prospects. Between his return to Sweden and the German invasion of Poland in September 1939, there is no question that Wallenberg's primary concern was to establish himself in a respectable, even high-level job; he did not, however, succeed. Nonetheless, in letters to friends and family he makes clear that though he failed to find the job he wanted, he enjoyed his bachelor life in Stockholm. And why not – he was a Wallenberg in Stockholm. Yet his frustrations continued to mount.

Though he was just one individual living in a small country on Europe's periphery, Wallenberg's connections to the family's international business empire made him especially well informed about Sweden and the world around him. Keeping trade open to Nazi Germany and Europe was essential to Sweden's economic health, even while the country's political leaders made clear their goal of keeping Sweden out of the impending war. During the war itself, Jacob and Marcus Jr kept their businesses flourishing even while extensively assisting government officials during a series of extremely complicated and important trade negotiations with the British and Germans. Jacob assisted negotiations with the Germans while Marcus Jr was often in London assisting that team's work.

In 1941, Raoul Wallenberg commenced his partnership with the Hungarian-Jewish immigrant Koloman Lauer, elements of which sent him travelling throughout the Nazi-occupied continent with some frequency. Yet in his letters written between 1937 and 1944, there is not a single word about the ever-worsening situation of Europe's Jews. Nor do those written between 1939 and 1944 offer any insight into what he thought either about the war itself, or the situation of the Jews. Here it is salient to again emphasize that readers of Sweden's newspapers between 1939 and 1945 were quite well informed about what was happening to Jews on the continent, as persecution evolved into ghettoization, deportation, and worse. From 1941 forward, even information about mass killing evolving into genocide reached Swedish newspaper readers.[49]

In fact, because of his privileged position, Wallenberg was probably better informed than most Swedes – even others of his social standing and education. He met frequently with his older cousins, and it is likely that they shared some information and insights with him. His continental travels during the war included a trip to Berlin in November 1942.[50] This was when the battle of Stalingrad was raging, and this trip through Germany, presumably by train, occurred during some of the worse months of the Holocaust. Between spring 1942 and spring 1943, deportation trains were traversing the continent from all directions, carrying millions to their deaths in the by now fully functioning Nazi death camps located in German-occupied Poland. Yet anything connected with such matters that he might have seen or heard of during these trips remained unremarked upon, in the available sources.[51] Even such important events as Sweden's quiet but newsworthy reception of some 1,000 Norwegian Jews in November and December 1942, who escaped deportation, as well as the country's very public role in the salvation of Danish Jewry in October 1943, are not commented upon by Wallenberg, either in response to newspaper reports indicating something was going to happen, or afterwards in the few letters we have from that period.[52]

In late 1941, one of Wallenberg's connections with Jacob paid off, and he was introduced to Lauer.[53] After coming to Sweden, Lauer set up a small import-export firm which was affiliated with Sven Salén, a prominent Stockholm businessman and shipper who was close to the Wallenberg brothers. It was successful enough to need another hand and, after being introduced, Wallenberg quickly became Lauer's valued partner. The Hungarian Jew recognized the talents of the energetic, well-connected young Swede, and made him a partner in the firm. Perhaps most important during the war was the gentile Wallenberg's Swedish passport, which allowed him to travel throughout Europe in order to conduct the firm's business of importing to Sweden foodstuffs from Hungary and elsewhere in Central Europe. According to Lauer, Wallenberg made at least two extended trips to the Hungarian capital before 1944. He spent most of February 1942 there, and stayed almost six weeks between early September and mid-October 1943.[54]

Wallenberg's last months in Stockholm were characterized, as with Sweden in general, by a striking normality. Though north-western Europe had not yet been invaded, everyone understood that it was only a matter of time. The Soviets were slowly but inexorably advancing towards Berlin after their great victories of summer and autumn 1943. Everyone in Sweden knew they had to sit tight a bit longer, and the war would be over. Though the general public did not grasp the full scale of the ongoing genocide, it was – as already noted – impossible for Wallenberg and all literate Swedes not to know that European Jewry was suffering a frightful onslaught – not just 'normal' wartime atrocities.

Interestingly, Wallenberg's calendar from the months before leaving for Budapest is filled with social events, dates with women, family gatherings and other activities normal for a man of his position and age. He went to work every day, and socialized at night and at weekends.

His last personal letter written before he departed for Budapest is an important one, as much for what it doesn't say as for what it does. Written on 28 February 1944 to his sister Nina, then living in Berlin with her diplomat husband, it is in many ways a typical letter penned by him. It is lengthy, articulate, personal and describes in detail things both familial and professional. It is worth quoting at length because it provides considerable insight into what was on his mind at the time, aspects of his ongoing business activities and conditions in Sweden:

> It is frightfully boring here without you, and the dinner table at home is straight out of a play by Strindberg ... This letter will be rather choppy, since it has been written on different typewriters, for we have been terribly busy. The boxcars with oranges keep rolling in, one after the other, and so far without any hitches or problems. The market has been flooded with oranges this past week, because too much is being imported from different places all at the same time, making prices plummet. Thank god all of ours had already been sold ... The rest of the business is not doing too well; there are constant problems with the poultry men. We have some other major projects planned, but it's too soon to tell whether they are feasible or not.
>
> The Falkmans had a magnificent dance with lots of pretty girls ... The following day, on the 19th, Gösta and Gittan gave a tremendously successful dinner party with Maj and Enzio, the Romanian minister ... a week later, Göran and Märta Crafoord had a dinner party, this one also very nice ...
>
> Yet another typewriter. Last Sunday ... I met up with Knut von Horn [who] works at the Ministry of Supply, as you know. During our walk, we talked about the way the supply situation is developing. We painted ourselves an alarming scenario, especially if there is peace in Finland. In that case, we guessed that we'd have a moral obligation to help them out, out of our own rations .... The painting was bleak even if there was no peace in Finland: in the event of a Russian attack we would have another half million refugees or more to feed ... I think that Central Europe is about to change political course again.
>
> A week ago, I sent a letter to *Dagens Nyheter* [Sweden's most important daily newspaper] suggesting that they do away with certain practices and change some of their permanent headings ... and yesterday I got a letter from Dehlgren, who thanked me for my kind interest ... Well, there is nothing more to report as far as I know, except to say that I hope that you'll be home for a visit, and the sooner the better. Best wishes, Raoul.[55]

As explained below, by mid-June Wallenberg had met with officials from UD and the American Legation who would first interview him, then invite him to accept the task which developed in negotiations between the Americans, Sweden's foreign office, and leaders of Stockholm's Jewish community. These sometimes confusing negotiations concluded with Wallenberg's departure from Stockholm on Friday, 7 July 1944. He would never return to Sweden, or to his family.[56]

EXAMINING WALLENBERG'S MOTIVES

One reason amongst many for re-examining Wallenberg is to better understand his reason(s) for accepting the task of going to Budapest, not least because his choice represents a moment when a 'bystander' chose to become a rescuer of Jews during the Holocaust.[57] Insight into his personal motivation can contribute to the discussion within Holocaust studies which seeks to understand who becomes a rescuer of his or her fellow humans during times of crises.[58] We shall therefore examine two central factors which figure prominently in the hagiographic and sometimes even scholarly literature, and are thought to explain his motivation to become a rescuer. Both can be proven to be essentially irrelevant, leaving more open the question of what exactly motivated him to leave the safety of Stockholm and go to Budapest.

One of the more fanciful theories given by the hagiographers, which seems to hold particular appeal for the reading and listening public, is the matter of his alleged 'Jewish blood' as a central motivating element. A survey of such assertions will be followed by an examination of what many authors (and others, such as filmmakers and politicians) purport to be Wallenberg's pronounced 'philo-Semitism', something which ostensibly caused him to feel an intimate solidarity with the suffering of Europe's Jews in the years and months before he went to Budapest.

These two issues can be seen as emblematic for the multiple methodological problems found in the most influential hagiographic literature. A complete review of these problems cannot be conducted here, but the critical reader will quickly see that much of this genre, which purports to be 'historical' literature, is characterized by a methodological shoddiness and sloppiness which is unacceptable in works purporting to be historical. The 'explanations', interpretations and conclusions found in these publications, about Wallenberg and his encounter with Holocaust history, are most often based on an arbitrary and scanty mix of fragmentary documentation, almost always without source citations. Perhaps most problematically from the historian's point of view, the most influential literature and representations about Wallenberg have relied largely on an uncritical acceptance of virtually everything found in survivor testimonies, memoirs, commemorative speeches, and so on, about Wallenberg. What has compounded these problems in the most influential publications is the failure of the authors to understand fundamental elements, both of the Holocaust at large and, more specifically and importantly, of what actually happened in Hungary and Budapest, and why. In short, this genre lacks credibility and is sometimes directly unreliable, yet such publications have been instrumental in shaping the commonly accepted understanding of Wallenberg, how and why he did what he did, and his place in Holocaust history.

The first issue, as noted, is the great importance which has been placed on his alleged 'part-Jewishness' or, as one writer put it, his 'dash of Jewish blood'.[59] This alleged and completely unprovable factor in his ostensible genetic makeup is said to have motivated him to save Jews. And again, when this somewhat bizarre assertion is made, we see in the literature the curious methodological mix of interviews (some done by the authors themselves, some repeated throughout the literature), fragments of letters or other documents, and other bits of purported evidence used by these authors to reach sometimes altogether different conclusions.

The claim generally starts with the notion that a very distant relative of Wallenberg was Jewish. There is general agreement that around the end of the eighteenth century, a German Jew named Benedicks emigrated to Sweden, establishing the maternal line of Wallenberg's family. H. Rosenfeld writes that Benedicks quickly became a financier to the Swedish court, while J. Bierman states that Benedicks became a court jeweller. Both agree that conversion to Swedish Lutheranism was almost immediate, as was marriage to a Lutheran Swedish woman.[60] This ostensible 'one-sixteenth' Jewishness inherited by Raoul Wallenberg is also mentioned in other accounts, with one current online source echoing the distasteful speculation noted above, that Wallenberg 'owned a drop of Jewish blood'.[61] Typically, there is no explanation of precisely how the 'dash' or 'drop' could make a difference, generations later during a genocide – but for many it seems important.

Tellingly, Wallenberg's sister Nina is quoted by Bierman as saying that the family grew up with no idea of their ostensible Jewish connection: 'not, I'm sure, because Mother wished to hide it, but because the Jewish ancestor was so far back and none of his descendants had been brought up in the ways of the Jewish people. So we didn't become conscious of this until the mid-thirties.'[62] Yet Bierman also

makes note of Wallenberg's 'one-sixteenth Jewish blood', claiming that
he was proud of it. A Swedish contemporary interviewed by this same
author related that when in 1930 they were in the army together,
Wallenberg told him that he was 'proud of his partial Jewish ancestry
and, as I recall, must have exaggerated it somewhat. I remember him
saying, "A person like me, who is both a Wallenberg and half-Jewish,
can never be defeated." '[63] This recollection concerns a distant conversation which took place several years before Wallenberg's sister said
that the family was even vaguely aware of their distant connection to
anything Jewish. In other words, the Jewish ancestry of the Wislings
(Wallenberg's mother's maiden name) was so distant as to be meaningless, except, it seems, in ex post facto interviews about Wallenberg.[64]
In the event, the history of Jews and Jewish life in Sweden leaves little
doubt that once converted, most if not all connections with Judaism
within the Wislings and other similar families with some sort of distant
Jewish connection would be quickly emptied of any effective relevance. Equally important, in post-agricultural (late nineteenth- and
early twentieth-century) Sweden, connections to Jewishness were publicly denied, particularly once a family such as the Benedicks or
Wislings had achieved any measure of social standing. Such trends are
known mostly to accelerate with each succeeding generation, something which remains true of contemporary Sweden.[65]

Continuing this trend Kati Marton, author of a popular book about
Wallenberg, cites a contemporary report (noted below) from Herschel
Johnson, the US envoy in Sweden. After meeting Wallenberg, Johnson
wrote that, 'He himself is half Jewish, incidentally'. In her book,
Marton concluded a key chapter entitled 'The Right Man', in the following way: 'Wallenberg [was] proud of his ancestry, but had probably
exaggerated his Jewishness. He was, in fact, only about one-sixteenth
Jewish.'[66] Seeming to buck the trend of claiming that Wallenberg's
putative Jewishness was significant, Rosenfeld concluded: 'Although
one of Raoul's maternal great-grandparents (earlier described in the
very same paragraph as a "great-great-grandfather") had been Jewish,
this was never a factor in his life and did not influence or affect his
later mission in Budapest.'[67]

There is no evidence whatsoever that any provable 'trace' of Jewish
blood, from either side of the family, influenced Wallenberg in any way,
including any notion – sound or silly – about Jewish 'blood', culture or
memory. It was uncommon in the extreme that an ethnic Swede, at any
time but certainly not during the first half of the twentieth century,
would voluntarily lay claim to any connection with Jewish culture or
religion – not least the Swedish-Lutheran haute-bourgeoisie to which
Wallenberg so securely belonged. Moreover, there is no evidence that

such a notion was genuinely considered by him – interviews decades later with contemporaries notwithstanding. On the contrary, the evidence strongly suggests that Wallenberg lacked any articulated or effective sense of connection with Jews, Judaism, or even what was happening to the Jews in Germany and Europe before 1944. As we shall see, Wallenberg's revealing correspondence does not offer the reader any evidence of solidarity with Jews, be it emotional, spiritual or cultural.

There is, however, one piece of evidence – mentioned above and used by Marton – from a contemporary source which tells us something of how Wallenberg apparently regarded himself in this respect. Significantly, it was expressed just prior to his departure for Budapest. In June 1944, when Wallenberg was negotiating with Swedish and American officials about the parameters of his mission, he met Herschel Johnson, the American envoy in Stockholm. After their second meeting, Johnson reported: 'There is no doubt in my mind as to the sincerity of Wallenberg's purpose because I have talked to him myself. I was told by Wallenberg that he wanted to be able to help effectively and to save lives and that he was not interested in going to Budapest merely to write reports to be sent to the Foreign Office. He himself is half Jewish, incidentally.'[68]

Was this rather exaggerated claim by Wallenberg incidental, or did it suddenly matter to him? And if so, why? It is easy to imagine that in his excitement at the prospect of his forthcoming task he did, as it were, burst out and say something that may have been in the back of his mind since being told by his mother that there was some sort of connection (although his sister Nina is not quoted as providing a context for the comment by their mother in the mid-1930s). Yet the question must be asked – did it matter in any significant way if he had any, to use the popular if distasteful jargon, 'Jewish blood in his veins'? What if anything does it contribute to our understanding of him and his motivations? Though authors of popular literature have written that they believe it was a decisive factor explaining his decision to undertake his task, there is – apart from the report by Johnson quoted above – no other contemporary evidence for the notion that Wallenberg perceived himself to be Jewish in any real sense, or that this played a role in motivating him to go to Budapest. It seems a standard practice of this genre to assert, either explicitly or otherwise, that 'because' he had Jewish blood, he particularly cared for Jews. This is not only empirical nonsense, it is morally objectionable. The reader is apparently to understand that because Wallenberg had some Jewish background, or 'blood', in him, it was in some way inevitable that an ambition to rescue Jews had evolved within him, and that it was only 'natural' for him to be concerned about Jews. Apparently all that was lacking up to that point in Wallenberg's life was the opportunity to do so. Most often such assertions are tied to his brief time in Palestine where, because he met some German Jews who fled Nazi Germany and succeeded in getting into Palestine, he developed a strong, even decisive feeling of solidarity with their plight – and wanted to do something about it. Indeed, it is sometimes asserted that after returning to Sweden from Palestine, he seemingly couldn't stop speaking about the Jews' situation. Such suppositions and speculative assertions may enhance a fictional narrative, but they are inappropriate in writing history.

What then did Wallenberg say about Jews, either in general, or about the accelerating suffering imposed on German Jews by Hitler's regime? On 3 April 1936, about a month after arriving in Haifa for his banking apprenticeship, Wallenberg wrote to his grandfather that he was among people 'of every possible nationality ... I'm thinking of learning Arabic instead of Hebrew, which is what everybody recommends even though Hebrew is the main language here, rising like a phoenix from the ashes.'[69] Then, after describing some daily activities, he wrote:

> The people at my boarding house are mainly German Jews and very nice and funny. One day, one of them told me in passing that her brother had been murdered by the Nazis. Otherwise, people here don't talk much about the past, but almost exclusively about the future of Palestine, in which everyone believes wholeheartedly – it would be a pity if they didn't, since Palestine is their home and the realization of a longtime [*sic*] dream.[70]

Concerning Wallenberg's alleged impressions after encountering these refugees, Marton wrote:

> For Wallenberg, Haifa in 1936 turned out to be an apprenticeship of a different sort. [Geman Jews] ... were streaming into Palestine ... Raoul met many of them through his Dutch mentor and in the kosher boarding house where he was a lodger. He listened to their stories ... It was Wallenberg's first exposure to the irrational and poisonous germ of anti-semitism ... He sat spellbound listening to [them] ... The impression this humbled segment of humanity made on him was to be permanent.[71]

Another author stated: 'Raoul left Palestine with a clear understanding of the extent and complexity of the 'Jewish problem' in Hitler's Germany ... Raoul spoke often – to those who were willing to listen – about the evil and dangers of Nazism.'[72]

And yet another wrote:

Among the people with whom Raoul had come into contact – and the experience seems to have made a lasting impression on him – were a number of young Jews who had fled from Hitler's Germany to Palestine. He had met them at the 'kosher' boarding-house in Haifa ... It was his first experience of the results of Nazi persecution and it affected him deeply – not just because of his humanitarian outlook but also, perhaps, because he was aware that he himself had a dash of Jewish blood.[73]

Even scholars have asserted this, as Eva Fogelman did in her book about rescuers of Jews during the Holocaust. 'He learned firsthand [from German Jewish refugees] the plight of the Jews. This awareness had tremendous impact in [sic] his willingness to help Hungarian Jewry.'[74] The three quotations given above, though phrased somewhat differently, are almost identical in meaning, and all are from interviews done at different times with Vivica Lindfors, a female contemporary of Wallenberg's. They all recount an evening in Stockholm some time in 1937, when Wallenberg and she had spent the evening dancing.[75] The aspiring actress was certain Wallenberg had taken her back to his office (or his grandfather's office in one account) to try to seduce her. Instead he spoke to her about some much more serious things: 'He spoke to me in an intense voice, very low, almost a whisper, of the terrible things that were being done to the Jews of Germany.'[76] Bierman quotes her as saying: 'He started talking very intensely about the Jews and Germany and about the horrors he had apparently seen.'[77] In the third version, Rosenfeld described Wallenberg not as whispering quietly and intensely but as 'haranguing me [the young girl] on the subjects of Nazism and the Third Reich. He spoke with much intensity about the developments in Germany. I was only sixteen then, and it was not the sort of thing that interested me. Moreover, I did not believe a word. In fact, I thought he was trying to seduce me.'[78]

If, however, Wallenberg was genuinely concerned about the persecution of Jews in Germany – whom he might have seen while travelling there – he made no mention of them in his correspondence from those particular months. By late 1936, Germany's Jews were increasingly subject to a variety of disorienting pressures and steadily escalating persecution. But, except for relatively rare instances when individuals might be mistreated in public by party members, police or members of the public, they were not during this time subjected to 'horrors' that might have been visible to a travelling Swedish businessman.

However, in the written evidence left behind by Wallenberg, both from his months in Palestine and for several years afterwards, one finds not a single expression of sympathy or empathy, either with the many Jews he met in Palestine, or their plight in Germany.[79] He comments several times on the Jews' situation in Palestine regarding their future prospects for the nascent state, but regarding Nazi persecution of Jews, not a single word can be found in his correspondence between 1935 and 1944. The 'absence' of this subject and its many corollaries is furthermore of interest because of the nature of his letter-writing. Wallenberg wrote about what was on his mind, and often offered to his reader an analysis of those political events which had caught his interest. His letters are expansive and interesting, but according to this body of evidence, the plight of Germany's Jews (and later other Jews) caught in the Nazi trap seems not to have caught his attention.

In stark contrast to the hagiographers' emphasis on Wallenberg's alleged strong reaction after hearing of the plight of German Jews while in Haifa, what stands out instead is the rhetorical distance he maintains when he does comment on Jews. There is no sign of the concern for Jewish suffering which the young Swedish actress and others seem to have remembered. There is no evidence of any real interest or connection, before June 1944, with the tragedy which engulfed European Jewry. There is no convincing evidence that before that year, Wallenberg placed any importance whatsoever, apart from some oral testimony given by people pleased to be interviewed decades after the war, on any perceived Jewish connection, nor any evidence that some distant Jewish 'blood' coursing through his veins made Jews or Judaism relevant for him in any way.

For instance, in his first letter from Palestine, written on 12 March 1936, Wallenberg concluded: 'The Jews here are afraid of the Arabs, who are beginning to wake up and dream of an empire. Poor people, they evidently have to adjust to being in a minority wherever they go.'[80] In the letter of 3 April cited above, Wallenberg devoted some lines to an analysis of the Yishuv's economy (the Yishuv was the name of the pre-state Jewish community), telling his grandfather:

> Because of this, their economy is rather fragile, but the Jews are firmly convinced that all will work out. They are used to suffering worse things than a financial crisis, so they don't care about the risks and, besides, they have no choice except to settle here. I never knew that so many Jews were as deeply and fanatically religious as many here are. To them, Palestine is much more than a mere refuge; it is the promised land, the land designated for them by God.[81]

A couple of weeks later he described one of his first trips outside of Haifa: 'Then we went to one of the new socialist Jewish colonies, located where the Jordan flows out of the lake. It was truly admirable … The Jews try as hard as they can to farm efficiently.'[82] In early July, he commented on the ongoing Arab riots:

The disturbances here are tapering off, but I will postpone my trip to Jerusalem ... there is still a curfew, and nobody is allowed in the street after seven o'clock, which should make life rather boring for those people, especially the young ones, who work until seven and then have to go home to their rooms without the chance to go to the movies or out for a walk. A sort of three months prison sentence for the poor Jews.[83]

Typically for this man empowered with considerable powers of observation, Wallenberg's admiration for the Zionist project was objective in tone, and evidences no sense of any particular personal connection. In the letter of 12 March cited above, he calls the Jews 'poor people', yet tells his grandfather:

They have boundless enthusiasm and idealism and these immediately strike you as the most common characteristics of Zionism. It is truly a gamble on their part to try to settle hundreds of thousands of Jews in this dry, stony little place surrounded by and already teeming with Arabs. They nevertheless are optimistic to a man, and were energy a guarantee for success the results would be excellent, for they seem to work practically around the clock.[84]

His references to 'them, or they' are telling. The meaning behind the use of such language should not be exaggerated, but it is clear that for Wallenberg the Jews were different and separate from him. Any analysis of his feelings and thoughts must be founded upon those words he says, or doesn't say. It is methodologically inappropriate to insert into his 'thinking' something poignant which is alleged to have motivated decisions made years later, when he was in Sweden or Budapest. His purported sense of solidarity with Jews seems more a result of the emotional hopes of the hagiographers rather than anything supported by the evidence. As we will see, when given the chance in Budapest, he did work ceaselessly to assist and save Jews. Nonetheless, prior to mid-1944, he did not pay particular attention or care particularly much about what was happening to European Jewry. Indeed, as noted above, he was more than happy to do business in Germany, years after Hitler's regime commenced its persecution of Jews, and particularly during a period when this torment and persecution worsened literally every day. Finally, however, there is nothing particularly unusual in the fact that he didn't mention this subject. Countless other Europeans of the same background at the same time also failed to mention, in their correspondence, newspaper articles and books, and so on, what was happening to the Jews.

WHY DID WALLENBERG GO TO BUDAPEST?

In the light, then, of what we actually know of what Wallenberg thought, felt and planned in 1944 for his future, we may ask: what were his motives for choosing to go to Budapest? He knew that there would be genuine risks in a city lying in the Red Army's path, but he also understood that he was accepting a mission that would be immensely challenging and probably quite exciting. Did he go because he was, as some have speculated, a paradigmatically altruistic person willing to sacrifice himself for the good of others? This is possible, but there is no written evidence to support this particular notion. There is, as we shall see, evidence to believe that he and his partner saw potentially profitable business opportunities available in Budapest. They knew that the war was coming to an end, sooner if not later, and that with its conclusion, business opportunities throughout Europe would be readily available. There is reason to believe that he left neutral Sweden because he felt that his professional opportunities had stalled, and that the Lauer enterprise was not commensurate with his status as a Wallenberg.

There seems no doubt that by spring 1944 he remained frustrated at being unable to practise what he seemed to enjoy most – architecture. Indeed, even when working for Lauer's firm, Wallenberg's personal letterhead still included the title 'architect'. It does seem likely that Wallenberg understood that the highly unusual yet felicitous set of circumstances and chance meetings, which led to his being asked by the Swedish and American governments to go to Budapest, offered a once-in-a-lifetime opportunity of extraordinary excitement and potential – one that he had to seize without regard for how it might influence his future. He had no way of knowing in any real detail what he would do in Budapest, or how he would do it, and he cannot have imagined how badly it would all end. One wonders what his grandfather would have thought about his carefully and expensively cultivated grandson accepting such an opportunity. Would he have approved, or would he have discouraged his grandson from accepting such a potentially dangerous, low-paid assignment?

What is certain is that his mother and grandfather had succeeded in raising and educating a man inclined to think well of others, to care about family and friends, and to do something positive – and profitable – with his life. It also seems certain that he was blessed with a good measure of personal courage. He had travelled widely in different, even exotic cultures, and clearly didn't frighten easily. This characteristic was much in evidence during the 'famous' hitchhiking episode, when he was hitchhiking in the States and was robbed by four men who picked him up. Afterwards he described the incident to GOW, writing of his own calm bravery:

> By now I had become very suspicious because of their questions about money, their lack of luggage, and the sudden stop ... Fearing the worst, I tried to keep a cool head so as not to make things worse ... When they had all my money, I decided it was their turn to show some goodwill, so I asked them to drive me back to the highway ... by this time they were the ones who were frightened, maybe because I was so calm. I really didn't feel scared; I found the whole thing sort of interesting.[85]

There is no reason to doubt this account of how his personal bravery brought him through this potentially dangerous episode. Eleven years later, he would often respond in a similar manner.

There is, however, no evidence to suggest that Wallenberg saw himself at any time before spring 1944 as either a philo-Semite or an incipient rescuer of the remnants of European Jewry. To make such an assertion is more fantasy than fact. On the contrary, his personal correspondence makes clear that his primary concerns in the months and years before going to Budapest were about his professional future. In fact, the strongest impression left by a close review of his personnel correspondence is that he was a perfectly normal young man, brought up in a life of considerable privilege, who was growing increasingly frustrated that his path forward was not what he expected. His social life was flourishing in 1944, but his professional life was not. A close perusal of his daily calendar reveals a man with many friends, both male and female, but with limited professional prospects which left him increasingly frustrated. There is no evidence of any articulated or demonstrated concern for what was happening to the Jews of Europe, or of Hungary. We must therefore conclude that apart from the recollections of a handful of contemporaries, related decades after the fact, there is no evidence that Raoul Wallenberg was in any way suffused with concern for the ongoing genocide of European Jewry. This seems to be a postwar construct of those who knew him. That said, it is equally clear that when an opportunity to actually do some good was granted him, he grasped it without hesitation. This historic choice can and should stand on its own.

NOTES

1. Both passages are in *Raoul Wallenberg: Letters and Dispatches 1924–1944*, trans. K. Board (New York: Arcade Publishing, 1995), pp.26–7. This collection contains letters not published in the original Swedish collection. All translations from Swedish to English from this collection are Board's, unless otherwise specified.

2. G.O. Wallenberg to R. Wallenberg (hereafter in this context GOW to RW, or vice versa), 26 August 1935, in ibid., p.1489.
3. F. Stern, *Einstein's German World* (Princeton, NJ: Princeton University Press, 1999), p.35.
4. See, for example, A. Lajos, *Hjälten och Offren: Raoul Wallenberg och judarna i Budapest* (Vaxjö: Svenska Emigrantinstitutets skriftserie, no. 15, 2003).
5. J. Bierman, *Righteous Gentile: The Story of Raoul Wallenberg, Missing Hero of the Holocaust* (London: Penguin, 1981), p.7.
6. Born in 1863, Gustaf Oscar Wallenberg was the second son of André Oscar Wallenberg, founder of the Wallenberg banking and business empire. This constantly expanding empire played a fundamentally important role in the development of the modern Swedish state. The Wallenbergs made an immeasurable contribution in Sweden's transition from a primarily agrarian economy to an industrial one. A fascinating personality in his own right, *Farfar* Gustaf came to play a very different role in Wallenberg family history than did his two even more influential brothers, Knut Agathon and Marcus Sr.
7. Originally published in Swedish as *Älskade farfar! Brevväxlingen mellan Gustaf & Raoul Wallenberg, 1924–1936* (Stockholm: Bonniers, 1987).
8. Much of this correspondence has never been used before.
9. RW to GOW, 7 November 1935, in Wallenberg, *Letters and Dispatches*, p.38.
10. GOW to RW, 11 May 1934, in ibid., pp.102–3, and GOW to RW, 30 October 1934, in ibid., pp.118–119.
11. Several of his university essays from an English class are in Riksarkivet (hererafter RA), Raoul Wallenberg Arkiv, Signum 1, vol. 8.
12. RW to GOW, 26 January 1935, in Wallenberg, *Letters and Dispatches*, p.130.
13. Much of what Wallenberg saw and thought while in South Africa is revealed in a lengthy article he published in autumn 1936 in a Swedish travel magazine, *Jorden runt*.
14. RW to GOW, 8 August 1935, in Wallenberg, *Letters and Dispatches*, p.145. In his next letter, Wallenberg wrote to GOW: 'I know that you object to my hanging around with Swedes, and I will remedy this bit by bit.' Going to the cinema was one of Wallenberg's favourite pastimes, something he did everywhere he went.
15. GOW to RW, 21 July 1935, in ibid., pp.140–1. Italics in the original.
16. RW to GOW, 26 August 1935, in ibid., p.147. The Swedish original is somewhat different. It reads: 'Själsligen har jag varit ganska trist de sista månaderna, även i Stockholm.' The translation should have read, 'Spiritually, I have been rather gloomy these past months, even in Stockholm.' Another more important line from this letter was completely expunged from the English translation: 'I själva verket har jag varit ganska nedbruten av att vara orsaken till en tragedi.' ('In actual fact I have been quite broken by being the cause of a tragedy.') See Wallenberg, *Älskade Farfar!*, p.163. No explanation for these editorial changes and purges are given by the editor or translator of *Letters and Dispatches*.
17. GOW to RW, 23 September 1935, in Wallenberg, *Letters and Dispatches*, pp.148–50. In the fourth paragraph of this extract, the English translation reads: 'But you must not give up your life.' The original Swedish is more emphatic.
18. Ibid., p.151.
19. As noted previously, Wallenberg's English was excellent, and he would often write in that language to his grandfather, particularly when a Swedish typewriter was unavailable. Why he wrote this key portion of this letter in English is unknown.
20. Ibid., p.151.
21. GOW to RW in ibid., p.154.
22. GOW to RW, 22 December 1935, in ibid., p.158.
23. GOW to RW, 4 February 1936, in ibid., pp.165–6.
24. RW to GOW, 28 February 1936, in ibid., p.168.
25. RW to GOW, 24 February, and RW to GOW, 28 February, in ibid., both p.167.
26. RW to GOW, 19 June 1936, in ibid., pp.183–4.
27. RW to GOW, 6 July 1936, in ibid., pp.186–7. 'Jacob W.' is his older cousin, the very powerful businessman.
28. RW to GOW, 20 January 1936, in Wallenberg, *Älskade farfar!*, p.180.
29. R. Wallenberg, *'Sydafrikanska intryck'* [Impressions of South Africa], *Jorden runt: magasin för geographi och resor*, 8, 2 (1936), pp.587–604.
30. Ibid., pp.589–90. He also noted: 'The coloured are children of the city with their own clubs and organizations which ape the whites in several aspects.'
31. Both Wallenberg's father and grandfather (GOW) were naval officers. It must have thrilled

him to see elements of the esteemed Royal Navy assembled like that for the first time in his life. While in Haifa the presence of British ships also drew his attention.

32. RW to GOW, 12 March 1936, in Wallenberg, *Älskade farfar!*, p.186.
33. News that Germany was persecuting its Jews was not new. The infamous Nuremburg Laws had been announced some six months before, while Wallenberg was in South Africa. These initial years of increasingly violent persecution of the Jews receive no mention in Wallenberg's correspondence.
34. RW to GOW, 12 March 1936, in Wallenberg, *Älskade farfar!*, p.187. There is no explanation for how Wallenberg could have imagined that a fleet stationed in the Mediterranean could have so quickly sailed to the North Sea.
35. RW to GOW, 19 June 1936, in Wallenberg, *Letters and Dispatches*, p.183. See the third epigram, at the beginning of this chapter, for the better-known comments from that same letter which are cited in several of the hagiographic accounts under review in this chapter.
36. RW to GOW, 19 June 1936, in ibid., p.182.
37. Both citations, RW to GOW, 6 July 1936, in Wallenberg, *Älskade farfar!*, pp.202–5.
38. Gustaf makes clear in one letter that although he had no objections to his grandson working in the Wallenberg sphere, he wanted him also to make contacts outside it. 'I want to eliminate any thought of acceptance based on your "being part of the family".' See GOW to RW, 22 December 1935, in Wallenberg, *Letters and Dispatches*, p.160.
39. RW to GOW, 12 October 1936, in ibid., pp.190–1. From about this date, this publication contains more correspondence, indeed the final letters, between the two of them.
40. RW to GOW, 19 January 1937, in ibid., pp.197–8.
41. See especially G. Nylander and A. Perlinge (eds), *Raoul Wallenberg in Documents, 1927–1947* (Stockholm: Stiftelsen för Ekonomisk Historisk Forskning inom Bank och Företagande, 2000), p.80.
42. R. Wallenberg to Nina von Dardel, 7 November 1938, in Wallenberg, *Letters and Dispatches*, p.202.
43. R. Wallenberg to J. Wallenberg, in Nylander and Perlinge (eds), *Raoul Walllenberg in Documents*, p.57.
44. Marcus Wallenberg Sr to R. Wallenberg, 23 November 1936, in ibid., p.36.
45. See, for example, P.A. Levine, 'Swedish Neutrality during the Second World War: Tactical Success or Moral Compromise?', in N. Wylie (ed.), *European Neutrals and Non-Belligerents during the Second World War* (Cambridge: Cambridge University Press, 2002). See also economic historian Sven Nordlund's, *Affärer som vanligt: Ariseringen i Sverige 1933–1945* (Lund: Sekel förlag, 2009).
46. Numerous recent studies have unequivocally established that virtually all aspects of Swedish commerce and culture maintained extensive contact and exchange with Germany throughout the Nazi era. The economy was highly dependent on trade with Germany and occupied Europe. Importantly, however, penetration of Nazi ideology into Swedish political life was limited. Though it existed, Sweden's domestic Nazi movement never gained any significant political or economic influence.
47. R. Wallenberg to G.O. Wallenberg, 12 December 1936, in Nylander and Perle, *Raoul Wallenberg in Documents*, p.39. The same letter is reproduced in Wallenberg, *Letters and Dispatches*, p.195.
48. R. Wallenberg to Nina von Dardel, 7 November 1938, in Wallenberg, *Letters and Dispatches*, pp.201–3.
49. See P.A. Levine, *The Swedish Press and the Holocaust*, unpublished MA thesis, Claremont Graduate School, Claremont, CA, 1987; and I. Svanberg and M. Tydén, *Sverige och Förintelsen: debatt och document om Europas judar 1933–1945* (Stockholm: Arena, 1997).
50. In early November he passed through Berlin, and picked up at Sweden's Legation (embassy) a letter addressed to Jacob Wallenberg. See the telegram from R. Wallenberg to J. Wallenberg, 9 November 1942, in Nylander and Perlinge, *Raoul Wallenberg in Documents*, p.90.
51. Swedish director Kjell Grede's feature film, *God afton Herr Wallenberg* (1989), begins with a depiction of Wallenberg on a train somewhere in Europe where he 'witnessed' the dumping of bodies from a deportation train. If this happened, which is unlikely, there is no documentation indicating his reaction to such a scene. It is more likely a figment of the director's imagination. It is, however, a telling example of how Wallenberg is represented as being 'concerned' about what was happening to the Jews. His own correspondence provides no evidence of such concerns.

52. On Sweden's role in those episodes of the Holocaust, see as P.A. Levine, *From Indifference to Activism: Swedish Diplomacy and the Holocaust, 1938–1944*, 2nd edn (Uppsala: Studia historica Upsaliensia, 1998).
53. There is an interesting irony to the fact that a Wallenberg ended up as partner with an immigrant, a Central European Jew, but that is a subject for another book.
54. K. Lauer to R. Philipp, 25 October 1955, in Raoul Wallenberg Archive, RA, Signum 1, vol. 6. This letter was written to a Swedish journalist who was one of the first to write about Wallenberg after the war.
55. RW to Nina Lagergren (née von Dardel), 28 February 1944, in Wallenberg, *Letters* and *Dispatches*, pp.205–8.
56. A complete biography of Wallenberg would have to use an even fuller range of sources than are used here, in order to explain more fully the man, his character and his place in Swedish society.
57. See, for example, D. Cesarani and P.A. Levine, *'Bystander' to the Holocaust: A Re-evaluation* (London and Portland, OR: Frank Cass, 2002).
58. See, for example, E. Fogelman, *Conscience and Courage: Rescuers of Jews during the Holocaust* (London: Cassell, 1995), and the earlier S.P. Oliner and P.M. Oliner, *The Altruistic Personality: Rescuers of Jews in Nazi Europe* (New York: Free Press, 1988). Wallenberg figures prominently in both volumes, which make many of the same mistakes about Wallenberg as does the hagiographic literature, including a complete misunderstanding of the political context from which his mission arose, and how he operated.
59. Bierman, *Righteous Gentile*, p.24.
60. H. Rosenfeld, *Raoul Wallenberg: Angel of Rescue, Heroism and Torment in the Gulag* (Buffalo, NY: Prometheus Books, 1982), p.23; and Bierman, *Righteous Gentile*, p.25.
61. See 'Raoul Wallenberg (1912–?)' on the website of the Jewish Virtual Library: A Division of the American-Israeli Cooperative Enterprise, www.jewishvirtuallibrary.org/source/biography/wallenberg.html. This is a paradigmatic example of how rumour and interpretive superficiality continues to exist.
62. Nina Lagergren quoted in Bierman, *Righteous Gentile*, p.25.
63. Professor I. Hedenius, quoted in ibid., p.25.
64. The genre's apparent compulsion to mention this purported 'one sixteenth' percentage of Wallenberg's 'blood' evokes distasteful echoes of the fateful discourse conducted throughout Europe, and North America in the 1930s and before to 'measure' Jewish blood. It seems that even otherwise rational people, including some Jews, find relevance in such an incalculable and meaningless 'measure' of blood.
65. A similar if later example can be seen in the history of the Bonnier family, prominent in Sweden for their achievements in the newspaper and publishing business from the late nineteenth century onward.
66. K. Marton, *Wallenberg* (New York: Random House, 1982), p.41. The author quotes Herschel Johnson, America's envoy in Stockholm during the war. More from this report in a subsequent chapter.
67. Rosenfeld, *Raoul Wallenberg: Angel of Rescue*, p.23.
68. H. Johnson to Secretary of State, 1 July 1944, no.2412 (section two), National Archives (hereafter NA), Washington, DC, Record Group (hereafter RG) 59, File 840.48 Refugees.
69. Though there is no evidence that he learned either language, his dexterity with foreign languages made plausible his early feeling that one of them could be learned during his planned time in Palestine.
70. RW to GOW, 3 April 1936, in Wallenberg, *Letters and Dispatches*, p.172. As far as I can discern, this is the only time in either this volume of letters, or the original Swedish edition, that Wallenberg wrote the word 'Nazi'.
71. Marton, *Wallenberg*, p.25.
72. Rosenfeld, *Raoul Wallenberg: Angel of Rescue*, pp.23–4.
73. Bierman, *Righteous Gentile*, p.24. The next line in this narrative is about Wallenberg's distant Jewish relative, Benedicks. Here we should note that the authors of what I consider to be hagiographic publications about Wallenberg often personalize him in a manner which raises problems for publications claiming to be historical rather than works of fiction. Quite often these authors refer to their subject as 'Raoul', creating for the reader a distinct feeling of familiarity, closeness, and even some intimacy with their protagonist. This tendency has often been matched by people who have come up to me after lecturing, referring in their questions or ideas about the evening's subject as 'Raoul', with a tone hinting

that they were in some fashion or another known to each other. Such fascinating manifestations of this peculiar connection to a figure from history leads one to reflect about how personality cults are created and sustained.

74. Fogelman, *Conscience and Courage*, p.336, n.6. Fogelman writes: 'Among Holocaust rescuers, Raoul Wallenberg is the most widely honoured individual', and says that he was 'larger than life'. See, respectively, p.352, n.15, and p.304.
75. There seems no question that Wallenberg enjoyed and was accomplished at social dancing!
76. E. Lester, *Wallenberg: The Man in the Iron Web* (Englewood Cliffs, NJ: Prentice-Hall, 1982), p.46.
77. Bierman, *Righteous Gentile*, p.28. Unfortunately, one gets the impression that this person's recollections are emphasized as important partly, if not primarily, because she went on to become – as this author and others have put it – 'a screen and stage actress of some international fame'.
78. Rosenfeld, *Raoul Wallenberg: Angel of Rescue*, p.24. The critical reader is given the feeling that she was saying something that she felt she was expected to say, and didn't want to disappoint her guests.
79. We may again note that in Sweden, news from neighbouring Germany about what was happening to the Jews was plentiful, detailed, and generally accurate.
80. RW to GOW, 12 March 1936, in Wallenberg, *Letters and Dispatches*, pp.170–1.
81. RW to GOW, 3 April 1936, in ibid., p.173.
82. RW to GOW, 20 April 1936, in ibid., p.176.
83. RW to GOW, 6 July 1936, in ibid., p.188.
84. RW to GOW, 12 March 1936, in ibid., p.171.
85. RW to GOW, 27 June 1933, in ibid., pp.91–2.

3

March 1944: The Holocaust in Hungary, An Overview

The Holocaust in Hungary was in many respects distinct from the tragedies that befell other Jewish communities in Nazi-dominated Europe ... [It] constitutes one of the most perplexing chapters in the history of the Holocaust. *It is a tragedy that should never have happened.* By the beginning of 1944 – on the eve of Allied victory – the leaders of the world, including the national and Jewish leaders of Hungary, were already privy to the secrets of Auschwitz ... The last major phase in the Nazis' war against the Jews, the Holocaust in Hungary is replete with paradoxes.[1] [Emphasis added.]

Ironically, it was the attempt of the Hungarian regime to shake off its alliance with Nazi Germany and make peace with the Allies that jeopardized [the Jews] ... The ghettoization process commenced with characteristic malevolence on the first day of the Jewish festival of Passover ... while [ghettoization] got under way, a triangular tussle developed between the Hungarians, the German Foreign Office and the RSHA [Reichssicherheitshauptamt] over their ultimate fate ... Kaltenbrunner and the RSHA aspired to annihilate the entire Hungarian Jewish population.[2]

THE HOLOCAUST'S PENULTIMATE CHAPTER

Within the panoply of horrors that was the Holocaust, the speed and brutality at which the 'final solution' occurred in Hungary represents one of most murderous episodes of the entire genocide. This is also one of the event's most complicated phases, replete with both significant similarities and often surprising deviations from what had happened elsewhere. Its perpetration has given rise to a number of 'iconic' scenes from Holocaust history, not least the photographs of selection taken on the (then) newly built 'ramp' at Auschwitz-Birkenau. The Hungarian Holocaust is one of the best documented and most extensively studied episodes, and has for decades attracted the interest of international scholars. In recent years, these studies have been complemented by a growing body of scholarship produced by Hungarian researchers freed from the ideological handcuffs under which they laboured during the Communist era.

The unprecedentedly rapid concentration, deportation and slaughter of hundreds of thousands of Hungarian Jews – orchestrated by the Germans and conducted by the Hungarians – took place after most of Europe's Jews had already been murdered, and with the world watching. Swiss historian Jean-Claude Favez has written that the Hungarian Holocaust was 'not only the last possible chapter in the Final Solution, [it was] also the first to take place more or less in the open, when the defeat of the Reich was no longer much in doubt'.[3] Indeed, while it was happening, British Prime Minister Winston Churchill described events in Hungary as 'probably the greatest and most horrible crime ever committed in the history of the world'.[4] Randolph Braham, still the episode's leading scholar and himself a survivor from Hungary, emphasized that the catastrophe was made all the more poignant because:

> In contrast to the illusions and rationalizations of the Jewish leaders and the unrealistic, if not quixotic, policies of the Hungarian government leaders, the Nazis and their Hungarian accomplices were realistic and resolute. They were resolved to carry out their racially and ideologically defined objective swiftly and unmercifully: the Final Solution of the Jewish question. Realizing that the Axis would lose the war, they were committed to winning at least the war against the Jews.[5]

What follows is a brief review of events, one which makes no claim to be comprehensive, but which is most salient to the aims of this study. The Swedish view of events will dominate. Though there is widespread agreement among historians that the Holocaust in Hungary can be usefully divided into three distinct phases, this chapter will not treat all three periods equally. Rather, the first phase will be discussed at greater length because it sets the stage for Swedish diplomacy during the second and third phase when Wallenberg was present, which then will be analysed in depth. Of course, even the events of 1944 have their own context.

THE DESTRUCTION OF HUNGARIAN JEWRY BEFORE JULY 1944

By late 1943, following the German demand that Hungary should do as other countries had done with their Jews, Adolf Hitler and his Nazi leadership were dissatisfied with Hungary's continuing refusal to deport its approximately 800,000 Jews. These demands were underpinned by a growing fear in Berlin that Hungary would withdraw its armies from the war against the Soviet Union. Hungary's reluctance to deport its Jews was in some ways surprising, given that the Magyar state had been the first in interwar Europe to pass an anti-Jewish law, a step which helped make such actions by other governments more imaginable. The infamous *numerus clausus* of 1922, which imposed a punitive quota on the number of Jewish students allowed to study at university, was described by one historian as 'merely the tip of the iceberg in [a] major upsurge of antisemitism in Hungary'.[6] By the late 1930s, Hungary's legislative mimicry of Nazi Germany's anti-Jewish laws confirmed public and government support for widespread anti-Semitic measures against its fellow citizens. Separate from the campaign against the Soviet Union, Hungary's resistance to joining the 'Final Solution' must have surprised Hitler. His anxieties concerning Hungary were complemented by the extent of that country's commitment to the 'crusade against Bolshevism', particularly as the war in the East began turning badly against the Germans. As time passed, the Hungarian government, headed by Regent Miklós Horthy, began looking ever more openly for a way out of its costly alliance with Nazi Germany.[7]

By March 1944, the Jewish population on Hungarian territory (which included tens of thousands of refugees from other countries, primarily Poland) constituted by far Europe's largest remaining Jewish population. To that date, they were able to continue their lives in relative safety, albeit burdened by a growing number of legislated discriminatory measures which made their lives more difficult and complicated. Though many thousands of Jewish men were forced into 'serving' in the so-called labour brigades and had died while 'assisting' their country's armed forces in the Ukraine, the country's leadership – particularly the mid-war government led by Miklós Kállay – resisted increasingly insistent German demands that its Jews be treated according to German policies and therefore deported to the death camps.

One irony of this situation is that in 1941, Hungarian authorities were directly responsible for the deaths of some 60,000 Jews during several infamous incidents in territories occupied by Hungarian forces. In August of that year, in the wake of Operation Barbarossa, Hungary's army joined German forces in perpetrating significant massacres in the southern Ukrainian communities of Kamenets-Podolsk, Stanislau and Horodenka, where approximately 15,000–16,000 Hungarian Jews were slaughtered.[8] In the northern Serbian town of Novi Sad, some 1,000 Jews were murdered by Hungarian forces, while both in that country and on the Eastern Front, approximately 42,000 male Jews died in the forced labour brigades.[9]

Though Hungary had resisted large-scale actions against its Jews, rhetorically at least the government maintained goals similar to the Germans. On 30 April 1941, Torsten Undén, Sweden's minister in Budapest, reported that Lázslo Bardossy, the (then) newly appointed prime minister, intended to bring his government's anti-Jewish measures more closely into line with that of Germany's.[10] The Swede wrote that for Hungary, 'Some such solution might well only be possible within the framework of a unified European adjustment, but until then, Hungary had to find its own way out'. Most important for the Hungarian government, he noted, was their need to define 'the concept Jew'. If the Hungarians succeeded in doing this, they would, he wrote sympathetically, be able to accomplish

> a complete removal of the Jews from the spiritual, political, cultural and educational circles important in social life, so that neither Jews, half-Jews or their fronts maintained any influence in economic life. On the other hand, it could not be ignored that the nation's almost one million Jews cannot be deprived of all possibilities of existence without creating severe economic and social consequences.[11]

The Swedish diplomat's troubling rhetoric aside, a felicitous change in Sweden's diplomatic representation in Hungary took place when in mid-1942, Undén was replaced by Carl Ivan Danielsson. Danielsson was a veteran diplomat who had served in Spain during the civil war, and who led the Budapest mission until the Russian occupation in early 1945. Danielsson became Wallenberg's boss, and happily had a decidedly more humane attitude towards Jews than did his influential predecessor.

Germany's pressure on Hungary concerning its Jews continued without notable success throughout 1943, even though the countries remained military allies. This cooperation, however, began to unravel after Hungary's army, deficient as an armed force in almost every useful and significant way, suffered a series of severe defeats on the Eastern Front. The catastrophic defeat delivered by the Soviets against the Hungarians in battles along the Don River in Ukraine in 1942 was followed months later by the rout of the Hungarians, Italians and Romanians in the Stalingrad region, facilitating the encirclement of German and Axis forces in that fateful city. These setbacks compelled Hungary's leadership to reappraise their collaboration with Nazi Germany. This, combined with its resistance on Jewish 'questions', were major factors leading to Hitler's decision in late February 1944 to occupy his erstwhile ally.

One example of this resistance to German demands came when Hungary refused to implement the 'yellow star', pointing out that Italy and Romania (two other German allies with their own disparate policies towards their Jews), had not done so. This resistance reached a certain apogee during Kállay's government, by which time it was well known in Hungarian government circles that Jews 'deported to the East' were being murdered, and that some neighbouring countries were treating their Jews harshly.[12] Though a series of discriminatory anti-Jewish measures were passed, Kállay publicly declared (somewhat remarkably) that 'the government will stand up against not only the destruction of the Jews, but against those who see the Jewish question as the only problem in this country'.[13] Hungarian historian Tamás Stark argued that 'Kállay attempted to circumvent German demands for more drastic actions against Jews by procrastinating in carrying them out and trying to gain time. His humanitarian and liberal convictions compelled him to do so, just as did his recognition that the goodwill of Britain and the United States was crucial in the foreign policy he was determined to follow.'[14] This wish to placate the Western Allies even while technically at war with them would continue throughout 1944. Historian Saul Friedländer believes that Kállay was prepared to 'slap the Nazi leader's face' with Hungary's refusal to deport its Jews.[15] This resistance, however, would have fateful consequences.

These consequences became manifest on Sunday, 19 March 1944, when German forces, including SS and Gestapo units, occupied Budapest. Though there remains some disagreement about Hitler's primary motive for the bullying and deceitful diplomacy culminating in his invasion, there is no doubt that Germany's leadership considered the presence of so many Jews still alive in the middle of Europe as an intolerable provocation. Ever since, historians have debated Germany's motives, but significantly Danielsson, Sweden's minister, had at the time no doubt. Germany invaded Hungary, he wrote, because of its 'inability or will to solve the Jewish problem according to the German pattern'.[16]

The Hungarians offered no resistance, and Budapest was quickly rife with both German Gestapo agents and their Hungarian colleagues hunting Jews and other political enemies. The immediate adoption of the 'yellow star' was ordered, with Danielsson reporting:

> The city itself is not occupied by German troops; they are encamped around [it]. On the other hand, Budapest is flooded with SS formations and Gestapo agents, and a merciless hunt is underway for leading Jews ... Diplomatic extra-territoriality has not been respected ... The city is calm but an extremely nervous atmosphere is noticeable, as so many feel unsure for their lives. The Legation is besieged by people, mostly Jews and Poles, who

are requesting asylum or seek a paper [from us] declaring that
they stand under the protection of the Legation.[17]

Though naturally enough Danielsson noted the situation in his
immediate proximity, for the most part in the weeks that followed,
most anti-Jewish actions took place not in the capital but throughout
the Hungarian provinces, including territories occupied since the
beginning of the war. This first phase of the Hungarian Holocaust saw
the rapid assembly, plundering, and (short-lived) ghettoization of more
than a half million Jews. In Budapest the Germans orchestrated the
persecutions, but in the countryside all anti-Jewish actions were organized and conducted by Hungarian authorities, particularly the provincial gendarmerie. Though its role has long been understood, new
research illuminates the critical role played by the highly militarized
gendarmerie, without whom the Germans would have been essentially
powerless to strike against the large Jewish population. Hungarian historian Judith Molnár has written:

> Eichmann and his colleagues needed the cooperation of the local
> administration and the police in addition to that of the gen-
> darmerie ... They needed above all exactly that militarily organ-
> ized, disciplined executive organization, whose members never
> asked questions but carried out their orders, whether these
> actions consisted of confiscating possessions, body-searches, mov-
> ing Jews into ghettos or brick-factories, or crowding them into
> freight cars.[18]

Commencing in mid-May, deportations from throughout Hungary
began northwards, primarily to Auschwitz-Birkenau. Through early
July, almost 440,000 Jewish women, children and (mostly) elderly men
were packed unmercifully into freight wagons, and shipped in inde-
scribably brutal conditions northwards through Slovakia into south-
western Poland. Each day, at the height of this frightful operation,
some 12,000 old men, women and children were sent on this hellish
journey. One historian has noted: 'The speed of deportations from the
Hungarian countryside following occupation was unprecedented ... At
no other point in the Nazi genocide were such a great number of Jews
deported, at such a rapid rate, from so many dispersed locations.'[19]
Another historian observed: 'This was the largest deportation operation during the entire Holocaust, totalling according to the Germans'
own figures, 437,402 Jews in almost 150 trains. Even the deportations
from Warsaw in the summer of 1942 could not match it in magnitude,
much less the complexity of the operation. All this was done under the
command of Adolf Eichmann.'[20]

Upon arrival, the victims tumbled from the wagons onto the infamous dun brown ramp, a space only recently completed within the confines of the camp itself, specifically designed to speed up the murder process. Following 'selection', those chosen to die immediately were moved into the nearby gas chambers. Their plundered bodies were then cremated either in the also recently repaired and improved crematoria, or in open-air pits. Those surviving the deportations and 'selections' were primarily thousands of women deemed fit enough by SS doctors for unendurable, often murderous slave labour.[21]

As noted, the removal of hundreds of thousands from throughout Hungary to the ramp at Auschwitz-Birkenau would have been impossible without wholehearted Hungarian assistance. Confronted with such facts, we may dismiss as fantasy one cliché invariably associated with Wallenberg. It is often said that 'He went to Hungary to save its Jews.' The tragic fact is that by the time Wallenberg arrived in Budapest, approximately 80 per cent of the country's Jews had already been deported and murdered. Of the approximately 1.1 million souls destroyed at Auschwitz-Birkenau, some 35–40 per cent of that total were, according to the latest research, Hungarian citizens.[22]

Another iconic moment from this phase of the Holocaust is the involvement of SS *Obersturmbannführer* (Lt Colonel) Adolf Eichmann. Though the enthusiastic Austrian had been a high-level bureaucrat in Germany's war against the Jews since the mid-1930s – he was, for instance, Heydrich's secretary for the infamous Wannsee Conference of January 1942, and had organized deportations to the death camps in Poland from throughout Europe – it was in Hungary that Eichmann reached the peak of his influence. Commanding in the field his own *Einsatzkommando* (special squad), Eichmann arrived in Budapest on Tuesday, 21 March. He immediately ordered the formation of a 'Jewish Council'. He seemed to enjoy verbally brutalizing its 'members' in his first meetings with them, and set in rapid motion the devastating persecution of the city's large Jewish population.[23] Before his departure to Budapest, SS *Reichsführer* Heinrich Himmler had ordered Eichmann to take his most experienced and dedicated 'desk-top' murderers with him, including such RSHA veterans of the 'Final Solution' as Theodor Dannecker, Dieter Wisliceny, Alois Brunner, Franz Novak, Hermann Krumey and others. Though consisting of between only 150 to 200 men, Eichmann's group had considerable experience in organizing mass deportations. Their expertise was immediately complemented by the enthusiastic cooperation of many within Hungary's political leadership, state and provincial bureaucracies, and the above-mentioned gendarmerie. Another dedicated Nazi sent to Hungary by Himmler was *Obersturmbannführer* Kurt Becher, appointed as the *Reichsführer*'s 'unofficial special envoy on economic affairs'. This intelligent and extravagant criminal would later clash with Eichmann, and would become part of Raoul Wallenberg's contact network in Budapest.

Throughout that spring, Germany's experienced team of Jew-killers guided their Hungarian collaborators through the by now familiar steps of identification and intimidation, isolation, robbery and plunder, assembly and ghettoization. These would be followed rapidly by massive deportations from the Hungarian provinces, already described above. In mere weeks, these perpetrators accomplished what had taken months and years elsewhere in Europe. Braham wrote: 'Eichmann's career was brought to a climax in Hungary, where [he] proved to be at his best. Having the benefit of years of experience in the deportation and extermination program as directed centrally from Berlin, in Hungary he finally had the chance to test his efficiency in the field.'[24] The economic annihilation of Hungarian Jewry was also accomplished during this period, an 'urgent' task accomplished by Germans and Hungarians, who had essentially completed it by the time the Russians arrived. It is useful to understand that this process in Hungary (and elsewhere) was not an anonymous, abstract process but, rather, the result of well-planned decisions taken by the nominal occupiers who empowered thousands of Hungarian officials and policemen to despoil their neighbours. Once these community leaders had fulfilled their lust for robbery, Hungarian civilians completed the process, stripping their neighbours of the little which remained. By the time the countryside was made 'judenrein', their possessions were already in the hands of their fellow, non-Jewish citizens. Hungarian historians G. Kádár and Z. Vági have written:

> The wealth and property of Hungarian Jews was expropriated at unprecedented speed and thoroughness even before the deportations began. The large number of people who were looted and the quantity of the wealth that was seized as well as the speed with which all this was done made the liquidation of the Hungarian Jews a unique chapter in the global history of the Holocaust ... By the spring of 1945, the 250,000 to 300,000 Jewish survivors had lost virtually everything, so in effect economic annihilation was even more successful than physical liquidation.[25]

DEPORTATIONS TO AUSCHWITZ-BIRKENAU ARE HALTED

The end of the first phase and start of the second coincides with the first days of July. By then, a variety of political factors – both domestic and international – convinced Horthy to order, on 6 July, the suspension of all deportations.[26] When considering aspects of mythic memory about Wallenberg and his role in Hungary, it is worth noting the rarely commented-upon fact that Horthy's unexpected decision preceded Wallenberg's arrival in Budapest on 9 July. The cessation of his government's genocidal collaboration with the Germans was *the* central factor in sparing the lives, at least for the time being, of more than 250,000 Jews. Without Horthy's belated decision, there simply would have been no Jews in Budapest for Wallenberg to assist. Here we see, not for the only time, events completely distinct from anything Wallenberg the individual could have done, said or thought playing a decisive role in shaping his story.

We may also note that had Eichmann convinced his Hungarian allies to do things as he wished, there would have been a different outcome, and Wallenberg (again) *would have had nothing to do* in Budapest. Eichmann had argued for a strike against the capital city's Jews first, before emptying the countryside. However, his key Hungarian collaborators, primarily State Secretaries László Baky and László Endre, argued for the reverse. They convinced the Germans that Hungary's security depended on moving first against the far larger numbers in the countryside, not least those in occupied Transylvania. By winning that argument, the by now familiar scenario was created, whereby the Jews from the countryside were deported first, with Budapest 'saved' for last.[27] This outcome of discussions between the perpetrators points to a crucial factor of the Hungarian Holocaust. In Budapest, and even more so elsewhere, the Germans had no choice but to accept the continuation of a significant level of Hungarian sovereignty – occupied Hungary was a very different situation in 1944 than, for example, occupied Poland or Belarus in 1941. Because the Germans lacked the manpower to carry out any large-scale operations against the Jews (in both Budapest and the countryside), the Hungarians had a considerable if not always decisive say in what happened, where and how, within their own borders.[28] If Hitler wanted to accomplish his dual goal of keeping Hungary in the war while exterminating its Jewish population, his representatives in the country could not simply run roughshod over their Hungarian colleagues. Historian Shlomo Aronson has pointed out that this situation resulted in 'A degree of Hungarian sovereignty observed by the Germans, at least on the surface ... it is clear that the Germans were not free to act in the capital without Hungarian consent, especially Horthy's.'[29] As we shall see, this particular circumstance was decisive in determining the effectiveness of neutral diplomacy in the months to come.

This second phase, which was relatively calm, was played out primarily in Budapest, and concluded with the onset of the deadliest

phase for the city's Jews. That third and fateful phase, which commenced on 15 October, was precipitated by Horthy and his government's tragically amateurish attempt to extricate the country from its
alliance with Germany. The goal was to switch to the Soviet side, as
their hated neighbours, the Romanians, had successfully accomplished
in late summer. Announced on the radio around midday by Horthy on
Sunday, 15 October, it failed completely. The result was the immediate
installation into power by the Germans of the *Nyilas*. Led by the apparently not overly intelligent Ferenc Szálasi, the *Nyilas* had long been
frustrated by the Germans' refusal to grant it the reins of power, despite
its allegiance to much if not all Nazi ideology. Since the March occupation, Germany's policy, as formulated by SS general and foreign ministry plenipotentiary Edmund Veesenmayer, had been to keep the more
moderate Hungarian nationalistic and royalist circles around Horthy in
power, rather than foist their own ideological allies onto the Hungarian
state. They did this only for practical considerations, primarily because
the Germans were desperate to keep Hungary's contribution to the Axis
war economy functioning, and they didn't trust Szálasi's *Nyilas* to
accomplish this. By October, Horthy's 'treachery' could no longer be
tolerated, and Veesenmayer was compelled to give executive power to
Szálasi's violent racists.[30] This change was disastrous for Budapest's
Jews, and ultimately fateful for Wallenberg himself.

For the Jews, this final phase was a nightmare of overcrowding and
near-starvation, random and sometimes mass killings, brutal labour
and, for many thousands, prolonged forced marches in winter weath-
er. After experiencing during the summer and autumn some faint hope
that they might survive until the Soviet army arrived, after 15 October,
some tens of thousands of Budapest's Jews were killed. Yet the numerical majority did survive, and finally, by the end of February 1945,
were liberated. As we shall see, it was also during this third phase that
Wallenberg 'entered' history. This is ironic in many ways because if
things had gone the way he planned, he would not even have been in
Budapest after the end of September. Events, however, put paid to his
plans.

THE BACKGROUND TO INTERNATIONAL DIPLOMACY IN BUDAPEST

Two important anomalies of the Hungarian Holocaust are of central
interest to this study, and are connected to the complex reality of how
sovereignty and political power were shared, shaped and contested
between the Germans and Hungarians. Firstly, and most important
for our concerns, is how and why diplomats of several nations and
international institutions tried to assist Jews in various ways in a

German-occupied country. Secondly, and directly related to this international effort, is the willingness of individuals at different levels of Hungary's national government, and Budapest's municipal authorities, to countenance either others helping Jews – the neutrals – or to make the even more unusual decision – during the Holocaust – to help Jews themselves.

The first of these anomalies is of greatest salience for this study. At no other time during the years of destruction do we see such visible, high-level and frequently effective aid given by European diplomats to help Jews survive the Nazis. The action of those 'on the ground', backed by their colleagues in their respective capitals, was from the beginning of the Hungarian Holocaust strengthened by the influential words of several world leaders who protested against events in Budapest – this had not happened since 1933 when Hitler came to power. In no other city during the war did a group of resident diplomats act in concert to assist Jews. They did so for a variety of reasons, and their activities were for all intents and purposes tolerated by the German perpetrators. Again, for a variety of reasons, from late 1942 forward, things were different in Budapest. As one scholar has noted:

> [The] activities ... of the international community ... created an atmosphere conducive to rescue work. [They] issued warnings and protests to the Hungarian authorities about the treatment of the Jews, extended official protection to Jews on Hungarian soil, and worked with local Jewish activists to rescue Jews from deportations and help keep them alive ... Owing in large measure to these activities, a majority of Jews residing in Budapest after the cessation of the first wave of deportations, in July 1944, survived.[31]

Yet in popular memory, and even in some scholarly accounts, it is believed that humanitarian diplomacy on behalf of Jews in Budapest either commenced with Wallenberg's arrival, or that it was moribund beforehand. Although it was highly unusual in wartime Europe for Jews to benefit from either the support of a sovereign government or to receive exemptions from Nazi anti-Jewish measures, in Hungary this occurred before 1944 with some frequency. In fact throughout the Nazi era, small numbers of Jews were consistently objects for negotiation by local officials, or foreigners able to help Jews from different nationalities. During the war some would be, as Yehuda Bauer has written, 'for sale', their lives subject to negotiations between representatives of sovereign governments and Germans officials. Moreover, as the inevitable end neared for Nazi Germany, there was an increased willingness on the part of some Nazi officials to negotiate for the lives of Jews, most prominently and most cynically Heinrich Himmler himself.[32]

Additionally, research has revealed in a way survivor testimony never could that virtually every type of activity conducted by Wallenberg in Budapest was done by others before his arrival, including his 'activation' or 'inspiration' of Jewish self-help. Hungarian historian S. Szita has demonstrated that Zionist groups in Budapest achieved much in terms of organizing assistance and, perhaps most importantly, establishing the notion within Hungarian officialdom that it was neither impossible nor unprecedented for someone, or some organization, to try to help Jews through negotiations with Hungarian civil servants, politicians and policemen.[33]

Before and during 1944, much of this activity originated with the Zionist group known as the Va'ada (Va'adat ha-Ezra ve-ha-Hatzala be-Budapest, the Budapest Relief and Rescue Committee). The various branches of this disparate group were led by such personalities as Reszö Kasztner, Ottó Komoly, Joel and Hansi Brand, Miklos (Moshe) Krausz and others. Wallenberg would come into direct contact with some of these individuals, while others helped pave the way for some of his much better-known activities. As Szita writes:

> By 1944, the Rescue Committee had gained significant experience in the employment of illegal tactics. Zionist principles lay at the root of the committee's resolve and performance; its operations were signified by several forms of resistance to persecution. Its primary resources could be identified as the cohesion and secrecy of its clandestine network of connections, its growing experience and prominence, and the financial support it received via Istanbul and Switzerland.[34]

Their activities included the frequent dispatch of detailed reports on the Hungarian situation to Allied governments and Jewish groups abroad; creating food depots in the city; organizing buildings and other locations as 'protected houses'; negotiating with and bribing Hungarian government officials for respite for some individual Jews (including obtaining release from work and concentration camps); and even convincing Swiss diplomats in Budapest to issue diplomatic papers intended to shield individuals and families from arrest and deportation. These operational precedents established vital banks of information and experience and created, it seems clear, a climate of relatively well-advertised activism on behalf of Jews that was in many ways tolerated by the authorities. However small-scale and clandestine these ideas, schemes and actions may have been, their existence meant that when Wallenberg arrived and the October crisis came to Budapest, he (and others) had 'street-smart veterans' to consult. The Swede used such hard-gained knowledge to great advantage when his time came.

Evidence of high-level Hungarian awareness of these activities can be seen as early as 1942. Hungarian historian L. Karsai quotes Hungarian Prime Minister Miklós Kállay, who in May 1942 wrote that he had heard of Jews, in Slovakian areas under Hungarian administration, who appealed to Hungarian officials for protection from anti-Jewish measures. The Jews sought documents indicating they were exempt from some measures, including deportations. The prime minister wrote to his interior minister: 'It strikes one that Hungarian municipalities issue certificates of residence one after the other for Jews who have for years been living in the territory of Czechoslovakia and/or Slovakia, have even acquired citizenship there, and would never dream of returning to Hungary were it not for the risk of deportation.'[35]

In his missive, Kállay pointed directly to a central issue which explains how neutral and other officials were able to extend protection to Jews who clearly had no previous, or de jure claim to the diplomatic protection of another nation. The protective value any such official document had depended entirely on a declaration of political interest by one sovereign entity to another. Such declarations took place at different bureaucratic levels in different cases and in different countries, often at the local level. This particular factor seems to have disturbed Kállay, as it would any politician keen to keep control of most matters from the centre of power. These crucial declarations of political interest form the core of what I have described as 'bureaucratic resistance', a political method used by the Swedes and others to protect Jews from the implementation of Nazi anti-Jewish policy, and which will be explained below in greater detail.

In fact, Kállay was reiterating to his colleague something that had already happened in Budapest. There we find as early as 1942 a willingness on the part of some officials to view the status of 'foreign Jews' differently from Hungarian Jews. Exemptions from discriminatory measures for some Hungarian Jews that were granted by representatives of foreign governments were accepted by Hungary, primarily those nations with whom the Hungarians sought good relations.[36] As Swedish-Hungarian historian Attila Lajos has demonstrated, the Swiss convinced the important domestic agency KEOKH, Hungary's National Central Authority for Control of Foreigners, to acknowledge the validity of protective papers issued to protect a few Hungarian Jews whom the Swiss considered as their nationals. Swiss diplomat Karl Lutz, stationed in Budapest from early 1942 (he would become an important colleague of Wallenberg's), negotiated then what would later become an issue of critical importance. This diplomatic manoeuvre established a critical precedent for neutral diplomacy in Budapest in 1944.[37] Lajos notes the cardinal importance of establishing this precedent:

already in 1942 Lutz pushed the question of whether the Swiss
Legation could issue Swiss emergency (protective) passports to
foreign citizens in Hungary from nations for which the Swiss
acted as protecting power, and who had lost their original passport. The intention for these passports was to demonstrate that
such persons stood under the protection of the Swiss Legation.
The Hungarian government accepted this Swiss request and
declared ... that they acknowledged these foreign protective passports, conditional upon the foreign legations in question applying
directly to KEOKH.[38]

The importance of this principle being accepted in Budapest is obvious,
yet it has until recently escaped the attention of historians, journalists
and hagiographers of Wallenberg. Lajos makes the additional and equally important point that 'The Hungarian government's willingness to
make a positive gesture toward the Allied states opened the possibility
for representatives of neutral states to issue such passes to a large number of Jews ... Recognition of [their] status as foreign citizens showed
itself to be crucially important for those Jews who obtained it.'[39]

INTERNATIONAL DIPLOMACY BEFORE WALLENBERG'S ARRIVAL

Some years ago, Israeli historian Asher Cohen concluded: 'Except for
a few individual cases, some well known, no significant aid or rescue
was rendered by non-Jews.' And that 'initially, there were no protests
or interventions on behalf of the Jews, either from inside Hungary or
from neutral countries, despite widespread knowledge of the deportations'.[40] Subsequent scholarship demonstrates that this is incorrect, yet
it provides the background to a brief consideration of international
diplomacy in Hungary prior to July 1944.

The Allies viewed Hungary as an integral part of the Axis coalition,
and were determined that it be defeated together with Germany. In the
war's grand strategy Hungary figured but little, yet it came peripherally
into Britain's focus as Churchill tried to convince the Americans to
allow the campaign in Italy to leap over the Adriatic into the Balkans
and push northwards. However, when Germany occupied Hungary in
March 1944, it acquired a greater level of attention from leaders and
diplomats of the Western Allies, the Vatican, the International
Committee of the Red Cross (ICRC) and, of course, the neutrals (primarily Switzerland and Sweden) to a much more significant degree
than before.

Though the Americans formally declared war on Hungary in 1942,
it was not until after March that the US government, and its newly

founded executive agency, the War Refugee Board (WRB), turned their attention to Hungary, and the now perilous situation of its Jews. The WRB was established only in late January 1944, tasked with saving and assisting the remnants of European Jewry. Prodded by the American press, John Pehle, the energetic head of the new agency, convinced President Roosevelt to broadcast a statement specifically warning the Hungarians not to harm its Jews, and threatening post-war retribution for those who collaborated with the Germans. On 26 June, President Roosevelt announced to the Hungarians: 'Hungary's fate will not be like any other civilized nation's ... unless the deportations are stopped.'[41] In this case, however, America's threats could be of only limited use – Hungary was a belligerent state and the US had no possibility of putting a WRB representative in place to provide humanitarian assistance. Indeed, though much has long been made, by many, of Wallenberg's connections with the Americans and the WRB, the evidence makes clear that this has been greatly exaggerated.[42] The Allies, in any case, believed that when hostilities concluded, Hungary would lie in the Soviet sphere, a factor which diminished their interest in what was happening there.

When viewing the Vatican's diplomacy in Budapest we see yet another illuminating anomaly. Historian John Morley has written: 'Hungary may be viewed as unique during the Holocaust because it was the only country in which Pope Pius XII intervened publicly on two occasions, and where the nuncio worked in collaboration with other diplomats.'[43] Led by Nuncio Angelo Rotta, Vatican diplomacy in Hungary differed markedly from the Vatican's overall, deplorably passive response to the Holocaust. Monsignor Rotta was diplomatic doyen in the city; he chose to expand gradually his initial notion of which Jews to help, and later contributed with an increasingly effective activism. Particularly after the advent of the *Nyilas* in October, Rotta's leadership of the city's handful of remaining diplomats became more noticeable, and in some instances made a difference.

Initially, however, Rotta's diplomatic aid to Jews was based on the morally problematic distinction made by the Roman Church between Jews who had been baptized and those who had not. Moreover, negative distinctions were sometimes made between those who had been baptized years earlier, and those who received an 'emergency' baptism. Morley writes that though Rotta protested against the panoply of anti-Jewish measures instituted after the occupation as 'inhumane and un-Christian' and contrary 'to the doctrine of the Gospel ... [He] did not protest against the intrinsic evil of the anti-Jewish decrees but asked only that "moderation" be used in enforcing them. This was a response typical of other Vatican representatives in the face of anti-Jewish laws and actions.'[44] Importantly, however, throughout the first phase of the occupation, Rotta kept the Vatican's Secretariat of State accurately informed of developments, including the imposition of the 'yellow star', and the dire situation in the countryside – including the onset of deportations – as well as that which he described as the 'excessive prudence' of Hungarian Catholic clerics in protesting actions against the Jews.

Rotta appealed directly to Hungarian officials, not waiting for approval from Rome before each decision he made. He was particularly disturbed by what he felt was the Hungarian government's failure to recognize what he called the 'value and effects of baptism', and accused them of 'injustice in refusing to make exemptions for baptized Jews'. Protests worded in this way made it clear to the government that his concerns lay not with all Jews, but primarily with those who were baptized. Addressing Horthy's executive council, Rotta protested: 'The simple fact of persecuting people for the sole reason of their racial origin is a violation of the natural law ... But to take anti-Semitic measures, without taking into account the fact that very many of the Jews by the reception of baptism laws have become Christian, is a grave offence against the Church.'[45] The nuncio did state, however, with admirable frankness: 'Everyone knows what deportation means in practice.' Yet no form of protest, at least until the summer, had much effect on either the Hungarians or their German mentors.

Throughout May and June, the sense of outrage contained in Rotta's messages to Rome increased. They resulted, for the first time since the slaughter of Europe's Jews began in 1941, in a clear and unambiguous public statement of protest by Pope Pius XII.[46] On 25 June, Pius authorized the transmission of a telegram in his name directly to Horthy. He appealed to the regent: '[To use] all possible influence in order to stop the suffering and torments which countless people are undergoing simply because of their nationality or their race.'[47] According to Morley, who was given access to Vatican documents denied other historians, Horthy replied on 1 July, telling Pius that 'he wanted to assure the Pope that he would do all possible [sic] to make sure that humanitarian principles would be maintained'.[48]

Subsequently, Horthy received yet another telegraphed appeal, this time from Swedish King Gustav V. A long-time admirer of Hungary, Gustav based his appeal for mercy for the Jews on the standards of Hungarian humanity, as well as long-standing Swedish and Hungarian ties.[49] While Gustav and the Pope appealed to Horthy's conscience, US president Roosevelt weighed in with a renewed threat of post-war punishment.[50] Though it is unknown which message weighed most heavily on Horthy, the combination clearly had an impact. As noted above, on

6 July he ordered that the deportations should be halted. Morley writes that Pius took particular pleasure in the ostensible effect he believed his appeal had, and ordered his diplomatic service to make sure the world knew of his telegram.

Throughout the Nazi period, the ICRC had for all intents and purposes failed to do anything for European Jews targeted by Germany. As one expert on the organization has written, the ICRC 'made no distinction between Jews and Aryans ... And where others did choose to make a distinction, it was unfortunately not up to the ICRC either to approve or disapprove of the laws enacted against Jews in consequence.'[51] Yet events in Budapest gradually roused the organization out of its indifference, albeit not for many weeks, and finally its representatives in Budapest acted. Led eventually by Swiss diplomat and businessman Frederic Born, by the end of the 1944 the organization was actively helping Jews, both on its own and in concert with the other neutrals. After a month in the city, Born wrote to Geneva: 'I know the extraordinary difficulties facing the ICRC, but the idea of standing by helplessly, powerless to do anything, is almost impossible to bear.'[52] One scholar noted that Born '[showed] organizational talent and an intense desire to aid the Jews ... He [also] requested a large sum of money for the necessary activities, and suggested that funds should be held ready in a special account.'[53] As Wallenberg and others would find out, money made a difference in Budapest.

Born maintained a flow of information to Switzerland about the treatment of the Jews, and he eventually joined his neutral colleagues in lobbying Hungarian officials to ease the ongoing cruelties. They were able to convince Hungarian officials to grant permission allowing official cooperation between the ICRC, the Hungarian Red Cross and Budapest's 'Jewish Council', something which contributed to the 'atmosphere of assistance' which existed, against the odds, in Budapest.[54] One result was the work of Ottó Komoly, a prominent Hungarian Zionist who established 'Section A' of the ICRC. In cooperation with some Christian rescuers, the ICRC eventually housed and assisted some 8,000 Jewish children.[55] Additionally and importantly, the organization abandoned its former apathy in working to obtain permission for official visits to camps and other locations where Jews were assembled. The Hungarians were told that allowing access would lessen the damage their reputation was suffering internationally. Equally as important, after the 15 October coup, Born and his assistants increased their cooperation with other neutral representatives, and contributed to sheltering and assisting Jews in Red Cross houses in both the 'international ghetto', and the larger, more central one established late in 1944. Braham concluded: 'By far the most important contributions of the [ICRC] to the Jewish community in Budapest were the sheltering of children and the safeguarding and supplying of Jewish institutions, including the ghetto, during the *Nyilas* era', including trying to protect, 'a large number of Jewish and non-Jewish institutions – hospitals, public kitchens, homes for the handicapped and the aged, research and scientific institutes, and shops'.[56]

Domestic factors also played a crucial role in bringing about Horthy's decisive shift in attitude. The activities of Interior Ministry State Secretaries László Endre and László Báky, the rabidly anti-Semitic, pro-German collaborators whose role in the fate of the Jews in the countryside was so crucial, finally caused sufficient irritation within the Executive Crown Council that Horthy moved against them. The two officials believed that their close ties to Edmund Veesenmayer were sufficiently strong, and they began plotting Horthy's overthrow. Fortunately they overplayed their hand, and officials loyal to Horthy caught wind of their plans. These officials roused the old admiral into action against the 'Lászlos' before they could move decisively against him.

Yet another factor in Horthy's volte face was that though he cared little for the Jewish multitudes in the countryside and would probably have been content to allow the deportation of most Jews in Budapest, he seems to have retained some sense of connection and allegiance to those prominent Budapest Jews with whom he felt a familiarity. In any case, Horthy's belated decisiveness – which had little to do with regret or humanitarian feelings – essentially ended the deportations to Auschwitz-Birkenau, even though many officials, German and Hungarian, believed that the 'job' remained unfinished. Though Eichmann's still-eager team was helpless without Hungarian manpower, they nonetheless succeeded in deporting some Jews out of the Budapest area in the days after the order to stop. Nonetheless, everyone in the city understood that the halt provided at least temporary salvation for the Jews, even though throughout August, Horthy did consider permitting the resumption of deportations.

Crucially, the halting of the deportations provided a diplomatic manoeuvring 'space' which the neutral diplomats used effectively. It gave them time to act within a political situation which in some ways was developing to their advantage, and it was into this complicated political situation that Wallenberg entered. Yet contrary to popular understanding, Wallenberg could do nothing for 'Hungarian Jewry'. The vast majority were already dead, or trying to survive the ordeal of the camps.[57]

'BUREAUCRATIC RESISTANCE' AND THE HOLOCAUST

In previous work, I have argued for the heuristic value of a theoretical concept which I described as 'bureaucratic resistance' against the implementation of Nazi racial policy. Arguing that this diplomatic response by the Swedes (and others) was a type of resistance which had previously escaped the attention of scholars, this theoretical notion evolved out of my study of the different forms of resistance against the Nazi regime. 'Bureaucratic resistance' was made manifest in UD's diplomatic response to the 'final solution' in many places, not just Budapest.[58] Though my first study concluded just as Wallenberg arrived in Budapest, the relevance of this concept to understanding his story is fundamental. This is not only because of Wallenberg's actual methods, but also because one particular document, the famed *Schutzpass* (protective passport), is one of the iconic symbols invariably connected to his story. This document, which he did not 'invent', plays a role in several of the myths about him. One sees a photocopy or representation of this document in most publications and other media about Wallenberg, and it holds a noteworthy place in collective memory about Wallenberg. Because it has come to symbolize a variety of his diplomatic efforts, the document has achieved virtually totemic status in common memory. For those survivors who themselves received this particular document, it remains a poignant symbol of salvation.[59]

Less well known is that documents similar to 'his' were issued by other neutrals, both before and after he arrived. Even less known is the fact that the *Schutzpass* was just one of several documents issued by the Swedes which were created in Budapest. Though Wallenberg was instrumental in creating *that* particular *Swedish* document, he did not 'invent' the *Schutzpass* in Budapest, nor had anything to do with establishing its all important protective utility there.[60] As noted above, long before Wallenberg arrived, Swiss diplomat Karl Lutz had created a Swiss document also called a *Schutzpass*, which was often issued as a 'collective' document, placing many individuals under the protection of just one piece of paper.

Because the concept of 'bureaucratic resistance' lies at the core of my argument explaining *how* Wallenberg and other Swedish and neutral diplomats were able to aid, assist and save some Jews, a brief review of its history and use is necessary. The use of documents to identify nationality – an identification which might bring protection to individuals and families, or which would identify their belonging to a group to be assaulted, deported or killed – was nothing new for Europe during the Second World War. However, prior to the First World War, such documents were far less common, something which facilitated movement within Europe and the vast waves of emigration from the Old World to the New. But 1914 put an end to such bureaucratic liberties and, ever since, movement between, and often within, nation states is dependent upon possession of a document issued by one's government. The physical possession of an official-looking piece of paper, stamped, sealed, or signed – and increasingly with photographs, although sometimes still without – became obligatory for travellers. As historian James Sheehan wrote: 'The borders over which Europeans had once moved with relative ease were now closely guarded; passports became essential for international travel. Enemy aliens faced internment or expulsion; foreigners were required to have new identity cards.'[61] Even for citizens within the borders of their native country, the successful outcome of an encounter with officialdom, particularly during times of crisis or war, was dependent on an individual possessing some document or another which was 'in order'.[62]

Holocaust literature is replete with stories of Jewish families (and in the first years of Hitler's regime, political refugees) waiting in anguish for their exit and entry visas, and frustrated by the costs and changing procedures of a frightening and Byzantine process. For German Jews during the 1930s, the insertion into their passport of a stamped and signed exit visa, accompanied by the indispensable entry visa to a country or territory of refuge, meant the difference between life and death. In 1938, before the war and the onset of mass murder, American journalist Dorothy Thompson stated with prescience: 'It is a fantastic commentary on the inhumanity of our times that for thousands and thousands of people a piece of paper with a stamp on it is the difference between life and death.'[63] Because 'bureaucratic resistance' worked as it did, particularly in Budapest as physically manifested by the various neutral documents, we can note the striking historical irony that one of history's most ideologically vicious regimes spared the lives of some few Jews based on paper documents of dubious legality. Such, however, was the European mentality during the 1930s and 1940s – a piece of paper held in one's hand could mean life, because it just might cause a threatening official to give way.

Before the systematic killing of Jews began in June 1941, tens of thousands of Jews and others were assisted and saved by possessing 'visas for life', issued by such diplomats as the Briton Frank Foley in Prague, Japanese diplomat Chiune Sugihara in Lithuania, Portuguese diplomat Aristides de Sousa Mendes in France and the American Varian Fry, also in France. In literature about these men, one often sees them compared with Wallenberg, often with specific reference to the use of documents.[64] Though after 1941, possession of only an entry visa was rarely sufficient for protection (soon after the war began,

Germany stopped issuing exit visas of any kind for Jews), physical possession of a passport or other document issued by a nation with which Germany maintained diplomatic relations could, and did, serve to protect. In Budapest, as we shall see, possession of a piece of paper could be the difference between life, deportation, or being shot into the Danube River.

In Sweden's case the historical ironies of this 'paper chase' are sharp, and relatively unknown. Prior to autumn 1942, the Swedish government resolutely erected 'paper walls' to keep Jews out. With the onset in late 1942 of the 'Final Solution' in Norway, through to the end of the war, Swedish officials no longer required that Jews should possess 'papers in order' to gain refuge. Interestingly, some of the same UD officials, who after 1942 were involved in issuing documents intended to protect Jews, were also part of Sweden's earlier and highly effective policy of keeping borders sealed solely through bureaucratic and diplomatic means. After the *Anschluss* but before *Reichkristallnacht*, several of these individuals were directly involved in the negotiations which compelled Nazi Germany – against the Nazis' own wishes – to mark passports possessed by German and Austrian Jews with a special stamp marking the holder as Jewish. Arguing that such a marking was necessary for the maintenance of Stockholm's 'refugee' policy, Swedish officials asked the Germans to produce a readily visible mark in passports which would allow their consular and border officials to recognize easily Jews who entered legations and consulates seeking entry visas, or when they showed up at border posts. Holders of passports branded with this infamous large, red 'J' were virtually certain to be denied entry visas by the Swedes. The successful conclusion of these negotiations in late 1938 meant that thousands of Jews could not obtain refuge in Sweden – even if they only wanted to transit the country on their way elsewhere. Also of interest is the fact that at the same time that officials in Stockholm were prodding their German counterparts to produce a special passport marking enabling them to distinguish Jews from 'Aryan' German travellers, Swiss officials were also engaged in negotiations with German officials, seeking exactly the same thing.

Today, the fundamental continuity of much of Germany's bureaucratic structure from Weimar to Nazi Germany is unquestioned. This traditional and powerful social force was staffed by thousands of men educated and employed long before Hitler came to power. It was their presence which made Germany's renowned bureaucracy function in 1942 much as it had functioned in, say, 1927 during the Weimar era. Whether throwing up bureaucratic barriers, allowing the regulated (and heavily taxed) flight of hundreds of thousands, or stripping Jews of their assets and homes, Germany's bureaucratic structure was remarkably consistent in form and function. It remained so when the goal was organized genocide. Because 'bureaucratic resistance' as conducted by the Swedes and others utilized existing bureaucratic structures and procedures, and because they maintained in their communications with German officials the formalized rituals, both verbal and written, of normative diplomacy, Swedish and other neutral diplomats were able to block, at some times and some places, the lethal implementation of Nazi racial ideology.

They were able to do this because even in Nazi Germany, and even amongst officials engaged in genocide, a space existed which could be exploited by another bureaucrat. This manoeuvring space within the global ideology of death was utilized throughout the Holocaust – in individual cases between 1941 and 1944 by Swedes in several cities in Europe, and then by Swedes and others on a literally massive scale in Budapest in 1944 and 1945. Historian Raul Hilberg noted: 'Every bureaucrat knows, of course, that open defiance of orders is serious business, but he also knows that there are many ingenious ways of evading orders. In fact, the opportunities for evading them increase as one ascends in the bureaucracy. Even in Nazi Germany, orders were disobeyed, and they were disobeyed even in Jewish matters.'[65] As sociologist Fred Katz observed:

> Bureaucrats do have considerable autonomy ... many forms of [which] are built into the structure of bureaucratic organizations. Such autonomy is part of the very fabric of bureaucracies ... When Nazi bureaucrats said they were merely following orders, they were hiding the fact that they had considerable amounts of autonomy.[66] [Because of the success of bureaucratic resistance, we can today speak not only of 'desk-top killers' during the Holocaust, but also of 'desk-top rescuers'.]

Because Swedish diplomats were recognized by their German counterparts as fully authorized officials carrying the mandate of their nation's sovereignty, Swedish diplomats were able to resist the full implementation of some Nazi anti-Jewish measures by injecting a credible claim into the available bureaucratic 'space'. They did this beginning in autumn 1942, first for some Norwegian Jews, and eventually for those of other nationalities. Help was given most often for an individual or family, and in the Swedish case, never for large groups of Jews. In Hungary, those negotiating with the perpetrators represented neutral nations which maintained diplomatic relations with both Budapest and Berlin. Crucially, throughout almost all of 1944, all parties endeavoured to maintain these diplomatic links. As a result, claims of political interest 'even' for Jews (something looked upon with some astonishment by German officials) were not founded upon one official 'pleading' for 'a Jewish life', but rather upon normative diplomatic precedence and mutually recognized bureaucratic procedure. By emphasizing to their counterparts – again, in Budapest but also in Berlin and elsewhere – that the Swedish government had a *political interest* in the welfare of an individual, or family, the Swedish diplomatic 'rescuer' minimized discussions about the 'racial value' of those they sought to protect. And though it was rarely stated directly, it was made clear to the putative perpetrator that he had a political and procedural interest in listening to the appellant; failure to grant their requests would disturb normal diplomatic relations, both between individual officials and, further on, between their nations.[67] Everything depended on the willingness of the neutral diplomat or official making an official, mutually recognized political claim for the protection of Jewish individuals, families, or groups. In Budapest, such political claims extended to buildings sheltering hundreds of Jews. We also know that there were some nationalities, primarily the neutrals, whom the Germans did not deport.

Essentially, the vital claim of political interest expressed by Sweden (and other neutral powers in Budapest) for Jews clearly of Hungarian nationality was made manifest through the ostensible transference of citizenship. Hungarian Jews were made into 'Swedes' by the mere issuance of a piece of paper, and upon that issuance, a claim was made that the person in question was now under the protection of Sweden, and therefore not liable to laws and measures endured by 'real' Hungarian Jews. In Budapest, physical possession of a 'foreign' document held by a person everyone knew was in fact Hungarian gave material evidence of the political interest of a foreign power in the treatment of the individual. This 'transfer of citizenship' made these 'former' Hungarian citizens eligible for the protections enjoyed by 'regular' nationals. When conducting 'bureaucratic resistance', Swedish diplomats placed their 'good offices' – in all its forms – between the perpetrator and victim. In Budapest the procedure was often remarkably ad hoc and definitely unprecedented in its scale. Sometimes it worked and sometimes it failed, but the direct result of this political minuet in Budapest, danced between Hungarians, Germans, Swedes, Swiss and others, was the shielding and saving of tens of thousands of Jewish lives.

Prior to 1944, the Swedes used this tactic in several cities to forestall the deportation of individuals and families, for they understood that if they could be kept from being forced onto a transport, there was a better chance of survival. Before Hungary, the Germans were in fact reluctant to deport citizens of nations with whom they maintained diplomatic relations. Indeed, even during the deportations from the countryside, there are accounts of neutral papers having some protective value, and that in at least several instances possession of such documents did keep some individuals from being loaded onto the cattle cars.[68]

In Budapest, between July 1944 and January 1945, the practice of 'bureaucratic resistance' reached its life-saving height. In that city's unique circumstances, 'bureaucratic resistance' became both theoretically more possible and practically more visible and effective than anywhere else during the Holocaust. It sometimes even manifested itself in physical, sometimes dramatic, circumstances. Wallenberg did on at least several occasions remove Jews from assembly points in Budapest and from death marches when, according to eyewitnesses, he and other diplomats loudly and publicly asserted their right as foreign diplomats to shield 'their citizens'.[69]

Interestingly, there is evidence that a rough hierarchy of the value of international protective papers existed, even among the *Nyilas*. Swedish 'bureaucratic resistance' tactics were enhanced because it was widely believed, by all sides, that they had a higher protective value than most other neutral papers. Braham has noted that Swedish papers gained this additional measure of protective value because of the country's favourable standing in the minds of Hungarian and German officials. This positive perception was particularly evident amongst Hungarian officials, due to the well-known humanitarian assistance their country received directly from Sweden after the First World War. This beneficial perception was enhanced because Wallenberg and the other Swedes negotiated far more often with Hungarian officials than German. Swedish diplomats and their requests were further aided by the fact that Sweden represented Hungarian interests in belligerent countries. On the other hand, as we shall see, by the end of December, Hungarian anger at Sweden's refusal to grant even de facto diplomatic recognition made all things Swedish more vulnerable to the anger of individual Hungarian officials who were in some way wronged by Stockholm, and thus determined to have their revenge.[70] Although Swiss papers had some of the same 'attributes' as Swedish documents, it seems the latter were in fact considered the most valuable. Vatican, ICRC, Spanish and El Salvadorian documents were all 'ranked' lower. In fact, things were made simultaneously both more difficult and easier for the Swedes because the persecutors themselves, particularly the Hungarians, failed to maintain a consistent response to the various documents. In describing the manner in which the Hungarian bureaucracy dealt with Swedish requests, one Swedish diplomat wrote that 'the left hand commonly does not know what the right hand is doing'.[71] These bureaucratic inconsistencies only deepened with time.

Additionally, there seems little question that the mere possession of an impressive diplomatic document issued by a foreign power had an important psychological effect on its bearer, even if it was forged. As one member of the Zionist underground remembered:

> The forged documentation in itself did not provide sufficient protection during street inspections ... [but they] had psychological value; it gave its holder the basis for a confident facade since anyone who did not appear natural and confident would not be saved even if he had a document in his pocket. [And] one needed to know which document to present and when to present it. During a street inspection, if someone took out a sheaf of papers, he was immediately suspect.[72]

In addition to the actual manner in which 'bureaucratic resistance' worked, there is another factor, also somewhat theoretical, which influenced attitudes in Budapest throughout 1944. Everyone, not least the sophisticated European bureaucrats who populate this study, understood by then that Germany was losing the war, later if not sooner. Unsurprisingly, this influenced in a positive direction some decisions taken by the perpetrators. Some years ago, German historian Hans Mommsen explained that integral to the success of anti-Jewish policies conceived and implemented by Nazi Germany was a process he labelled 'cumulative radicalization'. This notion demonstrates convincingly that with each step 'successfully' taken against the Jews, which had previously seemed morally impossible (if not unthinkable), the next, always more radical step was thus made easier to imagine and implement. With the piercing of each successive barrier of imagination, moral barriers deteriorated decisively. This psychological process – which was both collective and individual – was crucial, Mommsen argued, in bringing about the destruction of European Jewry. What Mommsen did not posit, but what the evidence makes clear did occur within the Nazi bureaucracy of destruction, is that this process also had an apogee. This peak was followed by a period of relatively lessening radicalism. This relative decline in the 'urge' to commit genocide can be seen in Budapest in the responses of both German and Hungarian bureaucrats, particularly the latter.[73]

As the war seemed to be reaching its inevitable conclusion, these murderous bureaucrats increasingly understood that those found responsible for the murder of Jews and others would be held to account by the victorious Allies. As historian Peter Black has pointed out, even Nazi officials at the highest levels were influenced by the tides of war. 'The loyal, somewhat realistic National Socialist was torn between his emotional and psychological need to keep the faith and a desire to insure his own personal survival ... the well-publicized intentions of the Allies to try Nazi leaders for war crimes moved some SS leaders to contemplate an alternative solution.'[74] Indeed, because of their lack of ideological conviction, Hungarian bureaucrats were even more susceptible to thoughts of post-war punishment. This made many of them even more amenable to negotiating with their neutral counterparts than were their German mentors. As noted, Wallenberg and the other neutral diplomats negotiated far more with Hungarian officials at different ministries and different ranks than they did with key German ideologues, most of whom seemed never to have lost their eagerness to kill Jews.

'Armed' with this method in Budapest, Wallenberg maintained and in some ways expanded 'bureaucratic resistance' to unprecedented and rarely repeated proportions. However, in order to fully understand exactly what he did and how he did it, we must survey in detail what his colleagues in Budapest had accomplished prior to the arrival in that city of the novice diplomat. In doing so, some of the more prominent myths about Wallenberg will be dispelled.

NOTES

1. R.L. Braham, 'The Holocaust in Hungary: A Retrospective Analysis', in R.L. Braham and S. Miller (eds), *The Nazis' Last Victims: The Holocaust in Hungary* (Detroit, MI: Wayne State University Press, 1998), p.27.
2. D. Cesarani, *Eichmann: His Life and Crimes* (London: William Heinemann, 2004), p.161 and p.168. RSHA is the acronym for Nazi Germany's main 'security' organization, responsible for planning and conducting the destruction of European Jewry. Organized and first led by Reinhard Heydrich, it was headed by Austrian policeman Ernst Kaltenbrunner, after the former's assassination in spring 1942, until the end of the regime.
3. J.-C. Favez, *The Red Cross and the Holocaust*, edited and translated by J. Fletcher and B. Fletcher (Cambridge University Press: Cambridge, 1999), p.238.
4. W.S. Churchill, cited in Braham, 'The Holocaust in Hungary', p.37.
5. R.L. Braham, 'Keynote Address', in R.L. Braham and B. Chamberlin (eds), *The Holocaust in Hungary: Sixty Years Later* (Boulder, CT: Social Science Monographs, 2006), p.xxiv.
6. A. Pók, 'Germans, Hungarians and the Destruction of Hungarian Jewry', in Braham and Miller, *Nazi's Last Victims*, p.49.
7. A naval officer during the Austro-Hungarian empire, Horthy led the counter-revolution of 1919 against the short-lived 'Soviet' government of Hungarian communists. Obtaining the position of regent, Horthy would be Hungary's head of state until late 1944.
8. T. Stark, *Hungarian Jews During the Holocaust and After the Second World War, 1939–1949: A Statistical Review*, trans. C. Rozsnyai (Boulder, CT: East European Monographs, 2000), p.14.
9. Braham, 'The Holocaust in Hungary', p.34.
10. During the war, and before, Sweden labelled its foreign emissaries 'ministers' rather than ambassadors. The building itself was a 'Legation' rather than an 'embassy'. Both older

terms, now anachronistic, are used throughout this study. Interestingly if entirely coincidentally, T. Undén was the brother of the more illustrious Östen Undén, then a high-level official in Sweden's government, and later long-serving foreign minister. More poignantly, it was during Östen's tenure as foreign minister immediately after the war that Sweden did little, if anything, to try to get Raoul Wallenberg released from Soviet custody.

11. T. Undén to C. Günther, no.86, 30 April 1941, Riksarkivet Utrikesdepartementet (Swedish National Archives, Stockholm, Sweden) 1920 års series (The Foreign Office's 1920 dossier series) (hereafter RA UD), Hp 1 Eu 581, folder 17.
12. L. Kársai, 'The Fateful Year: 1942 in the Reports of Hungarian Diplomats', in Braham and Chamberlin (eds), *Holocaust in Hungary*, pp.3–6.
13. M. Kállay, cited in ibid., p.13.
14. T. Stark, *Hungarian Jews During the Holocaust*, pp.15–16. Hungarian historian L. Kársai agrees with Stark's appraisal; see ibid., p.14.
15. M. Kállay, cited in S. Friedländer, *The Years of Extermination: Nazi Germany and the Jews, 1939–1945* (New York: Harper Collins, 2007), p.484.
16. I. Danielsson to UD, no.28, 23 March 1944, RA UD, Hp 1 Eu 58 2, folder 21.
17. I. Danielsson to C. Günther, no.58, 21 March 1944, RA UD, Hp 21 Eu 1094, folder 1.
18. J. Molnár, 'Gendarmes before the People's Court', in Braham and Chamberlin (eds), *Holocaust in Hungary*, p.148.
19. A. Cohen, 'The Dilemma of Rescue or Revolt', in Braham and Miller (eds), *Nazis' Last Victims*, p.125.
20. See Chapter 7 of Y. Lozowick, *Hitler's Bureaucrats: The Nazi Security Police and the Banality of Evil*, trans. H. Watzman (London and New York: Continuum, 2002). The figures, compiled by Edmund Veesenmayer, Germany's top official in Budapest, are given on p.253.
21. An oddity of the Hungarian Holocaust is that a significant proportion of men aged between their late teens and old age survived. Most of these survived while enduring the brutal conditions in the 'labour brigades'. Many such 'units' remained on Hungarian soil rather than being sent to the Eastern Front. In spring 1944, those older men and younger boys who remained in villages and cities were deported and murdered.
22. G. Kádár and Z. Vági, *Self-Financing Genocide: The Gold Train, the Becher Case and the Wealth of Hungarian Jews*, trans. E. Koncz, J. Tucker and A. Kádár (Budapest: Central European University Press, 2001), p.xxiii.
23. See Cesarani, *Eichmann: His Life and Crimes*, for a detailed description and analysis of Eichmann's tour of duty in Budapest.
24. R.L. Braham, *The Politics of Genocide: The Holocaust in Hungary*, revised and enlarged edn (Boulder, CT: Rosenthal Institute for Holocaust Studies Graduate Center/City University of New York Social Science Monographs, 1994), vol. 1, p.415.
25. Kádár and Vági, *Self-Financing Genocide*, pp.xxiv–xxv.
26. Though 7 July was for a long time the date considered by historians and others to be the day of suspension, Lászlo Kársai insists that the actual date is 6 July. Lecture by Dr L. Kársai, 1 March 2007, Open Society Archives, Budapest, Hungary.
27. Lecture by Dr L. Kársai, see n.26 above.
28. In fact throughout occupied Europe during the Holocaust, the Germans lacked the necessary manpower to do things all on their own. In the event, they were able to count on the assistance, virtually everywhere, of their fellow Europeans.
29. S. Aronson, *Hitler, the Allies and the Jews* (Cambridge: Cambridge University Press, 2004), p.220 and p.285.
30. The fact that the Hungarian government never completely lost political sovereignty over its country explains much about the ability of neutral diplomats to operate successfully in holocaustal Budapest. Much more on this in following chapters.
31. R. Rozett, 'International Intervention: The Role of Diplomats in Attempts to Rescue Jews in Hungary', in Braham and Miller (eds), *Nazis' Last Victims*, p.137.
32. The best analysis of this issue remains Y. Bauer, *Jews for Sale? Nazi–Jewish Negotiations, 1933–1945* (New Haven, CT: Yale University Press, 1994). See also Aronson, *Hitler, the Allies and the Jews*.
33. Much of the following information comes from S. Szita, *Trading in Lives? Operations of the Jewish Relief and Rescue Committee in Budapest, 1944–1945*, trans. S. Lambert (Budapest and New York: Central European University Press, 2005), pp.1–20.
34. Ibid., p.17.

35. M. Kállay, cited in Kársai, 'Fateful Year', p.9–10.
36. This particular theme, of Hungary's inclination to grant exemptions in order to further relations with other nations, gained acute prominence during the second half of 1944.
37. The diplomacy of Karl Lutz and the Swiss will be discussed in later chapters. In the meantime, we may note the historical curiosity that Lutz, like Wallenberg, had also spent time in both the United States and Palestine. Lutz represented Switzerland in both places while Wallenberg was still a student and apprentice banker.
38. A. Lajos, *Hjälten och Offren: Raoul Wallenberg och judarna i Budapest* (Växjö: Svenska Emigrantinstitutets skriftserie, no. 15, 2003), p.73.
39. Ibid., pp.73–4.
40. Cohen, 'Dilemma of Rescue or Revolt', p.125.
41. See www.scrapbookpages.com/BergenBelsen/bergenbelsen06.html.
42. For more on this, see Chapter 5.
43. J.F. Morley, 'Pius XII, Roman Catholic Policy, and the Holocaust in Hungary: An Analysis of *Le Saint Siege et les victims de la guerre, janvier 1944–juillet 1945*', in C. Rittner and J. Roth (eds), *Pope Pius XII and the Holocaust* (London and New York: Leicester University Press, 2002), p.156.
44. Ibid., p.158.
45. A. Rotta, cited in ibid., p.160.
46. Morley believes that this information, strengthened by a direct appeal from the American WRB, overcame the Pope's articulated reluctance to make a public statement.
47. Cited in J. Cornwall, *Hitler's Pope: The Secret History of Pius XII* (London: Viking, 1999), p.325.
48. Morley, 'Pius XII', p.164.
49. The telegram was delivered to Horthy on 3 July, and not by Raoul Wallenberg. Details of this highly unusual episode in Swedish diplomatic history are discussed in the following chapter.
50. Twice earlier, on 24 March and 12 June, the American government threatened Hungary with post-war retribution.
51. Favez, *The Red Cross and the Holocaust*, p.236.
52. F. Born, cited in ibid., p.237.
53. A. Ben-Tov, *Facing the Holocaust in Budapest: The International Committee of the Red Cross and the Jews in Hungary, 1943–1945* (Dordrecht, Boston and London: Martinus Nijhoff, 1988), p.449, n.32.
54. Rozett, 'International Intervention', p.142.
55. Ibid., p.142.
56. Braham, *The Politics of Genocide*, vol. 2, p.1211.
57. Though Budapest's Jews received this fateful reprieve, we should note that when the city was liberated in January/February 1945, approximately 60,000–65,000 Jews had either been murdered or died of disease, hunger or other causes.
58. See P.A. Levine, *From Indifference to Activism: Swedish Diplomacy and the Holocaust, 1938–1944*, 2nd edn (Uppsala: Studia historica Upsaliensia, 1998), Chapter 2, and passim. Studies published since 1996 have confirmed the existence and utility of this concept.
59. Many survivors have kept their *Schutzpass*, and are passing it as an heirloom to their descendents. Others have donated originals to public institutions such as Holocaust museums.
60. In fact, the document itself (it is uncertain where, and by which firm(s), the actual sheets were printed), is incorrect. As can be seen in plate no. 14, the Swedish national symbol, *Tre Kronor*, is upside down! Two crowns should top one, instead of the opposite as this renowned famous document shows it.
61. J. Sheehan, *The Monopoly of Violence: Why Europeans Hate Going to War* (London: Faber & Faber, 2007), p.82.
62. M. Marrus, *The Unwanted: European Refugees in the Twentieth Century* (New York: Oxford University Press, 1985), pp.92–4.
63. D. Thompson, cited in B.-A. Zucker, *In Search of Refuge: Jews and US Consuls in Nazi Germany 1933–1941* (Vallentine Mitchell: London, 2001), p.172. Much analysis of the American and British response to Nazi persecution of the Jews prior to 1939 centres around the story of 'paper walls' – bureaucratic barriers which kept Jews from obtaining refuge. See, for instance, D. Wyman, *Paper Walls: America and the Refugee Crises, 1938–1941* (New York: Pantheon, 1985).

64. Often called the 'Wallenberg' of their respective countries, the story of these men has received great attention as well. On Sugihara, see H. Levine, *In Search of Sugihara, The Elusive Japanese Diplomat Who Risked His Life to Rescue 10,000 Jews from the Holocaust* (New York: Free Press, 1996), and P. Rotner Sakamoto, *Japanese Diplomats and Jewish Refugees: A World War II Dilemma* (Westport, CT: Greenwood Press, 1998). Fry's story is told by S. Eisenberg, *A Hero of Our Own: The Story of Varian Fry: How One American in Marseille Saved Marc Chagall, Max Ernst, Andre Breton, Hannah Arendt, and More Than a Thousand Others from the Nazis* (New York: Random House, 2001), and by Fry himself, *Surrender on Demand* (Boulder, CT: Johnson Books, 1997).

65. R. Hilberg, *The Destruction of the European Jews: The Revised and Definitive Edition* (New York: Schocken Books, 1987), vol. 3, p.1024.

66. F. Katz, 'The Implementation of the Holocaust: The Behavior of Nazi Officials', in M. Marrus (ed.), *The Nazi Holocaust* (Westport, CT: Meckler, 1989), vol. 3, p.357.

67. In Norway, Swedish diplomat Claes Westring even succeeded in diplomatically shielding some Jews in internment camps, based on nothing other than the handing over of an application form for Swedish citizenship. See Levine, *From Indifference to Activism*, Chapter 7.

68. See Lozowick, *Hitler's Bureaucrats*, p.251. Lozowick writes that in some instances the Germans respected neutral papers in order to avoid protests by neutral diplomats in Budapest.

69. Such instances were, however, far less frequent than generally believed. More on this in subsequent chapters.

70. At Christmas, the Swedish Legation in Buda was attacked and plundered by *Nyilas* militia.

71. I. Danielsson to UD, Memorandum no.8, 17 May 1944, RA UD, Hp 21 Eu 1095, folder 4.

72. See D. Gur's testimony in R. Benshalom, *We Struggled for Life: Zionist Youth Movements in Budapest, 1944*, trans. O. Cummings and R. Rubin (Jerusalem and New York: Geffen, 2001), pp.141–2.

73. See Levine, *From Indifference to Activism*, especially Chapter 2.

74. P. Black, *Ernst Kaltenbrunner: Ideological Soldier of the Third Reich* (Princeton, NJ: Princeton University Press, 1984), pp.218–19.

4

April–May: Swedish Diplomacy in Budapest Prior to Wallenberg's Arrival

I hereby respectfully request that the Royal Foreign Office ask the Swedish Legation in Budapest to inquire about my wife's relatives; father, mother, brother-in-law, sister and nephew ... I have heard that in a similar case in Holland, those concerned whose relatives were Swedish citizens, temporarily received Swedish citizenship and therefore the possibility of receiving exit visas.[1]

Now King Gustaf has sent an appeal to Admiral Horthy in Budapest to use his influence to save Hungarian Jews from further persecution ... these methods are by now well known. It is known that Jews are transported in over-crowded freight cars. These transports take many lives ...[2]

SWEDISH DIPLOMACY DURING THE HOLOCAUST

One of the most enduring myths about Wallenberg is that Swedish diplomatic activity on behalf of Jews in Hungary began with his arrival on history's stage. The hagiographic publications and other forms of popular representation present Wallenberg as solely, and wholly, responsible for Sweden's diplomacy in Budapest. This is incorrect. Such simplistic narratives rely on the mistaken notion that he came into a diplomatic vacuum, filled it with the force of his charismatic personality, and single-handedly saved '100,000' Jews. Even some scholars have written that Sweden's diplomatic efforts commenced on 9 July 1944.[3]

As the editorial cited in the second epigraph above makes clear (as do many other sources), it was already a matter of public knowledge that the highest levels of Swedish society and government were involved in the effort to help Jews long before July. Even after the occupation, accurate information flowed out of Hungary. By mid-June 1944, newspaper readers in Sweden and throughout the Allied democracies knew quite a bit about the plight of Hungary's Jews. As noted previously, the world 'watched' as most Hungarian Jews were deported and exterminated, which was not the case with most previous episodes of the genocide of European Jewry.

Nor is there any doubt that Sweden's diplomatic activities to assist some Jews in Budapest began prior to the March occupation. Minister Carl Ivan Danielsson, assisted by his highly able and energetic younger colleague, First Secretary Per Anger, were active in assisting a few Jews. They did so using the diplomatic methods described in the previous chapter. Crucially, as will be shown, their ability (and subsequently Wallenberg's) to respond and help was led and directed by Undersecretary (*utrikesrådet*) Gösta Engzell, who headed UD's Legal Division.

Engzell was a paradigmatic Swedish civil servant – highly educated, well-schooled in Swedish consensus politics and protective of his country's interests. As I have argued previously, there is no doubt that this single government official was most responsible for reshaping Sweden's previously ungenerous and sometimes cruel response to the campaign against European Jewry. What makes Engzell's response after 1942 to the Nazis' war against the Jews even more fascinating is that he had earlier played a significant role in shaping the government's ungenerous response to the plight of German (and Austrian) Jews.[4] That notwithstanding, after Sweden quietly accepted in late 1942 those Norwegian Jews who managed to escape, Engzell crafted, with a firm and humanitarian hand, Sweden's response to the ongoing genocide – one visible both geographically and chronologically. Throughout 1943 and into 1944, he encouraged UD diplomats in Berlin, Prague, Vichy, Copenhagen and elsewhere to exploit a growing number of 'cases' where, these bureaucrats came to understand, their status as Swedish diplomats enabled them to intervene on behalf of some Jews. Sometimes they succeeded in securing their freedom or helped to ward off deportation. Sometimes they failed. The numbers of individuals involved in these unprecedented diplomatic efforts were always minimal, but the signal sent to the perpetrators, victims and bystanders alike was significant.

This series of individual efforts throughout 1943 blossomed into what became in early October 1943 Sweden's publicly declared acceptance of those Jews in Denmark able to flee to safety across the water of the Öresund. This dramatic event, one supported with quiet acceptance by Sweden's Prime Minister Per Albin Hansson and his cabinet, established an atmosphere within UD which made it possible for the nation's diplomatic apparatus to continue helping Jews when possible.

Meanwhile in Budapest, Danielsson and Anger were well informed both about what had happened elsewhere to Europe's Jews, and the vagaries of Hungary's accelerating persecution of its Jewish population. Benefiting from a surprisingly active daily press, denizens of Budapest could also read of the increasing political and military tensions between

Hitler's Germany and the Magyar nation. All were aware of the advances being made from both east and west by Allied armies. This situation further highlighted Hungary's many vulnerabilities.

SWEDEN'S BUDAPEST DIPLOMACY COMMENCES

In January 1944, two months before Hitler moved against his nominal ally, Danielsson sent a report to Stockholm stating: 'The Israelite portion of the population appears to fear above all a German occupation and subsequent Jewish persecution.'[5] Acting on this judgement and with Engzell's support, he and Anger began assisting at least one Jewish family. The criterion for providing help was sufficiently strong connections, personal or professional, to genuine Swedish citizens, or Swedish companies active in Hungary.[6] Contrary to previous policy and practice during the first years of the Holocaust, UD officials now made no attempt to shield from the public their efforts to help some Jews. That members of the public were aware of assistance being provided is clear from the ever-increasing numbers of letters received by UD containing desperate appeals and pleas for help for relatives, friends and business associates on behalf of Jews in Hungary. One appeal eventually came from as far away as Utah in the United States. These fascinating and often poignant documents – those penned by appellants and UD's many responses – put to rest any notion that Wallenberg was the sole innovator of Sweden's creative diplomacy on behalf of Budapest Jews. Indeed, Swedish diplomacy in Budapest was played out on a much broader stage than any single individual could have accomplished. The diplomacy conducted by Wallenberg and his colleagues, accompanied by other neutral diplomats doing similar things, became a nuanced and sophisticated blend of bluff, bravado, bureaucratic cleverness, and quiet but effective moral outrage.

One individual case which exemplifies Sweden's diplomacy in Budapest before Wallenberg's arrival is a 'minor' one – except of course for the family concerned. It is worth examining because it sheds light on the tactics and motivations which informed this diplomatic activity, and because it also illuminates the practice, precedent and circumstance which came to constitute much of Wallenberg's own activities.

Eva and Alice Eisman were two young women whose parents left Hungary before the war. Father Josef and his wife (who is unnamed in the documentation) arrived first in Denmark (it is unclear if they were considered refugees or not), and subsequently were amongst those Jews who fled to Sweden in October 1943.[7] Even though the parents left Budapest legally in 1938, for some reason Hungarian authorities refused to allow the daughters to join them, and the family remained separated for years. Naturally the parents lived in terror, fearing for their daughters' safety, and some three months after arriving in southern Sweden, Josef Eismann wrote to Gösta Engzell. 'The war is getting closer to Hungary now, and our fears increase that in spite of everything, our daughters may be deported.'[8] He continued: 'Here in Sweden we have received work ... We could live calmly if not for our daughters' sake. For more than five years we have suffered from the fear that our daughters would be deported and perish, and ... have never had a peaceful day or night. With the deepest respect I therefore request that our daughters Eva and Alice may receive all possible help so that they may leave Hungary and come to Sweden.'[9]

Meanwhile, the daughters learned that their parents were in Sweden, and contacted the Legation in Budapest. After receiving Josef's letter, Engzell wrote to Danielsson, instructing him to renew contact with the young women to inquire 'whether the fears of the parents are justified'. Engzell added: 'Because they are Hungarian citizens it hardly appears possible for the Legation to take any measures which would facilitate their departure from Hungary.'[10] Danielsson quickly replied that the women had again visited the Legation, telling him that they had spoken by telephone with their father, who informed them that an application for Swedish citizenship was submitted for them. This step, it was hoped, would induce the Hungarian authorities to permit them to leave. Meanwhile, Engzell accelerated the whole process and instructed Danielsson to issue emergency (*provisorisk*) passports for the daughters. Everyone involved now hoped that possession of documents indicating Swedish citizenship would enable German transit visas to be obtained and, with them, an assurance of safe passage to Sweden.[11] Yet nothing happened for several weeks, and on 19 March, the situation worsened radically.[12]

Josef Eisman understood well the meaning of the German occupation for his daughters, and on Tuesday 21 March he violated travel rules for refugees in Sweden and went to Stockholm to obtain an audience with Engzell.[13] As a result, the Under-Secretary immediately wrote to Danielsson, describing the father's 'desperate emotional state', and reiterating his authorization that emergency passports be issued to the two women.[14] In fact Danielsson had pre-empted this reminder, and on 23 March issued them the prized documents.[15] Then, a month later, the father received a letter from UD informing him that due to a bureaucratic 'mistake', Eva and Alice were already recognized *by Hungarian officials* as Swedish citizens! On 30 May, even after reading of the deportations taking place throughout Hungary, the (at least temporarily) relieved father sent a telegram to Engzell. Its poignant content illustrates the hope that thousands of Jews placed in paper as protection against murder. 'My daughters have been saved through your worthwhile help. With all our hearts my wife and I thank you and the Swedish state. We will never forget your great help and humanity.'[16]

Sadly, the father's relief was short-lived. On 1 June, Engzell cabled Budapest. '[J.] Eismann states that daughters are in danger. Can anything be done?' Some days later, before Danielsson could respond, Engzell again cabled Budapest. 'Eismann girls naturalized as Swedish citizens on 7th [*sic*] this month. Your assistance may stretch likewise to other close relatives in feasible fashion.'[17] Although Engzell's cable arrived in Budapest just as the deportations were (at least temporarily) stopped, it is unknown if the girls survived. Yet even so, we see in Engzell's telegram a sentence and sentiment which would contribute to the salvation of, at a minimum, thousands of others. Engzell's authorization that the Legation could also help 'other close relatives in a feasible fashion', enabled Danielsson, Anger and subsequently Wallenberg to continually throw the safety net they wove, in a 'feasible fashion', around an ever-increasing number of people.

THE LEGATION RESPONDS TO OCCUPATION

Though in the historical literature there remains some discussion about the Germans' exact motives for occupying their military and economic ally, as we have seen, Danielsson believed he understood why.[18] Some days after the occupation, Danielsson reported a public statement made by László Baky, the notorious anti-Semite appointed state secretary for political affairs:[19] '[Baky] wants to in the quickest manner, *with complete bureaucratic elimination*, solve all imminent questions and that [the new government] will not shy away from any necessary measures. He also declared that maintenance of his position is dependent on "the complete liquidation of all Jewish and leftist efforts" and that he is convinced that 'the government finally shall solve its enormous historical task.'[20] (Emphasis in original.) Per Anger did not doubt that with the German occupation, '[It] will be a very hard time now for the Jewish people'.[21]

By this point it was known around the world that Sweden was assisting Jews. As a result, from the first days of the occupation, the Legation was engulfed by Jews seeking diplomatic protection. Per Anger remembered that as soon as the Germans occupied the city:

> the Jews were also queuing up outside the Swiss, Portuguese, Spanish and Vatican [legations], but they came to us to start with ... we had perhaps more than the other countries [extensive] trade relations with Hungarian firms, Swedish firms with branches in

Budapest, [which] had managing directors and so on, many of whom were Jewish. We had contact with them before ... So it was natural for them, then, to rush to the Swedish legation ... and pray for help, ask for help.[22]

Anger also understood that virtually all other Legation activities would cease. 'From then on, of course, everything about trade or ordinary business with Sweden [was] put aside ... [everyone] in the legation concentrated on one thing ... To try to save people's lives.'[23]

Awareness of the government's willingness to help precipitated a virtual flood of letters to UD. Appeals came from anonymous refugee Jews, assimilated Swedish Jews and, with increasing frequency, gentile Swedes of high social, business and political station. Some appeals for distant relatives were even received from Jews living in the United States and elsewhere. Not surprisingly, this avalanche of appeals strained the relatively ad hoc procedures established by those few officials working on these issues within UD. This overload contributed to an increasing confusion about who could or could not be helped, who had received assistance and who was refused. As we shall see, this bureaucratic confusion would accelerate after Wallenberg's arrival, with both negative and positive consequences.

As previously noted, for both historic and contemporary reasons, quite a few Hungarian officials in both the national Budapest and city governments viewed Swedish humanitarian efforts with relative good favour. This factor was enhanced because throughout the war, trade relations between the two nations were extensive and mutually beneficial, with political relations basically stable. As also noted, Sweden represented Hungarian interests in those countries with which the latter was formally at war, and Hungarian officials even anticipated continued Swedish humanitarian assistance after the war.[24]

On 12 April, Engzell received an interesting letter of appeal from Vilmos Böhm, a prominent Hungarian Jewish refugee in Stockholm. Böhm, who during the war worked as a translator for Britain's Legation in Stockholm, was for a short time after the First World War Hungary's war minister, and a leading member of its Social Democratic Party. In the letter, Böhm requested assistance for several family members and other relatives, and his appeal was supported by a high-level official from Sweden's most important labour union, Landsorganisationen (LO). K.E. Jansson was secretary of the organization's 'division for refugee help', and as such he obviously felt it unnecessary to write what virtually became a 'standard' letter of appeal to UD.[25] A telephone call to Engzell and a single sheet, with the organization's letterhead, listing Böhm's relatives were sufficient to get these names immediately telegraphed to Budapest.[26] Additional evidence that Böhm's case was important came two months later when Valter Åman, another high-ranking politician in Stockholm's Social Democratic party, bypassed Engzell and wrote directly to Budapest, requesting further information about Böhm's relatives. Even in the growing chaos at the Legation, requests from important politicians did not go unnoticed, and Åman was answered almost immediately. Indeed, even though the politician had bypassed normal channels, his letter was accompanied by a sharp reminder from Stockholm that prominent officials remained concerned about Böhm's case.[27]

Another such appeal arrived from Wallenberg's business partner Koloman Lauer, who sent a list of seven relatives. His letter, written before Wallenberg was recruited for his task, was also short and to the point. It listed those relatives (or other individuals) in question, and named as references people likely to impress civil servants. In this case Lauer named his business partner – Raoul Wallenberg – as well as Sven Salén.[28] Appended to the appeal (another tactic which became common) was a letter of support from a prominent non-Jewish Swede, in this case one Erik Björkman, also a businessman. As if to dispel any notion that Lauer's appeal might be considered less worthy because the appellant wasn't born in Sweden, Björkman wrote that 'for a foreigner Dr Lauer has understood amazingly well what it means to live in Swedish conditions and accept a Swedish lifestyle, not least with regard to social questions'.[29]

Yet another appeal was received by UD which, again, represents scores of others sent to the government. It was sent not to Engzell, but directly to Foreign Minister Christian Günther. In a poignant historical irony, Professor Gunnar Dahlberg of Uppsala University's National Institute for Racial Biology (*Statens rasbiologiska institut*) appealed for help for some Jewish acquaintances in Budapest. Dahlberg wrote in his capacity as director, and used the institute's letterhead.[30] Coming from a fellow high-level civil servant, Sweden's top diplomat quickly instructed his men in Budapest to assist the professor's friends.[31]

One aspect of UD's help is more difficult to measure, but was undoubtedly of considerable emotional importance for those trying to survive, and for their relatives in Sweden. In late May, a Hungarian Jew practising medicine in Uppsala wrote to Engzell after succeeding in arranging emergency passports for his parents in Budapest:

> allow me to express a sincere thanks to UD and the Swedish Legation in Budapest for the whole-hearted and quick action. One function the protective letter will serve under all circumstances is to lessen worry and provide moral support for my parents. *For*

> *people who find themselves in their situation, the feeling of hav-*
> *ing a European state's support behind them has a significance*
> *scarcely less than life itself.*[32] [Emphasis added.]

Though most officials supported, at least tacitly, their government's
accelerating diplomacy in Hungary, there arrived a high-level protest
that helping Jews was not in Sweden's interests.[33] On 10 June,
Sweden's senior diplomat in Switzerland wrote that the situation in
Hungary was not as bad as some were saying, that UD was making a
mistake in getting involved, and that using diplomatic documents to
protect Jews was particularly inappropriate. Minister Przybyszewski-
Westrup suggested that it was common knowledge that 'Jews all
around Europe are, in their accustomed manner, trying to obtain citizenship in certain South and Central American republics, whose representatives gladly exercise philanthropy against hard cash'. Though this
experienced diplomat failed to specify what 'the accustomed manner'
of the Jews was, he did note that German officials were not allowing
themselves 'to be lured' into believing that bearers of such passports
were genuine citizens '[yet] ...strangely enough [the documentation is]
sufficiently respected so that the bearer at least is able to avoid the
worst forms of persecution, especially deportation eastward'. He had
information that such methods had been effective in Holland and
Belgium, and wrote that though such 'persecutions' in Hungary had
only just begun, 'such passports might mean salvation'. Meanwhile, he
urged his superiors to understand that if UD continued helping Jews in
this fashion, the negative consequences would be considerable: 'If our
diplomatic apparatus was to cooperate in such stories, there would be
serious problems which I don't believe should be minimized.'[34] No
response to the diplomat's protest was located, nor can it be ascertained if other officials agreed with Westrup's reasoning.[35]

Though Westrup tried to minimize what was happening in
Hungary, late May and June were in fact some of the most lethal weeks
of the entire Holocaust. On 2 June, Danielsson cabled that 'the situation in the Jewish question becomes more acute daily', adding that the
Legation had received word that deportations of Jews from Budapest
itself to Germany and Poland would soon begin, 'except for the 50,000
who will be closed into a ghetto'. Danielsson followed this ominous
news with two proposals. The first was that Sweden should, in a coordinated action with other neutral nations, try 'to save children, women
and [the] elderly. According to information available, unlimited financial support is available for this.' The second proposal was a request
from representatives of the Hungarian Red Cross that someone from
either SRK (Svenska röda korset, Swedish Red Cross) or Rädda barnen

(Save the Children) be sent to Budapest to conduct humanitarian work.[36] Stockholm responded four days later by saying that the Hungarian authorities should be informed of the 'gloom which characterizes the reaction of the Swedish people concerning the persecution of Jews now underway. Ascertain whether a Swedish initiative to rescue, for example, women, children and [the] elderly would lead to anything ... If so the proposal will be given a quick examination.'[37] Though diplomats in Stockholm continued using the word 'persecutions' when writing about events, they knew full well that something far more serious was occurring. In Budapest, Danielsson and Anger chose different words to explain the significance of the massive deportations they knew were occurring. On 14 June the following telegram reached Stockholm:

> According to reliable intelligence from various sources, deportation and extermination [*förintelse*] of the Jews accelerating. In eastern and southern Hungary the largest portion of Jews already deported primarily to extermination camp Kattovitz [*sic*]. Here in Budapest the order for Jews to concentrate in special houses expected this week. The Legation requests confirmation, in accordance with passport regulation 24, if following our own careful determination, emergency passports can be issued for people with connection to Sweden.[38]

Though indicating a wish to follow procedure, the two hard-pressed diplomats who unexpectedly found themselves surrounded by the maelstrom of genocide understood that a more drastic response was required. In effect they requested approval to issue at their discretion the most effective tool at their disposal – the emergency passports – without having to obtain approval for each individual case as was normal procedure. These documents (about which more below) indicated actual Swedish citizenship and were recognized as such both by German and Hungarian authorities. This request, which smoothed the way for Wallenberg's subsequent expansion of assistance activities, was approved early the next day by officials in Stockholm.[39] Importantly, however, it was not the only protective document issued by the Legation which became widely valued.

THE DEPORTATIONS REACH THEIR HEIGHT

For everyone in Budapest, the second half of June was dominated by the ongoing catastrophe of the provincial deportations. Jews in the city grew increasingly desperate, and the world continued to receive and react to news from Hungary. In Stockholm, an ever-increasing flow of information came to UD simultaneously to the recently commenced discussions about Wallenberg's possible appointment as ad hoc secretary to the Budapest Legation. Somewhat ironically, as will be shown in the next chapter, discussions about what he would do centred increasingly on a role as 'reporter' for Jewish issues, even though Danielsson and Anger were describing and analysing the destruction of Hungarian Jewry in great detail.[40] On 16 June, they reported that as of the week before, up to 420,000 Jews had already been deported, and that the Jews of Budapest would incur the same fate within several weeks. Their information was timely and accurate:

> all the captured Jews, men and women, children and elderly are loaded into cattle cars and transported partly to Germany and partly to the Polish General-government ... In Budapest the Jews are stripped of all their property. They now live 8–10 people in a single room.
>
> Those lucky enough for necessary labour are said to be transported to German industrial locations where they have a chance to be treated relatively well. The rest, on the other hand, children, weak women and the elderly are deported to the extermination camp at Auschwitz-Birkenau near Kattowitz in Poland.[41]

They were beginning to feel overwhelmed and though they wished to help as many as possible, they had to 'in the first place try to help those with connections to Sweden'. Noting their often frustrating negotiations with Hungarian and German officials, they wrote that their interlocutors constantly blamed the other nation's officials for the continuing deportations and persecutions.[42] In yet another report Danielsson renewed his appeal for immediate Red Cross intervention, reporting that 'stubborn rumours say that large numbers of transports [are] directed to Poland, where the human cargoes are exterminated by means of gas'.[43]

The manner in which Swedish diplomats negotiated with their German counterparts, about both individuals and principles, was illuminated in detail by Danielsson in a secret report written on 18 June. Because it captures the everyday details of how 'bureaucratic resistance' was conducted and reported by the Swedes before Wallenberg's arrival, it merits extensive citation. It demonstrates, among other matters, how these two Swedish officials (echoing their colleagues elsewhere) refused to take no for an answer. Moreover, their handling of these issues demonstrates the primacy of choices available to them, for there is no doubt that if they had chosen to report, for instance, that 'everything had been done' (in this case or that), or that 'there was nothing more to do', there was little or no likelihood that their superiors in Stockholm would either have reprimanded them or insisted they do more. Remarkably, in virtually every 'case' handled in a year of unprecedented stress, shock and increasing danger, Sweden's diplomats in Budapest almost always chose to continue trying to save people until it was impossible.[44]

This report begins by saying that because Danielsson and Anger had basically given up hope of receiving a favourable answer in the case of a man named Turai from the Hungarians, they turned to the Germans, obtaining a meeting with Theodor Grell, the Legation's *judereferent* (expert on Jewish 'matters'). Grell arrived in Budapest in March with Edmund Veesenmayer, specifically to help coordinate negotiations between the Germans and the Hungarians on issues directly related to the 'Final Solution'.[45] Grell was a classic 'desk-top' murderer, although the Swedes would not have thought of him in such terms:

> Grell said that he was very well acquainted with the Turai case; the Hungarian Foreign Ministry had again and again contacted the German Legation in the question. He regretted that he was not yet in a position to provide a definitive answer about his [Turai's] release. All such cases of Jews being naturalized after 19 March must of course always be sent to Berlin for appraisal. He hoped meanwhile that a favourable answer could be given within some weeks.
>
> In this connection Herr Grell touched upon questions concerning Swedish emergency passports, which, according to what he was able to understand, did not imply Swedish citizenship. A Hungarian Jew, named Kertész, who was arrested by the Germans, [was in possession] of such a passport (see our previous exchange of telegrams about this).
>
> Because this was raised we told [Grell] that this is a question of a person with close connection to Sweden who had applied for Swedish citizenship and for whom this would in the immediate future most likely be granted. We requested therefore that Kertész be released as soon as possible. Grell promised an answer to this issue, as with the others, as soon as possible.[46]

The dilatory tactics of Grell and other German officials would become distressingly familiar to Sweden's diplomats in both Budapest and Berlin. Interestingly, next day, the Legation cabled additional information received from the Hungarian government about its response to Swedish ideas for humanitarian assistance. In what must have been a very early-morning meeting, Danielsson was told by Deputy Foreign Minister Arnóthy-Jungerth that the matter would be handled next week by the Crown Council, but that 'it was scarcely possible that any

Swedish Red Cross action with a representative dispatched from Sweden was possible for the moment ... because of determined German opposition'.[47]

Later that same day, a written response was received from the government concerning the status and use of the emergency passports. The Swedes requested that Hungarian Jews who had 'merely' applied for Swedish citizenship should be treated immediately as if they already possessed Swedish citizenship. The government, however, 'with its deepest regrets' could not accede to any such request unless all individual cases were argued for in detail, such as why the petitioner wanted to take such a step![48] This document is interesting but, as it turned out, neither indicative nor descriptive of what actually happened. The Hungarian government and city authorities did in many cases consider, and to an ever greater extent eventually accept, that the mere fact of an application for Swedish citizenship was sufficient grounds for treating the person (and/or families) in question as a Swedish citizen. This is but one example of how during the Hungarian Holocaust, contradictory and seemingly 'unacceptable' political situations, concerning both individuals and 'principles', existed alongside each other, differing from one official to the other, from one week to the next.

This confusion was exemplified yet again the next day, when Danielsson again cabled Stockholm about an individual case. 'It is as good as impossible for the Legation to attempt, with any hope of success, to intervene in similar forthcoming cases, because we now learned privately about this and other matters that German authorities will not accept Swedish emergency passports for Jews.'[49] This would, happily, prove to be incorrect.

On 25 June Danielsson and Anger sent yet another highly descriptive report summarizing many of the details of their almost frenzied diplomacy. Addressed to Foreign Minister Günther, this particular document captures their sense of despair. At this point they clearly felt they were receiving little help from their colleagues in Stockholm. The immediacy of the information must have impressed and shocked officials there:

> When towards the middle of May the persecution of Jews began to reach huge proportions and ever more disgusting forms, the idea was put forth that Swedish intervention by the Red Cross and Save the Children would search for a path to assist at least children, women and the elderly ...
>
> To achieve this, cooperation was sought with the Hungarian Red Cross and with Jewish representatives who based their activities

within the Swiss Legation's B division. Before that, soundings were taken with the delegates of the International Red Cross [ICRC], which meanwhile quickly proved to be, for certain reasons, lacking in practical value.

Enduring the frustrating prevarications of the Hungarians was made even more difficult because Danielsson and Anger appear to have secured a promise of direct financial support from the American Joint Distribution Committee. They proposed again, with logic on their side, that long-time Swedish resident of Budapest, Valdemar Langlet, should be appointed as resident SRK delegate. This proposal was also supported by some Hungarian officials. Danielsson stressed that there would soon be very few Jews left to help if decisions were not rapidly made. 'Much valuable time is already lost, and if a final decision from either the Swedish or Hungarian side is not made before the end of the current month, these issues should be removed from the agenda and those poor Jews, who with their blood brothers' gold could have been assisted to get to neutral countries and eventually to America, may be considered beyond rescue [and] definitely lost.'[50]

Not surprisingly these reports and telegrams caused great concern in Stockholm, and some officials at UD, even the determined Engzell, began to doubt the protective value of the documents issued by the Legation.[51] Although Anger reported one incident in which a Jew was released from custody when he was able to produce a Swedish 'B' protective letter (*sky-ddsbrev B*), he despaired that little hope remained for Budapest's Jews. 'A change in the apparently irrevocable decision on the almost total deportation of Hungary's Jews appears ... to be unthinkable.'[52]

THE DESPERATION OF LATE SPRING 1944

Though the Swedes were well informed about what was happening, they didn't know that during June's final days, Horthy's Crown Council was debating whether or not to cease their government's murderous collaboration with the Germans, and to halt the deportations. As we have seen, these deliberations were motivated partly by the international pressures put on the country, and partly by the audacious but failed coup d'état of Baky and Endre. They had learned that Horthy was wavering and might move to stop them from finishing their task and deport Budapest's Jews. In fact, their machinations became known to leading officials around the regent, who had them arrested. A. Cohen wrote: 'The shift in government policy, which began at the meeting of the Crown Council on June 26 and continued at subsequent meetings into July, was marked first and foremost by the cessation of the deportations, but there were other aspects as well.'[53] On 6 July, the Hungarian government announced that the deportations would cease. As a direct result of these arrests, Eichmann and many of his staff left shortly thereafter, frustrated that they couldn't finish the job.

We have noted the protests and interventions made by US president Roosevelt and Pope Pius XII. These were known in Sweden, and during June several appeals reached King Gustav V, who also decided to address Horthy directly.[54] The king, who was politically quite influential, received government support in making a protest partly because of Sweden's history of positive relations with Hungary, and partly because during the war he still maintained some constitutional prerogatives. In this context, another myth about Wallenberg can be dispensed with. Some publications assert that Wallenberg met the regent, while others – even some contemporaries – have written that he personally delivered Gustav's appeal.[55] This was impossible, of course, because he had yet to arrive in Budapest, and the audience at which Gustav's telegram was delivered to Horthy took place on 3 July.[56] It would have been, in any case, unthinkable for a newly arrived, low-level diplomat to be entrusted with such a task when more senior diplomats were available. This myth has been repeated many times by both historians and journalists alike.[57]

In fact, instructions from the Palace in Stockholm arrived to Budapest on 30 June, and it took several days for Danielsson to obtain an audience with Horthy. The telegram, approved by UD, was signed by Gustav and transmitted for delivery in French:

> After receiving knowledge of the extraordinarily severe methods which your government is resorting to against Hungary's Jewish population, allow me to personally turn to Your Highness and in the name of humanity appeal that You take measures to save those who remain of that unfortunate people.
>
> This appeal is motivated by my old feelings of friendship for your country and by my genuine concern for Hungary's good name and reputation in the community of nations.[58]

Per Anger was also present, and he reported that Horthy understood and appreciated the king's appeal which, the Swedes were told, was similar to one recently received from the Pope. Horthy, they reported, 'regretted not having greater possibilities to hinder what was happening to Hungary's Jews ... [and said that] the Germans stand behind all the measures against the Jews'. Yet Horthy acknowledged that Hungarian officials 'were anxious to transport Eastern Hungary's Jews away because of the communist elements ... [and because] the

Jews had little in common with the Hungarian people'. Diplomatic practice prohibited a Swedish contradiction, yet Anger noted that Horthy had greeted them 'in an extremely personable manner, but he was very tired and deeply distressed over the recent events'.[59] What actual effect Gustav's intervention had on the decision taken by Horthy and the Crown Council is unknown, but it certainly contributed to the international pressure felt at that time by Horthy.[60]

Some have written that Gustav's message was meant to be kept secret, but the Swedes were in fact anxious to tell the world about this royal diplomatic intervention, so news of the meeting was soon broadcast around the world.[61] Two days later a prominent Swedish daily printed the leader cited in this chapter's second epigraph. Gustav's appeal was praised, and the editors' understanding of what was at stake was made clear. To expand upon the chapter's epigraph, we read:

> Now King Gustaf has sent an appeal to Admiral Horthy in Budapest to use his influence to save Hungarian Jews from further persecution ... these methods are by now well known. It is known that Jews are transported in overcrowded freight cars. These transports take many lives ... but even quicker methods are used, for example gas chambers. [It is known] that Germany's blessed leader is conducting a systematic extermination of millions of people in Europe.[62]

What follows is also interesting, with the editors addressing a difficult issue that hung over the conscience of most Swedes – their country's failure to contribute to the struggle against Nazism. Uncommonly, however, the editors connected the country's non-involvement in the fight against fascism to the ongoing extermination, making clear that these particular journalists understood that their nation's neutrality brought with it a feeling of moral ambiguity:

> At this point no one can be ignorant about this ... But there are surely some in a neutral country like Sweden where many people attempt to escape reality, who avoid reading about the horrible stories and refuse to believe them. They repress from their consciousness that which is incomprehensible, that which is outside the peaceful reality we see all around us. There is no other way of explaining the satisfied calm which prevails.
>
> Great cruelty is happening during this war, as all others ... women and children are bombed and maimed from the air. But none of this is so macabre as the systematic, industrialized mass slaughter of innocent people in German extermination centres.[63]

Following their audience with Horthy, Anger didn't mince words in

a report to Günther which described an assembly point just north of
Budapest – 'for all intents and purposes all the Jews in the country ...
have been deported either to Germany or Poland' – and said that Jews
from five small communities were sent to a nearby collection point. He
described his own recent visit:

> [which] largely confirms previous reports concerning the treat-
> ment of those interned ... 'the camp' lacks walls, a ceiling, beds
> and linen, etc. The interned were seen sitting on small bricks or
> earthen mounds without the slightest protection against either the
> sun or rain. Their natural needs are necessarily done on the
> ground in front of everyone. The local population formed a circle
> of curious observers around this arena guarded by Hungarian
> gendarmes.[64]

Still unaware that a decision to halt the deportations was imminent,
Anger analysed the effect that the international appeals and threats
addressed to Hungary's leadership might have. The threats of reprisal
issued by the US Congress on 27 June 'appears to have hardly had any
influence on the Hungarians in question', and 'the Holy See's appeal of
23 June even less'. Gustav's appeal is not evaluated. As noted earlier,
Anger concluded a couple of reports in evident despair.[65]

That same day he drafted yet another report describing the 'brutality
and cruelty the Hungarian gendarmes are guilty of'. Quoting sources
from the provinces, Anger wrote that 'several hundred gendarmes'
were so eager to get all the Jews of 'Sashalom east of Budapest' into
the town square for immediate deportation that they even grabbed sick
and recently operated-upon patients out of the Jewish hospital. 'This
episode should illuminate the treatment meted out by Hungarian
police forces in the countryside before [the Jews] are handed over to
the Germans.'[66]

Anger's sense of hopelessness was felt in Stockholm by Engzell, who
wrote to Danielsson with an emotional directness rarely seen in
Swedish diplomatic correspondence. This memorandum, drafted by
the individual most responsible for the positive evolution in Sweden's
response to the Holocaust, shows a sophisticated appreciation of the
political complexities prevailing in three capitals. It details the methods they were employing in an attempt to save at least some lives,
Engzell's growing frustration, and perhaps most importantly, his willingness to provide his colleagues in the field with the necessary autonomy needed to respond to the emergency. It merits extensive citation.
Arvid Richert was Sweden's long-serving minister in Berlin and a
key figure for most of the war in shaping Sweden's policies vis-à-vis
Nazi Germany:

Hungarian agreement in principle to a 'repatriation' to Sweden of Jews with connection to our country is of course a little bit of light in all this horror. Meanwhile, I assume that it will be altogether impossible for you to obtain German agreement ... It would be incredibly amazing if the opposite occurred. As you see from the enclosed letter, I have urged Richert to intervene ... [earlier, We] have protested to the Germans that a less favourable treatment of Swedish Jews than other Swedes is unacceptable, and a difference we refuse to recognize.

If, against all expectations, the journey [to Sweden] for some Jews might be arranged, I guess that several practical difficulties will arise. Travel costs are of course considerable, but it will probably be possible, if needed, to obtain some money through Americans for those suffering.

I want finally to touch upon the emergency passports and want to emphasise that we must be restrictive with them. Everyone wants one and it would be a debacle if we conceded too much. It is partially a matter of chance who gets them. We don't really know what good they do ... Much is a question of judgement which is difficult to decide from here ... But if you see in individual cases that such papers can save someone, we of course have nothing against your decision.[67]

Richert has sometimes been accused of being too willing to appease the Nazis, particularly in the war's first years, and he was consistently more reluctant than many of his colleagues to support Sweden's increasing assistance to Jews.[68] Engzell's memorandum to the still influential Richert (which was carried by Wallenberg for delivery on his way to Budapest) illustrates some important issues. Engzell addresses Richert in a firmer tone than normal, considering that the envoy was Engzell's institutional senior, if not formally his superior. This is yet another document containing illuminating detail about what the Swedes were doing and how they were seeking to work. Perhaps more importantly in a larger context, it demonstrates that some European diplomats were capable not only of a genuine desire to help keep some Jews alive, they were prepared to anger influential colleagues in doing so. Engzell's commitment to this goal would subsequently prove decisive for Wallenberg's activities:[69]

Since the new situation in Hungary began we have been heavily engaged in trying to save some Jews from there who have for different reasons connections to Sweden. The methods used have been primarily the same as used previously. Some have been made

Swedish citizens, others have received emergency passports, various types of protective papers, or entry visas. The overall effect in this whole thing has been dismal, yet quite a few have in this way been protected from deportation.

Danielsson has now informed us that in principle the Hungarian government has agreed to a 'repatriation' of those Jews with Swedish connections, depending on whether German officials there give their permission. According to the Hungarians, such permission should be obtained through the Swedish Legation in Berlin.

Previously Danielsson has provided the Hungarians with a list of 186 people. [He] also notes that 260 people have been given Swedish entry visas.

The type of connection to Sweden varies. In the first hand, apart from Swedish citizens, are [their] many close relatives, including relatives of Hungarians who have spent considerable time in Sweden. Then there are also some who have earned our attention, generally those who have worked for Swedish companies for longer periods. This number naturally includes family members.

We would be very happy to see the whole thing happen, but I must say that the prospects are not great. I have difficulties believing that the Germans will change their attitudes. In any case though it is possible that these poor people will, through our efforts, win some time, which always provides a glimmer of hope ... I request that you consider these possibilities. You can always informally report [to the Germans] what Danielsson has reported ... Time is running. Already around 450,000 Jews have been deported from Hungary and the remaining half million will probably disappear before 15 July. It is therefore desirable that something be done before that.[70]

It bears repeating that all of this took place prior to Wallenberg's assumption of his mission. It also bears reiterating that the world was keenly aware of Sweden's diplomatic activism prior to Wallenberg's arrival in Budapest. Further confirmation of this can be seen in a telegram received by Sweden's Legation in Washington, DC. Though somewhat hyperbolic and not entirely accurate, the 'Emergency Committee to Save the Jewish People of Europe' sent an appreciation of Sweden's diplomacy. Similar to many messages received in connection with Sweden's participation in the rescue of Denmark's Jews, the writer thanked the Swedish king for his appeal to Horthy, and the Swedish people for their 'unceasing efforts in behalf [sic] of the doomed Jewish people of Europe as evidenced in [Gustav's] plea to the Hungarian government. We fear that if action is not taken immediately, a million more Jews in Hungary and the Balkans will meet terrible death. Sweden's action again leads the way for all nations.'[71] From London's 'Religious Emergency Council' came similar expressions of gratitude, along with this pointed suggestion:

> A Declaration giving the Jews of Hungary the status of protected subjects of Sweden and/or offering them domicile in Sweden, might save many lives condemned to barbarous death ... In any event, it would serve as a crowning step to Sweden's persistent efforts to save whatever can be rescued from the destroyers of human lives, and might well encourage other States to take similar action.[72]

Further evidence that the world knew of the ongoing tragedy in Hungary is seen on 8 July, when in London *The Times* published a short yet detailed article entitled 'Hungarian Jews Fate: Murder in Gas Chambers'. Sources reported:

> the fate of more than 400,000 Hungarian Jews who were sent to Poland, mainly to the concentration camp in Oswiecim. According to this information the Germans on May 15 deported from Hungary 62 railway carriages filled with Jewish children, aged between two and eight years. Every day since, for a long period, six railway trains laden with adult Jews passed through the station of Plaszow, near Cracow.
> They were sent to Oswiecim, and most of them have been put to death in the gas chambers of that dreaded concentration camp ... Oswiecim is the biggest concentration camp in Poland. Conditions there are much worse than in the notorious camp in Dachau. In 1942 the Germans erected in Oswiecim gas chambers with installations enabling them to kill daily 6000 and even more of their victims ... In camps more than 2,000,000 Polish Jews have been murdered since 1939.[73]

Mention has been made of the many appeals received from individuals in Sweden on behalf of family, friends or business acquaintances in Budapest. The writers regularly pointed to existing connections with other leading Swedes, or said that the Jews in question were 'good, hard-working people'. It was for these and other reasons that the individuals in question had, as Engzell put it, 'earned Swedish attention'.[74] Even Foreign Minister Günther's wife Ingrid appealed on behalf of two Jewish families in Budapest.[75] Inexplicably, Engzell's response took a month, yet it again illuminates both his thinking and understanding of the prevailing situation. He explained that large numbers of Hungarian Jews had relatives in Sweden, and that it was necessary to maintain certain restrictions concerning help offered. Nonetheless, he wrote:

> we have asked the Legation to attempt to help these families. The Legation currently has approximately 450 such protectees [*skydds-lingar*]. In most cases, unfortunately, there is little chance to help. But we are conscious that all of our interventions provide at least some solace for relatives here and in certain cases [they] have helped, at least for some time. I hope sincerely that this will be the case now.[76]

Although Engzell's reflexive response was to attempt to maintain restrictions and follow established guidelines, there is no doubt that under the pressure of events, normative procedures fell away. What passed for policy was being adapted and adopted on the fly by those involved. Importantly, no evidence has been found which indicates any reproach of Engzell, either from his superiors at UD or from Prime Minister Per Albin Hansson's Cabinet. Engzell's activist diplomacy was approved, and the bureaucratic space he allowed Danielsson and Anger was subsequently exploited by Wallenberg. Richert's reluctance to press the Germans was not widely shared within UD, and most other officials who appear in the documentation were to all appearances eager to participate in activities which might lead to the saving of lives – even Jewish lives during the Holocaust.[77]

Interestingly, Engzell did not hide the fact that in many or even most cases, the Swedish government was powerless to help. In answer to one appeal, he wrote that he would have liked to offer more help, but had, with regret, to turn down the appeal because the person in question was not a Swedish citizen and therefore not eligible to receive a Swedish passport. The appellant was an academic at a prominent Swedish college, and Engzell informed him that his father-in-law had in fact already received a 'protective letter' (*skyddsbrev*) from the Legation, acknowledging that its protective value seemed most often a matter of chance. Engzell informed the appellant that further appeals on behalf of his father-in-law were futile, 'because the Legation had already done what it could'.[78]

HITLER'S OFFICIALS ON SWEDISH DIPLOMACY

Sweden's diplomacy in Budapest was naturally of interest to German officials. It is established in the literature that on occasion the Germans would exempt some Jews from deportation, or even treat them relatively better, if they possessed (however dubiously) citizenship from one of the European neutrals, some Central and South American countries, and even sometimes American or British citizenship.[79] The tendency to respect such exemptions increased as German defeats mounted, as did the willingness to negotiate with neutral diplomats. Though their eagerness to kill Jews scarcely abated during the war, some German officials were equally anxious to create post-war alibis.[80]

Throughout the spring and summer, Edmund Veesenmayer (who represented both Himmler's SS and von Ribbentrop's foreign ministry) wrote a series of reports about Swedish and Swiss diplomatic efforts which detail German irritation at the sometimes successful 'meddling' of neutral diplomats. Veesenmayer considered it 'unreasonable' that they had been successful in negotiating exemptions for Jews from deportations, from wearing the 'yellow star' or from other discriminatory measures. These reports also confirm that cooperation and collaboration with the Hungarians was less satisfactory in Budapest than it had been in the countryside, where it had been seamless. As noted, Eichmann and his men would have been helpless without Hungarian help everywhere, but this was particularly true in Budapest. One reason was that as soon as the military situation was deemed to have stabilized in March, most of the German troops who staged the occupation of Hungary went elsewhere.

In popular memory, the Germans decided and controlled everything in Budapest, leaving the Hungarians essentially as onlookers. The hagiographic literature on Wallenberg rarely takes into account the complex political situation prevailing in Budapest, where the Germans were not omnipotent. In the event, the most dedicated German and Hungarian perpetrators seemed to delight in assigning 'blame' to each other when their answers to neutral diplomats took time to answer, or were refused. As noted, when trying to obtain a decision concerning some detail or another concerning their assistance activities, the Swedes often complained that they were sent back and forth between 'responsible' Hungarian and German officials. Ironically, however, this cynical game of the perpetrators created some of the diplomatic space within which the neutrals were able to operate. We see evidence of this when on 20 June, Veesenmayer complained that 'because the coordination of the Jewish question in Hungary has entered an acute stage, interest from foreign powers in helping Jews has increased'. He also confirmed that Sweden's envoy assisted Jews by granting Swedish 'citizenship', 'to such Jews who have relatives in Sweden or long-standing business relationships ... in total this concerns some 300–400 Jews'.[81]

Per Anger's energetic work in the days before Wallenberg arrived was noted by Veesenmayer, and even publicized. On 5 July,

Veesenmayer reported that Budapest newspapers were writing that 'now as before [the Swedish Legation] is prepared to provide identification for possible departure from Hungary', but that Anger – he reported inaccurately – had 'clarified' for the Hungarian foreign ministry that reports of Jews receiving genuine Swedish passports were false.[82] More significant for understanding developments after Wallenberg's arrival is Veesenmayer's longer report dated two days later, which described the negotiations between Anger and one of his staff. Noting the small number of people involved, only 186 Jews, 'who unquestionably are Hungarian citizens but have connections with Sweden through (other) family members who have Swedish passports', Veesenmayer detailed the prevarications, lies and delays used by his fellow perpetrators as they remained determined to deport to their death as many Jews as possible, even as Anger negotiated for their protection. Veesenmayer was an experienced 'desk-top' killer who was angered and even offended by the mere notion that Jews warranted any protective political interest from the Swedes. Yet the prevailing political circumstances made it impossible for him to dismiss unilaterally their arguments and requests.[83]

Meanwhile, in Berlin, this and related issues were broached by Swedish diplomats in meetings with their German counterparts. On 11 July, L. Nylander, a mid-level diplomat at Sweden's Legation, reported on his long discussion with Eberhard von Thadden, the veteran Nazi diplomat who for years was an important cog in the bureaucracy of genocide functioning as part of Auswärtiges Amt (Germany's foreign ministry).[84] Instrumental in guiding the activities of other German diplomats as they coordinated the deportation and murder of Jews from throughout Europe with their colleagues in the SS, von Thadden's mendacious, prevaricating negotiating tactics were familiar to Nylander.[85] Using polite diplomatic language to justify mass murder, von Thadden patiently explained to the Swede why matters of concern to Stockholm were in essence out of his hands. There was, he said, 'unfortunately', little he or other German diplomats could do to accommodate the Swedes when it was 'actually' the Hungarians who exercised sovereignty over these issues. Cynically, he told the Swede that 'if the number in question had been some 10 or even 40 individuals it could have been arranged, but now [because the Swedes were seeking to help] "too many", the question must be decided upon the basis of principle (*grundsätzlich behandelt werden*), after normal and "requisite" discussions with the responsible security organs. "For his part, he didn't believe the Swedish requests could be granted".' Nylander concluded this familiarly fruitless discussion, ending his report with words similar to those of other Swedish colleagues who

had engaged German diplomats in discussions about saving a few
Jewish lives – and it represents a plank in the practice of 'bureaucratic
resistance'. Nylander wrote: 'Before leaving Herr von Thadden I
repeated my request for a favourable treatment of the question and a
speedy decision in a positive direction.'[86] Similarly futile negotiations
concerning the fate of tiny numbers of Jews in Budapest would continue in Berlin for the remainder of the year, with similar frustrations.

We may remind ourselves that the assault against Hungarian Jewry
was of considerable interest to the Western Allies, particularly the
Americans. On 3 July (again, just prior to the halting of the deportations),
high-level UD official Sven Grafström sent the American and British
Legations in Stockholm copies of several reports just received from
Budapest.[87] These uncensored accounts gave the Allies a comprehensive
view of Sweden's activities, and that of the other neutrals. This fact puts
to rest yet another myth about Wallenberg. The popular literature is rife
with speculation that he was arrested by Soviet troops and kept impris-
oned in the Gulag because he was an American 'spy', guilty in paranoid
Soviet eyes of passing information about events in Budapest to the
West. Danielsson's and Anger's reports were passed directly to the
Allies, something presumably known to Soviet diplomats in
Stockholm. Both of Wallenberg's senior colleagues were also detained
in early 1945 by Soviet troops when the city was liberated – yet they
along with several other Swedes who worked at the Legation were
released and sent home in April 1945. If the Soviets believed that
Wallenberg was a spy, it wasn't because he reported from Budapest to
US and UK diplomatic organs.

THE PROTECTIVE POWER OF PAPER

The importance of documents in providing, on occasion, a measure of
protection for endangered Jews has been discussed. One such document, 'Wallenberg's *Schutzpass*', is part of the ongoing discussion of
myths about him, and it is therefore necessary to explain more fully its
origins and use. Most writers and people interested in Wallenberg tie
him very closely to this ad hoc, hastily manufactured diplomatic document. It is also necessary to further describe some of the various protective documents, different from 'Wallenberg's *Schutzpass*', which
were issued by the Swedes and other neutrals. However, first it must
be emphasized that even those who obtained diplomatic papers issued
by neutral diplomats were by no means necessarily protected by mere
possession of a 'foreign' document. Particularly after the 15 October
Nyilas coup, possession even of a previously useful document was,
unfortunately, no guarantee of safety. They could and did work, but

not all the time. It was often, as Engzell said, a matter of chance.

The particular document so closely associated with Wallenberg was but one of a variety of neutral diplomatic papers in circulation both before and after the German occupation.[88] It has been noted that Swiss diplomat Karl Lutz issued a document which bore the rubric '*Schutzpass*' long before Wallenberg's arrival. Nonetheless, in popular memory, it is 'Wallenberg's *Schutzpass*' that has come to physically symbolize his and Sweden's diplomatic efforts. Though he was instrumental in creating Sweden's *Schutzpass,* which graphically was a particularly impressive document, its actual protective value was as mixed as the others. Moreover, as already noted, its protective utility, like all other such neutral documents circulating in Budapest in 1944, was based on a quasi-legal precedent accepted by Hungarian authorities long before he came to Hungary.

There seems to be no doubt that Raoul Wallenberg was responsible for the production of 'his' *Schutzpass*. He was an accomplished draughtsman, and clearly crafted it to impress authorities. He drafted it with considerable attention to 'bureaucratic' detail (much more so than the other ad hoc Swedish documents issued in Budapest), including an essentially 'nonsense number' for each individual document – at least it is a detail remembered by survivors. In essence, however, the document was a brash bluff. Anger remembers that '[he] saw our certificates for the visa, and he made it [a] more spectacular protective passport, in colour, in [the] blue and yellow Swedish colours, with the Swedish coat of arms'.[89]

Yet this iconic Swedish/Hungarian document was printed, for reasons unknown, with a serious mistake! Sweden's national symbol, most often produced in blue and yellow, is the *Tre Kronor* (Three Crowns), a royal symbol with its roots in the middle ages. Adopted officially in 1908 as the country's official symbol, it is the Swedish government's seal in all manner of media. Yet the actual *Tre Kronor* has always two crowns on top, one below, in a triangular form. The *Schutzpass,* however, has (in all versions viewed by the author, both in photos and directly), one crown on top and two at the bottom! It is odd, and impossible to explain, how a man as careful and attentive to detail as Wallenberg was could have allowed such a significant error to be committed.[90] The mistake is not commented upon in any official UD report from those months, nor remembered by Per Anger in a long interview. It was (again, inexplicably) replicated over at least several print runs during summer and autumn 1944. Interestingly, neither Hungarian nor German officials appear to have caught this mistake, as no evidence has been located to indicate that this error hampered its effectiveness.

Because neutral protective papers were critically important in

Budapest, and because that one document – the *Schutzpass* – typifies some of the heuristic problems connected to distracting myths about Wallenberg, it is helpful to see what Danielsson and Anger were doing with other documents they issued before Wallenberg arrived, and what they themselves understood about their effectiveness. We have seen that the two diplomats understood that the various documents they were issuing had a shifting and uncertain protective value, with some seemingly more effective than others. This uncertainty about the various documents increased throughout 1944, with (again) the Swedes and everyone else understanding that the most effective document, and therefore the most sought after, was an emergency passport (of whatever nation). This had a more authoritative look than others, it was harder to forge, its scarcity made it more desirable and the authorities knew that it was distributed more carefully than other protective documents. Another factor was that a document with the signature of a known neutral official (such as Danielsson or Lutz) was more valuable than one without, and that possession of any document with an actual Swedish or Swiss letterhead or inked stamp was more valuable than one without such accoutrements – regardless of the text on it. The flow of these documents became so great that the Swedes, Swiss and others feared that a potentially damaging 'paper inflation' threatened to damage the value of all types of neutral documents, even the most respected ones.

Just days before Wallenberg arrived, Danielsson and Anger described the problems of not understanding completely the protective value of their various papers, some of which they literally typed on the spot, on small pieces of low-quality paper:[91]

> Even though we have been, from the beginning, rather sceptical about the value of the different protective papers and letters [they have] been shown, in individual cases if the bearer has luck, to have been of assistance, yes ... sometimes even to have meant rescue at least for a while.
>
> One person who received a 'B' protective letter [*skyddsbrev*] told us later that he found himself on a street the other day where every Jew was stopped by the police and taken away, being told that they must help with clearing up bomb damage from the latest attack. He immediately showed the Swedish protective letter and due to this could proceed unhindered. Of approximately a hundred Jews stopped, only he and a doctor were allowed to go free.[92]

With the Swedes hesitant to issue too many emergency passports, terrified Jews clamoured for virtually any document they could get from the Legation. The desperate applicants, Danielsson wrote:

> understood that an emergency passport was unavailable, but
> they still requested a stamped certificate of any type ... and
> because the Legation does not want to completely deny those
> seeking help, a certificate has been issued saying, for example:
> 'It is hereby certified that the bearer has submitted an applica-
> tion to the Legation for Swedish citizenship' ... stamped with-
> out a signature.[93]

Per Anger remembered the potential danger of issuing too many
genuine documents, and the haphazard novelty of the others:

> We couldn't, of course, increase the number of emergency pass-
> ports ... that would have been a kind of inflation, and then those
> passports would have had no value. So instead I, or we [made up]
> this kind of certificate saying that the holder of this certificate has
> got a visa to Sweden, and ... until it is possible to travel to
> Sweden, he is under the protection of the Swedish government. I
> mean, it was that kind of a legal document, with stamps and all
> that ... [But it] had no base [sic] whatever in international law ...
> None.[94]

In a telegram sent on 5 July, Anger told Stockholm about a newspaper article which told of a Jewish bank director named Rapoch, who
attempted to escape a round-up by showing a Swedish document. But
the article, Anger reported, misidentified the actual document, a mistake which troubled him. 'The [information] was articulated in such a
way that the reader can form the impression that Swedish passports
can be obtained at the Legation in return for payment. Rapoch has, in
fact, received a protective letter B ... which in the article is described
as an emergency passport. The Legation has as a result of this article
formally protested with the Hungarian Foreign Ministry.'[95] The Swedes
knew that any perception amongst the public that protective documents could be purchased would severely diminish their protective
value, endangering lives even more.

A RESPITE FROM DEATH

Regent Horthy's decision to halt the murderous transports provided a
measure of respite, and even a modicum of hope, to Budapest's Jews.
This included, of course, the 450 Jews who up to that date enjoyed the
officially acknowledged protection of the Swedish government.[96]
Braham explains that Horthy took his decision for a variety of reasons
– none of them, however, deriving from any real abiding sense of

humanitarianism for the more than 250,000 Jews still alive in Budapest. Whatever the actual reason, Horthy's decision saved more lives than the combined efforts of the neutral diplomats in Budapest, or Allied representatives outside the country. Yet there remained many Germans and Hungarian officials, soldiers, bureaucrats and businessmen determined to achieve the 'goal' of a completely judenrein Magyar nation. It was these men with whom Raoul Wallenberg, aided by his colleagues, would do diplomatic battle between 9 July 1944 and 17 January 1945.

NOTES

1. Unknown to UD, 23 March 1944 (received), *Riksarkivet Utrikesdepartementet* (hereafter RA UD), Hp 21 Eu 1094, folder 2.
2. Editorial in *Aftontidningen*, 5 July 1944.
3. R.L. Braham has written that Sweden's diplomatic efforts began only in June, which is incorrect. See R.L. Braham, *The Politics of Genocide: The Holocaust in Hungary*, revised and enlarged edn (Boulder, CT: Rosenthal Institute for Holocaust Studies Graduate Center/City University of New York Social Science Monographs, 1994), vol. 2, p.1084, and R.L. Braham, 'The Holocaust in Hungary: A Retrospective Analysis', in R.L. Braham and S. Miller (eds), *The Nazis' Last Victims: The Holocaust in Hungary* (Detroit, MI: Wayne State University Press, 1998), p.39.
4. On this, see P.A. Levine, *From Indifference to Activism: Swedish Diplomacy and the Holocaust, 1938–1944*, 2nd edn (Uppsala: Studia historica Upsaliensia, 1998), and P.A. Levine, 'Attitudes and Action: Comparing the Responses of Mid-Level Bureaucrats to the Holocaust', in D. Cesarani and P.A. Levine (eds), *'Bystanders' to the Holocaust: A Re-Evaluation* (London and Portland, OR: Frank Cass, 2002), pp.212–36.
5. I. Danielsson to Foreign Minister C. Günther, no.23, 19 January 1944, RA UD, Hp 1 Eu 1095, folder 5.
6. A distinct connection with Sweden, either personal or professional, was the fundamental criteria for help being given. Importantly, however, the degree of such connections considered necessary diminished during the year until the concept became virtually meaningless.
7. See Levine, *From Indifference to Activism*, Chapter 11, on Sweden's role in providing refuge for almost 8,000 Jews in October 1943. Several hundred Jews without Danish citizenship are estimated to have been in that group.
8. Many have written that prior to the March 1944 occupation, Hungarian Jews remained unaware – sometimes even wilfully so – of what was happening elsewhere in Europe. Josef Eismann obviously did not believe that because the war was going badly for Germany, all would be well. His use of the word 'deportation' is significant.
9. J. Eismann to UD, 8 January 1944, RA UD, Hp 21 Eu 1094, folder 2.
10. G. Engzell to I. Danielsson, no.15, 14 January 1944, RA UD, Hp 21 Eu 1094, folder 2.
11. G. Engzell to Swedish Legation Budapest, 4 February 1944, RA UD, Hp 21 Eu 1094, folder 2.
12. Common Swedish bureaucratic process is to issue 'emergency passports' only to actual Swedish citizens, in the event that a passport is lost or stolen.
13. It says much about Engzell that he found the time to receive this desperate father. This was not the only case when this busy diplomat made time in his schedule to meet with individuals representing Jews in Budapest.
14. G. Engzell to I. Danielsson, no.213, 21 March 1944, RA UD, Hp 21 Eu 1094, folder 2.
15. I. Danielsson to UD, 23 March 1944, RA UD, Hp 21 Eu 1094, folder 2.
16. J. Eismann to G. Engzell, 30 May 1944, RA UD, Hp 21 Eu 1095, folder 4.
17. G. Engzell to Legation Budapest, no.203, 10 July 1944, RA UD, Hp 21 Eu 1095, folder 5. It is significant that Engzell instructed Danielsson to consider helping other family members now that the girls had been naturalized. Therefore, even other family members, at that point unidentified, were now eligible for assistance in the eyes of UD.

18. See Chapter 3, p.76, n.16.
19. Lázsló Baky and his equally vicious colleague Lázsló Endre both figure prominently in all accounts of the Hungarian Holocaust.
20. Danielsson to Günther, no.78, 28 March 1944, RA UD, Hp 1 Eu 582/21, folder 2.
21. Author interview with Ambassador Per Anger, March 1990, Uppsala University Library, Raoul Wallenberg Project Archive, no.C002, p.12.
22. Ibid., p.29.
23. Ibid., p.29.
24. These factors and others relating to Sweden and Switzerland's efforts to help Jews are detailed in a long memorandum sent from the Hungarians to the Germans on 27 June 1944. See Braham, *Politics of Genocide*, vol. 2, pp.874–7.
25. There developed eventually a virtual format for letters of appeal to UD. Because the situation in Budapest became so widely known, in subsequent months the letters of appeal became shorter and less emotional. The appellants understood that UD officials were fully briefed about what was happening, thus fewer rhetorical or emotional passages were used to 'convince' officials to help. Those listed in the letters were virtually assumed to be worthy or eligible for Swedish help, and outright rejections became rare. Many such appellants more or less adopted the format of a very brief letter, with the relevant names filled in. This was particularly the case with dozens sent to UD in the autumn by lawyers at a couple of prominent Jewish legal firms in Stockholm.
26. K.E. Jansson, 'Arbetarrörelsens flyktinghjälp to UD', 12 April 1944, RA UD, Hp 21 Eu 1094, folder 3.
27. V. Åman to Legation Budapest, 2 June 1944, RA UD, Hp 21 Eu 1095, folder 5.
28. K. Lauer to UD, 24 April 1944, RA UD, Hp 21 Eu 1094, folder 3.
29. E. Björkman to G. Engzell, 26 April 1944, RA UD, Hp 21 Eu 1094, folder 3.
30. Established in 1922 by the Swedish government and located at the author's Uppsala University, this institution was Europe's first nationally financed 'research' institute for eugenics and 'racial biology'. Swedish culture and science were intimately connected with the prevailing trends in the European-wide eugenics movement. This is an example of the legitimacy given to the pseudo-scientific mind-set of eugenics which facilitated the Holocaust. On this, see, for example, S. Kühl, *The Nazi Connection: Eugenics, American Racism and German National Socialism* (New York: Oxford University Press, 1994). In the 1930s, Gunwar Dahlberg, who was neither a racist nor an anti-Semite, replaced Herman Lundborg, the institute's first director. The latter was quite attracted to Nazi manifestations of eugenics, especially in connection to the indigenous *Sami* (Lappish) people in the north of Sweden.
31. G. Dahlberg to C. Günther, no.192/5080a, 15 June 1944, RA UD, Hp 21 Eu 1095, folder 5. Some days later a cable was sent to Anger in Budapest asking for news about the appellant's family. Högstedt to Anger, no.51, 6 July 1944, RA UD, Hp 21 Eu 1095, folder 6.
32. L. Porzolt to G. Engzell, no.192/4378, 25 May 1944, RA UD, Hp 21 Eu 1095, folder 4. As we will see, the psychological support which protective papers provided by Sweden and other neutral legations would only increase after the 15 October *Nyilas* takeover of the Hungarian government.
33. See, for example, Swedish minister in Bern Z. Przybyszewski-Westrup's memo to Sven Grafström, head of UD's political division on 7 June 1944. Przybyszewski-Westrup to Grafström, no.985, RA UD, Hp 21 Eu 1095, folder 5.
34. Z. Przybyszewski-Westrup to S. Grafström, 10 June 1944, RA UD, Hp 21 Eu 1095, folder 5.
35. It was characteristic throughout the years of murder for many Swedish diplomats and other officials to use word 'persecutions' (*förföljelser*), to describe what they knew was deportation and mass killing.
36. I. Danielsson to UD, no.157, 2 June 1944, RA UD, Hp 21 Eu 1095, folder 5.
37. S. Grafström to Legation Budapest, no.150, 6 June 1944, RA UD, Hp 21 Eu 1095, folder 5. Of course, everyone in Europe awoke that day to the news of the Normandy invasion.
38. I. Danielsson to UD, no.170, 14 June 1944, RA UD, Hp 21 Eu 1095, folder 5.
39. UD to Legation Budapest, no.165, 15 June 1944, RA UD, Hp 21 Eu 1095, folder 5.
40. See Chapter 5.
41. I. Danielsson to Foreign Minister C. Günther, no.127, 24 June 1944, RA UD, Hp 1/21 Eu 1095, folder 5.

42. This remarkable report was sent in the same Swedish diplomatic pouch containing a copy of the document which would come to be called the 'Auschwitz Protocols'. Recognized immediately as urgent, this now famous document was described by Danielsson as 'an account of the extermination camp Auschwitz, written by two Slovakian Jews who escaped from there'. It was given to the Swedes by members of Budapest's 'Jewish Council'. The pouch also contained a report from a woman who had escaped from Auschwitz. The manner in which Budapest's 'Jewish Council' dealt with and disseminated this information remains controversial. See, amongst others, Braham, *Politics of Genocide*, vol. 2, especially pp.806–50.

43. I. Danielsson to C. Günther, no.131, 30 June 1944, RA UD, Hp 1 Eu 583, folder 22.

44. It is likely that the report was actually drafted by Per Anger, in consultation with Danielsson, and then signed by the latter.

45. G. Kádár and Z. Vági, *Self-financing Genocide: The Gold Train, the Becher Case and the Wealth of Hungarian Jews*, trans. E. Koncz, J. Tucker and A. Kádár (Budapest: Central European University Press, 2001), p.215.

46. I. Danielsson to G. Engzell, no.447, 18 June 1944, RA UD, Hp 21 Eu 1095, folder 5. The fates of Turai and Kertész are unknown.

47. I. Danielsson to UD, no.179, 19 June 1944, RA UD, Hp 21 Eu 1095, folder 5. The telegram was sent at 08.07 that morning. Danielsson also proposed, for the first time, that the Swede Valdemar Langlet, a long-time resident of Budapest, be appointed delegate for SRK, a move which would have eliminated the need to obtain a German visa for a Swede dispatched from Stockholm. See Chapter 8 for more on Langlet.

48. Hungarian Foreign Ministry, 'Verbal note' 136/res. 6. 1944, 19 June 1944, German language copy in RA UD, Hp 21 Eu 1095, folder 5.

49. I. Danielsson to UD, no.185, 20 June 1944, RA UD, Hp 21 Eu 1095, folder 5.

50. I. Danielsson to C. Günther, no.128, 25 June 1944, RA UD, Hp 21 Eu 1095, folder 5. This letter was read widely within the government and sent to F. Rydman, head of SRK, and Archbishop Erling Eidem, head of Sweden's Lutheran state church.

51. G. Engzell to I. Danielsson, no.6, 5 July 1944, RA UD, Hp 21 Eu 1095, folder 6.

52. P. Anger to G. Engzell, no.15, 5 July 1944, and P. Anger to C. Günther, no.149, 5 July 1944, both RA UD, Hp 21 Eu 1095, folder 6.

53. A. Cohen, 'The Dilemma of Rescue or Revolt', in Braham and Miller (eds), *Nazis' Last Victims*, p.133. See also Braham's detailed description of these dramatic days in *Politics of Genocide*, vol. 2, Chapter 25.

54. King Gustav also had a series of contacts of a more dubious nature during the Nazi era, not least with Hitler himself during the mid-to-late 1930s. On this, see S. Thorsell, *Mein lieber Reichskanzler: Sveriges kontakter med Hitler's rikskansli* (Stockholm: Bonnier Fakta, 2006); and H. Arnstad, *Spelaren Christian Günther: Sverige under andra världskriget* (Stockholm: Wahlström & Widstrand, 2006).

55. For example Otto Roboz, head of Budapest's Jewish Orphanage for Boys, believed that this was the case. It is possible that such contemporaries contributed to this mistake when it was first published by Hungarian journalist and historian Jenö Lévai. Repeated many times since, it constitutes an element of the Wallenberg myth. It is, obviously, an appealing narrative titbit. See O. Roboz's memoir, published first in Hungarian in 1984, and translated into English that same year, *The Jewish Orphanage for Boys in Budapest During the German Occupation*, edited by A. Scheiber (Évkönyv: Central Board of Hungarian Israelites, 1983–84); also J. Lévai, *Raoul Wallenberg – hjälten i Budapest* (Stockholm: Saxon & Lindströms, 1948), p.41.

56. One journalist who has written about Budapest mistakenly called Wallenberg 'the envoy of the King of Sweden who operated in Budapest'. See the interesting but sometimes empirically problematic book about the fascinating Italian 'diplomat' Giorgio Perlasca, by E. Deaglio, *The Banality of Goodness: The Story of Giorgio Perlasca* (Notre Dame, IN: University of Notre Dame Press, 1998), p.154.

57. Several historians have also misunderstood and repeated mistakes regarding both the background of Gustav's appeal and the manner in which it was delivered. I have examined this episode in detail in my book, *From Indifference to Activism*, pp.273–5, and nn.112–17.

58. Both the French and Swedish versions are in RA UD, Hp 21 Eu 1095, folder 5.

59. P. Anger to C. Günther, no.143, 3 July 1944, RA UD, Hp 1/21 Eu 1095, folder 5.

60. In subsequent internal correspondence, including a report by Wallenberg, the Swedes believed that Gustav's intervention was key to Horthy's fateful decision.

61. At the bottom of the original telegraph are the instructions to the Budapest Legation to 'Telegraph when message delivered, publicizing here will take place.' RA UD, Hp 21 Eu 1095, folder 6.

62. *Aftontidningen*, 5 July 1944.

63. Ibid.

64. P. Anger to C. Günther, no.149, 5 July 1944, RA UD, Hp 21 Eu 1095, folder 6. This report, like many others, is notable for its wide distribution. After arrival it was sent to all important Swedish legations around the world; to the head of Sweden's Lutheran Church, Archbishop Erling Eidem; Chief Rabbi of Sweden's Jewish community Marcus Ehrenpreis; and other community leaders. More on both of these important Swedish religious leaders in subsequent chapters.

65. See note 52 above.

66. P. Anger to E. von Post, no.77, 5 July 1944, RA UD, Hp 21 Eu 1095, folder 6.

67. G. Engzell to I. Danielsson, no.6, 5 July 1944, RA UD, Hp 21 Eu 1095, folder 6.

68. For a different interpretation of Richert's ideas and influence, see K. Molin, 'Arvid Richert', in G. Artéus and L. Leifland (eds), *Svenska diplomatprofiler under 1900–talet* (Stockholm: Probus, 2001); and more generally, W.M. Carlgren, *Svensk utrikespolitik 1939–1945* (Stockholm: Allmänna förlaget, 1973).

69. Such bureaucratic support was decisive, as can be seen when comparing that received by Wallenberg from UD, and the lack of support Valdemar Langlet received from SRK. See Chapter 8.

70. G. Engzell to A. Richert, no.7, 5 July 1944 RA UD, Hp 21 Eu 1095, folder 6. This 'secret' memorandum was sent 'by courier' and distributed widely within the Swedish government.

71. G.A. Wechsler to Minister W.F. Boström, Washington, DC, 5 July 1944, RA UD, Hp 21 Eu, folder 6. The Germans, naturally enough, paid attention to the response to Gustav's appeal, including its reception in Sweden. See R.L. Braham, *Eichmann and the Destruction of Hungarian Jewry* (New York: Twayne, 1961), doc. 362, p.761.

72. S. Schonfeld, Executive Director of the 'Chief Rabbi's Religious Emergency Council' to C.O. Gisle, Swedish Legation (undated, but probably between 7 and 9 July), RA UD, Hp 21 Eu 1095, folder 6. Schonfeld hoped that their 'unorthodox suggestions ... may yet receive the sympathetic consideration of both his Majesty and the Swedish government'.

73. *The Times*, 8 July 1944, clipping in RA UD, Hp 21 Eu 1095, folder 6.

74. For a typical example, see the letter from Elsa Höglund, an official at Stockholm's City Hall to Engzell, appealing for assistance for a Mrs Margit Kertès of Budapest, no.225/222, 8 July 1944, RA UD, Hp 21 Eu 1095, folder 6.

75. Ingrid Günther's connection to these two families is not explained.

76. G. Engzell to *Statsrådinnan Fru* Ingrid Günther, 12 July 1944, RA UD, Hp 21 Eu 1095, folder 6. We may assume, however, that verbal communication on the matter took place in the interim between Engzell and Günther.

77. See, for instance, the letter from S. Högstedt to P. Anger, no.51, 6 July 1944, RA UD, Hp 21 Eu 1095, folder 6.

78. G. Engzell to Docent R. Jagitsch, Chalmers Technical College, no.987, 12 July 1944, RA UD, Hp 21 Eu 1095, folder 6.

79. See Levine, *From Indifference to Activism*, esp. Chapters 8 and 10. See also N. Eck, 'The Rescue of Jews with the Aid of Passports and Citizenship Papers of Latin American States', in *Yad Vashem Studies*, 1 (1957), pp.125–52.

80. Yehuda Bauer, *Jews for Sale? Nazi–Jewish Negotiations, 1933–1945* (New Haven, CT: Yale University Press, 1994), analyses some of these negotiations, including some which occurred in Hungary. This willingness to negotiate, for a variety of motivations, is analysed in S. Szita, *Trading in Lives? Operations of the Jewish Relief and Rescue Committee in Budapest, 1944–45*, trans. S. Lambert (Budapest and New York: Central European University Press, 2005). The case of SS official Kurt Becher is a particularly egregious case of a murderer successfully creating a post-war alibi by negotiating for the lives of a few Jews during the Holocaust.

81. E. Veesenmay to Auswärtiges Amt (hereafter AusAmt), 20 June 1944, Braham, *Eichmann and the Destruction of Hungarian Jewry*, doc. 324, p.695. This document also mentions various Swiss activities.

82. E. Veesenmayer to AusAmt, 5 July 1944, ibid., doc. 360, p.760.

83. E. Veesenmayer to AusAmt, 7 July 1944, ibid., doc. 363, p.762.

84. On this, see C. Browning's still valuable study, *The Final Solution and the German Foreign*

Office: A Study of Referat DIII of Abteilung Deutschland, 1940–1943 (New York: Holmes & Meier, 1978).
85. See Levine, *From Indifference to Activism,* esp. Chapter 10.
86. L. Nylander to G. Engzell, 11 July 1944, RA UD, Hp 21 Eu 1095, folder 6.
87. S. Grafström to H. Johnson and V. Mallet (respectively the American and British ministers in Stockholm), 3 July 1944, RA UD, Hp 21 Eu 1095, folder 6. Addressed to 'My dear Herschel, My dear Sir Victor', Grafström did ask, however, that if they used the information publicly, 'it is highly desirable that the source ... should not be mentioned'.
88. The Zionist underground in Budapest established fairly large-scale forgery operations which simultaneously aided and endangered the bearers of genuine neutral papers. This aspect of protective activities in Budapest will be reviewed in subsequent chapters.
89. Author's interview with P. Anger, p.45.
90. It is uncertain where and by which printing firm(s) in Budapest the actual sheets were printed. It appears to have been produced in print runs of at least several thousand sheets. See plate no.14.
91. A few specimens may be found in UD files.
92. P. Anger to G. Engzell, no.15, 5 July 1944, RA UD, Hp 21 Eu 1095, folder 6.
93. I. Danielsson to UD, no.118, 8 May 1944, RA UD, Hp 21 Eu 1094, folder 3.
94. Author's interview with P. Anger, p.31.
95. P. Anger to UD, no.214, 5 July 1944, RA UD, Hp 21 Eu 1095, folder 6.
96. P. Anger to UD, no.211, 3 July 1944, RA UD, Hp 21 Eu 1095, folder 6. Anger categorized the approximately 450 (the number was probably greater as some of the protective documents were intended for entire families) as having sufficiently strong connections with Sweden to be listed in a document submitted to Hungarian authorities. Provisional passports were held by 186, and about 260 had Swedish entry visas stamped on one type of document or another.

5

June: Myth and Fact: Understanding Wallenberg's Recruitment and Mission

Because it is obvious for us that current staff cannot devote time for this special task, consideration is being given to attach Raoul Wallenberg to the Legation. His good connections and knowledge of Hungary should therefore satisfy requirements. Cable immediately if any objections.[1]

Question of [Red Cross] delegate, your coded cable no.179, not current until further notice, since no objections to Raoul Wallenberg being attached Legation.[2]

SEPARATING MYTH FROM FACT

As noted in the introduction, the remaining post-war mysteries about Raoul Wallenberg are the following: why did the Soviet Union detain him and why was he, an accredited neutral diplomat, not returned by Stalin's government? Why did Wallenberg's own government not show much greater urgency in trying to obtain his release, particularly in the first months and years after his detention? Finally, and most poignantly, what, ultimately, was his fate? In spite of significant effort and expense by many dedicated individuals – not least Wallenberg's immediate family – and, quite belatedly, the Swedish and Russian governments, final and conclusive answers to these questions have remained frustratingly, even destructively, elusive.[3]

This study does not seek to answer those questions. They lie outside both its goals, and the competences of the author. However, their chances of ever being satisfactorily answered are increased by the two primary questions which are answered in this chapter. They are: for whom did Wallenberg work? And what did he and his employers – whoever they might have been – believe that this particular Swedish economic aristocrat could and should accomplish? In addressing these questions, which are also central to elements of myth around him, this chapter will describe and analyse the political and humanitarian intent of his mission as recounted in the relevant documentation. In doing so, several more of the foundational myths which have contributed to the popular misunderstandings of this chapter of Holocaust history will be dispelled. However, the central themes of this chapter can only be addressed after a brief review of other aspects of the humanitarian diplomacy conducted primarily but not exclusively by the United States, before and after Germany's March occupation of Hungary.

Events there presented a difficult challenge for the War Refugee Board (WRB), the small but dynamic executive agency established in late January by Franklin Roosevelt. The WRB was formed by Roosevelt in direct response to a devastating internal critique, by a group of second-tier US Treasury and State Department officials, of what they felt was the woefully inadequate response of their government to the genocide of the Jews.[4] They were outraged that their government had, to that date of the war, done virtually nothing to assist European Jewry. Their report persuaded Treasury Secretary Henry Morgenthau to convince his boss, the president, to do something – anything – to help European Jewry, even at that late date. Amongst the authors of the report was John Pehle, a young, gifted treasury department official, appointed interim head of the agency. His energy and competence enabled the agency to become, at least in some ways, one 'success story' of the Holocaust, and he remained its director almost until the end of the war.

Wasting little time, Pehle ordered representatives to take up diplomatic posts in the capital cities of the few remaining Europe neutrals, including Sweden. There, Iver Olsen, serving double-duty as both treasury and OSS (Office of Strategic Services) official, was already in place.[5] Bucking considerable odds, Pehle and his colleagues quickly established an effective presence within America's enormous wartime bureaucracy. Highly motivated, Pehle and his men succeeded in establishing effective cooperation with important government departments and agencies whose primary task was, after all, to successfully conclude a global war of unprecedented scale.[6] As a result, when Hungary was occupied, Pehle was able to respond quickly and effectively. Communicating through State Department channels, he requested those neutral governments still maintaining legations in Budapest to increase their delegations. He did so because he understood, almost instinctively, that the more neutral representatives on the ground, the better. Pehle's shrewd proposal is another example of how 'bureaucratic resistance' can work, for experience suggested that even the mere presence of diplomats able to report home gave at least some pause to the murderers. Pehle understood that a visible corps of diplomats in Budapest would make clear to the Germans that this time at least, mass murder would not occur in secret.[7]

In contrast, Great Britain showed far less interest in efforts to help Jews, and no agency similar to the WRB was established by London.[8] In fact, some British officials were disdainfully resentful of this American attempt to focus attention on the still-continuing continental campaign of mass slaughter and plunder conducted by the Germans. The request to increase representation was of course received by UD.[9]

THE WAR REFUGEE BOARD IN STOCKHOLM

The US Legation in wartime Stockholm was headed by Herschel Johnson, an experienced diplomat who maintained cordial relations with many leading Swedish officials and politicians, even during periods of tense relations. In what came to be called 'refugee matters', Johnson was ably assisted by the above-mentioned Olsen, a younger diplomat who figures significantly in the Wallenberg story. Olsen's position as a Treasury official points to the significant role that this US department, along with its British counterpart, the ministry of economic warfare, played in the war against the Axis. Treasury officials influenced important political and economic issues regarding both neutral and occupied Europe, and were central players in US–Swedish relations during the second half of the war on trade issues which lay at the heart of their bilateral relationship. Elements of this relationship were American fears that Sweden would become a 'safe haven' for German assets fleeing that country.[10] More widely known, as noted above, is the fact that Olsen was also resident agent for the OSS, America's newly established and very keen espionage bureaucracy, which evolved after the war into the Central Intelligence Agency (CIA). By spring 1944, Olsen had been in Stockholm for about a year, and received his new assignment, as WRB representative, from Pehle shortly after the agency began work in February. Though both Johnson and Olsen had many other onerous tasks filling their days, there is no doubt that they enthusiastically supported the WRB's mission, and worked energetically from Stockholm to give some measure of humanitarian assistance to Europe's remaining Jews.

They were aided by the fact that UD welcomed the establishment of the WRB. This positive reception was not surprising, because even though trade tensions between the two governments escalated throughout 1944, there was close cooperation on several humanitarian schemes. Important if not paramount in the minds of Swedish officials was the fact that they well knew that assisting American humanitarian initiatives gave them some much-needed diplomatic goodwill in

Washington. Such political capital with the world's most powerful nation was in short supply throughout 1943 and 1944 because of Sweden's stubborn refusal to cease supplying Nazi Germany with militarily vital raw materials and industrial products. By 1944, Allied impatience with Sweden was such that even Winston Churchill, long sympathetic to Sweden's particular geopolitical position, sought to bring pressure on Stockholm.

In March 1944, he told Victor Mallet, Great Britain's minister in Stockholm, that 'the Swedes must do more for us than keeping Sweden out of war. They must get in before the end.'[11] Though in the end no effective pressure was applied by either the British or the Americans to force Sweden to contribute militarily to the defeat of Nazi Germany, it was commonly understood in Stockholm that one way of 'getting in' which would not be a breach of neutrality was to increase humanitarian diplomatic activities, not least on behalf of Jews. Particularly after basking in the publicity gained by the country's highly visible reception of Denmark's Jews several months before, Swedish officials throughout the government had no doubt that there was considerable political goodwill to be gained by cooperating in schemes which helped the victims of the war. They knew that by helping Jews, there was a chance of lessening the occasionally brutal diplomatic pressure that the Allies, particularly the Americans, were putting on them. Therefore, when the WRB requested that Sweden strengthen its diplomatic presence in Budapest, Stockholm readily agreed – this American request also met a Swedish need.

When analysing diplomatic and/or humanitarian efforts conducted by sovereign nations which involve the citizens of other nations, it is always tempting to assign only – or even mainly – cynical explanations for positive decisions made. How does one measure, in the international affairs of a sovereign state, where political self-interest ceases and a genuine wish to help fellow human beings from a different nation begins? Most frequently, governments seem to help others only when they gain politically. Another frequent motive is when collective (or even individual) guilt – of one sort or another – is felt. Such guilt unquestionably existed in Sweden, and amongst individual Swedes of all stripes. The editorial in *Aftontidningen*, cited in the previous chapter, made clear that many Swedes did feel guilty, both for their nation's continuing trade with Germany and their non-contribution to the defeat of fascism. It also existed amongst officials at higher government levels. For instance, Foreign Minister Günther articulated this unease when he told Victor Mallet: 'You know that we Swedes feel a certain sense of shame when we look at our neighbours and brothers who are living under German oppression.'[12]

Sweden's humanitarian activities in Budapest (before and after Wallenberg arrived) were both practical and conceptual. They were conceptual in the sense that officials could point to a rather distinguished tradition of humanitarian assistance given previously to other nations and peoples, which was closely associated with the over 100-year-long tradition and policy of military neutrality. Though Sweden's response to Jewish humanitarian needs was hardly flawless even after 1942, it is again salient to note that politicians and civil servants alike were aware that some of their diplomatic efforts on behalf of Jews had become widely known in Europe and had garnered much praise.[13] Most if not all officials involved in these issues believed they were doing the right thing, and these initiatives caused little noteworthy internal dissent either within UD or the government at large. Moreover, humanitarian efforts in Budapest came at a particularly propitious point of the war; such initiatives were now more realizable than earlier in the war. By this time a stream of initiatives – some more fantastical than others – were produced by some governments and private, mainly Jewish, agencies. Crucially, there were some German and Hungarian officials who chose not to fight the political circumstances which made humanitarian initiatives on behalf of Jews possible. For some German officials, what was inconceivable in, say, Warsaw or Riga in past years, was now at least imaginable in Budapest in 1944. In sum, circumstances were favourable for Swedish officials to choose to help in Budapest, within the capacities of their traditions, politics and bureaucracy. Danielsson's, Anger's and Engzell's activities between January and July 1944 unquestionably set the necessary precedents for Wallenberg's historic diplomacy. We will now examine how this scion of Swedish business aristocracy came to take the place history offered him.

WALLENBERG'S RECRUITMENT

Throughout spring 1944, connecting threads of events and personalities came together, with practical considerations merging with conceptual ones. From Budapest came a formal request from Anger and Danielsson for more staff, as they struggled to cope with circumstances which could not have been foreseen, and for which the tiny legation staff was neither trained nor equipped.[14] Their request was strengthened when from Budapest the above-mentioned Valdemar Langlet began his persistent agitation that SRK (Svenska röda korset, the Swedish Red Cross) should also commence humanitarian work. Eventually he obtained the organization's appointment as representative in the city, overcoming considerable institutional sluggishness.

Later though, officials at both SRK and UD would come to regret this decision.[15] Per Anger remembers that the 72-year-old Langlet, a somewhat eccentric man with a fascinating life story, demanded repeatedly that an organization with SRK's history and capacity had to do something also in Budapest. Langlet insisted, said Anger, that 'we have to do more ... we can't stop now. We [must] have more people from Sweden to help us because we can't cope with this.'[16] According to Anger, Langlet is the person who first suggested that Count Folke Bernadotte, a leading official of SRK and member of Sweden's royal family, should be sent to organize efforts in Budapest. On 2 June, apparently motivated by Langlet, Danielsson endorsed a request from the Hungarian Red Cross asking that representatives of SRK and Rädda barnen (Save the Children) should be sent to help organize relief for the Jews.[17]

Meanwhile, in Stockholm, the country's Jewish leaders had been discussing what they could do to help their co-religionists in Hungary, motivated in part because their constituency had significant familial, business or other connections with Jews in Hungary. On 18 April, community official Norbert Masur summarized recent discussions for Marcus Ehrenpreis, the Jewish community's venerable and deeply respected chief rabbi. Historian Steven Koblik has argued that this letter illuminates the origins of Wallenberg's mission and appointment, and certainly Masur was more prescient about this than he could have imagined:

> We should try to find a prominent person, clever, with a good reputation, a non-Jew, who is willing to travel to Rumania/ Hungary, there to lead a rescue operation for the Jews. The person in question must have the confidence of the Foreign Ministry [UD], and be equipped with a diplomatic passport ... We must put a large sum of money at this person's disposal, for example 500,000 Swedish crowns.
>
> I think that through this plan several hundred people could be saved. The prerequisites are: the right man, support from UD, the money. The last is probably the least problem, for we can surely get most of it from the USA. Also, the support of UD should be possible to obtain, considering how ready our authorities now are to help ... I believe it is worth a try to carry out the plan. But there is no time to waste.[18]

It would be almost three more months, however, before any such mission would commence and, so far as is known, Wallenberg was neither in mind at this point, or part of these April discussions. But once these discussions became known within the tiny Jewish community, it is not surprising that someone like Koloman Lauer suggested

Wallenberg, as seems to have happened. Though Masur imagined that this person would operate in both Hungary and Rumania, in the event activities in the latter country were not considered.

Though Koblik is correct to assert that these proposals helped to outline further discussions, this was a period when Jewish leaders and activists in Palestine, Britain, North America, Turkey and elsewhere were casting about desperately for virtually any plausible scheme which might save the lives of, as Masur wrote, 'at least several hundred', let alone thousands. Hungarian historian Jenö Lévai suggests that the idea for establishing aid activities in Budapest came from Stockholm's Jewish leaders in a proposal to 'the Swedish government'.[19] This however is an exaggeration, and both historians misunderstood the manner in which UD operated, and the demonstrated fact that rescue activities had commenced, as we have seen, long before July 1944.

However, there is a document which brings Wallenberg into the picture several weeks earlier than previously believed. On 14 May, while serving in the reserve army, he wrote a short letter to army command, requesting permission that he should be allowed 'to go abroad'. He wanted to return to Hungary, 'in order to purchase food supplies both for export back to Sweden, and in order to distribute supplies for Hungarian Jews, through a committee which will be formed for this purpose'.[20] No details about who might serve on this committee are given. Earlier, of course, Wallenberg had twice visited Hungary on business for his and Lauer's import–export firm, Mellaneuropeiska Handels AB, so going to Hungary specifically for this purpose was nothing new for Wallenberg. But now, in mid-May, he suddenly asked the army for official permission to return to Budapest to help Jews there. Typically for Wallenberg, his request was forcefully made. 'This is a question about something which is extremely meaningful and which in real terms is a matter concerning life and death. It is therefore requested that a decision is made without delay so that a passport may be issued, [and] that a German transit visa shall not be delayed.' Interestingly, but contrary to what we will subsequently see regarding discussions about the length of time he might be in Hungary, in this request Wallenberg asked for permission to be abroad for six months, from 1 July until 31 December. When negotiating a few weeks later with UD officials, he seemed to think that a couple of months would be enough to accomplish what he had in mind. On 6 June, one month before he actually left Sweden, he was granted official permission to leave the country.[21]

It is also interesting that this letter mentions neither UD nor the Americans. What seems to have happened is that in late April or early

May, he was brought into ongoing discussions being held by Masur, Ehrenpreis and other Jewish community leaders, most likely introduced to the group by Lauer. They might well have been enthusiastic about him, as it was evident that Wallenberg met the qualifications outlined above. It seems most probable that these internal Jewish discussions were soon shared with UD and American officials, who listened sympathetically.

By mid-May, Jewish leaders had almost certainly met American diplomats for 'extensive discussions' about Hungary, but probably even more important was the 'lengthy discussion' Iver Olsen had on the evening of 18 May with Claes Westring, Sweden's consul general in Oslo.[22] Westring was stationed in Norway when the Germans and their Norwegian collaborators rounded-up and deported that country's tiny Jewish population in autumn 1942, and he undoubtedly briefed Olsen about his sometimes successful attempts to assist and rescue Jews threatened with deportation.[23] The tactics used by Westring in Norway that autumn were the beginning of what I have described as Sweden's 'bureaucratic resistance', and there is no doubt that he used these tactics effectively in negotiations with German and Norwegian officials.[24]

From the US came a cable on 23 May instructing Johnson and Olsen to again urge the Swedes to increase their representation in Budapest. 'Please urge appropriate authorities, in the interest of humanity, to take immediate steps to increase the numbers of Swedish diplomatic and consular personnel in Hungary ... Naturally, it is hoped that all means available to such ... representatives to persuade individuals and officials to desist from further barbarism will be used by them. The extent to which the Swedish government is cooperating should be reported to the Department immediately.'[25]

As noted, obtaining Swedish cooperation was not difficult, as can be seen in a telegram from Stockholm to Danielsson. It was sent on 6 June, that fateful day in the history of the war, and leaves little question of prevailing sentiments within UD. Danielsson was instructed:

> [to] make clear for Hungarian authorities the distress felt by Swedes created by the ongoing persecutions of Jews in Hungary. Investigate whether a Swedish initiative to rescue, for example, women, children and the elderly might lead to some result, and let us know if you are able to carry out such actions if they are approved by the Hungarians. If so, the proposal will be favoured with immediate attention.[26]

Three days later, Johnson met Permanent Undersecretary for Foreign Affairs (*Kabinettssekreterare*) Erik Boheman, who 'reacted favourably to suggestion of increasing Swedish representation at Budapest in hope that it might have some effect in saving threatened people and certainly in securing more detailed and accurate information in regard to conditions'.[27] Boheman, who had an excellent relationship with the Americans, gave a response to Johnson that was equally forthright and disingenuous. He had Danielsson's and Anger's up-to-date and accurate information arriving in a steady and reliable stream, so American pressure to establish a channel for obtaining reliable information was hardly necessary. Johnson's cable also contained Boheman's explanation for Sweden's controversial (for the Americans) decision to maintain diplomatic relations with the nominally sovereign Hungarian government administering the country:

> [Boheman] would like to make entirely clear that the only reason that Swedish government had consented to receive a Charge d'affairs of present regime in Budapest was in order to be able to continue Sweden's own representation in Hungary. He said that the [Swedish] government had flatly refused to give an agrement [sic] to a Quisling Hungarian Minister but that it had been felt here after much consideration that to refuse a Charge d'affairs would imperil the whole Swedish representation in Hungary and its possibility of assisting people in distress.

As we shall see, this particular issue assumed considerable importance after the *Nyilas* coup of 15 October. Johnson concluded: 'I will [soon] go back again to Mr Boheman and endeavour to get concrete suggestions from him as to what it may be practicable to do in Hungary as well as further expressions of his ideas regarding increased Swedish representation.'[28]

Three days later, Johnson again cabled Washington to report two items of interest. The first was of a conversation with Vilhelm (Vilmos) Böhm, who would come to play a minor role in the run-up to Wallenberg's recruitment. The Hungarian exile reviewed for Johnson the situation in Hungary as he understood it, and the American reported:

> [we] have found Swede who is going to Hungary in very near future on business trip and who appears willing to lend every possible assistance on Hungarian problem. Am having dinner with him on June 11 ... for purpose of exploring possibilities and to obtain in some measure his capabilities along those lines. Any instructions which would coordinate approach to Hungarian problem would be helpful.[29]

For some reason, this Sunday meeting with Johnson does not appear in Wallenberg's diary, although a meeting with Olsen and Lauer at Wallenberg's apartment was scheduled for four days later, on Thursday the 15 June.[30] This is the first time that Wallenberg's name appears in either Swedish or American documents in this context. Significantly, Johnson virtually repeats some of the formulations from Wallenberg's request for travel permission, so obviously they had communicated in some way – word got around fast in wartime Stockholm.

Also significant is Johnson's specific request for instructions from Washington about how a humanitarian mission endorsed by the US might be formulated. As we shall see, this request would be repeated, but it was never answered satisfactorily by Washington. Indeed, it is striking in the extreme that the American and Swedish diplomats involved in discussing Wallenberg's mission and drawing up guidelines for it appear never fully to have understood each other's ideas about exactly what Wallenberg would do in Budapest. They seemed to have had different ideas about what could, and could not, be accomplished, and seem never to have put on paper exactly what was being considered, or if agreement had been reached. This failure to communicate clearly led, unsurprisingly, to divergent understandings about the exact nature of the relationship between Wallenberg, Johnson and the WRB, and the Swedish government. Continuing discussions do not seem to have clarified matters. It is this highly unprofessional confusion which forms some of the groundwork for post-war confusion, which in turn has led to controversies and myths about a central element of Wallenberg's story: for whom was he working in Budapest?

Two more telegrams were sent from Stockholm during the afternoon of 21 June, only twenty minutes apart. The first, labelled 'urgent', was from Johnson to the State Department and John Pehle. The second was from Sven Grafström to the Legation in Budapest. Johnson's telegram is particularly important because it summarizes several key issues under discussion. Both cables provide insight into how Wallenberg received his appointment, and what was being discussed about what he would do. Johnson wrote:

> Mr Boheman has informed me that Mr Raoul Wallenberg will be appointed an Attaché to the Swedish Legation at Budapest for the specific purpose of following and reporting on situation with respect to persecution of Jews and minorities ...
>
> As Wallenberg's functions in Budapest will be purely official and he has for time of appointment severed all business connections, Boheman does not anticipate any trouble in his [Wallenberg] securing the necessary visa. He said if the visa is refused the Swedish Government will simply refuse in turn to receive the Hungarian Charge d'Affaires.

Mr Boheman made it clear that Foreign Office and his government are disposed to cooperate as fully as possible in all humanitarian endeavours and the appointment of this Attaché is
undoubtedly an evidence of official Swedish desire to conform to
the wishes expressed [by] Department.

Olsen and I are of opinion that war Refugee Board [*sic*] should
be considering ways and means of implementing this action of
Swedish government particularly with respect to financial support it may be possible to arrange for any concrete rescue and
relief progress which may be developed.[31]

It is obvious that the initial idea about Wallenberg's going to
Budapest on business, both to send foodstuffs back to Sweden *and* try
to engage in some assistance activities, had evolved into a situation
where he would officially be mandated to work at the Legation, thereby strengthening Sweden's staff as the Americans had requested. In
other words, this evolution served Swedish and American interests, it
was beginning to look like what the Jewish leaders had discussed in
April, and certainly was an exciting prospect for Wallenberg himself.

However, less progress was made on the matter of what exactly he
would do. This somewhat contradictory telegram certainly outlines
what the Americans imagined Wallenberg might do, yet it appears
that Boheman, again, was not completely honest with his American
counterpart. According to Grafström's telegram (and this is confirmed
by subsequent documents), Wallenberg's appointment was not yet
finalized:[32]

With reference to the special interest with which the Jewish question is being followed here, it is desirable that special reporting
occurs continuously, with proposals being made for suitable and
realistic humanitarian initiatives, even relief measures required
for post-war period. American legation here continuously giving
question considerable attention.

As we understand fully that current staff cannot spare anyone
for this special assignment, consideration is being given to attach
to the Legation Raoul Wallenberg, who with his good connections to Hungary should possess conditions required.

Telegraph immediately if any objections.[33] [Emphasis added.]

Danielsson had presumably met the presumptive diplomat during
his earlier business trips to Budapest, so he had his own impression of
Wallenberg. He also asked Anger, who remembered that 'Danielsson
asked me and I said, Well, I know him ... and I think this is an excellent solution. So we immediately answered that Raoul Wallenberg is

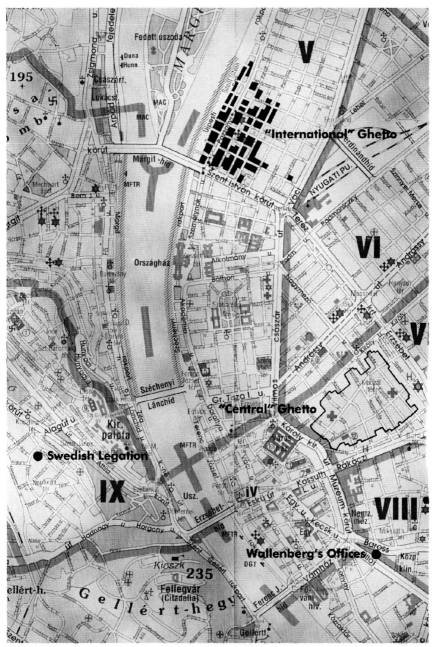

1. Central Budapest in 1944. Highlighted on this map are the 'international ghetto' and the 'central ghetto'. In Buda's 11th district, the Swedish Legation is illustrated, and in the 8th, on Ulloi ut 2–4. Wallenberg's offices in Post.

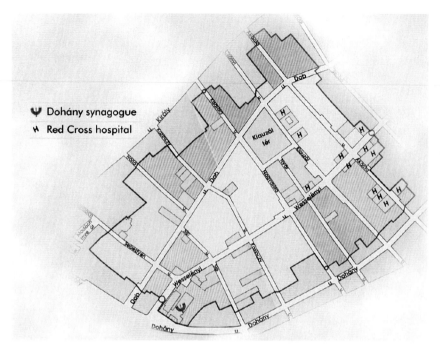

Key:
☪ Dohány synagogue
Ӿ Red Cross hospital

2. Budapest's 'central ghetto' with Swedish Red Cross hospitals and the Great Synagogue high-lighted.

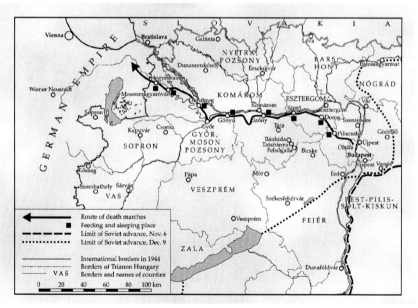

3. The map illustrates the route of the winter 'death marches' from Budapest to Hegyeshalom, November–December 1944.

4. Wallenberg, aged 3-4, with his highly influential paternal grandfather, Gustaf Oscar Wallenberg.. (Courtesy of The Jewish Museum, Stockholm and Karl Gabor.)

5. Wallenberg in his early teens. (Courtesy of The Jewish Museum, Stockholm and Karl Gabor.)

6. Wallenberg (to left), aged 23, with two Swedish friends in Cape Town, South Africa, during his business apprenticeship there. (Courtesy of The Jewish Museum, Stockholm and Karl Gabor.)

7. Edmund Veesenmayer, German Pleni-potentiary in Hungary, leaving the Royal Palace after providing Regent Horthy with his "letter of appointment", immediately after the March 1944 occupation. (Yad Vashem, Jerusalem.)

8. Veesenmayer was also an SS *Brigadeführer*. Directly responsible for the murder of hundreds of thousands of Hungarian Jews, Veesenmayer was found guilty of war crimes and sentenced in 1949 to twenty years imprisonment. In 1951 his sentence was reduced to ten years. That same year, he was released by the Americans due to 'ill-health'. He died in Germany in 1977. (Bundesarchiv Bild, Koblenz, Germany.)

9. A page from Wallenberg's diplomatic passport, stamped by UD, and issued a week before his departure to Budapest. The passport and other personal documents were returned by Soviet officials to Wallenberg's family in 1989. (Courtesy of The Jewish Museum, Stockholm and Karl Gabor.)

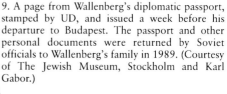

10. Another page from the passport. Note that Wallenberg's first name is misspelled, and that the period of validity was extended on 30 December by Per Anger. Expiration date was now 30 June 1945. (Courtesy of The Jewish Museum, Stockholm and Karl Gabor.)

11. Wallenberg's appointment's diary. It is open to the week after his arrival on Sunday 9 July. Note his lunch with Minister Danielsson, two meetings with Valdemar Langlet, and dinner with the Anger family. (Courtesy of The Jewish Museum, Stockholm and Karl Gabor.)

12. Wallenberg's telephone diary. Note Adolf Eichmann's telephone number. (Courtesy of The Jewish Museum, Stockholm and Karl Gabor.)

13. Wallenberg's Hungarian driver's license. He obtained it shortly after arrival, and it was valid until November. These documents were also returned to Wallenberg's family in 1989 by the Soviet Union. (Courtesy of The Jewish Museum, Stockholm and Karl Gabor.)

SCHUTZ-PASS

Nr. 68/96

Name / Név: Dr. Ladislaus Bálint

Wohnort / Lakás: Budapest

Geburtsdatum / Születési ideje: 23.VIII. 1891.

Geburtsort / Születési helye: Miskolc

Körperlänge / Magasság: 176 cm.

Haarfarbe / Hajszín: braun **Augenfarbe / Szemszín:** braun

Unterschrift / Aláírás:

SCHWEDEN   SVÉDORSZÁG

Die Kgl. Schwedische Gesandtschaft in Budapest bestätigt, dass der Obengenannte im Rahmen der — von dem Kgl. Schwedischen Aussenministerium autorisierten — Repatriierung nach Schweden reisen wird. Der Betreffende ist auch in einen Kollektivpass eingetragen.

Bis Abreise steht der Obengenannte und seine Wohnung unter dem Schutz der Kgl. Schwedischen Gesandtschaft in Budapest.

Gültigkeit: erlischt 14 Tage nach Einreise nach Schweden.

A budapesti Svéd Kir. Követség igazolja, hogy fentnevezett — a Svéd Kir. Külügyminisztérium által jóváhagyott — repatriálás keretében Svédországba utazik.

Nevezett a kollektiv útlevélben is szerepel.

Elutazásáig fentnevezett és lakása a budapesti Svéd Kir. Követség oltalma alatt áll.

Érvényét veszti a Svédországba való megérkezéstől számított tizenegyedik napon.

Reiseberechtigung nur gemeinsam mit dem Kollektivpass. Einreisewisum wird nur in dem Kollektivpass eingetragen.

Budapest, den 15. Sept.   1944

KÖNIGLICH SCHWEDISCHE GESANDTSCHAFT
SVÉD KIRÁLYI KÖVETSÉG

Kgl.Schwedischer Gesandte

14. A 'typical' Swedish 'Schutzpass'. Though designed by Wallenberg, Sweden's national symbol, 'Tre Kronor' (Three Crowns) is, inexplicably, inverted. The numbers in the upper-right corner are, so far as can be determined, meaningless. Issued exactly one month before the October *Nyilas* coup, this 'Schutzpass', like many others, was signed by Minister Danielsson, and only initialled by Wallenberg. Most important is the underlined sentence, which reads 'Until departure the aforementioned person and flat are under the protection of the Royal Swedish Embassy in Budapest'. This assertion by the Swedes (and other neutrals) had no basis in international law. (Courtesy of The Jewish Museum, Stockholm and Karl Gabor.)

15. Wallenberg at his desk, in conversation with some of his closest aides. It seems probable that the photograph was posed. (T. Verés Collection, Courtesy of USHMM Photo Archives.)

16. Wallenberg standing at his desk. It is unclear in which month the photograph was taken. (T. Verés Collection, Courtesy of USHMM Photo Archives.)

17. The Swedish Legation on Gellért Hill, with a municipal policeman guarding the main gate. The picture appears to have been taken in mid-autumn. (T. Verés Collection, Courtesy of USHMM Photo Archives.)

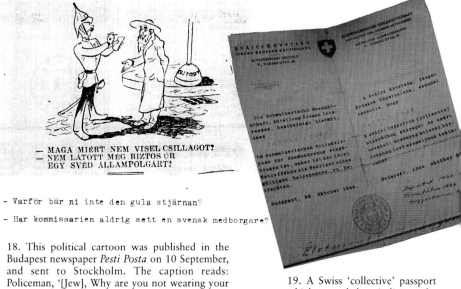

18. This political cartoon was published in the Budapest newspaper *Pesti Posta* on 10 September, and sent to Stockholm. The caption reads: Policeman, '[Jew], Why are you not wearing your Yellow Star?' The Jew answers, 'Has not the Officer ever seen a Swedish citizen [before]?' (Riksarkivet, Stockholm.)

19. A Swiss 'collective' passport which nonetheless indicates the name of one individual. (Author's photograph, taken at the Glass House Museum, Budapest.)

most welcome to come to Budapest.'[34] Danielsson cabled Stockholm, saying: 'No objections attachment Wallenberg.' Yet Wallenberg himself was not informed of this for several days; it was after all *Midsommar*, Sweden's revered holiday.[35]

The Americans were sanguine about the choice of Wallenberg, not least because he made a highly favourable impression on them. Olsen met Wallenberg at least twice – once for dinner alone on Monday 12 June, and then on 15 June, accompanied by Koloman Lauer, for a lengthy dinner and discussion at Wallenberg's Stockholm apartment.[36] Johnson met Wallenberg at least twice more, including lunch on 28 June at Bellmansro, one of Stockholm's most exclusive restaurants.[37] The veteran diplomat then wrote to Pehle: 'We are very favourably impressed with Wallenberg's ability to act intelligently and with discretion in carrying out any responsibilities that the WRB may delegate to him, and urge strongly that appropriate instructions be forwarded as soon as possible.'[38] Several days later, Johnson reiterated his confidence in the man who would adopt this unorthodox mission: 'There is no doubt in my mind as to the sincerity of Wallenberg's purpose because I have talked to him myself. I was told by Wallenberg that he wanted to be able to help effectively and to save lives and that he was not interested in going to Budapest merely to write reports to be sent to the Foreign Office.'[39]

The latter is in reference to what it seems the Swedes envisioned as Wallenberg's primary task – or at least a prioritized task which these habitually cautious civil servants were prepared to express on paper. It is difficult to understand Boheman's decision to wait even a few days to inform Wallenberg of the final decision concerning his appointment, because he and his colleagues knew full well what was occurring in Hungary. Indeed, during those last days of June, Boheman again spoke to Johnson, telling the American:

> information just received from Budapest concerning treatment of Jews is so terrible that it is hard to believe and that there are no words to qualify its description ... According to the evidence, these people are now being killed en masse by the Germans and large numbers are being taken to a place across the Hungarian frontier in Poland where there is an establishment at which gas is used for killing people.[40]

Two issues are important here. During the war, UD was a rather small institution within which officials frequently communicated informally either by telephone or through 'corridor' conversations. As a result, many issues which the historian might expect would be committed to paper were not – with all the advantages and disadvantages this implies. Boheman noted this in his post-war memoir: 'We knew each other so well that lengthy reasoning was seldom necessary and exchange of written messages between ourselves was never required ... We could all trust each other.'[41] As a result, presumptions of understanding regarding both policy and actual tasks were quite often just that, presumptions into which different understandings were easily made to fit. Because of the nature of bureaucracies, misunderstandings were not infrequent, even on issues of cardinal importance, and even between officials familiar with each other and working towards the same basic goals.[42]

Secondly, it is worth noting that there was ample precedent for UD to use such a person as Wallenberg on an ad hoc and loosely defined diplomatic mission. Throughout the war, both Jacob and Marcus Jr were members of negotiating teams which hammered out the essential trade agreements reached with the belligerents which enabled Sweden's economy to survive, and indeed flourish, during the war. Jacob worked the German side of negotiations, while Marcus Jr was a frequent guest in London; both provided invaluable assistance to their professional diplomatic colleagues. Earlier in the century, as we have seen, Wallenberg's grandfather Gustaf Oscar Wallenberg represented Sweden in Turkey and Japan. It was nothing extraordinary, therefore, for UD officials to entertain, and act upon, the prospect of someone such as Wallenberg working temporarily for the ministry, even on a mission of some sensitivity.

Interestingly, the British in Stockholm, who understood the Swedes much better than their American counterparts, were not so sure that Wallenberg would cut all business ties during his assignment. In a report sent on 3 July to London, an official wrote that 'the Swedish government have decided to attach to their Legation in Budapest, Monsieur Raoul Wallenberg, whose job it will be to deal with matters affecting the plight of Jews and persons whose lives and property are endangered by the Germans'. Describing something of Wallenberg's background and connections, the report then notes that Wallenberg 'has the reputation of being an intelligent, efficient and "rather smart" businessman'. The notation made subsequently by a British diplomat in Whitehall is particularly interesting: 'While I have no doubt that there is much truth in this and that the Swedes are actuated by the best of motives in this appointment, it does seem on the other hand that Wallenberg's firm will be able to profit by it to facilitate their business with the Hungarians.'[43]

More light is shed on Wallenberg's recruitment by another American document, this time from John Pehle's weekly summary of events dated 6 July, written for his boss and mentor, Treasury

Secretary Hans Morgenthau. In an opening section titled 'What we have done with respect to Hungary', Pehle wrote: 'We requested neutral powers and the International Red Cross to increase the size of their missions in Hungary. Sweden complied with our request and appointed a special attaché at Budapest who is in direct communication with our representative at Stockholm and has, in many ways, been extremely helpful to the Board.'[44] It is extremely unlikely that Pehle would, in a classified document, lie to his boss, and here we see direct evidence that the Americans understood Wallenberg to be a Swedish diplomat with links to the Board's activities. More evidence on this issue will be presented.

A final account of Wallenberg's recruitment comes from a source closer to him than any other: Koloman Lauer, his business partner. In two separate and highly detailed accounts written immediately after the war, the successful Hungarian-Jewish businessman gave his version of how Wallenberg was chosen. The first was addressed, for reasons unknown, to Marcus Wallenberg Jr.[45] The second is longer and even more detailed but undated, although its contents indicate that it was written some time later.[46] Though the two documents don't contradict each other, they give slightly different versions of Wallenberg's recruitment.

In the first, dated 20 April 1945, Lauer writes that in early June he had brought Wallenberg to the attention of Rabbi Ehrenpreis.[47] Then, in mid-June, he had introduced Wallenberg to Iver Olsen. We know that these meetings were influential in producing Wallenberg's appointment, particularly after Johnson discussed the matter with Boheman, and also that the connection between Wallenberg and the Americans was well known by friends and family. Yet for some reason Lauer concludes this letter with a request to the banker that he should 'treat my information about the American Legation in strictest confidence, since I have not been authorized to reveal anything about this'.[48] It is unclear why such a request was necessary in (presumably private) correspondence between two men who were more than casual acquaintances.[49]

Lauer's second and longer account adds much to our understanding of Wallenberg's time and activities in Budapest, as well as the issues under consideration in this chapter. Noting that his (Lauer's) company during the war was in the same building as the American Legation, he writes that the first time he introduced Wallenberg to Olsen was 'sometime at the end of April/beginning of May', although Wallenberg's own diary places these meetings in mid-June. Lauer says that the three discussed for some '8–10 hours' the situation in Hungary, which must be the 15 June dinner meeting mentioned above. Lauer then adds that the

following day, he contacted Sven Salén, the prominent shipper and
business associate of the older Wallenberg brothers (Salén also seems
to have assisted Lauer's business activities). Here we may note that
Lauer had, for perfectly understandable reasons, every reason to push
hard for Wallenberg to undertake some sort of rescue or assistance mission to Budapest. He had many family members there and was obviously desperate to help them in any way he could.

According to Lauer's longer account, it was Salén who contacted
Johnson, who then 'had lunch together with Raoul'. This account
places these meetings and discussions more than a full month earlier
than all other accounts.[50] Lauer also notes that very soon after the
lunch with Wallenberg, Herschel Johnson met Christian Günther to
discuss the matter. This is surprising, because Günther's name doesn't
figure at all in other accounts of this issue.[51] It is inconceivable, however, that Günther was not informed about Wallenberg's mission, or
that he did not, in the end, give it his approval.[52]

DEFINING WALLENBERG'S TASKS AND MISSION

The previous section has detailed Wallenberg's actual recruitment as a
somewhat distinct process from the parallel discussion which sought to
define what he would do in Budapest. In reality, of course, the two are
tightly intertwined. With his selection as special attaché apparently set,
what did his sponsor(s) plan, or believe, that Wallenberg would and
or could actually do in Budapest? As with many other issues already mentioned or still to be discussed here, the prevailing popular understanding
of the content and parameters of Wallenberg's mission has over the years
provided much fuel to the myth-making mill. This section will present
evidence for a more credible understanding of what the various parties
were thinking when they sent Wallenberg to Budapest. Included in this
account is the available evidence from Wallenberg himself.

We have seen that he told the Americans he was not interested in
going to Budapest 'merely to write reports', which it seems is what UD
officials nominally believed would be his primary task. The Swedes clearly understood that by agreeing to this appointment – thereby increasing
the Legation's staff, and designating Wallenberg to relieve Anger from
writing the desired 'special situation reports' – they had met American
requests without increasing substantially Sweden's diplomatic undertakings. They had good reason for believing this, because it is what the
Americans told them on several occasions. Wallenberg himself believed
that this is what UD wanted him to do; yet for him this was the minimum and apparently not particularly interesting task for the intelligent,
ambitious and adventurous businessman.

Johnson, as we have seen, felt comfortable describing to his superiors in some detail what Boheman had told him about the projected assignment; it was in Johnson's cable of 21 June that the parameters were outlined for the first time, as understood by high-level US and Swedish representatives: 'Mr Boheman has informed me that Mr Raoul Wallenberg will be appointed an Attaché to the Swedish Legation at Budapest for the specific purpose of following and reporting on situation with respect to persecution of Jews and minorities.'[53]

Numerous conversations between the principals occurred between mid-June and Wallenberg's 7 July departure in order to obtain, it may be surmised, a minimal degree of clarification – but little was committed to paper. What is certain is that as late as two weeks before his finalized appointment and departure, the two governments had quite different ideas about what Wallenberg should do. This failure to understand each other is evident in a message from Johnson to Pehle sent two days after the cable cited above. 'Legation ... is exploring with Swedish government all possible means by which further aid in the rescue and relief of victims of enemy persecution can be given by it. Foreign Office has not made reply before several days holiday commencing today but has promised prompt answer.'[54]

Yet Swedish officials still seemed to believe that Wallenberg had one primary task, which was to report from Budapest for two months. Then, according to their agreement with him, he would most likely return to Stockholm to tend to business matters.[55] Contrary to what many writers have asserted and to what is widely believed by the public, there is no evidence whatsoever that UD officials saw Wallenberg as a representative of the Americans, however unorthodox his recruitment had been. In the eyes of the Swedish government, Wallenberg was going to Budapest as a fully accredited Swedish diplomat. They expected him to adhere to established procedure while representing the country and ministry, and to follow Danielsson and Anger's directives. During his previous business travels in Nazi-occupied Europe Wallenberg had a regular passport. Now he was issued with a Swedish diplomatic passport.[56] Moreover, as we shall see in the copious documentation either produced by Wallenberg himself or about him, there is not the slightest hint indicating that any other Swedish diplomat connected to this story believed otherwise.

Now, at this decisive moment in his life, Wallenberg seems to have told the Americans that he had different ideas about what he wanted to do from those of his new employers. It seems likely that Wallenberg understood that the two governments had very different ideas about the exact nature of his forthcoming task(s) and, indeed, in light of what we know about him, it is certainly possible that he believed he could exploit such a gap – he was not a shy man. Wallenberg had spent some four years in the US, and during that time had met people from different occupations, segments and classes of American society. He surely understood the Americans better than his Swedish contemporaries did, including the men of UD. He knew how Americans operated, he had in the meantime gained experience in other cultures, and was known to be frustrated during his recent years in conservative, predictable Sweden.[57] Also, there is no reason to believe that he was permanently satisfied working for a minor business like Lauer's. We have seen that he told Johnson that he wished to do more than just write reports, which would be borne out almost immediately after arriving in Budapest.

In fact, on 28 June, Johnson wrote that Wallenberg believed the task of 'reporting' neither defined nor limited what he would try to do, and the American criticized UD's unwillingness to give Wallenberg a clearly articulated task beyond that:

> We should emphasize that the Swedish Foreign Office in mak-ing this assignment feels that it has cooperated fully in lending all possible facilities for the furtherance of an American pro-gram. It is not likely that [UD] will provide the newly appoint-ed attaché with a concrete program; but instead will probably give him rather general instructions which will not be suffi-ciently specific to enable him to deal promptly and effectively with situations as they develop in Hungary. The newly desig-nated attaché, Raoul Wallenberg, feels however that he, in effect, is carrying out a humanitarian mission in behalf [*sic*] of the War Refugee Board.[58]

There is no evidence that Johnson tried to discourage such thinking, perhaps because he thought the US might eventually gain some politi-cal advantage from being more closely associated with Wallenberg's hoped-for results. Nor does he seem to have discouraged the newly minted diplomat from thinking broadly. Johnson's cable continues: 'Consequently, he would like full instructions as to the line of activities he is authorized to carry out and assurances of adequate financial sup-port for these activities so that he will be in a position to develop fully all local possibilities. [We] urge strongly that appropriate instructions be forwarded as soon as possible.'[59] Yet again Johnson is appealing to Washington to provide a specific set of instructions, which obviously he had not received.

Several days later, and only five days before Wallenberg left Stockholm, Johnson again renewed his request for specific instruc-tions: 'Wallenberg, who is going to the Swedish Legation at Budapest as an attaché to handle refugee matters, was highly praised by Boheman who said that if our War Refugee Board could formulate some form of directive for him which the Foreign Office will be glad to transmit, it would be of great help to Wallenberg.'[60] It is this report in which Johnson mentioned Wallenberg's claim to be 'half-Jewish', for which there is no evidence. It is possible that while speaking with the American envoy Wallenberg simply may have become emotionally carried away in anticipation of his departure, but that is speculative. On the other hand, though this self-perception might have contributed to a desire to do more than reporting while in Budapest, there is no evidence that while there he either thought about this 'factor', or derived motivation from it. He was completely silent on the subject, as are all other sources from his six months in Budapest.

Interestingly, Wallenberg's appointment and the WRB's basic understanding of his tasks were made known to other agency representatives in Europe. On 4 July, Pehle cabled to his agents there:

> a neutral government is about to dispatch new attaché to its diplomatic mission Budapest. New attaché prepared to deal with Board's program through any available channels on practical basis as he is generally familiar with and has had extensive talks with Board's representative regarding immediate problems. He [is] also prepared to operate on Board suggested specific projects. You may desire, in line with your 3390 of May 27, that he undertake specific projects or contact specified persons. Please inform Board promptly if this is so.[61]

Confusion about what Wallenberg was to do is evident. The Swedes were not prepared to give him a concrete programme beyond writing reports and being visible. Pehle had given instructions that Wallenberg could not consider himself a representative of the WRB, but was 'prepared to operate on Board suggested specific projects'. Johnson's repeated requests for specific instructions seems to have been in vain. Indeed, Pehle seems to have believed that Wallenberg left for Budapest familiar with the WRB's essential tasks, and perhaps this is why the more specific set of instructions requested several times by Johnson was never sent. What is clear is that Wallenberg left for Budapest without a fully fleshed-out set of instructions, from either his own government or the Americans.

It can be noted that the nature of the WRB's operations, with its tone set by Pehle in Washington and practised in the field by his representatives, was to try virtually anything which seemed practicable and reasonably prudent. In the extraordinary circumstances in which the WRB was operating, this does not seem particularly problematic.

As for the Swedes, it was odd and irresponsible of UD officials to permit this untrained diplomat to proceed abroad without a detailed set of instructions on such a potentially controversial and sensitive mission, even if they trusted Danielsson and Anger to instruct and guide him. In sum, it seems most likely that Wallenberg left Stockholm determined to exceed his Swedish instructions. Perhaps even more importantly, he was most likely influenced by his discussions with Johnson and Olsen, who were, in turn, influenced by Pehle's instructions that virtually anything could at least be tried.[62]

It is also salient to note in this context that no evidence exists for believing that either the Germans or Hungarians understood Wallenberg as anything other than an accredited Swedish diplomat. If they had received information, in advance either of his departure or arrival, that he had an institutional connection, however surreptitious, with the Americans – either for espionage or humanitarian work – it is highly unlikely that Wallenberg would have been allowed to transit through Germany, or enter Hungary. And if Wallenberg had been refused a transit visa by the Germans – as they had refused one to Count Folke Bernadotte when his name was broached in connection with the SRK – or an entry visa to Hungary, then whatever the Americans, Swedes or Wallenberg himself hoped or believed he would do would all have been for naught. His status as a Swedish diplomat is what gained him access to Budapest.

Whichever understanding of Wallenberg's actual tasks prevailed when he departed is made even more difficult to establish conclusively in the light of the WRB's weekly report of 13 July 1944, one week after he arrived in Budapest. This 'Summary of Steps Taken by WRB with Respect to the Jews of Hungary' was an internal document not intended for sharing with other governments or for public release. In the section titled 'Operations from Sweden', we find the following:

> The Swedish Foreign Office has cooperated closely with our representative and has made available to him various official reports received from Swedish diplomatic personnel in Hungary. In addition, the Swedish Foreign Office has arranged to send Mr Wallenberg, a prominent Swedish businessman, to Budapest as attaché in refugee matters with the express purpose of saving as many lives as possible. The Swedish Foreign Office has gone so far as to indicate that Wallenberg would be available for any work the WRB might wish to assign to him. *We have, of course, cabled that, while Wallenberg could not act as the Board's representative nor in its name, he is free to communicate with our representative in Stockholm and to lay before him any specific*

proposals to aid the Jews of Hungary. Our representative has been instructed to lend every assistance possible to this mission.[63] [Emphasis added.]

This document confirms that the Americans understood Wallenberg to be a Swedish diplomat who could not act as their representative, but that he was available to them to assist in WRB-formulated rescue and assistance activities. Though it makes clear that the Americans felt a part of his mission was 'to save as many lives as possible', it is ambiguous, general rather than specific, yet it was what the agency had been established to do. That is, in this context, there is nothing unusual in Pehle seeking to involve a Swedish diplomat in their general activities. Nonetheless, why American instructions should be more detailed, if still broadly general, than Swedish instructions seems odd at best, and remains unexplained. Equally significant is what followed:

In the hope that rescue operations might be increased and developed from Sweden, we have sent a detailed program to Olsen suggesting the names of persons in Hungary who might be helpful in arranging rescues and we have indicated various escape routes which might be available from Hungary. We have arranged for private funds to be sent to Olsen to be used expressly for rescue operations from Hungary and we have indicated our willingness and eagerness to discuss any suggestion or program designed to help the persecuted people of Hungary.[64]

Yet the 'program' mentioned has never been located.[65] Most likely it was not a programme of action or instructions at all, perhaps just a list of names with some hastily written suggestions or thoughts. This explanation is supported by a WRB telegram sent on 23 June to Stockholm. Though it listed ten Hungarians believed to be prominent and potentially helpful, it is thematically vague in the extreme. Moreover, it is unlikely that up-to-date, correct information from Hungary was available to WRB officials in Washington. '[These names] ... have been suggested to us as [possible contacts] though nothing is known of their present views or associations, and if man in question is entirely reliable, you might consider asking him to talk with them. We believe them to have been given to us in good faith by persons deeply interested in the problem, but we cannot assure reliability of descriptions given.' The essential uselessness of the list is revealed when set against the situation prevailing in Budapest during those terrible weeks of early summer. For example, following two of the names we see severe caveats concerning their actual usefulness and reliability: 'Count or Baron Anton Szigrol or Szigray, said to be aristocrat with substantial means who is probably not in sympathy with excesses', while another name, 'Jenö Vasarhelyi, alleged to be president Kispet Textile Works [*sic*], who is in close collaboration with Germans but probably be willing to aid in exchange for compensation and future security assurances'.[66] This is hardly failsafe intelligence information which could be relied upon or realistically acted upon.

In my estimation there is one UD document which resolves any question about whom Wallenberg worked for, and which articulates what he was primarily going to do – at least as understood by the Swedish government. When Wallenberg left for Budapest, his 'employers' – that is, Boheman, Engzell, Grafström, von Post and Günther – took it for granted that Sweden's professional diplomats in Budapest would follow instructions and see to it that this untrained amateur would operate according to recognized norms, procedures and rules. They would also have taken for granted that his activities would promote primarily, if not exclusively, Swedish political interests. He was, after all, an accredited Swedish diplomat, and a Wallenberg. That the Americans might be pleased with this programme of potential action was evident to Swedish officials, which was of course partly their aim in permitting the mission to develop and commence. There can be no question regarding UD's motives – nothing could have forced the Swedes to engage Wallenberg at this highly particular time if they had not wanted to, or did not believe that their nation and government would obtain some useful political advantage.

This conclusion is supported by the fact that we know the men heading UD were very conservative bureaucrats, not given to risky diplomatic adventures, particularly at this late date in the war. They were not in the habit of supporting diplomatic 'wild cards'. The Swedes might not have sent Wallenberg to Budapest to 'save thousands of lives', but they certainly had nothing against it. And though the ministry attached significance to Wallenberg's appointment, neither it nor events in Budapest dominated or overshadowed the activities of its leadership.[67] They were very busy men whose primary task was not to save Jews or help the Americans. It was to see that Sweden's encounter with the dreadful consequences of the European war remained as they had been for some five years – safely at a distance. The Americans, I am convinced, believed sincerely that Wallenberg was travelling to Budapest as a bone fide Swedish diplomat. They were sincere in backing the sometimes idiosyncratic schemes hatched by WRB representatives, and Wallenberg's mission, however vaguely formulated, would also promote American interests. It might also, in the event, save some lives. This of course would redound to the credit of the Americans at an unknown later date.

Knowing what we do of Wallenberg's personality, and indeed of how he conducted himself once in Budapest, it seems justifiable to speculate that he departed from Stockholm with grander and more expansive ideas about what he was going to do than either his employers or background supporters envisioned. And though it is impossible to claim that we understand everything about his motives and goals, there is no doubt that he went to Hungary seeking to do more good than only helping to inform the world about what was happening to Jews in Budapest in the second half of 1944. Also important in this regard is the fact that no one really knew how Wallenberg's time in Budapest would turn out, or what he could – or could not – accomplish.

Dated 6 July 1944, the decisive memorandum cited below was sent not by normal diplomatic pouch (usually sent by normal post), but by courier. In fact, it seems most likely that the letter was carried by Wallenberg himself in a sealed envelope. The memorandum was drafted by Sven Grafström, a pro-Allied professional diplomat then serving as head of UD's critically important Political Division. It was addressed to Per Anger (Danielsson was on holiday that week, somewhat remarkably for such a critical time in the history of the country in which he was serving); it reads as follows:

Dear Chargé d´Affaires,

The Legation has already been informed ... that Mr Raoul Wallenberg has received the Ministry's mandate for two months as a member of the legation in Budapest to follow developments in the Jewish question and report to Stockholm. Mr Wallenberg should arrive in Budapest simultaneously with this letter. He shall report in the customary way as secretary of the legation. In all his work he shall naturally be subordinate to the head of the legation, whom he shall continually keep informed of his undertakings. I have strongly emphasized this to Mr Wallenberg, and you are charged as head of legation to monitor this, and ensure that it happens. [Jag har lagt herr Wallenberg detta på hjärtat, och det åligger Eder såsom beskickningschef att övervaka, att så sker.]

It appears suitable that he also establish close cooperation with Mr Langlet, who presently has been appointed representative of the [Swedish] Red Cross. However, Mr Wallenberg has no mandate from the Red Cross and may naturally not act in their name. Because the activity entrusted to Mr Wallenberg is of a special nature, and is extremely delicate, the support of the legation is of the greatest significance. Every 'encounter' [*intermezzo*] with the authorities should naturally be avoided, and I am counting on you, in this regard, to provide Mr Wallenberg with the required directives. Grafström.[68]

Written by a headstrong diplomat with a flair for language, this document strongly contradicts any notion that Wallenberg was working for anyone other than the Swedish government, or that high-ranking officials in UD believed otherwise. There is no reason to believe that Grafström was being less than completely honest with the younger Anger, or that he wanted Anger to 'read between the lines' in what is a clear set of instructions about how Wallenberg was to act, and to whom he was to report. Grafström emphasized with uncommonly strong language that Wallenberg was to obey all instructions given by Danielsson and himself.[69] Moreover, it is highly implausible, if not impossible, to imagine that the UD stalwarts involved in this matter would have approved, singly or together, any mission that would not serve, or might damage, Swedish interests. They simply would not have capriciously approved of Wallenberg acting as a 'secret' American agent. There is nothing in the careers of these professional diplomats which indicates that they would have approved such a controversial and potentially risky mission which, not incidentally, was going to be very public. They had no reason to subvert their own organization to serve some vague and undefined American interests, whatever the potential humanitarian benefit.

WALLENBERG DEFINES HIS MOTIVES AND MISSION

We can now turn to the sources which provide the clearest picture of Wallenberg's motives, which are two documents he wrote himself. They give a somewhat different picture from that sketched by either Swedish or American officials. Yet even they fail to provide fully conclusive answers to the questions under discussion. Though written by the central figure in this study, even these documents fail to define what he would actually do. Nor do they try to predict the situation in which he would act. In essence, it was impossible for everyone involved in these discussions to lay out a fully articulated, credible programme of action – there were too many uncertainties lying ahead.

Both documents recount conversations Wallenberg had with Vilhelm Assarsson, a senior diplomat who temporarily replaced Boheman for some days after the midsummer holiday. Although not listed in Wallenberg's appointments diary (perhaps he was too busy preparing to leave to remember to make those entries), it is clear that they negotiated face to face at least once in the days before Wallenberg's departure. Their aim – even at this late date – seems to have been to put on paper something which would define his mission. This included such 'practical' issues as how much he would get paid, how long he would stay, and more.[70] It is uncertain but likely that Gösta Engzell, the man who knew most about what was happening in Budapest, was present. That said, it is odd in the extreme that throughout Wallenberg's appointment process, the head of UD's legal division and the individual most directly responsible for Sweden's willingness and ability to help Jews seems uninvolved with the appointment, at least according to the available documentation.

Also of interest is the fact that these two documents were located not in Swedish government files, but in Koloman Lauer's private archive.[71] The letter of 6 July, the day before Wallenberg left Stockholm, provides us with his own understanding and interpretation of what lay ahead. Even though addressed to a high-ranking UD official, its substance lies far closer to what the WRB anticipated might happen than what the Swedes expected, or planned. Wallenberg wrote to Assarsson:

> In order that no misunderstandings might occur, allow me to confirm some of the things which were named during our meeting. It is hereby confirmed that I have a certain liberty to negotiate in accordance with the program which has been previously drafted by Professor Ehrenpreis, Mr Olsen, Dr Lauer and myself. Furthermore I have the right to use the resources [*medel*] which I carry [*medför*] for these individuals in a way which appears to me will most likely lead best to desired results, and which according to Mr Olsen and Professor Ehrenpreis in similar circumstances has shown to be necessary. Payments will in the main occur through middlemen [*göras genom mellanhänder*], so that my status as a Foreign Office official is not compromised [*så att icke min ställning som Utrikes-Departementets tjänsteman komprometteras*]. It is furthermore agreed that I may complete my employment after two months, that is 6 September, if I so desire ... Respectfully, R. Wallenberg.[72]

Wallenberg's reference to 'a program' drafted by himself and his interlocutors outside official government circles was unusual.[73] To think in this manner would have been in the spirit of the WRB, and his extensive discussions with both Johnson and Olsen would have reinforced such thinking. But it seems somewhat odd that Swedish officials would have accepted such an assertion without details being put on paper.

This 'official' memorandum drafted by Wallenberg is complemented by an undated memorandum (in Swedish, a *PM*, or *promemoria*), which is titled 'conversation with Permanent Undersecretary [*kabinettssekreterare*] Assarsson'. This fascinating document shows many things about Wallenberg, including a degree of confidence rather at odds with the fact that he was, after all, a relatively young man with no diplomatic experience who was about to engage in an unorthodox task for his own government. But Wallenberg was in no way a run-of-the-mill person. He did not lack self-confidence and clearly had a distinct sense of where he belonged in the world. He had his educational life and travels behind him, he knew the Americans and British backed him, and he was a Wallenberg.

The memo consists of nine typed bullet points, with the final two added in Wallenberg's handwriting. The first repeats his understanding that he departs with the freedom to negotiate some things on his own, without prior UD approval, '[and] that I will not be exposed to criticism from the Swedish side because of bribes which I make' ('och att jag icke kan utsättas för kritik från svensk sida på grund av mutor, som jag utdelat'). The word 'bribes' (*mutor*) was circled by someone, without explanation. It obviously made Assarsson, or someone else who read the original, uncomfortable.[74] Point two says that he (Wallenberg) takes it for granted that he can travel back to Stockholm when he chooses, without much ado, and that travel costs will be borne by UD. Point three is surprising, with Wallenberg asking which diplomatic rank he will hold when in Budapest. This is odd, because the rank of 'attaché' to describe his official position appears, as noted earlier, in several previous Swedish and American documents. Why was he unsure, at this late date, what his official rank would be? Point five states that he was advised by experts at the American and British Legations to inquire after several people, including some important members of the opposition, and he requests permission to do so. He notes advice given by 'Mr Böhm in the English legation', that under all circumstances he should try to establish a relationship with Hungarian Prime Minister Sztójay, and he asks if Assarsson thinks this possible.

The final two handwritten points are one word each in the original. Number 8 is *asylrätt* – right of asylum. Is Wallenberg asking to be given the authority to grant political asylum to individuals? This is unclear, but to claim such authority would have been, to say the least, unorthodox. The final point is *audiens* – audience, which seems to make reference to whether he could or should obtain an audience with, presumably, Hungarian Regent Miklós Horthy, which he never did.

Though these documents provide a convincing picture of what Wallenberg himself imagined he could or should be able to do, and what he thought might be necessary, neither can be considered an 'official' programme of action supported without hesitation by two governments.

He did meet again on 4 July with Jewish leader Norbert Masur, but what they spoke about is unknown, and it seems highly unlikely that Masur could have provided any sort of coherent 'programme' at this point.[75] Wallenberg had read through recent reports from the Budapest Legation, and Masur cannot have had information more up to date than that contained in them. More likely is that they simply discussed the situation again: what it might be possible to do, and perhaps even what they dreamed might be accomplished. Wallenberg was a determined man unafraid to 'think big', and it is easy to believe that he felt that his personality, experience and organizational abilities gave him a chance actually to accomplish something substantial. The evidence also provides scope to assert that, at this point in his life, he was impatient, perhaps even bored, with his situation, and that he saw this task as a grand, even possibly spectacular, adventure which would provide many future opportunities. Importantly, however, for any consideration of the myths which surround Wallenberg, it is worth noting that nowhere does he write that he thinks it possible to 'save Hungarian Jewry' from their final agonies, let alone 'rescue thousands of Jews' as a pre-determined point of action. Both documents, however, do make clear that he wanted to be successful, and that if he deemed it necessary, he would indulge in unconventional, perhaps even illegal methods to try to accomplish something useful.

UNANSWERED QUESTIONS

Many questions of central importance to the Wallenberg story are raised by an appraisal of the situation on the eve of his departure for Budapest. Among them are: what accounts for the lack of clarity about his mission, when lengthy negotiations between highly trained representatives of two sovereign nations had taken place? What explains the uncertainties, mixed understandings and even confusion surrounding the content of a diplomatic mission which, all knew, was, if not unprecedented, certainly not one to be readily found in the training programmes of Western chancelleries? Exactly why the Swedish government authorized such an unorthodox, ill-defined mission for an amateur outsider remains unclear. That they endorsed the American request to increase legation staff is undoubtedly true – it was also necessary to do so for their own reasons. But why Wallenberg wasn't provided with more detailed instructions from his new employers remains unclear. It may be that institutional logic and practice was brushed aside in the face of such a sensitive and difficult task as saving human lives during a genocide being conducted in the heart of a great European city under armed occupation.

There are no final answers to these questions. The most plausible answer is that Wallenberg seemed to be, for officials from both governments, the best man available at a time of momentous events and great horror. It is possible that individual and institutional fatigue among the men (both Swedes and Americans) who had worked so hard for so many years played a role in the somewhat amateur manner in which the appointment process was shepherded along. There can be no question that those involved in Wallenberg's recruitment perceived him as what he was: a serious, worldly and capable young man with a strong personality who came from a fairly uncommon background. Perhaps it was intuitive perception rather than cold political calculation which prompted these normally conservative bureaucrats to trust him more than they might have trusted other, less impressive, men. And though the actual framework and tactics for the mission may have resisted precise definition, there is no question that at this particular moment of the genocide and the war, those involved in 'refugee' questions – Swedes and Americans – knew and felt that something, anything, had to be done to help some Jews survive.

In countless ways between 1941 and 1945, the scale of the by then largely understood murder pushed to the side 'normal', or what might be called 'traditional', doubts which would normally prevail in conservative institutions. In this case, however, all who were involved in the process of recruiting Wallenberg, establishing an administrative and diplomatic basis for his position and defining his task, understood that something had to be done to assist Jews in Budapest. They clearly realized that circumstances had brought forth a man unusually suitable for having at least a chance of accomplishing something positive in such unprecedented circumstances.

Nonetheless, the question remains: was Wallenberg sent to Budapest 'merely' to report on a situation already being well reported, as the Swedes seem to have wanted and believed? Or was his task, as American officials in Washington seemed to believe, 'to save as many lives as possible'? I believe the answer lies less in Wallenberg's personal motives and more in the reality of the unprecedented situation which confronted Swedish and other neutral diplomats in Budapest. Historical research and analysis about the Holocaust makes it clear that for the most part, saving lives in Budapest in 1944 was less a matter of lofty humanitarian goals than the result of certain individuals choosing to act in a certain way at a certain time. Just as we know that during the Holocaust there existed 'desk-top' killers, we also know that some Europeans, in this case Swedes, chose to become 'desk-top' rescuers. In Budapest, the involvement and presence of a handful of neutral governments, officially represented by a handful of men who found themselves in unprecedented circumstances, utilized what during the Holocaust was a possibly unique political space in which something *could* be done – if the will to do it existed. When circumstances provided Raoul Wallenberg with a historic opportunity to act positively, there is no gainsaying the fact that he took full advantage of it. To his eternal credit, under circumstances when he could well have chosen to remain 'merely' a 'desk-top' rescuer, he decided that wasn't enough. We shall now review and analyse the essential details of what Raoul Wallenberg and his Swedish colleagues did in Budapest between July 1944 and January 1945.

NOTES

1. UD to Legation Budapest, no.175, 21 June 1944, *Riksarkivet Utrikesdepartementet* (hereafter RA UD), Hp 21 Eu 1095, folder 5.
2. UD to Legation Budapest, no.179, 27 June 1944, RA UD, Hp 21 Eu 1095, folder 5.
3. Following the dissolution of the Soviet Union, the Swedish and Russian governments established a 'Working Group' to answer the first three questions. By the late 1990s, Sweden established its own 'independent' commission to analyse its actions, or lack thereof, in the years following Wallenberg's detention. Both reports will be discussed in the epilogue. Since 1945, Wallenberg's mother Maj, brother Guy von Dardel and sister Nina maintained a tireless search for him. Their ultimately futile efforts have been complemented by journalists, documentarians, academicians and other individuals over the years. On this tragedy, see most recently the article by journalist Joshua Praeger, 'The Search for the Missing Holocaust Hero Began in 1945: The Unending Quest tore his family Apart', *Wall Street Journal*, 28 February 2009.
4. Literature about this chapter of Holocaust history is extensive. The best initial guide remains D. Wyman, *The Abandonment of the Jews: America and the Holocaust, 1941–1945* (New York: Pantheon Books, 1984).
5. The Office of Strategic Services was the secret intelligence agency established during the war by Roosevelt. It was the institutional predecessor to today's Central Intelligence Agency (CIA).
6. Author's interview with John Pehle, 4 September 1989, Washington, DC.
7. Israeli historian Robert Rozett wrote that the WRB also immediately contacted the Vatican, which was traditionally reluctant to help Jews. In this case, however, Washington was informed that 'instructions had already been given to the representatives of the Holy See in Hungary to do everything possible for the relief of the Jews'. For months, as noted in the previous chapter, this assistance was in the main limited to baptized Jews. See R. Rozett, 'International Intervention: The Role of Diplomats in Attempts to Rescue Jews in Hungary', in R.L. Braham and S. Miller (eds), *The Nazis' Last Victims: The Holocaust in Hungary* (Detroit, MI: Wayne State University Press, 1998), p.138.
8. In his weekly report of 29 May–3 June, Pehle wrote: 'While assurances of "warmest support and sympathy" have not been lacking, we have received little active cooperation to date from the British in connection with refugee rescue and relief.' National Archives [hereafter NA], Washington, DC, Record Group [hereafter RG] 59, File 840.48/6254.
9. A particularly useful review of the establishment of the WRB and its implications is T. Kushner, 'Rules of the Game: Britain: America and the Holocaust in 1944', *Holocaust and Genocide Studies*, 5, 4 (1990), pp.381–402. For specific studies of Britain and the Holocaust see, within a substantial literature, B. Wasserstein, *Britain and the Jews of Europe, 1939–1945* (Oxford: Institute of Jewish Affairs, Oxford University Press, 1988); and, more recently, L. London, *Whitehall and the Jews 1933–1948: British Immigration Policy, Jewish Refugees and the Holocaust* (Cambridge: Cambridge University Press, 2000).
10. See M. Lorenz-Mayer, *Safehaven: The Allied Pursuit of Nazi Assets Abroad* (Columbia, MO: University of Missouri Press, 2007).
11. W. Churchill, cited in L. Leifland, 'They Must Get In before the End: Churchill och

Sverige, 1944–1945', in M. Bergquist *et al.* (eds), *Utrikespolitik och historia* (Stockholm: Militärhistoriska Förlag, 1987), p.116. As will be shown, British officials in Stockholm played only a minor role in Wallenberg's recruitment, and Whitehall took a back seat to the Americans on issues relating to Swedish diplomacy and the Holocaust.

12. Ibid., p.119.
13. Sweden's cynical response to the ill-fated 'Adler-Rudel Plan' of 1943, which sought to perhaps save tens of thousands of Jewish children, is analysed in P.A. Levine, *From Indifference to Activism: Swedish Diplomacy and the Holocaust, 1938–1944*, 2nd edn (Uppsala: Studia historica Upsaliensia, 1998), Chapter 9. For a critical analysis of Sweden's domestic and often ungenerous response to those Jews who were able to gain refuge within the country, see K. Kvist-Gevert's new study, *Ett främmande element i nationen: Svensk flyktingpolitik och de judiska flyktingarna 1938–1944* (Uppsala: Acta universitatis Upsaliensis, 2008).
14. Author interview with Ambassador Per Anger, March 1990, Uppsala University Library, Raoul Wallenberg Project Archive, no.C002, p.26 and p.32.
15. See Chapter 8.
16. Author's interview with Per Anger, p.26.
17. I. Danielsson to UD, no.157, 2 June 1944, RA UD, Hp 21 Eu 1095, folder 5.
18. Cited in S. Koblik, *The Stones Cry Out: Sweden's Response to the Persecution of Jews, 1933–1945* (New York: Holocaust Library, 1988), doc. no.54, p.227.
19. J. Lévai, *Raoul Wallenberg – hjälten i Budapest* (Stockholm: Saxon & Lindströms, 1948), p.31.
20. The author thanks Nina Lagergren, Wallenberg's sister, for a copy of this remarkable document. Addressed *Till chefen för armén* (head of the army), 14 May 1944, from Sergeant no.1775 45/3C R.G. Wallenberg.
21. As noted in Chapter 2, Wallenberg enjoyed military service and was clearly highly competent. The document cited here carries a note from an army officer: 'From the point of view of this unit, Wallenberg is difficult to replace, because he is well-versed in the unit's conditions and knows the troops. [This request] can be granted only if a capable replacement can be made available.' Ibid.
22. H. Johnson to Secretary of State and WRB, 8 May 1944, NA, Washington, DC, RG 59, File 840.48/5992. Many such American documents were signed by Johnson, but when they concerned rescue and refugee activities conducted under the purview of the WRB, they were drafted by Olsen.
23. On this, see Levine, *From Indifference to Activism*, Chapter 7, pp.134–55.
24. Ibid., esp. Chapters 2 and 10.
25. C. Hull to H. Johnson and I. Olsen, 23 May 1944, NA, Washington, DC, RG 59, File 840.48/6139A.
26. UD to Legation Budapest, no.150, 6 June 1944, RA UD, Hp 21 Eu 1095, folder 5.
27. H. Johnson to Secretary of State, 9 June 1944, NA, Washington, DC, RG 59, File 840.48/6139.
28. Ibid.
29. H. Johnson to Secretary of State, 12 June 1944, NA, Washington, DC, RG 59, File 840.48/6273.
30. See R. Wallenberg's personal 1944 diary (calendar), RA, Raoul Wallenberg Arkiv, Signum 1, vol. 9.
31. H. Johnson to Secretary of State, no.2231, 21 June 1944, NA, Washington, DC, RG 59, File 840.48/6348.
32. It is a curious and unexplained omission in Boheman's memoirs that neither Wallenberg or virtually anything about Sweden's humanitarian activities during the war are mentioned. See his *På Vakt, kabinettssekreterare under andra världskriget* (Stockholm: Nordstedts, 1964).
33. S. Grafström to Legation Budapest, no.175, 21 June 1944, RA UD, Hp 21 Eu 1095, folder 5.
34. Author's interview with Per Anger, p.34
35. I. Danielsson to UD, no.191, 23 June 1944, RA UD, P 2 Eu, folder 1.
36. R. Wallenberg's 1944 diary, 12 and 15 June 1944, RA, Raoul Wallenberg Arkiv, Signum 1, vol. 9. This fascinating document has been little used by researchers to date. Amongst other issues, it reveals that Wallenberg had a very busy social life. The next evening, 16 June, he had dinner with a couple of friends in central Stockholm, noting that he was to wear semi-formal dress, and that either cognac or vodka (*brännvin*) would be the drink of the evening.
37. Ibid., 28 June 1944. That evening Wallenberg met, for the second day in a row, a woman

who was apparently his girlfriend at the time, 'Jeanette'. The previous evening he also met her unnamed parents.

38. H. Johnson to WRB, *no.* 2360, 28 June 1944, reprinted in D. Wyman, *America and the Holocaust* (New York: Garland Publishing, 1989–91), vol. 8, doc. no.22, p.54.
39. H. Johnson to Secretary of State, no.2412 (section two), 1 July 1944, reprinted in ibid., doc. no.11, p.34.
40. Ibid., doc. no.10, p.32.
41. Boheman, *På Vakt*, p.27. This method of communication characterized even official relationships with Allied diplomats, particularly Johnson and the Briton V. Mallet. They both worked ever closer with Boheman throughout the war, and all three men clearly trusted each other.
42. On this, see the new study of Foreign Minister Günther by H. Arnstadt, *Spelaren Christian Günther: Sverige under andra världskriget* (Stockholm: Wahlström & Widstrand, 2006). The title refers to the foreign minister's abiding love of gambling, both on horse racing and whilst playing bridge. Often during the war, when subordinate officials had business to conduct with him, he was located, even during working days, at north Stockholm's Solvalla racecourse.
43. Labouchere to Haigh, 3 July 1944, in Koblik, *The Stones Cry Out*, doc. no.64, pp.247–8.
44. J. Pehle to H. Morgenthau, 6 July 1944, reprinted in Wyman, *America and the Holocaust*, vol. 8, doc. no. 17, p.41.
45. In G. Nylander and A. Perlinge (eds), *Raoul Wallenberg in Documents, 1927–1947* (Stockholm: Stiftelsen för Ekonomisk Historisk Forskning inom Bank och Företagande, 2000), doc. no.48, pp.106–11.
46. 'Wallenbergaktionen', eight-page memorandum by K. Lauer, RA, Raoul Wallenberg Arkiv, Signum 1, vol. 6. Lauer made some corrections to this text.
47. J. Lévai interviewed Lauer for his book, and this description clearly influenced the description given therein.
48. See Nylander and Perlinge (eds), *Raoul Wallenberg in Documents*, doc. no.48.
49. Lauer was known to both Jacob and Marcus Jr, but seems to have had closer business connections to Jacob.
50. 'Wallenbergaktionen' memorandum (date unknown), RA, Raoul Wallenberg Arkiv, Signum 1, vol. 6, p.2. Lauer notes that he first met Raoul Wallenberg in the beginning of 1941, through an introduction by Sven Salén, stating that during the approximately three-and-a-half years of their business relationship they became 'best of friends [and] we often sat together in the evenings and discussed the future'. According to Lauer, Wallenberg made business trips to various countries, including Hungary, Romania, Switzerland and France.
51. Nor is another important meeting Wallenberg had at UD, probably on 5 or 6 July, entered into his diary.
52. The Foreign Minister was of course kept informed of events and staff in Budapest.
53. H. Johnson to Secretary of State, no.2231, 21 June 1944, NA, Washington, DC, RG 59, File 840.48/6348.
54. H. Johnson to Secretary of State, 23 June 1944, no.2277, NA, Washington, DC, RG 59, File 840.48 Refugees/6306. As noted earlier, the holiday referred to is Sweden's all-important *Midsommar*, during which time the country essentially shuts down. Throughout the war, important Swedish government officials would depart for the countryside during regular holidays and long summer breaks, often to isolated places without modern communications. This had an unequivocally negative impact on intellectual continuity regarding the discussion of issues, and thus on policy-making.
55. More on this below.
56. This document was on his person when arrested by the Soviets in January 1945 and returned decades later to his family. Today it is in Riksarkivet.
57. Sweden was then, and remains, a highly stratified and bureaucratized society in which individualistic patterns of work, particularly within government bureaus, are actively discouraged. As we shall see, Valdemar Langlet's humanitarian work was directly hampered by the 'bureaucracy's' reaction to his idiosyncratic personality and work habits.
58. H. Johnson to Secretary of State, 28 June 1944, no.2360, NA, Washington, DC, RG 59, File 840.48 Refugees.
59. Ibid.
60. H. Johnson to Secretary of State, 1 July 1944, no.2412 (section two), NA, Washington, DC, RG 59, File 840.48 Refugees.

61. Hull to Harrison and McClelland, 4 July 1944, no.2270, NA, Washington, DC, RG 59, File 840.48 Refugees/6156. Again, though 'signed' by then Secretary of State Cordell Hull, the memorandum was drafted and sent by John Pehle, which was common practice.

62. Pehle remembers that his agency did have considerable manoeuvring room, saying that even though President Roosevelt's interest in the agency waned once it was established, 'We had enough authority to do what we wanted so [that] we didn't have to go back that often.' Author's interview with John Pehle, 4 September 1989, Washington, DC.

63. 'Summary of Steps Taken by War Refugee Board with Respect To The Jews of Hungary', 13 July 1944, reprinted in Wyman, *America and the Holocaust*, vol. 8, doc. no. 7, p.20. There was, however, a touch of self-promotion in the report. By no means could Wallenberg have been described at that time as a 'prominent' businessman. His relatives were, but he wasn't. Pehle was trying to make his organization look more successful in the mind of the reader.

64. Ibid.

65. Why a document such as 'a detailed programme' would not have been found in UD archives cannot be known, for there can be no question that the document noted by Pehle would have been transmitted by the State Department to Johnson and Olsen in Stockholm. On this, see H. Feingold, *The Politics of Rescue: The Roosevelt Administration and the Holocaust, 1938–1945* (New Brunswick, NJ: Holocaust Library, 1970).

66. War Refugee Board to AMLEGATION STOCKHOLM, 23 June 1944, no.1246, NA, Washington, DC, RG 59, File 840.48 Refugees/6273. It is salient to note that all such communications were considered 'secret' and sent in the appropriate, ciphered format.

67. Prime Minister Per Albin Hansson was aware of activities in Budapest, and was 'copied' on reports from there, but there is no specific evidence that he was, at any stage, influential or even particularly interested in what was happening. Throughout the war, his primary concerns remained domestic and keeping Sweden out of the war.

68. S. Grafström to P. Anger, 6 July 1944, RA UD, P 2 Eu p.1. Interestingly, such detailed and firm instructions were not at all in evidence regarding the appointment of Valdemar Langlet of the SRK. It is also worthwhile noting that again, the time period of two months is stated.

69. Grafström's sentence – '*Jag har lagt herr Wallenberg detta på hjärtat*' – is a phrase and sentiment seen rarely if at all in UD documents from this period. Anger and Wallenberg knew each other from Stockholm, and from Wallenberg's visits, but they were not close. It is highly implausible that together they would have knowingly disobeyed clear directives provided by, in this case, Anger's professional superiors. Anger had chosen the foreign service as a career, and there is no evidence that he was willing to harm his future prospects by disobeying directives from above.

70. Perhaps Boheman was ill during the last days of June and early July. Just as likely is the possibility that he took an extended holiday after the *Midsommar* break. As a result, Wallenberg's final discussions with high-level UD officials were between himself and temporary (*tillförordnad*) Permanent Undersecretary (*Kabinettssekretare*) Assarsson. It is entirely possible that Assarsson was insufficiently briefed on the entire matter. It is a pattern of Swedish bureaucracies that the competent handling of complicated matters is damaged because of hasty or temporary personnel changes. Assarsson, who some months earlier had been expelled from the minister's post in Soviet Russia, does not appear anywhere else in this entire diplomatic episode, apart from reading some of the Budapest reports later in the year.

71. Though only one is dated, both were written by Wallenberg on 6 July. The dated letter is addressed to *Kabinettssekretararen*, unnamed but in all likelihood Assarsson, as his name appears in the actual memorandum drafted by Wallenberg. The undated document is entitled, by Wallenberg, 'Conversation with Permanent Undersecretary Assarsson' (*Samtal med kabinettssekreterare Assarsson*). These memoranda were obviously written by Wallenberg immediately prior to departure, which took place by train from Stockholm at 2.10 p.m. on 7 July. Both are in RA, Raoul Wallenberg Arkiv, Signum 1, vol. 6.

72. R. Wallenberg to *Kabinettssekreteraren* (unnamed), 6 July 1944, RA, Raoul Wallenberg Arkiv, Signum 1, vol. 6, attachment 1 (*bilaga* 1). These two documents were appended, in this document collection, to the extended account by Lauer of Wallenberg's recruitment, personality and mission written sometime in 1945. This somewhat straightforward but still slightly cryptic letter is, in many ways, a good example of how official Swedish culture communicates internally, and comes to agreements that are perhaps not as clear as desired.

73. It would be enlightening to know who within UD actually read Wallenberg's memorandum. Standard UD practice was that those who read a document minuted it. But to reiterate, this copy comes from Wallenberg's own files. No copy was found in UD files.
74. 'PM Samtal med kabinetttssekreterare Assarsson', undated, RA, Raoul Wallenberg Arkiv, Signum 1, vol. 6, *bilaga* 1.
75. R. Wallenberg's appointments diary, 4 July 1944, RA, Raoul Wallenberg Arkiv, Signum 1, vol. 9.

6

July: Wallenberg Arrives in Budapest

Wallenberg has received [the Foreign Office's] mandate for two months, as a member of the Legation, to report on developments concerning the Jewish question ... He will take up the post of secretary ... Naturally he is subordinate to the head of Legation in everything he does, the importance of which I have stressed for Mr Wallenberg.[1]

SAVING HUNGARY'S JEWS?

On 21 June, UD sent Danielsson a report about the discussions concerning Wallenberg's recruitment, asking if he had any objections to the young businessman with the famous name being assigned to the Legation. The workload which had engulfed the Legation ensured Danielsson's agreement, yet he looked at this unusual appointment of an outsider with some anxiety. According to Per Anger, it was quite a shock for the old-line diplomat to accept both the procedure by which Wallenberg was appointed and the relative independence he seemed to have negotiated from the mandarins of UD.[2]

Central to the many notions supporting the framework of myth around Wallenberg is the one which promotes the belief that he went to Budapest with a mandate to 'save Hungarian Jewry'. The hagiographic literature would have the reader believe that Wallenberg arrived in the city fully empowered and prepared to single-handedly save the lives of untold thousands. This is, of course, a powerful, almost redemptive narrative of belief and hope, but the realities of both his capabilities and the situation were quite different.

It is true that Wallenberg had an unusual degree of freedom to make his own contacts and to formulate plans and ideas, but it is not the case that he was free to do whatever he wanted. Moreover, the situation in Budapest simply would not permit any individual doing whatever he may have wanted to do. In fact, the evidence leaves no doubt that Wallenberg accepted the framework within which he would be operating. Yet he quickly became – perhaps not surprisingly, given what we know about him – an adept diplomat, almost a politician, capable of lobbying for what became his cause. That cause was to do whatever might be possible to ameliorate the plight of the city's Jews – but it wasn't to save Hungarian Jewry. In view of the tragic fact that well over half of Hungary's population of at least 800,000 Jews was by now either deported out of the country, or dead, there was nothing anyone could do to save them.

Moreover, contrary to Wallenberg's popular image, during the first months following his arrival he hardly became the 'Scarlet Pimpernel' of Budapest, nor an 'angel of rescue'. This type of activity, so closely associated with him, would have been both unwise and impossible. As we shall see, there is some truth to this image, but only after 15 October. It is equally certain that Wallenberg did not perceive himself in such romantic terms; he may have later on, but not in the beginning. Rather, he began his tenure in Budapest by getting organized, getting acquainted with the situation, and meeting those he already knew, as well as making many new contacts. Although he still didn't really know in detail what he would be doing, or what the situation would present him with, he did understand that without Danielsson's support, he would not be very effective. There is no doubt that he understood that the maintenance of proper relations with Minister Danielsson, First Secretary Anger and UD in Stockholm was essential if he was to be able to accomplish anything. Unsurprisingly, one of his first meetings after arriving was with Valdemar Langlet, who only recently had finally received a tepid endorsement from SRK (Svenska röda korset, the Swedish Red Cross). It is likely that the voluble Langlet expressed his deep frustrations with his situation (more on this in Chapter 8). Moreover, Wallenberg obviously understood that if any real good was to be done, he needed to be accepted as a credible figure by his forthcoming German and Hungarian interlocutors. Without the effective support of his colleagues, he might well be quickly discredited, vulnerable and ineffective. In wartime Budapest, had this happened, it would have become quickly known. To do anything, he required his diplomatic status and support network, and had he launched feverishly into ad hoc, unrealistic schemes, this support would quickly have waned. He had a lot to learn about a very complex situation, and he took the time to do so.

Though a picture of Wallenberg as a low-key bureaucrat belies the one held by most who have read or seen films about him, it is an ineluctable fact that without his politically recognized status as a diplomat backed by a neutral state, Raoul Wallenberg would have been powerless and dangerously exposed. Only by discerning the nature of the circumstances in which he arrived, and which were constantly shifting, and *then* applying his own personality and intelligence to the situation, could he really accomplish anything.

There was, in fact, little real danger that relations between UD and its new diplomat would become problematic as long as Wallenberg conducted himself according to established norms – which he did during these crucial first weeks. Moreover, officials in Stockholm were genuinely anxious to do what they could to help Jews in Budapest and, throughout his six months in the city, Wallenberg never had to overcome any real opposition to what he wrote, said and did. Thus we can dispense with another myth, that which claims that he had to fight simultaneously the Nazis and a turgid UD bureaucracy. The complex diplomacy in which he and his colleagues engaged between July 1944 and the city's liberation would have failed without solid backing from Stockholm, and there is no evidence that Wallenberg ever had to challenge an uninterested or moribund bureaucracy. Nor, despite what one film depicts, did Danielsson really try to hamper Wallenberg's activities or ideas.[3] On the contrary, Wallenberg's imagination and energy were magnified because he operated within a bureaucracy, not against it.

BUDAPEST IN CONTEXT

Before examining Wallenberg's activities during his first weeks in Budapest, it will be helpful to review briefly the geopolitical context which prevailed in Hungary and farther afield at midsummer 1944. This is necessary because the popular literature which forms the basis of much of the myth-making, and even some of the scholarly literature about Wallenberg, has largely failed to explain this essential context. What happened in Budapest was not an isolated affair, but rather part of a much broader ongoing, and vast, story.

Popular publications about Wallenberg all but ignore the fact that the political situation existing in Budapest that first week of July was quite different from that in March. The situation in which Wallenberg landed was one characterized by a growing crisis in German–Hungarian relations. The deportations had just been halted, against Germany's wishes; a new prime minister was soon to be appointed by Horthy; and the increasingly rapid advance of the Soviet Red Army into the east Balkans and Central Europe was capped by the end of the summer when Romania withdrew from the Axis, becoming the Soviet Union's awkward ally. In the west, the D-Day landings of 6 June had succeeded, although the American, British, Canadians and Poles fighting in Normandy had not yet achieved the decisive break-out into the rest of France. And though the imminent attempt of 20 July on Hitler's life was still a fortnight away, increasingly many Germans – soldiers, government officials and civilians – began to realize that final defeat was only a matter of time.

By this time, leaders of nations throughout Europe and the world had begun contemplating their own country's situation in the rapidly approaching post-war world – none more so than the Swedes. Per Albin Hansson's coalition government led a nation which had been spared the unfathomable physical and psychic damage endured by almost every other European nation. It presided over a people whose standard of living had risen during the war, and most Swedes understood that when the war ended, they would be in an enviable economic position. Economically, the country, including of course Jacob and Marcus Wallenberg Jr, looked to the future with confidence, knowing they would benefit enormously from helping to rebuild Europe. Non-belligerency had paid off. The Swedes also understood that Europe, and the world, would be dominated to an unprecedented degree by the two burgeoning superpowers – the United States and Stalin's Soviet Union.

In Hungary, the first days of July were, as we have seen, dominated by the drama of the halting of the deportations. Though Horthy's grip on power was in many ways uncertain, neither the Hungarian people nor the Germans were yet prepared to jettison the old admiral. Nonetheless, most Hungarian officials understood the game was up and began shifting their thinking accordingly. There remained a sufficient numbers of fanatics – nationalists and/or anti-Semites – who maintained a dream of both of Magyar greatness and a Hungary without Jews, but reality was rapidly closing in.

The history of the Holocaust is replete with seemingly inexplicable ironies and contradictions, and it continues to rankle many that the same man who bore profound responsibility for facilitating the Germans' ability to carry out the deportations to death by gassing of over 400,000 people during the preceding weeks now joined, in early July, the ranks of history of those who must be given some credit for saving many lives.[4] Historians of the Hungarian Holocaust are largely agreed that without Horthy's intervention, Budapest's Jews would almost certainly have been deported and murdered.

Survivors and historians alike agree that Horthy's anti-Semitism (of which there was no doubt) seemed less heartfelt when it concerned Jews in his capital city. The regent fully understood their importance to Hungary's economy, and over the years a few prominent Jews had entered his social circle. He appreciated 'his Jews', and when he finally understood that they too were threatened with death, he reasserted his authority and ordered the deportations to be halted. Horthy's abhorrent ambivalence is crystallized in a conversation he had with László Baky. Horthy is quoted as saying: 'I abhor the Communists and the Galician Jews – out of the country with them, out. But at the same time you must admit, Baky, there are some Jews who are just as good

Hungarians as you or I! For instance, take Chorin and Vida! I cannot allow them to be deported, but I don't mind about the others.'⁵Historian Randolph Braham concluded: 'With respect to the Jewish question, Horthy tried to soften the impact of his earlier stand ... he informed [Veesenmayer] that he had ordered the segregation of the converted Jews and that he would "soon" allow the deportation of more non-converted Jews from Budapest. He insisted, however, that the Jews must be treated better since their ill-treatment "went against the grain".'⁶

As the military situation rapidly worsened, more and more Hungarian officials in both the national and Budapest city governments became ever more aware of international opinion, and therefore more amenable to the neutrals' humanitarian diplomacy. As we shall see, this shift became more evident throughout the next few months, and it caused significant tensions with their German overseers. We see this in the Executive Crown Council's late June discussions, when one leading advisor emphasized to Horthy that 'no concessions could be made without the approval of the Germans, which in turn brought into question Hungary's sovereignty. [Imredy] suggested that the Germans be persuaded that it was also in their interest to have the neutral countries view Hungary as a sovereign nation.'⁷ One source of tension was the categories of exemptions for Jews which the Hungarians allowed, and which were resisted by the Germans. British historian David Cesarani has written: 'Veensemayer kept Berlin fully up to date and made sure that Eichmann respected the prerogative of the [Hungarian] Foreign Office to define exceptions according to nationality.'⁸ In the complex circumstances prevailing, it mattered greatly to the Hungarians what the Swedes, the Swiss, and other neutrals were thinking about them. They were also concerned with what the world at large thought of Hungary, and how current circumstances would affect post-war relations. One crucial effect of this was that, as the Regent and other leading government officials were notified of the humanitarian activities of the Swedes and others on behalf of Budapest Jewry, they made no attempt to stop them.

It is important to realize that even after Germany occupied Hungary, the latter's governing structure remained entirely intact. By this point of the war, Hitler's Germany did not have the administrative capacity to rule completely another nation.⁹ Few German troops remained in Hungary, and in July Veesenmayer had little if any immediate recourse to military coercion. This made the political situation in Hungary in 1944 far more similar to, for instance, that which prevailed in collaborationist Vichy France after 1940 than in subjugated Poland after 1939. Circumstances gave the Hungarians considerable but by no means complete autonomy on a range of issues, including, crucially, the 'Jewish question'. That is, by the summer, even while under German 'occupation', the Hungarians were able to handle their Jews as they wished, largely independent of German pressure.

In reality, within a broad sweep of Central and Eastern Europe, the Germans had no choice but to rely on local help to strike against Jews, and were therefore forced to acquiesce to some exemptions for some Jews from deportation. In Hungary (and other countries within what Holocaust scholar Raul Hilberg describes as a geographic 'arc' of destruction), the Germans were often forced for practical reasons to compromise when trying to reach their primary ideological goal – the complete destruction of each country's Jews.[10] Sometimes, noted in the scholarly literature but never fully analysed, there appeared within this 'arc' a crucial difference in the way the Nazis practised their racial politics than was the case, for instance, in Poland and eastward. Within this space, Hilberg concluded, 'the Germans were masters, but not absolute masters, powerful but not all-powerful'.[11] Observing this gap, American historian Charles Maier wrote: 'The conflicting sources of authority ... allowed oases of relative freedom, interstices where control was not absolute ... The war demonstrated that if foreign leaders – even of countries occupied by the Germans resisted, the Nazis left its Jews relatively undisturbed (if only, it was believed, for a while). In short, Nazi rule depended upon voluntary compliance.'[12]

Israeli historian Asher Cohen agreed that even though the ideology of destruction remained intact, the practice of persecution often did not.[13] Indeed, the situation in Europe had become so morally and politically distorted that the Hungarians were miffed that the Germans had 'allowed' Romania and Bulgaria to retain some of their Jews, while at the same time being subjected to unrelenting German pressure to 'transfer' all of their Jews. This formed part of the basis of their belated if still somewhat bold decision to defy the Germans and order the interruption (at least temporarily) of the deportations. For Braham, the Germans were compelled to 'subordinate their ideological drive to the concrete requirements of the continually deteriorating military situation of the Axis. The retention of Hungary in the Alliance and the full exploitation of its military and natural resources were vital considerations in the strategy of the Germans.'[14] Though the Germans maintained relentless pressure on the Hungarians to resume the deportations, the country's leadership exploited their relative autonomy, and used it to keep the Germans (and their *Nyilas* ally) at bay.

At the time, Sweden's diplomats were mostly unaware of these internal Axis tensions, and they despaired of saving any Jews. Indeed, around the time of Wallenberg's arrival, key Swedish officials were so pessimistic about achieving anything that there loomed a risk that the basis for Wallenberg's mission would be lost. In a long report written two weeks before Wallenberg's departure, Danielsson lamented the futility of most of their efforts. The Hungarian authorities would vaguely promise to respond to Swedish requests, but little would happen. Visits by Danielsson and Anger to their counterparts seemed scarcely to help, and the minister also complained that decisions taken by UD worsened chances for successful interventions, not least because Stockholm did not formally recognized the Sztójay regime: 'To obtain under such circumstances approval for even the most reasonable demands is, naturally, only possible with the greatest difficulties.'[15] We have already seen Anger's appraisal, written only two days before Wallenberg departed: 'Any change in the apparently irrevocable decision for the almost total deportation of Hungary's Jews appears ... unthinkable.'[16] Anger's analysis proved incorrect, but if it had been accurate, there would have been nothing for Wallenberg to do.

WALLENBERG ARRIVES IN BUDAPEST

At 13.50 on 7 July, Wallenberg boarded a train in Stockholm's Central Station, and departed for Berlin – he would never return to Sweden. Arriving the next day in Hitler's increasingly devastated capital city in time to have lunch with Arvid Richert, he also spent some time with his sister Nina and her husband (a junior diplomat at the Legation), and then left for Vienna at 17.21.[17] Three days before leaving Stockholm he had received permission to purchase a revolver, which he did. Part of the Wallenberg legend, it was of course highly unusual for a Swedish diplomat to equip himself in this fashion, and it is unclear why he did so, for it was unlikely to ever be genuinely useful.[18] More substantively, according to his diary, he met that same day with Norbert Masur, the Jewish leader involved in Wallenberg's recruitment, and with whom he undoubtedly discussed his upcoming mission.[19]

Wallenberg arrived in Budapest sometime on Sunday, 9 July, commencing a short residence at the famous Hotel Géllert on the Buda side of the Danube River. The hotel was close to the Swedish Legation, which was located about halfway up the Géllert hill. Losing no time, Wallenberg had lunch on Monday with Danielsson, dinner with Anger and his wife on Tuesday, and met Valdemar Langlet twice. His appointment's diary quickly filled with names, meetings, telephone numbers and addresses. Indicative of this effort to meet those in the city involved in assistance work, he soon met Miklós (Moshe) Kraus, the Zionist leader who was working closely with Swiss Consul Karl Lutz, and many others. The list of names given to Wallenberg by Vilmos Böhm led to meagre results, and has since been the subject of some debate. Hungarian historian Maria Ember concluded that most people on this list were either dead or in Gestapo custody by the time Wallenberg arrived, which demonstrates the difficulty for people outside Hungary of maintaining timely and useful intelligence which would actually help.[20]

Wallenberg's appointment's diary for 1944 stands out amongst those documents which, if carefully analysed, reveal much about the man. A careful review of his first months in Budapest reveals a wealth of interesting information, some seemingly of great importance, some apparently banal. Returned in 1989 to his family by Mikhail Gorbachev's government and the KGB, it enables us to track many of his movements in Budapest between July and December 1944, albeit by no means completely. It also tells us, as we have seen, something about whom he met and what he did in Stockholm during the first half of that year. Although difficult to analyse with complete accuracy, this essential and fascinating document will be referred to throughout the remainder of this study.[21]

For instance, soon after arriving in Budapest, he notes having to call Stockholm from the Legation, a detail significant enough to note then, but which is never repeated. Some of the names inscribed have become part of the Wallenberg legend, such as that of Elisabeth (Erzsébet) Nákó, a countess who would become his primary personal secretary, and whom he met at least twice during his first days in the city. Intriguingly, the telephone number of a 'Dr M' at Hungary's Ministry of Trade is noted, as is its address. Why Wallenberg made contact so quickly with this ministry is unclear, for its officials played no role either in the persecution of the Jews or in providing assistance or rescue. As will be shown in subsequent chapters, the evidence is clear that Wallenberg did not keep his promise given to the Americans and UD, to refrain from conducting business while in Budapest as an employee of Sweden's diplomatic service. The documentation makes clear that at the same time as he was engaged in historic rescue activities, he managed to keep an eye open to both immediately available business opportunities and post-war ones. There is no doubt that he used both his private and diplomatic contacts to promote his and Lauer's business interests. Needless to say, this element of his time in Budapest has never penetrated the hagiographic literature or other representations.

Maria Ember analysed Wallenberg's diary from the Hungarian perspective, providing biographical and contextual information about those whom Wallenberg met during these first weeks.[22] He immediately made contact with leaders of Budapest's Nazi-appointed 'Jewish Council', meeting Samu Stern and Dr Ernö Petö at its headquarters at 12 Sip utca. He visited that address on Tuesday, 18 July, meeting Petö at least twice. The next day Wallenberg met successively with Langlet; a Hungarian businessman named Bücher; Miklós Kertesz, a leading social democrat whose name he probably received from Böhm; and then, at 3.15 that afternoon, with 'SS'. Exactly what these letters mean is unclear. Although it probably meant Samu Stern, it could have been a representative of the German SS. Eichmann was still in Budapest, as were others, including Kurt Becher, Himmler's personal representative in the city, someone whom Wallenberg would eventually meet numerous times.[23] The telephone number of Veesenmayer's assistant, Theodor Grell, was soon entered into the diary's alphabetized listing, as were government ministries, Jewish hospitals, journalists and many others. Also included in this list is, naturally enough, Lajos Kelemen, the local representative for Wallenberg and Lauer's concern, Mellaneuropieska AB.[24] Perhaps most importantly during these early days, on Thursday morning, 20 July, Wallenberg met László Ferenczy, the Hungarian gendarme colonel whose whole-hearted collaboration with Eichmann was central to the murderously devastating effectiveness of ghettoization and deportation of Jews from the countryside. The address where Wallenberg met this mass murderer was just behind city hall, in an office with a sign reading, Ember reports, the grotesque euphemism 'International Warehousing and Shipment Corporation'.[25]

ONLY TWO MONTHS IN BUDAPEST?

With the framework of Wallenberg's initial activities in Budapest established, it is helpful to revisit the crucial question that has been taken for granted by virtually all previous commentators on Wallenberg. What was he actually to do in Budapest, and for how long was he to do it? Surprisingly, in the light of the sensitive nature of the mission, there is no doubt that even after arrival, among the principals there remained a striking lack of clarity. Nonetheless, Wallenberg left Sweden because discussions and expectations amongst the principals had reached such an advanced stage that it would have been politically untenable to cancel his departure. He understood that his government wished him to monitor and report on the situation, and that he had the backing both of his government and the Americans to engage in humanitarian activities. He had succeeded in negotiating a certain freedom of action to formulate assistance plans, and left Sweden believing that substantial sums of money from American sources would be available to facilitate putting his ideas into action. Yet remarkably, what he was to do, more than 'reporting', remained unclear.

The vague parameters of his mission notwithstanding, it is significant that he arrived intending to stay for only two months. It is significant because this illuminates an inherent and rarely noted contradiction between this anticipated period of time, during which virtually anything could happen, and what Wallenberg himself sought to do, or imagined himself capable of doing. Eight weeks is, after all, a very brief period of time in which to become organized and effective. Though there was some discussion of a 'concrete set of instructions' being given to him, this did not happen. This is confirmed when, only a couple of weeks after arrival, he renewed his complaints about not having received precise instructions from either his own government or the Americans. According to both Wallenberg and Lauer, the former left Stockholm without a clear idea of what the actual tasks were to be. Two weeks after Wallenberg began working in Budapest, Lauer, who was in frequent contact with his partner, wrote to the WRB's Iver Olsen. In section 'd' of this short letter, Lauer passed on information relating to Wallenberg's now-established office arrangements, noting that 'he intends to lodge some friends there since the Hungarian *Aussenamt* [foreign ministry] has declared it extraterritorial. *However, Mr Wallenberg is complaining over being left without instructions and money.*'[26] (Emphasis added.) Lauer's continuing involvement in contacts with the Swedish and American governments will be detailed throughout this book.

Nonetheless, all parties were agreed on at least several things. The first was that Wallenberg's mere presence would send a signal to the perpetrators, and the second was that if he did at least some of the necessary reporting, some of the burden on Danielsson and Anger would be lifted. Grafström's instructions are specific on this, and in this way Wallenberg did serve Swedish interests by fulfilling Allied wishes. The brief time period anticipated (again, contrary to the myth that he went to Budapest to 'save Hungarian Jewry'), is confirmed by other sources. In an undated letter from Lauer to Rabbi Ehrenpreis, Lauer wrote that he had proposed Wallenberg for the humanitarian mission being discussed in Stockholm Jewish circles. 'At my request Mr Wallenberg has declared himself prepared to stay in Budapest for two months, until the assistance activities can function on their own.'[27] Is this an indication of what Wallenberg himself anticipated, that he was going only to assist some Hungarians to set up a network of assistance activities, and then quickly return home after conducting some lucrative business arrangements, and receiving some acclaim? Oddly, his letter requesting release from his army unit put forth a period of six months abroad, but his subsequent discussions clearly indicate that he imagined being out of Sweden for only two months. An assignment of that approximate length matches discussions with the Americans, and, as noted, would have satisfied American requests that Sweden be publicly forthcoming in aiding Jews. We recall that Sweden agreed to the WRB's request to reinforce representation in Budapest partially to relieve pressure in other areas of their relationship.[28] Again, this need for such 'goodwill' was unquestionably linked to Sweden's highly contentious negotiations with the Allies to end all militarily important trade with Nazi Germany. This source of genuine tension between Sweden and the Western Allies ended only in November 1944, when shipments essential for Germany's war economy (and, not coincidentally, for the Swedes) was finally ended.[29]

Finally, this two-month period is mentioned several times by Wallenberg himself, both before departure and after arrival. The first time (as noted) was in the 'letter of agreement' negotiated with UD prior to departure: 'Furthermore it is agreed that I may finish my employment after two months, that is 6 September, if I should so wish.'[30] Perhaps even more significantly, Wallenberg twice mentioned to Lauer soon after arriving that he intended to return soon. As early as 18 July, he writes that he 'will try to come home for reporting as soon as possible', and shortly thereafter, on 24 July, that 'I hope to explain [some things] when during my visit in Stockholm.'[31] Why he would have needed to return to Stockholm so quickly 'for reporting' is unclear, for post and wire connections between Hungary and Sweden still functioned normally. Moreover, it seems odd that he would have planned to return to Stockholm so very soon after arriving in Budapest. What he was thinking when he wrote this cannot be known, but it is clearly at odds with an effective humanitarian mission.

Further evidence of his desire for a relatively hasty exit comes some weeks later. At the end of September he wrote to his mother that though the work of his 'B' department for humanitarian activities was coming to an end (something he expressed to UD as well), his anticipated and hoped-for departure was now delayed.[32] 'I had hoped to come home right after closing down the section, as they said. Unfortunately, my trip home seems to have been quite delayed, since the closing of the section is also taking a long time. At least, I'm going to try to go home via Germany and hope it won't take so long as if the trip had gone via Moscow–Haifa.'[33] This late-September letter was written, of course, two weeks before the shock of 15 October. In sum, the evidence is irrefutable that Wallenberg anticipated being back in Stockholm by mid-September, although exactly why he wanted and needed to return so quickly is unknown.[34] What he believed was possible to accomplish in such a short period of time also remains unclear. We may conclude, however, that it was circumstances, as much as any personal decision, which significantly lengthened Wallenberg's time in Budapest, and which irrevocably changed the course of his life.

WALLENBERG GETS ORGANIZED

What, then, did he do upon arrival? Some things have been described above, and though he engaged in an expanded range of activities and contacts somewhat unusual for a lower-level, apprentice diplomat, in the main Wallenberg's activities were more prosaic than dramatic. Though he was hardly confined to his desk, he did fulfil the one task clearly given him – to report on developments regarding the Jews in Budapest. We know also that he was positively enjoying the complex and challenging situation he found himself in. One month after arrival, he wrote to his mother:

> I have lived here through what are probably the 3–4 most inter-esting weeks of my life, even though we are surrounded by a tragedy of immeasurable proportions, and even though our days and nights are so filled with work that you are only able to react every now and then ... It is obviously extremely uncertain whether it will be possible to achieve a positive outcome, given that everything ultimately depends on the general situation.[35]

Contrary to popular myth, Wallenberg did not become, nor was he ever, a one-man show. Anger and Danielsson remained completely engaged, and – as noted – without their help and support, Wallenberg would have been far less effective. Nor did Wallenberg assume immedi-ate control of all activities connected to helping Jews, or become the sole reporter about them. His name does not appear in Swedish docu-mentation for several weeks, and WRB officials in Washington quickly lost track of him, although Iver Olsen in Stockholm obviously did not.[36]

Under normal circumstances it takes weeks, if not months, before a diplomat finds his or her feet in a new posting, and engages in sub-stantive work. In this regard, Wallenberg was unquestionably aided by his previous business visits to the city, which totalled some eight weeks in early 1942 and autumn 1943.[37] But Wallenberg was not an ordinary man, and he quickly demonstrated an understanding of the nuts and bolts of diplomacy which would have been impressive at any time. His first reports, which must have been approved by either Danielsson or Anger before dispatch, give witness to his powers of observation and organizational skills. Though he lacked formal diplomatic training, his initial reports demonstrate that he was well suited to his new role. His letters to his grandfather had long revealed his acute powers of obser-vation, and his intelligence and ease with foreign cultures and situa-tions now found full epistolary expression. He vividly described what he saw and heard – a process helped because he had, typically, prepared himself before departure by reading through many of the earlier Budapest reports.

A review of Wallenberg's initial reports prompts further reflection about the historical and heuristic value of the documents which form the heart of this study. They bring us, it may be asserted, as close to 'being there' as is possible decades later. The men drafting these documents were intelligent, educated, by nature curious, and trained to report clearly and concisely about what they were seeing and hearing. This felicitous combination of factors provides an unprecedented window, from a variety of perspectives, onto what happened in Budapest, and one feels little distance between what they saw and what we can read today. Of course these men chose to include or exclude certain information in their reports, but their training was to include what they decided was most important. They understood they were at the epicentre of a vast human drama as poignant and tragic as any in modern European history, and their reports are characterized by accuracy, emotional sobriety and professionalism.[38] Though these documents were written with Swedish interests and perspectives in mind, their accuracy is confirmed both from other contemporaneous documentation, and the research of historians who have explored other, non-Swedish perspectives. Of course these documents are not capable of giving a full, 100 per cent picture of what took place in Budapest, but no single source is capable of this. Equally certain is that they, like all historical sources, must be analysed with professional care and the insight provided by other sources, both primary and secondary. Moreover, their veracity then and utility today is greatly enhanced by the fact that their authors were secure in the knowledge that diplomatic practice prevented their reports being read by unwanted eyes. In fact, communications with Stockholm, both in the form of diplomatic pouches and coded telegraphs, remained normal until almost the end of December, when normal channels finally broke down.

In the context of research on the Holocaust, their authors had a particular position as they observed and reported what they saw and heard. These Swedish diplomats were neither perpetrators nor potential victims of the ongoing genocide – they had no intention (obviously) of perpetrating crimes, nor did they fear in any way becoming victims of the ongoing genocide, as survivors did. Their diplomatic status protected them (mostly) from fearing physical harm, at least until virtually the end of December 1944, when normal reporting could not in any case take place. This made them unafraid of engaging in close, careful and critical observation and analysis. This 'onlooker' status placed them in a situation possibly unique amongst those who recorded, at the time, and for one reason or another, Holocaust history as it unfolded. It is obvious that a study based on survivor accounts would tell a very different story, even about some of those aspects of Swedish and neutral diplomacy which are treated here. There is no question that these Swedish documents are a unique, and uniquely valuable, source which enables close description of this part of Holocaust history. Not incidentally, they are also uniquely valuable in removing the layers of myth which surround Raoul Wallenberg.

Wallenberg's first few reports will be treated in some detail, as they provide the clearest picture of what he did, thought and planned during this initial period. They add an illuminating level of detail (and sometimes amateurish analysis), about the general political situation and what was happening to the city's Jews, for which Anger did not have time. And because of who Wallenberg became, these reports have a poignant historical interest in their own right.

Wallenberg's first memorandum, dated 18 July 1944, was as lengthy as those Anger had written to date and, like most documentation produced by him, was rife with detailed information.[39] Appended to it was a list of names with annotation and analysis almost as detailed as the report itself. He was able to write such a detailed report so quickly because he clearly spent much of his first days informing himself of prevailing circumstances by reading translations of the local press, contacting (primarily) Hungarian officials from various ministries and meeting with people – Jews and non-Jews alike – who were willing to provide non-governmental information.

Wallenberg obviously wanted to impress those he knew would be reading this first report, which he also knew would be summarized in translation for the Americans and British. Yet there is no indication that he is addressing anyone other than UD officials. The language is quite officious, and it has a somewhat breathless, excited and perceptibly self-serious tone to it. Some of the information is already dated (and would probably have not been included if written by Anger or Danielsson), and there is some superficial analysis, though Wallenberg acknowledges when he is unsure or uncertain about something. He writes nothing about his own plans or thinking, nor is there any indication that after only eight to nine days 'on the job', he is impatient with his assigned task of 'merely' reporting. Yet in his first letter to his mother, he wrote: 'At the moment it looks as if our first venture within the framework of humanitarian work will be successful. Great difficulties still lie ahead, however, and I cannot yet believe that this first project will eventually succeed.'[40] Nothing is indicated about the 'first project', and it is odd that he wrote to his mother about it and not to UD.

The long report describes security measures taken to protect the identities of his informants, and several times he notes that he already has other sources at his disposal – 'my sources tell me', or 'my sources indicate', as if to prove the value of his newly established connections. The inexperienced diplomat relates virtually everything he has been told, which makes for fascinating reading but also for a much longer report than was the norm for Swedish diplomats, who generally favoured brevity and concision over length. Although here, again, many of Anger's and Danielsson's Budapest reports were exceptions to the normal pattern.[41] In general, diplomats who wrote overly long, unreadable or imprecise reports could fall into disfavour, but of course Wallenberg had, so far as is known, no ambition to be a career diplomat.

The plight of Jews already deported and in temporary ghettos is vividly described. Though Wallenberg uses the word 'persecutions' in the title, he knew full well that much worse was happening. To his credit, however, he avoids such phrases as 'it is too terrible for words', or 'words fail me in trying to describe' – phrases seen in some Swedish diplomatic documents describing the war against European Jewry. Instead he employs phrases such as 'disgusting' or 'incomparable brutality'. He provides information about terrible scenes related to him from an assembly camp at Békásmegyer and a deportation site in Kassa. The report also contains a short section titled 'Auschwitz, Birkenau and Waldsee', noting that everyone transported there except men and young women capable of working are 'killed'.[42] His familiarity with Budapest allows him to dismiss the pathetic arguments of those Hungarians who blamed the Germans for what was happening to the Jews. 'This, in any case, is untrue. Antisemitism is deeply rooted in Hungary.'[43] He describes fears of post-war retribution felt by some Hungarians involved in crimes against the Jews, and comments on rumours connected to why and how Jews are moved around the city into various dwellings and neighbourhoods. Relevant to later events is the observation that, so far, he knows of no forged or falsified identity papers available to Jews, because 'the printing houses are so well controlled that this path to rescue appears, for the moment, to be excluded'. At the same time that Wallenberg concludes that prevailing circumstances make it very difficult for Jews to flee, he also writes: 'The Jews in Budapest are completely apathetic and hardly do anything themselves to save themselves.' Indeed, again in contrast to those who have asserted that Wallenberg was motivated by some deep-seated emotional and/or 'blood' connection to a purported Jewishness, we find no rhetorical, ethnic or existential connection manifested with those whose plight he describes in such detail.[44]

Finally, just before concluding with a short but outdated description of the forced sale of the Weiss-Manfréd concern to the Germans,

Wallenberg touches upon a subject to which he would later return.[45] Noting that he is unaware of any cases in which someone was actually rescued from an internment camp (except for one instance mentioned earlier by Anger), he writes: 'In general, it appears that bribery occurs far less frequently than what one might have believed, not least because the whole assembly and transport procedure has been so mechanized, quick and impersonal that an outsider wanting to help has, quite simply, no chance of speaking with the camp commander.'[46] This four-page report concludes with a rather clear signature which would deteriorate under the stress to come.

The appended list includes some fifty-eight names of individuals and/or families who have been issued with emergency passports. Of course the list of names compiled by German industrialist Oskar Schindler and his Jewish assistants, collectively known as 'Schindler's List', has become one of the most famous documents from the history of the Holocaust – a demonstration not least of the power of film as creator of memory. Far less famous but no less poignant are the numerous lists drawn up in Budapest and Stockholm by Anger, Wallenberg, Engzell and others, which provide not only names but often other illuminating details about circumstances and fate. These documents shed even more light on the Holocaust than does the famous film, because of what they tell us about the potentialities for neutral diplomacy during the genocide.

On this particular list are a number of names which would become connected with Wallenberg's efforts, including Hugo Wohl, Gábor Forgács, Agnes Adachi (née Mandl) and others.[47] Most if not all of them had been named in previous correspondence, and many would be listed for the first (potential) transport of Jews to Sweden planned for later that month.[48] Its content indicates that it was assembled in some haste by Anger in response to an exchange with Stockholm, and all involved now realized that some sort of central or unified 'databank' of names of those receiving various Swedish (documentary) assistance was required. Anger asked Engzell for such a list, assuming that this was something centrally placed officials in Stockholm would draw up. Engzell informed him that, regretfully, they had neither the time nor personnel to undertake even such a relatively simple, but time-consuming administrative effort, though all agreed it was necessary.[49] This already existing bureaucratic disorder with name-lists would in subsequent months border on chaos, yet fortunately, these administrative lapses seem not to have actually hampered rescue and assistance efforts. Wallenberg and the others did not let themselves be overwhelmed by the blizzard of paper they were dealing with.[50]

The appendix itself contains a number of interesting notations, and has a different discursive character from Wallenberg's memorandum.

One annotation states that '[she] was in a forced labour detail which in most cases have been deported/a provisional passport [issued] by the Legation succeeded in getting her free and secure at least through the first of August'. Regarding one Eva Minkus, Anger noted: 'For this person the head of Legation has on his own authority issued a provisional passport, as mortal danger appeared imminent and marriage between her and a Swedish citizen is intended.'[51] The thrust of the diplomatic efforts expressed throughout is how the Legation has saved, and tries to save, Jews from deportation, internment, loss of property, wearing of the 'yellow star', and other measures of persecution and death. One long notation reads as follows:

> When issuing provisional passports without [UD's] explicit permission [*utan KUD:s särskilda bemyndigande*], the Legation has followed the principle of seeking to save from deportation or other measures from the authorities which according to experience is usually the first step towards deportation to unknown locations.
>
> In the beginning the Legation has attempted to 'bluff' with such a document, because it has been observed that certain authorities have shown a willingness to accept the Legation's issuance of a 'certificate' and [a Swedish] residence permit for the person holding an emergency passport. Supported by this certificate, the person in question has been freed from wearing the yellow star and from listing their property [for authorities]. He has even received normal rations ...[52]

It is difficult to find elsewhere such language used by a European diplomat during the Holocaust, and this evident eagerness to help Jews in Budapest highlights how far Swedish diplomacy had come since the 1930s. Finally, the appendix describes a type of behaviour by one Hungarian official which would become more common, the closer the Red Army came to the city. 'In certain cases this individual, in order to protect his own back, has requested written evidence of this attitude.'[53]

WALLENBERG'S FIRST ACTIVITIES

We have already noted that there were various factors motivating Wallenberg to accept the assignment fate handed him, and his personal desire to do something apart from 'merely' reporting cannot be doubted. Yet it is also true that the assignment came to Wallenberg at a time when he remained somewhat at a loose end about his professional future, even as his partnership with Lauer remained viable.[54] No doubt he considered the assignment exciting, and it is possible that he hoped or even anticipated that doing well in Budapest would advance his career prospects when returning to Stockholm – which, as noted, he fully anticipated doing. Wallenberg arrived in Budapest full of energy and ideas, and there seems little doubt that he thrived psychologically, even when under enormous pressure. He knew that going to Hungary was potentially hazardous (otherwise he wouldn't have purchased the revolver), but had every reason to be confident that for the most part, neutral diplomats had little to fear in occupied Europe.[55] However, though it cannot be doubted that he kept *his* ultimate goal in focus – helping as many people as his resources and circumstances permitted – evidence will be subsequently presented which confirms that both Wallenberg and Lauer saw this assignment as a chance to promote current and future business opportunities in Budapest and beyond. There is no question that Wallenberg, at a minimum – and as the British suspected – was watching for future business possibilities. This too contradicts some of the prevailing myths about the alleged purely altruistic nature of his motivations.

Wallenberg's second formal report is dated 29 July, and also contains two parts, both about three-and-a-half A3 pages. The first part is entitled 'Memorandum concerning assistance to Hungary's Jews', and the second 'Memorandum concerning the treatment of Hungary's Jews'.[56] The rhetoric in both is already somewhat toned down, demonstrating a calmer professionalism than did his initial report.[57] We see in this report the first indications of how Wallenberg imagined he might be of some assistance for the thousands of Jews appealing for Swedish help. Though some of his recommendations are naive and unrealistic, other proposals and ideas demonstrate the thinking that would soon result in concrete humanitarian assistance. The two documents, which contain detailed subcategories such as 'goals and means', 'official negotiations', and 'information activities/Jews self-help', demonstrate Wallenberg's considerable talent for organization, logical thinking and creativity. Moreover, in a sign that he was finding his feet, he did not shy away from suggesting forcefully to Stockholm what should and should not be done. Yet Wallenberg still gave no indication about how he would expand the ongoing diplomatic tactics used by the other Swedish and neutral diplomats.

In the section entitled 'Goals and means', he writes: 'To establish any final goal for assistance activity ... is impossible, because the situation changes every day. That which is important is to have available the financial and organizational means to be able to take advantage of every opportunity those measures [which are] demanded by the situation, hopefully without having to request permission [every time].' Though in his first report he suggested that bribery seemed less common than

believed, he had no doubt that, for a variety of reasons, quick availability of sufficient funds was vital. Wallenberg seems to have quickly
realized, and feared, that he might not have the freedom of action
which he believed had been given him in Stockholm, even though he
had yet to do anything which might have required specific permission.
It appears also that he was beginning to sense that Swedish activities to
date were proving inadequate, for later in the report he complains that
though 'very limited' assistance activity has been started, 'It is regrettable that those who were most interested in my coming here appear
not to understand that money is necessary. Here there is unlimited suffering which we need to alleviate.'[58] Wallenberg would frequently
return to these two themes – money and independence.

He confirms one of the primary reasons for UD authorizing his mission, writing that 'the Legation's permanent staff was, when I arrived,
completely exhausted'. In describing some of his own initial activities,
he informs Stockholm that he is using as voluntary help some Jews who
are exempt from wearing the 'yellow star', as the Swiss Legation had
done. Indeed, even the resident Gestapo unit employed Jews, because
so few Christians were available to help! Then, following prudent
bureaucratic procedure, Wallenberg reports that 'a telephone with
extensions is installed in the B-division's building, many thousands of
different stencilled forms printed up, and ... a half dozen typewriters,
desk, chairs, etc., borrowed from different quarters'. And, as an experienced businessman familiar with the social mores and graces of
European elite, Wallenberg also notes that 'as my private residence I
have rented a very beautiful house on top of the [Géllert] hill in order
to, on a suitable scale, be able to host [business meetings and dinners]'.[59]

Contradicting his own first report, Wallenberg notes that in several
cases a few Jews have been released from forced labour and internment
camps when able to show an emergency Swedish passport, which also
'liberated them from the obligation of wearing the star, which also
implies a great step on the way to rescue because curfew is also avoided,
and with it, other risks are also minimized'.

The next section repeats Wallenberg's strongly held belief that some
of the suffering endured by Budapest Jews was their own fault – the
result of their inability or unwillingness to help themselves. Yet he
immediately softens this opinion by noting the prevailing geopolitical
situation in Europe, and in fact expresses an almost intuitive understanding of the mass psychologies afflicting the Jews. Under the subtitle 'Informational Activities. The Jews Self-Help', Wallenberg writes
with emphasis:

> In some way we must get rid of the apathy about their own fate

which still   characterizes most Jews ... what is important is to exterminate the feeling [*utrota känslan*] among the Jews that they have been forgotten. The King's message was, in this context, of great utility. Similar messages from foreign institutions to their resident counterparts would [also] have great significance.

The mere fact that Swiss and Swedish legations have welcomed Jews, listened to them and registered them has encouraged them and others inclined to help. Even a successful repatriation action of limited scale or establishment of a Red Cross camp or financial assistance would, in my estimation, have its greatest significance through the fact that it would infuse hope into the breasts of a hundred thousand Jews and wake up the currently paralysed instinct for self-preservation.[60]

Finally, the report's penultimate paragraph contains some pointed criticism of propaganda broadcast to Hungary by the Western Allies: 'The Russian propaganda, which patiently emphasizes large themes and the love of peace, is considered to be better. If at least some promises could be given about future help to those who help Jews, [Allied] propaganda would surely do more good.' The report concludes with Wallenberg's opinion that publicity in foreign press about the situation 'has undoubtedly contributed to a considerable easing of the situation here'. This, of course, is what the Americans hoped when they asked the Swedes and others to increase their representation. Unfortunately, events would turn out otherwise.

After arriving, Wallenberg immediately established extensive communication with his business partner. In some ways this correspondence to Lauer duplicated what Wallenberg was reporting to UD, yet these early letters shed important additional light on what Wallenberg did in the beginning, and what he was thinking of doing. One aspect of this first phase not noted in previous literature about Wallenberg is the emotional pressure Lauer put on his younger partner to assist personally and immediately the Hungarian's widespread family. Lauer was naturally terrified about what might happen – or had happened – to members of his family, and before Wallenberg departed, Lauer briefed him about various family members. They spoke by telephone several times during those first weeks, and Lauer was clearly pressing his partner for news and results.[61] Wallenberg's first letter described his early contacts and efforts to help. He met Lauer's brother-in-law, but could find out nothing about Lauer's in-laws. Assuming they had been deported, Wallenberg wrote:

I am sorry to be unable to provide any comfort about this. It seems absolutely certain that your in-laws and Mrs Stein crossed the border at Kassa. Obtaining news from them from the other side, as long as they themselves don't write, is unfortunately completely excluded. I can't tell you how sorry I am to be unable to give you any better news. I can merely explain that everything humanly possible which can be done, has been done.[62]

Wallenberg then described some of his initial contacts, including a visit to the German Legation, the Hungarian foreign and interior ministries, and even the 'Traffic' department. Presumably he had gone there to obtain his Hungarian driver's licence, which he received, valid until 9 November 1944.[63] He then again reminded Lauer of the fundamental necessity of having sufficient funds and operational independence in order to accomplish anything of substance:

> Concerning general activities, naturally money is needed. This could merely be done if they pay into my account at Enskilda Bank.[64] I guarantee naturally that they will be paid back if I don't find any use for it. There is, for example, no possibility to work if I have to obtain approval for my anticipated plans for helping. I can't be bothered to telephone about this simply because UD wishes that everything shall go through them. I request therefore that a quick payment is made ... It all hangs upon this happening quickly. There are many to help and great suffering ...
>
> In general the money will go to individuals, the Red Cross, churches and private individuals who show themselves capable of helping Jews. On the other hand I doubt if much, perhaps a bit, shall be used for bribes. I don't much believe in this [method].

Why Lauer would remain a conduit to UD is unclear but, again, Engzell and others there had by now become accustomed to listening to many different people interested in what was happening in Budapest. UD files, however, are silent about Lauer's continued contacts. Nonetheless, during this early phase, Wallenberg clearly expected Lauer to smooth his way with the professionals in Stockholm:

> For several reasons I believe that we should avoid speaking too much by telephone because I am rather certain that due to my considerable activities, things will be noticed. Perhaps you can resume discussions with U.D. [*sic*] if something should go amiss. On the other hand, I am completely certain that it would be unfortunate if payments are made through U.D. [*sic*] because they must be much more formal than [required] if the thing happens privately.

Lauer next wrote on Monday, 17 July, to say that on the previous Friday, he had been granted Swedish citizenship, and he thanked

Wallenberg for help in this matter.[65] He passed on more details of various family members and relatives, including small children, begging Wallenberg: 'Do everything which is humanly possible to at least save someone from my family!' Lauer knew that Wallenberg's intentions were far broader than helping only his partner's family, and these urgent entreaties, however understandable, must have placed enormous emotional pressure on someone facing a completely unprecedented situation. Indeed, in his letter of 16 July to his mother, Wallenberg urged her to invite Lauer and his wife for dinner, because 'I have learned that his in-laws and evidently also a small child belonging to the family are already dead, i.e., that they have been shipped abroad from Kecskemet – and there they won't stay alive for long'.[66]

Nonetheless, Lauer was able to add some lighter thoughts:

> I have ordered cigarettes and coffee for you in Hamburg, which will be sent to your brother-in-law in Berlin, which he can surely forward to you. We all are well, but miss you very much, and will be happy when you finally have accomplished your mission and return to us. I assure you, an executive in Mellaneuropeiska [their trading company] is better off than either a legation secretary or councillor![67]

In Wallenberg's short reply of 24 July, typed under the Legation letterhead, the main theme is what he believes he can get done, so long as he receives sufficient funds and is free to use the money as he decides. Asserting that Sweden's humanitarian undertaking in Hungary cannot be considered finished when the much discussed repatriation to Sweden of some 649 Jews is accomplished (it never occurred), Wallenberg wrote that he looked forward to explaining his ideas 'during my visit to Stockholm'. As noted earlier, the phrasing makes it clear that it was his intention to return to Sweden relatively soon, something which must have influenced his overall thinking and planning.[68]

MONEY AND BRIBERY

Wallenberg's time in Budapest would be characterized by frequent requests to Stockholm for ever larger amounts of money. For instance, in his letter of 18 July to Lauer, he wrote:

> I beg you to try to arrange it so that I am able to dispose of the Pengö [Hungary's currency during the war] without inhibitions. I may be mistaken concerning my choice of people, but I do believe that I have some contacts that are to be regarded as serious ... Later I will return to the possibilities of bribing successfully

German or Hungarian officials and departments. I believe such
advances are often used for blackmailing the people concerned.

Obviously in normal Swedish diplomatic practice, bribery would be
unthinkable and prosecutable, and Per Anger remembered with some
anxiety that Wallenberg stressed this tactic, even though he had already
written about being unsure if it really worked. At one point,
Wallenberg asserted that money supplied by him to his contacts would
be used to purchase fake baptismal certificates and identity cards. Yet
again, in his 24 July letter to Lauer, Wallenberg stressed: 'It is necessary that I have money in order to be able to operate.'

It is of interest that these and many other documents mention a
variety of sources of funds. Sometimes they are Hungarian pengő
received locally, and sometimes from Swedish Jewish, American
Jewish, or American government sources. During these months, the
only government apparently unwilling to commit itself to increased
financial outlays for humanitarian help was Sweden's. UD did agree to
a monthly salary of 2,000 Swedish kronor for Wallenberg, but otherwise it seemed quite miserly about extending special funds to help with
assistance work in Budapest. Indeed, still remaining in the archives
from these months are scores of invoices sent to individuals in Sweden
for costs incurred by UD when the ministry provided telegraphic facil-
ities for contacting family members, other relatives, friends for whom
assistance was requested, etc.[69] Issues connected to Wallenberg's frequent concentration on obtaining sufficient funds 'in order to function' may be regarded in both a positive and negative light, and will be
further explored in subsequent chapters.

In conclusion, there is no question that Wallenberg's first weeks in
Budapest were extraordinarily busy and filled with ideas, meetings
with a variety of contacts, memoranda, personal letters, and more. He
obviously threw himself into his mission, and felt that he was doing the
best he could. His feverish activities in July and August were fundamentally important to his ability to function effectively afterwards,
because in the event he did not return to Stockholm in September. His
work habits and personality all set the stage for the far more ad hoc,
at times even desperate diplomacy he and other diplomats were compelled to practice after the *Nyilas* coup of 15 October. His repeated
requests that large funds be made rapidly available highlights how
quickly he came to operate in an unconventional manner, even though
such unorthodox financial doings made some at UD anxious.
However, though this was undoubtedly the case, there is no evidence
that Engzell, Danielsson, Anger or other UD officials tried to alter or
put a stop to his ideas about how best to use assistance funds. Nor is

there any evidence that they tried to keep in check the youthful energy that had been unleashed in Budapest. Whatever Wallenberg may have had in mind upon arrival, events completely outside his control would determine both what he did, with whom, and how, although, as noted above, the anticipated brevity of his stay must have influenced his early thinking. It certainly disproves any mythical contention, so often noted by the hagiographers, that he arrived in Budapest determined 'to save Hungarian Jewry'. Assisting and saving even some hundreds or 'merely' a few thousands was also a noble goal.

NOTES

1. S. Grafström to P. Anger, no.66, 6 July 1944, *Riksarkivet Utrikesdepartementet* (hereafter RA UD), P 2 Eu, folder 1.
2. Author interview with Ambassador Per Anger, March 1990, Uppsala University Library, Raoul Wallenberg Project Archive, no.C002, pp.23–4. Wallenberg met Danielsson on previous business trips to Budapest, something which must have eased the latter's concerns.
3. Director Kjell Grede's 1989 film, *God afton Herr Wallenberg* (Good Evening, Mr Wallenberg), has a scene which represents Wallenberg as confronted by Danielsson, as if the latter was against the former's humanitarian work. This notion is not supported either by reports written by both during that time or by other evidence. Though Danielsson may have been sceptical of some of Wallenberg's methods, there can be no question that he fully supported the effort.
4. Though the deportations were halted, Eichmann, using almost pathetic yet still lethal trickery, managed in mid-July to organize the dispatch of at least two more trains to Auschwitz.
5. J. Lévai, *Black Book on the Martyrdom of Hungarian Jewry* (Zurich: Central European Times, 1948), p.113. In fact Horthy was lying, for he had allowed the deportation of many prominent Jews from Budapest, but only after their assets had been confiscated either by the Germans or the Hungarians themselves. See S. Szita, *Trading in Lives? Operations of the Jewish Relief and Rescue Committee in Budapest, 1944–1945*, trans. S. Lambert (Budapest and New York: Central European University Press, 2005), especially Chapter 8.
6. R.L. Braham, *The Politics of Genocide: The Holocaust in Hungary*, revised and enlarged edn (Boulder, CT: Rosenthal Institute for Holocaust Studies Graduate Center/City University of New York Social Science Monographs, 1994), vol. 2, p.884. The situation would drastically change again after the 15 October *Nyilas* coup.
7. Former Hungarian Prime Minister Bela Imrédy, cited in Braham, *Politics of Genocide*, p.877.
8. D. Cesarani, *Eichmann: His Life and Crimes* (London: William Heinemann, 2004), p.173.
9. On Nazi Germany's remarkable failure to effectively govern the European nations they conquered militarily, see M. Mazower's new study, *Hitler's Empire: Nazi Rule in Occupied Europe* (London: Allen Lane, 2008).
10. In fact, similar circumstances prevailed for several nations in Central and Eastern Europe which were in what Raul Hilberg has described as a 'semi-circular [geographic] arc of destruction, extending counter-clockwise from Norway to Romania'. See R. Hilberg, *The Destruction of the European Jews: The Revised and Definitive Edition* (New York: Schocken Books, 1987), vol. 2, p.543.
11. Ibid., p.545.
12. C. Maier, *The Unmasterable Past: History, Holocaust and German Identity* (Cambridge, MA: Harvard University Press, 1988), p.94.
13. A. Cohen, 'Pétain, Horthy, Antonescu and the Jews, 1942–1944: Toward a Comparative View', in M. Marrus (ed.), *The Nazi Holocaust: Perspectives on the Holocaust* (Westport, CT: Meckler, 1989), vol. 4, pp.63–100.
14. Braham, *Politics of Genocide*, vol. 2, p.882.
15. I. Danielsson to C. Günther, no.127, 24 June 1944, RA UD, Hp 21 Eu 1095, folder 5. This long report was shared with both the Americans and the British.
16. P. Anger to C. Günther, no.149, 5 July 1944, RA UD, Hp 21 Eu 1095, folder 6.

17. Friday, 7 July 1944, R. Wallenberg's appointment's diary, RA, Raoul Wallenberg Arkiv, Signum 1, vol. 9.
18. On 30 June, Wallenberg received his Swedish diplomatic passport. Travelling on this would presumably have ensured that he would not be searched by either the Gestapo or German customs police, allowing him to transit with the weapon.
19. The entry for 4 July reads '*Am. nationaldag*', meaning surely the American Fourth of July celebrations, to which he had presumably been invited as a result of his recent contacts with American diplomats. Yet it was then crossed out, presumably indicating that he was unable to attend the annual American celebration to which prominent Swedes are traditionally invited.
20. M. Ember, *Wallenberg Budapesten* (Budapest: Városháza, 2000), p.3.
21. The diary's usefulness in tracking whom he met diminishes towards the end of the year, most likely due to the crush of events. It concludes, of course, on 31 December, and it is unknown if Wallenberg began using a new diary for 1945 before being detained by the Soviets.
22. For biographical details about Hungarians whom Wallenberg met or obtained information from, see Ember, *Wallenberg Budapesten*, passim.
23. There is no reason to believe that Wallenberg would have known who Adolf Eichmann was, apart from the Austrian's specific role in Budapest. Contrary to the depictions of the hagiographers and filmmakers, the evidence indicates that they did not actually meet. They were aware, however, of each other's activities. See Chapters 11 and 12.
24. Somewhat surprisingly for such an accomplished draughtsman, Wallenberg's handwriting was sometimes nearly illegible. Some names and notations are almost or completely unreadable, a tendency which got worse as stress, fatigue and the rush of events took their toll.
25. Ember, *Wallenberg Budapesten*, p.33.
26. K. Lauer to I. Olsen, 24 July 1944, RA, Raoul Wallenberg Arkiv, Signum 1, vol. 6. Written in fluent English, this letter summarizes much of Wallenberg's early activity.
27. K. Lauer to M. Ehrenpreis, cited in J. Lévai, *Raoul Wallenberg – hjälten i Budapest* (Stockholm: Saxon & Lindströms, 1948), pp.33–5. The letter is most likely from some time in early-to-mid-May.
28. Sweden was the only neutral which increased its representation in Budapest in response to this American request.
29. It must be noted that forcing Sweden to cut trade with Nazi Germany was far more important to Roosevelt's diplomats than assisting some distant Hungarian Jews. Throughout 1944, Stockholm and Washington were engaged in increasingly rancorous negotiations, during which the Americans sought to convince the Swedes to finally cut off all militarily important trade with Nazi Germany. Throughout that year, the Americans cajoled and the Swedes resisted. On this, see P.A. Levine, 'Swedish Neutrality during the Second World War: Tactical Success or Moral Compromise', in N. Wylie (ed.), *European Neutrals and Non-Belligerents during the Second World War* (Cambridge: Cambridge University Press, 2002), pp.304–30.
30. R. Wallenberg to *Kabinettssekreteraren* Assarsson, 6 July 1944, RA, Raoul Wallenberg Arkiv, Signum 1, vol. 6.
31. R. Wallenberg to K. Lauer, 18 July 1944, *bilaga* 7, and RW to KL, 24 July 1944, *bilaga* 8, both RA, Raoul Wallenberg Arkiv, Signum 1, vol. 6.
32. It remains to be established with any lasting credibility what dangerous espionage the novice, non-Hungarian-speaking diplomat might have accomplished in that short time.
33. R. Wallenberg to Maj von Dardel, 29 September 1944, in *Raoul Wallenberg: Letters and Dispatches 1924–1944*, trans. K. Board (New York: Arcade Publishing, 1995), p.275. The potential return route noted, 'Moscow–Haifa', is hard to understand, and remains unexplained.
34. This experienced traveller, who had spent years abroad, could hardly have been homesick, or uncertain of his ability to function in a foreign country.
35. R. Wallenberg to Maj von Dardel, 6 August 1944, in *Wallenberg: Letters and Dispatches*, pp.273–4. In this letter he also tells of the much appreciated, impromptu birthday celebration arranged for him by his secretary, Countess Nákó.
36. John Pehle does not remember hearing of Wallenberg after his appointment, nor through much of 1944. Author's interview with J. Pehle, 4 September 1989, Washington, DC.
37. See A. Lajos, *Hjälten och offren: Raoul Wallenberg och judarna i Budapest* (Växjö: Svenska

Emigrantinstitutets skrifserie, no. 15, 2003), p.113. In spite of the weeks he had spent in Budapest on business trips, Wallenberg did not speak any Hungarian. His excellent German would have more than sufficed for communicating with most Hungarians, particularly in Budapest.

38. The overall accuracy of their reporting has been confirmed subsequently many times in numerous sources and publications.

39. 'Memorandum concerning the persecution of Hungarian Jews', and 'Memorandum 11 – concerning emergency passports issued by the Legation in Budapest for persecuted Jews', both 18 July 1944, RA UD, Hp 21 Eu 1095, folder 6.

40. R. Wallenberg to Maj von Dardel, 16 July 1944, in *Wallenberg: Letters and Dispatches*, p.273.

41. As one diplomatic historian has written, 'the art of diplomatic writing was to say, in the proper order, everything that needed to be said and nothing beyond that'. See G. Craig, 'On the Pleasure of Reading Diplomatic Correspondence', *Journal of Contemporary History*, 26, 3 (1991), pp.369–84.

42. Wallenberg used the conjugated Swedish verb *att avliva*, which has a different connotation from, for instance, 'murdered'. 'Waldsee' was the imaginary location some deported Hungarian Jews were forced to mention in 'postcards' they were compelled to write, which were then sent back to Hungary by the Germans in an attempt to deceive those remaining in the country.

43. 'Memorandum concerning the persecution of Hungarian Jews', 18 July 1944, RA UD, Hp 21 Eu 1095, folder 6.

44. Also of interest is this passage: 'In principle the Social Democratic party is friendly to Jews but practically paralysed and hardly in a condition to do anything. I don't know anything about the Communist Party's attitudes or activities.'

45. On this episode in the Hungarian Holocaust see, most recently, G. Kádár and Z. Vági, *Self-financing Genocide: The Gold Train, the Becher Case and the Wealth of Hungarian Jews*, trans. E. Koncz, J. Tucker and A. Kádár (Budapest: Central European University Press, 2001), pp.195–208.

46. 'Memorandum concerning the persecution of Hungarian Jews', 18 July 1944.

47. It is of considerable interest that a number of the names on this list are those which appear in literature about Wallenberg as his aides. Some have been interviewed by oral historians over the years, have published something themselves about Wallenberg, and are recognizable to any student of Wallenberg.

48. Through the remainder of the year, the Swedes would continue trying to organize a transport of Jews from Hungary to Sweden, but they failed. German intransigence proved too difficult to overcome.

49. G.Engzell to P. Anger, no.61, 18 July 1944, RA UD, Hp 21 Eu 1095, folder 6.

50. Additionally, this organizational disorder makes it almost impossible to know with certainty who, and how many people, actually received the various types of Swedish documents. It is also impossible to know in each individual case whether or not the documents – including the *Schutzpass* – contributed to a positive outcome. More on such lists in subsequent chapters.

51. In more normal times, of course, the mere prospect of marriage to a Swedish citizen would not be sufficient grounds for issuing a government document denoting Swedish citizenship!

52. The words 'bluff' and 'certificate' are in quotation marks in the original document, the latter word only the first time.

53. This remarkable document concludes by noting that one official at KEOKH, the Hungarian government's alien control agency, had shown an unexpected willingness to assist the Swedes in aiding Jews with papers. Anger also learned that, 'no.24, Fru Kamarás, has committed suicide'.

54. Though as noted in Chapter 2, Jacob and Marcus Jr remained reluctant to fully integrate their younger cousin into their business empire, Wallenberg's personal financial situation was never insecure.

55. It was of course impossible to know that Budapest would suffer such a destructive siege as that which commenced in late December. Yet so far as is known, no Swedish diplomat was killed in occupied Europe during the war, although diplomats and staff were exposed to great dangers in cities such as Warsaw, London, Berlin, Moscow and, of course, Budapest.

56. Both no.173, 29 July 1944, RA UD, Hp 21 Eu 1092, folder 1.

57 Amongst other items of interest in the annex is his exaggerated claim, which he says has

been 'confirmed', that King Gustav V's appeal to Horthy was 'the direct cause' for the cessation of the deportations. He also notes the beginning of popular opposition both to the government itself and its anti-Jewish actions.

58. Only a week later the WRB's Olsen, on a visit to Svante Hellstedt at the Foreign Office, made 50,000 kronor available 'for Sweden's work for the rescue of Jews in Hungary'. Wallenberg's name is not mentioned in this memorandum. *Promemoria* (PM) no.2300a, 5 August 1944, RA UD, Hp 21 Eu 1096, folder 8.

59. 'för att i lämplig omfattning kunna representera'. There is testimony in oral histories of the period suggesting that Wallenberg received from some Budapest Jews financial assistance in kind, such as houses, offices and vehicles. In return, it is most likely these individuals and their families received Swedish assistance of some type or another, as also happened with Valdemar Langlet.

60. 'Memorandum concerning help for Hungary's Jews', no.173, 29 July 1944, RA UD, Hp 21 Eu 1092, folder 1. Also of interest here is his proposal that an appeal from Erling Eidem, Sweden's archbishop, would also be useful. More on this in the following chapter.

61. As will be seen in Chapter 11, such pressure from Lauer would continue.

62 R. Wallenberg to K. Lauer, undated, RA, Raoul Wallenberg Arkiv, Signum 1, vol. 6. Although undated, the content makes clear that it was written soon after arrival

63. This document, with a picture of him obviously taken in Budapest, was also returned to the family in 1989 at the same time as the already-mentioned diplomatic passport. A copy is in RA, Raoul Wallenberg Arkiv, general.

64. Enskilda Bank was the family bank and naturally the one Wallenberg used.

65. Wallenberg, before leaving, had supported in writing Lauer's application for citizenship.

66. R. Wallenberg to Maj von Dardel, 16 July 1944, in *Wallenberg: Letters and Dispatches*, p.273.

67. R. Wallenberg to K. Lauer, undated, RA, Raoul Wallenberg Arkiv, Signum 1, vol. 6.

68. R. Wallenberg to K. Lauer, 24 July 1944, RA, Raoul Wallenberg Arkiv, Signum 1, vol. 6; and RW to KL, 18 July 1944, ibid. which is in German, indicating that it was dictated to one of his staff, a pattern that would continue. The figure of '649 Jews' was also used by Lauer in a letter to Olsen.

69. The standard price seemed to be 4kr per telegram. Bills for payment can be found in several files, including RA UD, Hp 21 Eu 1096, 1095, 1098, and others.

7

Summer 1944: Per Anger, Archbishop Erling Eidem and the 'Everyday' Politics of Genocide[1]

Dear Mrs. Günther, Regarding your letter concerning assistance to two Jewish families in Budapest, Ledofsky and Szalkay.

Because of the large number of Hungarian Jews who have through relatives connections to Sweden, unfortunately we must observe certain restrictions in who we help. We have however requested that the Legation try to help these families named. The Legation has currently about 450 such 'protectees'. Unfortunately, [helping them] has been shown in most cases to be futile. But we are aware that every one of our interventions provides a certain comfort for relatives and acquaintances here [in Sweden] ...

> G. Engzell to Ingrid Günther (wife of Sweden's Foreign Minister), 12 July 1944[2]

A TEMPORARY REPRIEVE?

It is impossible to exaggerate the importance of the halting, in early July, of the deportations to Auschwitz. One historian labelled it 'a sensation', and there seems no question that most people in Budapest – apart from the still very determined perpetrators – breathed a sigh of relief.[3] Yet whatever sense of relief may have been felt remained tentative, largely because the array of severe discriminatory measures against the Jews was not eased. The Germans were equally surprised and displeased by Horthy's move, which included his wish to sack Prime Minister Sztójay's pro-German government and replace it with one more closely aligned with himself and other Hungarian nationalists. The Germans naturally resisted, and Sztójay lasted in office several more weeks.

Throughout July, divisions within Hungary's government persisted, with some leading officials determined to maintain their genocidal collaboration with the Germans. Sztójay and others supported the Germans' wish to resume the deportations, while others, including

Deputy Foreign Minister Mihály Arnóthy-Jungerth, argued that such a radical solution of the 'Jewish question' would have 'grave consequences for Hungary after the war', and that Hungary's interests were best served by distancing themselves from the campaign of murder.[4] There seems little doubt that the combination of foreign and domestic pressures, combined with highly unfavourable military developments, were making a deep impression on many Hungarian officials within both national and municipal bureaucracies. In fact, Jungerth-Arnóthy not only kept his colleagues in the cabinet informed of what the neutrals were doing, he urged the Swedes, Swiss and others to continue their assistance and rescue attempts. Horthy himself, though, largely responsible for the suspension of the deportations, maintained contact with Edmund Veesenmayer, even discussing the possibility of their resumption.

In Berlin, high-ranking officials, all the way up to Hitler, were informed by Veesenmayer of the Swedish and Swiss efforts. It is clear that, because of the fragile balance of power in Budapest, Veesenmayer had no choice but to tolerate neutral diplomacy on behalf of Jews. Nonetheless, he chose not to even attempt to crack down on them. He could have harassed and distracted neutral diplomats with his security forces, or put more pressure on Hungarian authorities to do something, but there is no evidence of this.[5] Instead, he sought instructions from Berlin, which urged him to reject the various rescue schemes promoted by the neutrals.[6]

Also throughout July, Anger and Danielsson exploited the gaps created by German–Hungarian dissent, and continued negotiating with both. The immediate goal was to secure the rescue of the Jews, for whom they had assumed direct responsibility. The longer-range goal, which included increasing cooperation with the other neutrals, was to create an umbrella of diplomatic activism under which at least some might survive. This goal was closely linked to the approach of the Red Army. This chapter will analyse these efforts, highlighting the work and diplomacy of Per Anger, the now veteran chargé d'affaires during Wallenberg's six months in Budapest, and a man equally anxious to do what he could to help those in need.

PER ANGER CONFRONTS GENOCIDE

Some of Anger's activities in spring and early summer have been described previously, including his and Minister Danielsson's audience with Horthy on 3 July. That first week in July also saw continuing efforts to obtain the necessary permissions for the organization and departure of a 'Swedish' train with Hungarian Jews possessing emergency passports.

This particular effort, in which we see characteristic Swedish activism hindered by typical German and Hungarian obfuscation, and bald lying about who was responsible for the final decision, resulted in tactical failure. Yet even this episode of failed diplomacy is of interest and importance.

Anger had been concentrating on trying to organize Hungarian exit visas and German transit visas for just under 200 individuals (the numbers vary in different documents). His efforts were encouraged and supported by Engzell, who urged their colleagues in Berlin to help remove German resistance, although he was sceptical that this would succeed. On Wednesday, 5 July, the day before Horthy ordered the deportations to be halted, Anger visited the German Legation, trying to push them to accept the notion of a 'repatriation train', and he requested the necessary transit visas. Anger's requests were met by Councillor Grell's typical unwillingness to give a straight answer to any request concerning Jews, saying that such decisions were made in Berlin. Comparing his efforts with ongoing Swiss negotiations to get 7,000 holders of 'Palestine certificates' out of Hungary, Anger wrote that 'in spite of extended negotiations with Hungarian and German officials, permission for this emigration [effort] has not been received'.[7]

Veesenmayer's account of, and conclusions from, the meeting between Anger and Grell are illuminating. The methodically murderous plenipotentiary noted that 186 Hungarian Jews had received Swedish entry visas and 'certificates', and were the subject of approaches by Anger to the Hungarian foreign ministry and the German Legation, with officials at both claiming it was the other one which made any final, binding decisions. The diplomatic minuet which characterized many such meetings between German perpetrators and Swedish officials is described:

> My colleague [Grell] confined himself to taking notes of the explanation, pointing out to the Swedish chargé d´affaires that in any case the Jews in question are not Swedish citizens but Hungarian citizens, for whom unquestionably the Hungarians are responsible and not the Swedes. The chargé finally said that his visit was solely informational and that he reserved for himself a more formal move as soon as he received further instructions ... from his government.[8]

Hitler was informed of these efforts and responded that he was prepared to grant to the neutrals the lives of small numbers of Jews, so long as the Hungarians agreed to deport the hundreds of thousands remaining in Budapest. On 10 July, von Ribbentrop telegraphed Veesenmayer, telling him that Hitler agreed to the repatriation of the Swedish and Swiss groups:

> The offers from the Swedish, Swiss and American governments
> [WRB] can be fulfilled, and we assume that the governments con-
> cerned are going to bring the Jewish groups ... into their countries
> ... However, we can only agree to this concession on condition
> that the removal of the Jews to the Reich that was temporarily
> stopped by the Regent is now going to be immediately and as
> quickly as possible completed.[9]

There is no evidence that Swedish diplomats were aware, as they
continued their negotiations to rescue those few people, that they were
being drawn into a grossly immoral exchange.

The Swedes' efforts continued parallel to negotiations conducted by
the equally tireless Karl Lutz, the Swiss consul with whom Wallenberg
would subsequently closely cooperate. The Swiss diplomat lobbied to
get some of the thousands of Jews on his 'Palestine Lists' to the Yishuv
through either Romania or Turkey.[10] The Germans, however, were
even less inclined to grant these exemptions because of their wish to
continue currying favour with the Arabs. Notionally at least, it seemed
that some Jews protected by neutral diplomats would be allowed to
leave so long as the overall goal of emptying Budapest was achieved.
This is another example of some diplomatic manoeuvring space being
created, which was subsequently used. In fact, there was the precedent
of Jews being allowed to leave which had been established within the
Eichmann–Kasztner negotiations.[11]

Establishing actual lists of Jews with connections to the neutrals, in
this case regarding the hoped-for repatriation train, was an increasingly time-consuming task for many diplomats and officials in Budapest,
both neutral and Axis. The Swedes, as noted earlier, were losing track
of all the names in their rapidly increasing paper flow, and confusion
was growing about exactly how many people were in question.
Ironically, this problem worsened when colleagues at other Swedish
legations in Europe sent names to UD after learning of the unorthodox
methods and decisions occurring in Budapest. On 8 July, a diplomat in
Bern wrote to Engzell, saying that a Swedish woman in Geneva, who
was married to a Hungarian citizen, had asked for assistance for her in-
laws living in Hungary:

> I don't know exactly if the Legation in Budapest is giving visas in
> such a case, but I received during our conversation before my
> departure [from Stockholm] the impression that [you] at home
> are trying whatever is possible in some way through the Legation
> in Budapest to help Hungarians with connections to Sweden ... I
> therefore permitted myself to inform Fru Salgo that her father [in
> Sweden] should contact your division ...[12]

On 14 July, Anger telegraphed Stockholm asking for complete lists of names of those who had applied for assistance, both in Hungary and Sweden.[13] Engzell answered four days later, writing that he understood that the staff was overwhelmed, and 'it would be a great joy if the plan [repatriation] to save them could be carried out'. He then answered Anger's appeal for more organized information:

> we are glad if something can be achieved ... Lately we have been generous with assistance and accepted all applications. Unfortunately though we have not from the beginning made lists. We have only made a card catalogue with 'primary' names and other applicants. We must unfortunately therefore deny your request for control lists. We don't know who has been put onto the Legation's lists. In some cases [the applicant's] relatives are numerous and we've only telegraphed a few names [to you]. It would be extremely time-consuming work to make up such a list here.[14]

A breakthrough in the repatriation train negotiations appeared possible when, on 13 July, Engzell received a telegram from Danielsson saying that Arnóthy-Jungerth had requested a meeting. The high-ranking Hungarian told Danielsson that '[the] Hungarian government accepts Sweden's proposal for Red Cross rescue work for children, women and elderly. Simultaneously [he] confirmed that the Hungarian government permits the repatriation to Sweden of the approximately 450 Jews in question. And after negotiations with German officials, [they] appear to have unexpectedly granted permission for rescue work and transit through Germany.'[15] Several days later, Anger added that it seemed the Hungarians 'appear to be making great efforts to ease the treatment of the Jews'.[16]

On 17 July, Anger wrote excitedly to Stockholm: 'Quite unexpectedly both Hungarian and German authorities have acceded to transport home to Sweden for those Jews on our lists ... this hit the Legation like a bomb.' Only two days earlier, the Hungarian Foreign Office had informed the Swedes that there was little chance of this outcome. 'The change came therefore very suddenly; it appears to be one of the consequences of the Regent's recent interventions to soften the measures against the Jews.'[17] As with many of the documents under analysis, this two-page report informs us about numerous matters. Anger noted that things were developing so quickly that Hungarian authorities had not been notified of the specific nature of an individual's connection to Sweden. One list of names was demanded so quickly that such information was included, yet Hungarian authorities seemed unconcerned with what had been, to this date, essential information. This is evidence that bureaucratic chaos on the perpetrator's side was also on the increase, something which proved both favourable and disadvantageous in the attempt to save lives.

Noting that many from the list had most likely already been deported to either Poland or Germany, Anger offered the officials at KEOKH (Hungary's National Central Authority for the Control of Foreigners) help to find some of these individuals. Anger, who surely discussed these matters with Wallenberg, stressed to Stockholm that there was no time to waste. Though exact transport details had not been worked out with the relevant authorities, the departure would be facilitated, Anger believed, if he was allowed to issue a 'collective passport', much, he said, as the Swiss had done for those theoretically bound for Palestine. Reading this, Engzell wrote, '*Ja!*' (Yes!).[18] On 20 July, he cabled that 'a collective passport may be issued for the Jews'.[19]

What the Swedes in Budapest could not have known, even though their colleagues in Berlin and elsewhere had experienced these standard Nazi negotiating tactics, is that the Germans had no intention of letting these Jews depart. It was virtually standard operating procedure for Nazis such as Eichmann (and there were many others like him) to 'promise' something concerning Jews which they had no intention of delivering. Some days earlier, the German Legation in Budapest had sent a report to Berlin complaining, both about what the Swedes were seeking to do, and that many of the Jews now obtaining Swedish protection were even less 'qualified' than had previously been the case. In Berlin on 11 July, a mid-level Swedish diplomat met with Eberhard von Thadden, the notorious AuswärtigesAmt official. As usual, the Nazi diplomat claimed virtually as a right the freedom to place Jews outside the law and society:

> I have visited Councillor von Thadden, for whom I explained in detail our viewpoints on the question of Jews in Hungary. [He] received a report on the actions of our Legation in Budapest with information about those Jews. Meanwhile, he made the principled objection that neither he as a German nor I as a Swede were legally authorized to deal with this matter, which was a domestic Hungarian matter ...
>
> For his own part, [von Thadden] believed it likely that the Swedish request presented would not be accepted. In particular this applied for those Jews who have no relatives in Sweden, but only are representatives for Swedish business or industrial companies. It is preferable [he said] to release a little Jewish haberdasher rather than the big business and industry Jews, who always showed themselves to be the most dangerous and most antisocial elements.[20]

Then, just a week after the ostensible German decision to grant transit, Eichmann wrote to Berlin from Budapest: 'we will, for as long as possible, draw out the ongoing efforts for some Jews to emigrate so that after the evacuations resume, all possibilities for emigration are choked off'.[21] In other words, Eichmann hoped not only to finally deport the remaining masses, he had every intention of killing those Jews currently under neutral protection. In reality, however, Eichmann's July frustrations caused him to leave Budapest mid-month, going to lurk elsewhere in Hungary and hoping that Horthy would change his mind, so that Budapest's Jews could also be sent to die in Birkenau's gas chambers.[22]

Two other relatively minor issues are of interest from these days, and both continue the process of unravelling the skein of subsidiary myths which envelop Wallenberg. The first is the notion that the Legation's contacts with Budapest's Jewish community, not least with its Nazi-formed 'Jewish Council', began only after he arrived. In fact, its members had earlier sent a copy of the 'Auschwitz Protocols' to UD through the Legation, and now, on 18 July, they sent a two-page appeal directly to King Gustav, thanking him for his appeal to Horthy, and requesting increased Swedish humanitarian aid in material and political form. The letter, signed by three leading members of the 'Council' – *Hofrat* (court councillor) Samu Stern, Ernö Petö, and Dr Karl Wilhem – was unlikely to be sent to Sweden's king through the good offices of a young, inexperienced diplomat who had taken up his position only days before.[23] Their trust in Danielsson and Anger is evident, as the latter ended his covering letter with the notation that the men of the council requested that the king would, as soon as he read it, burn the part with their names and the stamp of the 'Council'.[24]

The second matter is that even outside of Budapest, Sweden's diplomatic activities on behalf of Jews were widely known before Wallenberg became a noticeable part of existing efforts. On 21 July, UD received an aide-mémoire from Britain's Foreign Office, asking the Swedes 'to use their good offices to do what they can to protect the under-mentioned Hungarian subjects whose relative, Mr Paul Ignotus, works in a British government department'.[25]

SWEDEN'S PRELATE FAILS TO UNDERSTAND

The many studies analysing the response of Germany's Catholic and Protestant Churches to the persecution and genocide of the Jews have no counterpart in Swedish historiography, where the overall response of Sweden's State Lutheran Church to the Holocaust remains largely unknown.[26] Though the circumstances in which Sweden's clergy found itself was obviously fundamentally different from that faced by their colleagues to the south, they did have to respond ethically and spiritually to some of the same weighty questions and ethical dilemmas.[27] We see an example of this in the sometimes poignant exchange of correspondence which took place between Erling Eidem, archbishop (and head) of Sweden's State Lutheran Church, and several officials at UD, primarily Sven Grafström, then interim head of the political division. An examination of this correspondence sheds important light on attitudes informing the intellectual and cultural milieu prevailing in Sweden during the Second World War, and helps us to understand otherwise hidden elements of UD's response to events in Hungary, and elsewhere earlier.

Throughout the period under study, and particularly as the year wore on, Engzell and others frequently sent copies of official government documents (including reports stamped 'secret'), as well as correspondence between diplomats, appeals for help received, and so on, to leading members of Sweden's government and relevant society. By mid-July, the 'ccs' on documents about Jewish issues included Archbishop Eidem. In response to one of them, at the height of his summer holiday, the archbishop sent a three-page, handwritten letter to Sven Grafström from the countryside near the university town of Uppsala.[28] After first thanking him for sending reports about events in Budapest, the clergyman wrote: 'My heart has been warmed by the measures and efforts undertaken to help by UD's leadership, but the violence against those poor people and their fate have given me nightmares day and night.' One of Eidem's reasons for writing was to describe the telegram he had just received from Rabbi Isaac Herzog of Jerusalem, a leading figure in the Yishuv. Herzog requested that Eidem make a public protest and appeal to Hungary's leaders for mercy for the Jews. Eidem provided his own answer to the plea: 'A special appeal from me would not reach those responsible and wouldn't be of any significance. [And] to start a church "protest-action" would, so far as I understand, be inappropriate and would probably hurt matters.' Herzog's other request was that two prominent Hungarian rabbis and their families be rescued: '[Herzog] proposes that they be invited to Uppsala University to give lectures in Talmud and Rabbinica.'[29] In two earlier instances, wrote the archbishop, he had failed in his attempts to help Jews, and now he asked Grafström for advice about contacting the university's leadership.

Eidem's mildly sympathetic but unimaginative reception of a desperate appeal from a renowned Jewish spiritual leader reveals the archbishop's failure to understand the scale of the disaster which overtook Hungary's Jews, as well as pointing towards one of the irresolvable

moral dilemmas created for bystanders to genocide. Eidem continued:
'Two more viewpoints: It might expose both rabbis to greater risks if
they were to receive a foreign invitation. And furthermore: It makes
me uneasy to try to save these two spiritual leaders, when their con-
gregations cannot be helped.'[30]

Grafström immediately answered the archbishop's 'very friendly
letter'.[31] Oddly, he agreed that direct contact with the Hungarian rabbis would probably cause them harm (and of course neither of them
could know if the rabbis and their families were even alive), even
though Grafström knew perfectly well of the many direct contacts
between Swedish representatives and literally hundreds of Hungarian
Jewish citizens which had occurred. No reports that the fact of mere
contact brought reprisals have been found. Grafström brought up the
recently suspended deportations, writing (unsurprisingly), that in UD's
judgement, 'There is surely no question that the King's appeal has had
great significance.' Eidem was informed that Sweden's Red Cross delegate (unnamed) was taking measures to help Jews in concentration
camps: 'for this work there is money available, also from American
quarters'. It is worth noting that Grafström did not name Wallenberg
as part of the recently increased assistance efforts. Perhaps even more
surprising was an initiative hitherto unmentioned in UD documents:
'Furthermore, the Swedish government has instructed the Legation in
Budapest to provide entry visas for *all* Jewish children in Hungary.'
(Emphasis added.)[32] He wrote of the ongoing efforts to get the 'repatriation train' out of Hungary, because 'according to information from
Budapest, Hungarian exit visas and German transit visas have been
arranged for this group'. The letter concludes with a sentiment which
was widespread in UD: 'This is perhaps not so much, but I believe I can
say that we here have taken all measures which in the current circumstances have been reasonable and possible.'

The Archbishop, in turn, quickly thanked Grafström for all the
information, which he forwarded to Jerusalem. Revealingly, he also
thanked the diplomat for confirming his own thinking, and relieving
his moral doubts: 'Now I feel calmed because You, Head of the [Polit-
ical] Bureau, in your letter explained that you shared my understanding. It creates such anxiety to receive such cries for help and not be
able to take any direct actions that would help individuals.' Then,
however, the archbishop gives further evidence that even by this late
date, he scarcely understood the nature of Nazism. Agreeing with
Grafström that everything which could be done was being done, the
archbishop wrote: 'One cannot understand that an occupying power
[Germany] which itself is struggling with so many great difficulties,
seems able still to carry out what appears to be such an unnecessary

series of violent measures.'[33] This striking failure to understand the
nature and purpose of a genocidal regime occupying a sovereign nation
(a failure shared by untold millions of other Europeans), and to realize
the nature of the now over three-year-long, often visible campaign of
murder against European Jewry, is partially explained by, in this case,
Eidem's temporal proximity to the event – the Holocaust was not yet
understood in such profound terms. Yet a spiritual leader of Eidem's
stature might have been expected to acquaint himself better with information available to him from UD, if he had shown more curiosity. Such
information would have only complemented that frequently available
in the public domain. Indeed, just three days earlier, the influential
Stockholm daily *Svenska Dagbladet* published an interview with a
German diplomat claiming that his country was not treating Jews inhu-
manely. The journalist wrote: '[The German] underscored that the
Jews themselves bore responsibility for the situation they are in.
Germany considers the Jews a belligerent, warring power, against
which Germany is fully justified to take determined defensive measures
against.'[34] Some weeks later Eidem would have occasion, seemingly
reluctantly, to revisit this matter.

Ironically, the same day that Grafström confirmed Eidem's unfortunate belief that a public protest by the leader of Sweden's Church
would be a mistake, Per Anger telegraphed Stockholm recommending
that precisely such a public appeal be made from Sweden to Hungary's
Protestant bishops.[35] Such an appeal would be helpful, the diplomat in
place argued, not least because it would strengthen Horthy's position
vis-à-vis the Germans. Anger even proposed that specific figures about
the number of Jews deported should be part of any such clerical
appeal.[36] Wallenberg, in his long report of 29 July, would propose virtually the same thing. He wrote: 'I return therefore to the proposal
about a telegram from the Archbishop to [Hungarian] bishops, a proposal made also from clerical quarters here.' He also emphasized: 'It is
quite certain that publicity in international press has contributed greatly
to an easing of the situation here.'[37] It is unknown why Grafström did
not make this information known to Eidem.

On 3 August Eidem again wrote to UD, this time to First Secretary
Östen Lundborg, also thanking him for previous correspondence.
Writing that 'thoughts about those poor Jews in Hungary leave me neither day or night', Eidem added that he had now had time to reflect
about whether or not to send a telegram, protesting at the treatment
of the Jews, to Hungarian evangelical bishops, a proposal he had
recently received from 'from private clerical quarters' in Sweden:

This proposal appears to me more complicated than it did in the beginning. In the first place it appears particularly uncertain if such a telegram from me would be delivered to the Hungarian bishops in question. Moreover I must say that I feel it hard to direct such an appeal to them, as this might expose them for a not inconsiderable danger when it is uncertain that their protest would lead to anything positive.

These circumstances make me rather doubtful about accepting the proposed plan. My caution is not based on any indifference, which I hardly need to tell you.[38]

Why Grafström and other officials did not reassure the archbishop that their colleagues in Budapest were urging that exactly such an appeal be made, and that it had the potential to do some good, is not known. It is clear, however, that in this case, the archbishop allowed his caution to trump – easily it seems – his sense of moral outrage. He concluded incorrectly that public or 'private' protest would do more harm than good. We know today, and others knew then, that such an appeal would have had some impact, but the archbishop decided otherwise. Koblik's analysis of Eidem's and the Church's response is persuasive. He argued: 'Eidem opted to remain silent primarily for political and social reasons. As a high-ranking figure in Sweden's government, he felt a responsibility to support the government's foreign policy.'[39] But Swedish policy in Budapest was, to state the obvious, to do as much as possible for Hungary's Jews, and not to allow caution, institutional inertia or previous patterns of response to prevent a positive humanitarian reaction. Yet Sweden's foremost Christian leader decided that remaining silent and doing nothing was the best response. Koblik concluded:

[Eidem] would not take the moral leadership in public for which his office provided the opportunity. There was no physical danger to his person, as there was to religious leaders in Germany ... When faced with the dilemma of defending the church as a social-political institution or sustaining [its] role as the moral leader of society, Eidem chose to be a bureaucrat rather than a religious figure.[40]

It is impossible to disagree with Koblik's conclusion that Eidem's tepid, even somewhat cowardly response to appeals for help constitutes a glaring moral failure by Sweden's most internationally prominent religious leader during the Holocaust.

'SPACES OF DEATH' IN BUDAPEST

One of the many inhumane measures taken against Budapest's Jews in the shadow of the deportations was the ghettoization process they endured in June and July. These forced movements within the city, which were very different there from those in other European cities, have long been subject to misunderstandings by historians and others – misunderstandings which have contributed to some of the layers of myth which envelop the Wallenberg story. This misunderstanding is hardly unsurprising, considering the fact that even Wallenberg and his usually well-informed colleagues themselves misunderstood what was happening on the streets of the city in which they operated, and precisely why city officials were ordering the Jews to leave their homes to be concentrated in other buildings. Because these confusing developments had a significant impact on subsequent Swedish assistance efforts, it is helpful to review the issue.

In his previously discussed memorandum of 18 July, Wallenberg commented on the forced movement of Jews within Budapest. In this case he essentially reported incorrect but widely spread rumours:

> In this connection it can be mentioned that in certain quarters it is believed that the presence of Jews [throughout the city] would imply some protection against [Allied] bombing. In these circles it appears to be the belief that the Jews are spread out on purpose in approximately 2,600 'Jew houses' everywhere in Budapest instead of being assembled in a ghetto, and that for the same reason those Jews in labour service are forbidden from seeking shelter during bombing raids.[41]

By using Hungarian sources, British historian of historical geography Tim Cole is able to give us a better understanding in this instance of what actually happened in Budapest than Wallenberg's report or other Swedish sources do. His work helps us to understand the implications of a pernicious process consciously created by those Cole illuminatingly labels as 'doctors of space'. These men made cruel decisions about human living quarters based primarily on ideologically based notions that 'strict' boundaries in time and space had to be established between Jews and non-Jews.[42] Cole argues that important aspects of the 'Final Solution' in general, and certainly the many instances of ghettoization – particularly in Budapest – were carefully planned:

> by a multitude of architects, engineers, and cartographers [implementing] smaller architectural and spatial solutions ... planning and implementing ghettoization was, in part at least, an act of urban planning [by] Budapest municipal officials [in what] amounted to a physical reshaping of the city in 1944–1945. It is within such activities, which took place over many days and weeks, that one can detect some of the 'everyday politics' of genocide.[43]

Today, Holocaust historians understand that the genocide was not 'one' plan conceived and planned in Berlin and implemented identically all over Europe. Rather, the actual event consisted of many cognate 'local' genocides which occurred in particular ways in different places at different times throughout Nazi-dominated Europe; time and place were often more decisive in determining the timing and character of ghetto-creation rather than one 'master plan'.[44] Affirming Christopher Browning's conclusion that ghettoization in Poland 'was in fact carried out at different times in different ways for different reasons on the initiative of local authorities', Cole emphasizes that this was especially the case even within the relatively limited confines of municipal Budapest:[45] 'With the restructuring of the spaces of the urban and rural environment ... the Holocaust emerges as a profoundly spatial historical event. The relationship between "Nazi" and "Jew', between "Perpetrator" and "Victim" was constructed in, and *through*, space. Annihilating the "Jew" was a spatial process from start to finish.' (Italics in the original.)[46]

Understanding the relationship between perpetrator and victim also influences our understanding of the 'bystander'; most particularly those neutral diplomats we are studying. Cole points out:

> ghettoisation [involves] both the creation of spaces of 'Jewish absence' and the creation of spaces of 'Jewish presence', with the 'doctors of space' making specific decisions at specific times. Holocaust ghettoisation ... is about the drawing of boundaries (whether physical facades or imaginary dividing lines) which separate 'Jews' from 'non-Jews'. The boundary created by ghettoisation acts as both a means of inclusion and a means of exclusion.[47]

Cole further notes that 'territoriality is about the exercise of power through the control of space', with the result, surely unplanned by the perpetrators and perhaps unique to Holocaust history, that in the specific circumstances of Budapest:

> territoriality was central to attempts to rescue 'Jews' and not simply destroy 'Jews'. Thus territorial solutions were being proffered by both the *Nyilas* puppet government *and* a host of neutral powers with legations in Budapest ... the adoption of territorial solutions by [the neutrals] was about continuing a tradition in which territoriality had played a central role in controlling the city's 'Jews' ... central to territoriality is the drawing up and policing of borders, *to exclude the territorial transgressor.*[48] [Emphasis added.]

The rumour-based 'analysis' by Wallenberg and others of the alleged effects of American bombing became, according to Cole, the dominant post-war interpretation explaining how ghettoization occurred in Budapest. Dispersal for protection was, however, not the primary motivation of those municipal officials who, importantly, made their decisions independent of German influence. 'When ghettoisation was implemented ... there was little mention of geostrategic concerns' (i.e. using the Jews as shield against the American bombers), but rather ghettoisation was implemented in order to realize both antisemitic goals and to achieve material gains for the city's non-Jewish population.' Cole cites acquisitive municipal officials who pushed for ghettoization because it would result in the 'freeing up [of] a large number of flats and their allocation for [residents] without flats'. It was, officials argued, '[that] because of their material strength, the Jews live in exaggerated housing conditions', and that after this internal shifting of populations, the Jews would be 'in flats more suitable to their proportion and social values'. Exactly how Jewish 'social values' differed from those of their fellow urban residents was not explained by those making the decisions. Ghettoization also had the added value of ending alleged shortages faced by 'Hungarian workers'.[49] The consequences of these base material motivations, a part of the Holocaust from its beginnings and a central part of the destruction of Budapest Jewry, had direct impact on what the neutral diplomats could, and could not do.

Importantly, the erroneous post-war explanation for what underlay ghettoization in Budapest is particularly relevant for our concerns in the period after the deportations ceased. Moreover, they are (again) important for our understanding of what and how Wallenberg did what he did in the prevailing circumstances, and also in helping us see more elements of myth about him.[50] Keeping Cole's ideas about spatiality in mind is useful in understanding how neutral diplomats were able to help Jews in some buildings in particular areas of Budapest, and why they were unable to help others elsewhere. He also provides a clearer sense of the actual physical geography of the 'Jewish houses', the 'international ghetto', railway stations and other places of assembly and deportation. This holds as well for the weeks after late November, when the order came to form a 'central ghetto' in the heart of Pest. These spatial relationships increase our understanding of where Wallenberg moved throughout the city – not least after 15 October. As we try to trace and understand his movements after that date, when his presence and visibility meant so much to so many, we understand what the physical distances and artificially created spatial boundaries prescribed by the 'doctors of space' meant for his activities. A critical result of the proscribed ghettoization process was, Cole writes, 'in a shift of "Jewish" population from the periphery to the centre'. This new pattern of occupancy had implications for the survival of thousands of people.

Though some still survived elsewhere, the vast majority of Jews were now housed in the districts closest, on either side of the city, to the Danube River.[51]

The second factor concerns a central myth about Wallenberg. It is often said that his personal intervention halted the destruction of the short-lived 'central ghetto' in Pest, thereby saving the lives of some 70,000 souls entrapped there. Though there is little, if any, reliable evidence supporting this notion, in common memory his name is inextricably linked to the ghetto's salvation. As with so many other individual episodes of the Holocaust in Budapest, such a misunderstanding distorts what actually occurred, and hinders rather than facilitates a better understanding of what Wallenberg actually did.[52]

Understandably, the Jews of Budapest believed that what they heard throughout the spring and early summer about the various 'moving' directives was a prelude to deportation. They had no reason to hope otherwise, not least because this outcome was sought by those anti-Semitic municipal officials who hoped to repeat in their city what had been accomplished throughout the country. Only Horthy's intervention prevented this from happening. Nonetheless, the suffering endured by hundreds of thousands of innocent people forced from their homes by administrative fiat, leaving behind most of what they owned and held dear, and forfeiting all that they had inherited from generations of family life, was bad enough. Moreover, in thinking about the context in which orders to relocate were received, we may note that this massive and inevitably chaotic remaking of the city's demographic map came about two weeks after the D-Day invasion – which, of course all were aware of – and about two weeks before Wallenberg arrived – which they were not. One Jewish leader described what he saw:

> June 24 fell on a Saturday. Budapest was the scene of such a sight as not seen for centuries. The children of Israel carried their bags and their baggage, pieces of furniture and articles for personal use, whatever they needed most, by carriage, handcarts, and wheelbarrows, and those who found nothing better, bundles on their back, to the houses indicated ...[53]

A FATEFUL JULY ENDS

The remainder of July saw feverish diplomatic activity by Swedish diplomats in Budapest, Stockholm and Berlin on behalf of the Jews of Budapest. Simultaneous with efforts to secure the release of the promised transport was the dispatch of ever-lengthier lists with names of Jews, which Swedish diplomatic posts literally around the world had received from a wide array of appellants.[54] On Monday, 24 July, Stockholm telegraphed more names, saying that '[we] have in every case where some form of connection to Sweden has been demonstrated accepted applications for protection. We doubt these lists can be increased further.'[55] Coordination between the Swedish missions in Budapest and Berlin now became especially important:

> Hungarian exit permission has now been received for our list of Swedish Jews, with 91 people given provisional passports ... Yet in spite of German promises, there is danger the matter will be drawn out in time, therefore request that Legation in Berlin immediately contact again German authorities about this question ... The Legation has received masses of new applications from Jews who have, in the majority of instances, connections to Sweden. Request information whether [you] in Sweden are prepared to accept more Jews.[56]

The next day Stockholm reversed its decision and sent another two dozen names for the Legation's lists, putting even more pressure on Legation staff.[57] Though Anger reported that Hungarian authorities seemed willing to accept the asserted connections to Sweden, German officials were not so forthcoming. On 27 July, Anger wrote with some sadness and sarcasm that a German note 'confirmed our suspicions that [they would] sooner or later sabotage the seemingly accepted plan for Jews to travel to Sweden'. Rather than accept the approximately 600 names now on Swedish lists for transit through Germany, Nazi diplomats said that each and every name had to be 'tested'. And again the Swedes were told that the neutral repatriation schemes would be allowed only if the Hungarians then made all remaining Jews available to the Germans for forced labour 'duty'. However, Anger wrote that in growing contrast to the Germans, Hungarian officials were demonstrating an increasing willingness to accommodate Swedish requests, even releasing some arrested Jews based merely on the assurance that, 'they were on our repatriation lists'.[58] He also informed Stockholm: 'Possibilities for the lodging of people on our lists in special houses or camps is being discussed with the appropriate authorities.'[59] This is one of the first indications about those Jews who would be housed in what came to be called the 'international ghetto'.

Anger's understanding of German attitudes was correct. On 29 July, Veesenmayer telegraphed von Ribbentrop with a long report describing his frustration with Hungarian reluctance to strike again against the Jews: 'I answered [Sztójay] that it was intolerable for us to wait any longer and I suggested that now 50,000 Jews should be transferred to some camps outside of town in order to send them to the Reich. This is necessary because the Jews in Budapest are getting cheeky again and because the halt in the evacuation of the Jews was harmful to the authority of the Hungarian government.' How Budapest Jewry demonstrated their 'cheekiness' to the German plenipotentiary is not made clear, but how the Swedes and other neutrals were engaging in effective negotiations with the perpetrators on behalf of some of the 'impertinent' Jews is. Veesenmayer continued:

> The Swedish Legation completed a list of a total of about 650 people who have been awarded Swedish citizenship for family or business connections to Sweden or who have been approved for entry into Sweden. For the first group of about 100 people the Swedish Legation has submitted regular and provisional Swedish passports and filed an application for obtaining German transit visas. The Swedish Legation asked for the granting of a collective passport for a much larger group that is going to be handed in [soon] ... All involved agree that included in the new operation are only those Jews still living in Budapest.
>
> In the same context, the local Spanish Legation has also filed an application for making possible the emigration of one Hungarian Jew and the Portuguese Legation for nine Hungarian Jews ... All these operations have been discussed in the Hungarian Foreign Ministry as well as between members of the [neutral] missions and us.[60]

In a vivid demonstration of how far Sweden's response to the Holocaust had evolved since the war began and, even more so, internal UD notions of what was 'allowable', on 26 July a dramatic change in Sweden's position was cabled. 'We here are prepared to accept all Jews from Hungary with connections to Sweden, your no.235.'[61] Equally surprising was Stockholm's notification to Danielsson that they were prepared to organize shipping and air transport to Sweden for the Jews on UD's list – 'government agencies and organizations here are prepared to organize reception of those without any means of support'.[62] This too is a dramatic change from how Sweden's government and, indeed, society normally thought about refugees; if they wanted refuge in Sweden, they could not rely on the government to fund it. It may be noted that the policy of refugees having to find or fund their own living had been for decades Swedish social policy towards refugees of all stripes, particularly Jews.

The month ended with UD sending ever more names to Budapest, many the consequence of stories and information in daily newspapers, which then created a new flood of applications. And though many of these names had no apparent connection to Sweden at all, officials chose not to refuse these applications. Telling one appellant that even though these (new) people were unlikely to receive much help from the overwhelmed Legation, Svante Hellstedt wrote to Danielsson that 'we here must leave it completely to the discretion of the Legation to decide what might possibly be done'.[63] By this point of the war, diplomacy on behalf of Hungarian Jewry constituted a significant element of UD's activities, and for those involved in events in Budapest, trying to save Jews was now an everyday activity.

Though by the end of July Wallenberg had been in the city for some three weeks, he had not yet assumed a particularly prominent role in assistance activities. This would happen in August, even though by that time he had reached the virtual halfway mark of his anticipated stay. Yet from the day he arrived, Wallenberg accelerated his activities, becoming more acquainted with the Hungarian and German officials who remained determined to kill as many Jews as they could before the Red Army arrived, and gradually more visible to the city's Jews. However, before resuming our focus on Wallenberg's role in Sweden's historic diplomacy, the next chapter will examine another ad hoc Swedish diplomat whose name and achievements have been all but ignored by historians and hagiographers alike. He was Valdemar Langlet, who had finally in late June gained his official appointment as representative for SRK (Svensak röda korset, Sweden's Red Cross). Like his colleagues, his daily task also became that of helping Jews survive the Holocaust.

NOTES

1. This chapter title is inspired by Professor Randolph L. Braham's magisterial study, *The Politics of Genocide: The Holocaust in Hungary*, revised and enlarged edn, 2 vols (Boulder, CT: Rosenthal Institute for Holocaust Studies Graduate Center/City University of New York Social Science Monographs, 1994).
2. G. Engzell to Mrs I. Günther, no.37, 12 July 1944, *Riksarkivet Utrikesdepartementet* (hereafter RA UD), Hp 21 Eu 1095, folder 6.
3. A. Handler, *A Man for All Connections: Raoul Wallenberg and the Hungarian State Apparatus, 1944–1945* (Westport, CT: Praeger, 1996), p.60.
4. Braham, *Politics of Genocide*, vol. 2, p.870.
5. In the autumn, when circumstances forced Veesenmayer to retreat from Budapest, he handed the keys of some German buildings to the Swedes. There were even instances of German troops tasked with protecting Swedish diplomats against the *Nyilas*.
6. Wagner, Inland II, to Ribbentrop and Steengracht, AusAmt, 29 June 1944, in R.L. Braham, *The Destruction of Hungarian Jewry: A Documentary Account* (New York: Pro Arte for the World Federation of Hungarian Jews, 1963), doc. 325, p.697.
7. P. Anger to G. Engzell, no.16, 5 July 1944, RA UD, Hp 21 Eu 1095, folder 6.
8. E. Veesenmayer to AusAmt, 7 July 1944, in Braham, *Destruction of Hungarian Jewry*, doc. 363, p.762.
9. J. Ribbentrop to E. Veesenmayer, 10 July 1944, in ibid., doc. 326, p.700.

10. The Swiss Legation represented British, and thus Palestinian–Jewish, matters. Lutz's achievements remain in need of scholarly analysis. Swiss author T. Tschuy's *Dangerous Diplomacy: The Story of Carl Lutz, Rescuer of 62,000 Hungarian Jews* (Grand Rapids, MI: W.B. Erdmans, 2000), is a work of unreliable hagiography echoing similar publications about Wallenberg. Equipped with a foreword by the esteemed Simon Wiesenthal, this book raises many of the issues discussed in Chapter 1. Similarly to the number of '100,000' being applied to Wallenberg, Tschuy's claim that Lutz is directly responsible for saving 62,000 Jews is, equally, a completely unreasonable exaggeration. One wag has noted there were eventually more Jewish lives saved by neutral diplomats in Budapest than actually live there.

11. See S. Szita, *Trading in Lives? Operations of the Jewish Relief and Rescue Committee in Budapest, 1944–1945*, trans. S. Lambert (Budapest and New York: Central European University Press, 2005), especially Chapter 6. Szita's book contributes much to our understanding of the still-controversial Kasztner story.

12. M. Bagge to G. Engzell, no.39, 8 July 1944, RA UD, Hp 21 Eu 1095, folder 6. Another such example is from 10 July, when the general consul of Denmark's government-in-exile sent a name to Engzell, asking for assistance.

13. P. Anger to UD, no.24, 14 July 1944, RA UD, Hp 21 Eu 1095, folder 6. This lack of organization would burden subsequent assistance efforts.

14. G. Engzell to P. Anger, no.61, 18 July 1944, RA UD, Hp 21 Eu 1095, folder 6. Engzell informed Anger that it was his understanding that such a transport could be financed by the Jews themselves but, if not, 'there are possibilities of asking the Americans here for a contribution'. This again raises the question of why the Swedes were not willing to even consider providing the necessary funding themselves.

15. I. Danielsson to G. Engzell, no.221, 13 July 1944, RA UD, Hp 21 Eu 1095, folder 6. Arnóthy-Jungeruth added that as Hungary was now acting in a 'humanitarian manner', he hoped Sweden's press would be more positive to his country.

16. P. Anger to UD, no.229, 16 July 1944, RA UD, Hp 21 Eu 1095, folder 6. This coded cable arrived late that evening, and provides an example of how information from Budapest was shared with government and private officials. It was read by Foreign Minister Günther, and was immediately sent to several cabinet ministers, as well as to Rabbi Ehrenpreis. Anger added that since the deportations had ceased, 'only some individuals have been taken away'.

17. P. Anger to G. Engzell, no.86, 17 July 1944, RA UD, Hp 21 Eu 1095, folder 6.

18. Anger noted that the transport would most likely need a diplomatic escort, 'either someone from the Legation or possibly the International Red Cross could accompany it'.

19. UD to Legation Budapest, 20 July, RA UD, Hp 21 Eu 1096, folder 7.

20. L. Nylander to G. Engzell, no.50, 11 July 1944, RA UD, Hp 21 Eu 1095, folder 6.

21. A. Eichmann to RSHA, 24 July 1944, in Braham, *Destruction of Hungarian Jewry*, doc. 328, p.705. The subject line of this document is 'the final solution [*Endlösung*] of the Jewish question in Hungary'.

22. Y. Lozowick, *Hitler's Bureaucrats: The Nazi Security Police and the Banality of Evil* (London and New York: Continuum, 2002), p.264.

23. All three men play important roles in the story of Budapest's Holocaust.

24. P. Anger to C. Günther, no.158, 18 July 1944, RA UD, Hp 21 Eu 1095, folder 6. The three requested this because of fears of reprisals 'against Hungary's surviving Jews, if it became known that [the Council] had sought out contact abroad'. This particular request was not respected.

25. Foreign Office, through British Legation Stockholm to UD, 21 July 1944, RA UD, Hp 21 Eu 1096, folder 7.

26. Steven Koblik's landmark 1987 essay on Erling Eidem and Sweden's Lutherans remains one of the only analyses. See S. Koblik, *The Stones Cry Out: Sweden's Response to the Persecution of the Jews, 1933–1945* (New York: Holocaust Library, 1988), Chapter 3. Two newer publications studying some aspects of the Church during these years are A. Jarlert, *Judisk 'ras' som äktenskpshinder i Sverige: effekten av Nürnburglagarna i Svenska kyrkans statliga funktion som lysningsförrättare 1935–1945* (Malmö: Sekel, cop., 2006); and J. Perwe, *Bombprästen: Erik Perwe på uppdrag i Berlin under andra världskriget* (Stockholm: Carlssons, 2006).

27. The Swedish Lutheran Church's relationship with its German counterpart is historically a particularly close one, and throughout the Nazi era there were constant visits back and

forth between clergy and lay members of the Churches.

28. E. Eidem to S. Grafström, 20 July 1944, RA UD, Hp 21 Eu 1096, folder 7.
29. Church headquarters are also in Uppsala, something which Herzog obviously knew.
30. E. Eidem to S. Grafström, 20 July 1944, RA UD, Hp 21 Eu 1096, folder 7. Eidem ends the letter with apologies for writing by hand, explaining that he is in the countryside on holiday, as is his secretary.
31. S. Grafström to E. Eidem, no.311, 21 July 1944, RA UD, Hp 21 Eu 1096, folder 7.
32. It is highly unlikely that Grafström unilaterally proposed such an idea, although no evidence of previous discussions about it have been located. Its existence is confirmed, however, when on the next day Engzell informed the Legation in Washington of the hoped-for transport of 'approximately 700 Jews', and 'Furthermore, the Legation in Budapest has received permission to issue visas for Jewish children'. UD to Legation, Washington, DC, no.395, RA UD, Hp 21 Eu 1096, folder 7.
33. E. Eidem to S. Grafström, no.1513/44, 24 July 1944, RA UD, 1096, folder 7. Eidem was now armed with secretarial help, and the typed letter addressed Grafström as 'dear friend' (*käre vän*).
34. *Svenska Dagbladet*, 21 July 1944.
35. At about the same time, Hungary's Catholic clerics were discussing the release of a pastoral protest letter, but these internal discussions bore little fruit. See Braham, *Politics of Genocide*, vol. 2, pp.1215–19.
36. P. Anger to UD, no.233, 21 July 1944, RA UD, Hp 21 Eu 1096, folder 7. The source of Anger's information was a Hungarian railroad authority official stationed at Kassa in northern Hungary. Research confirms that the information received by Anger was remarkably accurate. On this see Szita, *Trading in Lives?*, pp.39–42.
37. 'Memorandum concerning help to Hungary's Jews', 29 July 1944, pp.3–4, RA UD, Hp 21 Eu 1092, folder 1.
38. E. Eidem to Ö. Lundborg, no.1570/44, 3 August 1944, RA UD, Hp 21 Eu 1096, folder 8.
39. Koblik, *Stones Cry Out*, p.114.
40. Ibid., pp.114–15.
41. 'Memorandum regarding the persecution of Hungarian Jews' [PM beträffande de ungerska judeförföljelserna], 18 July 1944, RA UD, Hp 21 Eu 1095, folder 6. Paradoxically in this case, Jews were perceived by their Gentile counterparts both as 'human shields', and as bringing punishment upon the city as punishment for their 'treacheries'.
42. T. Cole, *Holocaust City: The Making of a Jewish Ghetto* (New York and London: Routledge, 2003). The following section is indebted to Cole's important study.
43. Ibid., p.2
44. See, for instance, U. Herbert (ed.), *National Socialist Extermination Policies: Contemporary German Perspectives and Controversies* (New York: Berghahn Books, 2000). The major advances in understanding the extermination of the Jews as represented in this volume are important and in some ways a 'typical' example of the gap between scholarship and the lay public.
45. C. Browning, cited in Cole, *Holocaust City*, p.31.
46. Cole, *Holocaust City*, pp.18–19. For the author's explanation behind his idiosyncratic use of quotation marks throughout, not least around the word 'Jew', see pp.44–8.
47. Ibid., p.37.
48. Ibid., pp.41–2.
49. Ibid., p.124.
50. The internal movement of Jews in Budapest analysed by Cole took place largely in the weeks before Wallenberg arrived.
51. Cole, *Holocaust City*, p.164.
52. The details of this will be discussed in Chapter 12.
53. Cited in Cole, *Holocaust City*, p.166.
54. On the last day of July, two more lengthy lists were dispatched to Stockholm. One of these was eight typewritten pages long with 143 names and notations. See no.174 and no.175, both I. Danielsson to C. Günther, 29 July 1944, both RA UD, Hp 21 Eu 1096, folder 8.
55. UD to Legation Budapest, no.225, 24 July 1944, RA UD, Hp 21 Eu 1096, folder 7.
56. P. Anger to UD, no.235, 24 July 1944, RA UD, Hp 21 Eu 1096, folder 7.
57. UD to Legation Budapest, no.227, 25 July 1944, RA UD, Hp 21 Eu 1096, folder 7.
58. P. Anger to G. Engzell, no.145, 27 July 1944, RA UD, Hp 21 Eu 1096, folder 8. This report was sent to previous recipients outside the foreign office, and to Count Folke Bernadotte

of the Swedish Red Cross and Gunnar Josephson, chairman of Stockholm's Jewish Community (Mosaiska församling).

59. P. Anger to UD, no.238, 27 July 1944, RA UD, Hp 21 Eu 1096, folder 7.
60. E. Veesenmayer to foreign minister of the Reich, 29 July 1944, in Braham, *Destruction of Hungarian Jewry*, doc. 204, p.461.
61. UD to Legation Budapest, no.228, 26 July 1944, RA UD, Hp 21 Eu 1096, folder 7.
62. UD to Legation Budapest, no.235, 28 July 1944, RA UD, Hp 21 Eu 1096, folder 7.
63. S. Hellstedt to I. Danielsson, no.79, 29 July 1944, RA UD, Hp 21 Eu 1096, folder 7.

8

August: Valdemar Langlet and Carl Ivan Danielsson, the Forgotten Swedes

> I am anxiously awaiting report wheteer [*sic*] you have been able to rescue my children stop I understand that Swedish visa or passport can effect their rescue and plead that you grant this to them this is the time to do something because tomorrow may be too late stop I hope and pray that you will answer the prayers of a mothers [*sic*] broken heart.
>
> Mrs Elizabeth Buchinger, Brooklyn, NY, 14 August 1944, to King Gustav V.[1]

RECOVERING OTHER SWEDISH HEROES

As discussed in Chapter 1, analysis of historical memory and its significance has received much attention from scholars in Holocaust studies, and much more is understood today about the causes and consequences of this complex process than was the case only a decade or so ago. Central to this development is a deeper if still imperfect understanding of how collective historical memory is formed, including the need to ascertain distinctions between private and public memory. It is relevant to ask, even if no final answer can be given, why some things, events or individuals from Holocaust history gain prominence in contemporary collective memory, while other, seemingly similar, phenomena or people slip unnoticed or unstudied into the past. It also seems worthwhile to ask whether, in some fashion, collective memory works differently for those considered 'villains' than it does for 'heroes'.

Why, for instance, does Wallenberg occupy such a prominent place in Holocaust memory when others who were in Budapest, and who faced the same dangers and essentially did the same things, are virtually unknown to posterity outside a limited circle of descendants and admirers? Why do names such as Valdemar Langlet, Angelo Rotta, Karl Lutz, Giorgio Perlasca, Gernaro Verolino, Fredrich Born and Angel Sanz-Briz not evoke the same sense of admiration and awe as Wallenberg's? Indeed, according to one scholar, even some contemporaries of Wallenberg believed that he was receiving too much credit as events unfolded, unfairly overshadowing others who were also saving lives.[2] Closely connected, of course, to the question of how some people or things are remembered is why certain things or people are essentially forgotten. Does the explanation in this case lie in the fact that Wallenberg is commonly believed, however inaccurately, to have saved the largest number of people, or perhaps because he tragically disappeared into the Gulag while the other men lived long after the war, sometimes doing their old job, then fading into retirement, old age and obscurity?

Those mentioned above are all considered heroes by various people or groups, and we know of no efforts to consciously diminish or denigrate any of them within some ostensible hierarchy of fame and heroism, yet Wallenberg's fame far eclipses the others; and none occupies in any way the symbolic role in Holocaust memory that Wallenberg does, either in their own countries, or internationally.[3] As with other elements of this story, this manifestation of collective memory has contributed to a distortion of common understanding of how the handful of neutral diplomats active in Budapest worked together, and has added a few layers of distorting myth to Wallenberg's story.

Sweden too has its 'unknown heroes': a small number of men and several women who contributed to the country's humanitarian achievements in Budapest during 1944. This small group includes the three career diplomats, Minister Carl Ivan Danielsson and First Secretary Per Anger, and Undersecretary Gösta Engzell, all of whom have figured prominently throughout this study, with the first two invariably mentioned in accounts of Wallenberg.[4] Mention has been made previously of the central fact that without the support of these three men, Wallenberg would have been far less effective, if not wholly so. Yet the three have been largely forgotten by the Swedish public.[5] Other names connected to the Swedish story in Budapest are the young diplomats Lars Berg, Yngve Ekmark and Göte Carlsson, and two young administrative assistants at the Legation, Margareta Bauer and Berit Brulin. Asta Nilsson was an experienced aid worker sent to the city in August by SRK to assist Valdemar Langlet. Though his name has already been mentioned in previous chapters, this chapter will focus upon the work and significance of Langlet, a fascinating if still marginal character in Swedish and Holocaust history. Yet by focusing on him, some essential details and contexts of the Holocaust in Budapest which have been 'lost' in Wallenberg's shadow will be illuminated.

Valdemar Langlet was an experienced journalist and traveller who, by the early 1930s, found himself settling into an extended residency in Budapest. In 1944, at the unlikely age of 72, circumstances thrust the worldly Langlet into a role he could hardly have imagined, and for months he engaged in extremely strenuous and stressful humanitarian work. Assisted by his Russian-born and much younger wife, Nina, both became rescuers of Jewish lives, and others, during Budapest's Holocaust.[6] Though his presence in Budapest has been noted by some historians, it has never been explored or analysed. Langlet's activities preceded Wallenberg's, eventually paralleling his and that of other neutral diplomats. Sometimes coordinating and sometimes clashing with Wallenberg and the other Swedes, Langlet remained in Budapest through liberation, resuming humanitarian activities as soon as it was feasible. It is interesting that for some reason, those who encountered, heard of, or worked for Langlet have been far less active in promoting his memory than those in similar positions vis-à-vis Wallenberg.[7] This brief survey may perhaps awaken further interest for a more thorough look at the life, accomplishments and sad ending of this other extraordinary, idiosyncratic, and brave Swede who became an unexpected diplomat during the Holocaust.

VALDEMAR LANGET, THE ECCENTRIC DIPLOMAT

The only publication in Swedish about Langlet is amateur historian Björn Runberg's *Valdemar Langlet, Räddare i faran*.[8] An ex-employee of SRK, Runberg explored the archives of the very organization which authorized Langlet's activities, motivated by what he described as SRK's 'shameful neglect' of Langlet while he was still alive, and of his legacy.[9] Runberg's contention that the decades-long emphasis on Wallenberg has kept Langlet unfairly in the shadows is evident in his book's subtitle, *'Wallenberg was not alone'*.[10]

Langlet was born in 1872 to an haute-bourgeois, professional family, and received a high-level education and the funds to travel widely. He was a stylish, highly intelligent and temperamental man who, it seems clear, shared some significant characteristics with Wallenberg. Both travelled extensively as young men, were adept at languages and learning, and had contacts with the highest levels of Swedish society, although Wallenberg far more.[11] As a young man, Langlet travelled widely in Tsarist Russia, Asia and Central Europe, learned Esperanto (he formed Sweden's first and Europe's second club to promote the language), and had for many years a successful journalistic career in Sweden. Later, Langlet and Nina, his second wife, journeyed throughout the Balkans, eventually settling in Budapest in 1931 – a residence which would end only in 1945. Langlet learned Hungarian, enabling him to work as a clerk at Sweden's Legation in 1938, and later as temporary cultural attaché. While doing so he established contacts 'with certain authorities, the press and cultural figures'.[12] By 1944, Langlet had lived in Budapest for sixteen years, eventually obtaining a position at Budapest University as lecturer in Scandinavian languages. He had also established an extensive network of local contacts which would aid his wholly unexpected months as a humanitarian aid worker.[13]

Langlet was a charismatic personality whose long experience in the city was an obvious resource, yet one which for some reason UD and the quasi-governmental SRK were at first reluctant to utilize. Runberg writes that Langlet felt emotionally unable to stand by and do nothing when persecution and murder engulfed his beloved city, and he lobbied both Swedish and Hungarian officials, trying to kick-start a programme of assistance under the aegis of SRK.[14] As with most personal accounts, Langlet's book about Budapest is a problematic source, albeit colourful and well-written. In it, he claims to have been the Legation's officer in charge of 'Jewish questions', but there is no evidence in UD files that he performed this function, either officially or otherwise.[15] A man surely accustomed to working in his own way, Langlet's strong personality, eccentric habits and lack of bureaucratic discipline came to irritate high-level officials in Stockholm at UD and SRK. Even amongst his more sympathetic colleagues in Budapest, Per Anger remembered: '[Langlet] wanted to save the whole world, which led him into difficulties and made it also difficult for us sometimes to [help] him, and to save his ... people who were under the Red Cross.'[16] Though Langlet's work was appreciated, his unwillingness to subordinate himself to Danielsson and Anger caused severe clashes with his Budapest colleagues and the two Stockholm bureaucracies. It appears also that the situation was aggravated by some of his personal habits. Clearly a loose cannon in the eyes of his more conventional colleagues, suspicions, however unfair, about Langlet's work methods and effectiveness caused tension and bad feelings amongst men working for the same thing. The result was a weakening of his ability to accomplish what he set out to do. Among other problems, Anger believed that Langlet had 'very little in the way of practical judgement in approaching the problem'.[17] Years later, Anger remembered:

> [Langlet was] very strong in his belief that something must be done very quickly, and this old man with his experience from Hungary and all that ... of course you listened to him ... [But] he got into trouble, you know ... [you] should try to be more strict and limit more the categories of people you help.
>
> [Stockholm told him] ... you have to coordinate your efforts with the Swedish legation, you have to be ... under the command of the Swedish minister. They pointed this out many, many times. But it was very difficult to control him, I must say. And he saved people's lives, no doubt about it. But at the same time he risked the whole operation in floating about like he did.[18]

Though Langlet and Wallenberg cooperated in some ways, there was dissonance and even some competition in their working relationship. However determined to help, both were inexperienced diplomats, and their ideas and methods did not always meld. It is likely if not certain that they met during Wallenberg's earlier business trips to Budapest, but in any case Langlet would certainly have known who Wallenberg was before the latter's arrival. A proud man who knew that his appointment as SRK delegate was not greeted in official Stockholm with unqualified enthusiasm, one can imagine that Langlet took umbrage easily. He was forced to accept that after all his years in Budapest and his connections to the Legation, it was the younger man who was granted formal diplomatic status and supported by funds unavailable to Langlet, and both issues were apparently a source of some tension between the two.[19] Though Wallenberg mentions Langlet in his reports, he did not follow instructions to cooperate closely with him and may well have envied the older man's local contacts and ability to communicate with friend and foe directly in Hungarian.[20] Langlet mentions and praises Wallenberg is his account, but by no means describes in any detail his contacts or cooperation with him.

Disorganized and unorthodox though he may have been, there is no doubt that Langlet took on his daunting challenge with a wholehearted desire to do the best he could. Like Wallenberg, he was personally inspired by the work, and his letters and reports from this period burst with energy, ideas, passion and even a bit of self-aggrandizement. In both a positive and negative sense, it made a man in his twilight years feel needed and important again. And no wonder; he had lived an eventful, even colourful life to that point, and was keenly aware that fate placed him in the middle of a historic tragedy.

As noted, Langlet and his wife stayed in Budapest well into 1945, resuming their humanitarian work as best they could after the fighting ceased. Shockingly, however, their energy and commitment for the welfare of others went without reward or even much apparent praise from SRK. According to Runberg, they returned to Stockholm in difficult financial straits, having left Budapest with nothing, and were in no way helped to resettle in Sweden by the organization they so capably served. According to Nina Langlet, they were ordered by SRK to return to Sweden, even though 'In Sweden all that awaited him was different kinds of miseries, primarily displeasure from his superiors.'[21] Langlet immediately wrote his account of things, which was published in 1946, but otherwise he and his wife slipped from public view. While there is no evidence that SRK sought to distance itself from the Langlets' efforts, Runberg says the organization did little if anything even to publicly acknowledge their efforts. According to Nina Langlet, amongst the most mystifying things was that when they gave their reports to SRK, these were refused, and handed back![22] Why their noble work seems to have embarrassed an organization dedicated to such work is unclear, but when Langlet died in October 1960, he was very much a man forgotten by his country.[23]

Regarding another issue which is similar to Wallenberg's case, it is unlikely that the number of lives saved directly by Langlet can ever be empirically established. There is no doubt, however, that he saved many lives, assisted thousands more, and deserves to be remembered far more widely than he is today.

LANGLET'S EFFORTS

As we have seen, in the weeks following the March occupation, Danielsson and Anger struggled to keep up with the situation, and had by late spring requested reinforcements. The original idea to meet this request was that a representative of SRK should be sent from Stockholm. Langlet wrote that he came up with the idea himself, exploiting his asserted position in the Legation, his previous contacts with the Hungarian Red Cross; and he even raised the idea in discussions with the high-ranking officials in Hungary's foreign ministry.[24] According to Runberg, Langlet proposed to Stockholm in May that SRK vice-chairman Count Folke Bernadotte, a member of Sweden's royal family and a leading figure in the organization, be appointed as special delegate. The Germans scuttled this high-profile appointment by refusing to grant him a transit visa, although it appears that Bernadotte himself was reluctant, saying that he was too busy.[25]

In any case, Danielsson and Langlet conferred, and the former proposed to UD that the long-time resident might be a suitable interim representative. Langlet, wrote Danielsson, 'has worked with the Hungarian Red Cross. Request that query be made to [SRK] board for this as temporary measure until something more definite can be organized.'[26] Danielsson seems to have regretted the proposal almost immediately. Nonetheless, two days later on 21 June, permission was received to grant Langlet interim authorization until other arrangements could be made.[27] This was in reference to the ongoing discussions concerning Wallenberg's appointment, which had not yet been finalized. It is worth noting in this context that when American minister Herschel Johnson cabled Washington on 21 June about ongoing negotiations concerning Wallenberg's mission, he also wrote: 'It is likewise intention of [Swedish] Foreign Office to secure if possible an appointment as representative of other Swedish Red Cross for Professor Maltet [sic], a Swede who is now teaching in University of

Budapest. Professor Maltet [*sic*] will not be connected with Swedish Legation but will co-operate closely with Wallenberg.'[28] Johnson can only have obtained such a reading of the situation from Boheman, who seems already to be putting distance between UD and Langlet.[29] This apparently immediate chilling of relations between UD and Langlet is even harder to understand in view of the fact that Langlet's appointment was readily accepted by the Hungarians, who wished for him to cooperate with the Hungarian Red Cross, and to be supported at the highest levels of the government. His appointment, Randolph Braham wrote, was confirmed by Deputy Foreign Minister Arnóthy-Jungerth, and 'acknowledged with a pledge of cooperation by Gyula Ambrózy, the head of Horthy's Cabinet Office'.[30]

Ironically, this early summer period may have been when SRK's leadership paid the most attention to what its organization could do in Budapest. Rather shockingly, for the remainder of 1944, Langlet's work seems to have been of scant interest to SRK. It not only failed to authorize a salary for his work, it also chose not to provide what he needed most – funds to operate. Evidently, Langlet had already in mid-May begun operating on his own, weeks before his official mandate was confirmed. Without permission, he had issued letters of protection (*skyddsbrev*) bearing the organization's symbol and his signature. Langlet seems to have fashioned his *Schutzpass* after the Swiss 'collective passport' already in limited circulation.[31] When recounting after the war why he did this, Langlet wrote: '[Officials in Stockholm] protested against our boldness in issuing, without authorization from [Sweden], the "protective letter" which looked like a passport. I answered that we didn't request permission because I was sure we would be told no.'[32] There seems little doubt that he had grown frustrated and impatient with Stockholm's refusal to give him an answer about his appointment; nor is there any question that this premature, unauthorized action cannot have pleased the conservative and hesitant SRK. In this case at least, it is entirely understandable that SRK would be displeased, even shocked, that a document apparently authorized by them actually wasn't. These actions increased the underlying scepticism about Langlet, and may account for SRK's unwillingness to finance the operation in a realistic and responsible manner. It is hard to imagine the organization's board taking similar decisions had Bernadotte gone to Hungary. Moreover, there is evidence indicating that Langlet understood his original mandate as directing him not to help Jews at all, but only 'so-called Aryans'.[33]

Langlet tried to assist Jews in the same fashion as the other neutral representatives did – by issuing protective documents which placed the individuals or families named under the protection of the issuing legation or organization – and the 'protective' letters drawn up and issued by Langlet and his many Jewish assistants were similar in form and content to other neutral documents. According to Runberg, by January 1945, Langlet and his Jewish assistants may have distributed up to 20,000 to 25,000 such documents, a figure which seems a considerable exaggeration, but which nonetheless points to the Legation's frequently voiced concerns throughout 1944 that 'document inflation' could damage assistance efforts.[34]

Langlet's initial phase of activities is, unsurprisingly considering its unauthorized nature, sparsely documented. Knowing what we do about his personality, it is not surprising that a man of his age and experience, supported by far greater knowledge of Budapest and Hungarian society than any other Swedish diplomat, would assert himself. Though Anger was critical of some of Langlet's more unconventional ideas and methods, he gave him great credit for bravery and initiative, particularly in the first weeks after the occupation. Cooperation with the Legation seems initially to have been relatively smooth, but deteriorated rapidly in July after the deportations were halted. In fact in late June, although Langlet was already deeply engaged in assistance activities, his appointment was, for at least a couple of days, terminated. This happened because negotiations with Wallenberg had entered their final phase, with Engzell then telegraphing Budapest on 27 June , instructing the Legation to cancel Langlet's mandate.[35] Yet only the next day, another telegram was sent saying that because Wallenberg's departure had been delayed (with no explanation given), Langlet remained authorized to represent SRK and lead its activities.[36] One cause for the delay and hesitation in formalizing Langlet's appointment may have been his lack of discretion in contacting people in both Budapest and Stockholm. Again prematurely, he informed them of his work, and beseeched them to do something to help him. Several times he urged his contacts in Sweden to lobby UD and SRK directly, in order to obtain an increase in their support for his activities. Such unorthodox requests, particularly in conservative wartime Sweden, cannot have been appreciated by the traditional bureaucrats of either organization.

Word of Langlet's activities obviously got around Stockholm, and on 6 July, Koloman Lauer wrote to 'my good friend Valdemar', and pleaded with Langlet to help 'Mr Wallenberg' find his in-laws and their daughter and help them come to Sweden. He wrote that he had 'come to know Raoul Wallenberg during the last three years, and who is a decent and good hearted man who will certainly do everything in his power to help'. This letter concludes with something that may have inflated Langlet's self-image, making him even more difficult for the other Swedes to deal with: 'You have no idea how many people here in Sweden are praying to God that he may protect you, so that you can continue with your work in the name of humanity. Those friends whom I have spoken with think of you with deep gratitude.'[37]

Any doubt that Langlet's manner and methods were creating problems is dispelled by Anger's cable of 7 July to UD. It read, 'Thankful for message when Wallenberg is expected here as Langlet is unsuitable and Legation is in general overwhelmed with work.'[38] Obviously the perception had grown that Wallenberg would 'replace' Langlet, yet Wallenberg had by this date received his appointment as 'first secretary' to the Legation, and not as SRK representative. This is further evidence of the imprecise discussions between individuals and organizations which led to ongoing confusion regarding the specificity of tasks, titles, institutional responsibility, and more. This was a confusing time, demanding great powers of bureaucratic improvisation, but it does seem deplorable that clearer communication failed to occur on these important issues. UD's failure to communicate important issues clearly and directly with its diplomats in Budapest would come to haunt Wallenberg, and complicate the decades long post-war search for him.

In several extraordinary letters to prominent individuals in Stockholm, Langlet made clear that he saw his task as far weightier than did his superiors in Stockholm.[39] Another example of his manner of communication can be seen in a letter to a Mrs Annie Fischer-Tóth and a Professor Kinberg. In it, Langlet scathingly criticized them for inaction, accusing them of making it more difficult to help Fischer-Tóth's mother and sister:

I wrote already several weeks ago a detailed ... letter to Prof. Kinberg in response to his telegram about your mother and sister, and I can hardly express my amazement that I haven't heard back from you. You know of course that your mother and sister hang in mortal danger everyday! I have done everything in my power to help them, but it doesn't help when their closest [relatives] sit, apparently, with their arms crossed.

With your status in [Sweden] it wouldn't have been difficult at all for you and Kinberg to arrange an emergency passport at UD. I am unable to do this here on my own, merely give a worthless assurance of an entry visa, in the event that a [repatriation] takes place.

It is 'quarter to 12', and if you don't immediately do that which I have proposed, you may be assured that never again will you see your mother and sister. I apologize for the hard words, but on Sunday they will go to the ghetto and with that their fate – immediate deportation and destruction – is assured. I have, for the sake of you, great artist, done more for them than for most of my other protectees. And what have you yourself done? At least here I know of nothing. [Signed] with profound misery to you, Valdemar Langlet.[40]

Letters containing outbursts like this, which had been passed on by the recipients to UD, surely diminished whatever remaining confidence the mandarins of UD and SRK had in Langlet's judgement and actions. The letter itself is minuted, noting that a telegram concerning it was sent to Budapest the next day, but this was not located. Creating further consternation was Langlet's letter written to a Bruno Reichwald, who also forwarded it to UD. In it, Langlet urged Reichwald to directly lobby officials at UD. Langlet wrote: 'As Red Cross delegate I am able to help [your friends] home to us [in Sweden], but for that permission is needed from UD. It would then be necessary for you, at UD, for example through my friend attaché C.F. Högstedt, to make appeals that the Legation is authorized to issue visas for them.' Langlet must have had a feeling that his position was in some jeopardy, because he urged Reichwald to act quickly, not because of the threat of immediate deportation, but because 'it can happen that in August, someone "puts a stick in our wheels". Therefore, whatever you do, do it soon!'[41] It didn't take long before Danielsson was instructed to firmly admonish Langlet for dispatching such 'particularly ill-conceived letters to relatives of Jews in Hungary resident here'. Engzell's aide S. Hellstedt wrote:

> We here are completely convinced that Lektor Langlet is provid-ing the Legation with great services, and that through his knowl-edge about local conditions and people [he] is most useful, and neither do we doubt that he is doing his best to help those poor, needy people ...
>
> Would it not be suitable to ask that when the occasion presents itself, [you] make clear for Langlet the altogether unnecessary irritation that his temperamental writings cause amongst the already stressed relatives of victims of Hungary's Jewish actions.[42]

Naturally, there was enormous pressure on Langlet, and it began to show in his correspondence. The pressure may have been caused partly by the location of his office and reception rooms, which were located on Lonyai *utca* (street) in the heart of Pest. Differing from the location of the Legation and Wallenberg's primary office, which were on Buda's

Géllert heights at a remove from the central city, Langlet's location exposed him to considerable psychological pressure because of the endless visits by desperate Jews and many others, appealing for help for themselves and their families. They were pleading for help from someone they assumed had the full financial and institutional backing of a well-known and respected international organization, and could-n't have known that Langlet was struggling daily with a severe lack of funds and institutional support in Stockholm. In a letter to a friend in Stockholm, Langlet acknowledged this pressure, telling him: 'As you [know] I have currently have other difficulties to deal with than my issues with my publishers ... those issues will have to wait until I tear myself a bit from the difficult job I accepted and which deprives me of every thought of holiday and the longed for journey home. Unfortunately, it pains me that I long so deeply'.[43] And though he seemed to do his best to ignore the criticism he was receiving from Stockholm, he was clearly frustrated, and his work hampered, by the minimal material and psychological support SRK gave. Finally, anoth-er factor complicating Langlet's position was the apparent tension between himself and Wallenberg regarding money. On at least one occasion, Lauer in Stockholm became concerned that money trans-ferred through SRK might not reach Wallenberg, He wrote to Wallenberg: '10,000 crowns [that] has been transferred through Red Cross to Langlet ... [sum] is to be placed at your disposal, for it would not be right if the distribution of the amounts is done by several people, it has to remain concentrated with one person. Please let me know if you have received the sum.'[44]

Sixty years ago (and still today), Swedish society was as imbued with notions of hierarchy as any other European society. People were not free simply to speak to or contact anyone they wanted, particularly if the matter at hand was likely to be difficult, or cause either individual or institutional anxiety – at least not if they expected results. Moreover, Langlet was not a Wallenberg. On 27 July he wrote a letter of appeal directly to a member of Sweden's royal family on behalf of three young girls which was very badly received by SRK's leadership. The somewhat disjointed letter also brought up other matters, includ-ing Langlet's apparently unilateral attempts to organize 'two larger Red Cross train transports, but I have in many cases great difficulty in finding accommodating Swedish homes which are open for a guest from here'. Langlet requested that King Gustav himself be contacted with thanks for his telegram to Horthy, and then informed his reader about support he had received from someone, which had freed him, one reads with some surprise, from the obligation of helping 'exclu-sively so-called Aryan persons in the work which SRK has entrusted me with!'[45] Much is unclear here, particularly the apparent allegation being made by Langlet that his original mandate from SRK was in fact to help only gentiles rather than Jews. In the light of some recent publications and journalistic investigation, this possibility cannot be excluded.[46] SRK's growing irritation with Langlet can also be seen in the memorandum of 11 August to Budapest: 'SRK's board has requested, through Baron Steirnstedt, that [communications] regarding the Hungarian Jewish question and similar issues be as a rule directed only to Secretary-General Rydman, and not to Prince Carl or Count F. Bernadotte.'[47]

Throughout July and August, Langlet sent a stream of reports to SRK as well as pleading, almost haranguing letters to private individuals, some of great social prominence. It is impossible to question his profound desire to help those in need. It is possible, however, to question the manner in which he acted, not least in a strategic sense. Unquestionably, his unorthodox entreaties came to negatively influence his tactical ability to engage in the range of humanitarian activities in which he was engaged. Had Stockholm supported him, it is far more likely that he would have received more support, including financial.

Langlet's reports are fascinating documents. Highly untypical of Swedish diplomatic documents and characterized by a florid style and quite emotional pleading, they are hastily written cries for help in the name of individuals, newly established orphanages, and food kitchens.[48] They are filled with insistent proposals and urgent requests for more personnel and money, and sometimes even included brief political analyses. This correspondence illuminates a man utterly committed to helping others, but one who had no monopoly on wisdom, effectiveness or motivation. Sadly, the conclusion is unavoidable that his apparent 'lack of control' did hamper if not actually damage his desire to help as many people as possible survive. It is not unlikely that if officials in Stockholm had had more confidence in him, there might have been a greater willingness to provide the necessary financial and institutional support his work so obviously required. It is impossible to know how much more effective he would have been. What is also remarkable is how much he still seems to have accomplished as he established food kitchens, orphanages, shelters for Jews of all ages and, of course, issued documents designed to protect.

Langlet's contacts in Sweden all seem to have been people of status, and he cajoled them to put pressure on Engzell and UD to obtain action – mainly in the form of Stockholm sending a name, or names, to Budapest, with some sort of protective measure then conducted on behalf of this person, or family. But Langlet was pushing hard on an open door. There was no resistance to any of his suggested measures, as we have seen. Perhaps his communication with Danielsson, Anger and Legation staff deteriorated so quickly that he had no idea what was happening at the Legation, but this seems highly unlikely. As we shall see, Danielsson actually defended Langlet from some of Stockholm's pressure and complaints. Perhaps he simply got too emotional when writing his letters of appeal.

The significance of this is obvious; for one of the few times in the history of the Holocaust, representatives of a European nation were doing virtually everything they could to help as many people as they reasonably could. They needed no convincing to keep trying harder, and what might have seemed 'unreasonable' earlier during the genocide was now deemed politically possible and morally desirable. We see these noble sentiments encapsulated in a very few words sent by telegram sent on 26 July to Budapest: 'We here are prepared to accept all Jews from Hungary with connections to Sweden.'[49] To the lasting credit of these men, they kept expanding and making ever less important to the point of non-existence the 'necessary connection to Sweden' which ordinarily would have had to exist if these people were to receive Swedish help. Those involved clearly understood that circumstances dictated a different 'bureaucratic' reality than would ordinarily be the case.

Relations between Langlet, Danielsson, and Stockholm deteriorated throughout August, and a turning point was reached by the middle of the month. On 8 August, Danielsson was again told it was necessary for Langlet to be reined in and even reprimanded. This rebuke was the result of the many waves he had caused, culminating in his unsolicited proposal that Prince Carl himself contact the Germans directly in his capacity as chairman of SRK to try to win agreement for the transit of Langlet's 'trains'. According to court officials, Langlet's proposal 'has greatly disturbed Prince Carl, as this can most certainly not be considered within Langlet's competence to make such a proposal. Both SRK's board and we here are worried that Langlet, in his well meant eagerness to help Jews, instead rushes about in a manner which can damage the Red Cross and [this] rescue effort.'[50]

A minor myth about Wallenberg is that he was unreasonably restrained by Danielsson in the former's attempts to be creative and bold with rescue proposals and efforts. The evidence, however, does not support this. Indeed, it may well have been Langlet instead of Wallenberg whom some survivors of Budapest thought of when speaking of this. Langlet was sending to Stockholm virtually every idea which came to mind, without an effective internal filter, and this proved to be a mistake. Everyone was making things up in an effort to help, but Langlet, as judged by his superiors, seems to have gone too far.

On 23 August, Engzell telegraphed Budapest, ordering cooperation between the International Committee of the Red Cross (ICRC), Langlet and the Legation. He asked Danielsson with some impatience exactly how Langlet, Wallenberg and the Legation were coordinating their activities, and how they were financing them. He tersely informed the minister that SRK was considering replacing Langlet: 'The Red Cross is considering sending a suitable and competent person as representative to lead the assistance work. What is your response?'[51] It seems strange that Engzell would ask how Wallenberg was financing his operations, since he himself was involved in all aspects of Wallenberg's work, but at this point in time, confusion about various financial details was increasing, and we have already noted some instances in which a lack of procedural effectiveness led to some internal UD confusion.

Danielsson responded with precision and authority. Cooperation with the ICRC's representative, he told Engzell, was already underway:

> *Secundo:* Langlet's and Wallenberg's decisions and actions taken following consultation with the Legation. They work with their own collected resources, Langlet to date 100.000 pengö, Wallenberg a bit more ... More staff always welcome. Langlet, with his knowledge of Hungarian conditions and knowledge of Hungarian, I consider to be suitable leader. We hope though that Asta Nilsson's promised help is realized.[52]

Danielsson's support for Langlet seems to have satisfied Stockholm. However the notion that Langlet acted only after consulting with Danielsson and Anger was more a hope than a reality. Cooperation between Langlet and the Legation would continue to worsen – a situation made ever more difficult because activities meant that the Swedes' humanitarian work became less a matter of planning than an improved response to circumstances far out of their control.

However disorganized or non-bureaucratic Langlet may have been, it is impossible to exaggerate how difficult the circumstances were in which he was operating. A comprehensive yet awkward organization had sprung up virtually overnight, which was staffed by scores of people (a few were paid – most were Jewish volunteers) whom Langlet cannot have personally known or vetted. He received critical help from his indefatigable wife Nina, and everyone involved had to keep track of a growing number of locations, vehicles, negotiations with various Hungarian ministries and agencies, inspections, and so on. The punishing schedule and stress would have daunted anyone, let alone a man of Langlet's years. None of this can have been helped by the deterioration in relations with his superiors and colleagues.

A constant complaint voiced by Langlet both during the operation and afterwards was, as already noted, the severe lack of operating funds. As he began his activities he believed that substantial local funds would be made available to him, but this seems not to have happened.[53] He certainly believed that he could have done more good with more money.[54] Writing years later, Nina Langlet remembered this as one of the greatest difficulties: 'SRK's board, which appointed Valdemar Langlet, failed to provide either money or a uniform to him. Our assistance activities were only possible because of the assistance we received from Hungarians in the form of grants and the practical work done by our brave and warm-hearted staff.' According to her, it was only Asta Nilsson, the veteran Rädda barnen (Save the Children) aid worker just arrived from Stockholm, who received a salary.[55] It in unknown why SRK or UD refused to provide the necessary financial assistance to Langlet's operation, or even pay him a salary. We have seen that on several occasions, Engzell, Grafström or other UD officials noted that American money was available to the Legation, for repatriation trains and other things. Yet no one seems to have proposed that some of this American money might fund Langlet's activities. There seems little question that had the Americans received a request for such assistance, they would most likely have made available some of their substantial funds for Langlet's work. On the other hand, it would seem reasonable to conclude that Langlet would have heard, through his many contacts in Stockholm, both that American money was available and that Wallenberg would be receiving some. But no evidence has been found in UD files that he considered going directly to the Americans. Indeed, Langlet was angered by the knowledge that Wallenberg was supported by American and other monies: 'I never found out where Wallenberg's money [came from], because on that point he observed a strange silence, in spite of otherwise good cooperation with us. But it was obvious that he had access to quite considerable reserves.'[56]

From almost the start of his operations, Langlet pleaded with Stockholm for administrative help, and his bitterness at not receiving more of it permeates his contemporary reports and his post-war account. Sadly, yet another blow to Langlet's morale came when the long-awaited Asta Nilsson finally arrived at the end of August. Nilsson worked after the First World War for Save the Children and was directly affiliated with SRK. Why it took so long for her to arrive is unknown, but Langlet's frustration at the situation became worse, as they seemed to have clashed almost immediately. The Langlets post-war perception was that 'help' had arrived in the guise of a somewhat lazy and arrogant woman who refused to take orders from him.[57] Per Anger wrote: 'Unfortunately, later in their cooperation Asta Nilsson and Langlet clashed. Because they were both Red Cross representatives, a dualism arose and Asta Nilsson refused to take orders from Langlet. The problem was solved by having them both report directly to the mission, who [*sic*] did their best to coordinate their activities.'[58] According to Björn Runberg, Langlet enjoyed so little confidence amongst Stockholm officials that even before leaving for Budapest, Nilsson was directed to report not to her nominal boss, but to either Danielsson or SRK in Stockholm.[59] Problems between the two mounted, and that must have damaged both their collective and individual work.

It is sometimes claimed that Wallenberg and Langlet didn't know what the other was doing, but this is untrue. They seem to have met when one or the other deemed it necessary (we can remember that Wallenberg had a meeting with his older colleague on his first working day in July), and they do at least mention each other in reports. Nonetheless, their cooperation was never as close as probably anticipated, and surely should have been, given the nature of their activities and their goals. Langlet's brief description of their cooperation is restrained at best, and sometimes demonstrates, as we have seen, some frustration and even bitterness about Wallenberg. Though Wallenberg received instructions to coordinate his activities with Langlet, he seems not to have made more than a perfunctory effort to do so. Yet there is no question that until the end of the year, they remained aware of each other's activities. Danielsson and Anger seem not to have kept Langlet as informed of things as they should have, for instance in the matter of negotiations being carried out in Stockholm and Berlin regarding the obtaining of permission for their 'repatriation train'.[60] We have seen that in common memory it is Wallenberg who 'invented' the *Schutzpass* – but Langlet claims that Wallenberg got the idea from him. In the end, however, they seemed to have respected each other and certainly, after the war, Langlet remained concerned about Wallenberg's fate, in spite of his own very real difficulties.[61]

Langlet's personality and eccentricities seem also to have hurt his relations with Hungarian officials. In a report written shortly after they arrived back in Stockholm from the USSR, Danielsson and Anger revealed, without using Langlet's name, their distress at having to work with him and the negative consequences of his methods.

SRK's activities expanded considerably, with a continually growing number of offices, refugee houses, and so on, with more people and locations which in one way or another were placed under Red Cross protection. Meanwhile, it became increasingly difficult for its leadership to keep this organization together:

After the appearance of the Szálasi regime, relations between the Red Cross and relevant authorities became undeniably more tense, and virtually every day incidents with the Arrow Cross party occurred. The Legation managed usually to intervene and deal with these questions, but our work was, because of this, made much more complicated due to difficulties in exercising effective control over Red Cross activities, which in a number of cases were not made known in advance to us.[62]

DANIELSSON, THE VETERAN DIPLOMAT

While continuing to observe Langlet's activities, we can broaden our view and also focus on the man who had the difficult task of restraining Langlet's enthusiasm and lack of discipline, and Wallenberg's welcome, but inexperienced, presence. In popular accounts of Wallenberg, Minister Carl Ivan Danielsson is usually noted as being there, but has never been adequately described, let alone studied. When he has appeared in either books or films, it has been as either an insignificant marginal presence or, more problematically, as a negative influence on Wallenberg's dynamic diplomacy. Neither assertion is supported by the memory of those who served with him, or the relevant documentation. On the contrary, there is every reason to believe that Wallenberg and Danielsson complemented each other. Rather than being an obdurate conservative force, he showed a pragmatic willingness to conduct a flexible and creative diplomacy during an extraordinary moment in history.

This study argues that Wallenberg engaged in an effective method of diplomacy built on precedents established by his nominal UD colleagues. It is reasonable to conclude that if Danielsson, for whatever reason, had chosen to inhibit Wallenberg, or failed to support him, the novice diplomat would have been far less effective. Indeed, for a number of reasons, Danielsson might well have reacted negatively to Wallenberg. If he had raised objections to 'a Wallenberg' working out of his Legation, this inevitably would have delayed the start of the mission. Had he done so, he would not have been, by any measure, the first European diplomat during the Hitler era to make excuses or advance rationalizations 'explaining' *why* Jews could not be helped 'at this time, for this reason'. A diplomatic veteran of Spain's Civil War, amongst other assignments, Danielsson is sometimes remembered as a nationalistic conservative, which is hardly odd for someone of his social and educational background. He arrived in Budapest in 1942, replacing (thankfully one might add) the even more conservative Torsten Undén. Undén had views on Hungarian Jewish matters that would have been cause for genuine concern had he remained Swedish minister in Hungary in 1944.[63] When the occupation took place, Danielsson reacted calmly and with purpose, quickly adapting to the radically new situation in which he found himself, one for which neither his training nor long experience could possibly have prepared him. He stood at the centre of events in Budapest, and his decision to help other human beings when it lay within his capacity to do so was crucial for the success of Swedish diplomacy in Budapest. It was also within his professional and ultimately defensible capacity to have reacted otherwise. But he did not, and his personal bravery and leadership are worth remembering.

Danielsson was UD's only highly experienced minister who served through both war and genocide simultaneously, yet he has escaped the attention of Swedish historians. The only other civil servant of his rank in a somewhat similar situation was Arvid Richert, whose long tour in Berlin has been described and analysed.[64] Richert and his staff also witnessed elements of the murder of the Jews when they viewed the assembly and deportation of the city's Jews, and were well aware of much else that happened to the Jews in Germany and elsewhere in Europe.[65] Though they endured the Allies' aerial bombardment of Hitler's capital, they did not experience the 'street-level' cyclone of war and genocide which engulfed Budapest. It is an enduring tribute that Sweden's diplomats in Hungary maintained, so far as is known, a remarkably calm and effective professionalism in a situation they could never have anticipated when taking up their assignments. Nonetheless, when serving in Budapest Danielsson was in his 60s, and his frequent absences from the Legation suggest that the pressure and stress took its toll.

Lars Berg was an apprentice diplomat when sent to Budapest in August to help with the administrative burdens created by Sweden's maintenance in Hungary of the 'national interests' of other nations, including the Soviet Union. In his account published shortly after the war, the inexperienced Berg described Danielsson:

> Minister Danielsson received me in a polite but reserved way, as might be expected from a diplomat of the old school towards a very young colleague ...
>
> [His] stiffness and slight arrogance I thought, at the time, was exaggerated, but which I would later learn to admire. [He] was that day similarly reserved and correct as I would later see him during American air attacks, hunted by Arrow Cross militia, or

starving in an underground cave. Not even sitting in the back of a
Russian truck in freezing cold did he lose an ounce of his dignity.[66]

Per Anger worked closest to Danielsson for some three years, and
remembers him as 'a courageous man'. The veteran envoy gave the young
Legation secretary (who arrived in Budapest late in 1942) considerable
independence and responsibility, a tactic that would pay dividends
throughout 1944. Yet Anger remembers that Danielsson was rather
shocked that an outsider like Wallenberg should be given first diplomatic
status and then such freedom of action: '[Danielsson] slowly or step by
step became convinced that this was the only way to do it, to save people.' Nor was the minister averse to breaking rules, even international
law when necessary. Anger continued: 'it was remarkable to see how
Wallenberg came every day to him with heaps of protective papers ...
and he signed them ... without any comments ... Danielsson understood this situation, so when he was asked once [about] a paper which
was false, and was asked if that was his signature, he said, "Of course,
I've signed that ... of course".'[67]

Danielsson's flexibility and far-sightedness was not restricted to
acceptance of the unconventional Wallenberg. Rather than support
Stockholm's efforts to sack Langlet, or have him pushed to the side,
Danielsson defended him. He assured Engzell that although troubled
by some of Langlet's actions, it was necessary to understand the old
eccentric. It is significant that rather than circumscribe Langlet's
actions because of Stockholm's criticism, the cagey Danielsson proposed that Langlet should be allowed to continue with his work – however upsetting and unorthodox it was to some in Sweden – and we
have already seen his complaints about Langlet afterwards.
Danielsson's attitude is brought into even sharper relief if we imagine
the likelihood that most of his UD colleagues would probably have
decided otherwise. Danielsson kept Langlet in business because it was
both impractical to stop him under the circumstances, and because if
more rather than fewer Jews were to be helped, it would have been the
wrong decision. On 10 September, he wrote to Engzell the following
covering letter for a very long report submitted by Langlet:

> it is a consequence of Langlet's good heart and impulsiveness that
> we don't communicate with each other in all questions ... for
> instance, [we] had no idea he was issuing a type of protective doc-
> ument [*skyddsbrev*] to his protectees until one day he showed an
> example to me. We were confronted with a *fait accompli*, and [I
> told him] how dubious I found the Red Cross continuing with the
> issuance of such documents.

Circumstances [however] are such that the Hungarian Interior

Ministry is completely accepting such identification papers, and because the rescue activities of the Red Cross should, under prevailing circumstances, be made as effective as possible ... it is inadvisable for any restrictions being placed on them by the Legation.[68]

Langlet's lengthy report covered by Danielsson's supportive letter deserves its own niche in the contemporaneous recording of Holocaust history. Similar to Wallenberg's reports, Langlet's provide a detailed, even intimate window into the thinking and emotions of an interesting person responding to extreme circumstances. As with the reports by Wallenberg, Anger and Danielsson, Langlet's provides a thumbnail sketch of how denizens of mid-century European society responded to a genocide happening within view. Simultaneously mundane and fascinating, this seven-page report contains elements of political analysis (unwanted by Stockholm), descriptions of bureaucratic procedures and problems, humanitarian passion, financial banalities and necessities, personal intrigue, complaints and human fatigue. In a disorganized but gripping flow of consciousness, Langlet provides a compelling hotchpotch of history. He defends his flailing attempts to get under control his rapidly expanding assistance apparatus, now consisting of almost a score of buildings, an expanding motor pool, orphanages and scores of volunteers – or at least enough to satisfy his superiors. For instance, echoing Swedish charity campaigns, Langlet writes that only a few Swedish kronor are needed to feed one Hungarian child in pengö for one month, and then complains that the Legation's concentration on helping only Jews survive will become obsolete when the Soviet army arrives. Such details may seem unimportant in the vast context of a continent-wide genocide, but in fact the opposite is true.

For our purposes, Langlet's comments about his protective papers and Wallenberg are particularly interesting. Describing his primary location at Baross utca 15, Langlet writes that they are trying to limit hours when accepting new applications for protective papers. He continues:

The central office naturally takes care of the 'petty cash box' and accounting, as well as all routine daily matters. There are issued, after checking all individual details, protective letters in the form of identity cards with a photograph, number and the usual passport information; these cards, which fit into a wallet, are approved by the Ministry of the Interior contingent on confirmation. Therefore they can give some protection against arbitrary detentions by subordinate police forces, both domestic and foreign.

This report on SRK's quite well organized work in Hungary should not conclude, however, without a brief note about the unbelievably expansive work, occurring parallel to but without much 'connection', being conducted by the Legation's B-division led by legation secretary Raoul Wallenberg, assisted by several hundred unpaid assistants. It is limited, theoretically in any case, to Jewish people who have family or business connections with Sweden, and planned at its start to facilitate their departure from Hungary and entry into Sweden.[69]

It bears repeating that contained within these apparently mild words was the ongoing salvation of human lives. For the remainder of 1944, Langlet worked ceaselessly if with increasing disorganization and chaos. Many a gate and doorway in Budapest was adorned with the identification plaque of SRK. In cooperation with Wallenberg, he arranged the complicated delivery of life-saving supplies to many locations, an operation which became ever more difficult with each passing week. His energy seemed endless, even if his adherence to strict organizational procedures sometimes failed. It is also bears repeating that Langlet accomplished all of this working for an organization whose sole reason for existing was to engage in humanitarian work, but which refused to provide him with any funding, and which grew increasingly impatient with his personal idiosyncrasies. Shamefully, after the war, SRK recognized Langlet's accomplishments briefly and only with reluctance, and then allowed his memory and deeds to fade into obscurity.

IVER OLSEN AND THE *WRB* IN STOCKHOLM

These personalities and details of diplomacy described above were, of course, in a context of continuing high-level, government-to-government negotiations and, more importantly, the course of the war itself. The summer of 1944 was a disastrous period for Nazi Germany and its allies, and the situation would only continue to deteriorate. Nonetheless, as August ended with Hitler suffering one political and military defeat after another, Nazi determination to keep killing Jews never slackened in Budapest, or anywhere else in the dictator's rapidly shrinking area of control.

Geopolitically, the key event concerning events in Budapest occurred late in August, when Romania left its alliance with Nazi Germany and capitulated to the onrushing Red Army. It was obvious to everyone that it was only a matter of time before Stalin's juggernaut pierced Transylvania – which under Hungarian occupation had been one of the regions most ruthlessly emptied of its considerable Jewish population – and surged into Hungary's hard-to-defend, open plains. Romania had been one of Germany's key partners in the genocide's first two years, and its army and police forces were responsible for more Jewish deaths during the Holocaust than any other besides those of the Third Reich. Yet Marshal Antonescu's government calculatingly refused German demands to deport and murder the large Jewish population of 'Old Romania'. The switch to the Soviet side was rapid and effective, and the Hungarians were particularly dismayed at the seeming improvement in the situation suddenly now enjoyed by their archrivals, and worried about how it would impact on how the Soviets treated them. The Romanians were of course eager to take whatever political advantage they could from their lapsed allegiance to Nazi Germany.

Per Anger's last political report of July noted that *Nyilas* leader Ferenc Szálasy continued to agitate for inclusion into Horthy's government and against the tenuous security enjoyed by the Jews. Anger also noted that Hungary's government was showing signs of instability:

> Many signs are visible of an internal dissolution within state organs. Officials are taking improvised and often contradictory measures. Highly placed officials have in surprising numbers requested leave 'for illness' and the leading posts are mainly occupied by new people who have received these positions as political payoffs rather than competence. Economic life is suffering enormously from the political situation. The elimination of the Jews from business life has in the main paralyzed both industry and trade.[70]

Meanwhile, in Berlin throughout July and August, Swedish Legation staff continued trying to secure German approval for the repatriation. An early August letter to Stockholm summarizes the situation:

> In spite of my repeated attempts at the German foreign ministry, I have been unable to obtain a decision regarding the German stand about the Jews in question in Hungary.
>
> One well informed official in this matter has told me that the question of the departure of the 'Swedish' Jews out of Hungary is closely connected to the issue of Hungary's general Jewish policy [*judepolitik*]. According to my source, Hitler has decided that all Jews in Hungary must be unconditionally removed ... among others, the Swedish king's telegram and the Pope's appeal to Horthy created great German displeasure. According to my source,

the matter of the 'Swedish' Jews departure from Hungary and permission to transit Germany is conditional on Hungarian acceptance of German demands for treatment of the Jews.[71]

Meanwhile, the 'politics of genocide' continued between the Swedes, Americans and British, parallel to the Americans and Hungarians communicating through Switzerland, informing each other of positions taken regarding Budapest's Jews. It has been noted earlier that one motive for Sweden's abiding engagement in helping Jews in 1944 was Stockholm's belief that humanitarian activities provided Sweden with a chit to counterbalance, at least partially, the ever-increasing pressures applied by the Western Allies to make Sweden stop trading with Nazi Germany. In increasingly bitter negotiations, Swedish negotiators maintained that international law gave them the legal right to fulfil their agreements and corporate contracts with Nazi Germany. The Allies vainly tried to convince the Swedes of the morally problematic nature of a Scandinavian democracy continuing to supply a genocidal, fascist regime with militarily vital supplies. In these negotiations we see a caustic irony; a nation whose diplomatic apparatus was devoting more and more energy to saving Jews was simultaneously seeing its most important politicians and business leaders – including the powerful Wallenberg brothers – pushing back hard against Allied demands for an immediate complete cessation of trade.

Nonetheless, Sweden's assistance to Jews in Budapest produced the hoped-for political profit. Both Herschel Johnson and Victor Mallet (Britain's minister in Stockholm) wrote letters to their capitals, praising Sweden. Both were well aware of – and Johnson had been actively involved in – Wallenberg's recruitment, and both Legations regularly received Anger's earlier reports, as well as Wallenberg's. One direct result of the Allies' satisfaction was the announced willingness to ship more food to Sweden, in spite of the general blockade which still prevailed. In a joint démarche of 13 July sent to UD, the Allies were crystal clear:

> The Government of the United States and His Majesty's Government in the United Kingdom desire to express again their admiration for the humanitarian policy followed by the Swedish Government in affording asylum to refugees both child and adult from Denmark, Norway and other areas under German domination and wish to renew assurances previously made that should the Swedish Government so desire, [we] are ready to give prompt and sympathetic consideration to requests for increases in Swedish blockade quotas in order to ease the burden on Swedish resources resulting from the temporary care of refugees ...

received under the liberal and humanitarian Swedish policy in this regard.[72]

For the Americans, events in Hungary were the concern primarily of the WRB, and it relied on Sweden for reliable information to help formulate its plans and policies for Hungary. In his weekly summary report of 7–12 August, John Pehle informed Treasury Secretary Hans Morgenthau: 'In view of the widely differing versions received from various sources regarding the changed attitude of the Hungarian government, we have requested Minister Johnson and Board Representative Olsen in Stockholm to obtain for us clarification of a number of questions through the Swedish Legation in Budapest.'[73] In a two-part report sent on 25 July, Johnson wrote: 'Following information has been received indirectly from Wallenberg in Budapest.' He related German attitudes about releasing Jews, the general political climate and the possibility of deportations resuming. He noted different schemes being considered by Wallenberg and other neutrals, and, finally, specific information about the Swede's activities and plans: 'Wallenberg reports that he rented a 16 room office which, because of its extra-territorial nature, has given him the opportunity of providing asylum for several prominent Hungarian rabbis and religious leaders. He also reports that he expects to be back in Stockholm for a few days at the end of the month.'[74]

Sweden soon received another small pay-off of 'goodwill' from the Americans. Food supplies to Sweden would be increased, 'pursuant to the recently reported commitment by the Hungarian authorities to the International Red Cross that Jewish children under ten years old who have necessary visas may leave Hungary'.[75] Though the British government objected both to the establishment of the WRB and some of its operations, regarding Budapest they acted mostly in concert with the Americans. On 2 August, British Chargé Montagu-Pollock wrote to UD's Rolf Sohlman that his government maintained its endorsement of July's appreciative sentiments: 'This Legation has now been instructed by the Foreign Office to let you know that needless to say this offer also applies in respect of Jewish children from Hungary whose admittance into this country the Swedish government are so generously endeavouring to facilitate.'[76] Cooperation on humanitarian matters continued a week later when the Americans again approached UD with a rather remarkable if subdued acknowledgement that its own earlier, highly restrictive policies towards Jews fleeing Hitler was now definitely reversed:

> The American Government is hopeful that the Swedish Government will be able promptly to agree to advise enemy

governments that Sweden is willing to allow the entry into Sweden, with or without transit visas, of any person to whom an American immigration visa was issued on or after July 1, 1941. The Legation is authorized to state that any such persons so admitted will be adequately maintained and that any who may be found not qualified for the issue of a visa will be evacuated [to the US] as soon as possible.[77]

Contact between the Americans and Swedes also occurred directly between two of the men involved in this story. Per Anger had returned to Sweden in early August with his wife and young child, eager to move them out of harm's way. In preparation for this visit, Wallenberg dictated a brief memo to his colleague about some of the issues he wished Anger to raise when at UD. He began the memo by noting what Anger already knew, that the Germans were not likely to allow any transport of Jews out of Hungary, and that as a result, rescue efforts should be concentrated within the country. And then, somewhat shockingly, Wallenberg stated: 'By the way, it is not in Sweden's interest to accept too many Jews.'[78] The remainder of the memo consisted of Wallenberg's recommendations about how best to proceed with other ideas and plans. Then he wrote something equally interesting, as we continue our consideration of existing myths. 'It has to be emphasised that it is not possible to rescue everyone from wearing the star or to take them into a camp. We take the view that none of our measures are to be used on a large scale, because then they would attract too much attention. The Germans might then force the [Hungarian] authorities to stop making such concessions towards us.' So instead of seeking to 'rescue all Hungarian Jewry', he actually understood after a few weeks experience that there were practical limitations to what could and should be done. In the event, he and his colleagues would end up assisting many thousands more than they ever imagined would be the case.

During his approximately two weeks in Stockholm, Anger briefed his colleagues, and had what must have been a most interesting lunch with Iver Olsen. Anger seems not to have written a report about it, but Olsen did:

I had lunch with the First Secretary of the Swedish Legation in Budapest, who is here for a short while. He is a fine chap and had many interesting comments to make. He said Wallenberg is working very hard and doing everything possible ... He considers the situation in Hungary far from settled ... [and] is very sceptical as to the possibility of bringing to Sweden the 2,000 odd Jews who, up to now, have been issued Swedish papers.[79]

Of the many interesting things reported by Olsen, this last was one of the most surprising, for this particular figure for the number of Jews protected by the Swedes is not seen elsewhere. Anger could have meant the total number, including family members, now protected in some way under a general umbrella of Swedish protection, rather than a specific number of protective papers – of whatever variety – actually issued. 'This chap is positive that the only real constructive move to be made just now is to get as many Jews as possible into Swedish camps, and then extend the Swedish protection to as many others as possible. I thoroughly agree and that is why I am so anxious to press the Swedish Red Cross in this matter.' Olsen may have misunderstood, because no proposal existed for the Swedes to establish camps outside the city. Rather, Anger may have been referring to the buildings under Swedish protection in what was by now called the 'international ghetto'.

Interesting as well, when attempting to understand the reaction of contemporaries to the horrors of the Holocaust, is something Anger told Olsen about his own ability to actually believe some things happening in Budapest. Anger, who had also served in Berlin when, not incidentally, deportations to the East began in 1941, had to that date written much about what he had seen and witnessed. Yet he still felt the need to tell Olsen that 'even he did not believe some of the atrocities until he himself was an eye-witness'. Anger then related something noted earlier by Wallenberg, which was clearly the prevailing belief within the Legation. The Jews, he indicated, were completely apathetic, and this made it more difficult to help them. 'He lamented very much the total lack of courage among the Hungarian Jews, since they could do so much to help themselves even when they knew it was only a matter of a short time before they would be killed.'[80]

Some days later Olsen sent a memorandum to UD with questions about 'principal uncertainties', and a quiet directive to Wallenberg. The questions were about the possible resumption of deportations; food supplies for Jews; what, if any, realistic possibilities of departure from Hungary existed; and other matters: 'If Wallenberg could clarify all points for guidance of Department and Board, it would be deeply appreciated. It appears, leaving it to Wallenberg's discretion ... that the main emphasis should be placed now on inducing appropriate Hungarian circles to maintain and strengthen newly reported relaxation of Jewish regime ... and apply such relaxation to all Jews in Hungary without exception.'[81] This memo indicates that Olsen understood some things about prevailing circumstances, but not others. This, however, cannot be considered surprising, for no one involved had ever been in this situation before, and most things were being made up as they went along.

The American public was also aware of Sweden's activities in Budapest, which were publicized around the world, including Gustav's appeal to Horthy.[82] Months earlier, Sweden's role in the salvation of Danish Jewry had been widely publicized and praised in the US. Now, from March 1944 onward, UD received numerous direct appeals from people in the US for help for relatives in Budapest. Several were in fact sent directly to the king, and one telegram sparked his personal interest, and is another interesting example of the 'everyday politics of genocide', on several levels. The 14 August cable from Elizabeth Buchinger of Brooklyn, New York is cited in this chapter's epigram. On the telegram itself is a minute from one of the king's aides: 'Given by His Majesty the King to UD. His Majesty the King desires to obtain information, in order to personally respond to telegram.' The next day, UD cabled the Legation: 'At request of King, cable situation Buchinger children.'[83] No word came from the Legation, so on 19 August, another cable was sent to Budapest: 'Desirable to immediately receive answer our 255, [regarding] Buchinger children, as King seeks to hear the issue's situation.'[84]

The Legation answered on Wednesday 23 August: 'Your coded cable 255. Hungarian police investigation without result to date. Endre taken away from Szombathely. Regarding Eva and Imre, no police message. Legation will try through its own investigation to discern children's fate.' The king was immediately informed.[85] In fact, the children were most likely already dead. Szombathely is in western Hungary, and that province was emptied of its Jews weeks before, with virtually all residents sent to Auschwitz-Birkenau. The king's reaction to this incomplete information is not known. Also in the files is evidence of the king's interest in the fate of a Hungarian-Jewish tennis player and her mother. The king, known worldwide for his passion for tennis, instructed his aides to inform UD that he wished for a tennis player named Koermoeczy to receive Swedish protection. On 14 September, Budapest cabled Stockholm with the information that she, and her mother, had 'received Swedish protective passports'.[86]

Genuine appreciation for Sweden's humanitarian actions came this time from the highest American levels in an early September letter from Johnson to Foreign Minister Günther. The letter raises no other issues, and there is no reason to think that the Americans were engaging only in diplomatic sophistry. Even though things were a long way from over in Budapest, Johnson was instructed to communicate American satisfaction with Sweden:

> I have the honor to inform Your Excellency that I have received instructions from my Government to express to the Swedish

20. The 'Glass House' factory in the heart of Pest used by Swiss diplomats and Zionist activists in their assistance activities. Probably photographed in mid-autumn, those Jews in the queue must have been waiting for hours, with numerous municipal policemen in attendance. (Author's photograph, taken at the Glass House Museum, Budapest.)

21. A Swiss 'Schutzpass', issued for an individual and his wife, and signed by Karl Lutz. Note that the document's holder is an American citizen, and that it was issued in April, months before Wallenberg's arrival. (Author's photograph, taken at the Glass House Museum, Budapest.)

22. Karl Lutz, Swiss diplomat and colleague of Wallenberg. (Author's photograph, taken at the Glass House Museum, Budapest.)

23. Ferenc Szálasi, head of the *Nyilas* Party and Hungary's self-styled 'Führer', on what is believed to be 16 October, entering the Royal Palace for his installation as prime minister. (Courtesy of USHMM Photo Archives.)

24. Szálasi greeting a German soldier on the same day. Note the Hungarian army officer standing behind him. (Courtesy of USHMM Photo Archives.)

25. Budapest Jews at an assembly point, probably in late November or early December in preparation for a 'death march' towards the Austrian border. It is believed that the figure with his hands behind his back is Wallenberg. Note also the municipal policemen in negotiations with Wallenberg and others. (T. Verés Collection, Courtesy of USHMM Photo Archives.)

26. Another photograph from that same occasion. The Hungarians guarding the assembled Jews could be Hungarian soldiers. Verés took such photographs secretly, hiding what he called his 'beloved Leica' camera under his scarf. (T. Verés Collection, Courtesy of USHMM Photo Archives.)

27. Another 'secret' photograph taken by T. Verés, this time male Jews being marched out of Budapest on a 'death march'. Note their large bundles. (T. Verés Collection, Courtesy of USHMM Photo Archives.)

28. Jews assembled on a city street, guarded by *Nyilas* militia, most likely in preparation for a 'death march'. (Yad Vashem, Jerusalem.)

29. *Nyilas* militiamen guarding the Swedish Legation on Gellért Hill, probably in late December. (Courtesy of USHMM Photo Archives.)

30. A photograph taken in Buda in early 1945 by Karl Lutz showing the extent of the destruction in Budapest. The picture looks towards the hills from which the Soviet Red Army rained artillery fire on the city. (Yad Vashem, Jerusalem.)

31. A block of flats that in 1944 was in the centre of the 'international ghetto'. In these buildings, dozens of Jews were forced to exist in a single room. (Author's photograph.)

32. A corner of a block that in 1944 was in the centre of the 'international ghetto'. Today, one street is named in honour of Wallenberg. (Author's photograph.)

33. The wall-mounted memorial to Wallenberg on Wallenberg utca in what was the 'international ghetto'. Note that even in this representation of Wallenberg, the 'Schutzpass' in his hands has the Tre Kronor (Three Crowns) inverted. (Author's photograph.)

34. The Swedish Legation on Minerva utca, on Buda's Gellért Hill, today. (Author's photograph.)

35. The memorial plaque mounted on the wall of the (former) Swedish Legation. The text reads, 'The Royal Swedish Legation 1944. In this building, envoy Carl-Ivan Danielsson, and Legation Secretaries Raoul Wallenberg and Per Anger conducted a comprehensive rescue action during which thousands of persecuted Jewish lives could be saved.' (Author's photograph.)

36. The building on Benczúr utca in Pest where it is believed Wallenberg spent his last night as a free man. Note the damaged memorial plaque mounted on the wall. Today it serves as the Austrian Embassy. (Author's photograph.)

37. 'The Snake Killer, or Wallenberg Memorial Statue'. Located in St Stephen's Park near the 'international ghetto', the original statue was by Pál Pátay. Commissioned after the war by Jews saved by Wallenberg, it was due to be unveiled in April 1949. The night before the ceremony, security forces removed it from the pedestal. Eventually it was mounted in front of a pharmaceutical factory in Debrecen, with no explanation of its origin or meaning. It remains there to this day. The replica (pictured) was unveiled in 1999. (Author's photograph.)

Government the utmost appreciation of the Department of State
and the War Refugee Board for the invaluable humanitarian services rendered by the Government of Sweden in connection with
the Hungarian situation. Please accept, Excellency, the renewed
assurances of my highest consideration.[87]

It should be noted that Wallenberg was not mentioned by name, indicating that the Americans knew that things were far more than a one-
man show.[88]

The Americans' appreciative tone regarding Budapest (and later the
'White Buses') would characterize until the end of the war Stockholm's
relations with the Allies on humanitarian issues. The same tone did not
prevail, however, on the issue of trade, which was of much greater
importance to the Allies. Sweden's continuing rejection of demands for
an immediate cessation of trade with the Nazis created severe tensions
which ended only when Per Albin Hansson's government decided, quite
belatedly in November, to finally cut off all essential trade with Hitler's
rapidly shrinking empire. Bitterness resulting from Sweden's stubborn-
ness regarding its trade with Nazi Germany would come to overshad-
ow Swedish–American relations for some years after the war, when the
immediacy of humanitarian issues had faded away into memory.

WALLENBERG IN MID-SUMMER 1944

Though a relative stability characterized the situation until about
mid-August, persistent rumours of renewed deportations flourished,
deepening the anxiety felt by everyone. While Danielsson and Anger
continued operating much as they had, Wallenberg accelerated the pace
of his activities. He took his obligation to report seriously, knowing that
his memoranda were also sent to the Western Allies. Though they were
already getting shorter, they remain for these weeks fascinating windows into the details of the Hungarian Holocaust.

Far more organized than Langlet's distracted and florid memoranda,
Wallenberg's first report in August is, compared to his earlier reports,
concise and lacking both the artifice of his July reports and their amateurish speculation. Not surprisingly, Wallenberg understood the situation in August much better than when he arrived. He also had far less
time to write lengthy descriptions designed as much to impress as to
inform. He began: 'Since the last report, hardly any change in the situation has occurred.'[89] Though the situation was calmer since the deportations had been halted, the daily terrors to which Budapest's Jews were
subjected had not. He described several particular incidents, then
wrote: 'Today and yesterday the city has been full of Gestapo-inspired

rumours that the large "*aktion*" against the Jews would now occur. I have not yet been able to confirm them.'

Though Langlet may have had better local connections, Wallenberg's position and name gave him access to much higher-placed officials and individuals. He reported on meetings with Horthy's son Nikolaus, who, Wallenberg wrote, asked him for an anonymous memorandum stating the ways in which the Swedes were helping Jews. He also met Interior Minister Jungeruth, who continued to lie to the young diplomat about Hungarian actions and aims: '[He] said that he would welcome a large number of Jews leaving for Sweden and confirmed that before they left they could live in special houses under Swedish protection. The decision in principle to deport Budapest's Jews remained in place, but efforts were underway to obtain assurances from the Germans that no harm will come to them.'

We next see an account of the (again) seemingly mundane details of bureaucracy and organization that have seldom played a role in accounts of Wallenberg, but which were crucial if he was actually to be able to help people:

> The B-section's personnel are now 40, organized into a reception, registration, treasury, archive, correspondence as well as the transport and housing sections, each of them enjoying its own, competent leadership. In another neighbouring building a six room flat has been rented.
>
> The total number of requests [for protective papers] received is approximately 4000. The reception was closed some time ago in order to go through and check them. New, printed letters of protection [*skyddsbrev*] and passport papers will be sent out as soon as the requests have been approved.

Precisely as a genocide takes place in steps, without a necessarily precise 'final goal' articulated in advance, so does its response. The final paragraph of Wallenberg's report, headed 'Establishing of a camp', is particularly interesting. It illustrates not only the paradoxical blend of the ordinary with the extraordinary, but also the fact that in many ways, even in this extraordinary situation, Wallenberg and the other diplomats trying to save human lives still thought, at least at this stage and about some things, in relatively conventional terms. To offer 'costs and compensation' for ostensible damages suffered was a proper and conventional way of looking at circumstances, at least for a European businessman like Wallenberg – even during a genocide:

> On probably Wednesday or Thursday [9 or 10 August] we will empty the rented flats at Pozsony utca 3, which is a Jewish

building, of its current inhabitants and instead house there an equal number of Jews who are under the Legation's protection. It would be eminently desirable to be able to pay the moving costs and small damages to those Jews who in this way have to suddenly leave their homes. Afterwards a nearby building on the same street will be turned into a Swedish assembly camp [*sammelläger*]. On average one can count with about 100 people in every building.[90]

It seems that by helping some Jews find shelter, others were being cast out, again, onto the street. This report illuminates the paradoxical fact that by helping those Jews fortunate enough to receive some form of Swedish protection, Wallenberg was likely to expose other Jews to greater danger, for there was no certainty that those forced to leave a building taken over by the Swedes would find further shelter in the 'international ghetto'. The unintended, almost inevitably negative consequences of genocide penetrated every level of activity in Budapest that year, although it is uncertain if Wallenberg himself reflected on such issues.

Perhaps paradoxically – or perhaps not – it seems that the harder Wallenberg worked, the more he seemed to enjoy himself. He had established himself comfortably and could concentrate on the myriad and vivid tasks he was suddenly wrestling with in a wartime city pulsing with nervous energy and danger. In a matter of weeks he had gone from a somewhat aimless position as a minor Stockholm business man, albeit a Wallenberg, to a position which conferred profound practical and moral responsibilities upon him. He had made his presence known both in official circles and amongst Budapest's Jews, and there seems no doubt that his presence and basic task quickly became known amongst the population. Even if it was unclear how he would actually 'save' many Jews, the perceptible increase in Swedish diplomatic activity that Wallenberg set in motion and made visible gave some Jews increased hope. Otto Salamon, a Budapest survivor, remembers that there was an expression that Jews would use during the war after hearing of some good news:

We called it 'Zsidó Vitamin' news. 'Zsidó' is Hungarian for Jewish [and] any news potentially of benefit to the Jews was deemed as Jewish Vitamin. So what was Zsido Vitamin news? When we heard that there was an attempt on Hitler's life. That the Allies were winning the war ... And soon after Wallenberg arrived in Budapest in July, the word quickly spread that there was some Swedish Christian doing wondrous thing for the Jews of Budapest and so he too became a Zsidó Vitamin news.

And this Zsido Vitamin news, indeed, became a reality when my mother sought him out and obtained from him the 3 Schutz-Passes that enabled us to live in one of his safe houses.[91]

It seems fair to assume that Wallenberg himself received emotional sustenance and energy from being able to help, so directly and palpably, scores of people in such evident need. Though the notion should be resisted that Wallenberg was in any way 'born' to be a rescuer of Jews during the Holocaust, there is no question that he was a genuinely caring individual brought up to treat other people well. Everything we know about him allows us to surmise that he was highly cognizant of his new situation, and intended to make the most of it. He probably did reflect upon the fact that historical forces, far beyond the influence of any one individual apart, perhaps, from the German Führer, provided him with what he clearly understood was a unique personal and existential opportunity. Reference has already been made to Wallenberg's 6 August letter to his mother, expressing both his exhaustion and exhilaration. In it he also described his work, writing, 'It is obviously extremely uncertain whether it will be possible to achieve a positive outcome, given that everything ultimately depends on the general situation.' He acted as if he knew he was making history.

Yet, busy and distracted as he was, Wallenberg remained conscious of his class and family, telling his mother: 'Budapest, which used to be so gay, has changed completely. Most of the ladies from the better families have left the city, and the men are all at the front. Business is utterly paralyzed. It is becoming almost completely politicized.' Ever the dutiful son, Wallenberg described the birthday celebration given 'by my very capable secretary, Countess Nako', and also told his mother: 'I have rented a very beautiful 18th century house on the castle hill with gorgeous furniture, and a lovely little garden.'[92]

Also casting a shadow over Wallenberg's activities at the time was the possibility, at least, that the end of his stay in Budapest was in sight. Evidence indicating that he himself might end his stay in Budapest after only two months has already been cited, and there seems no question that a return to Stockholm, at least for some days, remained a distinct possibility. Further indication of this can be seen in a long letter from Lauer to Wallenberg written over several days in late August. In it, Lauer mentions three times an imminent visit by Wallenberg to Stockholm, including discussions with UD and Iver Olsen about his humanitarian activities, and in order to discuss business opportunities which, this letter makes clear, the two had discussed and modestly pursued during Wallenberg's first weeks in Budapest.[93] Whether he would have actually returned if events had run a different course cannot be known, and there is no comment on such an eventuality. Everything depended, as Wallenberg quite evidently understood, 'on the general situation'. The prospect of a September departure from Budapest appears nowhere in UD records, apart from his original 'terms of work' agreed in early July. But the Americans seemed also aware that his return to Sweden was imminent.[94] It is hard to imagine, however, that such a timescale did not affect his planning and decisions during those early weeks of what would become six full months in the city. Indeed, as we shall see, he soon reported to Stockholm that by mid-September he anticipated that his 'B' division would be dissolved (*avvecklad*), although it is difficult to understand why he believed that his work, and that of his division, was nearing completion.

Engzell and other officials in Sweden continued to be swamped with scores of requests for assistance, and throughout July and August, numerous lists with dozens of names left Stockholm. Keeping track of the many names and increasing numbers became increasingly difficult. On 9 August, Danielsson read: 'In the event that those people for whom assistance has been requested are already on your lists, I kindly apologize; We are namely so over loaded with work here that a proper checking of these lists cannot be conducted.'[95] Stockholm's inability to keep track of names being sent to Budapest unquestionably contributed to an aspect of Wallenberg and Langlet's work which was criticized both then and afterwards – that of 'protective paper inflation'. UD also contributed materially to this problem by notifying Budapest that previous criteria for determining sufficiently strong 'connections to Sweden' did not apply any more.[96] This fortuitous 'problem' played havoc with strict bureaucratic procedure. It is also likely, however, that it led to dozens if not hundreds more people receiving some sort of neutral paper. Possession of a stencilled form bearing the seal of the Swedish government seal, with a stamp and perhaps a photograph, could, and sometimes did, lead to an increased chance of survival – something which now looked increasingly possible as the Red Army moved westward.

In fact, this departure from strict bureaucratic convention did not unduly disturb Engzell and his staff; they continued to demonstrate full confidence in their colleagues in Budapest. We may again note that officials in Stockholm could have chosen otherwise, not least by insisting on maintaining the right of final judgement on all applications for assistance. To have done so would have been far truer to long-prevailing bureaucratic tradition in Sweden than what was actually happening. Sometimes, bureaucracies react to a crisis by becoming even more restrictive – this is not how UD reacted. Though everyone concerned understood that they were involved in a loosening of procedures which

in normal times might well have led to a reprimand or even discipli-
nary measures. Engzell and his colleagues understood that these were
not, in any way, ordinary times:

> As you see, [in this list] there are several cases where the connec-
> tion is only from friends in Sweden. Yet as the situation continues
> to develop, we have in the meantime decided not to refuse such
> requests, but rather send them to you to decide if, in your judge-
> ment, something can be done. However if you should consider
> that this expansive attitude [*sic*] on our part risks those cases
> where closer connections [to Sweden] exist, please tell us as we
> would then, naturally, try to dam up the flow of those seeking
> assistance.[97]

So far as can be ascertained, at no time did Danielsson ever request
that the flow of names from Stockholm should be slowed or halted
only because the connection to Sweden was more tenuous than opti-
mally desired, or because of their work load.

In viewing these events, it is important not to lose sight of the day-
to-day physical and psychological pressures being endured not just by
the victims, but also by those providing assistance. In mid-September,
Danielsson wrote to UD telling of the almost continual air raids the
city was enduring from the Americans and, increasingly during the
nights, from rapidly approaching Soviet forces: 'All work at the
Legation is suffering greatly from these daily alarms.' Yet they perse-
vered, and many in Budapest, and not only Jews, turned to the Swedes
for protection:

> Requests for asylum have been made by members of the royal fam-
> ily, relatives to [Horthy], leading industrialists as well, finally, of
> personal friends with strong connections to Sweden. I have
> answered these negatively, but a situation can occur when one
> stands confronted by a *fait accompli* where those in question are
> confronted by genuinely mortal danger are given entrance to the
> Legation.[98]

Though August had been considerably calmer than previous
months – and how could it not have been when compared with the
volcanic violence which had torn through Hungary, and the country's now decimated Jewish population – the atmosphere was anything but placid. Eichmann and his men were no longer leading
events, but remained lurking in the background, hoping for another
shift by Horthy. They almost got their wish, as there are indications
that some time during the last week of August, the regent told the
Germans they could act to 'remove' all Jews from the city. This didn't

happen because in the end, Veesenmayer was ordered by Himmler to refrain, at least for the moment, from ordering Eichmann back into action.[99]

Langlet, Danielsson, Anger and Wallenberg continued their increasingly expansive activities on behalf of thousands of Jews, and many others. We shall see that though in some ways September also enjoyed a relative calm, though the city's population was now spending hours in bomb shelters as the Americans increased their sorties over Budapest. All eyes, of course, were looking eastward, monitoring the progress of the Red Army. Everyone also understood that as long as the Germans remained in Hungary, the some 200,000 to 225,000 Jews clinging to life in Budapest remained gravely threatened.

No artificial historical theory has successfully dethroned the individual from the summit of historical explanation, and this chapter has focused on the thinking and choices made by ordinary men acting in extraordinary times. Though large and impersonal social and political forces played important roles in shaping Holocaust history, it was the choices of identifiable men who made the Holocaust happen. In looking at the actions of men like Valdemar Langlet and Carl Ivan Danielsson, we see the real good which can result from decisions taken by an individual. As September commenced, Sweden now had in place a group of exemplary diplomats. The manner in which they acted and the decisions they made continue to illuminate important aspects of the 'everyday' history of the Holocaust.

NOTES

1. Telegram from E. Buchinger, Brooklyn, NY, to King Gustav V, Stockholm, 14 August 1944, *Riksarkivet Utrikesdepartementet* (hereafter RA UD), Hp 21 Eu 1096, folder 9.
2. Historian T.D. Kramer quotes György Gergely, a Hungarian who worked for the Swedes and the International Red Cross, as lamenting the fact that 'populist – often exaggerate – assessments of the Swedish diplomat's attainments have obscured the greater achievements of the Swiss Consul, Charles Lutz, and the valuable work of the Vatican's representatives, Nuncio Angelo Rotta and his secretary Monsignor Gennaro Verolino'. T.D. Kramer, *From Emancipation to Catastrophe: The Rise and Holocaust of Hungarian Jewry* (New York and Oxford: University Press of America, 2000), p.239.
3. In one measure of historical memory recognizing what happened in Budapest, all those mentioned have been recognized as 'Righteous Among the Nations' by Israel's Yad Vashem Memorial Authority. To be given this award, a certain amount of research and verification of their achievements must be accomplished. The award is given either to the individual or his/her family in a public ceremony.
4. Both Danielsson and Anger have been named, in the early 1980s, as 'Righteous Among the Nations', while Engzell has not received this honour.
5. See Per Anger's own short account, *With Raoul Wallenberg in Budapest: Memories of the War Years in Hungary* (Holocaust Library: New York, 1981), and the hagiographic book by E.R. Skoglund, *A Quiet Courage: Per Anger, Wallenberg's Co-Liberator of Hungarian Jews* (Grand Rapids, MI: Baker Books, 1997). It is no coincidence that both books have Wallenberg's name in the title.
6. Both were honoured by Yad Vashem as early as 1965. Both died in obscurity in Sweden.

7. There is, however, the Valdemar Langlet General School and Adult Education Centre in Budapest.
8. Both V. Langlet and his wife wrote books about their experiences. See V. Langlet, *Verk och dagar i Budapest* (Stockholm: Wahlström & Widstrand, 1946); and N. Langlet, *Kaos i Budapest: bertättelsen om hur svensken Valdemar Langlet räddade tiotusentals människor undan nazisterna* (Vällingby: Harrier, 1982). Both are discussed in subsequent chapters.
9. B. Runberg, *Valdemar Langlet: Räddare i faran: Wallenberg var inte ensam* (Stockholm: Megilla-Förlaget, 2000). Professional Swedish historians have ignored Langlet completely.
10. Author's interview with B. Runberg, 15 August 2000, Stockholm, Sweden.
11. Of course, the two were a generation apart in age. Langlet was 72 in 1944; Wallenberg was 32.
12. T. Undén to P. Westrup, 13 May 1938, RA UD, P 2 Eu, folder 1. Undén was made Sweden's minister in Budapest after the Legation in Vienna was closed in the wake of March's Anschluss.
13. Runberg, *Valdemar Langlet*, pp.13–17.
14. Ibid., p.71; V. Langlet, *Verk och dagar i Budapest*, pp.44–7. This is also Per Anger's memory of what Langlet did in May and June.
15. V. Langlet, *Verk och dagar i Budapest*, p.44. Somewhat boastful, chronologically uneven and without any sources given, Langlet's book is more useful as a description of his own memories than as a reliable historical guide.
16. Author interview with Ambassador Per Anger, March 1990, Uppsala University Library, Raoul Wallenberg Project Archive, no.C002, p.25.
17. In mid-August, Per Anger visited Stockholm, during which time he met Iver Olsen. In the latter's letter to the WRB about the conversation, the Swede expressed some severe reservations about Langlet which were unlikely to ever make it into a diplomatic document. I. Olsen to WRB, 14 August 1944, reprinted in D. Wyman, *America and the Holocaust* (New York: Garland Publishing, 1989–91), vol. 8, p.11.
18. Author's interview with Per Anger, pp.34–5.
19. V. Langlet, *Verk och dagar i Budapest*, p.54.
20. Wallenberg, however, was fluent in German, the Magyar capital's widely used second language.
21. N. Langlet, *Kaos i Budapest*, p.190.
22. Ibid., p.175.
23. Runberg notes that on two occasions when it would have seemed perfectly appropriate for SRK officials to highlight Langlet's work, they ignored it completely. See Runberg, *Valdemar Langlet*, p.64 and p.72.
24. V. Langlet, *Verk och dagar i Budapest*, pp.46–7.
25. Runberg, *Valdemar Langlet*, p.19.
26. I. Danielsson to UD, no.179, 19 June 1944, RA UD, Hp 21 Eu 1095, folder 5.
27. UD to I. Danielsson (no number), 21 June 1944, RA UD, Hp 21 Eu 1095, folder 5.
28. H. Johnson to Secretary of State/WRB, Pehle, no.2231, 21 June 1944, NA, Washington, DC, RG 59, File 840.48/6348.
29. Braham mistakenly labelled Langlet as 'a member of the Swedish Legation'. See R.L. Braham, *The Politics of Genocide: The Holocaust in Hungary*, revised and enlarged edn (Boulder, CT: Rosenthal Institute for Holocaust Studies Graduate Center/City University of New York Social Science Monographs, 1994), vol. 2, p.1234.
30. Ibid., p.1234, and p.1282, n.117.
31. Runberg, *Valdemar Langlet*, p.19.
32. V. Langlet, *Verk och dagar i Budapest*, p.78.
33. See note 37 below.
34. As noted, one of the primary concerns of Swedish diplomats (and others) was that this blizzard of both legitimate and forged documents would negate their effectiveness, through a type of 'inflation'.
35. UD to I. Danielsson, no.179 (Stockholm), 27 June 1944, RA UD, Hp 21 Eu 1095, folder 5. This seems odd, in light of the fact that Wallenberg was going to Budapest as a UD diplomat, not an SRK representative. The documentation offers no explanation for Engzell's apparent confusion.
36. UD to I. Danielsson, no.183, 28 June 1944, RA UD, Hp 21 Eu 1095, folder 5.
37. K. Lauer to V. Langlet, 6 July 1944, RA, Raoul Wallenberg Arkiv, Signum 1, vol. 6.
38. P. Anger to UD, no.216, 7 July 1944, RA UD, P 2 Eu, folder 1.

39. See, for example, Langlet's letter of 16 July to B. Reichwald, RA UD, Hp 21 Eu 1096, folder 8.
40. V. Langlet to Mrs Annie Fischer-Tóth, c/o Prof. Kinberg, Saltsjöbaden. This letter was registered at UD on 18 July 1944, RA UD, HP 21 Eu 1095, folder 6. See also a similar letter from Langlet to Paul Krueger, 5 August 1944, RA UD, Hp 21 Eu 1098, folder 13.
41. V. Langlet to B. Reichwald, 16 July 1944, RA UD, Hp 21 Eu 1096, folder 8. Langlet concludes the letter: 'With best wishes and in hope that we meet, when I am home from all the crazy work which envelopes me.'
42. S. Hellstedt to I. Danielsson, no.77, 29 July 1944, RA UD, Hp 21 Eu 1096, folder 7.
43. V. Langlet to E. Bladh, 5 August 1944, RA UD, Hp 21 Eu 1096, folder 9. Bladh worked for the prominent publisher, Nordstedts & Sons. Why this particular letter was passed on to UD is unclear.
44. K. Lauer to R. Wallenberg, 21 August 1944, RA, Raoul Wallenberg Arkiv, Signum 1, vol. 6.
45. V. Langlet to Her Royal Highness Princess Sybilla, 27 July 1944, RA UD, Hp 21 Eu 1096, folder 9. Langlet also asked Princess Sybilla's husband, Prince Carl, to telegraph Danielsson directly, even though, he noted somewhat dryly that 'the Minister himself is currently enjoying leave'.
46. 'The White Buses' was SRK's famed relief expedition to several German concentration camps in spring 1945, and was the organization's other significant humanitarian enterprise on the continent during the war. Infinitely more costly than any funds Langlet may have wanted, the expedition was led by Count Folke Bernadotte. For decades there has been an air of controversy about it, with rival claims and conclusions being cast about. For the two 'sides' see, most recently, S. Persson, *'Vi åker till Sverige': de vita bussarna 1945* (Rimbo: Fischer & Co., 2002), and I. Lomfors' critical new analysis, *Blind fläck: Minne och glömska kring Svenska röda korsets hjälpinsats i Nazityskland 1945* (Stockholm: Atlantis, 2005).
47. S. Hellstedt, 'Memorandum concerning relations UD–SRK', 11 August 1944, RA UD, Hp 21 Eu 1096, folder 9.
48. Reports written in this style were almost certain to raise eyebrows and anxiety in official Stockholm, and unquestionably contributed to the distrust which negatively affected Langlet's efforts.
49. UD to Legation Budapest, no.228, 26 July 1944, RA UD, Hp 21 Eu 1096, folder 7.
50. S. Hellstedt to I. Danielsson, no.97, 8 August 1944, RA UD, Hp 21 Eu 1096, folder 8.
51. G. Engzell to Legation Budapest, no.269, 23 August 1944, RA UD, Hp 21 Eu 1097, folder 10.
52. I. Danielsson to UD, no.269, 28 August 1944, RA UD, Hp 21 Eu 1097, folder 12. Asta Nilsson was the experienced aid worker soon to arrive in Budapest to assist Langlet. They would clash shortly thereafter.
53. V. Langlet, *Verk och dagar i Budapest*, p.53
54. Langlet, ibid., p.56.
55. N. Langlet, *Kaos i Budapest*, pp.13–14.
56. Ibid., p.54 and p.72.
57. Ibid., pp.60–2.
58. Anger, *With Raoul Wallenberg in Budapest*, p.55.
59. Runberg, *Valdemar Langlet*, p.81.
60. V. Langlet, *Verk och dagar i Budapest*, p.72.
61. After the war, Langlet remained interested in Wallenberg's fate. See, for instance, his correspondence with K. Lauer in RA, Raoul Wallenberg Arkiv, Signum 1, vol. 6, January 1948.
62. I. Danielsson and P. Anger, 'Memorandum concerning activities in the Budapest Legation immediately before and after the Russian occupation', 2 May 1945, RA UD, P 2 Eu, folder 1.
63. See P.A. Levine, *From Indifference to Activism: Swedish Diplomacy and the Holocaust, 1938–1944*, 2nd edn (Uppsala: Studia historica Upsaliensia, 1998), Chapter 11. Historians are not trained to speculate broadly. Yet the thought that Undén might have been the one to formulate Sweden's diplomatic response in Budapest gives cause for deep reflection about the role of the individual in history.
64. Richert figures centrally in W. Carlgren's thorough but politically tilted *Svensk utrikespolitik 1939–1945* (Stockholm: Allmäna förlaget, 1973). Danielsson's role in Budapest has failed to attract the attention of Swedish historians.
65. Richert's intervention on behalf of hundreds of Dutch Jews deported to Mauthausen in

1941 in response to protests in Holland was most interesting. See Levine, *From Indifference to Activism*, pp.118–20.

66. L.G. Berg, *Boken som försvann: Vad hände i Budapest* (Arboga: Textab Förlag, 1983), p.12. Originally published in 1949, Berg's account describes activities at the Legation and in Budapest between August 1944 and March 1945. Bizarrely, after being placed on sale in 1949 in several Stockholm bookstores, every copy mysteriously disappeared. In the foreword to the 1983 version, Berg wrote: 'The book received attention in the Swedish press and was in bookshop windows as soon as it came out. But after only some days it disappeared completely, both from shops and the publisher. Why, and after whose intervention? I have still not to this day been able to discover why.'

67. Author's interview with P. Anger, pp.22, 25 and 46.

68. I. Danielsson to G. Engzell, 10 September 1944, RA UD, Hp 21 Eu 1092, folder 1. This letter, as well as Langlet's report, was sent to S. Rydman of the SRK.

69. V. Langlet to SRK, report no.3, 9 September 1944, RA UD, Hp 21 Eu 1092, folder 1.

70. P. Anger to E. von Post, no.177, 28 July 1944, RA UD, Hp 1 Eu 583, folder 22. Anger also provides some interesting observations about the immoral manner in which 'Aryanization' of Jewish assets occurred in Budapest.

71. L. Nylander to S. Hellstedt, no.133, 4 August 1944, RA UD, Hp 21 Eu 1092, folder 1. As was generally the case, this letter was read by *Kabinettssekretarare* Boheman, and Grafström, head of the political division.

72. Copy of joint demarché, 13 July 1944, RA UD, Hp 21 Eu 1092, folder 1.

73. 'WRB's Report for Week of 7 to 12 August, 1944', reprinted in D. Wyman, *America and the Holocaust* (New York: Garland Publishing, 1989–91), vol. 8, p.50.

74. H. Johnson to Secretary of State, no.2779, 25 July 1944, in Wyman, *America and the Holocaust*, vol. 8, pp.56–7. This is another indication that Wallenberg considered a return to Sweden soon after he arrived in Budapest.

75. American Legation Stockholm to UD, no.489, 1 August 1944, RA UD, Hp 21 Eu 1092, folder 1.

76. W.H. Montague-Pollock to R. Sohlman, no.36/46/44, 2 August 1944, RA UD, Hp 21 Eu 1092, folder 1.

77. American Legation Stockholm to UD, no.492, 4 August 1944, RA UD, Hp 21 Eu 1096, folder 8. A copy of this demarché was quickly sent to both Berlin and Budapest.

78. R. Wallenberg to P. Anger, 6 August 1944, RA, Raoul Wallenberg Arkiv, Signum 1, vol. 6. No copy of this important document was located in UD's files. This is yet another piece of evidence that Wallenberg did not in fact identify with Jews in any pronounced or particular way.

79. I. Olsen to WRB, 14 August 1944, reprinted in Wyman, *America and the Holocaust*, vol. 8, pp.11–12.

80. Ibid.

81. I. Olsen to UD, no.250/435, 24 August 1944, RA UD, Hp 21 Eu 1097, folder 11.

82. UD to TT, 'Utrikespolitiska institutet & Statens informationsstyrelse', texts of King Gustav's telegram to M. Horthy and the latter's response, 10 August 1944, RA UD, Hp 21 Eu 1096, folder IX.

83. UD to Legation Budapest, no.255, 15 August 1944, RA UD, Hp 21 Eu 1096, folder 9.

84. UD to Legation Budapest, no.262, 19 August 1944, RA UD, Hp 21 Eu 1097, folder 10. The language used in this 'royal' telegram is particular: 'då Konungen låtit efterhöra ärendets läge' [since the King seeks to hear of the issue's situation].

85. Legation Budapest to UD, no.261, 23 August 1944, RA UD, Hp 21 Eu 1097, folder 10.

86. Legation Budapest to UD, no.309, 14 September 1944, RA UD, Hp 21 Eu 1099, folder 16. This again was the most desired document, with a protective power greater than Wallenberg's *Schutzpass*. The king's interest paid off.

87. H. Johnson to C. Günther, no.518, 2 September 1944, RA UD, Hp 21 Eu 1098, folder 13.

88. In January 1945, Wallenberg would be directly thanked by the American government. See Chapter 12, epigram.

89. R. Wallenberg to UD, 'PM beträffande de ungerska judarna' [Memorandum concerning Hungarian Jews], 6 August 1944, RA UD, Hp 21 Eu 1096, folder 8.

90. Ibid.

91. O. Salamon, email to author, 10 December 2007.

92. R. Wallenberg to M. von Dardel, 6 August 1944, in R. Wallenberg, *Letters and Dispatches 1924–1944*, trans. K. Board (New York: Arcade, 1995), pp.273–4. He concluded the letter with wishes to 'Nina, Father and Guy'.

93. The question, and significance, of whether Wallenberg conducted business in Budapest, which would have been a violation of his 'terms of agreement' with UD, will be discussed below.

94. See note 74 above.

95. S. Hellstedt to I. Danielsson, no.103, 9 August 1944, RA UD, Hp 21 Eu 1096, folder 8.

96. S. Hellstedt to I. Danielsson, no.102, 9 August 1944, RA UD, Hp 21 Eu 1096, folder 8.

97. S. Hellstedt to I. Danielsson, no.88, 4 August 1944, RA UD, Hp 21 Eu 1096, folder 8.

98. I. Danielsson to UD, no.323, 19 September 1944, RA UD, P 2 Eu, folder 1.

99. E. Veesenmayer to Auswärtige Amt, 24 August 1944, doc. 213; and E. Veesenmayer to von Ribbentrop, 25 August 1944, doc. 214, both in R.L. Braham, The *Destruction of Hungarian Jewry: A Documentary Account* (New York: Pro Arte for the World Federation of Hungarian Jews, 1963), pp.480–1.

9

September: The Calm before the Storm

As soon as the Russians arrive in Budapest, the only way for Raoul to come to Sweden goes through Russia. Such a journey is tiresome and all the formalities will take a very long time. If you consider it appropriate, I would be most grateful if you would intervene with [UD] in order to permit Raoul to return home soon. I am morally responsible for his journey, since I am the one who persuaded him to take on his mission.

Koloman Lauer to Jacob Wallenberg[1]

I'd like to be able to praise Raoul Wallenberg, but alas, I'm unable to ... the people [he] saved ... were wealthy Jews, those of high intellectual level, foreign speaking people with ... international ties ... Nobody in my community were saved by Swedish Papers [sic].

Naomi Reuki, Budapest survivor[2]

BUDAPEST'S 'INDIAN SUMMER'

As the punishing vortex of deportation, forced relocation and constant fear waned slightly for Budapest Jewry, Germany's retreat on both the Eastern and Western Fronts accelerated. Against all expectations, the last days of summer were a period of an eerie and anxious calm for the Jews clinging to survival. Some survivors remember it as a kind of 'Indian summer', several weeks of unexpected relief from the horrors of recent months. Some historians have attributed this change in the atmosphere to a relative calming of the political cauldron, describing it as a period of 'relative stability', 'slackening tension', even political 'tranquillity'.[3] One Swedish diplomat, Lars Berg, remembers those weeks almost as an idyll, when the work (at least of his division of the Legation) wasn't too pressing, and wartime Budapest remained a place where sumptuous dining and entertainment were still available.[4]

Most of the city's Jews were vaguely aware that the deportations remained stalled, and all hoped that the newly installed Lakatos government would not renew the assault on them. Then as throughout the war, Hungarians of all stripes had regular access to information, mainly through the continued existence of a lively if not genuinely free press; and a growing awareness that Hitler's fall was a matter of time increasingly influenced the city's atmosphere. Though parts of the city had been targets for American bombers, for the most part, the war had, to date, physically spared Budapest. Yet many also feared the fact that Stalin would soon be dictating Hungary's future.

For Hungary's government, August and September were characterized by Horthy's inability to decide critical issues. One day he would move to replace Sztójay, the next decide to leave him in office. Although the aging Regent never caved in entirely to Veesenmayer's pressure, he gave many around him the impression of a leader about to collapse. It took him weeks to finally remove Sztójay, and replace him at the end of August with General Géza Lakatos, who was more loyal to Horthy than to Hitler. One of the most important consequences of this change was the removal of several government ministers who served German interests more than Hungarian. In fact, one plank of Lakatos's new programme was to call a halt to government-sponsored persecutions of Jews. As Braham wrote: 'With the inauguration of the Lakatos government, the anti-Jewish pressure in Budapest eased.'[5] Veesenmayer was appalled by the composition of the new government, yet circumstances didn't allow him, yet, to depose Horthy. The German plenipotentiary was aware of moves by the Hungarians to emulate their Romanian neighbours and abandon the Axis, yet still chose not to strike.

This confusing confluence of factors and figures caused historian Andrew Handler to summarize the bizarre political situation with a descriptive complaint: 'The chronicler of the events that took place in Budapest in the latter half of August stands bewildered attempting to line up the pieces of the political jigsaw puzzle. No configuration of preconditions could have extricated Horthy from the credibility gap he was widening and deepening with every declaration, with every deed.'[6] Yet Veesenmayer concluded that, on balance, allowing Horthy to remain in place would better serve German interests, which continued to include the final destruction of Hungary Jewry. Informants kept the Germans aware of everything discussed by Horthy and his cabinet, including their ostensibly secret discussions with the Allies about quitting the alliance with Germany, and suing for peace. Most importantly at this stage, Veensenmayer decided not to press for Lászlo Szálasi, the fanatic nationalist and anti-Semitic leader of the *Nyilas*, to assume executive power.

Most salient for our concerns is the fact that Deputy Foreign Minister Arnóthy-Jungerth remained in place. Throughout 1944, it was above all the foreign ministry among government and city agencies which was most amenable to facilitating the rescue and assistance work of the neutrals. Arnóthy-Jungerth understood the relative political advantage gained in allowing the neutrals to continue their ongoing efforts, even if he did not necessarily sympathize with them.[7] We may remind ourselves of the simple but critical fact that had the Hungarian government decided to declare all neutral representatives personae non gratae, all humanitarian work would have ceased, and all of them, including Wallenberg, would have been forced to leave the city. Had officials in the ministry agitated for the closing down of neutral legations, this most likely would have happened. In this context it is noteworthy that the foreign ministry was even prepared to confront the Germans with petitions for the return of a few Jews who had been deported, it was argued, 'illegally' or 'by mistake'. These few individuals had received government exemptions, and therefore, argued the Hungarians, could not be treated as most other Jews.[8] There were by now widely acknowledged exemptions given to a few Jews who had 'earned' them, giving them, at least nominally, some protection against some discriminatory measures. Prominent amongst the categories of exemptions were the various papers issued by the neutrals. Also important were those exemptions which became known as 'Horthy exemptions'.[9] In addition, we see that in the midst of the overwhelming hostility of much of the population, 'many decent ordinary Hungarians' helped Jews obtain exemptions, and sheltered some Jews or created hiding places for them. There was, wrote Randolph Braham, a feeling amongst many Hungarians that it was all right to help some Jews, some of the time.[10] The Germans, of course, maintained pressure throughout the late summer to resume the deportations, even referring to the Swedish and Swiss protective efforts to 'bargain' with the Hungarians; if the latter procrastinated in resuming the killings, then at least they 'should' get some Jews to ship away. As Braham concluded: '[The Germans] tried to exploit the issue of Jewish emigration under the Swedish and Swiss schemes as a lever to pressure the Hungarians ... In view of their considerably weakened state by the end of August ... they were no longer in a position to impose their will. Nevertheless, for tactical reasons, they insisted on at least a token resettlement of 1000 Jews.'[11]

Several issues of central importance to this study are illustrated in an extraordinary political cartoon published on 10 September by the Budapest newspaper *Pesti Posta*. In it, an Orthodox Jew, readily identifiable because of his garb and facial hair, is confronted on a city street by a Budapest policeman. The policeman is depicted issuing this individual with a penalty citation because he 'dared' to appear in public without a visible 'yellow star', as required by law. In the caption, the policeman asks the Jewish man: 'Why are you not wearing the yellow star?' The Jew dares to respond, asking the policeman in return, 'Has not Herr Policeman ever seen a Swedish citizen before!'[12] In this street-level representation we see several pertinent issues raised, with perhaps the most important one being the manner in which the official is hindered from harassing his interlocutor because both understand that the latter is protected and represented by a third-party political authority requiring respect – the neutral governments. We learn that the decisive moment of decision in this 'encounter' is influenced not by force, fear or intimidation, but rather by mutually recognized symbols – both negative and positive. Far more generally in the context of the Holocaust at large, when a Jew was confronted by an authority, such a 'successful' outcome was rare indeed. It demonstrates that among Hungarian low-level officialdom, it was widely known that those thousands of Jews who had obtained some type of exemption, or were able to dwell in a building covered by a neutral legation, had acquired a modicum of protection which most would not violate.[13]

Yet as September wore on, military and political events conspired to create yet another tragic irony of Holocaust history. At the same time that noticeable numbers of Jews actually enjoyed significant support from elements of their nation's bureaucracy as well as from some fellow citizens, they would shortly be subjected to some of the worst random urban violence of the entire Nazi period. In this increasingly fraught and confusing situation, Wallenberg and the other Swedes continued their efforts to help as many innocent people as they could.

WALLENBERG AND MONEY – AGAIN

In Wallenberg's second report of 29 July, he raised an issue which became a prominent and sometimes problematic thread through his time in Budapest – the matter of money. Identifying it as an issue is simple, as it is raised many times in the documentation. Fully understanding its importance to his mission is a much more difficult task, as is discerning its exact meaning for the ongoing discussion about myth. 'What is important', he wrote, 'is to have the pecuniary and organizational means in order to be able to take at any moment those measures which the situation demands, preferably without having to ask for permission ... It is regrettable that those most interested in my trip here appear not to understand that money is necessary. There is limitless suffering to try to lessen.'[14] As we have seen, before leaving Stockholm he demanded from UD, and apparently received, permission to use money for bribes. He knew from reading Langlet's initial reports how important the availability of funds was, not only for potential bribes but, more practically, for the purchase of food, office equipment, petrol and other necessary supplies. The issue is difficult to analyse because of the incomplete and at times opaque nature of the relevant documentation, yet it is clear that Wallenberg's requests for more money became ever more insistent. His demands even created some conflict with the WRB's Iver Olsen, who did in fact channel funds to Wallenberg, but who insisted that some sort of bookkeeping be done.[15]

We see something of Wallenberg's position with regard to money, and his worry that normal organizational procedure would slow his ability to act, in an early letter to Lauer:

> Concerning [my] general activities, naturally money is needed. This can happen only if it is transferred to my account at Enskilda Bank. I guarantee of course that it will be paid back if I have no use for it. But there is no possibility of operating, for example, if I have to first obtain authorization for the possible assistance plans that I have. I can't be bothered to telephone about this because UD wants that everything should go through them. I ask you therefore to see to it that payments be made and that I be advised. The rest I will see to. The precondition meanwhile is that this happens quickly.
>
> The money will in general go to individual people, the Red Cross, churches as well as private individuals who have shown an ability to help Jews. On the other hand I doubt if anything, maybe though a little, will go towards bribes. I don't really believe in this too much. If however some negotiations in this direction are needed I will let you know.
>
> The donated money I have already received has been used mainly for administrative costs for the large office, but it is perhaps possible that UD can come up with a name for which they can pay for this, and if so that even this money will be free to be used for support.
>
> I am altogether certain that it would be unfortunate if payments were made through UD because they of course must be much more formal [about things] than would be the case if the thing happens privately.[16]

In his next letter to Lauer, Wallenberg again referred to the difficulties involved in obtaining sufficient cash, and cutting through the red-tape around it: 'I beg you to try to arrange that I am able to dispose of the Pengö sum without hindrance ... There is [here] a problem in arranging means of payment, so it is difficult to get hold of Pengös.'[17]

At least during August and September, Lauer acted as a conduit for exchanges of information, ideas and complaints between Wallenberg and Swedish and American officials. Lauer was in frequent contact with both, and it may be remembered that the offices of Mellaneuropieska and the American Legation were in the same building in downtown Stockholm, at Strandvägen 7.[18] There seems no doubt, as we shall see, that Iver Olsen used Lauer to communicate with Wallenberg, thereby bypassing official Swedish channels. Two weeks after Wallenberg arrived, Lauer wrote Olsen a lengthy letter, providing the American with additional news and information from Wallenberg, with whom he spoke by telephone the previous day. The issue of money figured prominently, and it became an issue of some contention (through Lauer) between Wallenberg and the Americans. In addition, there is further evidence that Wallenberg left Stockholm feeling that he had received insufficient guidance from either the Swedes or the Americans.: 'Mr Wallenberg is complaining about being left without instructions and money ... Mr Wallenberg implores you to give him a message as soon as possible how much money he could have at his disposal ... It is of great importance that UD should send official instructions by wire to the Swedish Legation ... authorizing them to deal with the Hungarian government regarding this action.'[19] That same day Wallenberg wrote to Lauer again, emphasizing his need for money, suggesting some solutions about how Swedish kronor could be exchanged for Swiss francs in Switzerland, and then transferred 'in the normal way' to him in Budapest.[20]

In an internal memorandum which Wallenberg wrote to Per Anger (who was in Stockholm at the time), Wallenberg discussed at length the subject of money, its potential uses and abuses, the problems of obtaining pengö, and the difficulties of organizing the more desirable transfer through Switzerland of crowns into francs. Clearly the issue was problematically complicated. Several times, Wallenberg broached contradictory ideas, including his belief that some Jews required financial compensation because they were being forcibly removed from dwellings in order to make room for other Jews (this will be discussed later). Yet he notes that this might have a positive psychological effect on all Jews in the city: 'this would at the same time serve as compensation and would undoubtedly make quite an impression of the population as a demonstration of human dignity, and it would emphasize abroad that we are accustomed to respecting the rights of Jews. For this 600,000 pengö would be used.'[21]

Tensions over money between Lauer, Wallenberg and the Americans evidently increased, and seem to have boiled over several weeks later. On 5 August, Olsen visited UD, telling his counterparts that 50,000 Swedish crowns were now available 'for the rescue of Jews in

Hungary'. Yet, remarkably, he also told them that he was unsure if it should be used by Wallenberg or by SRK.[22] Five days later, Olsen again contacted UD, and complained to an aide of Engzell's. The aide wrote to Engzell that Olsen 'had heard' that Wallenberg was using money for administrative costs which the Americans hadn't agreed to; that the Americans believed UD should be covering these costs; if this was true, he continued, '[Olsen] is sure that The War Refugee Board (?), which provides the money, would not like this. I believe I have been able to reassure Olsen, that as the money was given for "relief work" amongst the Jews, it will not be used for anything else.' The question mark is in the original, and seems to indicate that this official, who worked closely on these issues with Engzell, was unfamiliar with the WRB.[23]

On 21 August, Lauer began a very long and sometimes emotional letter to Wallenberg, which, it seems, was not concluded and dispatched until a week later.[24] This document is a complex jumble of information, questions, pleadings, contacts to make in Budapest, internal intrigues, financial figures and schemes, personal financial problems Wallenberg had left behind in Stockholm, and more. Most immediate for our concerns is what Lauer wrote about Wallenberg's money problems. Although the Americans had provided some initial funding for his operations, now, on 23 August, Olsen had abruptly decided not to pass on another payment:

> Today [Olsen] was to give another 50,000 crowns which he promised me last week. Today he refused to pay this sum, saying he was not able to make it available because he does not get any reports from you. He has only received one copy of your reports to UD from a private person ... Tove Filse. I consider this to be an excuse, and to be honest I am now very tired of the whole affair. I faithfully and honestly forwarded the letters I have received from you, and which actually do not contain that much. I myself have not read a single report from you. I consider it to be very desirable that you come to Stockholm to talk about several matters here on the spot. I enclose a copy of my letter to [him].[25]

Obviously this was a tense time for everyone, and Lauer clearly had become frustrated. He was distraught over his family's fate, and perhaps felt more in the middle of things he couldn't control than he had anticipated. People who knew him in Stockholm (and presumably their friends, and their relatives, and others) were inundating Lauer with requests to contact Wallenberg directly to ask for help for relatives and friends. Lauer held them off, creating, he wrote, a considerable amount of anger, even enmity, and 'because of this we probably gained many enemies'.[26] One source of frustration for Lauer was that Wallenberg's sponsors –

American, Swedes, Swedish Jews and others – wished for a clearer picture than they had of what the novice diplomat was doing with his money. This seems odd, given that this was only a few weeks since he arrived, and after he had in fact provided some detailed information in his UD memoranda about expenses and costs. It is possible that his sponsors were getting cold feet about the scale and risks of Wallenberg's ongoing mission, and that its highly unorthodox origins and foundations were causing anxiety. Even Rabbi Ehrenpreis pressed UD to get Wallenberg to report more precisely about how money received to that date had been used. 'The Professor', Lauer wrote, wanted only to help finance the transport of some Jews to Sweden, and was sceptical about what Wallenberg was doing in Budapest. Lauer added: 'I completely share [this] opinion of these people. You probably won't receive here much gratitude for your work [there].'[27]

The enclosed letter to Olsen referred to above was Lauer's emotional defence of Wallenberg. The two had spoken by telephone earlier, and Lauer was clearly offended by the nature of some of Olsen's queries. It reveals what these men were thinking and feeling as they all tried, however differently, to help Jews in Budapest. Because it is so illuminating, and so at odds with the fuzzy and always positive generalizations about Wallenberg's mission which characterizes the hagiographic literature, it merits extensive citation. Lauer wrote to the American:

> I revert to our conversation today ... I want to draw your attention to the fact that Mr Wallenberg is working very hard, often 16 and 17 hours, to be able to bring real help. It is a physical impossibility to write reports to several persons under these circumstances, he simply has to concentrate on UD, and it is not his fault that you have not received them from UD.
>
> As I have learned from Mr. Wallenberg's communications, he urgently needs about 600,000 Pengö for lodging 2000 people in the houses rented by him, i.e. about 100,000–200,000 Sw. Crowns. Mr. Wallenberg will only spend this money for the above mentioned purpose and for relief purposes, as agreed upon.
>
> If you have no confidence in Mr. Wallenberg, it certainly would be better you told me this, so that he could finish his work at [sic] Budapest and return. Please understand that Mr. Wallenberg not only gives all his time and efforts [sic] to bring relief to the sufferers, but also under certain circumstances risks his life.
>
> I myself feel a certain moral obligation with regard to the action, and therefore I am very anxious that Mr. Wallenberg shall not go on with his work at [sic] Budapest unless he is in favour of your confidence and help. I hope you do not misunderstand me ...[28]

The understandable tensions evolving may have been heightened by the fact that both Wallenberg and Lauer clearly were anticipating the former's return to Stockholm in early-to mid-September, and that time was running out for them. It will be remembered, in his own negotiations with UD, that Wallenberg had requested, a priori, an end to his mission at approximately this point in time if he wished. This is confirmed three times in the long letters from Lauer to Wallenberg cited above, the third being when, on 26 August, Lauer wrote to Wallenberg that 'your arrival in Stockholm is welcome for the following reasons: Abetryck, Håkansson, Seenels legal process'.[29] Further confirmation is given by Per Anger, who remembers that at exactly this period, Wallenberg was feeling that he had done what he set out to do: 'So Raoul Wallenberg at [the] ... end of August, September, he prepared his trip back to Sweden ... He thought he had done his job and it was now ... what could he do more in Budapest?'[30]

Confirmation that Wallenberg himself saw his work nearing its end is found in his report to UD of 12 September, which he concluded with a section headed 'The dissolution of the Jewish Division: Due to the [current] political situation, until further notice, reception [of applications] will definitely conclude on Sunday the 17th this month, and as work diminishes, personnel will be released. Meanwhile, the issuance of protective passports [*skyddspass*] continues because it is considered that there are certain risks that pogroms will occur in connection to the German withdrawal from Budapest.'[31]

Olsen, who took Lauer's complaints seriously, had no substantive reason to entertain doubts about what Wallenberg was doing. On 28 August, Lauer opened up a new account at (the Wallenberg family's) Enskilda Bank, and 50,000 Swedish crowns were made available to Wallenberg.[32] American approval of Wallenberg's activities was reconfirmed just a few days later when Olsen received a cable from Washington: 'JDC is remitting to you $100,000 under Treasury license for use in Hungary under Wallenberg's supervision and at his discretion.'[33] In Budapest, Danielsson informed UD that suitable methods for transferring funds to Wallenberg were now in place, yet even those which was available were not being completely used: '10,000 [Swedish crowns] received to date, only partially used. Accounting to occur afterwards. 50,000 received remain in Enskilda Bank account.' In light of Wallenberg and Langlet's endless complaints about the lack of funds, it seems remarkable, and remains unexplained, how at this date a portion of available funds were unused, with some returned at the end of the war to the Americans. Also of interest is the minute Engzell inscribed on the original telegram. He noted that because Wallenberg's special account was now open, no more money was to be channelled through Lauer, and that Olsen would be informed of this.[34]

Thcsc figurcs wcrc confirmed some days later by Wallenberg him-self, in his first report, it seems, written specifically to Olsen and the Americans. Dated 12 September and written in his still excellent English, this is yet another document which sheds light on several cen-tral issues in the Wallenberg saga with what might be called an 'illumi-nating confusion'. Illuminating because of the exact details he gave about some central issues, and confusing because so many of those issues have been conflated, confused and distorted in the most influ-ential hagiographic literature and representations about Wallenberg.[35]

He described the Legation's primary protective activities to that date as the distribution of 'protective passports'. With this he meant all the various documents distributed by the Legation, even before his arrival, and not what are today known as *Schutzpässe*. But now, 'it is planned to start a humanitarian action including the distribution of food-stuff [*sic*] and money'. This is the first document informing us that holders of Swedish papers in Budapest were also to receive a cash distribution, although exactly for what is unclear. 'A small department for the distribution of money to the holders of protective passports has been opened ... Rules for the distribution of money and food-stuff [*sic*] will be worked out on the basis of the experience of the first distribu-tion.' Then, rather candidly, Wallenberg noted what may have been a cause of concern for those in Stockholm, although how they were informed about what follows is unclear. But obviously his Stockholm patrons had been informed, and Wallenberg addressed these concerns, along with others:

> A considerable part of the expenses till now has consisted in giving dinners and lunches for various influential officials, particularly the officers responsible for the Jewish questions. During one of these dinners the promise was given to liberate all those Jews, who were interned and who held Swedish protective passports and to free up to 4,500 Jews who held Swedish protective passports from the Jewish star.[36]
>
> As for the further funds, placed at the disposal of the Jewish action, none of this money has been distributed, but it will prob-ably in large part be invested in food-stuff [*sic*].
>
> No money has been used for bribes but certain gifts of sardines has [*sic*] been distributed. No money has been used to pay dam-ages to those Jews, who we had to have ousted from their apart-ments in Pozsonyi-Street, which was to have been transformed in a [*sic*] Swedish ghetto. This plan was never carried out due to the changes in the general situation.

Considering the genuinely stressful circumstances within which everyone was operating, it is not surprising that amongst the principals, there reigned considerable confusion about some very important things. No one really seemed to know exactly how much money was in question, where precisely it was coming from, and what it was being used for. This must have caused some anxiety amongst those ultimately responsible for things, even if they did take into account that the prevailing circumstances caused some normative administrative procedures to be accorded less priority than normal. There seems no question that everyone involved was genuinely trying to be as effective as possible.

The day after Wallenberg wrote that report, UD's Svante Hellstedt again received Olsen, who was anxious about several matters. In a letter to Danielsson, Hellstedt wrote that Olsen had told him that more money was to be made available for 'Mr Wallenbergs [sic] activities amongst the Jews', but that he needed more information if this was going to happen. Olsen knew that Wallenberg needed about another 120,000 Swedish crowns, but he (Olsen) was very eager that all funds be channelled through UD, and no longer Lauer.[37] Then, on 26 September, Olsen deposited another 200,000 Swedish crowns into Wallenberg's account at Enskilda Bank.[38]

Although the money Wallenberg received is impossible to trace in detail, he did provide some information about it, at least to Lauer, who remained in contact both with the Americans and UD. In one of his last personal letters to Lauer, written on 29 September, Wallenberg (contradicting Danielsson) noted that he had depleted most of the funds received, and that they had been used for a variety of things. The largest sum, 500,000 pengö, he gave directly to the 'Jewish Council', as well as to a bombed-out children's home. Wallenberg had become, especially in the days before the *Nyilas* takeover, a source of direct financial support for a number of groups and organizations. This has escaped the notice of historians and chroniclers, and must have placed even more personal pressure on him.

Indeed, this stress can only have been deepened as he contemplated what his own situation would be, after he had completed – as he saw it – his mission:

> I am doing what I can to get back home quickly. But you can't understand how difficult it is to wind-up such a gigantic organization. As soon as the invasion arrives, this [process of] completion will take place by force. As long as there is no invasion, our activities are welcome and necessary. It is very difficult to simply stop [the work]. I will try to come home a few days before the Russians come marching in.[39]

As he had before and would again, Wallenberg asked Lauer to contact Jacob Wallenberg about his employment possibilities within the empire, although why he didn't address his elder cousin directly is unknown. He concluded by repeating something he had already told Lauer by telephone: 'Finally, I want to ask you to talk to Jacob Wallenberg and ask him, if he is very angry that I am staying here for such a long time and if I may thus lose my chances to continue the work started at Enskilda Bank.'[40] That same day Lauer wrote to Jacob Wallenberg, addressing in poignantly portentous words circumstances which neither of them could have known would come to pass:

> Last week I spoke with Raoul over the telephone. He asked me to inquire of you whether his services are needed here in Stockholm in connection with Enskilda Bank's building plans.
>
> Apart from this, in view of Raoul's own existence, it would be highly desirable that he get here as soon as possible in order to resume his activities with the firm.
>
> As soon as the Russians arrive in Budapest, the only way for Raoul to come to Sweden goes through Russia. Such a journey is tiresome and all the formalities will take a very long time.
>
> If you consider it appropriate, I would be most grateful if you would intervene with [UD] in order to permit Raoul to return home soon. I am morally responsible for his journey, since I am the one who persuaded him to take on his mission.[41]

It remains unclear to what extent the availability of money, or lack thereof, affected Wallenberg's operations. It is clear that he had substantial sums available, yet in the circumstances they could never be enough. Gaps in the evidence makes a complete review of Wallenberg's financial activities virtually impossible to accomplish. This problem is compounded for the period after 15 October, when the many disruptions caused by the *Nyilas* ascendency ended both any chance and real need that proper accounting procedures would be maintained. After that date, few involved continued to press Wallenberg to account, in detail, for the flow of money. We may, however, conclude this review of Wallenberg and the funding connected to his mission by noting what Minister Danielsson wrote to Stockholm, just days before disaster again descended on Budapest:

> Transfer of Olsen's money is best done by transferring amounts to Wallenberg's special account at Schweizerischer Bankverein, Zurich. From this payments are made to various secret accounts, belonging to private individuals and companies ... Wallenberg has already received and for the most part used this amount in pengö

... Because the need for money is so great, request immediate decision in principle concerning these Swiss transactions.[42]

The next day he cabled Stockholm again, urging that immediate transfers of new funds be made. 'If transfer is not authorized immediately, assistance activities must be diminished.'[43] To his credit there seems no doubt that even Danielsson, the old-line diplomat, considered the lapse of established procedures acceptable – it was necessary and urgent if people were going to receive assistance. Money received from American Jews and the US government, complemented by local sources, played a central role in Wallenberg's ability to assist Jews in Budapest. Equally, there seems no doubt that whatever reservations government officials and others might have had about Wallenberg's exact use of every crown, dollar or pengö, or irritation about his repeated requests for more money, his activities continued to enjoy the support of those interested in his work.

SWEDISH DIPLOMACY CONTINUES

Naturally, Wallenberg's money issues were contiguous with the Legation's ongoing diplomatic activity, which continued at a feverish pace. The month had begun, as we saw, with a new government appointed by Horthy. It contained politicians and soldiers from across the political spectrum, something which ensured a continuing wrestling match within the Crown Council about how much, or how little, to accede to German demands to resume, in one form or another, the deportations.

For Sweden's government, the month commenced in a most positive fashion when the Americans again officially thanked Stockholm for its humanitarian efforts. Minister Johnson wrote to Günther: 'I have received instructions from my Government to express to the Government of Sweden the utmost appreciation of the Department of State and the War Refugee Board for the invaluable humanitarian services rendered by the Government in connection with the Hungarian situation.'[44] Similar evidence of bettered relations with Great Britain would also be delivered, again, later in the month to UD.[45] Additional words of praise continued to reach Sweden from private Jewish organizations, when early in September, the British section of the World Jewish Congress cabled Rabbi Ehrenpreis, expressing not only what members of the organization felt then, but something which would burnish Sweden's post-war reputation in the United Kingdom and Europe (at least among those unaware of the more problematic aspects of Sweden's dealings with Nazi Germany). 'I ought to say', the letter read, 'that we are all deeply grateful to the Swedish government for the noble part they have played, not only in giving asylum to refugees, but also with regard to the Jewish position in Hungary. Sweden's sympathy, help and interest have been of the greatest encouragement to us.'[46]

These words of support combined to do two things for Sweden's politicians and civil servants. As noted earlier, although it is always tempting to ascribe cynical explanations to any political words or gestures connected to humanitarian issues, it is also important to understand the positive consequences such political posturing could bring. Direct praise like this from the soon-to-be-victorious Allies was very important to a government trying to chart the country's post-war course. Not unimportantly, it encouraged those officials dealing directly with humanitarian issues in both Stockholm and Budapest, a mental boost surely helpful in the face of such dismal and saddening difficulties.

It is worth noting that not only Jews sought Swedish diplomatic protection. There remained a small number of 'genuine' Swedes in Budapest, and the Legation had to plan for their assistance in the event of an emergency. This emergency was, of course, the prospect of a massive Soviet assault on a city which, if the Hungarians stayed in the war and the Germans, or rather Hitler, decided that Budapest should be defended, it would be. Others seeking Swedish protection included, Danielsson wrote, 'members of the royal family, relatives of Horthy, prominent businessmen [and others]. I have answered them in the negative.'[47]

During the first week of the month, Danielsson had what must have been an interesting meeting with Lakatos's new foreign minister, the anti-Nazi Gusztáv Hennyey, who was known to be sympathetic to the Swedes.[48] The meeting began with the Hungarian thanking Sweden's government for its willingness to assume protection of Hungarian interests in the now hostile Romania, something which was in fact a mixed blessing for Danielsson, as it added to the Legation's growing responsibilities. Hennyey then told Danielsson that the 'Jewish problem' would now be 'given a national solution, but in humanitarian forms'. Claiming that the Hungarians were now 'standing up' to the Germans' constant pressure to renew deportations, Hennyey said that the new government intended to move 'the majority of Budapest's Jewish population to suitable internment camps and that all capable of working would be put into war-work'. He then acknowledged that all Jews enjoying Swedish protection would continue to be freed from the obligation of wearing 'the star' while in dwellings designated Swedish, in anticipation that travel to Sweden would soon occur. Danielsson concluded, without comment: 'The Foreign Minister considered it necessary to add, that since the situation had eased for the Jews, they had become significantly more secure and cocky in their behaviour. Their reliability was doubtful, which under the current difficult circumstances compelled the government to keep very strict control over them.'[49] Danielsson also reported the persistent rumours that Hungary would soon end its alliance with Germany and request an armistice with the Soviet Union.[50]

We have noted previously the iconic status of numbers connected to the mythology surrounding Wallenberg, most prominently that of '100,000'. In fact, there are considerable statistical difficulties in establishing with any real certainty the actual numbers of Jews saved by Wallenberg, assisted by him, helped by Langlet, or who received some form of assistance from the Legation more generally. Indeed, one of the most effective forms of protection for individual Jews was being able to remove the 'yellow star' and move about – not least to obtain rations and black-market food. Thousands did this either 'legally' after receiving one type of exemption or another, while many others dared to remove it from their garments. These numbers are impossible to even estimate with any accuracy.

However, another number frequently associated in the literature for those helped by the Swedes is 4,500, a number which has misled even otherwise careful scholars, causing them to make mistakes about Swedish activities in Budapest, and another example of how the failure to use Swedish documents has led to distortions and myth-making. This figure was the one desired by the Hungarian government in an attempt to limit the numbers receiving Swedish assistance, but it is clear that the Swedes went far beyond such an artificial and, in the circumstances, impossible limitation. Interestingly, accurate statistical information is not available even in the Swedish archives. This is because, for instance, numbers mentioned in one document which seem to be referring to one set of figures concerning a specific point in time or situation is then referred to in another document by a different number. The following examples must suffice to illuminate the great uncertainty which accompanies any attempt to determine a final and wholly credible number of people assisted by the Swedes, or even to ascertain which type of protective document is being referred to, with specific regard to one number or another.[51]

On 12 September, Danielsson sent the following coded telegram to Stockholm listing some of the important numbers in question. Importantly, this cable summarizes much of Wallenberg's paperwork up to that date:

> Between 10 August and 10 September approximately 5,000 protective passports [*skyddspass*] have been issued, with 2,000

already given out. Protective passports are not the same as emergency passports, [see] our #189. In total we have received applications for protection from 9,000 Jews, with about 190 emergency passports distributed. Because now protective passports [*skyddsbrev*] provide the possibility of removing the star and staying in Budapest, the emergency passports should for the moment be issued only to Jews only in exceptional instances.

The impending, possible change in the situation has brought again a virtual siege of the Legation by a large number of politically neutral people who fear for their lives and request the Legation's protection. May [we] in threatening situations try to assist some by issuing either a [Swedish] entry visa or emergency passport?[52]

Less than a week later, in an internal memorandum, Gösta Engzell, the one man who with certainty read everything coming out of Budapest, and who, as we have seen, was the driving force in Stockholm for all that was occurring, gave different numbers from those just received from Budapest:

The press has previously reported information about the on-going action from the Swedish side concerning the protection of Jews in Hungary ... The number of applications for such 'protective passports' is up to more than 11,000 and to date the Legation in Budapest – where these matters are dealt with by a special section which works with voluntary personnel numbering around 100 people – has issued approx. 3,000 protective passports. These numbers of course clearly show that the requirement for close connection to Sweden is no longer strictly maintained.

Recently the Hungarian authorities have requested that the Swedish action be limited to 4,500 people ... From the beginning we have hardly counted on receiving German transit visas for the journey from Hungary to Sweden, at least not for any larger numbers, and even these haven't been granted.[53]

Another factor which makes it difficult to establish the actual number of Jewish individuals affected by Sweden's assistance and rescue activities is (again) the growing number, and growing length, of lists of names being sent back and forth. The previously noted confusion experienced within UD during the height of the deportations from the countryside continued in September in both Stockholm and Budapest. This confusion was compounded because the relevant documents contain the names both of single individuals and of individuals listed with 'family members', and even this practice was extremely inconsistent.

For instance, on 9 September, Hillel Storch, a Latvian Jew who would become increasingly involved in Sweden's late war-efforts to help Jews, sent two lists of names received by the organization he represented, the World Jewish Congress. This list alone (which was compiled from diverse sources) had several dozen names, as did another one received in mid-September by UD which contained some thirty-five listings, with dozens of individual names.[54] From Budapest came lists of names that made a pretence of some numerical order, but this seemed more a ruse than any genuine 'bookkeeping' of names and numbers. It begins with the number '5009', and then falls into numerical disarray. No attempt was made to alphabetize such lists. These are but several of the literally scores of examples which confirm the difficulty of arriving at any sustainable final number of people who received Swedish diplomatic protection – and this was still prior to 15 October.[55]

By the end of the month, Engzell was compelled to sorting the names received onto 'strong' (*stark*) and 'weak' (*svag*) lists. This difference was meant to indicate the degree and strength of the individual's, or family's, connection to Sweden, which was the determining factor. Yet, as we have seen, with the passage of time, this ordinarily vital judgement became virtually meaningless. Dozens of names on both types of lists lay far outside the guiding parameters which were once in place. In effect, Engzell and the others made the practical yet moral decision not to exclude virtually any names from the lists being produced – not if they felt that this act might help a person, or family, survive.[56] The documentation makes clear that names were put on lists, sometimes with the single word 'assist' (*bistå*) on top, without any other explanation, argument or information. As noted previously, Schindler had 'his list', but the Swedish diplomats involved in rescue work during the Holocaust in Hungary had numerous lists with ever-increasing numbers of names on them.

Even the Germans were throwing figures around for the number of Jews receiving Swedish help. On 27 September, Grell and Veesenmayer of the German Legation reported to Auswärtiges Amt on the activities of the Swedish, Swiss and Portuguese Legations:

> [The Swedes have] so far almost 6,000 people who applied for naturalization [but] there are rumours that the Swedish government only approved the entry into Sweden of a very small number that was even less than the number of 400 emigrants approved by [us]. When issuing the protective passports, the Swedish Embassy has assumed and also informed the applicants that upon issuance of the passport they were also granted an

entry visa. Because of this, the Swedes find themselves in a bit of a predicament.[57]

The Swiss are reported as having 7,000 Jews under their protection who seek emigration to Palestine, and the Portuguese as having issued 900 protective passports, with twelve exit visas approved by the Germans.

Reference has already been made to Wallenberg's lengthy report of 12 September, including his response to questions transmitted to him from the Americans in Stockholm.[58] It is in many ways a repeat of his previous ones, although shorter. It was sent along with two annexes drafted in response to Olsen's request for information about Wallenberg's activities – questions which, for some reason, Engzell thought were 'more or less odd'.[59] It began with Wallenberg's appraisal that 'Since the last report was sent, the situation has changed numerous times, without any final clarity appearing.'[60] Though much of the report recapitulates and summarizes information sent in the preceding weeks, it is a compelling document, for as with his other reports, it illuminates in detail much of the daily persecution, humiliation and torment being visited upon the Jews of Budapest. The immediate threat of deportation had receded, but life bore little semblance to normality.

After describing the relative advantages enjoyed by Jews who had received some form of Swedish help, Wallenberg then suggested something which seems to have displeased his superiors in Stockholm: 'It would be advantageous for the Swedish Jewish action if the easing of measures against the Jews was publicized in the Swedish press. This is because the Hungarian authorities, eager to show the world their good will, have motivated their relaxation of measures with reference to [such publicity].' In lukewarm terms, Wallenberg also noted the limited cooperation with Valdemar Langlet and his SRK activities, including 'cooperation concerning obtaining houses and other spaces'.

Knowing that the number of people 'employed' by his section had raised some eyebrows, Wallenberg felt it necessary to explain why:

> The number of those seeking help is enormous. Thousands of applications are received and checked. In order to explain the necessity of the large organization [built up], it can be added that the majority of the personnel have on several occasions had to work for 24 hours without halting.
>
> Another reason that so many people are needed is the fact that new orders or ultimatums from the authorities make it necessary, sometimes in only days or maybe even only hours, to conduct enormous amounts of work.[61]

As noted above, the report's final section was headed with the words 'The dissolution of the Jewish section'. This proves that Wallenberg believed, at least on one level, that his work was done, allowing him to anticipate a return to Stockholm. He had obviously been thinking much about this, and presumably looked forward to it. Of interest also is the report's second annex. Entitled (in English) 'Reply to questionnaire', Wallenberg listed rationed foodstuffs such as milk, sugar and meat; Jews received 'one-third of the Christian ration'. This was followed by a longer list including butter, rice and flour, for which, he wrote, 'there was no Jewish ration. However, in general Jews do not suffer from shortage [*sic*] of food as they seem to be able to procure the necessities of life on the black market.' In a 'bullet' list of information given, 'e/' says: 'As far as the Swedish action is concerned, there is no difference between children and grown-ups.' Noting also his extensive lobbying activity with Hungarian authorities, he believed that, as a result, 'Some of these authorities have consented partially to disregard existing laws.' This report to the WRB concluded with the following: 'The idea of organizing special Jewish ghettos in one part of Budapest for approx. 4,500 Jews was quite near to execution but had to be abandoned because of the changed attitude in government circles and the friendlier treatment of Jews protected by Sweden.'

This study has argued that Wallenberg's mission and tactics must be seen, at least partly, within a rather unique Swedish political context, and that outside this context, any understanding of his achievements is a distorted one. This is again visible at the end of September, where we see a particularly vivid example of exactly how far the government and people of Sweden had come in their response to Nazi Germany's war against European Jewry. This author's earlier work demonstrated that Undersecretary Gösta Engzell, the man at the centre of Sweden's response, epitomized and motivated his ministry's dramatic shift from – as previously characterized – 'indifference to activism'.[62] Since then, other Swedish scholars have analysed the role anti-Semitism played in Swedish policy towards Jewish refugees. For instance, in response to the 'refugee crisis' which drastically worsened following Hitler's March 1938 Anschluss with Austria, Sweden raised its political barriers to Jewish entry, making it all but impossible for more than a handful to obtain sanctuary. Late that year, Engzell responded to a colleague who was deeply worried that Sweden would soon suffer 'an invasion of Jews'. Engzell wrote: 'Naturally, [UD] is very restrictive concerning Jewish emigrants', and '[We] are very conscious about the danger of a growing anti-semitism here and [we] have well seen small signs already.'[63]

Now, in September 1944, one of Engzell's aides wrote to Budapest regarding a case which in many ways exemplifies how UD came to learn of Jews in trouble, and how it sought to help them. The rhetoric employed by this Swedish official could not be more different from that used in 1938. It began when Erik Kockum, a prominent Swedish businessman, rang Engzell's legal division, asking that a protective paper should be issued for an acquaintance of his in Budapest, a 'Chief Executive Foeldiak'. Kockum then wrote to UD's Rolf Sohlman: 'I don't want to neglect to rapidly thank you for your friendliness in arranging a protective passport [*skyddspass*] for Foeldiak. Even though one has gradually become accustomed to all the persecutions of Jews, one is in some way especially moved when it concerns someone [previously] met, even if only briefly. In accordance then with your proposal, I will today cable him according to your copy, and I hope that the thing can be arranged.'[64]

Sohlman immediately contacted the Legation in Budapest, and the next day responded to Kockum. His response shows just how far he and other Swedes had come in their reaction to 'all the persecutions of Jews':

> Brother [*Broder*], As per your letter of the 27th of this month, may I hereby confirm, that the Legation in Budapest is authorized to provide a protective passport [*skyddspass*] for direktor Foeldiak, *naturally under the assumption that the person in question is a Jew.* If this is not the case, the Legation, in accordance with its instructions, must return the question to the ministry. In principle, protective passports for non-Jews can only be considered in exceptional cases and with the presumption that [he] has in one way or another close connections to Sweden.[65] [Emphasis added.]

Obviously Wallenberg decided not to return to Stockholm during the latter half of September, and his last report of the month was written on 29 September.[66] That particular Friday at the end of the month must have been calm, because he also found the time to write a fairly long letter to his mother. Now, almost three months into his mission, this four-page report continues to display the qualities of observation, analysis and understanding which characterize almost all of Raoul Wallenberg's correspondence and writing. Ironically, now just two weeks before the fateful 15 October, the first line says: 'Since the last report the situation has improved somewhat.' Even when describing essential 'legal' matters involving Jews and the Hungarian authorities, he writes with an impressive precision, clearly still taking his task of reporting with great seriousness. Virtually every line in this report, like so many other Swedish reports from Budapest, contains a plethora of tragically commonplace details which make up both individual and collective Holocaust narratives, documenting the destruction of individuals and communities. Some of them may seem trivial or innocuous, yet they constitute part of the literature of destruction.

Wallenberg reported on the thousands of Jews sent out of Budapest for forced labour on defence installations, and of hostile relations between the Germans and Hungarians. Diplomatic if not dramatic interventions are described, which gained freedom from arrest for a few individual Jews, as are the difficulties of getting letters past the censors for dispatch to applicants for protective papers. In yet another illustration of why the numbers of people assisted by the Swedes are so difficult to establish, Wallenberg gives similar yet still varying numbers to those Engzell had used just days before:

> No new applications were accepted after 16 September. Therefore, the [Jewish] division's final closure can currently take place as soon as the pending cases, about 8,000, which have not yet been evaluated regarding the granting of protective passports, are processed. According to current plans, there should be about 4,500 protective passports to be issued. Of these, about 2,700 are already distributed.[67]

More problematically but not surprisingly, he reports in some detail incidents where, it appears, Swedish papers are being sold for money. This was allegedly done by some employees of the Legation but all, he writes after investigating, are exonerated. He is pleased that all his volunteers, plus their families – about 300 people – are exempt from wearing the 'yellow star'. Finally, he praises the work of the division (and implicitly his own), saying that some Jews were released from internment camps because 'The officials responsible for these orders of release were thoroughly lobbied [*bearbetats*].' Not incidentally, there is evident deterioration in the quality of his signature – fatigue and stress were surely taking their toll.

Yet he found the time and energy to dictate a letter to his beloved mother. Expressed in much the same style of his correspondence years before with his grandfather Gustaf, Wallenberg provides a vivid description of what he was doing and how he was feeling. The entire letter is of great interest, not least for what he says about meeting an unnamed representative of Heinrich Himmler. After describing the effects of the constant air raids, Wallenberg writes: 'Despite this, everything is moving along very well. I gave some nice dinner parties for various officials who are important to my work.' Wallenberg then describes his activities to his mother:

Our operation has been very effective so far. I have a staff of about 115 people, all of whom are working very hard. My own day consists mainly of seeing people who work here and who need to be given various instructions. Also people who bring me news ...

I also travel around in my [car] and visit various officials. I enjoy these negotiations very much. They are often extremely dramatic. [Recently], I went to a detainment camp on the Austrian border. The commandant refused to receive me at first, then he allotted me five minutes, and finally, after negotiating for four hours, I managed to have eighty people released the very same day and sent to Budapest. It was quite a moving sight.[68]

I had hoped to come home right after closing down the section, as they said. Unfortunately my trip home seems to have been quite delayed, since the closing of the section is also taking a long time.[69]

For Wallenberg and the Swedes – in both Budapest and Stockholm – September ended with more applications for assistance arriving than ever before. Engzell, whose decisions seemed always supported by his superiors at UD, continued to respond in a practical and non-bureaucratic manner. During this entire period he allowed Danielsson great leeway in making important decisions, and maintained this attitude even as things got ever more complicated. Engzell's stance, which could well have been different, reflected fully his desire to save lives during the Holocaust:

I have herewith the honour of sending to you a list in three copies of applications received by the Ministry for assistance for Jewish individuals in Hungary. The connection to Sweden appears to be, in these cases, of the type for which assistance in some form may be provided, if according to your judgement there exists possibilities to save those in question.[70]

Saving Jews in Budapest, as we have repeatedly seen, was not only the desire and work of one man.

WALLENBERG DOES BUSINESS IN BUDAPEST

There is another aspect of Wallenberg's activities in Budapest which has to date escaped notice, but which could conceivably have affected his work there. It has often been surmised but never proven that Wallenberg engaged in activities separate from his humanitarian mission, generally thought to be some type of espionage for one country, or agency, or another.[71] This assertion remains a mere theory because of the lack of credible and convincing evidence.

There is, however, evidence suggesting that he may have engaged in another activity unconnected to his official function. In this case it is of a type which comes as no surprise, if one considers Wallenberg's background and circumstances before accepting his mission. It appears that while in Budapest, Wallenberg made at least some effort to either conduct business then, and/or to create future business opportunities for himself, Lauer and possibly even the Wallenberg empire. This will be discussed later. Connected to this, but ostensibly even more mundane, are questions arising from information related to Wallenberg's life back in Stockholm, and what his future would be back home after completing his tasks. These may at first glance appear uninteresting, but they are connected to the creation and maintenance of some myths about him.

Questions about what Wallenberg would have done in Stockholm (or elsewhere), had he returned home – as all involved had every reason to believe he would – are absent in the literature or other representations. Yet issues concerning life after Budapest were unquestionably present for him while he was there. It is perfectly natural that Wallenberg should plan or imagine his life after the war ended, even while engaging in his humanitarian work. This concerns us here because this issue illuminates again the powerful tendency to view and understand Wallenberg's story as somehow apart from, or outside, 'normalcy'. And this tendency has contributed to the general inability or unwillingness to understand him as a 'normal' man. This in turn has contributed to the important historical distortions already discussed.

The point bears repeating that even for Holocaust heroes, good history must trump historical fantasy. It must again be emphasized – however obvious it seems – that Wallenberg was a man with ordinary goals, hopes, fears and worries. The evidence leaves no doubt that he planned to resume his life, which meant, in his case, a search for professional and personal happiness. He certainly was concerned about future opportunities within the Wallenberg sphere, as we saw in one letter to Lauer asking his partner to contact his cousin Jacob. One means of doing so was by looking into and pursuing business ideas while in Budapest. Exactly what he would have been doing in, for instance, July 1946, or March 1947, cannot of course be known, but there is nothing nefarious in asserting that while on his humanitarian mission, Wallenberg also engaged in business. After all, he needed to make a living, and it appeared most likely that he would do this as a businessman.

Such an understanding of Wallenberg neither contradicts, nor should it obviate, the prevailing image of an energetic young man working with enormous energy and imagination to help others. It will be remembered that his grandfather's training was not intended to develop an altruistic rescuer of other human beings in a time of crises, but rather to educate a man who would enter business and make money, albeit in an honest and decent way. When considering Wallenberg today, we should not forget that in 1944 he had his whole life ahead of him. Therefore there is nothing extraordinary about him devoting some of his time in Budapest to think about and plan for a future in the post-war world of Swedish, European and world business. Such mundane matters are not what is generally considered when heroes are remembered, but in the case of Wallenberg, it is a fact. Importantly I think, it provides an opportunity to reflect that an almost unavoidable 'ordinariness' existed within the same man who was doing extraordinary things. Moreover, this seems to be the case with most rescuers of Jews during the Holocaust, gentile and Jewish.

As the evidence is considered, it may be remembered that Wallenberg pledged to UD's leadership that he would cut all ongoing business ties 'during the period in question'.[72] Not only did he not do that, he also left behind, naturally – as documents from the Lauer collection prove – bills to pay, including rent on his apartment. In fact, the day Wallenberg left for Budapest, he and one Eberhard Håkanson signed a legally binding business agreement, rather prosaic in content. Before leaving, Wallenberg decided to invest with Håkanson in the printing and distribution (for profit, it was hoped) of two business catalogues. Although only a small venture between the two men, it indicates both that Wallenberg had some capital to use in pursuing his own ideas, and that he conducted normal business up to the very day that he left.[73] Lauer's letter of 21 August to Wallenberg reported ongoing discussions involving the legal firm Justitia, and a man named Mr Pettersson – 6,000 Swedish crowns were in dispute.[74] On 25 August, Lauer told Wallenberg that the dispute was being solved because part of the amount had been recovered: 'So don't worry, after all the [total] amount might well be paid soon.'[75]

More salient for our concerns is the fact that Wallenberg, while serving Sweden's foreign ministry, used his correspondence and telephone conversations to discuss with Lauer both ongoing and future business ventures. In many respects their extensive correspondence is clear and easy to interpret. Regarding these business issues however, the documentation, while making it clear that business was discussed, is less clear about actual outcomes and concrete future plans.

Lauer seems to have initiated most of the discussion of business while Wallenberg was in Budapest, but it is clear that Wallenberg remained deeply interested, even concerned at times, about some of his ventures in Sweden. He took time to think about them and discuss them with his business partner, even – remarkably enough – after the *Nyilas* takeover. A minor piece of evidence in this regard may be seen, although this is speculative, in one of the first entries Wallenberg made in his appointment's diary after arriving. Next to the entry 'Trade Ministry' is a 'Dr M' and his telephone number. Why Wallenberg would be in contact with Hungary's ministry of trade so soon after arrival, in view of the nature of his mission, must remain a matter for speculation – but that contact information is there.[76]

Far more certain evidence about this is found in the long letter written by Lauer between 21 and 28 August (discussed above), where a long paragraph, under the heading 'Manager Sternberg', discusses the Linum flax spinning mill (presumably in Budapest) that Sternberg had directed for twenty years: 'I believe that it is our duty to make it possible for such a person, who could set up a new industry here, to enter Sweden ... We are trying to get Sternberg an emergency passport and afterwards we think he could set up a factory here. Anyway, it would be interesting if you could talk to him already and ask him to draw up plans for a hemp-spinning mill and to hand them over to you.'[77]

During most of Wallenberg's time in Budapest, the two discussed *Banankompaniet* (The Banana Company), which appears to have been a new venture for them. Telegrams were exchanged between the two, using the company's name, and on 29 September, Wallenberg wrote to Lauer, asking him, 'If possible, please forward the enclosed letter to Ahlén & Holm Corp, Stockholm. I am very happy about the transition to The Banana Company which I have planned for a long time. This corporation will definitely have certain advantages because of this transition, and I thank you so much for your confirmation, given by telephone, that our agreement will continue to function.'[78] On this occasion Wallenberg again asked Lauer to contact Jacob Wallenberg to ask him 'if he is very angry that I am staying here for such a long time and if I therefore have lost my chances to continue the work started at the Enskilda Bank'.

Then, on 28 October, just two weeks after the *Nyilas* chaos engulfed Budapest, and when Wallenberg struggled most of the day to help Jews and was in some danger himself, Lauer addressed a letter several pages in length, which dealt almost exclusively with business matters, to 'Legation Secretary Raoul Wallenberg'.[79] It began by thanking Wallenberg for two letters of 12 and 22 October, in which Wallenberg had clearly asked him some questions about ongoing affairs, 'which I [Lauer] will answer as follows'. He told Wallenberg that the matters connected with The Banana Company are taking up most of his time, making it almost impossible to attend to matters connected to their older joint company, Mellaneuropeiska AB (sometimes, as here, referred to as Meropa). Lauer noted that a final agreement with Sven Salén concerning The Banana Company cannot be entered into, 'until your situation is fully known and I have a hundred percent certainty that you will be my colleague with BK. I wanted to first see if you and I have sufficient capacity to deal with BK's business.' Lauer then noted that BK has a future potential 'to sell bananas worth eight to twelve million crowns'.

After detailing some other aspects of this venture, including buying raisins in California, and items from the food giant Kellogg in America, Lauer wrote the following:

> Everything depends on how we build up our sales organization ... Can you possibly investigate in Budapest if you can find a competent person who understands fruit conserves, who has practical knowledge and long experience – if so, try to get him for us! Equally we need a man who understands baking ... If you would find such especially competent people, we would try to obtain entry visas for them. CEO Soor of the Manfred-Weiss corporation can surely advise you about this urgent need. But don't forget that producing common marmalade is not the same as producing baked goods.

Lauer continued by describing a number of ongoing issues, including troubles with business connections in Paris created because there was no one who could travel there to deal with the problems. Then Lauer wrote something remarkable, particularly when seen with hindsight:

> We have conducted several negotiations with Russian trade representatives here in Stockholm. If you can't get away in time [before the Russian invasion], then you will have to travel through Russia, Moscow, and it would be good if you could investigate possibilities for us while there. I enclose copies of our correspondence with the Russian trade representatives. Meanwhile I have ordered 1,000kg of caviar for Christmas, if it arrives in time.
>
> It is not altogether impossible that I can also come to Moscow while you are there, but I can't promise for sure because the formalities imply certain difficulties.

The business part of this extraordinary letter concludes with Lauer informing Wallenberg: 'But, as I have already several times said. The greatest hindrance is that I can't take care sufficiently of urgent

Meropa business, and we run the risk of being separated from these interesting and profitable business opportunities.' The final instance of Lauer writing to Wallenberg about business, at least in the available documents, was on Wednesday, 15 November. In a poignant yet playful tone, he chided Wallenberg about losing his business sensibilities because he had become a diplomat: 'Have you, since becoming a diplomat, completely forgotten what is customary within the world of business? I predict that we will have much to do and that I will have to scold you ... in order for you to lose the diplomatic habits.'[80]

There is no doubt that business issues interested and engaged Wallenberg simultaneous to his humanitarian actions in Budapest, but the available evidence does not allow larger conclusions to be drawn. Clearly he violated his promise to UD not to engage in any business activities while there, which, it will be remembered, was something British officials suspected he might do. Presumably it became known to others in the city that he was making contacts with individuals on a purely business basis, but if or how this affected his diplomacy is unclear. Perhaps thinking about his future business opportunities at home was a welcome distraction from all the misery and stress Wallenberg was facing. What is certain that neither he nor Lauer felt any qualms about discussing business in the midst of a genocide. It also demonstrates that even heroes think about their future while negotiating with murderers.

DID WALLENBERG MEET ADOLF EICHMANN?

One of the more prominent myths about Wallenberg which has become a staple of the hagiographic literature is his alleged meeting and confrontation with the infamous SS *Obersturmführer* Adolf Eichmann. Eichmann was, of course – not least after capture in 1960 – one of the most widely known of the major Nazi criminals. As we have seen, he also played a major role in the destruction of Hungarian Jewry. For the concerns of this study, however, Eichmann's role is far less central, as he had little if anything to do with shaping the German and Hungarian response to neutral diplomacy; the internal dynamics of German politics and policies in Budapest and Berlin ensured that Eichmann was reduced mainly to railing in frustration about what the neutrals were doing. On the other hand, in the context of narrative drama it is understandable that such an 'exciting' element as Eichmann – so evidently a villain, with Wallenberg the hero – has been given such a prominent role. Scholars, on the other hand, have given this story little if any credence, and have attached no significance to it.

Nonetheless, because this 'encounter' is so prevalent in the hagiographic framework around Wallenberg, it is necessary to present, even briefly, evidence which reconfigures this element of myth in the Wallenberg saga. In fact, according to the available evidence, this part of Wallenberg's story is more connected to the problematic issue of him conducting business while in Budapest than it is to his humanitarian diplomacy. That troubling issue is made more fraught if, as the data suggests, Wallenberg may have attempted, or at least considered, conducting business with Kurt Becher, another SS officer who was, as recent research has demonstrated, Heinrich Himmler's influential and effective personal representative in the Nazi plundering, both of the general Hungarian economy and in the economic destruction of Hungarian Jewry. Wallenberg and Becher met, the evidence shows, at least a handful of times.

To return first to the Eichmann myth, we shall review their alleged dinner meeting, during which Eichmann, the quintessential 'desk-top' killer, was challenged by Wallenberg in ways both practical and moral to such an extent that it shook the Nazi's allegiance to his cause, and to the killing of Jews. In fact, it seems all but certain the two never met in Budapest, but if they did, it was not over good food and drinks, followed by lengthy discussion. Even more unlikely is the possibility that Wallenberg could have had any moral influence on such a decadent and committed killer as Eichmann, or that he made Eichmann 'feel guilty' about what he had been doing to Jews for years.

There are two sources for the 'dinner myth', and both have been used to expand upon and embroider that which did not happen. The first and most influential source comes from the lengthy description of the 'encounter' by Lars Berg, the junior Swedish diplomat sent to Budapest in August. First published in 1949 in his original Swedish account, and then years later in both Swedish and English, Berg's text unfortunately doesn't provide an exact date for what he purports was a long and bibulous dinner, but the reader can contextualize it to sometime in September.[81] Regrettably, much of this first-hand account has a novelistic feel to it, encumbering it with much implausible embellishment and making it a far less reliable account than it otherwise might have been. Two other historians who have examined this issue have also dismissed Berg's account of this purported meeting as both implausible and certain not to have occurred.[82] The second source is Wallenberg's letter to his mother of 29 September, already referred to: 'A few days ago I had invited some very interesting big game, namely Himmler's representative ... Unfortunately, something came up at work at the last minute and [it] prevented him from coming. He is quite a nice man who, according to what he himself says, will soon shoot himself.'[83] In this English-language publication, Eichmann's name is given in brackets, but no source is given for this information. Hungarian historian Szabolcs Szita, on the other hand, is sure that it is Becher to whom this letter refers, and this seems most likely.[84] There exists, however, a possibility that they did encounter one another in late November or early December during one of Wallenberg's forays to the Hungarian–Austrian border to rescue 'Swedish' Jews forced to march from Budapest. In his last report, written on 8 December 1944, Wallenberg reported that the effort had to be broken off because of 'the threats of violence from the Germans in Eichmann's *kommando*'.[85] Eichmann himself was often present when Jews were 'handed over' by the Hungarians at the Hegyshalom border crossing, but even if they did encounter each other during this episode, they certainly would not have had a long, discursive tête-à-tête, as has been imagined by some authors.

One source which might be expected to reveal the existence of such an important encounter is Wallenberg's appointment's diary, which provides the best if still fragmentary evidence of whom he met, and when. When studying his habits regarding this diary, we can surmise it is likely that he would have entered Eichmann's name, had they in fact met. But Eichmann's name is found only in the diary's telephone listings and was entered soon after Wallenberg's July arrival. There is some difficulty in reading Wallenberg's handwriting, which wasn't good in any case, and had deteriorated further under the circumstances. On the other hand, there is no question that Wallenberg met, or was scheduled to meet, SS *Obersturmbannführer* (Lt Colonel) Kurt Becher at least six times. According to Wallenberg's diary, the first scheduled time was Saturday afternoon, 9 September.[86] This is interesting because, according to an extensive study about Becher by Hungarian historians G. Kádár and Z. Vági, Becher was Himmler's personal representative, 'responsible for promoting SS economic interests in Hungary and who in that capacity orchestrated and personally benefited from the expropriation of vast amounts of Jewish wealth'.[87] Furthermore, amongst the many aspects of the Hungarian Holocaust which 'stand out' within the tragic entirety of the event, the authors demonstrate that

> The wealth and property of Hungarian Jews was expropriated at unprecedented speed and thoroughness even before the deportations began. The large number of people who were looted and the quantity of the wealth that was seized as well as the speed with which all this was done made the liquidation of the Hungarian Jews a unique chapter in the global history of the Holocaust.[88]

Importantly for our concerns, Becher had, according to Kádár and Vági, nothing at all to do with the physical destruction of the Jews: 'neither Becher nor his office had anything to do with the [Final Solution], every phase of which was directed by a different SS Main Office ... [though] his organization was irrelevant from the point of view of the [Final Solution], Becher was in connection with the process by negotiating with various Jewish groups and riding the side-waves of deportation'.[89] Wallenberg does not figure at all in this detailed study, apart from in a single footnote unrelated to Becher's economic activities.[90] On the other hand, Szita writes that Becher negotiated with Wallenberg and other neutral diplomats in late November about some rescue issues.[91] Yet Wallenberg's last meeting with Becher, at least as entered in his diary, was scheduled for the evening (19.00) of 3 November.[92] Becher's name does not appear in any Swedish official documents, nor in anything written by Wallenberg, apart of course from his diary.[93]

We can conclude only that Wallenberg seems to have met a number of times with someone who was one of the most influential SS men in Budapest during the Hungarian Holocaust, but who had little or nothing to do with the activities of the neutral diplomats. As for Becher himself, Szita wrote: 'Becher was a pragmatic and cynical National Socialist, one with whom it might be possible to conduct business even after the war.'[94] Kádár and Vági concluded that he was 'a highly intelligent, unscrupulous realist and cynic, who in the face of Germany's imminent military defeat recognized that belonging to the Nazi establishment could cause him serious problems after the end of the war ... He ... escaped punishment in all prosecutions brought against him, and in [Bremen] in 1995 died at the age of 86, a multi-millionaire.'[95] The available evidence, it should be emphasized, reveals nothing about what Wallenberg and he discussed.

Wallenberg did meet other 'desk-top' killers in Budapest, including – at least four times – Colonel of the Hungarian Gendarmerie László Ferenczy, one of the men most directly responsible for the rounding-up and deportation to their deaths of hundreds of thousands of Jews. He also met, on numerous occasions, another prominent Hungarian official named Nándor Batizfalvy, the interior ministry official who, according to Braham, 'provided the legislative framework for the expulsion of the "alien" Jews from Hungary in 1941'.[96] Batizfalvy's position within KEOKH made him a particularly important, if somewhat unsavoury, connection for the Swedes.

It is clear that Wallenberg's efforts to establish as broad a contact network as possible paid dividends. Of course, all of those he met had their own reasons for meeting with him, with all seeking the greatest possible advantage for their own interests. It was a time of great tension and cynicism, and obviously Wallenberg was capable of manipulating people for his own interests. Every sentient person in the city was aware of the extent of the ongoing neutral diplomacy, with all meetings and negotiations conducted in the shadow of the Red Army's inexorable if sometimes slow advance. Moreover, for those with an eye not only to survival but to the post-war world of European business, it was evident that the acquaintance of a Swedish diplomat named Wallenberg was an asset which might pay off well one day.

SWEDES, JEWS AND GERMANS

We have seen that Anger, Wallenberg and Langlet sometimes referred to what they felt was the harmful apathy afflicting Budapest's Jews, and their apparent unwillingness to 'help themselves'. Though this may have been true regarding the majority of the population, particularly in the occupation's first months, it is not a sufficiently accurate appraisal of the community's Jewish leadership, some of whom were compelled by Eichmann to serve on the 'Jewish Council'.[97] In fact, several of Wallenberg's first and most valuable contacts were with individuals 'serving' on the 'Jewish Council'. Men such as Samu Stern, Károly Wilhelm and particularly Ernö Petö (whom Wallenberg met frequently) were his and the other neutrals' natural allies. As Randolph Braham has written: 'the Jews of Budapest argued that what had happened in the provinces could not possibly happen in the supposedly civilized capital, in full view of foreign diplomats'.[98] In fact, Wallenberg's good relationship with the 'Council' was crucial in making him more effective.

Their knowledge of local needs and circumstances helped guide Wallenberg through the bureaucratic thicket of Hungarian officialdom. They understood the often tense state of relations between the Germans and Hungarian leadership, and there seems little question that Wallenberg (and the other neutral diplomats) benefited from their guidance in exploiting the tensions between the erstwhile allies. Budapest's Jewish leadership showed a degree of political skill and shrewdness, taking advantage (particularly from the summer onwards) of political opportunities which scarcely existed for their counterparts in other 'Jewish Councils' which had existed and then been destroyed in Nazi-occupied Europe. The split within the 'Council' and community caused by Reszö Kasztner's rescue efforts was unfortunate, but it seems not to have negatively affected cooperation with the Swedes, who were not involved with Kasztner's and his Va'ada's activities before 15 October. Kasztner himself did not remember in his post-war report any particularly noteworthy cooperation with Wallenberg and the neutrals, although he describes their activities, and praises Wallenberg, Lutz and some others.[99]

The 'Council' was obviously eager to cooperate with Wallenberg, not only because he eventually decided to provide it, as we have seen, with direct financing. Perhaps just as significant was the vitally important psychological support the Jews derived from knowing that they were not entirely on their own. One gets the impression that Wallenberg and the leaders of the Jewish community cooperated and functioned quite well together, even if the community was riven with conflicts and controversies. There was, of course, sound logic in the creation of close cooperation with the neutral diplomats, but that was no guarantee it would actually happen. Indeed, speaking of the men with whom Wallenberg cooperated, historian Yehuda Bauer concluded poignantly that although men such as Stern, Freudiger, Wilhelm and Petö 'hated each other's guts, by and large, as Jewish leaders mostly do, most of them tried their best'.[100] This included putting aside their differences and rivalries and cooperating with newcomers such as Wallenberg.

Moreover, there was a second tier of Jewish leadership which was, according to historian Asher Cohen, neither passive nor apathetic:

> The emergence of a relatively young leadership within the Council is of considerable significance. These were lower-echelon workers who were influenced by Zionist activities and were not prepared to agree to everything proposed by the older generation ... The Jewish leadership in Budapest, perhaps under the influence of Zionist activity, gradually and hesitantly began to develop a more independent and more dynamic line of action.[101]

Tragically, this evolution took place only during the summer after the deportations were halted, yet coincided with Wallenberg's arrival. It seems reasonable to surmise that when he met some of these younger men, he found people less suspicious of foreigners and more willing to create a system of cooperation with an outsider. This activist cooperation manifested itself not least in the organization of soup kitchens, orphanages, shelters for the elderly, impromptu schools and other cultural activities. These essential if small-scale and unglamorous activities were led by men such as Ottó Roboz and Ottó Komoly. They were Zionists who, with their colleagues, may well have heard from Wallenberg his sympathies for the Zionist project he had admired while in Palestine in the previous decade. All manner of cooperation and mutual support between these men and Wallenberg would become particularly urgent after 15 October.

Nonetheless, there were significant divisions within the Jewish community, divisions which left, for some survivors, legacies of deep bitterness and resentment. Like most Jewish communities which suffered the agonies of Nazism, Budapest's community was by no means unified even as it struggled to survive. Existing social and political hierarchies were exacerbated by the extreme crisis caused by impending doom, and of course not everyone within the community was able to exhibit solidarity with their co-religionists. It is only natural that those receiving protection (of whatever form), such as the Swedes and other neutrals were providing, would be targets of resentment from those who were unable to obtain exemptions, protective papers, shelter, or other forms of neutral assistance.

This chapter began with a letter written in the early 1990s by a Budapest survivor who found it impossible to join the ranks of those praising Wallenberg. In that letter, Neomi Reukei accused Wallenberg of helping only community elites, causing resentment between those Jews who received Swedish protection and others who did not. She also wrote: 'The district where I lived with my family, Obuda (the third) a small but strong community of about 5000, perished totally ... Nobody in my community was saved by Swedish papers.' And that because of this, 'I would like to praise Raoul Wallenberg, but alas, I'm unable to do so.'[102]

Hers was unlikely to be a solitary experience, although there is no widespread evidence that Wallenberg and the Swedes discriminated against poorer or less assimilated Jews. The charge that her family and community found it difficult if not impossible to obtain Swedish protection may have an element of geography within it. Obuda was relatively distant both from the Swedish Legation on Géllert Hill in the eleventh district, and from Wallenberg's other important location(s), established at almost the other end of the city in Pest's eighth district. It seems certain also that highly assimilated Jews (who formed the vast majority of Budapest Jewry) may simply have known how to contact and press neutral diplomats for some measure of protection and other protective measures which Orthodox Jews lacked. More generally, as J. Lévai has written, there was resentment amongst many Jews in Budapest against those with greater resources: 'difficulty was caused by the obvious fact that the wealthy Jews were able to save their lives in a number of different ways, whereas the poor ones were unable to do anything whatsoever'.[103] The variation in Swedish assistance available to different social classes has been confirmed by recent research. Swedish historian Laura Palosuo concludes that 'people who obtained access to protected houses in the International ghetto and could thus escape the labour service system, the [central] ghetto, and the death marches often belonged to upper social classes'. She adds, however: 'During the autumn, the neutral legations differentiated less between individuals seeking help, and the social background of the protected became more diverse.'[104]

On the other hand, Wallenberg himself most likely caused problems with his 'housing' scheme from early August. He had fairly advanced plans to assist some Jews at the apparent expense of others, something which was bound to cause resentment – even if he did not anticipate such a reaction. His report of 6 August concluded with a paragraph titled 'The Establishment of a Camp'. His idea was to use an apartment building already designated a 'Jewish house', on Pozsonyi utca 3, as a 'Swedish house'. The building lay in a neighbourhood in the fifth district which evolved into what came to be called the 'international ghetto'. As we have seen, Wallenberg proposed that this Jewish house

> [should] be emptied of its current inhabitants and instead, house there an equal number of Jews who are under the Legation's protection. It would be greatly desirable to be able to pay moving costs and limited damages to those Jews who have to in this way suddenly leave their homes. Afterwards, nearby houses on the same street will be turned into a Swedish assembly camp. On average, one should be able to count on approximately 100 people in every building.[105]

Even though the plan was not realized, it is quite probable that those who might have been affected had heard about it. The presence of hundreds of Jewish volunteers in Wallenberg's division surely guaranteed that no secrets could be kept about plans or ideas.

We have seen that Wallenberg reported to Stockholm suspicions that Swedish papers were being sold and purchased from Legation offices. Though he 'exonerated' the accused, it seems far more likely than not that at least some authentic Swedish papers were bought and sold.[106] The buyers and sellers who constituted such a 'market' would inevitably be those with connections and/or sufficient remaining financial resources to purchase them. Swedish documentation, perhaps naturally enough, makes no mention of the notion that in some way the Swedes, and Wallenberg, were favouring Jews who were more affluent than others. Per Anger makes no reference to different classes of Jews receiving a more favourable reception than others, but in such a situation there are bound to be those more able to call upon the attention and services of foreign diplomats in such an unstable situation. Indeed, seemingly protecting himself against such charges, Wallenberg wrote, in a rather fulsome letter to Iver Olsen: 'It has been my objective all the time, to try to help all Jews ... I have worked on the hypothesis that those, who were no longer under the obligation to carry the star, would help their fellow suffers [sic].'[107] Additionally, Wallenberg comments on

the social cleavages within the Budapest community, writing disdainfully about '[the] small stream of particularly unpleasant people, mostly of high social status, who elbow their way into my office'.[108]

By the very nature of things, those who benefited from Sweden's
humanitarian assistance would be targets of resentment for those who
did not. The daily persecutions, humiliations and death threats
imposed by Hungarian and German authorities naturally worsened
any existing fractures in social solidarity – this is human nature.
Moreover, it was inevitable and unavoidable that neither Wallenberg
and his colleagues, nor Sweden's government could help everyone.
What was new was that in holocaustal Budapest there were outsiders
trying to help. It is therefore necessary and appropriate to emphasize
who in fact does bear the responsibility for unpleasant fractures in
social solidarity. That responsibility does not lie upon Wallenberg or
the other Swedes for having to 'choose' to help some but not others;
nor upon Jews 'pushing' their way upstairs at the Swedish Legation,
desperate to obtain help for themselves and their families. It lies, naturally, upon the perpetrators. It was they who chose to do what they
did – the vast majority of Jews in Budapest (and elsewhere during the
Holocaust) had no choices. The responsibility for the breakdown in
social solidarity amongst some Jews in Budapest rests with those who,
in spite of the accelerating 'difficulties' they were encountering in
achieving their malignant goal of eliminating Budapest's Jewry, never
stopped trying. We may conclude this survey of the key month of
September by looking at a secret report sent from T. Grell to Berlin on
29 September. It illuminates without ambiguity what the perpetrators
thought of those seeking to save lives:

> Following events at the local Swedish Legation, which I have pre-
> viously reported, Councillor von Chopey at the Hungarian
> Foreign Ministry spoke with me to explain the following.
>
> At the moment there is great indignation within Hungarian cir-
> cles about the behaviour at the <u>local Swedish Legation</u> regarding
> the indiscriminate and unlimited issuance of <u>Swedish protective
> passports for Hungarian Jews</u>, all the more so [because] the
> Swedish Legation is said to have formally made demands for spe-
> cial protection for these Jews in a rather arrogant note. [von
> Chopey] said he ensured that, in return, the Swedish Legation
> was clearly reprimanded in an even harsher note.
>
> The Hungarian side has the impression that when issuing these
> protective passports and demands for protecting [Jews], the
> Swedes and Swiss do not really seek to achieve actual departures
> of Jews from Hungary in order to accommodate Jews in their

countries, but rather do this only in order to get high marks from the English and Americans ...

Therefore the Hungarian authorities request ... that the Germans now actually grant the visas which have been requested for scheduled groups of Jews, and that these countries be forced to accommodate these groups of Jews. Concerning Sweden, Chopey knows with certainty that at the Swedish Legation, only 14 entry permits were approved.[109] [Underline in the original.]

As autumn began, Wallenberg and his colleagues believed, not without reason, that things might remain relatively calm at least until the expected and much feared Soviet onslaught. They also believed, and rightly so, that they had actually accomplished something – but their challenges would escalate exponentially within a fortnight. For after 15 October, they would find themselves confronting, and in the middle of, another unexpected and radically violent situation which would test them in ways they had never imagined. For Wallenberg and his colleagues, the *Nyilas* coup of 15 October represented a hazardous leap into the unknown.

NOTES

1. K. Lauer to J. Wallenberg, 29 September 1944, reprinted in G. Nylander and A. Perlinge (eds), *Raoul Wallenberg in Documents, 1927–1947* (Stockholm: Stiftelsen för Ekonomisk Historisk Forskning inom Bank och Företagande, 2000), p.101.
2. N. Reukei, 14 July 1990, correspondence to Raoul Wallenberg Project, Uppsala University Library, Raoul Wallenberg Project Archive.
3. R.L. Braham, *The Politics of Genocide: The Holocaust in Hungary*, revised and enlarged edn (Boulder, CT: Rosenthal Institute for Holocaust Studies Graduate Center/City University of New York Social Science Monographs, 1994), vol. 2, p.1222; A. Handler, *A Man for All Connections: Raoul Wallenberg and the Hungarian State Apparatus, 1944–1945* (Westport, CT: Praeger, 1996), pp.63–4; A. Cohen, *The Halutz Resistance in Hungary 1942–1944* (Boulder, CT: Social Science Monographs, 1986), esp. Chapter 8; and R. Rozett, 'International Intervention: The Role of Diplomats in Attempts to Rescue Jews in Hungary', in R.L. Braham and S. Miller (eds), *The Nazis' Last Victims: The Holocaust in Hungary* (Detroit, MI: Wayne State University Press, 1998), p.143.
4. L.G. Berg, *Boken som Försvann: Vad hände i Budapest* (Arboga: Textab Förlag, 1983), p.12.
5. Braham, *Politics of Genocide*, vol. 2, p.919.
6. Handler, *A Man for All Connections*, p.63–4.
7. Importantly, Arnóthy-Jungerth remained in office until 15 October.
8. Braham, *Politics of Genocide*, vol. 2, p.904.
9. Thousands of these exemptions were issued directly by the Royal Palace for (amongst other things) distinguished military service during the previous war.
10. Braham, *Politics of Genocide*, vol. 2, p.906.
11. Ibid., p.922.
12. *Riksarkivet Utrikesdepartementet* (hereafter RA UD), Hp 21 Eu 1098, folder 15. The image drawn of the Jew contains some typical anti-Semitic features often found in European cartoons about Jews, which is hardly surprising (see plate no.18).
13. After 15 October, members of *Nyilas* were far less inclined to respect this 'agreement'.
14. R. Wallenberg, 'Memorandum concerning help to Hungary's Jews', 29 July 1944, RA UD, Hp 21 Eu 1092, folder 1.
15. Per Anger remembers that Wallenberg had no problems in obtaining sufficient funds for his

activities. 'He managed to get what he wanted, I think.' However, Anger, who was given the task by UD, after the war, of tracing and analysing the money trail through transfer documentation, eventually gave up in frustration. Author interview with Ambassador Per Anger, March 1990, Uppsala University Library, Raoul Wallenberg Project Archive, no.C002, p.54.

16. R. Wallenberg to K. Lauer, date unknown, but clearly written shortly after arriving in Budapest. RA, Raoul Wallenberg Arkiv, Signum 1, vol. 6.
17. R. Wallenberg to K. Lauer, 18 July 1944, RA, Raoul Wallenberg Arkiv, Signum 1, vol. 6. Cryptically, Wallenberg added, in his own handwriting: 'Langlet's 1,000,000 Swiss francs were of course unavailable.' Exactly what this referred to is uncertain, and as noted in Chapter 8, Langlet often complained bitterly about a lack of funds.
18. This address is one of the finest in the city, and about a ten-minute walk from UD.
19. K. Lauer to I. Olsen, 24 July 1944, RA, Raoul Wallenberg Arkiv, Signum 1, vol. 6.
20. R. Wallenberg to K. Lauer, 24 July 1944, RA, Raoul Wallenberg Arkiv, Signum 1, vol. 6.
21. 'PM für Gesandtschaftssekretär Anger', 6 August 1944, RA, Raoul Wallenberg Arkiv, Signum 1, vol. 6. This document was previously discussed in Chapter 2. It was dictated in German, and sent to Anger in Stockholm. Wallenberg concluded this report to his senior colleague by saying that 'there are so many problems and there is such a crush of people here that it is in fact physically impossible to do any reports. I do not want to talk too much by telephone because this humanitarian action has already caused quite a sensation in certain circles.'
22. *Promemoria* (PM), S. Hellstedt, 5 August 1944, RA UD, Hp 21 Eu 1096, folder 8.
23. PM, S. Hellstedt, 10 August 1944, RA UD Hp 21 Eu 1096, folder 9. The 'question mark' seems to indicate that Hellstedt didn't know about the WRB. If so, this might be another example of how bad internal UD communications actually were, Boheman's assertion notwithstanding. This, however, is more speculative than certain.
24. K. Lauer to R. Wallenberg, 21–28 August 1944, RA, Raoul Wallenberg Arkiv, Signum 1, vol. 6. The archived photocopy of these letters runs from one sheet to another on the dates cited. They appear to be one letter, but it is possible that they were sent out separately between those dates.
25. Ibid., p.6.
26. Ibid., p.8.
27. Ibid., p.10.
28. K. Lauer to I. Olsen, 23 August 1944, RA, Raoul Wallenberg Arkiv, Signum 1, vol. 6.
29. K. Lauer to R. Wallenberg, 26 August, RA, Raoul Wallenberg Arkiv, Signum 1, vol. 6, p.9.
30. Author interview with P. Anger, p.49.
31. 'Report about the Hungarian Jews', R. Wallenberg, 12 September 1944, RA UD, Hp 21 Eu 1092, folder 1.
32. Lauer signed the formal request using Wallenberg's initials, which obviously wasn't a problem in the family's bank. 28 August 1944, RA, Raoul Wallenberg Arkiv, Signum 1, vol. 6.
33. Copy of no.83 WRB to AMLEGATION Stockholm, 8 September 1944, in D. Wyman, *America and the Holocaust* (New York: Garland Publishing, 1989–91), vol. 8, doc. no.23, p.55. JDC is the Joint Distribution Committee, one of the most important Jewish philanthropic agencies in the United States.
34. I. Danielsson to UD, no.279, 4 September 1944, RA UD, Hp 21 Eu 1097, folder 13.
35. 'PM First report regarding the use of funds, placed at the disposal of the Jewish action', 12 September 1944, RA UD, Hp 21 1092, folder 1.
36. It is unclear if Wallenberg is writing about German or Hungarian officials. In the context, however, he is probably referring to his frequent lunches and dinners with Hungarian officials.
37. S. Hellstedt to I. Danielsson, no.179, 13 September 1944, RA UD, Hp 21 Eu 1098, folder 15. The phrase cited was written in English, not Swedish.
38. Copy of letter from Olsen to Stockholms Enskilda Bank AB, 26 September 1944 (5 October 1944 to WRB), from War Refugee Board Archive, Sweden, Box 72. Copy graciously provided by Meredith Hindley.
39. R. Wallenberg to K. Lauer, 29 September 1944, RA, Raoul Wallenberg Arkiv, Signum 1, vol. 6.
40. Ibid.
41. K. Lauer to J. Wallenberg, 29 September 1944, in G. Nylander and A. Perlinge (eds), *Raoul Wallenberg in Documents, 1927–1947* (Stockholm: Stiftelsen för Ekonomisk Historisk Forskning inom Bank och Företagande, 2000), p.101.

42. I. Danielsson to UD, no.397, 10 October 1944, RA UD, Hp 21 Eu 1092, folder 1.
43. I. Danielsson to UD, no.406, 11 October 1944, RA UD, Hp 21 Eu 1092, folder 1.
44. H. Johnson to C. Günther, no.518, 2 September 1944, RA UD, Hp 21 Eu 1098, folder 13. Günther responded with a courteous letter of thanks several days later. C. Günther to H. Johnson, no.564, 5 September 1944, RA UD, Hp 21 Eu 1098, folder 13.
45. R. Sohlman to W.H. Montagu-Pollock, 18 September 1944, RA UD, Hp 21 Eu 1092, folder 1.
46. A.L. Easterman, World Jewish Congress, to Rabbi M. Ehrenpreis, 6 September 1944, RA UD, Hp 1099, folder 17.
47. I. Danielsson to UD, no.277, 4 September 1944, RA UD, P2 Eu.
48. Braham, *Politics of Genocide*, vol. 2, p.919.
49. I. Danielsson to C. Günther, no.214, 6 September 1944, RA UD, Hp 1 Eu 583, folder 8.
50. I. Danielsson to UD, no.281, 7 September 1944, RA UD, Hp 1 Eu 583, folder 22.
51. This is an example of how the historian or chronicler can be mislead by oral testimony. If the Swedes, who themselves were issuing the protective documents, sometimes got confused about exactly which type of paper was being applied for, issued or received, it is easy to understand confusion in remembering, decades later, exactly which type of document was received. Yet oral testimonies have in the main determined the popular picture of how the Swedes used their protective documentation.
52. I. Danielsson to UD, no.289, 12 September 1944, RA UD, Hp 21 Eu 1092, folder 1. This cable arrived in Stockholm the next day.
53. PM (draft), by G. Engzell, 19 September 1944, RA UD, Hp 21 Eu 1092, folder 1. Regarding the number of employees, the number first given in the draft was 250. It was then crossed out and replaced with 100. Numbers mentioned in the hagiographic literature for Jewish volunteers are generally much higher.
54. Both 9 September 1944, RA UD, Hp 21 Eu 1098, folder 14. On 14 September, Storch sent another list to UD, noting that the organization was willing to cover all costs associated with finding the individuals in question, and for their possible stay in Sweden. H. Storch to S. Hellstedt, 14 September 1944, RA UD, Hp 21 Eu 1099, folder 16.
55. Lists from Budapest, arrived at UD 16 September 1944, RA UD, Hp 21 Eu 1099, folder 16.
56. There are numerous documents with such lists, and the indications 'strong' or 'weak', in RA UD, Hp 21 Eu 1097, 1098, 1099, passim.
57. T. Grell and E. Veesenmayer to AuswärtigesAmt, 27 September 1944 (NG-4985), in R.L. Braham, *The Destruction of Hungarian Jewry: A Documentary Account* (New York: Pro Arte for the World Federation of Hungarian Jews, 1963), doc. 331, p.711.
58. I have analysed this specific report at length in 'One Day during the Holocaust: An Analysis of Raoul Wallenberg's Budapest Report of 12 September, 1944', in *Holocaust Studies: A Journal of Culture and History*, 11, 3 (Winter 2005), pp.84–104.
59. G. Engzell to P. Anger, no.142, 29 August 1944, RA UD, Hp 21 Eu 1097, folder 12.
60. 'Report About the Hungarian Jews', 12 September 1944, RA UD, Hp 21 Eu 1092, folder 1.
61. Because of the extent of the work, his section had recently moved again. 'The reception is still in the house Minerva utca 1A ... all internal administration is taken care of at Tigris utca 8A, which is totally occupied by the section. The house has ten rooms and a cellar.'
62. See P.A. Levine, *From Indifference to Activism: Swedish Diplomacy and the Holocaust, 1938–1944*, 2nd edn (Uppsala: Studia historica Upsaliensia, 1998), especially Chapters 4 and 5.
63. Ibid., pp.100–1.
64. E. Kockum to R. Sohlman, no.159, 27 September 1944, RA UD, Hp 21 Eu 1099, folder 18.
65. R. Sohlman to E. Kockum, no.141, 28 September 1944, RA UD, Hp 21 Eu 1099, folder 18.
66. 'Report About the Hungarian Jews', 29 September 1944, RA UD, Hp 21 Eu 1092, folder 1. While most of his correspondence by this time was dictated to his secretary/secretaries in German, including some personal letters home, this report was written by him in Swedish. Interestingly, there is a notation that seven copies of it were made, indicating increased distribution within the government and, as was the case with a lot of the correspondence coming out of Budapest, to other individuals, including Rabbi Ehrenpreis and Gunnar Josephson, leaders of Stockholm's Jewish community.
67. Ibid. It is interesting that Wallenberg uses the Swedish word *skyddspass* and not the better-known *Schutzpass* when referring in the report (and elsewhere) to the most common protective documents distributed by the Swedes.

68. This is the only available evidence stating that Wallenberg conducted such rescue activities before 15 October.
69. R. Wallenberg to Maj von Dardel, 29 September 1944, in R. Wallenberg, *Letters and Dispatches 1924–1944*, trans. K. Board (New York: Arcade Publishing, 1995), pp.274–5.
70. G. Engzell to Legation Budapest, no.258, 29 September 1944, RA UD, Hp 21 Eu 1099, folder 18. At the top of this letter was the notation 'strong list'.
71. This issue will be addressed in the Epilogue. Most recently, see W. Agrell, *Skuggor runt Wallenberg: Uppdrag i Ungern 1943–45* (Lund: Historiska media, 2006); and previously, B. Schiller, *Varför ryssarna tog Wallenberg* (Stockholm: Natur och kultur, 1991).
72. R. Wallenberg to E. Boheman, 19 June 1944, in Wallenberg, *Letters and Dispatches*, p.233.
73. 'Between Mr Eberhard Håkanson and Mr Raoul Wallenberg, both of Stockholm, the following agreement has been reached this day.', 7 July 1944, RA, Raoul Wallenberg Arkiv, Signum 1, vol. 6.
74. K. Lauer to R. Wallenberg, 21 August 1944, RA, Raoul Wallenberg Arkiv, Signum 1, vol. 6.
75. Ibid., 25 August 1944.
76. R. Wallenberg's appointment's diary, on the page for '13 July 1944', RA, Raoul Wallenberg Arkiv, Signum 1, vol. 9.
77. K. Lauer to R. Wallenberg, 21 August 1944, RA, Raoul Wallenberg Arkiv, Signum 1, vol. 6.
78. R. Wallenberg to K. Lauer, 29 September 1944, RA, Raoul Wallenberg Arkiv, Signum 1, vol. 6.
79. K. Lauer to R. Wallenberg, 28 October 1944, RA, Raoul Wallenberg Arkiv, Signum 1, vol. 6. The following citations are all drawn from this long document, unless noted otherwise.
80. K. Lauer to R. Wallenberg, 15 November 1944, RA, Raoul Wallenberg Arkiv, Signum 1, vol. 6. This is a partial letter, with only the 'p.s.' section of it in this file.
81. L.G. Berg, *Boken som Försvann; Vad hände i Budapest* (Arboga: Textab Förlag, 1983), pp. 20–2. In English, *The Book That Disappeared: What Happened in Budapest* (New York: Vantage Press, 1990).
82. A. Lajos, *Hjälten och Offren: Raoul Wallenberg och judarna i Budapest* (Växjö: Svenska Emigrantinstitutets skrifserie, no. 15, 2003), p.150; and M. Ember, *Wallenberg Budapesten* (Budapest: Városháza, 2000), pp.71–7 (translation for author by A. Szónyi).
83. R. Wallenberg to Maj von Dardel, 29 September 1944, in Wallenberg, *Letters and Dispatches*, pp.274–5.
84. S. Szita, *Trading in Lives? Operations of the Jewish Relief and Rescue Committee in Budapest, 1944–1945*, trans. S. Lambert (Budapest and New York: Central European University Press, 2005), p.147, n.41.
85. R. Wallenberg, 'Report Concerning the Situation of the Hungarian Jews', 8 December 1944, RA UD, Hp 21 Eu 1092, folder II.
86. Entry for 9 September 1944, in R. Wallenberg's appointment's diary, RA, Raoul Wallenberg Arkiv, Signum 1, vol. 9. The last time Becher's name appears is, ironically, 15 October. It is unknown if they actually met on that fateful day.
87. G. Kádár and Z. Vági, *Self-financing Genocide: The Gold Train, the Becher Case and the Wealth of Hungarian Jews*, trans. E. Koncz, J. Tucker and A. Kádár (Budapest: Central European University Press, 2001), p.xix.
88. Ibid., pp.xxiv-xxv.
89. Ibid., p.193.
90. Ibid., p.270, n.212.
91. Szita, *Trading in Lives?*, p.134. This discrepancy cannot be satisfactorily reconciled.
92. Entry for 3 November 1944, in R. Wallenberg's appointment's diary, RA, Raoul Wallenberg Arkiv, Signum 1, vol. 9.
93. See Chapter 10 for further discussion about Wallenberg's contacts with Becher and those around him.
94. S. Szita, *Trading in Lives?*, pp.133–4. Szita continues: 'It is accurate to qualify Becher's flight before the swiftly approaching Red Army as a well-planned and methodically executed "departure", in preparation for which he virtually emptied the three villas that he had occupied, removing all furniture, decor and everything else that could fit through the doorway.' For some reason, Becher was vigorously defended by Reszö Kasztner in post-war testimony.
95. Kádár and Vági, *Self-financing Genocide*, p.258.
96. Braham, *Politics of Genocide*, vol. 2, p.965.
97. Highly emotional controversies continue about what the leadership of Budapest's 'Jewish

Council' knew about Auschwitz and Nazi policies of genocide before and during the occupation's first months. They are, however, separate from the concerns of this study.

98. Braham, *Politics of Genocide*, vol. 2, p. 893.
99. R. Kasztner, *Der Bericht des jüdischen Rettungskomitees aus Budapest 1942–1945*, copy in Joint Distribution Committee Archives, New York City, folder SM no.18, especially pp.117–19 and pp.125–6.
100. Y. Bauer, 'The Holocaust in Hungary: Was Rescue Possible?', in D. Cesarani (ed.), *Genocide and Rescue: The Holocaust in Hungary 1944* (Oxford and New York: Berg, 1997), p.208.
101. A. Cohen, *The Halutz Resistance in Hungary 1942–1944* (Boulder, CT: Social Science Monographs, 1986), pp.132–3.
102. N. Reukei, 14 July 1990, correspondence to Raoul Wallenberg Project, Uppsala University Library, Raoul Wallenberg Project Archive.
103. J. Lévai, *Black Book on the Martyrdom of Hungarian Jewry* (Zurich: Central European Times, 1948), p.316.
104. L. Palosuo, *Yellow Stars and Trouser Inspections: Jewish Testimonies from Hungary, 1920–1945* (Uppsala: Studia Historica Upsaliensia, 231, 2008), pp.235–6.
105. R. Wallenberg, 'Memorandum concerning the Hungarian Jews', 6 August 1944, RA UD, Hp 21 Eu 1096, folder 8.
106. There was massive forgery of Swedish and other neutral papers.
107. R. Wallenberg to I. Olsen, 12 October 1944, *War Refugee Board's Final Report*, p.738, FDR Library, Hyde Park, NY. Copy graciously provided by Meredith Hindley.
108. R. Wallenberg to Maj von Dardel, 29 September 1944, in Wallenberg, *Letters and Dispatches*, pp.274–5.
109. Memorandum by T. Grell, submitted by E. Veesenmayer, no.053, 29 September 1944, in Braham, *Destruction of Hungarian Jewry*, doc. 367, p.768.

10

October: Raoul Wallenberg Enters History

I can assure you that I am fine. The times are extraordinarily exciting and nerve-racking. We keep working and struggling on, and that is the main thing ... Dozens of people are standing around me, everyone with pressing questions, so that I don't know to whom to reply and advise first ... [I] send ... kisses to all of you.

> Raoul Wallenberg to his mother, Maj, 22 October 1944[1]

... we got the call that the whole house was taken ... the whole house was empty except one guy sitting at the desk ... Wallenberg told me (I was his interpreter) ... 'Ask him where the people are from the house.' And the guy said to me ... poker-faced, 'They are in the Danube, swimming'. So Wallenberg said, 'Ask him why'. So I asked him why. He said, 'Because they were dirty Jews'. So that was it. We were late arriving there.

> Thomas Verés, Wallenberg's photographer, late October 1944[2]

THE *NYILAS* ACHIEVE POWER

Around midday on Sunday, 15 October 1944, Miklós Horthy made a dramatic radio announcement declaring that Hungary had agreed to an immediate armistice with the Soviet Union. For everyone in Hungary, it seemed for a moment that the war had ended. For Budapest's Jews, the broadcast allowed them a moment of hope that they had survived. Tragically, Horthy's manoeuvre was 'ill-conceived and inadequately prepared', and it failed. The announcement marked the end of his conservative nationalist government, and the assumption of power by the *Nyilas*, the extreme right-wing 'Hungarist' movement. Led by Ferenc Szálasi, an ex-army officer and radical anti-Semite, his own announcement later that same day that he was now in charge marked the beginning of what is generally described as the third and final phase of the Hungarian Holocaust.[3] Veesenmayer's patience had run out, and he immediately installed Szálasi. It also marked the moment which signifies what may be described as Raoul Wallenberg's entry into history. If Hungary had successfully concluded an armistice with the Soviet Union, it is highly likely that Raoul Wallenberg would have remained, within Holocaust history and memory, 'merely' an ad hoc diplomat who bravely assisted many Jews in Budapest for a couple of months, and who then returned home to resume his life. If Hungary's leadership had been more competent and the Germans less ruthless, Wallenberg probably would have remained similarly 'forgotten', along with his other diplomatic colleagues: an obscure but honourable footnote to Holocaust history.

Interestingly, the profusion of popular and scholarly literature about Wallenberg during this period makes it a particularly well-known episode of the Holocaust.[4] The hagiographic literature invariably concentrates on Wallenberg, with all other individuals and contexts consigned, incorrectly, to supporting or background roles. Many of the elements of this phase, not least that of the Jews endangered by the radical street violence of *Nyilas* thugs, has generally come together as a compelling narrative shaped by Wallenberg's own, individual actions – as if he alone determined what happened during those last months of 1944. This is, of course, historic nonsense for many reasons, not least because such representations either largely misunderstand or ignore the complicated political context prevailing within the city until it was overrun by the Red Army in the first weeks of 1945, first Pest and then Buda. Similarly, most historians have misunderstood the essential details of what Wallenberg and the other Swedes did. Both factors have distorted the common understanding of Wallenberg, and contributed to the web of myth which distorts a proper understanding of his actual achievements.

This is Wallenberg's 'Scarlet Pimpernel' period, when hagiographers and film directors emphasize moments of physical bravery on Wallenberg's part as he (so it is depicted) fearlessly confronted *Nyilas* thugs, gendarme officers, and sometimes even German soldiers and diplomats. This is the period when he seemingly spent entire days rushing around the city, never sleeping in order to always be on call to intervene in an attempt to save Jewish lives. As we shall see, there were instances when he did rush to a location where Jews were assembled, or when the *Nyilas* did break into a 'yellow star' house and he was called to help. But the frequency of these encounters has been exaggerated. At times Wallenberg was in some physical danger from the perpetrators, but he was more likely to be a random victim of Soviet artillery than to be shot by a *Nyilas* thug.

In fact, most of what Wallenberg did between 15 October and 17 January remained similar to what he had been doing. The situations which continued to dominate his time and consume his energy were less a matter of confrontations on the street, at railway yards or on the Danube's quay, and more of the quieter business of negotiations with Hungarian and sometimes German officials. Such meetings may be less dramatic than the act of leaping upon a boxcar and passing out protective passports to desperate hands, yet they probably protected many more people. The reality of the political struggle for the survival of the city's Jews between the Germans, *Nyilas* and the neutral diplomats determined their fate more than anything Wallenberg himself could have possibly done.

It is therefore misleading to speculate about how many Jews Wallenberg himself saved. It would be more faithful to the historical truth if the number of Jews assisted and saved by the staff of the Swedish Legation (and others) could be accurately established. Aided by their many Hungarian (voluntary) staff – mostly Jews but also some Christians – they all sought to assist as many people as possible – primarily but not exclusively Jews. What branded Wallenberg in the memory of survivors during this phase is that, far more than the other neutral diplomats, he was seen by many who did survive. These individuals have testified about what they saw, but they cannot have known about the often intense negotiations between the neutrals and the perpetrators. They never saw Danielsson, Wallenberg and their colleagues negotiate with such officials as the new *Nyilas* Foreign Minister Kemény, or Interior Minister Vajna, or Gendarme Colonel Ferency. Any narrative of those weeks which maintains a solitary focus on Wallenberg distorts our picture of his activities, and those of the other neutral diplomats also seeking to save lives.

15 OCTOBER 1944

Historian Krisztián Ungváry, the leading expert on what would become the 'Battle for Budapest', writes: 'in reality the fate of Budapest was determined by Germany military policy ... The persecuted Jews saw the advancing Soviet troops as their saviours. The rest of the population, however, had gloomy forebodings.'[5] The extent to which military events decided the fate of the city's Jews, and everyone else, is rarely noted in the hagiographic literature. As Ungváry points out:

> The battle for Budapest was one of the longest and bloodiest city battles of the Second World War. From the appearance of the first Soviet tanks on the outskirts of the capital until the capture of Buda Castle, 102 days passed ... the three-month siege ... engulfed 800,000 non-combatants and was so vicious that comparisons

with Stalingrad began to appear even in contemporary soldiers' writings. The inhabitants of Budapest were never evacuated and 38,000 died alongside a similar number of Hungarian and German military personnel ... The casualties of the attacking Red Army, with some 80,000 dead, bring the grand total close to 160,000.[6]

It is therefore necessary to place the work of neutral diplomats, as well as the fate of the city's Jews, within the context of the Red Army's advance. Against expectations, the defence mounted east of Budapest by Hungarian and German forces succeeded for a time. As late as 20 October, Soviet forces were only some 100 kilometres from Pest, yet it took many more weeks for the city's encirclement to be completed. As Ungváry writes: 'While the awareness of approaching defeat and the terror perpetrated by the [*Nyilas*] government increasingly fuelled the people's desire for an end to the ordeal, the [Hungarian] army still possessed substantial energy reserves. This was one of the reasons why the siege of Budapest was to prove so long and bloody.'[7]

Alongside the failure of Horthy's government to coordinate its political movements with Hungary's military leadership, the failed attempt to extricate the country from its alliance with Germany was due to the fact that Veesenmayer and his staff knew what was being planned. Jenö Lévai wrote: 'Veesenmayer already knew about the plans of the Regent and the Government since September 11th ... On the 26th, [he] flew to German Headquarters and saw Hitler ... On his return he told Szálasi that the Führer had decided to remove the Regent and that he, Szálasi, was to be regarded as the only reliable factor.'[8] The Germans' patience with the old admiral had run out, and when he moved on 15 October, so did Veesenmayer. Throughout that Sunday, and into the next day, confusion reigned about who was in control. Immediately after Horthy's radio broadcast, the Germans and their *Nyilas* protégés acted, gaining control of the radio station, and broadcasting Szálasi's own proclamation that the party now ruled the country. Importantly, the army's leadership – a mix of right-wing Horthy loyalists, *Nyilas* sympathizers and pro-German admirers – had long been indoctrinated by anti-Soviet propaganda, and it now ordered its troops to continue 'the struggle against Bolshevism'.

R.L. Braham describes aspects of that fateful day:

> As on March 19 ... the people were overcome by a collective sense of helplessness, compounded by apprehension about the impending changes engendered by years of vicious anti-Communist and anti-Jewish propaganda. The passivity was heightened by the fact that it was a Sunday and the factories were

closed. The only visible jubilation, however short-lived, came from the Jewish community and from some of the traditionally anti-Horthy and anti-*Nyilas* elements.[9]

Survivor testimonies describe the joy felt after Horthy's radio announcement, followed almost immediately by the crushing realization that in fact neither the war nor their plight had ended. And from that day, until the defeat of German and Hungarian forces in Budapest, the Jews' situation would worsen. The nominal shield of protection which had prevailed since early July was now gone, replaced by the radical *Nyilas* who filled the airwaves with vicious anti-Semitic propaganda, and whose intent was to incite party members to persecute and kill those Jews they could find. Hundreds were killed on 15 and 16 October, with many committing suicide in despair at the new situation. In locations throughout the countryside, hundreds of Jewish men in forced labour brigades were also slaughtered. Braham concluded:

> October 15, 1944, will undoubtedly go down in history as one of Hungary's darkest days. By its end, the Horthy era had ended – along with the 'historical' Hungary, with its mixed feudal-bourgeois socioeconomic structure ... The *Nyilas* coup finally enabled the radical Right to assume power and to enjoy the glory of the Hungarist State, though under constant military pressure, until almost the end of the war.[10]

It is important to note the fact that, simultaneous with the widespread violence inflicted upon Jews, on streets and in cellars by *Nyilas* members in the days following the failed armistice, the new Hungarian 'führer's' 'programme', however quixotic and even bizarre, considering the military situation, was not the same as his German mentors. The *Nyilas* were racist and violent, with the party and its ragtag militia using the situation to inflict as much pain, humiliation and death as they could. But neither the party's leaders nor their programme was ideologically annihilationist. Though they had adopted important elements of Hitlerian ideology, their own 'final' goal was to purge Hungary of its Jews, not caring what happened to them afterwards. Murdering each and every Jew, as the Nazis sought to do, did not interest Szálasi. More important for the party's quite eccentric leaders – long frustrated by their inability to depose Horthy and the conservative nationalists – was, as Ungváry writes, 'the creation under Hungarian leadership of a federal state called the Hungarist Carpathian-Danubian Great Fatherland, which was to comprise Hungary, Slovakia, Vojvodina, Burgenland, Croatia, Dalmatia, Ruthenia, Transylvania and Bosnia'.[11] This fact created a more differentiated political situation within the city, which directly influenced the ability of the neutral diplomats to continue acting, as it provided an opportunity for their negotiations on behalf of Jews to continue.

According to László Karsai, 'Szálasi was merely an antisemite. He knew no inferior and superior races; he merely hated the Jews ... In his own view, Szálasi was not *antisemitic* but *asemitic,* working for a Hungary completely free of Jews.'[12] Szálasi's programme stated explicitly that the Jews: 'Shall perform labour service for the Nation inside the country; their treatment shall be determined by their behaviour; their legal status shall be regulated by law; no difference shall be made between one Jew and another. When the war is over, all Jews shall be removed from Hungary to a place to be determined by international agreement. The Jew shall never be allowed to return to Hungarian soil.'[13]

In reality, even after 15 October, and even in the midst of much confusion, there remained important continuities in Hungary's governing structure. The discontinuities manifested themselves in the deadly yet mainly random violence of the *Nyilas,* many of whom were young men and teenagers incited by mid-level party fanatics. The continuities, on the other hand, could be seen within ministries and city administration, which, although nominally directed by the *Nyilas,* were still staffed by many non-party officials. Echoing Hitler's attitude towards the 'wild violence' perpetrated in Germany by the SA in the early 1930s, Hungary's Nazis now sought for the state to maintain its monopoly of violence towards the Jews, and in fact some of them feared the developing anarchy on the capital's streets. Contradicting some of their own propaganda, Hungary's new leaders declared that the state was determined to decide alone the fate of the Jews, and the extent of the violence against them. Already, on 16 October, Gábor Vajna, the government's new, 'notoriously antisemitic' minister of the interior, had issued a long public proclamation 'as regards the Jewish question':[14]

> I order all officials of the civil administration and all police officers to do their utmost to safeguard and maintain good order, discipline and public safety ... For the solution of the Jewish question detailed instructions will be issued and carried out. Nobody shall take upon himself the right to act as a despotic and arbitrary judge of the Jews, as the solution of this question is the business of the State.[15]

Of significance during this period is the persistence of the grandiose and wholly improbable goals maintained by the *Nyilas* leaders, even as the Red Army continued its ultimately unstoppable advance. Seemingly unconnected to reality, Vajna and his colleagues appeared to believe that they, and not Stalin's legions, would determine what would happen in Budapest.

Of interest for our concerns is what he proclaimed about those Jews under neutral protection:

> Emphatically I wish to warn all Jews and those who serve their interests, that every authority in the State is keeping a close watch on their activities ... In this respect I do not differentiate between Jews belonging to the Catholic, Protestant or Israelite Churches; I deal only with the Jewish race. I will not acknowledge the validity of safe-conduct or foreign passports issued by whomsoever to Hungarian Jews ... we will tolerate interference from nobody, whether in Hungary or abroad. No person of Jewish blood should therefore allow himself to think that he can violate the decrees and laws of the Hungarian State with the assistance of foreigners.[16]

However, as will be shown, the prevailing realities did not allow Vajna to act unilaterally. It is of considerable importance that in this particular matter, and in the first days after the coup, the combined protests of the neutral diplomats convinced the *Nyilas* government to rescind his directive.[17] As a result, most neutral documents 'regained' some protective value, although they continued to vary in their actual effectiveness.[18] Nonetheless, one manifestation of how Hungarian Nazis sought to separate Jews from other Hungarians can be seen in the continued willingness of some Hungarian officials, including some *Nyilas* officials, to maintain some exemptions for some Jews – exemptions of a sort unthinkable under Hitler's racial anti-Semitism. As Braham writes: 'In contrast to the *Nyilas* mobs which contained large numbers of armed adolescents, many among the official leadership continued to differentiate between various categories of Jews. The "protected" categories included most of those who were originally covered by the special exemption system introduced by the Horthy regime.'[19] What this meant for the Swedes and other neutral diplomats, as we shall see, was that even while street violence occurred, they still had officials whom they could lobby.

We shall also see how the Swedes in particular exploited the fact that the new regime considered formal diplomatic recognition from the neutrals a matter of great urgency. This would provide them, at least in their own minds, with the international legitimacy required for the implementation of their Hungarist programme. Karsai concluded: 'Szálasi's intention to secure international legitimacy for his regime strongly influenced his decisions.'[20] Naturally, these diplomatic issues were invisible to the city's remaining Jewish population of between 150,000 and 200,000.[21] It is significant that even as violence swept the city, some city police – both officers and patrolmen – chose to not join in the rampage. Contrary to common perceptions, Karsai found that 'In this initial period of the Arrow Cross regime, Jewish houses ... guarded by disciplined policemen, still provided genuine refuge for the inhabitants. Some of these police officers, fully aware that the Germans would lose the war, saved the lives of many Jews by protecting – on orders from their superiors – Jewish houses such as the Jewish Council headquarters on Síp Street.'[22] However, the weak *Nyilas* government was unable to achieve what Hitler and Himmler had achieved, and street violence against the Jews would continue, albeit with some hindrances. Wallenberg and the other Swedish diplomats would provide some of those barriers, however incomplete they were, until the only violence in the streets was the accelerating battle between German and Hungarian troops, and Soviet forces.

Immediately after 15 October, the Germans – who in Jewish matters remained entirely dependent on their Hungarian collaborators – resumed their efforts to purge Budapest of its Jews. However, by this point their goals were ostensibly different from those of the summer of extermination, for no longer were the Jews to be sent to their immediate death in Auschwitz. Now, as Veesenmayer explained to the Hungarians, 50,000 Jews were needed for labour for various projects in the Reich. These included what came to be known as the *Jägerstab* project, and for building defence systems along the Hungarian–Austrian border.[23] Though this 'project' clashed with Szálasi's stated goal that the Jews were to be kept in Hungary for slave labour, the Hungarian 'führer' was in no position to contradict his German benefactors. Though Eichmann left Budapest around the end of September, he remained hovering in its environs, waiting for another opportunity to resume his work.[24] He soon found it.

Here we may dispense with yet another myth about Wallenberg, connected in this case with Eichmann. It is common to read in the popular literature about Wallenberg that among his deeds, he 'stopped deportation trains leaving for Auschwitz'.[25] This, again, is historic nonsense. Horthy ended the summer's deportations before Wallenberg arrived, and in autumn 1944, SS *Reichsführer* Heinrich Himmler ordered Birkenau's gas chambers to be dismantled in the wake of the *Sonderkommando* uprising of 7 October. As a result, they were unavailable to Eichmann or anyone else after the coup of 15 October, or by the time the November–December deportations, generally described as the death marches, began.

Nonetheless, Eichmann was 'delighted' at having the chance to finish his 'Hungarian project', and immediately negotiated with Vajna for the removal of a first group of Jews, which he intended would be quickly followed by others.[26] The partial destruction of Hungarian rail networks had made the Germans even more dependent on Hungarian manpower than before, and part of the Nazis' negotiating ploy was to assure their counterparts that if the Hungarians organized the large-scale deportations (on foot) demanded, the Germans would grant the neutrals transit visas in order for 'their Jews' to actually leave the country. As Braham concluded: 'The objective ... of course, was to induce the Szálasi government to agree speedily to the other part of the agreement originally suggested by Hitler – the extension of the Final Solution program to all other Jews.'[27]

THE SWEDISH LEGATION BEFORE THE COUP

When analysing Swedish diplomacy during this phase, it is useful to understand the perspective of the Swedes and of other neutral diplomats as they confronted the new situation. We have noted that in many ways they were in a unique position in Holocaust history. They were observing at first hand a particular kind of persecution and death engulfing thousands of people around them, and were working (and thinking and feeling) in the midst of a genocidal maelstrom. Their diplomatic status, which was fully recognized by all sides, made threats against them unlikely, and provided them with relative security from physical harm.[28] Nowhere else in Nazi-occupied Europe during the Holocaust did accredited diplomats have quite the same position or opportunity. Different from most 'bystanders' to the Holocaust, these 'ordinary' Europeans officials were compelled to make choices which were in no way hypothetical. They could 'stand by', or they could intervene on behalf of people who sought their help.[29] Had they chosen to remain relatively passive, it is highly unlikely that any of them, including Wallenberg, would have suffered subsequent professional disadvantage. On the other hand, had they made that choice, and stayed, as it were, behind their desks, they might have had to answer to their consciences, as did most others who comprise the category of 'bystander'. The manner in which they responded tells us not only about these men themselves, but also much about the possibilities which existed even for other 'bystanders' to genocide.

We have noted that September had been relatively calm politically, but in the days before 15 October the Swedes were very busy. On 3 October, Danielsson informed Stockholm that the Germans were losing patience with Horthy. He wrote that pressure on the Hungarians was increasing, 'to resume the persecution of the Jews. The German government is said to now be prepared to apply force to back up their words. Vesenmayer [*sic*], who on Sunday visited German headquarters, has today returned. The 4th or 5th of October are said to be critical days.'[30] More significantly, on Thursday, 12 October, Danielsson was summoned to an audience with Prime Minister Lakatos, an indication of the importance the Hungarians placed on their relations with Sweden. Obviously knowing of Horthy's forthcoming request for the armistice, Lakatos asserted that his government had 'regained full sovereignty'. He asked Danielsson if this now provided the necessary conditions for Sweden's government to grant full diplomatic recognition. The Swedes' refusal to grant recognition in March had remained particularly irritating to the Hungarians and, in the weeks to come, it would become central to Swedish–Hungarian negotiations, even subsequent to the impending change of government. It is noteworthy that even after March, though Stockholm had not granted Sztójay's diplomats full status, the Hungarians chose to give Swedish representatives (including of course Wallenberg in July) all diplomatic rights. During the meeting itself, Lakatos explained why Hungary was unable to act as quickly and unilaterally as Romania did, in severing the alliance with Germany: mainly because Hungary was actually occupied by German troops. Lakatos ended the conversation by asserting that under his government, 'initiatives had been taken for a more humanitarian policy towards the Jews'.[31]

Also of interest in these first days of October is further evidence of how far afield news of Sweden's Budapest diplomacy had reached, even before the new crisis. In Stockholm, a news agency reported that 'Jews were promised Swedish passports' by a gang of profit-seeking swindlers, while from Sweden's Legation in Buenos Aires came a telegram that a local Hungarian newspaper had printed the names of fifty Jews who were 'under the protection of the Legation in Budapest'.[32] From Jerusalem came yet another desperate plea for help from the Yishuv's chief rabbi to Marcus Ehrenpreis, who forwarded the telegram to UD. It read: 'Latest news danger deportation to extermination of remnants Hungarian Jews. Acutely please petition King Church and Government not to rest in face cruellest tragedy in story of man make every effort save last remnants.'[33] That same day, Herzog again telegraphed Archbishop Eidem with an almost identical text, although there he wrote: 'Warmest thanks your noble effort Hungarian Jewry.' Erling also sent his telegram to UD.[34] There is no indication that these two Swedish religious leaders put any new urgency into advocating a particular course of action.

For Wallenberg's part, the days before the coup seemed to have been dominated by telegraphed exchanges with UD about getting more money, in ever larger amounts, as quickly as possible; his request for early October was for 150,000 Swedish crowns, a substantial sum. In looking at these exchanges, we may return to the question of which institution, or country, was actually his employer. In the telegrams from Stockholm, which were drafted by senior UD officials, there is nothing whatsoever to support any other conclusion than that they considered him an employee, however temporary, of UD. There is nothing in the language used to suggest that these officials sought to create an institutional or bureaucratic distance from him or his trans-actions. Normally this could have been sensitive territory, yet there is no sign of an institutional anxiety.[35] Similarly, there is no hint that either Danielsson or Wallenberg saw the latter as anything other than a (temporary) Swedish diplomat.

Thursday, 12 October, was a particularly busy day for Wallenberg. He had meetings from morning to evening, including one with Dezsö Billitzer, an aide to Ottó Komoly, a leading Zionist who by this time was a member of the 'Jewish Council', and an important figure in the community's assistance activities.[36] That same day he drafted, amongst other documents, his last report to UD before the coup, a long letter to Lauer and another one (discussed previously) to Iver Olsen. The report to UD (in Swedish, which means Wallenberg must have drafted it himself over a period of some hours) begins poignantly, in view of what would happen on Sunday: 'Since the last report the situation has improved somewhat.' As detailed as his previous reports, this docu-ment remains characterized by its matter-of-fact tone and bureaucratic language. One section notes: 'A [sub-]division has been organized in order to assist the move of *skyddspassjudarna* [literally, protective pass Jews] into Aryan buildings. Among those working in this section are bank directors Makai and Lany from Credit Bank, Swedish citizen Mr Sixten von Bayer, as well as some high-society women [*några damer ur societeten*]. The section has an office with four rooms.'[37]

He wrote that due to 'rising optimism' among the Jews, some are 'by themselves removing the Star of David'. He described negotiations with German diplomats (including the fact that the 'deportation com-mando' had left for Berlin), the freeing of some Jews from Hungarian internment camps, his preparations with Valdemar Langlet to open a new hospital, and ongoing and increasingly broad cooperation with '[Langlet], the International Red Cross, the Zionist's Organization, and the Jewish Council'. Noting also the increasing poverty of the Jews, the report concludes by explaining the matter of protective passports being sold: '[The] explanation is that it was discovered that a convict-ed murderer, who naturally had no connection to the Legation, pro-duced about 40 protective passports, incidentally of extremely bad quality, and sold them for about 3–4,000 pengö each.'[38]

Wallenberg's letter to Lauer (which was dictated in German), begins by again telling his partner: 'Unfortunately, it does not look like it will be possible to leave here quickly. The operation is too big and it seems impossible to wind it up.' Most of the letter replicates what is in the UD report, but the penultimate paragraph does not:

> Again I ask you to tell me something about the state of affairs at the Banana Co., and if you have spoken to Jacob Wallenberg, so that I know what is going to happen with me and Huvudsta if I don't come home, let's say within the next 3 weeks. I will try to organize the division in a way that it will be possible for me to leave 1–2 days before the Russians [come in] ... On the other hand, if I leave too soon something could happen in my absence, which might not if I were here.[39]

Several times during the first days of October, Engzell sent lists of names which had been received by UD from a variety of sources. The phrasing he used in one letter is repeated several times in others, repeating his confidence that Danielsson, Anger and Wallenberg would use their judgement wisely about who could, and who could not, be helped. On 10 October, in connection to a full page of names, Engzell wrote that 'the connection to Sweden appears in these cases to be of the type that assistance [*bistånd*] in some form can be given, such as according to your judgement possibilities exist that in this way, those concerned may be saved'.[40] Yet not every name received was sent with a positive recommendation. In a limited number of cases, Engzell, or someone else in Stockholm, told Budapest that the application for assistance – generally in the form of a protective passport – was rejected.

The previous diplomatic efforts conducted by UD with Nazi Germany officials have already been mentioned. It is relevant in this context to note that even as events in Budapest dominated 'refugee' issues within UD for most of 1944, efforts to aid Jews elsewhere continued, making what was happening in Budapest distinctive but not unique. We are reminded of this when we see that on the day after the *Nyilas* coup, Arvid Richert (Sweden's minister in Berlin), wrote to Engzell with a summary of recent efforts to discern the fate or safety of a dozen or so Jews from Norway, Prague and elsewhere:[41]

> Because von Otter has previously taken care of our 'Jewish issues' [*judeärenden*], I thought it appropriate that before his departure, he visit Councillor von Thadden [at Inland II] at Auswärtiges Amt in order to 'freshen up' these matters. Certainly these are for all practical purposes already decided in the negative, but we wanted of course to not leave any efforts undone in the hope that at

least on some point a positive outcome might result ... [The discussions] produced no immediate results, and von Otter's impression of von Thadden's general attitude was no more favourable than before. In the meantime we shall continue our efforts.[42]

Finally, on the Friday before the coup, Engzell telegraphed Budapest asking for the exact number of 'protective passports' issued to date, and also wondering if the entire effort would be endangered if more than the authorized 4,500 'such passes' (allowed by the Hungarian government) were issued, in the event that the prevailing situation changed, '[because] according to rumours from various sources, it appears that deportation of Hungarian Jews will happen'.[43] This confirms that Engzell, even before the drastic turn of events of 15 October, was open to the possibility that more papers than were officially authorized might be issued if the situation warranted it. Supported yet again by Engzell's flexible attitude, his Budapest colleagues would quickly make use of the diplomatic leeway authorized by their boss.

WALLENBERG REACTS TO THE COUP

For several members of the Legation, 15 October began at one of the city's railway stations, where Per Anger, Lars Berg and Göte Carlsson were seeing to the departure of members of the city's Swedish 'colony'. These long-time residents had decided, in consultation with the Legation, that the time had come to leave the city, and by coincidence it was planned for that morning. However, while there, news of Horthy's radio speech swept through the station. The diplomats faced the dilemma of whether to send their countrymen off in a situation of great uncertainty, or to keep them in Budapest.[44]

For Wallenberg, this new phase was scheduled to begin with another meeting that Sunday with SS officer Kurt Becher; they had most recently met the previous Wednesday afternoon. It is unclear what time they were to meet, or if the appointment was actually kept. Nor can it be known from the available evidence what they intended to discuss. What can be said, however, is that while Wallenberg had scheduled meetings on previous Sundays, it was not always his custom to do so.[45] Here we may again note that Becher's name does not appear in any documents written by Wallenberg, either diplomatic or personal, apart from the appointment's diary. This is curious, because it was standard procedure for UD diplomats to report the names of those they met. For instance, in a matter 'peripheral' to events in Budapest, it was reported to Stockholm that between 15,000 to 18,000 Hungarian Jews were said to be in work camps near Vienna. Attempts to help in some way, which also involved Sweden's Berlin Legation, were foiled, not least because 'Obersturmbaufürer [sic] Krumey could not or rather clearly does not want to protect them against the threatening winter conditions.'[46] It seems reasonable to assume that if Wallenberg met Becher in an official capacity, the German's name would have appeared in documents. Becher, on the other hand, mentioned in one post-war testimony that he negotiated for some Jews, 'with the Swedish Legation for our share [of] this quota'.[47] The person with whom he negotiated, however, is not named. Another interesting name entered into Wallenberg's diary, presumably scheduled before the events of 15 October, was a meeting at the Hotel Ritz, at 14.00, with a 'v. Scholtz'. Although it is uncertain, this could have been an Abwehr agent who had been in contact, months earlier, with Rezö Kasztner, and whom Wallenberg would (if in fact it is the same person) invite to dinner at his home, late in December.[48] For the remainder of this week Wallenberg's diary is empty, although he was of course extremely busy.

One telling example of how a scholar who has not used Swedish sources described incorrectly Wallenberg's activities both before and after the coup (to be differentiated from his understanding of Hungarian circumstances) can be seen in A. Handler's *A Man for All Connections*. Ironically, in one of the few publications about Wallenberg by a professional historian, Handler makes numerous mistakes. He writes: 'The meagre sources of information concerning his activities and whereabouts in the last ten days of ... Horthy's rule offer no evidence of the extent to which Wallenberg was aware [of things].'[49] On the contrary, we have already seen how well informed the Swedes were, and how illuminating Wallenberg's report of 12 October was. This makes even odder Handler's assertion that in the days immediately before 15 October, 'for reasons only known to him, [Wallenberg] chose to remain silent'.[50] Handler then mistakenly places Wallenberg at the railway station supervising the departure of the Swedish group (noted above) 'until late in the evening', but this is contradicted by both Anger's and Berg's accounts, which indicate that the group departed early in the afternoon. Then, compounding this misunderstanding, Handler asserts that Wallenberg was preoccupied with 'time-consuming administrative procedures' related to a matter with which, in fact, Wallenberg had nothing to do. The result, asserts Handler, was that 'Wallenberg spent much of the first of the two day spectacle that ended the Horthy era ... indoors. The absence of relevant sources makes it difficult to speculate about the extent to which Wallenberg realized the nature and implications of the events of October 15 and 16.'[51] Such misunderstandings, which are perhaps minor in character but indicative of larger conceptual misunderstandings, are common even in brief descriptions of Wallenberg by historians.

In fact, Wallenberg and his fellow Swedish and other neutral diplomats understood very well the nature of what had happened that day. Moreover, as Wallenberg himself reported to Stockholm a week later, he did not stay 'indoors' as chaos descended upon Budapest. 'The entire first day the undersigned had to travel around the city on a woman's bicycle on streets filled with bandits in order to tie things together. The second day was given over to moving [my division's] personnel who found themselves in danger to safer hiding places and with a sack to carry around foodstuffs for them.'[52] Exactly what Wallenberg did for the remainder of the week is nowhere described in such detail, but he was in no way passive. He understood the extent of the crisis, and he and his colleagues struggled to respond. There seems no doubt that when he wasn't helping his staff, he was making use of the extensive network of contacts he had up to that point, in order to communicate with leading officials of the new government.

On Wednesday, 18 October, Danielsson telegraphed Stockholm, giving his appraisal of the new situation and informing UD that they had been told 'Swedish protective documents issued for Jews after the 30th of March not respected by the new government. All Jewish personnel exposed to mortal danger. The Legation is besieged by Jewish people who are seeking asylum, which we do not consider, with reference to our situation, to be able to give.'[53] Though communication by telephone might also have occurred that week, Stockholm's first telegraph to Budapest was sent on 19 October. The Legation was instructed to remind Hungarian officials of King Gustav's earlier appeal on behalf of Hungarian Jews, and that the king, and the Swedish government, 'assume that those Jews who have received Swedish protective passports are spared, and that a quick response is expected. You are free to tell [the Hungarians] that if this wish is not fulfilled then you see no possibility of continuing your activities.' In a handwritten addition to the telegram's draft, Engzell added for transmission: 'Naturally no recognition from the Swedish side if obligations [not met].'[54] Yet the Swedes quickly learned that even Interior Minister Vajna's tough public stance towards Jews under neutral protection was not necessarily the only thinking underway within the new regime. In Danielsson's first letter to UD (which, in an example of the still well-functioning communications between the two countries, was written on the 21 October, and received only four days later in Stockholm), he virtually mocked the Hungarian 'führer's' seriousness. Proclamations from other ministers, including the new foreign minister, Baron Kemény, were also forwarded. Danielsson also informed UD that 'particularly interesting for Sweden' was

Interior Minister Vajna's declaration that although 'at the moment he wants to remove all value from the protective documents issued for Jews by the Legation, [we] have in the meantime learned privately from foreign ministry [sources] that this is not true'.[55]

Further evidence of Wallenberg's effective networking is seen in Danielsson's next cable to UD: 'Our only contact to date with new Hungarian government has taken place informally [through] Wallenberg, who has had two conversations with Foreign Minister Baron K. [Kemény] concerning Jews under Swedish protection.'[56] Repeating that there were already signs that Swedish documents would, in the main, be respected, Danielsson then went directly into the issue which would in some ways dominate their relations with the Hungarians for the remainder of Wallenberg's time in the city: whether or not Stockholm would recognize the new regime. Danielsson wrote: 'What will likely be decisive in this matter is to what extent the diplomatic connection between Sweden and Hungary remains.' The Legation had already received notice from Kemény that he quickly expected full diplomatic recognition, and Danielsson clearly hoped that Stockholm would change its stance. For the first of numerous times, Danielsson suggested to UD that if 'its' Jews were to be protected and their efforts were to continue, the Hungarian regime would have to be officially recognized, or at least placated sufficiently, so that relations between the two countries would not be cut. Danielsson continued to repeat this argument until it became virtually a plea. Two days later, Danielsson notified UD that Vatican Nuncio Angelo Rotta had informed him that the Vatican would establish full diplomatic relations with the new regime, 'in order not to risk his Christian activities or their assistance activities for baptized Jews. Regarding the assistance activities of other countries for Jews, [Kemény] explained that the government was prepared to respect these providing that normal diplomatic relations be maintained.'[57] The maintenance of this argument, against the expressed wishes of superiors in Stockholm, is yet more evidence of Danielsson's and Anger's abiding desire to maintain their humanitarian efforts, for they could well have argued and acted otherwise.

Valdemar Langlet also had to confront the challenges of the tumultuous new situation. His operation had continued to expand – however chaotically – through August and September, and in some ways Langlet was even more active, right in the midst of Pest, providing immediate food or shelter, than were his Swedish colleagues. Like Wallenberg, he also 'employed' scores of Jewish and non-Jewish volunteers.

Now, after 15 October, the long-standing problem of financing these activities became urgent, if he and his operations were to continue.

Langlet requested that Danielsson should contact both UD and SRK's leadership, asking for more money, a necessity which must have greatly pained this proud man, particularly when he knew how relatively well financed Wallenberg's activities were. In a coded telegram sent to Stockholm on 21 October, Danielsson wrote: 'Langlet requests that the following is sent to Red Cross board: Thanks for gift of medicine, request response whether or not preparations being made for, during winter months, guaranteed assistance concerning previously requested financial support.'[58] Taking more than a week to respond, SRK's leadership sent a message that must have caused him considerable dismay: 'Inform Langlet [that] government money for continuing assistance activity to be received if such [need] is to be found possible and necessary.'[59] How the board of the SRK did not come to the obvious conclusion that the need was there and that it was possible to send funds safely to Budapest (as obviously Wallenberg's operation was doing) is not known, but clearly, even the urgency of the crisis did not prompt SRK's leadership to overcome its perceived difficulties with Langlet. This highly respected organization clearly chose not to help Langlet help others to an extent well within their capabilities.

For the first forty-eight hours after the coup, we know that Wallenberg was compelled to dash around the city, locating and rescuing members of his large staff and their families who had either fallen into the hands of *Nyilas* militia, or were too frightened to leave their hiding places. Literally and figuratively, this gave a segment of the city's population a quite different view of him than existed before. Though his exact movements cannot be tracked during subsequent weeks, the impact on his reputation as a man of action – both at the time and ever since – was enormous. What is clear, however, is that the bulk of his time during the second half of October was largely spent doing what he had been doing for the last three months. He contacted officials – primarily Hungarian and Jewish, but also some German – whom he already knew. He must have made dozens of phone calls, and continued to write reports. In his discussions with representatives of the national and municipal authorities, he was encountering men who for the most part continued to respect the idea that those Jews provided with protection by neutral diplomats were in a different, if still vulnerable category.

In other words, after the 15 October and for much of the remainder of the year, Wallenberg functioned, for the most part, more as a bureaucrat and diplomat than as a dashing 'Scarlet Pimpernel'. This was wise of him, because there is no doubt whatsoever that he and the other neutral diplomats remaining in Budapest were more effective by continuing their negotiations with those officials, including the

Budapest police, with the power to influence events. More lives were saved in Budapest through these contacts than by rushing about the city confronting episodic outbreaks of murderous violence. This more subdued image of Wallenberg goes against the grain of much of the witness testimony, popular literature and cinematic representations, but it is borne out by the contemporary documentation.

We have already noted Wallenberg's three-page report of 22 October. Drafted in Swedish under conditions of great stress and fatigue, it is yet another highly descriptive document written with precision and insight, and is another important Swedish contribution to the Holocaust's literature of destruction.[60] Relating information collected from a variety of sources, Wallenberg describes murders committed by Hungarian militia men within city limits and by SS troops outside Budapest. Weeks before the death marches of November commenced, Wallenberg was told of Jewish men between the ages of 16 and 60 sent for 'labour service' (*arbetstjänst*) towards the front lines.

One such column was seen by an eyewitness on the way towards Gödöllö:

> Those marching are very badly treated and a dead sixty-year old Jew lay by the roadside covered with newspaper and had obviously been beaten. Beginning tomorrow all remaining men and additionally women between 16 and 40 years are used for clearing rubble. In certain cases those holding protective passports have been attacked by armed bandits and their documents torn up. To date no reports of any deaths amongst those possessing protective passports.

It may seem obvious, but is worth noting that such a report cannot be written in haste, nor the information it contains collected in only some minutes. Composed in grammatically correct Swedish and well organized, such a document can only be completed over a period of hours – that is, when Wallenberg had to be sitting at a desk working and not hurrying about the city. Moreover, this document demonstrates the continuing importance of 'bureaucratic resistance'. One result he reported, and for which he claimed direct credit, was the annulment of a directive stating that even minor violations of certain anti-Jewish measures would be punished by death.[61]

Indeed, not only was Wallenberg calmly proud of what he, his colleagues and the many Jews serving in his 'volunteer' staff had accomplished in the days since the coup, he seemed positively to be enjoying himself. There is no doubt that Wallenberg's well developed sense of adventure, often demonstrated in earlier years, was alive and well, and that despite the extremely trying circumstances, he was thriving.

Having such a strong sense of himself and his abilities must have been a considerable asset under the circumstances. This chapter's first epigram was penned by Wallenberg that same evening in a letter to his mother. It is a document which illuminates Wallenberg the man as much as his official reports do:

> Today you only get these lines written in haste. I can reassure you that I am fine. The times are extraordinarily exciting and nerve-racking. We keep working and struggling on, and that is the main thing, however.
>
> Right now we are sitting by candlelight trying to prepare the diplomatic pouch. There is a power outage – that is all we need in this great mess. Dozens of people are standing around me, everyone with pressing questions, so that I don't know to whom to reply and advise first.
>
> I hope all is well with you, and I swear solemnly that you will get a more detailed account next time. I will stop for today and send my best wishes and kisses to all of you.[62]

MORE MYTH AND HISTORY

We have seen that Wallenberg, sometimes accompanied by Per Anger, had met with *Nyilas* Foreign Minister Kemény for negotiations. In this connection, yet another minor myth about Wallenberg may be put to rest, one which has through the years remained noticeable in the common picture of Wallenberg. An essential element of a mid-1980s film starring the American actor Richard Chamberlain was an alleged romantic link between the Swede and Kemény's wife, Elisabeth. Although denied by the baroness herself in an interview with journalist John Bierman in the early 1980s, I have heard about this obviously appealing dramatic notion scores of times after giving lectures about Wallenberg.[63] Contrary to cinematic myth, the 'glamorous' baroness was pregnant, and presumably in no condition to have an affair with the dynamic Swedish diplomat who did, by her account, charm her. Though according to his diary they met at the Gellért Hotel soon after Wallenberg arrived, that was their only scheduled meeting.[64] There is no evidence that their acquaintanceship played any significant political role.

However, Wallenberg's appointment's diary gives some clues about something which seems a genuine mystery. Though from 15 October until the end of December the diary becomes somewhat less useful as a source, it continues to provide important evidence of whom he was at least planning to meet. These include his meetings with *Obersturmbannführer* Kurt

Becher, and the SS man's recently acquired friend and apparent confidant, Hungarian businessman Vilmós Billitz.[65] Between September and late November, Wallenberg met the two of them about a dozen times: Becher at least five times, and Billitz a handful of times – at least as recorded in the Swede's diary. We have noted that the two historians who have studied Becher most closely confirm the SS officer's post-war account that he had little or nothing to do with anti-Jewish activities, either directly or through Hungarian allies.[66] Becher's greatest 'success' in Hungary as Heinrich Himmler's direct representative (and one strongly supported by the *Reichsführer*, a critical factor in the internecine battles of the SS), which furthered the economic interests of the SS, was the forced sale of the Weiss-Manfréd industrial concern to the SS.[67] At the time of the March occupation, Hungarian economic bureaucrats were unable to keep Becher from wresting the concern from Hungarian control, something which continued creating great tension between the Germans and Hungarians. Most interesting in this connection is Billitz, who was a well-known Budapest businessman, and a director of one of the concern's companies. Billitz eventually became quite close to the German, even accompanying the SS officer to Switzerland in November to meet with Jewish and American representatives.[68] Billitz, like Becher, also had, so far as is known, nothing to do with measures for or against Jews. According to Wallenberg's diary, his last scheduled meeting with Becher was for 3 November, but this cannot have taken place because Becher was already in Zurich the day before.[69] The last scheduled meeting with Billitz was for Friday, 24 November. These many meetings are of interest because they must have taken both time and attention from what is commonly believed to be Wallenberg's literally round-the-clock efforts to save Jews. The questions today are obvious: why was Wallenberg meeting so frequently with these two men, and what can these numerous meetings have been about? We may be sure that people in high-pressure circumstances such as these men were do not meet time and again unless something substantive is being discussed, and unless their individual interests are in some way being addressed and advanced. Moreover, such meetings were bound to be met with curiosity in different quarters and organizations, and might well have made Wallenberg less effective than he otherwise would have been. In combination with the time necessary to discuss, write and think about (as he did) possible business ventures with Koloman Lauer, it becomes clear that the rescue of Jews was not Wallenberg's sole priority. Currently there is no further evidence available which would shed further light on these potentially significant but unexplained meetings, and the matter must be left for future research.[70]

We may conclude this brief discussion about Wallenberg's possible business ventures by referring again to suspicions raised in late June by the British that Wallenberg would most likely try to conduct business while on his diplomatic mission.[71] American officials were probably less familiar with the Wallenberg empire, which – though it had strong ties in the US – still conducted business predominantly in Europe. On the other hand, the British well understood the tenacity with which family members pursued business and profit at the highest financial and political levels, something virtually dictated by what might be called the family's 'mindset'. That state of mind and those fundamental goals are confirmed yet again in a recent biography of Jacob Wallenberg, whose lifelong task was described as 'first and foremost to administer the inheritance of previous generations, to guard the family's position in Swedish industry and to shape the family's fortune'.[72] Raoul Wallenberg's education (apart from studying architecture in the United States) was shaped to follow family traditions, and we have seen that he was particularly close to, and influenced by, Jacob. Both before and during his time in Budapest, Wallenberg was extremely anxious to become more involved with central elements of the family's business empire, but he evidently failed. As we have seen, one of the reasons Wallenberg was given his mission was his earlier established contacts in Budapest, all of which were business contacts. Now, with the post-war era looming and with Wallenberg anticipating a return to Stockholm and to his and Lauer's business, he may well have begun exploiting those contacts, even as he carried on with his diplomatic and humanitarian activities. In fact, it would have been more surprising if the ad hoc diplomat had not been on the lookout for post-war opportunities, although this meant breaking his promise to UD and the Americans not to do business while in the city. Where these contacts might have led had he not been taken into Soviet custody can only be the subject of guesswork.

OTHER NEUTRAL DIPLOMATS IN BUDAPEST

Meanwhile, Wallenberg's and the Swedes' diplomatic activities continued unabated until the end of October. One important feature of this period was the increased cooperation between those neutral diplomats remaining in Budapest. This group, which included among others Swiss diplomats Karl Lutz, Harald Feller and Friedrich Born, Italian adventurer Giorgio Perlascas and papal representatives Angelo Rotta and Gennaro Verolino, and Hungarians such as Georges Mantello, constitutes (along with the Swedes) a fascinating group of men who, again, when given the chance to save some Jews through diplomatic means, made the most of it.[73] Anger remembers that Wallenberg was particularly important in pushing for increased collaboration: 'Our closest connection was of course with the Swiss, the whole time. We had more or less daily contact ... so that was very important ... Wallenberg was very much a driving force to get us together, to get these neutral [legations] together, and making joint interventions to the [Hungarian] Foreign Office about the Jewish situation ... [which] were written in the names of all of us.'[74] Lutz, who had been in Budapest since 1942, and Wallenberg were frequently in contact, with the latter visiting Lutz's office on a number of occasions. More experienced leadership for the group than Wallenberg's was provided by Nuncio Rotta, Danielsson, Lutz and Born, representative of the ICRC (International Committee of the Red Cross). Importantly, the remaining hesitation exhibited by the non-Swedes (apart from Lutz) to helping Jews now completely disappeared, and their efforts became wholehearted. Anger was particularly struck by the activism of Monsignor Gennaro Verolino, Rotta's assistant, whom he described as 'a courageous young man'.[75] Almost as importantly, this handful of diplomats now had the full support of their own governments and institutions, which was not necessarily the case before the October crisis. As historian R. Rozett has written: 'autumn's [activities] and the first few weeks of 1945 rested on the pillars of international concern, wide cooperation between international diplomats and Jews, and the approaching Soviet conquest. These factors combined to impede the completion of the destruction of Hungarian Jewry.'[76]

Contrary once again to popular conceptions of Wallenberg's alleged unilateral achievements, whatever pressure he and the Swedes were capable of exerting on Hungarian authorities was decisively strengthened by cooperation between the neutrals. Their effectiveness was, in turn, enhanced because even top-level *Nyilas* officials, starting with Szálasi and Kemény, remained willing to meet with the diplomats. This sent important signals to government, party and municipal officials at mid- and lower levels, who in turn, were in direct contact with the municipal police and *Nyilas* functionaries. If, for instance, a police sergeant knew that his superiors were in contact with the neutral diplomats, this increased the chances that the documents issued by neutral legations would be respected by him or his men. On occasion, even street thugs would hesitate in assaulting a Jew carrying neutral documents when it was known that high(er)-level officials remained interested in such matters. None of this, however, guaranteed the effectiveness of these documents if the immediate, 'street-level' perpetrator was sufficiently determined to commit murder and mayhem.

The presence of others in Budapest who contributed in some ways to the survival of Jews should also be noted. There are countless descriptions from Budapest survivors that the *Nyilas* takeover provided thousands of Hungarian gentiles with the opportunity to persecute, torment, rob and murder the city's Jews. Historians concluded long ago that without the murderous collaboration of many civilians, things would not have happened as they did. It should not be forgotten, however, that many individuals in Budapest chose to help their fellow Jewish citizens in a variety of ways. For instance, Wallenberg's volunteer staff of Jews is invariably mentioned in accounts, but little is said (or known) about the dozens of Hungarian gentiles who assisted with Valdemar Langlet's disparate operations.[77] Individual members of both the Catholic and Protestant clergy protested both publicly and privately, with some hiding Jews, especially children, in monasteries and cloisters.[78] It is important also to note that 'ordinary' people in Budapest helped in different ways; individual Jews or families were hidden in 'Aryan' buildings, and food was provided for, and shared with, Jewish friends and neighbours. These 'deviations' from the far more widespread patterns of events in Budapest must also be part of the Wallenberg story.

NEWS OF WALLENBERG'S ACTIVITIES SPREAD

Not surprisingly, the strains of the new situation created tensions within the Legation. There was, of course, the pure physical stress of working so many hours under the emotional pressure of trying to assist and save lives. UD's refusal to recognize Szálasi's government was a source of tension, as was, it seems, the fact that others on the staff harboured some resentment about Wallenberg's relative freedom of action. Though Lars Berg was a genuine admirer of Wallenberg (he observed him closely for some five months), he criticized Wallenberg in his memoirs: '[Not always in Budapest] did I appreciate all his measures, for some of them, from a purely Swedish interest, were sometimes potentially dangerous. Within the Legation we had some very tough arguments from which, I must add, Raoul always won because of his powerful intelligence ... [however], the leadership of a legation must always lie with the minister.'[79] Nonetheless, it appears that Danielsson and Anger chose not to inform Stockholm of these internal disputes.

On the other hand, Danielsson was informed of tensions in Stockholm about Wallenberg's activities, and they came from a surprising source – those who supported Wallenberg's recruitment. On 31 October, Engzell, having a chance to include a last-minute memorandum before the dispatch of a diplomatic pouch, expressed some long-held worries about Wallenberg's financial activities:

I would like to, in haste, bring up a question which I raised with Anger during his [August] visit here, and which appears to me to be somewhat unclear. When people have turned to us concerning financial aspects of our help to Jews, that is, the financing of Wallenberg's activities, they have generally said that they assume that it is the ministry and Legation which is responsible for the accounting, and overall activities. We have of course seen Wallenberg's brief [numerical] columns of this business, but have no possibility of judging [their accuracy].

I only want now to make you aware of these concerns held by some (for example, Ehrenpreis, the American refugee attaché Olsén [*sic*], and others), and would very much like to hear, when possible, your understanding of this matter. I would like to add, that this [query] implies no suspicions about Wallenberg's handling of these matters.[80]

Perhaps even more surprising than the fact that suspicions were raised against Wallenberg by his nominal patrons, is that UD's career diplomats didn't allow these suspicions to cause them to restrict what Wallenberg was trying to do. After all, this strong-willed, amateur diplomat was representing their institution, government and nation during a period of great uncertainty about how and when the war would end. It is possible that the strains of the war years on Günther and his closest aides gave them less time and made them less inclined to exercise normal control. However, Wallenberg's autonomy was limited to measures regarding direct assistance to Jews, and not larger political issues, such as the accelerating fight about recognition of the *Nyilas* regime.

We may conclude this chapter by noting that Sweden's goal of gaining favour with the Western Allies for their humanitarian diplomacy, and consequently relieving other political pressures, continued to be achieved. On 31 October, the British Legation in Stockholm sent yet another note to UD expressing Great Britain's appreciation for what Sweden was doing in Budapest: 'Please tell Ministry FA [Foreign Affairs] that we fully understand reasons for this contact with de facto authorities and much appreciate this attempt to save Jewish lives.'[81] Also from Stockholm came a report to Washington from American Minister Herschel Johnson to WRB chief John Pehle. It summarized for the WRB what 'Willenberg' (*sic*) and the Swedes were accomplishing in Budapest, with largely American funding. Dated 30 October, this two-page memorandum provided many of the details contained in Wallenberg's latest reports. Johnson recapitulated for his government the themes of pre-coup optimism, then post-15 October despair: 'First report reflected considerable optimism as to local situation with respect to Jews ... The report of October 22 reported extremely unfavourable developments.' Importantly, even this detailed and confidential document gives no basis for believing that the Americans thought of Wallenberg as anything other than a Swedish diplomat working for UD. It echoes British sentiments of approval for Sweden's activities, and concludes with the following: 'It appears Wallenberg is throwing his full energy into his task and doing remarkably well considering enormous difficulties. Olsen thinks official recognition by WRB of Wallenberg's efforts, which would be forwarded through the Foreign Office well justified. Swedish Government continuing to make extremely strong representations to Hungarian Government regarding treatment of Jews.'[82]

NOTES

1. R. Wallenberg to M. von Dardel, 22 October 1944, in R. Wallenberg, *Letters and Dispatches 1924–1944*, trans. K. Board (New York: Arcade Publishing, 1995), p.276.
2. Author's interview with Thomas Veres, 28 August 1989, New York City, in Uppsala University Library, Raoul Wallenberg Project Archive, no.C507, pp.35–6.
3. R.L. Braham, *The Politics of Genocide: The Holocaust in Hungary*, revised and enlarged edn (Boulder, CT: Rosenthal Institute for Holocaust Studies Graduate Center/City University of New York Social Science Monographs, 1994), vol. 2, p.946.
4. Israeli and other Western historians have covered the period extensively since at least the late 1970s. In the last decade or so, a new generation of Hungarian historians – freed from the constraints of communist ideology – have made major contributions to our understanding of the Hungarian Holocaust.
5. K. Ungváry, *Battle for Budapest; One Hundred Days in World War II*, trans. L. Löb, (Swindon: BCA/I.B. Tauris & Co. Ltd, 2003), p.3.
6. Ibid., p.xi. Ungváry also notes: 'Berlin fell within two weeks and Vienna within six days, while Paris and the rest of the European capitals – apart from Warsaw – saw no fighting at all.'
7. Ibid., p.6.
8. J. Lévai, *Black Book on the Martyrdom of Hungarian Jewry* (Zurich: Central European Times, 1948), p.337.
9. Braham, *Politics of Genocide*, vol. 2, p.950.
10. Ibid., p.948 and p.951.
11. Ungváry, *Battle for Budapest*, pp.2–3.
12. L. Karsai, 'The Last Phase of the Hungarian Holocaust: The Szálasi Regime and the Jews', in R.L. Braham and S. Miller (eds), *The Nazis' Last Victims: The Holocaust in Hungary* (Detroit, MI: Wayne State University Press, 1998). p.104.
13. Braham, *Politics of Genocide*, vol. 2, p.945.
14. Ibid., p 955.
15. See the proclamation by G. Vajna, cited in Lévai, *Black Book*, p.343.
16. Ibid., p.343.
17. Braham, *Politics of Genocide*, vol. 2, p.956.
18. There seems little question that the actual protective value of the variety of neutral papers (and their forgeries) in circulation differed from one day to the next. In the hagiographic literature, it is asserted that 'Wallenberg's *Schutzpass*' guaranteed safety. In reality, it did not guarantee the non-arrest or safe passage of an individual or a family.
19. Braham, *Politics of Genocide*, vol. 2, p.900.
20. Karsai, 'Last Phase of the Hungarian Holocaust', p.105.
21. Exact numbers were impossible to know. Braham concluded that within the city, some 160,000 Jews were in 'yellow star' houses or in hiding. Some 150,000 Jewish men were separated from their families and kept in forced labour brigades. Interestingly, some could

on occasion leave their units and visit the city. Braham, *Politics of Genocide*, vol. 2, p.952.
22. Karsai, 'Last Phase of the Hungarian Holocaust', pp.106–7.
23. The Jews were to be used to dig massive underground caverns in which, it was imagined, jet aircraft could be produced, safe from Allied bombing attacks. On this, see Braham, *Politics of Genocide*, vol. 1, pp.396–7.
24. Braham wrote that Eichmann had left Hungary, something which Eichmann himself later testified was incorrect. Braham, *Politics of Genocide*, vol. 2, p.956. See also Eichmann's own testimony to the Israeli police in *Eichmann Interrogated: Transcripts from the Archives of the Israeli Police*, trans. R. Manhei (New York: Farrar, Straus & Giroux, 1983), p.242.
25. To take but two of many possible examples, see E.R. Skoglund, *A Quiet Courage: Per Anger, Wallenberg's Co-Liberator of Hungarian Jews* (Grand Rapids, MI: Baker Books, 1997), p.120; and, even more problematically, 'Raoul Wallenberg', 8 June 2008, Wikipedia (on the internet).
26. D. Cesarani, *Eichmann: His Life and Crimes* (London: William Heinemann, 2004), p.189.
27. Braham, *Politics of Genocide*, vol. 2, p.958.
28. On the whole, these neutral representatives were safe from assault from *Nyilas* militia. Nonetheless, they were exposed, as was everyone else in Budapest, to injury or death from bombing or shelling.
29. For a more theoretical discussion of this issue, see P.A. Levine, 'On-Lookers', in P. Hayes and J. Roth (eds), *The Oxford Handbook of Holocaust Studies* (Oxford: Oxford University Press, forthcoming).
30. I. Danielsson to UD, no.377, 3 October 1944, *Riksarkivet Utrikesdepartementet* (hereafter RA UD), Hp 21 Eu 1092, folder 1.
31. I. Danielsson to UD, no.410, 12 October 1944, RA UD, Hp 21 Eu 1092, folder 1.
32. STB news agency, 3 October 1944, and from Winther, Swedish Legation Buenos Aires, no.895, 5 October 1944, both RA UD, Hp 21 Eu 1092, folder 1.
33. C. Herzog to M. Ehrenpreis, 8 October 1944, forwarded to A. Assarsson, UD, RA UD, Hp 21 Eu 1092, folder 1.
34. E. Eidem to UD, 10 October 1944, RA UD, Hp 21 Eu 1092, folder 1.
35. See, for instance, S. Grafström's letter of 12 October to Stockholms Enskilda Bank, RA UD, Hp 21 Eu 1092, folder 1.
36. R. Wallenberg's appointment's diary, RA, Raoul Wallenberg Arkiv, Signum 1, vol. 9. Komoly and Billitz obviously provided Wallenberg with close contacts to much of the Jewish community's assistance activities, which, although hampered after 15 October, continued to provide essential assistance to thousands. See Braham, *Politics of Genocide*, vol. 2, pp.1118–22.
37. R. Wallenberg, 'Report about the Hungarian Jews', 12 October 1944, RA UD, Hp 21 Eu 1092, folder 1.
38. Ibid. Each paragraph of this report provides illuminating detail about the Holocaust in Hungary.
39. R. Wallenberg to K. Lauer, 12 October 1944, RA, Raoul Wallenberg Arkiv, Signum 1, vol. 6. Huvudsta was then, and still is, a prominent Swedish property firm.
40. G. Engzell to Legation Budapest, no.280, 10 October 1944, RA UD, Hp 21 Eu 1100, folder 19.
41. See P.A. Levine, *From Indifference to Activism: Swedish Diplomacy and the Holocaust, 1938–1944*, 2nd edn (Uppsala: Studia historica Upsaliensia, 1998), especially Chapter 10.
42. A. Richert to G. Engzell, no.336, 16 October 1944, RA UD, Hp 21 J 1050, folder 14.
43. UD to Legation Budapest, no.424, 13 October 1944, RA UD, Hp 21 Eu 1092, folder 1.
44. P. Anger, *With Raoul Wallenberg in Budapest: Memories of the War Years in Hungary* (Holocaust Library: New York, 1981), pp.63–4; and L.G. Berg, *Boken som Försvann: Vad hände i Budapest* (Arboga: Textab Förlag, 1983), pp.30–1. The group arrived some days later safely in Sweden.
45. A survey of his diary shows that of the fourteen Sundays between 16 July and 15 October, Wallenberg scheduled meetings on half of them. On most of those days, only one meeting is indicated.
46. S. Hellstedt to A. Richert, no.701, 13 October 1944, RA UD, Hp 21 Eu 1092, folder 1.
47. Testimony of Kurt Becher, February 1946, 'Re: Instructions to record facts and probable assumptions regarding questions and persons connected with Jews in Hungary', in Braham, *The Destruction of Hungarian Jewry: A Documentary Account* (New York: Pro Arte for the World Federation of Hungarian Jews, 1963), doc. 438, pp.895–905.

48. According to Braham, *Politics of Genocide*, vol. 2, p.1081, Scholz (Wallenberg spelled the name as Scholtz) was an Abwehr agent who compromised himself through contact with Budapest Jews and who, as a result, may have been co-opted by SS Intelligence. By this point of the war of course, Himmler's SS and RSHA had virtually eliminated the Abwehr, subsuming its operations into theirs. S. Aronson identifies Scholz as a purported Gestapo official also 'described as the head of Abwehr Station Budapest'. See S. Aronson, *Hitler, the Allies and the Jews* (Cambridge: Cambridge University Press, 2004), p.191.

49. A. Handler, *A Man for All Connections: Raoul Wallenberg and the Hungarian State Apparatus, 1944–1945* (Westport, CT: Praeger, 1996), p.77.

50. Ibid., p.78.

51. Ibid. Strangely, Handler goes on to conclude that there is 'no evidence that during the first three months of his stay in Budapest [Wallenberg] had acquired familiarity with Hungary's political system, the leaders and programs of political parties, law-enforcement authorities', etc. The evidence presented in the present study completely contradicts such a conclusion. Handler made these mistakes because he relied upon other historians who also failed to use Swedish sources.

52. R. Wallenberg, 'Secretary of the Legation', 'Report about the Hungarian Jews situation', 22 October 1944, RA UD, Hp 21 Eu 1092, folder 1.

53. I. Danielsson to UD, no.428, 18 October 1944, RA UD, Hp 21 Eu 1092, folder 1.

54. UD to Legation Budapest, no.453, 19 October 1944, RA UD, Hp 21 Eu 1092, folder 1. That same day, this same information was cabled to Sweden's legations in Berlin, London and Washington.

55. I. Danielsson to C. Günther, no.9, 21 October 1944, RA UD, Hp 21 Eu 1100, folder 20.

56. I. Danielsson to UD, no.438, 22 October 1944, RA UD, Hp 21 Eu 1092, folder 1.

57. I. Danielsson to UD, no.440, 24 October 1944, RA UD, Hp 21 Eu 1092, folder 1. It is worth noting here that in Danielsson's perception, the Vatican was still helping only Jews who had converted, and had undergone a so-called 'emergency' baptism.

58. I. Danielsson to UD, no.434, 21 October 1944, RA UD, Hp 21 Eu 1092, folder 1.

59. S. Rydman, SRK to UD, 30 October 1944, RA UD, Hp 21 Eu 1092, folder 2. The telegram was sent on 1 November.

60. R. Wallenberg, 'Report about the Hungarian Jews situation', 22 October 1944, RA UD, Hp 21 Eu 1092, folder 1.

61. Ibid., p.3.

62. R. Wallenberg to Maj von Dardel, 22 October 1944, in Wallenberg, *Letters and Dispatches*, p.276. These lines from this letter complement those in n.1 of this chapter. It was dictated in German to a staff member.

63. J. Bierman, *Righteous Gentile: The Story of Raoul Wallenberg, Missing Hero of the Holocaust* (London: Penguin Books, 1981), p.78. Though Bierman's book is better than most of this genre, his account of Baroness Kemény's role and its alleged significance is a typical hagiographic mix of interviews given some decades after the period, in a dramatic tone which seeks to convince the reader of the account's 'authority'. In a section several pages long, Bierman writes about the interview, but fails to provide virtually any other sources for many important details. In the interview, the baroness is quoted as responding, after being asked if they were 'lovers': 'Ridiculous ... I was very pregnant at the time I knew him and although he was very charming he was not nearly as good looking as my husband.'

64. R. Wallenberg's appointment's diary, RA, Raoul Wallenberg Arkiv, 2 August 1944.

65. V. Billitz is not to be confused with Dezsö Billitzer, a mid-level official active within the Jewish Community's assistance activities, and a close friend of Otto Komoly.

66. What he may or may not have done on the Eastern Front, at which he served extensively as part of an SS unit, is a different subject.

67. By this period, severe conflicts within the SS (Nazi Germany's 'state within the state') involving the organization's economic branch, the WVHA, and its 'security' branch the RSHA, had reached new heights.

68. See G. Kádár and Z. Vági, *Self-financing Genocide: The Gold Train, the Becher Case and the Wealth of Hungarian Jews*, translated by E. Koncz, J. Tucker and A. Kádár (Budapest: Central European University Press, 2001), p.213 and pp.251–6.

69. Ibid., p.255.

70. Questions connected to these issues have also been posed by G. Rydeberg, archivist of UD, in his 2006 survey of recent research about Wallenberg, *Raoul Wallenberg: Historik och ny forskning* (Stockholm: UD publikationer, 2006), pp.8–9.

71. See Chapter 5, n.43.
72. See H. Modig's review of H. Lindgren's new biography of Jacob Wallenberg, in *Historisk tidskrift*, 2 (2008), pp. 273–5.
73. On G. Mantello, see Braham, *Politics of Genocide*, vol. 2, pp.1270–1. On the neutrals actions in general, see ibid., Chapter 31.
74. Author interview with Ambassador Per Anger, March 1990, Uppsala University Library, Raoul Wallenberg Project Archive, no.C002, p.67.
75. Author's interview with Per Anger, p.67. In 2004, the Swedish state educational institution Living History Forum (*Forum för Levande historia*) awarded Verolino with its annual Per Anger Prize for his humanitarian efforts in Budapest in 1944.
76. R. Rozett, 'International Intervention: The Role of Diplomats in Attempts to Rescue Jews in Hungary', in Braham and Miller (eds), *Nazis Last Victims*, p.149.
77. N. Langlet, *Kaos i Budapest: bertättelsen om hur svensken Valdemar Langlet räddade tio-tusentals människor undan nazisterna* (Vällingby: Harrier, 1982), pp.13–14.
78. On this, see Braham, *Politics of Genocide*, vol. 2, pp.1190–8.
79. Berg, *Boken som Försvann*, p.14.
80. G. Engzell to I. Danielsson, no.233, 31 October 1944, RA UD, Hp 21 Eu 1100, folder 20.
81. H. M. Pollack to UD, no.252, 31 October 1944, RA UD, Hp 21 1045, folder 2.
82. H. Johnson to Secretary of State (WRB), no.4416, 30 October 1944, in D. Wyman, *America and the Holocaust* (New York: Garland Publishing, 1989–91), vol. 8, doc. no. 26, pp. 60–1.

11

November–December: Death, Despair and Heroism

My dear Mr Wallenberg ... We have followed with keen interest the reports of the steps which you have taken to accomplish your mission and the personal devotion which you have given to saving and protecting the innocent victims of Nazi persecution ... I think that no one who has participated in this great task can escape some feeling of frustration [that] our efforts have not met with complete success ... [Yet] it is our conviction that you have made a very great personal contribution to the success which has been realized in these endeavors.

John Pehle (WRB) to Raoul Wallenberg, 8 December 1944[1]

Under current circumstances, with Budapest in the centre of military actions, the [Budapest] Legation has no possibility of continuing its humanitarian activities. In fact, [UD] has no current contact of any kind with the Legation.

UD, Stockholm, to Swedish Legation, Washington, 4 January 1945[2]

GENOCIDE IN BUDAPEST

As the first terrifying fortnight of the *Nyilas* era ended, the single factor which meant the most for Jewish survival – the arrival of the Red Army – appeared dismayingly distant. Hungarian and German forces surprised everyone with their effective defence, continuing to hold back the advance of Marshal Malinovsky's Second Ukrainian front. On 1 November, Malinovsky believed that Budapest would be taken within three days, yet not until almost eight weeks later, in late December, would the city finally be encircled and besieged.[3] Even then, it would take almost another two months before the entire city was liberated, and the mass killing of Jews by *Nyilas* militia and their collaborators finally ended. Nor would the desperate plight of hundreds of thousands of other Hungarians improve until the fighting stopped.

Inevitably, the Germans' goal of completing the destruction of Hungarian Jewry was given new life by the *Nyilas* coup, and both

Veesenmayer and Eichmann immediately plunged with determination into action to finish 'the job' that they had almost completed by early July. Their task, however, was made much more difficult by Himmler's late-October decision to destroy the gas chambers and crematoria at Auschwitz-Birkenau in the wake of the *Sonderkommando*'s uprising of early October. Yet Hitler and Germany's leadership in Berlin and Budapest remained determined to deport Budapest's Jews into the still-deadly 'universe' of the concentration camp system, ostensibly for labour. As we shall see, they sought to accomplish this by using the now familiar tactic of 'giving' the neutrals those few thousand Jews who had obtained protective papers and exemptions, in order to prompt the Hungarians to facilitate the deportation of the remaining Jews, who numbered still some 200,000 souls. German dependency on Hungarian manpower to destroy those Jews remained acute.

Though Szálasi's Hungarist ideology did not 'require' the physical destruction (at least on Hungarian soil) of the Jews, persecution, impoverishment and widespread murder continued unabated – as did typical Nazi attention to destructive detail. R.L. Braham reported:

> On November 3, the Szálasi government issued a sweeping decree under which the remaining Jewish property was confiscated 'for the benefit of the State'. Theoretically, it was to be used for financing war-related expenditures and the implementation of the anti-Jewish laws. Exempted from confiscation were only a few strictly personal items such as wedding bands, religious artifacts, textbooks, and drugs, plus a two-week supply of food, fuel, and a nominal amount of cash.[4]

Within city limits, the only thing ameliorating the torment of the Jews remained the work of the remaining neutral diplomats, who redoubled their efforts. The point has been made that Swedish diplomacy was made far more effective through increasing collaboration with the other neutrals, and this remains true until the end of this period. However, just as this study is unable to offer much voice to the memories of survivors of the Holocaust in Budapest, it is also unable, for reasons of space, to offer a full, comparative analysis of the accomplishments and failures of international diplomacy in Budapest.[5] Instead, these collaborative efforts will be noted in this study's penultimate chapter, where they appear in immediate connection to Swedish activities and initiatives. Increasingly, however, the heroic efforts of Wallenberg and the other neutral diplomats were overtaken by the despair, destruction and death which enveloped the Hungarian capital.

DID WALLENBERG SAVE 100,000 JEWS?

Though the hagiographic literature about Wallenberg would have the reader believe that he was always rushing about the streets from threat to threat and location to location, there is little actual evidence that this was the case. Contributing to this distorted picture is the fact that around the time of the coup, Wallenberg had shifted his primary operation from the Legation in Buda to an office in Pest. He established his headquarters in Ulloi utca. 2–4, in the heart of Pest, near the edge of the eighth district, making him more visible than before.⁶ In fact though, this period continued to be dominated far more by normative diplomacy than by Wallenberg, Anger or anyone else rushing about saving individuals or groups of Jews. Though this did sometimes occur, their negotiations with Hungarian (and sometimes German) officials remained far more effective in helping Jews than in anything else. During the first two weeks of November (and almost to the end of the year) Swedish diplomacy continued the pattern of diplomatic activism demanded by the situation.

Everything that Wallenberg and his colleagues did between 15 October and January 1945 was overshadowed by two immediate issues, with a third looming in everyone's mind. Though rampant, random and often deadly, *Nyilas* street violence did not yet dominate the Swedes' actions and possibilities, and relatively normative diplomacy remained predominant. The second factor, noted earlier, was the knowledge that sooner rather than later the Soviets would liberate Budapest, although no one could know exactly when that would happen. The third factor was Germany's looming defeat. Though the autumn's military operations in north-west Europe began with the failure of Operation Market-Garden, and with it the hope that the Anglo-American armies would cross the Rhine into Germany before Christmas, there still prevailed the basic understanding that Hitler's defeat was inevitable. Few observers, including the Swedes in Budapest, could have guessed that in fact so little progress would be made on either the Western or Eastern Front through the end of 1944.⁷

In November, the refusal of UD officials in Stockholm to grant any form of recognition to the Szálasi regime began more and more to influence what Swedish diplomats could and could not do. In fact, the day before the mid-October coup, UD cabled Budapest that because (then) Prime Minister Lakatos admitted to Danielsson that Hungary remained 'completely occupied' by German troops, for Sweden there could be no question of recognizing his government, or Szálasi's successor Nazi regime. Nor was there any question of Stockholm accepting an official Hungarian representative, a decision which in late

December had especially unpleasant consequences.[8] Here we may note again that one factor which gave the Swedes some leverage on Szálasi's regime not enjoyed by the other neutral delegations (several of which did recognize the Szálasi regime) was the fact that Stockholm was the protecting power for Hungary amongst the belligerent powers, most importantly in the United States and United Kingdom, although not for the USSR.[9] In fact, not all neutral legations stayed after the coup, with at least two deciding to leave the city.[10]

It has been demonstrated that regardless of Wallenberg's personal qualities and motivations, had he not been an accredited Swedish diplomat, he would have been powerless to help anyone. This point is emphatically confirmed when viewing Danielsson's role during this period. If he had not fought his superiors in Stockholm on the matter of recognition as tenaciously as he did, the Swedes, including Wallenberg, would have been forced to leave the city. Danielsson left Stockholm in no doubt that that if some sort of recognition wasn't granted to the *Nyilas* regime, all humanitarian activities on behalf of Jews would be forced to cease. If, in such a circumstance, Wallenberg had wished to stay (which, given what we know, seems unlikely), he would not have been allowed to. Even if he had tried to stay, he would have been wholly ineffective, while placing himself in genuine danger. As long as some Hungarian officials continued to care about this issue, it worked to the Swedes' advantage. Danielsson played this card with great skill, keeping a deeply contentious question open for weeks. In the face of enormous pressure, he held at bay until late December any final Hungarian decision about Sweden's representation in the country. Danielsson was not alone in conducting such delicate diplomacy. Per Anger remembers that he too played the diplomatic game, one in which, even in a genocidal situation, egos played a significant role:

> I was very much involved with Kemény, because I could visit the Foreign Office very easily, and so Raoul and I very often had meetings with Kemény ... I flattered [him] and said, 'Oh, you are absolutely one of the outstanding foreign ministers in modern time, and you will be perhaps the first ambassador to Sweden, because we want to recognize your government very soon.' I [said] things which I never had any authorisation to say, but that was the only way to negotiate.[11]

In the event, November commenced on a positive note. At the same meeting in late October when Danielsson reminded the new foreign minister of King Gustav's earlier appeal requesting 'humanitarian treatment of the Jews', Kemény gave the Swede the encouraging news that the government had in fact decided to 'respect the previous government's undertakings in regard to Jews under Swedish protection'. This was of fundamental importance if Wallenberg and the Swedes were to achieve anything, and it was quickly reported to key individuals in Stockholm (both Swedish and Allied), and to Sweden's Legations in Berlin and London.[12] The wide circulation given to this particular memorandum points to another important aspect of Sweden's diplomacy in Budapest. Since late 1942, Stockholm's efforts on behalf of some Jews scattered throughout Europe was not limited to the efforts of individuals, but rather became – and remained – official policy conducted by several legations, especially Berlin. Though there is evidence of reluctance by several individuals to help Jews, there is no question that Sweden's foreign policy apparatus genuinely tried to accomplish something on behalf of those few Jews left alive in Europe. Though these disparate efforts may have failed to accomplish all that was hoped for, their moral importance must be acknowledged.

Yet the chaotic nature of the situation prevailing in early November is seen in Danielsson's report that despite official Hungarian confirmation that Swedish (and other neutral) papers would be respected, 'the public announcement of this on the radio has not yet penetrated to party functionaries, who still on a daily basis are guilty of attacks even against Jews holding Swedish protective papers [*skyddspass*]. The Legation has however managed in numerous cases, through direct intervention, in creating a more correct situation.'[13] This last sentence seems to describe incidents when either Wallenberg or another Swede – most likely Per Anger – did confront directly a situation, or an individual, whose outcome and or intent was to harm any Jew(s) who enjoyed Swedish protection. What, exactly, such episodes looked like, or how often they actually happened, is impossible to know from the documentation. When mentioned, they are not described, nor do they identify which Swede 'directly intervened'. Exactly where or how intervention occurred, how many Jews were involved, and how many might have been directly released to safety, or even perhaps taken (by a *Nyilas* functionary, or a municipal policeman) to a Swedish protective house, is not specified. This lack of documentary clarity provides the opportunity to return to a key issue in the mythology around Wallenberg – namely, the highly emotive matter of 'how many Jews Wallenberg saved'.

Previous accounts have not attempted to conceptualize and genuinely understand what it actually meant to 'rescue' or 'be saved' in Budapest. At its core, this is a discussion about definitions, and trying to understand more completely what actually happened in Budapest. How can or should 'rescue' be precisely defined in this highly particular context? For instance, should an individual 'rescue' be put into the 'positive' numerical column, because of direct intervention by Wallenberg one day, when perhaps the next day or week that individual may well have been hauled to the Danube's quay and shot dead? Or because during one 'episode' a perpetrator may have recognized the validity of a Swedish document, reinforced by Wallenberg's physical presence, when in a subsequent episode, another, more wilful perpetrator chose not to respect that same document, with murder the result? Did Wallenberg (and the other Swedes) 'save' more Jews by 'direct intervention', or were more 'rescued' through the negotiations which convinced Hungarian officials to revalidate the neutral protective documents which that same official had earlier declared invalid? Indeed, in the interests of precision, we may ask if Wallenberg 'saved' more people by direct intervention, or by purchasing foodstuffs to be stored in locations accessible to Jews and not plundered by Hungarian or German soldiers? Perhaps his attention to critical issues of hygiene in 'Swedish houses' actually saved more Jews from death by disease than he did along the route to Hegyshalom?

Estimates of the numbers of Jews who found shelter in 'Swedish houses' are just that, estimates which tell us nothing about the length of time 'x' number of thousands found temporary shelter (for days or weeks), or 'rescuing' shelter until the Soviet occupation. Nor do such imprecise speculations take into account the number of people forcibly removed from Swedish shelter. Moreover, who is to be given primary responsibility for the shelters of the 'international ghetto' coming into existence – Wallenberg, Danielsson, Anger, Lutz, Rotta – or the Hungarian 'doctors of space' analysed by Tim Cole? How is the 'counting' to occur if some individuals found shelter in a Swedish house, but were then removed or ordered from a 'protected' building and sent on the deportations (by foot) to the Austrian border? We have only approximate numbers about how many died during these 'death marches', along the route, or in the (thoroughly inadequate) shelters provided in Hegyshalom. Nor do we have any idea how many 'Wallenberg Jews' either died or survived once they entered the Reich's camp system. Nor have we any idea how many who possessed Swedish papers were subsequently murdered.[14] No sufficiently credible combination of explanatory factors can be identified which explains the 'numerical' outcome of a series of diverse incidents, nor is there a credible approximate count of how many Jews Wallenberg did directly 'save' through courageous, physical intervention, from either an urban assembly point, a brickyard, or a death march. It may have been dozens, or perhaps hundreds – it is impossible, with the available documentation, to provide even a 'guesstimate'. The various figures given by the Swedes themselves between March and December are limited;

they differ according to the type of paper received and/or other type of assistance given, and are even sometimes contradictory.

What can be said with certainty, however, at least according to evidence apart from the decades-old memories of some survivors, is that Wallenberg never 'leapt onto' the roof of a freight car bound for Auschwitz, in order to pass out handfuls of *Schutzpässe*. Indeed, even imagining such a scene, the question must be asked: what type of Swedish protective document would have been wildly distributed at such an alleged occasion? Were they *Schutzpässe*, or emergency passports, or perhaps only a 'protective document' (*skyddsbrev* A or B)? Which ones were more or less effective during such a remembered incident? Belonging to any discussion of numbers is the matter of whether or not Wallenberg can be 'credited' with saving the tens of thousands of Jews huddled in the 'central ghetto'.[15] Furthermore, the matter of sheer blind luck in explaining some instances of Jewish survival in Budapest, as elsewhere during the Holocaust, may be raised – and into whose numerical 'credit column' of souls 'saved' are they to be put?

The essential point here is that obtaining specific numbers for how many Jews Raoul Wallenberg 'saved' is in fact impossible, and in my judgement can never be credibly established within a useful numerical framework. Nor can his *exact* influence in the survival of 'x' number of individuals ever be adequately determined, at least not in a manner which will add to our understanding of how he did help, in one way or another, some people to survive. This issue of numbers, it seems clear, has lost its empirical utility and moral value. It should, I think, cease to be a part of discussions about why Wallenberg is important to us, and to the history and memory of the Holocaust. What is essential, as this study has argued throughout, is to understand the tactics and motivations displayed by Wallenberg and his colleagues which, we know for certain, did contribute to the relief and survival of a significant number of human beings.

A BLIZZARD OF PAPER

The relative value of the protective papers issued by the Swedes and other neutral diplomats, has already been discussed from several points of view. We have seen that the idea of a *Schutzpass* was conceived not by Wallenberg, but by Karl Lutz late in 1942, thereby establishing a vital precedent which would find its full expression in the second half of 1944. Indeed, even the numbers 'saved' or 'shielded' or 'assisted' by Lutz himself cannot be credibly established, not least because his form of protective paper was issued not only for individuals, but also for families and even larger groups. Although, in the case of the Swedes, the number of 4,500 individuals allowed by the Hungarians to receive some form of protective document is noted several times in the documentation, analysis shows that this particular number had mixed meanings at different times for different participants in the ongoing multilateral negotiations.

Complicating further any discussion of numbers 'saved' is the fact that all the neutral papers, including Swedish documents, were forged in large numbers by young Jews, primarily those involved in the different Zionist groups. Indeed, the production of forged, official-looking neutral documents was another form of 'bureaucratic resistance', and such forgeries were produced on a considerable scale. One young Zionist activist, David Gur, wrote about both the quantities of forged documents in circulation and the necessity for calm in the face of life-threatening pressures:

> The forged documentation in itself did not provide sufficient protection during street inspections ... [it] had psychological value; it gave its holder the basis for a confident facade – since anyone who did not appear natural and confident would not be saved even if he had a document in his pocket. One needed to know which document to present and when to present it. During a street inspection, if someone took out a sheaf of papers, he was immediately suspect. The rank and file Christian citizen had nothing more than a residence permit and identity card.[16]

In his study of Budapest's Zionist resistance, which was particularly active in forging Swiss protective papers, Asher Cohen wrote: 'It is not possible to ascertain ... with any degree of certainty how many Swiss protective passes were circulated by the Resistance. The number apparently ranged between 100,000 and 125,000. It is even more difficult to estimate how many Jews owe their lives to these [forged] passes.' This widely known inflation of protective documents in circulation – and this was another phenomena which occurred in Budapest and nowhere else during the Holocaust – had, however, a significant cost: 'It appears that the mass circulation given to the protective passes [by the Resistance] gradually reduced their value and their dependability in the eyes of the Hungarian [authorities]. Against the background of the conditions then rampant in Budapest, it is impossible to verify these matters with any degree of accuracy.'[17]

In fact the Swedes were themselves not above forging protective papers. Late in December, during an incident with a *Nyilas* man, Lars Berg was given a document from German military authorities stating that Swedish diplomats were under their protection. After receiving it, Per Anger decided that duplicating it would be a good idea, and proceeded to do so: 'this [German] general gave Berg a paper where it was stated that the holder of this paper is under the protection of the German government. And we duplicated that in many, many copies ... everyone got a copy of that paper.'[18]

Meanwhile, the Germans' typical tactics of delay and obfuscation regarding neutral efforts to obtain the departure of small groups of Jews was demonstrated yet again early in November. A Swedish diplomat went to AuswärtigesAmt in Berlin in order to discover if it was true, as they had been informed by the Hungarians, that the Germans had actually granted permission for a train of some 400–500 'Swedish' Jews to transit Germany on their way to Sweden. Eberhard von Thadden, whom we have encountered previously, had been for many months Sweden's interlocutor in the prolonged negotiations for transit permission. Yet when the latest developments were described to him, according to the Swede, he feigned 'complete ignorance' of the entire question, let alone the claim that progress had recently been made in the trilateral negotiations.[19] In fact, Berlin continued to instruct Veesenmayer to convince the Hungarians neither to allow such trains to leave, nor to permit the neutral legations to issue any more protective documents than were authorized prior to 15 October.[20]

These matters of securing the departure of even a few Jews, cooperation with the Swiss, and the increasingly acute issue of whether or not to recognize Szálasi's government were all subjects raised in a cable Danielsson wrote on 8 November. Describing the situation for the Jews as increasingly one of 'terror, brutality, confiscated ration cards and forged, official-looking neutral documents – deteriorating conditions in general', Danielsson requested with some urgency:

> [that Stockholm should] show its seriousness, by pressing Berlin for transit visas for the immediate departure of some 150 people. [Hungarian] government renews its question regarding recognition. From the viewpoint of saving Jews it is desirable that some formal acknowledgement might be shown, as on 15 November, annulment planned of status for protective paper Jews [*skyddspassjudar*], making them equal with all other Jews. Informal query made to Hungarian authorities whether circumstance [may apply] if Legation remaining [in Budapest] would be seen as de facto recognition of new government.[21]

Engzell answered the next day, telling Danielsson that so long as the word 'recognition' was not used with the Hungarians, it was acceptable for the Legation to promote the notion that its continued physical presence should be thought of by the Hungarians as constituting de facto recognition.[22]

Also taking some of Danielsson and Anger's time and energy were continuing difficulties with Valdemar Langlet and his unwieldy operation. These were described to Stockholm, with UD (and therefore SRK as well) being informed that at least a portion of the problems were caused by Langlet's methods and behaviour. In Langlet's defence, it can be readily noted that some of his problems were caused by the fact that most participants in the ongoing drama(s) knew that Langlet's operation did not enjoy the same support from its Stockholm base as did the Legation's. Danielsson wrote that *Nyilas* militia were violating SRK locations 'on a daily basis', yet, luckily, interventions by Legation staff (again unnamed) continued to solve the many 'local' situations. However, clearly frustrated with the old academic, he added:

> The Legation's work with these questions is meanwhile seriously complicated by the difficulty of controlling Langlet's activities. These are currently of considerable proportion with continually growing number of locations and employees who issue protective papers, etc. in the name of the Red Cross, of which in general the Legation is not informed of in advance. Langlet has now been seriously admonished that in all important questions [he must] seek the advice of the Legation.[23]

Indeed, SRK's shocking disinterest in providing genuine support for Langlet's efforts is again made visible in a letter of 7 November by its chief, Prince Carl, to Rabbi Ehrenpreis. Written as a response to an appeal received from Ehrenpreis, this disingenuous 'diplomatic' letter reeks of an unjustified self-satisfaction for the institution. Claiming credit for Langlet's and Asta Nilsson's ongoing humanitarian struggle in Budapest, the prince then wrote that, in the event, there was nothing more he or his organization could do at the moment. Specifically, he rejected Ehrenpreis' idea of contacting a German prince (the Count of Sachsen-Coburg-Gotha) directly, because, he argued, 'experience shows that such an approach will lead to nothing ... Meanwhile I am of the opinion that currently it is not possible to take any new measures to assist the unfortunate Jews in Hungary ... I regret that I cannot give you a more favourable answer to the question you posed to me.'[24]

It is worth considering, however, whether the lack of trust shown in Langlet by SRK was in some ways justified, as he came in for – yet again – very sharp if still reluctant criticism from Danielsson. Informing Engzell that because of their own workload, Legation staff were having great difficulties in exercising effective control over Langlet, Danielsson used rather harsh language about someone he obviously respected: 'Mostly the Legation has in the most important questions been confronted with a *fait accompli* by Langlet, but in order not to jeopardize things, been forced to accept his obviously well meant but scarcely thought-through actions. He has had difficulties in keeping his activities within reasonable proportions.'[25] As a possible, if belated, solution to this problem, Danielsson assigned Yngve Ekmark, a young Swedish diplomat who had left Belgrade some weeks before and ended up staying in Budapest, as 'commissioner' for Langlet, but it is unclear what actual effect this move had.[26]

Danielsson's report – one of the last written letters (to be differentiated from the still-functioning coded telegram system) which made it out of Budapest to UD – also contains one of the few descriptions of the work done by another unknown hero of Sweden's efforts in Budapest, Asta Nilsson. We have earlier noted that she was an experienced aid worker sent by Rädda barnen (Save the Children), and assigned to do what was possible to help. Danielsson wrote: 'Additionally, cooperation between Langlet and Asta Nilsson has not been the best. [She] is however currently putting in a most worthwhile work in saving and helping children and now has [set-up] a number of children's homes for approximately 1,700 children.'[27]

Much of November and December was characterized by changes in the daily situation and, consequently, changes in what the Swedes could do to best maintain the considerable assistance they were providing to their growing number of charges. Because Wallenberg, Danielsson and Anger were able to maintain effective contact (at several institutional levels) with Kemény's ministry, they understood the acutely ad hoc, increasingly chaotic circumstances which prevailed within the government. For instance, on 12 November, Danielsson cabled Stockholm to say that negotiations with the foreign ministry had resulted in an ostensible increase in the number of protective documents they could issue, although they understood that this could well change.[28] Also mentioned for one of the first times is that the holders and beneficiaries of the 4,500 'protective passports' known to have been issued would be moved into segregated housing, along with approximately 12,500 'other Jews'. This is in obvious reference to the rapidly expanding 'international ghetto', now firmly established in Pest's fifth district, close to the bank of the Danube.[29]

Although it is never stated explicitly in the extensive exchange between Danielsson and Stockholm regarding the issue of recognition, it seems clear that UD's primary reason for its intransigence on the issue was its desire not to anger the Anglo-Americans, who were against any diplomatic moves which favoured an Axis member. It has been noted several times that underlying – but not dominating – Swedish diplomacy in Budapest was Stockholm's desire to curry much-needed favour with Washington and London. In early November the

Americans again echoed recent British praise. The 'sincere appreciation of the US government for the Swedish government's humanitarian activities' was again sent, pleasing senior Swedish politicians and officials. Also of interest is the specific mention of Wallenberg's activities, indicating that even though Iver Olsen had some anxieties about how Wallenberg was accounting for his American funds, the WRB representative still communicated to Washington his favourable understanding of what the young Swede was doing. The Americans' praise for him was unambiguous, expressing their 'sincere' appreciation for 'the ingenuity and courage which Mr Wallenberg has shown in rendering assistance to persecuted Jews'.[30]

However, not all top UD diplomats were of the opinion that Sweden's humanitarian work was having the desired effect with the Americans. Though Sven Grafström, head of UD's political division, did not at any time try to hamper activities in Budapest, he did complain in his diary that nothing seemed to help improve relations with the US: 'The Americans are not nice towards us. All of our successive measures in favour of the Allies hasn't helped us one bit ... the State Department, we hear, uses severe language against us ... [they] consider us a nation out for profit, and nothing else.'[31]

Another issue causing Danielsson increasing concern was the anticipated evacuation of Szálasi's government from the capital towards western Hungary. A plan was under consideration to flee before the final Russian offensive, and officials were beginning to insist that the neutral diplomats should accompany them. Though it was announced that any Hungarian official not obeying this order was liable to be executed (according to what the Swedes were told by their interlocutors at the foreign ministry), the Hungarists were essentially powerless to force the neutrals to move with them. When the issue was first raised with Stockholm, Danielsson received a curt response from UD that 'in the event of the government's departure, you shall stay in Budapest', something which pleased Danielsson and aided Wallenberg.[32] As noted above, the minister sought to use this circumstance as a way of convincing the Hungarians that the Legation's continued presence was tantamount to de facto recognition. Though Stockholm partly accepted this reasoning, the unrelenting refusal to accept in Stockholm any sort of official Hungarian representation ultimately undermined Danielsson's credibility, and damaged assistance activities. In any case, he reported, the Hungarians were demanding that, at a minimum, one representative of the Legation should be evacuated with the government. Refusal to do this would be considered 'a hostile act' on the part of the Swedish government.[33]

This was a vital argument Danielsson was pursuing, and he kept at it because he knew (and had communicated) that without satisfaction of some sort, the Hungarians would shut down all Swedish activities. Here it may be noted that a temporary diplomat of Wallenberg's status could not have engaged his superiors in this almost insubordinate fashion, and the veteran diplomat's determined refusal to accept what was a clear decision made by his superiors was, at a minimum, highly unusual. Undaunted, Danielsson immediately responded with an even longer explanation, including a virtual plea that some public gesture by Stockholm was quickly needed. After another meeting with Kemény on 10 November, Danielsson commenced a lengthy telegram by noting, without comment, the foreign minister's assertion that the recent change in government was in fact conducted according to Hungary's constitution. Danielsson added the salient fact that his colleagues from the Vatican and Turkey (which had maintained its representation in Budapest) were urging the Hungarians to view their continued presence as de facto recognition. He again appealed vigorously to UD that accepting some form of Hungarian representation in Stockholm was absolutely necessary, otherwise 'our entire Jewish assistance activities [*judehjälpaktion*] will be lost ... if no form of recognition is granted'.[34]

This telegram then concluded with a proposal from Danielsson that is surprising in the extreme, and not noted elsewhere in publications about Wallenberg. Insisting that the government's departure was imminent, the Hungarians increased pressure on the Swedes, yet Danielsson and Anger pushed back. Eventually, the Swedes proposed that rather than the entire staff evacuating westwards, only one representative should leave the city – something which it appears several of the other neutral legations had agreed:

> The foreign minister has insisted that the Legation be represented when the government evacuates [Budapest]. He told the resident Portuguese chargé d'affaires that if he, against the government's wishes, stays in Budapest, there can no longer be an official guarantee of protection of extraterritoriality. In this case it appears unavoidable, with regard to, among other things, the many interests represented by [our] Legation in Hungary, that some gesture must be made. [Therefore] I propose that Wallenberg be detached to the government when it leaves the capital city – this because in any case the Legation's Jewish activities [*judeaktion*] will be, in the main, concluded when the Russians invade.[35]

The seriousness of Danielsson's proposal was underscored when, even before Stockholm had a chance to react, he and Anger informed Kemény's colleagues that it was their intention that Wallenberg would join the planned evacuation. This time Danielsson stressed to his superiors that not only would activities on behalf of the Jews be halted, but the safety of the entire staff would be jeopardized. UD swiftly answered, expressing some amazement that it was Wallenberg who had been suggested: 'Is it really suitable that Wallenberg be detached to the government? Is he not best needed in the period between the evacuation [of the government] and before the Russians arrive?' Yet despite Stockholm's surprise and uncertainty, Danielsson was again given autonomy to take the decision he thought best.[36] Why Wallenberg was proposed as Sweden's link with the soon-to-depart government, and not, for instance, Lars Berg or Yngve Ekmark, is a mystery which the available sources do not solve. Danielsson's partial explanation, that circumstances themselves would soon put a stop to all humanitarian activities, is both unconvincing and somewhat surprising in view of all his previous supportive decisions regarding Wallenberg.

Yet just two days later, on Wednesday, 15 November, Stockholm was again informed that Danielsson had in mind Wallenberg's departure from Budapest, this time in connection with the still hoped-for transport of 150 Jews to Sweden. UD was told by telephone: 'The front is closing on the city. Artillery fire and flames visible from the city.' Just as importantly, the Hungarians had informed them that the way was now clear for the departure of the 150, and could essentially occur at any time. However, agreement from relevant German officials in Berlin still had to be secured, because (as it was typically phrased) certain 'formalities' remained unresolved. If things worked out, the Legation representative accompanying the group would be Wallenberg, who 'is the only one available [to accompany] a possible transport, because the other two proposed are fully occupied'.[37] The names of the other two in question are not given, but a logical guess would be Berg and Ekmark – Danielsson would never have countenanced losing Anger under the circumstances. Evidently he had concluded that circumstances allowed for Wallenberg's departure, although exactly why he came to such a seemingly inappropriate, even unwise decision is not known. He needed no reminding that those Jews under Swedish protection needed all the help they could get, nor did the minister ever cease his efforts to help. Yet it seems odd, at best, under the circumstances that he had twice proposed Wallenberg's departure.

Of course, Wallenberg didn't accompany the Hungarians when they evacuated, nor did the transport materialize. This new knowledge, however, makes it easy to imagine that had Wallenberg been compelled, for whatever ultimate reason, to leave Budapest before the Russians arrived, his own life would have turned out very differently.

Twice – at least potentially – fate determined that he would remain in Budapest. This knowledge changes nothing about our understanding of Wallenberg's diplomacy, but it does heighten the sense of tragedy felt when contemplating his fate after 17 January, 1945.

THE STRUGGLE TO SAVE LIVES ACCELERATES

It is difficult today to grasp the dizzying range of political and practical complications prevailing in Budapest at that time about all issues, including the fate of the Jews. The diplomatic battle between neutrals and perpetrators continued unabated, with – again – all participants in the drama aware that the approaching Red Army meant that all political and personal goals, all means and plans, were but fragile notions of what should or might happen. Yet meetings, memoranda, reports and planning did continue in this fascinating diplomatic minuet between three governments – Swedish, Hungarian and German. Unsurprisingly, those German diplomats and officials remaining in Budapest, still led by Veesenmayer, never stopped trying to inflict as much violence and death upon the surviving Jews as possible before they were forced to evacuate. It is incorrect to assert, however, as the hagiographers do, that this was a period when 'Wallenberg battled Eichmann' (who wasn't even in the city much at this point), or that the Swedes 'battled the Nazis' in any singular fashion apart from their energetic diplomacy. Nevertheless, it is important not to lost sight of the fact that those dozen or so European men who conducted neutral diplomacy during these weeks were, increasingly, risking their own lives to help Jews during the Holocaust.

As November wore on, the level of contact between the neutrals and the Szálasi government began to diminish, but the latter retained its need to maintain positive contacts with those diplomats remaining. As A. Cohen noted: 'the neutral missions still commanded considerable prestige. They were almost the only elements which enjoyed general confidence in the Hungarian capital at that time.'[38] As a result, leading figures in Szálasi's government, not least Minister of the Interior Vajna and Foreign Minister Kemény, remained susceptible to appeals made by the neutrals. In their efforts to influence these *Nyilas* party leaders, they invoked the prestige of their own countries and institutions, including that of several of the ad hoc neutral 'representatives', such as the 'Spaniard' Giorgio Perlasca and the 'Portugese' Count Pongrac.[39] Importantly, these worldly diplomats did not appeal to any sense of shame they believed might be felt by the perpetrators, or express their own deep sense of moral outrage at what they were

witnessing.[40] Rather, while describing in detail what they knew about
the continuing outrages, they appealed for an easing of the atrocities
being inflicted on the Jews by referring to promises already given, and
by stressing that the reputation of the Hungarian people and nation,
both then and in the future, would be damaged if such treatment continued.

However, even if the neutrals could have exercised even more influence on Hungary's leadership, it was not always the case that high-
level decisions and directions which were in some way 'favourable' to
Jews were effectively translated into a reduction of street-level persecutions, brutality and murder. When Rotta and Danielsson met Szálasi
on 17 November, they dared to inform him about the ongoing atrocities, pointing out (no doubt in another attempt to flatter the ego of
Hungary's 'führer') that in comparison, Mussolini was far more effective in controlling his followers from committing abuses and atrocities.
They told 'the Leader of the Nation' that 'the operations of these
[party functionaries] gives the impression that behind the legal government there is another government [and] the responsible government is covering the activity of irresponsible people and thus creating
a general feeling of uncertainty among Hungarians and foreigners'.[41]
Though in the end their influence was bound to be limited, there can
be no question that things would have been much worse without the
tireless efforts of Budapest's neutral diplomats. And again, considering
the increasingly dangerous circumstances in which these men found
themselves, they could well have chosen the easier option of going to
the safety of bomb shelters, or leaving the city. In the study of genocide, such examples of why some people chose *not* to be bystanders
must be highlighted.

The new leaders of Hungary had another group of persuasive interlocutors and, throughout November and as far into December as was
technically feasible, Edmund Veesenmayer and other top German officials in Budapest and Berlin remained determined to empty Hungary
of its remaining Jews. Now, however, they sought to convince their
Hungarian collaborators that the desired methods for murdering these
Jews would be different from those used previously. As part of a general trend in Nazi treatment of Europe's few remaining Jews,
Budapest's Jews, like others, would be exploited for their 'labour',
rather than killed outright at the conclusion of 'transport'. For true
Nazis this was an ideologically distasteful shift, but one necessitated by
the acute need for labour within the still largely intact German industrial and agricultural economy of Hitler's Reich. Nonetheless, for
those Jews sucked into the consequences of a policy which some have
called 'annihilation through work', this still offered at least a chance of

survival. Its implementation in Budapest would take the lives of many thousands of Jews – mostly victims of the infamous 'death marches' of late November and early December – but it also contributed to the fact that well over 100,000 Jews in Budapest would survive the departure of the Germans' civilian leadership, and the terror of the *Nyilas*.

The Germans were responsible for ordering the death marches to the Austrian border but, as with the massive deportations earlier in the year, without Hungarian manpower and logistical help, they would have been powerless to accomplish them.[42] The actual manner in which those marches took place ensured a high mortality rate for those forced out of Budapest. Veesenmayer, Grell, Eichmann and other leading Germans in the city knew well that few of the elderly or children could march for days without food or shelter and survive, nor would they be useful 'labour' even if they reached the dispersal points established at the Hegyshalom crossing-point into Austria. They also understood that it was improbable that those 'injected' into what remained of the Nazi concentration camp system would survive. Nonetheless, Veesenmayer and his aides argued as vociferously for the new policy as they had for the old. The only thing standing in the way of its full implementation were 'technical difficulties', and the continuing efforts of the neutrals.

Therefore, it is no surprise that the Germans did what they could to hamper the Swedes and others throughout November and December. We have seen how reluctant Berlin was to approve the departure even of a few hundred Jews to Sweden, and the inability of Swedish diplomats to obtain approval even for a limited transport. Concerned by a report from Budapest about the neutrals' efforts to increase the numbers of protected Jews, on 16 November, von Ribbentrop wired Veesenmayer urging him to insist to his Hungarian counterparts that any such increase was unacceptable because 'only great problems would arise and concessions by the neutral states in the question of recognition [of Szálasi's regime] could hardly be expected'.[43] Days later, Veesemayer again complained to Berlin that Szálasi would no longer approve of further transport on foot of the Jews needed for 'labour', and that in any case, those arriving at the border were unfit for the desired purpose. He also complained that within the 'special ghetto for holders of protective passports', thousands of forged documents had been discovered, 'for which the Swiss Legation apologized, pointing to the disastrous conditions within their offices for emigration run by Jewish employees'. Regarding 'Sweden Jews', he described receiving 'a remarkable report' that Sweden's government had requested that Switzerland accept transports of 'its' Jews holding 'Swedish protective passports', because 'as reported in the past, the Swedish government is not inclined to allow entry into Sweden even of those issued its passports'.[44] Veesenmayer also noted the involvement of the neutral legations in Szálasi's change of position, illustrating further how closely the participants in this three-sided diplomacy were aware of each other's activities.

Having looked briefly at the highest levels of ongoing diplomacy during this period, we may return our focus to Wallenberg himself. What was he doing during these weeks; who was he meeting; and, in essence, what did he think and feel as he viewed the tragedy swirling around him? Answers to such questions are harder to discern than previously, because he now had little if any time to write. He was unable to write his customary letters to friends or family, and there is a gap in his personal correspondence between late October and early December. For instance, it is unknown what he thought of Danielsson's proposal that he either be sent westward with the fleeing government, or should potentially accompany the transport of 'Swedish' Jews, though Danielsson and Anger must have discussed this with him.

The value of Wallenberg's diary as a source has been noted, but for the period after 15 October, its value diminishes. The turmoil naturally affected how he planned his days, and it is certain that he was unable to organize his time in his customary fashion. Though there are many days which are completely blank, or which contain only one entry, there is no reason to suppose that he was in any way idle during those November and December days when nothing was 'scheduled'. Wallenberg continued to arrange meetings with, for example, members of the 'Jewish Council', the treacherous Lászlo Ferency, Becher's friend Billitz, his Swedish colleagues, and others. Also, following his own earlier recommendations, he continued to meet with Hungarian journalists, confirming his persistent belief that publicizing the plight of Jews was one way of helping them. For instance, on Monday, 13 November, he scheduled a meeting with a journalist at *Pesti Hirlap*, a prominent Budapest newspaper. This meeting took place, not incidentally, following a lunch meeting with Kemény.[45] In his diary, 10 December carries a notation unlike any other seen during his time in Budapest. At 09.00, he was to meet one 'Lederer [who] wants money'. This was followed by a meeting with both 'Ferency [and] (Hegedüs)', then he was to go on immediately to a street address (Mór utca 2. II), although no name is given.

Already noted are Wallenberg's interesting but unexplained contacts with 'v. Scholtz'. The first was on 16 October (the day after the coup) at the Hotel Ritz, and the second for 'dinner at home' (written in English) at 20.30 on Thursday, 28 December. Again, we cannot know the content of these apparent meetings, but it is intriguing that Wallenberg met this man twice, particularly at the end of December, when the city had been finally cut off and was enduring radical violence and chaos. Indeed, this second scheduled meeting chips away at yet another minor myth about Wallenberg, one connected to his last weeks in Budapest. The hagiographers invariably relate the dramatic 'fact' that during these final weeks Wallenberg was constantly on the move, never sleeping in the same place. This particular notation from 28 December, and others, suggest otherwise.

One frequent contact Wallenberg had during this time was with Nándor Batizfalvy, a police officer working for KEOKH. Ironically, Batizfalvy had previously lent his talents to (as Braham wrote) 'providing the legislative framework for the expulsion of "alien" Jews from Hungary in 1941', something which led to the death of many thousands. Wallenberg met him either alone or in the company of others, including the murderous Gendarme Colonel László Ferency, at least half a dozen times during November and December. It seems that Batisfalvy grew to regret his involvement in persecuting Jews, and was now, during this period, using his position and contacts in several ways to help Wallenberg and other neutral diplomats. For instance, he informed them of the inhuman conditions being endured by the tens of thousands forced onto the roads out of Budapest towards Austria during the infamous death marches.[46] Another contact of significance was with the municipal official named Hegedüs, who was in charge of sanitation in Budapest and whom Wallenberg met at least several times (at least once, as noted above, with Ferency).[47]

The content of these meetings is not reported by Wallenberg in Swedish documentation, but they do shed light onto another important aspect of Wallenberg's activities. We can surmise that he met such people to discuss matters of hygiene and sanitation, perhaps in connection with the Jews living in 'Swedish houses' in the 'international ghetto' or in the later established 'central ghetto'. The horrific crowding endured by ghetto inmates, however short-lived, inevitably created conditions with potentially catastrophic effects and quickly accelerating levels of mortality. The collapse of sanitation and hygiene in ghettos and other assembly points during the Holocaust killed hundreds of thousands of Jews just as quickly and 'efficiently' as a perpetrator's bullet. In Budapest the maintenance of some measure of sanitation was absolutely vital if disease was not to prove fatal to thousands, and Wallenberg could well have supplied Hegedüs, and other municipal authorities with whom he had contact, with the funds necessary for the maintenance of some sanitary standards. If this was the case, then this decidedly 'undramatic' form of assistance may have contributed to the survival of as many or more Jews than others forms of 'rescue' conducted by Wallenberg.

Close contact with municipal and lower-level national government officials not allied with or relatively uncommitted to the *Nyilas* regime was essential to Wallenberg's activities. This contact and cooperation occurred not only with food and sanitation experts, but also with city police forces, many of whom did provide invaluable assistance to neutral diplomats, including Wallenberg. Such cooperation can be seen in the eyewitness testimony of Thomas Verés, the young photographer who sometimes accompanied Wallenberg around the city and who took several of the most well-known photographs of Wallenberg, including the staged photograph taken in his office surrounded by his closest staff. In early January 1945, Verés was caught in a *Nyilas* raid while sheltering in a Swedish house in the 'international ghetto'. As the house was being emptied of most Jews, many of whom were among Wallenberg's voluntary staff and their families, one woman managed to quickly call the Swede, who was nearby. Verés remembers:

> I was in the house ... ready to be led to the Danube. I told somebody next to me, I said ... 'Look, the only thing what you should do before they start shooting, let's go down on [our] stomachs, you know, and try to jump in the Danube.' So anyway, there we were standing, suddenly he showed up with a truckload of policemen, regular Budapest policemen. And he came, and he spoke to the Hungarian Nazi leader there, the [*Nyilas*] guy, and everybody was released.[48]

In this particular episode of direct, personal intervention by Wallenberg, we see that he was far more effective due to the presence of numerous (and presumably armed) city police who had received instructions to help him – for there is neither evidence nor any reason to believe that groups of such civil servants would have helped merely at the request of the foreign diplomat. They were helping Wallenberg because of the political contacts he had established, contacts which can only have come about through calm negotiations in someone's office well before the incident in question. Otherwise that manpower would not have been available to him when quickly needed.[49]

More evidence of direct intervention by a member of the Legation came from Budapest on 16 November: 'Envoy Danielsson telephoned at 12.45 to say that Legation [members], in order to try to save people with Swedish passports who have been arrested in large numbers, have had to directly and strongly intervene in several situations.'[50] From this we can know that on at least several occasions, a member of the Legation went to what was an emergency situation somewhere in the city (the locations are not specified), asked which of the Jews arrested were in possession of Swedish protective documents, and demanded that the *Nyilas* men release them. It appears from Danielsson's description(s) that these interventions were not always successful, but that even when they failed to gain everyone's release, it was felt that such efforts should continue.[51] There seems little question that in the majority of such episodes it was Wallenberg who rushed to intervene, for neither Anger or Berg claim to have done this on more than several occasions. Wallenberg's efforts were helped by his physical proximity to most such incidents, because this was the period when he was largely in Pest, and not at the Legation in Buda. Although we can be sure neither of how many times such dramatic interventions actually occurred, nor of how many people were saved from death because of such interventions, there is no question that they did happen. It is from such episodes, which took place over a period of weeks and were viewed by many Jews, that Wallenberg's reputation for physical intervention comes. We can be certain that knowledge of such dramatic interventions, regardless of exactly how many, were spoken about, and thus his reputation grew. However, it must again be emphasized that were Wallenberg not by now a well-known figure, known to have good political connections in the city, he would most likely have failed to effect rescue, and would have been in even greater danger than was inherent in the situations he confronted.

At this juncture we may ask why descriptions of such interventions found in the Swedish documentation differ from the predominating view offered by survivor testimony. The first answer is that such a 'prejudice' within the Swedish documentation is to be expected in documents composed by diplomats trained to say as much as they could in as few words as possible. As we have seen in scores of documents, when Danielsson, Anger and Wallenberg had essential details to report, they did not shy away from doing so. We have seen the many (inherently dramatic) descriptions of events, discussions, or people they met. Were they being modest about what were, in fact episodes of great drama and danger or, rather, did they not have that much to report in the way of such 'cinematic' moments? These men were perfectly aware of the historic nature of the events they were caught up in, and they were not immune to the emotions of the moment. Yet, regardless of the emotional strain they were all under, they continued to meet their professional obligation of providing their government with the most objective and informative description of what was happening. This gives their descriptions (sometimes first-hand, at all other times from sources who were direct and/or recent witnesses and participants) an exceptional degree of credibility.

Differing from this, and a factor which explains some of the difficulties of using survivor testimony to explain complicated political situations, is that the survivors' range of vision and overall understanding of the situation they were enduring was actually extremely limited. Survivor testimony (in its various forms) will always be essential and irreplaceable in the writing of Holocaust history – but not in the writing of each and every aspect of Holocaust history. The diplomats cited so liberally in this study were in an extraordinary position in numerous ways to both observe and *understand* much, if not all, that was happening during the months of 1944 under analysis. On the other hand, the individual survivors' memories – most often recorded after decades of being filtered by their subsequent lives – is dominated by what they remembered, in often constrained, confusing and terrifying circumstances, specifically to them, or to those around them. As a result, for instance (as noted above), when Verés and others saw a truckload of municipal policemen suddenly appear in the company of a neutral diplomat, they cannot have understood or been present at the event's antecedents, or genuinely understood afterwards why that truckload of policemen suddenly appeared to save their lives.[52] Indeed, how could they, when the acute drama of their own immediate survival, or that of family or friends, was paramount to what had just happened to them?[53] There were, of course, many instances when Jewish survivors wrote down what they had just lived through, or seen – in Budapest and elsewhere. But again, the Swedish documents used throughout this study are the best sources to describe and analyse the actions and decisions of Wallenberg and his colleagues.

It is noteworthy, even for a diplomatic historian, that the existing descriptions of 'dramatic' rescues by Wallenberg or someone else are far fewer and shorter than are the reports and cables discussing the contentious recognition issue. This surely is the case because even when the 'street-level' perpetrator held the lives of his putative victims in his hands, it was the political elites, of all sides, who decided the fate of the majority of Budapest's Jews. It is certain that if the 'average' *Nyilas* functionary or youthful thug determined to murder Jews had not been acting within a wider political context, the survival rate of Budapest Jewry would have been dramatically lower. This decisive context was described, analysed and reported as it happened by Wallenberg and his colleagues.[54]

WALLENBERG DAY BY DAY

The emotional and physical burdens on Wallenberg and the other Swedes had increased enormously after the coup – and continued to increase, as did the danger from the escalating air and ground bombardment. Legation staff were also feeling more isolated and cut off from home. As communications between Budapest and Stockholm became more difficult, the frequency of personal communications with families and friends also lessened. Though Wallenberg had little time to write to his family or to Lauer as before, there are several letters which do shed light on at least some of what he was thinking and feeling during his final days and weeks in Budapest.

On Friday 24 November, Koloman Lauer wrote his last known letter to his business partner. Lauer was probably as well informed as anyone about what Wallenberg was enduring. Yet he chose to continue putting emotional pressure on Wallenberg, with urgent appeals that time should be spent inquiring about friends or relatives. Perhaps even more striking is that at this remarkable juncture, Lauer still sought to conduct business as usual. Beginning with 'dear Raoul', he requested that Wallenberg should find and speak to a businessman named Soor in order to clarify, for Lauer, several questions of great importance. It is possible that these questions were some sort of code, meant to hide other issues but, in the light of the nature of their correspondence and the vigour with which they had been pursuing business opportunities, this seems unlikely. More probable is that as experienced European businessmen, they knew that the end of the war was going to present important business possibilities that simply could not be ignored – even in the midst of a genocide.[55] Lauer asked:

> What are the intentions of Manfred Weiss, when the income for the tomato purée has been invested in Svenska Globus?[56] Why have these shipments been sent to Svenska Globus and not to BK [The Banana Company]?[57]
>
> Was Engineer Balint of Manfred Weiss the contact for dealing with the consignments of tomato pureé and goose liver? Has director Soor negotiated these questions with him?

Lauer then increased the pressure, stressing to Wallenberg: 'It is of the greatest importance that we get all of these questions answered, and I request that you make a record of director Soor's answers and ask him to sign it, get it legitimated at the Legation, and send it to us.' Requesting that Wallenberg get such a document legitimated by someone at the Legation speaks against this being some sort of secret code, as Lauer also requested the same of another conversation that Wallenberg was to have with someone named Gyarmaty.

Lauer then related some business and personal news from Stockholm:

The first bananas, about 20 tons, have arrived in Sweden and created quite a stir, because according to the decision [of the author-
ities], they can only be distributed to hospitals and children's
homes. But we intend to get a licence for another 100 tons, which
will be sold in stores. On [other] business fronts, nothing new. I
have sent your part of the shipment of bacon from South America
to your mother, including your Christmas present [to her] in the
form of a turkey, bananas, and cocoa powder.[58]

Though they may have spoken by telephone in the interim, exactly
what Wallenberg thought about most of this letter is not known,
although at least some of it was answered in his last letter to Lauer,
written (that is, dictated) in German, under the Legation letterhead,
and dated Friday, 8 December.

That day appears to have been relatively calm for Wallenberg, who,
the previous evening, had found time to have dinner with Per Anger. The
two knew each other from Stockholm before the war, had met and
worked together in Budapest before 1944, and had been working with
great closeness and some success in the remarkable months since July.
Indeed, it is no wonder that Per Anger dedicated much of his post-war
life, both professionally and personally, to finding his friend and colleague. On the same day that he wrote to Lauer, Wallenberg also drafted
a lengthy report to UD (discussed below), as well as the last known letter to his beloved mother.

The letter to Lauer began with the familiar request to understand
that he currently had little if any time to write, and would probably not
have time to write again.[59] He told Lauer that some relatives were now
employed at the Legation and that they were well. Then, in a mild
rebuke to his partner – who should have understood the situation and
not pressed Wallenberg about individual matters, as he had done in the
letter of 24 November – he told Lauer that he simply no longer had
the time to ascertain the fate of specific individuals: 'My work load is
so great that I cannot deal with personal tragedies anymore. I employ
340 people and [many] other temporary workers. There are more than
700 people living in my offices.' Then, almost as an afterthought,
Wallenberg added: 'The work is incredibly interesting.'

Next he raised an idea which has since caused speculation in discussions about why the Soviets detained him. 'I have a plan for after the
Russians occupy [the city], since I won't be able to get home [immedi-
ately] anyway, about forming a group which will help the Jews reclaim
their assets.' Exactly what he meant is unclear, nor does he say in any
detail how he might go about helping Budapest's Jewish survivors
recover some of their property and other assets, but it is striking that at

this tumultuous stage of affairs, he was thinking about lending some of his time and talents to such an endeavour. Wallenberg then again made clear that in spite of the violence all around him, he continued to feel a genuine liking for his task: 'The situation in the city is extremely adventurous. Bandits hang around the streets, beating people up, shooting people dead and torturing others. Amongst my staff there have been 40 cases of arrest, assault and brutal treatment. On the whole though, we are in a good mood and enjoying the fight. Unfortunately I have no more time for writing and so I ask you if you want to know more, contact [UD].' Poignantly and pragmatically, the letter concludes with yet another appeal that Jacob Wallenberg should be contacted about potential job prospects after he returned to Stockholm: 'Finally I ask you once again to inquire with Jacob Wallenberg about my position at Huvudsta, as I have now been away so long. I request a telegraphic answer. Kind regards, yours, R Wallenberg.' It is remarkable that he still found the emotional energy to worry about his personal future.

The letter was sent to Stockholm by one of the last diplomatic pouches out of Budapest, but Lauer did not forward the query to the banker until Tuesday, 19 December. He informed the elder Wallenberg:

> [Raoul] intends to stay in Budapest a couple of months after the Russian occupation of the city and to form an international group for the restoration of Jewish assets; he assumes that in any case he can not depart so soon, if the [return] journey has to be through Russia. At the same time he has asked me to ask you, what will happen with his place in Huvudsta, since he will be there [in Budapest] for another few months and absent [from Huvudsta] … I would be most grateful for an answer as quickly as possible.[60]

It is unclear why Wallenberg chose not to communicate directly with his cousin, nor is there any known correspondence by either Jacob or his brother Marcus Jr to their younger cousin while Wallenberg was in Budapest. Jacob Wallenberg took three weeks to answer Lauer, possibly because the Christmas and New Year holidays intervened. Yet on 22 December, Lauer (who may have spoken with Jacob), chose to wire Wallenberg in Budapest: '[Your] presence at building firm's project not necessarily required stop. Have referred architect Wahlman to bank manager Jacob Wallenberg stop. Ask your urgent telegraphic notification regarding Gustavsson affair stop. Wish you all the best, Happy New Year and expect your return to our company with pleasure stop. Greetings to Anger.'[61]

This information must have been a blow for Wallenberg, whose goal of finding a suitable position at the centre of the family empire had for years been a priority. Why Lauer wrote this, including the equally dismaying information that he had recommended another architect (which was, of course, Wallenberg's formal training) to the banker for this project is not known. Equally striking is Jacob Wallenberg's answer to Lauer, dated 8 January, which states the opposite of the cable to Budapest: 'Some time ago I received your letter of 19 December, and thank you for your kind Christmas and New Year's greetings, which I warmly return to you. Concerning the question about Raoul Wallenberg and Huvudsta, I may inform you that this [position] will remain open until further notice.'[62] Why Jacob did not communicate directly with his younger cousin is not known, but it is highly unlikely that Wallenberg received Jacob's more favourable answer – for by that date he had only eight days of freedom remaining to him.

That same Friday, 8 December, Wallenberg was able to write to his mother. As it is the last known letter written by him, it merits extensive citation. Some of what he wrote to Lauer is repeated:

> I really don't know when I'll be able to make it up to you for my silence. A diplomatic pouch leaves today, and once again all you get from me are a few lines written in haste.
>
> The situation is risky and tense, and my workload almost superhuman. Thugs roam the city, beating, torturing, and shooting people. Among my staff alone there have been 40 cases of kidnapping and beatings. On the whole we are in good spirits, however, and enjoying the fight.
>
> I sent a telegram in which I said that I was agreeable to taking over the Lagergrens' apartment. The conditions were as follows. My own apartment must be let through a rental agency, something to which Mr. Eriksson must first give consent. [Let the movers] handle the move ... I don't want anyone to have to bother ...
>
> We can hear the gunfire of the approaching Russians ... day and night. Since Szálasi came to power, diplomatic activity has become very lively. I myself am almost the sole representative of our Legation in all government ministries. So far, I've been to see the foreign minister about ten times ... the minister of the interior twice, the minister of supply once, the minister of finance once, etc.[63]
>
> Food is very scarce in Budapest. We managed to stockpile a fair amount ahead of time, however. I have a feeling that it will be

difficult to leave after the [Russian] occupation, so I doubt that I will get to Stockholm until around Easter. But this is idle speculation ... At any rate, I will try to return home as soon as possible.

It is simply not possible to make plans at the moment. I really thought that I would be with you for Christmas. Now I must send you my best wishes ... by this means, along with my wishes for the New Year. I hope the peace so longed for is no longer so far away.

The enormous amount of work makes the time pass quickly, and I am often invited to late-night feasts of roast suckling pig and other Hungarian specialties.

Dearest Mother, I will say good-bye for today. The pouch must be readied. Greetings, tender and heartfelt kisses to you and the whole family ... Lots of kisses to Nina and the little girl.[64]

If we are to understand Wallenberg, it is important to grasp that in spite of the pressure he was under, and in spite of the pain and horror he was witness to, he continued to enjoy his tasks and to thrive emotionally. He was surely helped with all of this by the full support and genuine affection of the many Jews with whom he worked closely. That affection was expressed to him with some genuine gallows humour by his staff in a poignant Christmas present he received from them. It was a parody of the elaborate blue and yellow *Schutzpass* so closely associated with Wallenberg, which they entitled *Der Schutzpass in der Kunstgeschichte Julklapp, 1944* (the Protective Passport in the History of Art of Christmas Presents).[65] It is a remarkable testament to Wallenberg's spirit and that of his Hungarian colleagues that they were able, at that dark hour, to find humour in their work of trying, and often failing, to save human lives.

THE 'INTERNATIONAL GHETTO'

Amongst the many important developments around the middle of November, for Wallenberg and the others, was the establishment of what came to be called the 'international ghetto'. The scheme was adopted by most of the other neutral legations, and by the end of the month, somewhere between 15,000 and 20,000 Jews were moved into the Uj Lipotváros neighbourhood of the fifth district, which was designated by Hungarian authorities for use by the neutrals. They, and not the neutrals themselves, made the bulk of assignments for 'protected houses'. Resident German authorities had nothing to do with this development, apart from reporting about it to Berlin.

As with other elements of Jewish persecution in Budapest, this development was a deviation from how Jews elsewhere in Eastern Europe had been treated. The 'international ghetto' was not a closed-off, sealed area, but was instead a well-developed urban neighbourhood consisting mostly of modern four- to six-floor apartment houses.[67] The buildings making up the ghetto were designated by Hungarian authorities as under the protection of the neutral powers, based on the internationally recognized concept of 'extraterritoriality'. This made them, at least in theory, the sovereign territory of Sweden, Switzerland, the Vatican, and so on, and thus 'immune' from violations by the host authorities.[67] Tim Cole reports that up to 122 apartment buildings were designated for the use of the neutrals in this neighbourhood, of which some thirty-one were Swedish. 'Spread over a limited number of streets in [the fifth district], individual houses were assigned to specific neutral legations, and [sometimes] shared by two legations ... The International ghetto houses were centred on Pozsonyi ut., which formed the core of this ghetto ... On this street, all of the yellow-star houses were designated for use by "protected Jews", with the majority designated for use by those under Swedish protection.'[68] Another deviation from what had happened elsewhere during the Holocaust is the fact that in some cases, buildings were boldly declared 'neutral territory' by the legations themselves, without prior agreement of the Hungarian authorities. According to Swedish and other sources, the mid-November establishment of the 'international ghetto' led to the concentration of 'some 15,600 Jews holding genuine protective passes [being] assigned to apartments that had previously housed only 3,969 ... it was not unusual for a two-room apartment to contain 50 to 60 persons'.[69] The scale of the Legation's undertaking must have caused considerable consternation at UD.

Though the Jews housed in the 'international ghetto' were in some ways better off than those Jews still sheltering elsewhere, contrary to common perceptions, the area was not necessarily safer for those 'protected' Jews lodged in these buildings.[70] They were better off largely because they were able to receive somewhat more regular food supplies, including some from stores established by Wallenberg and Langlet. And though the buildings were given a measure of protection from municipal police forces assigned to this task, *Nyilas* militia often invaded these specific buildings, 'searching' for false neutral papers. Kristian Ungváry writes:

> The International Ghetto was far more dangerous than the 'ordinary' ghetto – which was created a little later in the VII district – because the proximity of the Danube Embankment and easy

access to the houses encouraged the Arrow Cross to perpetrate bloodbaths ... it became clear that many protection papers were forged. These houses were searched as a priority, and because it was difficult to distinguish between genuine and forged documents, many people were deported indiscriminately.

The marauders also justified their violations of extraterritoriality by claiming that Jews with neutral papers still possessed some assets. As a result, many sheltering in this neighbourhood were violently removed from the buildings and robbed of what little they had left. Hundreds were then taken to the Danube and shot into the freezing river waters.[71]

Fortuitously for the neutrals' efforts, Szálasi (and his colleagues) remained almost irrationally covetous of international diplomatic recognition for their dominion over the Magyar nation. But they would agree to meet the neutrals only if they believed there was something to be achieved. This sufficed to keep doors open for Wallenberg, Lutz, Rotta and the others, well into December. Danielsson had judged the situation correctly, and in all likelihood explains his near-insubordination over this issue.

This continuing high-level access was epitomized by what must have been a singularly fascinating if not bizarre audience granted on 17 November by 'The Leader of the Nation', as Szálasi insisted on being called, to Papal Nuncio Rotta and Danielsson. The diplomats' primary goal for the meeting, which lasted longer than expected, was to hand over a memorandum of joint protest concerning the treatment of the Jews.[72] Indicative of the close manner in which the neutrals were cooperating during this period, the lengthy and detailed protest note was drafted two days before by Danielsson, Rotta and other neutral diplomats at a meeting at the nuncio's residence.[73] The two senior diplomats requested that Szálasi should do something to ameliorate the treatment of the Jews, particularly those now being subjected to the atrocities of the death marches. Just as Per Anger did when meeting Kemény, the Swede and Italian shrewdly appealed to Szálasi's vanity, choosing not to criticize him directly. The minutes of the meeting, several pages long, record:

> When the neutral legations raise their voice in this issue, they do so in the interest of Hungary's good [international] relations as they fear that the manner in which the Hungarian government is currently treating its Jews might stain Hungary's honour. [Therefore] when protesting in this fashion, they are also representing Hungarian interests ... The [neutral] legations have no other aim

than to decrease human suffering and to increase the assistance given to the victims of the war. If the Hungarian government is prepared to take respectful and humane measures regarding the matter of the Jews, then in due course it will promote in the future helpful measures to be taken towards the Hungarian people.[74]

Though Szálasi had agreed to this audience, his impatience with having to hear these protests is apparent. He concluded their extended meeting by telling Rotta and Danielsson that he would no longer be available to them: 'The question of the Jews is regarded as completely settled in its international aspects, and [I] can no longer be at the disposal of foreign legations regarding this question.'[75] He then insisted that all further communications go directly to the foreign ministry. For some reason Danielsson had arrived late, but he did not fail to inform the Hungarian 'führer' that threats had been made against both himself and Wallenberg. Adding diplomatically that he, Danielsson, did not believe such threats, he nonetheless insisted that it was unacceptable for the physical safety of diplomats to be threatened. Szálasi responded with equal diplomatic courtesy but, as events would show, disingenuously: 'The Leader of the Nation reassures the Swedish Minister that his personal safety is completely taken care of ... He [Szálasi] will discern where such rumours come from, and should they discover that there are such plans, he will take care of those villains. If the rumours are not true, however, he will take equally harsh action against those starting such rumours.'[76]

It is worth noting Rotta's increasingly active diplomatic role after 15 October. Previously his concerns lay primarily with baptized Jews, but now he sought to use the Vatican's prestige on behalf of all threatened Jews. For instance, there is no evidence that those finding shelter in the six apartment buildings in the 'international ghetto' designated for Jews holding Vatican protective papers were only 'baptized' Jews. Most importantly, as doyen of the city's remaining diplomats, Rotta exercised ever more active and effective leadership within the group, and towards the Hungarian government. He sent a steady flow of information to Rome about the plight of the Jews, though Pope Pius XII again chose to remain silent, refusing to publicly condemn *Nyilas* atrocities.[77] This is in accord with the Pope's dismal pattern of response to the Holocaust. Vatican historian John Morley discovered that Rotta sought to convince the Pope that public protests should occur, even if they would be in vain. Rotta, Morley wrote, 'observed that there was little hope among the diplomats of any positive result from this intervention because of the "fanatical hatred" of the Arrow Cross toward the Jews, but they viewed their effort as a gesture appealing to

Christian and civil conscience'.[78] Rotta's explanation for what motivated his appeal is interesting, because nowhere in Swedish diplomatic correspondence from these weeks is their motivation to help Jews articulated. Danielsson, Anger and Wallenberg seem by that point to have taken it for granted that it was the correct thing to do, even if they sometimes failed.

This period also saw an increase in the activities of the ICRC. Generally reluctant throughout the Holocaust to intervene on behalf of Jews threatened with persecution and extermination, the period after 15 October finally saw the organization cast aside at least some of its diplomatic ennui. Led by Fredric Born and Hans Weyermann, admirable efforts were made to assist some Jews, both unilaterally and in conjunction with the other neutrals. They took responsibility for the denizens of two buildings in the 'international ghetto', and established other locations in the city which they adorned with the organization's shield, declaring them protected places. As Jean-Claude Favez wrote:

> From September onwards they handed out letters of protection to their (increasingly numerous) Jewish aides, and after 15 October they stepped up the policy, issuing these so-called passports to any Jew claiming a connection, however tenuous, with the delegation, so that within a few weeks 15,000 people were in possession of such documents. After putting their signboards up on Jewish hospitals, clinics, hostels and soup kitchens, the delegates began responding to requests from the Hungarian authorities and civic leaders to take under their protection a growing number of public buildings in the capital.[79]

Another intriguing character helping Jews during this period was Giorgio Perlasca, a veteran Italian fascist who in mid-November convinced the departing Spanish Chargé d'Affaires Sanz Briz to issue him with Spanish citizenship papers in order to be able to assist Jews. In conversation many years later with an Italian journalist, Perlasca said: 'Sanz Briz then asked me to stay on at the embassy office and help out with the effort to protect the Jews. I was happy about it. I was glad to be able to do something useful. I had them fill out a certificate identifying me as a member of the embassy staff. And that's how I started my work.'[80] K. Ungváry writes of Perlasca:

> The most daring rescues, perhaps, were accomplished by Giorgio Perlasca, the 'Spanish chargé d'affaires'. Perlasca was actually an Italian citizen who had been interned on 19 March 1944 because of his anti-German views. After escaping he took refuge in the Spanish Embassy, where he joined life-saving missions. The

Arrow Cross tolerated the actions of the embassy, hoping that the Szálasi regime would be recognised by the Spanish dictator Franco. The Spanish chargé Angel Sanz-Briz had firm instructions to the contrary. He sent enthusiastic but meaningless statements to the Arrow Cross Foreign Ministry, where the truth remained unrecognised for a long time ... Until the closure of the encirclement he [Perlasca] constantly supplied the Foreign Ministry with misleading information and even resorted to blackmail, claiming that several thousand Hungarian hostages could be found in Spain if anything happened to his protégés. By the time his activities came to an end the number of Jews under his protection had grown from 300 to 5,000.[81]

For reasons unknown, Swedish sources are completely silent about Perlasca's activities.

DANIELSSON BATTLES STOCKHOLM

November and December saw Swedish diplomacy in Budapest reach its activist height. High- and mid-level negotiations were conducted with both Hungarian and German officials, exchanges of memoranda and telegraphs continued with UD, food stores were established (primarily by Wallenberg), and more. For Danielsson, the last weeks of the year remained dominated by his continuing efforts to effect a change in Stockholm's decision not to recognize Szálasi's regime; he continued to make it patently clear to UD officials that without some gesture on the part of Sweden, more Jewish lives would be lost.

On 16 November he cabled Stockholm, stating: 'Our negotiating position with Hungarian authorities particularly difficult, because they are clearly waiting for a message regarding accepting a representative for the new government in Stockholm. As capture of Budapest by Russians much delayed, the possibilities to achieve results through [continued] delay increasingly small. Uncertain whether under such circumstances Hungarian side will recognize Jews with protective papers. The Szálasi party is quickly utilizing [its] remaining time to mercilessly liquidate remaining Jews in Budapest.'[82] At least twice, Danielsson requested that UD's stance in the question, and its negative and fatal consequences for the Jews, should be brought to the attention of the WRB's Iver Olsen. This, however, was a serious misjudgement on his part, because he seemed unaware that one of the primary reasons for Stockholm's refusal to grant recognition was to placate the Americans. This was particularly necessary when Sweden was finally, this very month, cutting its trade with Nazi Germany.[83]

Danielsson's professionally hazardous efforts to effect a change in UD's stance regarding the recognition issue continued in yet another strongly-worded cable to Stockholm. The cable was sent on 23 November at 13.25, and arrived at UD at 18.00:

> A Hungarian employee within our Jewish activities [*judeaktionen*] who knows Foreign Minister Kemény personally had a conversation yesterday with him about Sweden's activities in the Jewish question. During the meeting the minister regretted the failure to recognize [the government] and explained with anger that he intended to summon Sweden's minister [and say] that if no form of recognition is obtained within a definite deadline, then all Jews under Swedish protection ... will be drowned in the Danube.
>
> Therefore I dare to again request that, in order to save these Jews from a certain death, if I cannot be authorized to explain for the minister that the fact that the Swedish government has not recalled its Legation in Hungary may be considered as *de facto* relations between the two governments. I have just this moment been summoned to meet the minister. Even a modest acknowledgement from the Swedish side in the question of recognition would most certainly make possible the saving of an extremely large number of Jews. Request therefore due to the question's extreme importance for Jewish assistance activities, that [Iver] Olsen be briefed about the above.[84]

Read by most of UD's senior leadership, even this urgent request was not granted. One copy in the files carries a notation that Olsen was not informed about Danielsson's request that the American should be briefed.[85] UD's inflexibility was made worse by the failure to answer Danielsson for some three weeks. Yet even in the face of Stockholm's silence, Danielsson still didn't give up. He met with Kemény again on 24 November, with the latter comparing the favourable treatment received by resident Legation staff with 'the disdain shown by Swedish authorities'. Kemény pointedly reminded his guest that Sweden had no difficulties, years before, in recognizing Germany's Nazi government.[86] That same day, Danielsson sent another cable, saying again that a decision was urgently needed: 'If Sweden genuinely wants to save its Hungarian Jews, cannot the Swedish government adopt a similar stance [as the other neutrals], which should in fact not lead to any negative consequences, because the story of the Hungarian Nazi government is soon finished.'[87] Wallenberg, Anger and Berg were aware of Danielsson's battle on this issue. It is equally certain that knowledge of Stockholm's intransigence did not help them either politically or morally in their fight to save Jews.

This long-drawn-out issue was finally resolved, in writing, on Wednesday, 13 December. Why it took so long to send a final answer to Danielsson is unclear, but in the event it was, as can be seen below, weak, unhelpful yet unequivocal. Danielsson, who was negotiating with the Szálasi regime, had probably realized that reference to longer-range Hungarian interests was not of central interest to the *Nyilas*. In any case, Danielsson also understood that giving the Hungarians nothing would most like result in reprisals against Legation staff:[88]

> We hereby confirm that Swedish government does not intend to recognize Szalasi [*sic*] government. You should seek to keep the question from developing further, and emphasise the extremely regrettable impression not only in Sweden but throughout the world by evacuations of Jews from Budapest, which we assume means also Jews with Swedish protective passports. If the question of cutting diplomatic ties is raised, you may, if you find it suitable, remind [the Hungarians] that Sweden is the protecting power for Hungarian interests in eleven countries, among them the US, British Empire, Romania and Argentina.[89]

Though UD mandarins must certainly have discussed Danielsson's series of urgent telegraphs, no evidence of such a discussion has been found. Obviously, however, they neither agreed with him, nor shared his sense of urgency. To date they had relied on his judgement on a series of very sensitive issues, but not this time; perhaps they saw it as a larger geopolitical matter of greater importance than what was happening in Budapest itself. Fears that the US would react in a genuinely problematic fashion over this issue seem greatly exaggerated for two obvious reasons. The matter concerned a Swedish mission which the American government had not only been following closely, but was peripherally assisting. There was more than enough goodwill built up between the two governments regarding humanitarian efforts, and the relationship could easily have tolerated some stress in this regard. Had UD adequately explained to Johnson and Pehle (and their bosses at the State Department) why they felt it was necessary to grant some measure of recognition to the *Nyilas* regime, they undoubtedly would have received American approval, if perhaps only informally. The second reason is that the Americans were satisfied that Sweden had finally decided to end militarily important trade to Nazi Germany. The deeply unimaginative diplomacy conducted in this matter by Günther and his advisors is evident in their decision not to support Danielsson on the recognition question. Their stance jeopardized the safety and work of their own diplomats, and put the lives of thousands into mortal danger.

The response by Szálasi's *Nyilas* was immediate, and violent.

Describing the incursions and (limited) looting of several SRK locations as 'atrocities', Danielsson left Stockholm in no doubt about the cause and effect:

> Privately, an official at the [Hungarian] foreign ministry told us that the attacks against SRK are merely the beginning of the liquidation of Swedish activities. It is believed that a large number of Jews are in Swedish houses illegally ... The cause of these actions against Swedish activities was primarily the insulting treatment of Hungarian diplomats in Stockholm as well as the repeated assertions in the Swedish press that Szálasi is crazy.[90]

Additionally, there is no doubt that the late-December assault on and plundering of the Legation itself was a direct result of this decision. Locations connected to both Langlet's and Wallenberg's operations suffered numerous violations of extraterritoriality, something which the other foreign legations avoided, apart from on one occasion in November when a location under the protection of the Nuncio was invaded, but not plundered.

In his 1981 memoir, Per Anger wrote that UD's intransigence did cause much trouble: 'There is also not a shred of doubt that it was [UD's] action in expelling [Szálasi's] representative and the Swedish government's stiff-necked unwillingness to recognize the Szálasi regime that set off the operation against our legation.'[91] Anger also recalled Danielsson's many telegraphed pleas trying to convince Stockholm of the extreme hazards caused by their inexplicable policy. Anger's bitterness is not far from the surface:

> It is hard to find an explanation for this stiff-legged policy, through which not only the legation's existence but also, above all, the lives of our Jewish charges were placed in danger. It can hardly have been out of consideration for the Allies that we refused to recognize Szálasi. They would certainly have accepted an explanation by Sweden that recognition of the Arrow Cross was necessary in order to save the Jews.[92]

How many lives were lost as a result of UD's intransigence on this issue cannot be known.

SWEDEN'S DIPLOMATS UNDER ASSAULT

In late November, *Nyilas* authorities made the decision to concentrate all unprotected Jews into another segregated area, this time in the city's centrally located seventh district, one end of which was anchored by the famous Dohány Synagogue. The formal decision was taken on

21 November and, a few days later, Stockholm was informed that 'a central ghetto for 80,000 Jews' was to be formed.[93] By 2 December, the transfer of Jews into that tiny part of Pest was virtually complete. As K. Ungváry writes: 'On 10 December the area was closed off with wooden boards, leaving only four exit gates. About 60,000 people were packed into 4,513 apartments, sometimes 14 to a room. According to plans, all the Jews – with or without protection papers – were eventually to be brought there.'[94]

One of the greatest challenges for Wallenberg and his allies in the 'Jewish Council' was to provide enough food for the survival of their charges, and others. The 'official' ration permitted ghetto inmates was only some 900 calories a day, so any supplement which could be provided by Wallenberg, Langlet, the ICRC and others was critical for the survival of Jews in both ghettos. Though wartime conditions prevailed, not until the city was actually cut off was food generally unavailable – if sufficient funds for purchases from the black market were available. This increased Wallenberg's urgent need to receive ever-larger sums from Stockholm, which had become increasingly difficult. Danielsson cabled UD, reporting that the 'Jewish Council' alone was requesting 500,000 pengö a day for the purchase of food, and that Wallenberg now needed the enormous sum of 450,000 Swiss francs.[95] Though a steady if irregular stream of smaller amounts had reached him up until now, it had become necessary for all transfers to go through Switzerland, and it is unknown if this sum was either made available to him or reached him. What we do know is that the larger figure made officials in Stockholm very nervous – perhaps understandably – and they were unwilling to use the Legation in Bern to help facilitate the transfer.[96]

It seems clear that, in the main, Wallenberg used his funds to purchase foodstuffs, clothes and limited amounts of medical supplies. Allegations of any significant use of bribery remain unsubstantiated. Fortunately, according to Danielsson and Anger, Wallenberg was not entirely dependent on money transferred from Stockholm. He was helped, even at this late date, by funds provided by Budapest Jews. This fact provides further evidence contradicting the claim made by some that the Jewish community was unwilling to help itself. They also reported that between 14 and 23 December, a large part of the stored foodstuffs was looted by *Nyilas* functionaries.[97] As they wrote less than six months after the events in question: 'From the middle of December, the ability of the Legation to assist Jews worsened radically ... [the Szálasi government] explained that they would respect the Swedish protective passports only on the condition that the Swedish government recognized the new Hungarian government. Because the

Swedish side did not desire such a step, great difficulties were created for the Legation's assistance activities.'[98]

By the last week of December, diplomacy in Budapest was coming to an end, with escalating threats from *Nyilas*, against Swedish activities and localities, overshadowing everything Wallenberg, Anger, Langlet and the others were trying to do. Incursions into buildings storing food and other supplies organized by Wallenberg and Langlet became an almost daily affair, and these now irreplaceable supplies were often carted away. Even a formal diplomatic meeting on 23 December between (probably) Wallenberg and Deputy Foreign Minister Vöczköndy was overshadowed by the threat of Hungarian violence against Sweden's diplomats. Vöczköndy was deeply resentful of the way he had been treated some months earlier in Stockholm, and he now urged the Swedes again to evacuate with the government because, he cynically explained, 'of difficulties for the government to ensure the safety of diplomats after the evacuation'.[99] Though there is no evidence of actual physical violence against any Swedish diplomat, even at this late date, they – not only Wallenberg – often found themselves in situations that were threatening and had the potential to turn out badly.[100]

In fact, the Swedes, with the exception of Wallenberg, who spent most of his time in Pest, would soon be forced into circumstances from which it was impossible to help others. From the morning of 24 December, when the Legation was heavily assaulted by the *Nyilas*, ensuring their own survival fully occupied them until the terrible Battle of Budapest reached its actual conclusion.[101] The final words of the last communication from Sweden's Legation in Buda included a personal message: '[point] 3. Attachés Anger and Wallenberg request that a message be passed to, respectively, Mrs Anger and Wallenberg's parents/Dardel/, that they are well and send warm Christmas greetings.'[102] UD's final cable to Budapest, sent on Christmas Day, returned the families' greetings to them, but the message was not received.[103]

1944 COMES TO ITS END

The various post-war accounts of 24 December are virtually identical. Early in the morning of Christmas Eve – which is generally for Swedes the most peaceful and relaxing day of the year – the Legation was invaded by party members and militia, as well as some city policemen.[104] This gross violation of international law, which ended all Swedish diplomatic activity, apart from Wallenberg's, began at 05.30, when a villa under Swedish protection was invaded. Right next door to the Legation on Gellérthegy, this opulent building had housed Finland's Legation, and was then used by Wallenberg for his work. In their joint 'after action' report, written soon after they had returned in April 1945 to Stockholm, Danielsson and Anger described the scene:

> many armed *Nyilas* men and [police] detectives had forced their way into the [Finnish] house. Three staff members went there immediately to try to intervene, but were arrested with the motivation that the government had given orders that all members of the Legation were to be taken [westward] to Szombathely. Next, both secretaries were arrested, while the Legation was plundered. The Finnish house was almost completely [ransacked] and from the main Legation [building], food, clothes and the staff's personal effects [were taken].
>
> That afternoon began the Russians final offensive against Budapest, with units penetrating the city's northwest neighbourhoods. During the resulting confusion the staff under arrest managed to get free. Both female employees were taken to the city's ['central'] ghetto, but were freed almost immediately with the help of the International Red Cross. The Russian ring around Budapest was then sealed closed, and with that, the possibility of the Legation still managing to communicate ceased.

In the wake of the raid, there was little if anything legation members could do, apart from trying to secure their own survival. Following the plundering of the Legation, Danielsson, Anger, Berg and the others spent most of the next two months sheltering from the battle thundering around them in different locations, enduring many of the same privations and terror endured by hundreds of thousands of Hungarian civilians. Like Wallenberg, they would be detained by Soviet troops. Unlike Wallenberg, this group all returned home. Treated almost immediately by Russian troops and officials with full diplomatic courtesy, several were interrogated, albeit mildly, at different times either during their initial detention or in the weeks to come. The group consisted of Ivar Danielsson, Per Anger, Lars Berg, Margareta Bauer, Birgit Brulin, Yngve Ekmark, Göte Carlsson and D.P von Mezey, the Legation's long-serving Hungarian staff member.[105]

Ironically, this group would travel virtually the same route that Wallenberg most likely had already travelled. But their final destination was, happily for them and their families, Stockholm. While in Moscow they visited their colleagues resident in Stalin's capital, including Swedish Minister Staffan Söderblom. Danielsson even met with a Soviet foreign ministry official to explain what the Swedes had been doing in Budapest.[106] Travelling in a comfortable railcar through Russia, and then back by boat to Sweden, they were, of course, enormously relieved to have survived to tell their story. They also started their enquiries about what had happened to their colleague, Raoul Wallenberg. Per Anger remembers their arrival by boat from Finland early on the morning of 18 April 1945:

> On the quay our families and relations met us, among them Raoul Wallenberg's mother, Maj von Dardel, who was nursing a faint hope that, in spite of everything, her son might be among us. We never suspected then that when we had passed through Moscow Wallenberg was there, confined in Lubyanka Prison ... The Swedish press was anxious to hear about our experiences ... on the way to the Foreign Office's press bureau Söderblom's words came back: 'Remember – not one harsh word about the Russians!'[107]

The history of Sweden's Legation in Budapest during the Holocaust had come to an end. Many, if not most, of their achievements, failures and heroic efforts would fall into obscurity, overshadowed for many reasons by the history, memory and mythology of Raoul Wallenberg. We shall now turn our attention to the last weeks and days of Wallenberg's time in Budapest, and of his life as a free man.

NOTES

1. J. Pehle to R. Wallenberg, 8 December 1944, copy in *Riksarkivet Utrikesdepartementet* (hereafter RA UD), Hp 21 Eu 1092, folder 3. The letter was sent to US Legation, Stockholm, to be forwarded 'to Mr Wallenberg when it is practicable to do so'. Wallenberg never saw this letter.
2. UD Stockholm to Swedish Legation Washington, no.34, 4 January 1945, RA UD Hp 21 Eu 1100, folder 23.
3. See K. Ungváry, *Battle for Budapest: One Hundred Days in World War II*, trans. L. Löb (Swindon, UK: BCA/I.B. Tauris & Co. Ltd, 2003), Chapter 1.
4. R.L. Braham, *The Politics of Genocide: The Holocaust in Hungary*, revised and enlarged edn (Boulder, CT: Rosenthal Institute for Holocaust Studies Graduate Center/City University of New York Social Science Monographs, 1994), vol. 2, p.962.
5. Such a study remains to be written, and would most likely require the efforts of a group of historians from different countries.
6. The office on Ulloi utca became Wallenberg's primary, but not sole, working location in Pest. All district designations are from 1944. The Legation itself, located on Gellérthegy (Gellért Hill), was physically relatively isolated.
7. Throughout November, Swedish diplomats in Budapest, Berlin and Stockholm all believed that the fall of Budapest was only a matter of days, something which must have influenced their thinking. See, for example, the Berlin Legation's telephone message to Stockholm, from Budapest, of 9 November. RA UD, Hp 21 Eu 1092, folder 2.
8. UD to I. Danielsson, no.429, 14 October 1944, RA UD, Hp 895, folder 2.
9. By this time, Swedes represented Hungarian interests in over a dozen nations, mostly in the Western hemisphere.
10. I. Danielsson to UD, no.46?(*sic*), 3 November 1944, RA UD, Hp 21 Eu 895, folder 2. He reported that the Portuguese chargé d´affaires had already left, with Spain's minister scheduled to leave that day.
11. Author interview with Ambassador Per Anger, March 1990, Uppsala University Library, Raoul Wallenberg Project Archive, no.C002, p.60.
12. S. Hellstedt, UD (circular) memorandum, 28 October 1944, RA UD, Hp 21 Eu 1100, folder 20.

13. I. Danielsson to UD (coded telegram), no.456, 31 October 1944, RA UD, Hp 21 Eu 1092, folder 2. Coded telegrams were used more so than previously because of the diminishing regular postal and diplomatic pouch communications.
14. In one instance remembered by Thomas Veres, Wallenberg's photographer, a friend of Veres, was rescued from a deportation assembly site and put by Wallenberg and Veres into a safe house. The man decided, however, that he had to visit his fiancée and, while walking there, was taken by *Nyilas* thugs, and never seen again. See the author's interview with T. Veres, Uppsala University Library, Raoul Wallenberg Project Archive, no.C507, pp.50–1.
15. This question is discussed in Chapter 12.
16. See D. Gur's testimony in, R. Benshalom, *We Struggled for Life: Zionist Youth Movements in Budapest, 1944*, trans. O. Cumming and R. Rubin (Jerusalem and New York: Geffen, 2001), pp.141–2.
17. A. Cohen, *The Halutz Resistance in Hungary 1942–1944* (Boulder, CT: Social Science Monographs, 1986), p.193.
18. Author's interview with P. Anger, p.69.
19. A. Richert to S. Hellstedt, no.381, 2 November 1944, RA UD, Hp 21 Eu 1092, folder 2. In spite of their frustrations, Sweden's diplomats in Berlin continued to lobby their German counterparts, both verbally and in writing, in increasingly fruitless attempts to actually get at least some Jews out of Hungary to Sweden.
20. Wagner to Veesenmayer, 16 November 1944, in R.L. Braham, *The Destruction of Hungarian Jewry: A Documentary Account* (New York: Pro Arte for the World Federation of Hungarian Jews, 1963), doc. 334, p.717.
21. I. Danielsson to UD, no.476, 8 November 1944, RA UD, Hp 21 Eu 1092, folder 2.
22. UD to Legation Budapest, no.511, 9 November 1944, RA UD, Hp 21 Eu 1092, folder 2. The rapid exchange of telegrams demonstrates the excellent links still connecting Stockholm and Budapest during the first half of November.
23. I. Danielsson to UD, no.483, 9 November 1944, RA UD, Hp 1 Eu 583, folder 23.
24. Prince Carl to M. Ehrenpreis, no.194, 7 November 1944, copy to UD, RA UD, Hp 21 Eu 1100, folder 21.
25. I. Danielsson to G. Engzell, no.491, 9 December 1944, RA UD, Hp 21 Eu 1092, folder 2.
26. Although both Langlet and his wife Nina hint in their memoirs at some of these difficulties, they do not describe the extent of them, nor the damage Langlet's methods clearly caused.
27. I. Danielsson to G. Engzell, no.491, 9 December 1944, RA UD, Hp 21 Eu 1092, folder 2.
28. Again, the document in question here is labelled, in Swedish, a protective 'passport' (*skyddspass*), but it was not an actual emergency passport. Those were rarely issued during these final weeks. It is most likely the *Schutzpass* that is being referred to at this stage, although this is unclear.
29. I. Danielsson to UD, no.498, 12 November 1944, RA UD, Hp 21 Eu 1092, folder 2. Also noted in this short telegram is one of the first notifications that *Nyilas* functionaries and militia were planning to attack the Swedish and other neutral legations.
30. American Legation Stockholm to UD, 8 November 1944, RA UD, Hp 21 Eu 1092, folder 2.
31. S. Grafström, *Anteckningar 1938–1944*, edited by S. Ekman (Stockholm: Samfundet för utgivning av handskrifter rörande Skandinavians historia, 1989), p.618 and p.620.
32. S. Grafström to Legation Budapest, no.502, 4 November 1944, RA UD, Hp 21 Eu 1100, folder 20.
33. I. Danielsson to UD, no.485, 10 November 1944, RA UD, Hp 21 Eu 895, folder 2. Danielsson also noted that the other neutrals were planning to send a representative westward, in the event that a complete evacuation of diplomatic staff did not occur.
34. I. Danielsson to UD, no.490, 11 November 1944, RA UD, Hp 21 Eu 895, folder 2.
35. Ibid.
36. UD to Legation Budapest, no.529, 13 November 1944, RA UD, Hp 21 Eu 895, folder 2. The telegram, written by Eric von Post, who had served for several years in Berlin, stressed again that there could be no question of Sweden accepting any representative of the Szálasi government.
37. 'Telephone message from Berlin ... message from Budapest', 15 November 1944, RA UD, Hp 21 Eu 1092, folder 2.
38. Cohen, *Halutz Resistance in Hungary*, p.187.
39. I. Danielsson to UD, no.500, 15 November 1944, RA UD, Hp 21 Eu 1092, folder 2.
40. According to J. Lévai, they did however articulate their 'obligations dictated by humanity and Christian love in expressing their deep sorrow' about the cruelties of which they

learned. See the memorandum of 17 November cited by Lévai, and signed by the Swedes, Vatican, Swiss, Spanish and Portuguese representatives, who all met at the Nunciature on Wednesday, 15 November. In J. Lévai, *The Black Book on the Martyrdom of Hungarian Jewry* (Zurich: Central European Times, 1948), pp.358–9. No copy of this important joint note of protest was found in Swedish archives.

41. 'Royal Hungarian Ministry of Foreign Affairs, Department of Politics, Minutes of the visit of Apostolic Nuncio Rotta and Swedish Minister Danielsson to the Leader of the Nation on 17 November 1944', copy in Uppsala University Library, Raoul Wallenberg Archive, document collection. Translation by A. Szónyi.

42. The long columns of helpless women, elderly and children marching westward from Budapest were guarded exclusively by Hungarian soldiers and *Nyilas* militiamen. Those who survived were turned over to the Germans only at the border.

43. H. Wagner to E. Veesenmayer, 16 November 1944, in Braham, *Destruction of Hungarian Jewry*, doc. 334, p.717.

44. E. Veesenmayer to AusAmt, 21 November 1944, in ibid., doc. 242, p.532. No evidence supporting Veesenmayer's allegation against Sweden has been located.

45. R. Wallenberg's diary, 13 November 1944.

46. Braham, *Politics of Genocide*, vol. 2, p.965.

47. Ibid., p.977.

48. Author's interview with T. Verés, pp.52–3 (see note 14).

49. Verés also remembers how closely Wallenberg worked with city officials, 'Not Jews. Higher up from the government, the [city] government, you know ... who had high positions and they worked for us.' Ibid., p.51.

50. 'Telephone conversation with Berlin', received Stockholm 15.45, 16 November 1944, RA UD, Hp 21 Eu 1092, folder 2.

51. See point 'c' in another telephoned report, this time by Per Anger, from Budapest through Berlin on 17 November. Within two hours that afternoon, Anger telephoned Berlin twice with reports. RA UD, Hp 21 Eu 1092, folder 2, and Hp 1 Eu 583, folder 23.

52. A valuable discussion of this difficult issue is by historian M. Roseman, 'Surviving Memory: Truth and Inaccuracy in Holocaust Testimony', *Journal of Holocaust Education*, 8, 1 (Summer 1999).

53. These reflections are based on the author's extensive experience in interviewing survivors of the Hungarian Holocaust, and in studying in detail their testimonies, and comparing and contrasting them with contemporary documentation.

54. The few survivor or contemporaries' testimonies used in this study are from individuals who had direct contact with and knowledge of Wallenberg's activities. As noted previously, to have used survivor testimonies extensively would have made this a very different book.

55. K. Lauer to R. Wallenberg, 24 November 1944, RA, Raoul Wallenberg Arkiv, Signum 1, vol. 6. It is not known when Wallenberg received the letter, but it must have been fairly quickly, as he answered some of Lauer's questions exactly two weeks later, on 8 December.

56. It is probably no coincidence that on that same day, 24 November, Wallenberg was scheduled to meet with Vilmos Billitz, Kurt Becher's Hungarian partner and friend, and a former high-ranking executive within the Weiss-Manfréd concern.

57. There are no known details about the company, Svenska Globus.

58. K. Lauer to R. Wallenberg, 24 November 1944, RA, Raoul Wallenberg Arkiv, Signum 1, vol. 6.

59. R. Wallenberg to K. Lauer, 8 December 1944, RA, Raoul Wallenberg Arkiv, Signum 1, vol. 6, *bilaga* 14.

60. K. Lauer to J. Wallenberg, 19 December 1944, in G. Nylander and A. Perlinge, (eds), *Raoul Wallenberg in Documents, 1927–1947* (Stockholm: Stiftelsen för Ekonomisk Historisk Forskning inom Bank och Företagande, 2000), p.104.

61. K. Lauer, 'Banankompaniet Mellaneuropieska handels AB', to R. Wallenberg, Swedish Legation, 22 December 1944, RA, Raoul Wallenberg Arkiv, Signum 1, vol. 6. It is unclear what the 'Gustavsson affair' refers to.

62. J. Wallenberg to K. Lauer, 8 January 1945, in Nylander and Perlinge, *Raoul Wallenberg in Documents*, p.104.

63. This is somewhat of a boast by Wallenberg, since he well knew that Danielsson and Anger also frequently visited government ministries and officials. Indeed, Wallenberg never obtained an audience with Szálasi himself, which Danielsson did at least once.

64. R. Wallenberg to M. von Dardel, 8 December 1944, in Wallenberg, *Letters and Dispatches*,

pp.276–8. Wallenberg's sister Nina, who has been referred to previously, had recently given birth to 'the little girl'. She was named Nane, and became a lawyer, painter and, eventually, the wife of Kofi Annan, former secretary-general of the United Nations.

65. In RA, Raoul Wallenberg Arkiv, Signum 1, vol. 8. How this poignant gift made it back to Stockholm is unknown.

66. Not each and every one of the hundreds of ghettos in Eastern Europe were 'sealed off' as, for example, the Warsaw ghetto was, but most did not allow free movement in and out.

67. Though eventually there were almost daily violations of this 'extra-territoriality' by *Nyilas* militia, there is no question that a measure of protection was obtained for those Jews able to find shelter in this area.

68. See T. Cole, *Holocaust City: The Making of a Jewish Ghetto* (New York and London: Routledge, 2003), pp.205–6. In addition to the Swedes and Swiss, other houses were designated the 'territory' of the Vatican, Portugal, Spain, the Swedish Red Cross and the International Red Cross (ICRC).

69. Braham, *Politics of Genocide*, vol. 2, p.975.

70. By the end of November, conditions in both the 'international ghetto' and the now established 'central ghetto' were so bad that it can hardly be said that the Jews 'lived' there. It is more accurate to understand their tortuous hours and weeks as a mere clinging to existence in the fragile hope of surviving until the Red Army came.

71. Ungváry, *Battle for Budapest*, p.246. For details about the 'international ghetto', see also Braham, *Politics of Genocide*, vol. 2, pp.971–6.

72. The most detailed but now somewhat dated description of the neutrals' collaborative efforts remains, Braham, *Politics of Genocide*, vol. 2, Chapter 31.

73. I. Danielsson to UD, no.500, 15 November 1944, RA UD, Hp 21 Eu 895, folder 2. Clearly wishing to let UD know of the willingness of other nations to recognize the Hungarist regime, Danielsson used this telegram to describe the efforts of Angel San Briz, the Spanish chargé d'affaires, to engage his fascist government in protecting Jews. Also noted in this telegram is the fact that 'the Russian threat against Budapest has eased somewhat', yet another indication of the tenacity with which German and Hungarian forces were still fighting the Red Army. They would, disastrously, continue this fight weeks later within the besieged environs of Budapest itself.

74. Memorandum of visit by Apostal Nuncio Angelo Rotta and Swedish Minister Danielsson to the Leader of the Nation on 17 November 1944, copy in Uppsala University Library, Raoul Wallenberg Archive, document collection.

75. Ibid.

76. Ibid.

77. M. Phayer, *The Catholic Church and the Holocaust, 1930–1965* (Bloomington and Indianapolis, IN: Indiana University Press, 2000), pp.108–9.

78. J.F. Morley, 'Pope Pius XII, Roman Catholic Policy, and the Holocaust in Hungary: An Analysis of *Le Saint Siege et les victims de la guerre, janvier 1944–juillet 1945*', in C. Rittner and J. Roth, (eds), *Pope Pius XII and the Holocaust* (London and New York: Leicester University Press, 2002), p.169.

79. J.-C. Favez, *The Red Cross and the Holocaust* (Cambridge: Cambridge University Press, 1988), trans. J. Fletcher and B. Fletcher, p.249. K. Ungváry reports that Born gave out only '1,300 identity cards serving as letters of safe conduct'. See Unváry, *Battle for Budapest*, p.243.

80. E. Deaglio, *The Banality of Goodness: The Story of Giorgio Perlasca* (Notre Dame, IN: University of Notre Dame Press, 1998), p.76. In yet another example of how writers have misunderstood Wallenberg and his mission, Deaglio labels the Swede 'the special envoy of King Gustav'. The Swedish king had nothing to do with Wallenberg's appointment or mission. See ibid, p.68.

81. Ungváry, *Battle for Budapest*, p.243. R.L. Braham describes Perlasca's feats in *Politics of Genocide*, vol. 2, pp.1241–4.

82. I. Danielsson to UD, no.507, 16 November 1944, RA UD, Hp 21 Eu 1092, folder 2.

83. See P.A. Levine, 'Swedish Neutrality During the Second World War', in N. Wylie, *European Neutrals* (Cambridge: Cambridge University Press, 2002).

84. I. Danielsson to UD, no.525, 23 November 1944, RA UD, Hp 21 Eu 1092, folder 2.

85. See copy of telegram no.525, same date, in RA UD, Hp 12 Eu, folder 1.

86. I. Danielsson to UD, no.533, 26 November 1944, RA UD, Hp 21 Eu 1092, folder 2.

87. I. Danielsson to UD, no.534, 26 November 1944, RA UD, Hp 21 Eu 1092, folder 2.

88. Hungarian authorities had already pressured the Swedes that week by unleashing a *Nyilas* assault on Langlet's Red Cross activities. Several of his locations were attacked, but he was not harmed.

89. UD to Legation Budapest, no.612, 13 December 1944, RA UD, Hp 21 Eu 1092, folder 2.

90. I. Danielsson to UD, no.601, 18 December 1944, RA UD, Hp 21 Eu 1092, folder 2.

91. P. Anger, *With Raoul Wallenberg in Budapest: Memories of the War Years in Hungary* (New York: Holocaust Library, 1981), p.111.

92. Ibid., p.112.

93. I. Danielsson to UD, no.535, 26 November 1944, RA UD, Hp 21 Eu 1092, folder 2. It is immaterial that the figure stated proved to be somewhat greater than the actual numbers involved.

94. Ungváry, *Battle for Budapest*, p.247.

95. I. Danielsson to UD, no.535, 26 November 1944, RA UD, Hp 21 Eu 1092, folder 2.

96. S. Grafström to Stockholms Enskilda Bank, no.3152, 27 November 1944, RA UD, Hp 21 Eu 1092, folder 2.

97. I. Danielsson and P. Anger, 'Memorandum Concerning the Activities of the Swedish Legation in Budapest around the period prior to and after the Russian Occupation', 2 May 1945, RA UD, P 2 Eu, p.3. This eleven-page report drafted by the two diplomats is a particularly valuable source for understanding the final weeks of Legation activities. It also recounts the treatment they and other Swedish diplomats received during their detention by the Soviets before they were able to return to Sweden in April 1945.

98. Ibid., p.3.

99. Ibid., p.4.

100. Swiss diplomat Harald Feller was detained and roughed up by *Nyilas* thugs late in December. When they released him, he was told to tell the Swedish minister that similar treatment was almost a certainty. No Swedish diplomat, including Wallenberg, was ever beaten by Hungarians.

101. Historians agree that *Nyilas* functionaries and militia did little actual fighting against the Soviet invaders. Their atrocities against the Jews would end only when most were too frightened to be out on the treacherous streets. Their hunting of Jews, which they continued during the early part of the fighting with almost complete impunity, required them to move about the city.

102. Telephoned message, from Budapest through Berlin to Stockholm, no number, 23 December 1944, RA UD, Hp 21 Eu 1092, folder 3.

103. UD to Legation Budapest, no.643, 25 December 1944, RA UD, Hp 21 Eu 1092, folder 3.

104. Swedes celebrate Christmas Eve more noticeably than they do Christmas Day.

105. Similar 'after-action' reports to that recorded by Danielsson and Anger were also drafted by Berg, Bauer and von Mezy. See RA UD, P 2 Eu.

106. There is some historical irony in this as well. Staffan Söderblom had assumed his post only a few months earlier, and would retain it through the first years of Wallenberg's detention. He played a central role in the Swedes' scandalous handling of this matter between January 1945 and July 1947.

107. Anger, *With Raoul Wallenberg in Budapest*, p.146.

12

January 1945: The End of Diplomacy and Freedom

In your [meeting] with Swedish Foreign Minister it should be made clear that this Government considers that frequent and extended visits of Swedish Consuls ... where Jews are concentrated constitute one of the most effective means of preventing their further extermination. This method proved its efficacy in Budapest where, thanks to the presence of Swedish personnel, many lives appear to have been saved.

J. Pehle to H. Johnson, 19 January 1945[1]

THE LAST WEEKS

Raoul Wallenberg's last weeks as a Swedish diplomat in Budapest were different than the preceding ones. Circumstances compelled him to work far more on his own than before, and by all accounts he became a tour de force of personal diplomacy. This is the period when he was seen by many survivors, and their memories have largely shaped common memory of Wallenberg. If he sought adventure by going to Budapest, he certainly found it during his final weeks there. Nor is it a coincidence that this is when Wallenberg's most outstanding personal qualities and characteristics are on frequent and public display. From the historian's perspective, this period is when the surviving documentary record of his activities becomes increasingly scarce. Yet there is important documentation from these weeks, telling us something about Wallenberg at this time, and this will be analysed in a manner which should, in subsequent popular publications and representations, complement the existing oral testimonies and memoirs about Wallenberg. This mix of perspectives will show Wallenberg practising bureaucratic resistance in a singular, decisive and, indeed, historic fashion.

EICHMANN THREATENS WALLENBERG

It is noteworthy that even by this late date and under extreme circumstances, he took his role as a recorder of events seriously. His final report is similar to previous ones – well organized, clearly written and a fount of information and insight into the history of the Holocaust in Budapest and western Hungary during the last weeks of 1944. Dated 8 December, it began again with classic diplomatic understatement. 'Since the last report, the circumstances of Hungarian Jews have worsened further.'[2] In describing the still ongoing death marches, he recounted what he saw himself, and information received from others. His description of the suffering of some 40,000 Jews is vivid. 'Many have died', he wrote, and 'those not able to continue marching are shot. At the border they are taken control of with blows and brutality by men in SS – *Spezialkommando Eichmann*, and then sent for hard labour on border fortifications.'[3] Turning to Budapest, he noted the now 'catastrophic' difficulties in obtaining sufficient food for his charges. He reported rumours of an imminent pogrom against the 'central ghetto', demonstrating that his sources remained effective: 'SS organs in the city are said to have received orders not to conduct any systematic slaughter of Jews.' The rumoured pogrom did not take place, and there is no evidence that SS units contributed to the murderous anarchy then underway.

Describing the re-formation of his staff in the difficult days after the October coup, Wallenberg noted with muted pride that successful negotiations with the Army Ministry resulted in the return to Budapest of some 15,000 Jewish men who had been trapped in forced labour battalions. Then Wallenberg provided for the first time some numbers of those whom either he or his staff managed to save directly from deportation sites in Budapest, or at the 'march' routes' terminus: 'Some 200 ill people have been collected in rescue vehicles from deportation assembly points. Through interventions of one type or another, from railcars or other [modes] of transport, some 2,000 people have been returned, about 500 from Hegyshalom. This [effort] must unfortunately be halted, after Germans in the *Eichmannkommando* have threatened violence.' Jews sheltering in Swedish houses, he wrote, had better circumstances than those in other buildings in the 'international ghetto', but he doesn't explain why. The report concluded by noting, again without explanation, that Jews holding Swedish protective passports had fared the best of all those with neutral papers: 'Only 8–10 have been shot to date in Budapest and its surroundings.'[4] This report (which, of course, no one knew would be his last) was widely distributed within Sweden's political elite; even King Gustav received a copy.[5]

In popular representations of Wallenberg, great weight has been given to his 'battle' with Adolf Eichmann. By the autumn they clearly were aware of each other, but any 'fencing' they did was through bureaucratic channels. If Wallenberg had actually met Eichmann during his interventions at the border, he almost certainly would have specifically noted this, and not just mentioned the *Eichmannkommando* as he did. However, threats were made by Eichmann against the Legation, and Wallenberg specifically. These gave rise in late December to an interesting exchange between German and Swedish diplomats which, it appears, reached the highest levels of Hitler's Reich. More important than the actual incident, however, is the light this throws upon the attitudes of the German perpetrators. These exchanges illuminate how, even when faced with defeat, there remained a determination to continue the genocide of the Jews for as long as possible.

The episode under discussion began on 15 December, when Danielsson cabled: 'The head of the *SS-kommando* for solution of the Jewish problem, here, General [*sic*] Eichmann, has told a [local employee] that he intended to have the Jew-dog Wallenberg shot.'[6] Even though this was second-hand information, Danielsson obviously took it seriously, as did Wallenberg's UD colleagues, who considered it an unacceptable breach of diplomatic protocol. Arvid Richert in Berlin was informed, and he decided upon a highly unorthodox Sunday visit to Auswärtiges Amt in order to make a formal protest. Equally unorthodox was his subsequent visit to the home of Envoyé von Erdmannsdorff, where the Swede told his interlocutor that Eichmann and another SS officer had threatened to 'shoot the "Jewish dog" Wallenberg, legation secretary and member of the well known Wallenberg family'.[7] Erdmannsdorff, an old-line Prussian civil servant, told Richert that he should bear in mind the expression, 'dogs that bark don't bite', and promised to cable Germany's Legation in Budapest immediately for clarification. Richert then asked another diplomat to inform Walter Schellenberg, the infamous SS *Brigadeführer* (Brigadier General) – one of the highest ranking members at that time in the RSHA – about the Swedish protest. This apparently happened, and Schellenberg cabled SS chief Heinrich Himmler about the matter. It appears that Himmler decided to intervene, and may even have ordered Eichmann to be admonished.

The next step in this diplomatic minuet was Richert's letter to Stockholm of 23 December, drafted after meeting Erdmannsdorff again. The German confirmed that the verbal threat – 'the Jewish dog Wallenberg would be shot' – had been made, but that it was not to be taken seriously. In fact, said Erdmannsdorff, the unfortunate phrase came only after many complaints were lodged against the 'inappropriate' activities of the 'Jewish Office' of Sweden's Budapest Legation, and 'especially Secretary Wallenberg'. Richert preserved for posterity the text received from German officials in Budapest (which must have been one of their last, as all civilian officials who could leave the city were doing so in great haste). Wallenberg had been threatened, the cable read, because 'in a very unorthodox way, he had done something [to assist] those Hungarian Jews who had been taken to the border for labour. It is equally clear that, using completely illegal methods, [he] attempted to remove those Jews from work there, which had been legally authorized, by distributing protective passports.' Erdmannsdorff added that however unconventional Wallenberg's activities may have been, 'under no circumstances was such an expression as the one used to be excused'.[8] It seems highly unlikely that a senior diplomat such as Erdmannsdorff would have offered such an apology to Richert in a matter of significance for Swedish–German relations without Himmler's approval. Eichmann was, after all an SS man, and Erdmannsdorff knew that Schellenberg had briefed Himmler about the matter.

Thus we see that even at this late stage of the war, with only some four months remaining until the genocide of the Jews would finally end, senior AuswärtigesAmt diplomats (a ministry which remained throughout the Nazi era staffed primarily by non-Party civil servants), continued to conduct themselves according to the ethos of the SS when dealing even with Swedish diplomats. They truly believed, or at a minimum continued to argue for, the notion that it was *legal* to kill Jews, through hard labour, so long as it had been authorized by one office or another. Also evident in this exchange is the desire of the two countries' diplomats to maintain correct diplomatic protocol in their bi-lateral contacts. (Sweden never formally severed diplomatic ties with Hitler's Germany.) Strange as it might seem today in a society with far fewer operative norms and formalities, we see that even as Europe endured the final agonies of war and genocide, normative diplomacy maintained both its customary status in relations between nations.

WALLENBERG'S LAST CHRISTMAS

R.L. Braham has written: 'The reign of terror that had begun with Szálasi's assumption of power ... went almost completely out of control after the beginning of the Soviet siege. Gangs of armed *Nyilas* roamed Budapest ... [attacking] ... Jews huddled in their shelters, cellars, and homes outside the ghetto, in the "international ghetto", and in the large ghetto. Their attacks became increasingly daring and ever larger in scale.'[9] Because of this, Eichmann was not the only perpetrator with whom Wallenberg had to deal during those last weeks; and throughout December (and perhaps into January), he continued to meet Colonel Lázslo Ferenczy and N. Batizfalvy from the interior ministry – sometimes together. Such meetings with distasteful people were necessary if

Wallenberg was to continue to have any chance of being able to call upon police resources to aid him in resolving the now almost daily emergencies. We have seen that the refusal to recognize Szálasi's government caused such liaisons to be far less effective for Wallenberg. Nonetheless, there is evidence that even after the government's order to assault the Swedes was issued, Wallenberg and the other Swedes were still able sometimes to call upon police protection, for themselves and their charges. Indicative of these important contacts is the fact that the last entry in Wallenberg's personal diary was for a meeting at 10.00 on Friday, 29 December with 'Löcsey'. This was undoubtedly István Löcsey, a member of *Nyilas*, who had recently been appointed by municipal authorities as 'ministerial counsellor in charge of Jewish affairs'.[10] Löcsey (also rendered as Löcsei) had sufficient authority to try to protect the Jews in the ghetto, which he utilized on at least several occasions. Once he tried to facilitate the movement of food into the ghetto, when *Nyilas* militia tried to halt and plunder the shipments. Whether or not the meeting actually took place is unknown, but the fact that Wallenberg was still trying to meet a figure like Löcsey illustrates how well the Swede understood the situation.[11]

In addition to his meetings with Hungarian authorities useful to him, he also seemed to maintain social contacts as well. One of the most poignant entries is for Sunday, 24 December. It was Christmas Eve, and Wallenberg was scheduled to celebrate the holiday first with Margareta Bauer, and later that afternoon at Lars Berg's residence, undoubtedly with other members of the Legation, but of course these celebrations were made impossible by the *Nyilas* assault on the Legation. Where Wallenberg spent his last Christmas as a free man is unknown, although he was scheduled to meet someone at 14.00 on Christmas Day.[12]

DID WALLENBERG SAVE THE 'CENTRAL GHETTO'?

It is impossible to trace Wallenberg's actual whereabouts during his last two weeks in Budapest. J. Lévai recounted that Wallenberg was almost in constant motion between New Year's Day and 17 January 1945, and historians and hagiographers have continued to rely heavily on Lévai's various accounts that he published so quickly after the war.[13] Apart from oral sources however, it cannot be confirmed that Wallenberg – as the dramatists and journalists would have it – had to sleep in a different location every night, constantly evading *Nyilas* efforts to halt his diplomatic activities. The explanation is probably a practical one: after Christmas he had little if any access to Buda, where his rented villa was – so he had to sleep elsewhere most of the time.[14] Yet, on 28 December, we find the entry in his appointment's diary – noted in the previous chapter – for 'dinner at home with Scholtz' (the German agent). The dramatic notion that he was constantly on the move because of danger should receive even less support in light of the fact that Hungarian authorities did not seek his arrest, nor was he a 'hunted man', constantly threatened with arrest or death by *Nyilas*. Had this been the case, he could not have continued to visit relevant officials, nor would he have been able to move about Pest as he seemed to do – he was after all, by this time, a very well-known figure. Indeed, Hungarian historian S. Szita has written: 'Gendarmerie Chief Inspector István Parádi attended to Wallenberg's personal protection and prevented numerous operations against Jews.'[15] There is every reason to believe that Wallenberg was able to maintain a certain level of diplomatic activity – at least on an ad hoc basis – almost until he left Budapest. Lévai describes significant activity by Wallenberg, a conclusion supported by K. Ungváry.[16]

The last remaining episode of diplomacy in which Wallenberg is thought to have played a significant role concerns the *Nyilas* plan to assault the 'central ghetto'. Most salient for this study is to obtain, if possible, an answer to the question: was Raoul Wallenberg personally responsible for saving the ghetto, with its approximately 60,000–70,000 inmates, from destruction? In the hagiographic literature and films, he is usually given sole or virtually primary responsibility for successfully intervening with German and/or *Nyilas* officials and saving the ghetto from destruction. With this deed he is given what might be called 'numerical credit' for this, the ghetto's ostensible salvation.[17] There is no question that a major assault on the ghetto was planned for the last hours before the Russians completed their occupation of Pest, and most relevant accounts depict Wallenberg as aware of and involved in efforts to hinder the raid. But there is broad agreement among historians that his role was considerably more limited than that widely depicted in popular representations. Contemporary Swedish sources tell us nothing about this episode.

This study has provided evidence by which Wallenberg's actual deeds may be understood and thought about with more precision than has generally been the case. This need for precision applies also to the question of whether Wallenberg (or any one person for that matter) 'saved' the ghetto from (as Lévai wrote) 'annihilation'. In order to give any useful answer, it is important in this context to ask what such 'annihilation' would actually have entailed at that time and at that place. Certainly the *Nyilas* conducted regular raids against locations where Jews sheltered, including into the ghetto, and Jews were being killed literally around the clock in the days before liberation. We know that senior *Nyilas* officials planned a concentrated assault, but could they have actually destroyed the ghetto, and murdered tens of thousands before the Soviets arrived? Disturbing as the question may be, we have to ask also if they could actually have physically erased the 'central ghetto' with the military and explosive resources they had access to at this late date. No evidence exists to indicate that there were plans to dynamite and destroy the scores of buildings, something which would have ended the area's function as a nominal sanctuary. In fact, the ghetto's denizens could not have been 'annihilated' by the *Nyilas*, but of course thousands might have been killed if a pogrom-like rampage had taken place.[18]

If the 'destruction' of the ghetto was a logistical impossibility, Wallenberg cannot have 'saved' it. Nor could *Nyilas* count on sufficient German help. Historians G. Kádár and Z. Vági concluded that 'we know for certain that the commanders of German units defending Budapest cared little about the ghetto or the Jews (which does not of course exclude individual excesses being committed). The Wehrmacht and the *Waffen-SS* instead were focusing all their attention on military operations and the enemy.'[19]

The ghetto was not assaulted, and those who would surely have died in a massive raid were spared. What then was Wallenberg's role in the significant achievement which was the halting of the *Nyilas* assault? In a word, the role he played was made possible by his recognized diplomatic authority, and not his personal presence or intervention. All credible accounts agree that the decision of *Nyilas* member and police officer Pál Szalai to betray the *Nyilas* plans to *Wehrmacht* General Schmidhuber (rendered by some as Schmidthuber), was the critical act in this particular drama. Schmidhuber happened to be in the City Hall's bomb shelter with Szalai.[20] At the same time, Szalai was able, through a friend, to inform Wallenberg, who was contacted by telephone. Wallenberg obviously thought rapidly, and according to Szalai's postwar testimony, threatened Schmidhuber with post-war retribution in a quick return message.[21] The key action in stopping the impending attack was taken by Schmidhuber, who not only ordered the assault to be halted, but also decided to arrest some of the individuals due to lead it. Some cinematic fantasies show Wallenberg dramatically confronting Schmidhuber late at night, threatening him with post-war retribution, but there is no credible account that places Wallenberg at City Hall that Tuesday afternoon, 16 January, when Schmidhuber began placing orders. There seems no question that Schmidhuber was swayed by Szalai's appeal to have the assault stopped, but we will never know to what extent Wallenberg's threat may or may not have influenced Schmidhuber's decision to intervene, as the latter was soon killed in battle.[22] Szalai testified in court shortly after the war:

368 Raoul Wallenberg in Budapest

> Also in the City Hall shelter at the time was ... Schmidthuber ... I asked him whether he was aware of the operation planned for the ghetto, and I also informed him that members of his unit were among those mobilized in the Royal Hotel. I warned him that according to Wallenberg's communication, if he did not prevent this crime he would be held responsible and would be called to account not as a soldier but as a murderer. Thereupon [Schmidthuber] summoned the *Nyilas* member [and the German, who would have led the assault] ... He further summoned Vajna and Police Commissioner Kubissy, whom he ordered to prevent this crime ...[23]

K. Ungváry describes the events in the following way:

> With Wallenberg's agreement Szalai warned ... Schmidhuber, the German commander of Pest, that he would be held responsible for the actions of his subordinates. Schmidhuber promptly summoned Vajna and the German and Hungarian initiators of the plan, arrested an SS sergeant and forbade the pogrom. To ensure that his order was obeyed he sent his Wehrmacht soldiers into the ghetto.

Widespread perceptions notwithstanding, Raoul Wallenberg did not directly 'save' the approximately 70,000 Jews in the ghetto. However, it seems that his prestige as a neutral diplomat played a role in influencing the thinking of the one individual who was able to guarantee its safety. We may be certain that the warning to Schmidhuber, an educated European who had already seen untold death and destruction, was understood, and that some fear of future retribution played a part in motivating that particular German not to have the deaths of more Jews on his conscience. We may also be sure that Wallenberg's belief that justice would be imposed on the killer(s) after the war is yet another example of his humanity and vision.[24] The ghetto was finally liberated by Soviet troops on 18 January.[25] The previous day, Raoul Wallenberg had been deprived of his liberty when he was detained by other Soviet troops.

WALLENBERG ENCOUNTERS STALIN'S ARMY

By the morning of 17 January, 1945, Raoul Wallenberg must have been emotionally and physically exhausted, although he seems to have retained his sense of humour. The primary account of Wallenberg's last days in Budapest, one used by historians and hagiographers alike, is J. Lévai's. It is built on interviews or statements given to him in the first year or so after the end of the war by at least a handful of men who saw and spoke with Wallenberg between 13 and 17 January. It also contains facsimiles of some UD documents.[26] Though Lévai did not provide source notes, there is no question that his account benefits from chronological and linguistic proximity to the events and personalities spoken about. Lévai reports some vivid scenes and memorable quotes from his interviews, and what was recounted about Wallenberg in his final hours as a free man. Some elements, it must be said, are less plausible than others, and even within these half-dozen or so recollections there are some minor but telling discrepancies.[27]

According to Lévai, László Petö, a 'Jewish Council' official, was the last person in Budapest to speak with Wallenberg. Petö remembers that Wallenberg was in 'great humour' on the morning of 17 January, when he met up with the Swede as he was preparing to leave the city, with a Soviet escort, for Debrecen in Eastern Hungary. Petö's memory of Wallenberg's mood is seconded by another source, and it is entirely plausible, knowing what we do about Wallenberg. He had fought a tremendous battle, Pest was now secure in Soviet hands, and he surely anticipated with some joy returning in the near future to his family and home.

Wallenberg was going, he told Petö and others, to meet with Soviet Marshal Malinovsky, an 'appointment' which must have been arranged through Wallenberg's other recent contacts with Soviet soldiers. Petö told Lévai that Wallenberg was going to Soviet headquarters to discuss Budapest's reconstruction. However, the notion that a minor Swedish diplomat (even one with the illustrious Wallenberg name) would be allowed to present to a Soviet marshal whose armies were still engaged in massive combat operations a reconstruction plan for Budapest, one allegedly designed for immediate implementation, is a rather dubious one. Its lack of realism seems uncharacteristic for Wallenberg, as does its political naivety. He was, after all, a sophisticated man who had learned an enormous amount during the last six months, and he must have understood that a Soviet marshal was hardly likely to simply meet him and then put into motion plans presented by a junior Swedish diplomat to rebuild, immediately, Budapest's Jewish community. Surely he must have known that functionaries of Stalin's government did not function that way?

Interestingly, several of those who assisted Wallenberg most closely, men such as Max Fleischmann, Hugo Wohl, Vilmos Forgács and Paul Heggedys, did try to continue their 'division's' humanitarian activities in the wake of the Russian occupation. They constituted the core of Wallenberg's indispensable 'local' help before he was detained, and were aware of a large sum of pengö available for continued relief activities.

They were, however, not allowed to continue this work, because, according to Lars Berg, 'Seen from the Legation's perspective and with regard to the Russians, continuing humanitarian activities which bene-fited only Jews could no longer be justified. Instead, all assistance activities should be gathered under one roof, most suitably SRK.'[28]

We do know that at some time on Wednesday, 17 January, probably about midday, Wallenberg left Pest for Debrecen. He was accompanied by his chauffeur, Vilmos Langfelder, and their car was escorted by a squad of Red Army officers and soldiers. According to Petö, Wallenberg said, speaking in German: 'They were ordered here for my sake, but I don't know if they are here to protect me or to guard me. I don't know if I am [their] guest or their prisoner.'[29] Wallenberg bid farewell to Petö, and then drove south-east on Aréna ut., out of the city. He and Langfelder were never seen again by anyone who was not in the employ of Josef Stalin's Soviet state.

Thus ended the history of Swedish diplomacy in Budapest and, with it, a chapter of Holocaust history. Wallenberg worked ceaselessly to give hope, assistance and often life to so many. Tragically, he would never enjoy the fruits of his labours. The humanitarian who had con-tributed to the redemption of so many thousands of other lives, would be robbed of the remainder of his own.

NOTES

1. J. Pehle (WRB) to H. Johnson, American Legation Stockholm, no.106/293, 19 January 1945. Franklin Delano Roosevelt Library, Hyde Park, NY, War Refugee Board Collection, Sweden, Box 31, 'cooperation with other governments'. Meredith Hindley graciously pro-vided this document.
2. R. Wallenberg, 'Report Concerning the Situation of the Hungarian Jews', 8 December 1944, *Riksarkivet Utrikesdepartementet* (hereafter RA UD), Hp 21 Eu 1092, folder 2. Sent along with this report is a fascinating organizational chart detailing the various offices active within, and under, his 'main office'. The precision of the drawing suggests that he did it, although this is uncertain. On this graphic the royal Swedish *Tre Kronor* shield is cor-rect.
3. It was common during the Third Reich, in both the Wehrmacht and the SS, for special or temporary ad hoc units to be given the name of its commander. That Wallenberg used the name 'Eichmann' in describing that unit positioned in Hegyshalom does not make it cer-tain that Eichmann was there when Wallenberg was. He could well have been told the name of the unit by one of the officers or soldiers he encountered on a rescue expedition to the Hungarian border town.
4. All quotes above, R. Wallenberg, 'Report Concerning the Situation of the Hungarian Jews', 8 December 1944, RA UD, Hp 21 Eu 1092, folder 2.
5. The king seems to have followed events in Budapest with continuing interest since he was asked to communicate with Horthy in June. He instructed his aides to follow at least sev-eral individual cases, although what he specifically thought about these matters is unknown.
6. See document no.78, I. Danielsson to UD, 15 December 1944, in S. Koblik, *The Stones Cry Out: Sweden's Response to the Persecution of the Jews, 1933–1945* (New York: Holocaust Library, 1988), p.270. There are several problems with this translated document, including the fact that it is highly unlikely that Danielsson (or Anger, who may have written the cable) would have got Eichmann's rank so badly wrong, just as it is unlikely that Eichmann would

ever have presented himself as occupying a higher rank than he possessed.

7. A. Richert to E. von Post, no.1698, 17 December 1944, RA UD, Hp 21 Eu 1092, folder 3.
8. A. Richert to E. von Post, no.1778, 23 December 1944, RA UD, Hp 21 Eu 1092, folder 3.
9. R.L. Braham, *The Politics of Genocide: The Holocaust in Hungary*, revised and enlarged edn, 2 vols (Boulder, CT: Rosenthal Institute for Holocaust Studies Graduate Center/City University of New York Social Science Monographs, 1994), vol. 2, pp.997–8.
10. Ibid., p.987.
11. Ibid., p.989 and p.1004.
12. On 26 December, Wallenberg was to celebrate the fiftieth birthday of someone named Pagango.
13. There are many accounts which use Lévai extensively.
14. As late as 28 December, Wallenberg did plan on at least one 'dinner at home' with the German, Scholtz.
15. S. Szita, cited in K. Ungváry, *The Battle for Budapest: One Hundred Days in World War II*, trans. L. Löb (Swindon, UK: BCA/I.B. Tauris & Co. Ltd, 2003), p.262. See also n.129, p.306.
16. See J. Lévai, *Black Book on the Martyrdom of Hungarian Jewry* (Zurich: Central European Times, 1948), pp.410–17; and Ungváry, *Battle for Budapest*, p.248, and Chapter 8, passim.
17. This issue is, for some reason, one of the most frequently asked about, when I have lectured publicly, and even in discussions with some Holocaust historians. The figure is basically the Jewish population of the two Budapest ghettos: '30,000' in the 'international ghetto', '70,000' in the 'central ghetto'.
18. One rumour circulating was that the Germans were planning to destroy the ghetto through aerial bombardment, but this was impossible as the Luftwaffe no longer had this capability. See Braham, *Politics of Genocide*, vol. 2, p.1005. Lévai also cites this rumour.
19. G. Kádár and Z. Vági, *Self-financing Genocide: The Gold Train, the Becher Case and the Wealth of Hungarian Jews*, trans. E. Koncz, J. Tucker and A. Kádár (Budapest: Central European University Press, 2001), p.234. Their account of this episode does not even mention Wallenberg.
20. Ungváry, *Battle for Budapest*, p.249. Ungváry has studied the military personnel and units involved more closely than any other historian. He renders Schmidhuber a *Wehrmacht* general, not an SS *Brigadeführer*, as is often the case.
21. In interviews with Lévai after the war, Szalai said that his cooperation with Wallenberg was, over several weeks, intensive and often successful. See J. Lévai, *Raoul Wallenberg – hjälten i Budapest* (Stockholm: Saxon & Lindströms, 1948), pp.191–4.
22. Schmidhuber was killed on 11 February when trying to break out of Budapest with his troops. See Ungváry, *Battle for Budapest*, p.184.
23. Testimony of P. Szalai, cited in Braham, *Politics of Genocide*, vol. 2, p.1006.
24. He can hardly have known any details about what the Allies were planning for post-war war-crimes trials.
25. Buda's agonies, for the Jews there and everyone else, continued for another month before the final destruction of Hungarian and German forces.
26. By 1948, Jenö Lévai had published three highly detailed books about the Holocaust in Hungary, the Budapest ghettos and Wallenberg. The last of these, titled in English, *Raoul Wallenberg's Adventurous Life, Heroic Struggles, and the Secret of His Mysterious Disappearance* (Budapest: Magyar Téka, 1948), was quickly translated into Swedish, and published as *Raoul Wallenberg – hjälten i Budapest*. Unfortunately, this edition, by a distinguished Stockholm publishing house, does not give any publishing information about Lévai's original volume, sources used, nor a translator's name. How he obtained Swedish documents cited in this book remains a mystery.
27. Lévai, *Raoul Wallenberg – hjälten i Budapest*, pp.241–5.
28. L. Berg, 'Individual Account, provided by Lars G. Berg, attaché at the Swedish Legation, Budapest, for the period 13/2–15/3', RA UD, P 2 Eu, p.4.
29. Dr L. Petö, cited in Lévai, *Raoul Wallenberg – hjälten i Budapest*, p.245.

Epilogue
17 January 1945: Wallenberg Leaves History and Enters Myth

On 15 January, the Pest side [of the city] fell into Russian hands and contact with the Legation's humanitarian division ... was broken. According to information received, the division's chief [Wallenberg] had achieved contact several days earlier with Russian troops, and he was observed shortly after the fall of Pest together with Russian officers. However, since then, he has not been heard from.

Danielsson's and Anger's May 1945 Report[1]

SWEDEN'S SHAMEFUL RESPONSE TO WALLENBERG'S DETENTION

When Buda was finally captured by the Red Army in late February 1945, Danielsson, Anger and the other Swedes who had been hiding in that part of the city were detained by Soviet troops. Following this, they were dispatched upon a path through Bucharest, Ukraine and Moscow, similar to that on which Wallenberg had been sent. Indeed, while in Moscow they were permitted to meet their colleagues at the Legation in Moscow. This group of Swedish diplomats was returned to Stockholm by the government of the Soviet Union in mid-April – but Raoul Wallenberg never was. Their return home marks the beginning of the search for Wallenberg, one which for some, even to this day, is not over.

This epilogue will not attempt to review the decades-long efforts undertaken by dozens of individuals from many countries in what can well be labelled 'the search for Wallenberg'.[2] To adequately survey this effort would be another book entirely. What can be stated, however, is that the failure of Sweden's government to achieve Wallenberg's release is undoubtedly one of the great political and moral scandals of the country's modern history, and there remain many unanswered questions about why much more was not done to bring him home. Though still no final, definitive answer can be given about Wallenberg's ultimate fate, what seems most likely is that he was murdered by the KGB in July

1947. 'Sightings' of him in subsequent years, allegedly in various locations scattered throughout Stalin's 'Gulag Archipelago', have never
been sufficiently verified in order for them to be considered genuine.

The demise of the Soviet Union twenty years ago provided an
opportunity both to explore archives previously closed and to speak to
individuals involved in Wallenberg's detention and interrogation. Two
major investigations have been commissioned by Sweden's government; the first, in cooperation with Boris Yeltsin's first Russian government, was carried out in the 1990s. Crucially, both have failed to
answer the two primary questions surrounding Wallenberg's disappearance: why was he detained, and what was his ultimate fate? In the
preface to the first inquiry, titled 'Report of the Swedish-Russian
Working Group' and published in 2000, a high-ranking UD official
wrote: 'Unfortunately, we still do not have a complete, legally tenable
account of Raoul Wallenberg's fate or the reasons for his arrest, despite
the tremendous efforts of everyone involved. Documents appear to
have been destroyed, key persons have died or are either unable or
unwilling to remember. It is not therefore possible to close the Raoul
Wallenberg file.'[3]

In tracking what is commonly known as 'The Raoul Wallenberg
Case', UD officials have created, since 1945, the largest accumulation of
files in the ministry's history, but to no avail in answering the critical
questions. The second Swedish inquiry, the results of which were published in 2003, was an analysis of what Sweden's political and diplomatic
leadership did and – far more importantly – did not do in trying to
obtain Wallenberg's release. Entitled 'A Diplomatic Failure: The Raoul
Wallenberg Case and Sweden's Foreign Affairs Leadership', this highly
detailed but somewhat tendentious examination of the failed efforts to
discern Wallenberg's fate, the reasons for his arrest, and why more was
not done diplomatically to obtain his freedom – particularly in the first
critical months and years of his detention – is a deeply damning account
of the indifference, incompetence and failed professionalism of some key
individuals within the highest ranks of Sweden's government. This
'Eliasson Commission' report details a feckless and shockingly passive
bureaucracy far too ready to accept inadequate explanations from a
powerful neighbour. It does, however, seek to paint the young businessman as a representative not of Sweden's government, but of America's –
that is, of the WRB.[4] There seems little question that the political imperative driving the commission's work was a determination to provide
cover for the Swedish government, by creating the impression that a primary explanation for Sweden's indifference was that UD officials
'believed' Wallenberg was the responsibility of the American government, and not their own. The evidence presented throughout this study

dismisses this contention. Indeed, when discussing any aspect of Wallenberg's disappearance, it must be remembered that he was not just an 'ordinary' Swede – he was a Wallenberg. It is as if an ad hoc American diplomat with the name of Rockefeller had been kidnapped by a foreign power, with the detainee's standing making no difference as to how hard the government worked to get him back. The quiescence of Sweden's government for many years remains essentially unexplained and quite impossible to understand.

From the moment when Wallenberg failed to return, his mother, stepfather, sister, brother, Per Anger and many others engaged in tireless efforts to discern his fate, tragically without success. On the other hand, over the decades little seems to have been done by the most powerful Wallenbergs, Jacob and Marcus Jr. Though they provided a modicum of financial support for some time to Wallenberg's immediate family for their search, they signally failed to push the government harder in those first years; nor do they ever really seem to have utilized their positions and power to push or cajole the government into pressing the Soviets to reveal why their younger cousin was detained, or what happened to him. This is yet another essential element of mystery surrounding the whole affair, and about which much more research is required.

Of course, one of the primary theories about why Wallenberg was detained revolves around the notion that he was a spy; some have claimed he was an American spy, others a Nazi spy, and so forth. The copious UD documentation utilized in this study does not even hint at anything like this. On the contrary, the relevant documents make it abundantly clear that in 1944, everyone at UD considered Wallenberg a fully accredited if still ad hoc diplomat. This is what they wrote, thought and acted upon while his humanitarian activities in Budapest were being planned, and when they were underway. As we have seen, the other Swedish diplomats in Budapest did virtually identical things as Wallenberg, and they were, as noted, sent back to Sweden. Therefore the notion that Wallenberg was a spy – for anyone or any government – remains an unproven, irresponsible and tendentious theory which should be finally dispensed with.

THERE IS MORE TO KNOW ABOUT WALLENBERG

The primary goal of this study has been to contextualize and demystify the achievements of one individual who is essentially a minor figure in Holocaust history, but who has evolved into a major figure of Holocaust memory. In doing so, no attempt has been made to minimize in any way Wallenberg's historic deeds, but rather to understand

them more completely. The point has been made, and it bears repeating, that I feel a deeper understanding of Wallenberg's achievements
will enhance our appreciation of them, not diminish them. To understand him as a real man, and not as some mythical 'angel of rescue'
honours him far more, I am convinced, than does a continuation of the
dominating and distorting myth-making about him. His actual life and
deeds are, in fact, more interesting than fictitious tales about him.

Nonetheless, even this study has not been able to answer all questions about Wallenberg and his work, and more research about him, his
life and his diplomatic colleagues in Budapest remains to be done. Not
least, a methodologically sound oral history, using the literally hundreds of interviews from Budapest survivors, should be a priority.
Important oral historical information exists in archival collections in
Sweden, Israel, the United States, Australia and elsewhere.
Additionally, there remains the need for a truly comparative study of
the full range of humanitarian activities conducted by neutral diplomats in Budapest. This would further contextualize Wallenberg, and
help us better understand a unique chapter of Holocaust history.

In conclusion, the following may be said. One of the primary motivations for this study has been to understand how and why diplomacy
can make a difference during an episode of genocidal violence. There
are vital historiographical, moral and psychological issues relevant to
any consideration of Wallenberg's achievements, and if we are to be
true both to the history of his achievements and to the meaning of his
memory, we must remember him for how he lived, not how he died.
We must hope that there will be, today and in the future, individuals
like Raoul Wallenberg who are intent on making a difference in the
lives of others. Mythical 'angels of rescue' are unlikely to turn up when
we really need them.

NOTES

1. I. Danielsson and P. Anger, 'Memorandum Concerning the Activities of the Swedish
   Legation in Budapest around the period prior to and after the Russian Occupation', 2 May
   1945, *Riksarkivet Utrikesdepartementet* (hereafter RA UD), P 2 Eu, p.6. For some reason,
   neither Wallenberg nor anyone else is named.
2. The morally admirable but almost obsessive interest shown by a number of individuals over
   the years in determining Wallenberg's fate in the Gulag could well be the subject of yet
   another book about the impact he has had on the memory of the Holocaust.
3. *Raoul Wallenberg: Report of the Swedish–Russian Working Group, Ministry for Foreign
   Affairs*, New Series 2: 52 (Stockholm: Elanders Gotab AB, 2000). See the preface by Hans
   Dahlgren, then state secretary for foreign affairs, p.7.
4. *Ett diplomatiskt misslyckande: Fallet Raoul Wallenberg och den svenska utrikesledningen,
   kommissionen om den svenska utrikesledningens agerande i fallet Raoul Wallenberg*, Statens
   offentliga utredningar 2003, 18 (Stockholm: Elanders Gotab AB, 2003).

Bibliography

Document Collections

Braham, R.L., *Eichmann and the Destruction of Hungarian Jewry* (New York: Twayne, 1961).

Braham, R.L., *The Destruction of Hungarian Jewry: A Documentary Account* (New York: Pro Arte for the World Federation of Hungarian Jews, 1963).

Wyman, D., *America and the Holocaust,* a thirteen-volume set documenting the editor's book, *The Abandonment of the Jews* (New York: Garland Publishing, 1989–91), vol. 8.

Archival Collections

National Archives, Washington, DC, Record Group 59.

Raoul Wallenberg Project Archive, Uppsala University Library, Uppsala, Sweden.

Raoul Wallenberg Arkiv, Riksarkivet (RA) (Sweden's National Archives, Stockholm, Sweden).

Utrikesdepartementets 1920 års series, RA (National Archives, Stockholm, Sweden).

Books and Articles

Agrell, W., *Skuggor runt Wallenberg: Uppdrag i Ungern 1943–45* [Shadows around Wallenberg: Mission in Hungary 1943–45] (Lund: Historiska media, 2006).

Anger, P., *With Raoul Wallenberg in Budapest: Memories of the War Years in Hungary* (Holocaust Library: New York, 1981).

Arnstad, H., *Spelaren Christian Günther: Sverige under andra världskriget* [The Player: Christian Günther and Sweden during the Second World War] (Stockholm: Wahlström & Widstrand, 2006).

Aronson, S., *Hitler, the Allies and the Jews* (Cambridge: Cambridge University Press, 2004).

Bartov, O., 'Reception and Perception: Goldhagen's Holocaust and the World', in G. Eley (ed.), *The 'Goldhagen Effect': History, Memory, Nazism – Facing the German Past* (Ann Arbor, MI: University of Michigan Press, 2000), pp.33–87.

Bartov, O., Grossman, A. and Nolan, M., *Crimes of War: Guilt and Denial in the Twentieth Century* (New York: New Press, 2002).

Bauer, Y., *Jews for Sale? Nazi–Jewish Negotiations, 1933–1945* (New Haven, CT: Yale University Press, 1994).

Bauer, Y., 'The Holocaust in Hungary: Was Rescue Possible?', in D. Cesarani (ed.), *Genocide and Rescue: The Holocaust in Hungary 1944* (Oxford and New York: Berg, 1997), pp.193–209.

Bédarida, F., 'Historical Practice and Responsibility', in F. Bédarida (ed.), *The Social Responsibility of the Historian* (Providence, RI: Berghahn Books, 1994).

Ben-Tov, A., *Facing the Holocaust in Budapest: The International Committee of the Red Cross and the Jews in Hungary, 1943–1945* (Dordrecht, Boston and London: Martinus Nijhoff, 1988).

Berg, L.G., *Boken som försvann: Vad hände i Budapest* [The Book which Disappeared: What Happened in Budapest] (Arboga: Textab Förlag, 1983).

Bierman, J., *Righteous Gentile: The Story of Raoul Wallenberg, Missing Hero of the Holocaust* (London: Penguin Books, 1981).

Black, P., *Ernst Kaltenbrunner: Ideological Soldier of the Third Reich* (Princeton, NJ: Princeton University Press, 1984).

Bloxham, D. and Kushner, T., *The Holocaust: Critical Historical Approaches* (Manchester: Manchester University Press, 2005).

Boheman, E., *På Vakt: kabinettssekreterare under andra världskriget* [On Guard: Permanent Under Secretary during the Second World War] (Stockholm: Nordstedts, 1964).

Braham, R.L., *The Politics of Genocide: The Holocaust in Hungary*, revised and enlarged edition, 2 vols (Boulder, CT: Rosenthal Institute for Holocaust Studies Graduate Center/City University of New York Social Science Monographs, 1994).

Braham, R.L., 'Keynote Address', in R.L. Braham and B. Chamberlin, (eds), *The Holocaust in Hungary: Sixty Years Later* (Boulder, CT: Social Science Monographs, 2006).

Braham, R.L. and Miller S. (eds), *The Nazis' Last Victims: The Holocaust in Hungary* (Detroit, MI: Wayne State University Press, 1998).

Brown, G., *Courage: Eight Portraits* (London: Bloomsbury, 2007).

Browning, C., *The Final Solution and the German Foreign Office: A Study of Referat DIII of Abteilung Deutschland, 1940–1943* (New York: Holmes & Meier, 1978).

Browning, C., *Nazi Policy, Jewish Workers and German Killers* (Cambridge: Cambridge University Press, 2000).

Carlgren, W.M., *Svensk utrikespolitik 1939–1945* [Swedish Foreign Policy 1939–1945] (Stockholm: Allmänna förlaget, 1973).

Cesarani, D., *Eichmann: His Life and Crimes* (London: William Heinemann, 2004).

Cesarani, D. and Levine, P.A., *'Bystanders' to the Holocaust: A Re-evaluation* (London and Portland, OR: Frank Cass, 2002).

Chesshyre, R., citing J. Bierman, *Guardian*, 17 January 2006.

Cohen, A., *The Halutz Resistance in Hungary 1942–1944* (Boulder, CT: Social Science Monographs, 1986).

Cohen, A., 'Pétain, Horthy, Antonescu and the Jews, 1942–1944: Toward a Comparative View', in M. Marrus (ed.), *The Nazi Holocaust: Perspectives on the Holocaust* (Westport, CT: Meckler, 1989), vol. 4, pp.63–100.

Cohen, A., 'The Dilemma of Rescue or Revolt', in R.L. Braham and S. Miller (eds), *The Nazis' Last Victims: The Holocaust in Hungary* (Detroit, MI: Wayne State University Press, 1998), pp.117–35.

Cole, T., *Holocaust City: The Making of a Jewish Ghetto* (New York and London: Routledge, 2003).

Cornwall, J., *Hitler's Pope: The Secret History of Pius XII* (London: Viking, 1999).

Craig, G., 'On the Pleasure of Reading Diplomatic Correspondence', *Journal of Contemporary History*, 26, 3 (1991), pp.369–84.

Deaglio, E., *The Banality of Goodness: The Story of Giorgio Perlasca* (Notre Dame, IN: University of Notre Dame Press, 1998).

Eck, N., 'The Rescue of Jews with the Aid of Passports and Citizenship Papers of Latin American States', *Yad Vashem Studies*, 1 (1957), pp.125–52.

Eichmann Interrogated, Transcripts from the Archives of the Israeli Police, edited by Jochen von Lang in collaboration with Claus Sibyll, translated from the German by Ralph Manheim, introduction by Avner W. Less (New York: Farrar, Straus & Girous, 1983).

Eisenberg, S., *A Hero of Our Own: The Story of Varian Fry: How One American in Marseille Saved Marc Chagall, Max Ernst, Andre Breton, Hannah Arendt, and More Than a Thousand Others from the Nazis* (New York: Random House, 2001).

Ember, M., *Wallenberg Budapesten* [Wallenberg in Budapest] (Budapest: Városháza, 2000), partial translation for author by A. Szónyi.

'Ett diplomatiskt misslyckande: Fallet Raoul Wallenberg och den svenska utrikesledningen, kommissionen om den svenska utrikesledningens agerande i fallet Raoul Wallenberg [A Diplomatic Failure: The case of Raoul Wallenberg and the leadership of Sweden's foreign affairs: The Commission investigating Sweden's foreign affair's leadership concerning the case of Raoul Wallenberg], Statens offentliga utredningar 2003, 18 (Stockholm: Elanders Gotab AB, 2003).

Favez, J.-C., *The Red Cross and the Holocaust*, edited and translated by J. Fletcher and B. Fletcher (Cambridge:Cambridge University Press, 1999).

Feingold, H., *The Politics of Rescue: The Roosevelt Administration and the Holocaust, 1938–1945* (New Brunswick, NJ: Holocaust Library, 1970).

Fogelman, E., *Conscience and Courage: Rescuers of Jews during the Holocaust* (London: Cassell, 1995).

Fry, V., *Surrender on Demand* (Boulder, CT: Johnson Books, 1997).

Grafström, S., *Anteckningar 1938–1944* [Diary 1938–1944], edited by S. Ekman (Stockholm: Samfundet för utgivning av handskrifter rörande Skandinavians historia, 1989).

Gur, D., testimony in Benshalom, R., *We Struggled for Life: Zionist Youth Movements in Budapest, 1944*, translated by O. Cummings and R. Rubin (Jerusalem and New York: Geffen, 2001), pp.141–2.

Handler, A., *A Man for All Connections: Raoul Wallenberg and the Hungarian State Apparatus, 1944–1945* (Westport, CT: Praeger, 1996).

Herbert, U. (ed.), *National Socialist Extermination Policies: Contemporary German Perspectives and Controversies* (New York: Berghahn Books, 2000).

Hilberg, R., *The Destruction of the European Jews: The Revised and Definitive Edition*, 3 vols (New York: Schocken Books, 1987).

Jarlert, A., *Judisk 'ras' som äktenskpshinder i Sverige: effekten av Nürnberglagarna i Svenska kyrkans statliga funktion som lysnings-förrättare 1935–1945* [Jewish 'Race' as Marriage Barrier in Sweden: The Effect of the Nuremberg Laws in the Church of Sweden's National Function in the Act of Marriage 1935–1945] (Malmö: Sekel, cop., 2006).

Kádár, G. and Vági, Z., *Self-financing Genocide: The Gold Train, the Becher Case and the Wealth of Hungarian Jews*, translated by E. Koncz, J. Tucker and A. Kádár (Budapest: Central European University Press, 2001).

Karsai, L., 'The Last Phase of the Hungarian Holocaust: The Szálasi Regime and the Jews', in R.L. Braham and S. Miller (eds), *The Nazis' Last Victims: The Holocaust in Hungary* (Detroit, MI: Wayne State University Press, 1998), pp.103–16.

Karsai, L., 'The Fateful Year: 1942 in the Reports of Hungarian Diplomats', in R.L. Braham and B. Chamberlin (eds), *The Holocaust in Hungary: Sixty Years Later* (Boulder, CT: Social Science Monographs, 2006), pp.3–16.

Karsai, L., Lecture, 1 March 2007, Open Society Archives, Budapest, Hungary.

Katz, F., 'The Implementation of the Holocaust: The Behavior of Nazi Officials', in M. Marrus (ed.), *The Nazi Holocaust: Historical Articles on the Destruction of European Jews* (Westport, CT: Meckler Corp, 1989), vol.3, pp.353–72.

Koblik, S., *The Stones Cry Out: Sweden's Response to the Persecution of the Jews, 1933–1945* (New York: Holocaust Library, 1988).

Kramer, T. D., *From Emancipation to Catastrophe: The Rise and Holocaust of Hungarian Jewry* (New York and Oxford: University Press of America, 2000).

Kühl, S., *The Nazi Connection: Eugenics, American Racism and German National Socialism* (New York: Oxford University Press, 1994).

Kushner, T., 'Rules of the Game: Britain, America and the Holocaust in 1944', *Holocaust and Genocide Studies*, 5, 4 (1990), pp.381–402.

Kvist-Gevert, K., *Ett främmande element i nationen: Svensk flykting- politik och de judiska flyktingarna 1938–1944* [A Foreign Element in the Nation: Swedish Refugee Policy and Jewish Refugees 1938–1944] (Uppsala: Acta universitatis Upsaliensis, 2008).

Kwiet, K., 'Anzac and Auschwitz: The Unbelievable Story of Donald Watt', *Patterns of Prejudice*, 31, 4 (October 1997), pp.53–60.

Lajos, A., *Hjälten och offren: Raoul Wallenberg och judarna i Budapest* [The Hero and Victims: Raoul Wallenberg and the Jews in Budapest] (Växjö: Svenska Emigrantinstitutets skriftserie, no.15, 2003).

Langer, L., *Using and Abusing the Holocaust* (Bloomington and Indianapolis, IN: Indiana University Press, 2006).

Langlet, N., *Kaos i Budapest: berättelsen om hur svensken Valdemar Langlet räddade tiotusentals människor undan nazisterna* [Chaos in Budapest: The Story of How the Swede Valdemar Langlet Saved Tens of Thousands of People from the Nazis] (Vällingby: Harrier, 1982).

Langlet, V., *Verk och dagar i Budapest* [Work and Life in Budapest] (Stockholm: Wahlström & Widstrand, 1946).

Lawton, C.A., *The Story of the Holocaust* (New York: Franklin Watts, 1999).

Leifland, L., 'They Must Get In before the End: Churchill och Sverige, 1944–1945', in M. Bergquist *et al.* (eds), *Utrikespolitik och historia* [Foreign Policy and History] (Stockholm: Militärhistoriska Förlag, 1987), pp.113–43.

Lester, E., *Wallenberg: The Man in the Iron Web* (Englewood Cliffs, NJ: Prentice-Hall, 1982).

Lévai, J., *Raoul Wallenberg's Adventurous Life, Heroic Struggles, and the Secret of His Mysterious Disappearance* (Budapest: Magyar Téka, 1948).

Lévai, J., *Raoul Wallenberg – hjälten i Budapest* [Raoul Wallenberg – The Hero of Budapest] (Stockholm: Saxon & Lindströms, 1948).

Lévai, J., *Black Book on the Martyrdom of Hungarian Jewry* (Zurich: Central European Times, 1948).

Levi, P., *The Drowned and the Saved* (London: Abacus, 1988).

Levine, H., *In Search of Sugihara, The Elusive Japanese Diplomat Who Risked His Life to Rescue 10,000 Jews from the Holocaust* (New York: Free Press,1996).

Levine, P.A., *The Swedish Press and the Holocaust*, unpublished MA thesis, Claremont Graduate School (Claremont, CA, 1987).

Levine, P.A., *From Indifference to Activism: Swedish Diplomacy and the Holocaust, 1938–1944*, 2nd edn (Uppsala: Studia historica Upsaliensia, 1998).

Levine, P.A., 'Attitudes and Action: Comparing the Responses of Mid-Level Bureaucrats to the Holocaust', in D. Cesarani and P.A. Levine, *'Bystanders' to the Holocaust: A Re-evaluation* (London and Portland, OR: Frank Cass, 2002), pp.212–36.

Levine, P.A., 'Swedish Neutrality during the Second World War: Tactical Success or Moral Compromise?', in N. Wylie (ed.), *European Neutrals and Non-Belligerents during the Second World War* (Cambridge: Cambridge University Press, 2002), pp.304–30.

Levine, P.A., 'One Day during the Holocaust: An Analysis of Raoul Wallenberg's Budapest Report of 12 September, 1944', *Holocaust Studies: A Journal of Culture and History*, 11, 3 (Winter 2005), pp.84–104.

Levine, P.A., 'From Archive to Classroom: Reflections on Teaching the History of the Holocaust in Different Countries', in M. Goldenberg and R. Millen (eds), *Testimony, Tensions and Tikkun: Teaching the Holocaust in Colleges and Universities* (Seattle, WA, and London: University of Washington Press, 2007), pp.116–33.

Levine, P.A., 'On-Lookers', in P. Hayes and J. Roth (eds), *The Oxford Handbook of Holocaust Studies* (Oxford: Oxford University Press, forthcoming 2010).

Levy, A., *Nazi Hunter: The Wiesenthal File* (London: Robinson, 2002).

Linnea, S., *Raoul Wallenberg: The Man Who Stopped Death* (Philadelphia, PA: Jewish Publication Society, 1993).

Lomfors, I., *Blind fläck: Minne och glömska kring svenska röda korsets hjälpinsats i Nazityskland 1945* [Blind Spot: Memory and Forgetting Regarding the Assistance Activities of Sweden's Red Cross in Nazi Germany 1945] (Stockholm: Atlantis, 2005).

London, L., *Whitehall and the Jews 1933–1948: British Immigration Policy, Jewish Refugees and the Holocaust* (Cambridge: Cambridge University Press, 2000).

Lorenz-Mayer, M., *Safehaven: The Allied Pursuit of Nazi Assets Abroad* (Columbia, MO: University of Missouri Press, 2007).

Lozowick, Y., *Hitler's Bureaucrats: The Nazi Security Police and the Banality of Evil* (London and New York: Continuum, 2002).

Maier, C., *The Unmasterable Past: History, Holocaust and German Identity* (Cambridge, MA: Harvard University Press, 1988).

Marrus, M., *The Unwanted; European Refugees in the Twentieth Century* (New York: Oxford University Press, 1985).

Marton, K., *Proceedings: Stockholm International Forum on the Holocaust: A Conference on Education, Remembrance and Research* (Stockholm: Graphium Norstedts, 26 January 2000).

Mazower, M., *Hitler's Empire: Nazi Rule in Occupied Europe* (London: Allen Lane, 2008).

Modig, H., 'Jacob Wallenberg 1892–1980, by Håkan Lindgren', *Historisk tidskrift*, 2 (2008), pp.273–5.

Molin, K., 'Arvid Richert', in G. Artéus and L. Leifland (eds), *Svenska diplomatprofiler under 1900–talet* [Profiles of Swedish Diplomats during the Twentieth Century] (Stockholm: Probus, 2001).

Molnár, J., 'Gendarmes before the People's Court', in R.L. Braham and B. Chamberlin (eds), *The Holocaust in Hungary: Sixty Years Later* (Boulder, CT: Social Science Monographs, 2006), pp.137–52.

Morley, J.F., 'Pius XII, Roman Catholic Policy, and the Holocaust in Hungary: An Analysis of *Le Saint Siege et les victims de la guerre, janvier 1944–juillet 1945*', in C. Rittner and J. Roth (eds), *Pope Pius XII and the Holocaust* (London and New York: Leicester University Press, 2002).

Mundy, S., 'State of the Arts: Is Culture a Source of Closer Unity or Further Division among Europeans?', *Time*, Special Issue (Winter 1998–1999).

Nordlund, S., *Affärer som vanligt, Ariseringen i Sverige 1933–1945* [Business as Usual: Aryanization in Sweden 1933–1945] (Lund: Sekel förlag, 2009).

Nylander, G. and Perlinge, A. (eds), *Raoul Wallenberg in Documents, 1927–1947* (Stockholm: Stiftelsen för Ekonomisk Historisk Forskning inom Bank och Företagande, 2000).

Oliner, S. and Oliner, P.M., *The Altruistic Personality: Rescuers of Jews in Nazi Europe* (New York: Free Press, 1988).

Palosuo, L., *Yellow Stars and Trouser Inspections: Jewish Testimonies from Hungary, 1920–1945* (Uppsala: Studia historica Upsaliensia, 231, 2008).

Persson, S., '*Vi åker till Sverige*': de vita bussarna 1945 [We're Going to Sweden: The White Buses 1945] (Rimbo: Fischer & Co., 2002).

Perwe, J., *Bombprästen: Erik Perwe på uppdrag i Berlin under andra världskriget* [The 'Bomb Priest': Erik Perwe's Mission in Berlin during the Second World War] (Stockholm: Carlssons, 2006).

Phayer, M., *The Catholic Church and the Holocaust, 1930–1965* (Bloomington and Indianapolis, IN: Indiana University Press, 2000).

Pók, A., 'Germans, Hungarians and the Destruction of Hungarian Jewry', in R.L. Braham and S. Miller (eds), *The Nazis' Last Victims: The Holocaust in Hungary* (Detroit, MI: Wayne State University Press, 1998), pp.45–54.

Praeger, J., 'The Wallenberg Curse; The Search for the Missing Holocaust Hero Began in 1945. The Unending Quest Tore His Family Apart', *Wall Street Journal*, 28 February 2009.

Report of the Swedish–Russian Working Group, Swedish Ministry for Foreign Affairs, New Series 2: 52 (Stockholm: Elanders Gotab AB, 2000), available in both Swedish and English.

Robóz, O., *The Jewish Orphanage for Boys in Budapest During the German Occupation*, edited by A. Scheiber (Évkönyv: Central Board of Hungarian Israelites, 1983–84).

Roseman, M., 'Surviving Memory: Truth and Inaccuracy in Holocaust Testimony', *Journal of Holocaust Education*, 8, 1 (Summer 1999), pp.1–20.

Rosenfeld, H., *Raoul Wallenberg, Angel of Rescue: Heroism and Torment in the Gulag* (Buffalo, NY: Prometheus Books, 1982).

Ross, Z., *Thomas Cook's Guide to Sweden* (Peterborough: T. Cook Publishing, 2008).

Rotner-Sakamoto, P., *Japanese Diplomats and Jewish Refugees: A World War II Dilemma* (Westport, CT: Greenwood Press, 1998).

Rozett, R., 'International Intervention: The Role of Diplomats in Attempts to Rescue Jews in Hungary', in R.L. Braham and S. Miller (eds), *The Nazis' Last Victims: The Holocaust in Hungary* (Detroit, MI: Wayne State University Press, 1998), pp.137–52.

Runberg, B., *Valdemar Langlet: Räddare i faran – Wallenberg var inte ensam* [Valdemar Langlet: Rescuer in Danger – Wallenberg Was Not Alone] (Stockholm: Megilla-Förlaget, 2000).

Rydeberg, G., *Raoul Wallenberg: Historik och ny forskning* [Raoul Wallenberg: History and New Research] (Stockholm: UD publikationer, 2006).

Schiller, B., *Varför ryssarna tog Wallenberg* [Why the Russians took Wallenberg] (Stockholm: Natur och kultur, 1991).

Schult, T., *A Hero's Many Faces: Raoul Wallenberg in Contemporary Monuments* (London: Palgrave Macmillan, 2009).

Sheehan, J., *The Monopoly of Violence: Why Europeans Hate Going to War* (London: Faber & Faber, 2007).

Skoglund, E.R., *A Quiet Courage: Per Anger, Wallenberg's Co-Liberator of Hungarian Jews* (Grand Rapids, MI: Baker Books, 1997).

Stark, T., *Hungarian Jews During the Holocaust and After the Second World War, 1939–1949: A Statistical Review*, translated by C. Rozsnyai (Boulder, CT: East European Monographs, 2000).

Stern, F., *Einstein's German World* (Princeton, NJ: Princeton University Press, 1999).

Svanberg, I. and Tydén, M., *Sverige och förintelsen: debatt och document om Europas judar 1933–1945* [Sweden and the Holocaust: Debates and Documents about Europe's Jews 1933–1945] (Stockholm: Arena, 1997).

Szita, S., *Trading in Lives? Operations of the Jewish Relief and Rescue Committee in Budapest, 1944–1945*, translated by S. Lambert (Budapest and New York: Central European University Press, 2005).

Thorsell, S., *Mein lieber Reichskanzler: Sveriges kontakter med Hitlers rikskansli* [My Dear Chancellor: Sweden's Contacts with Hitler's Reichschancellery] (Stockholm: Bonnier Fakta, 2006).

Tschuy, T., *Dangerous Diplomacy: The Story of Carl Lutz, Rescuer of 62,000 Hungarian Jews* (Grand Rapids, MI: W.B. Erdmans, 2000).

Ungváry, K., *Battle for Budapest: One Hundred Days in World War II*, translated by L. Löb (Swindon, UK: BCA/I.B. Tauris & Co. Ltd, 2003).

Wallenberg, R., 'Sydafrikanska intryck' [Impressions of South Africa], *Jorden runt: magasin för geografi och resor*, 8, 2 (1936), pp.587–604 in Uppsala University Carolina Library.

Wallenberg, R., *Letters and Dispatches 1924–1944*, translated by K. Board (New York: Arcade, 1995).

Wallenberg, R. and Wallenberg, G.O., *Älskade farfar! Brevväxlingen mellan Gustaf & Raoul Wallenberg, 1924–1936* [Dearest Grandfather! The Exchange of Letters between Gustaf and Raoul Wallenberg, 1924–1936] (Stockholm: Bonniers, 1987).

Wasserstein, B., *Britain and the Jews of Europe, 1939–1945* (London and New York: Institute of Jewish Affairs/Oxford University Press, 1988).

Wästberg, P., 'Wallenberg hedras med nya skulpturer' [Wallenberg is Honoured with a New Sculpture], *Svenska Dagbladet*, 6 May 2001.

Wines, M., 'Tale of Swede, Savior of Jews, Adds to Puzzle', *The New York Times*, 22 October 2000.

Wyman. D., *The Abandonment of the Jews: America and the Holocaust, 1941–1945* (New York: Pantheon Books, 1984).

Wyman, D., *Paper Walls: America and the Refugee Crises, 1938–1941* (New York: Pantheon Books, 1985).

Websites

'Raoul Wallenberg', Wikipedia, 8 June 2008.
www.chgs.umn.edu/visual_Artistic_Resources/Public_Holocaust_Mem
   orials/Raoul_Wallenberg_Memorial.html.
www.Amazon.co.uk/Raoul-Wallenberg-Sharon-Linnea/dp/customer-
   reviews/08, 3 April 2008.

Index

Names of publications beginning with the letters 'A' or 'The' will be filed under the first significant word. Page references to endnotes will be followed by the letter 'n'. The letters 'R.W.' stand for Raoul Wallenberg'

A

Adachi, Agnes, 179
Adler-Rudel Plan (1943), 160n
Aftontidningen, 135
Åman, Valter, 107
Ambrózy, Gyula, 218
Anger, Per, 230, 245, 302, 338, 348, 355; genocide, confronting, 192–7; and Langlet, 137, 215, 218, 223, 227, 327; and Olsen, 236–7; and Swedish diplomacy, Budapest, 102, 103, 105, 109–16, 121, 126, 136; as 'unknown hero', 213; and Wallenberg, 142–3, 146, 147, 150, 153, 164, 170, 175, 178, 179, 311, 341
Ann Arbor, University of Michigan in, 39
Anschluss (1938), 54
anti-Jewish policies, 54, 55, 82; in Hungary, 74, 75, 76, 86
Antonescu, Marshal, 233
apathy of Jews, alleged, 182–3
Arab Uprising (1936), 49
architecture, R.W.'s love of, 66
Arnóthy-Jungerth, M., 111, 192, 195, 218, 251–2
Aronson, Shlomo, 80
Arrow Cross *see Nyilas* (Arrow Cross)
'Aryanization' of Jewish assets, 54
Assarsson, Vilhelm, 154
asylum, right of, 156
'Auschwitz Protocols', 129n
Auschwitz-Birkenau: halting of deportations to, 79–81, 89, 126–7, 167, 191–2; ramp at, 72, 78; *see also* deportations
Axis coalition, 85

B

Báky, László, 80, 89, 105; and Horthy, 167–8
The Banana Company (*Banankompaniet*), 274–5

banking career of R.W., 41, 44, 46, 49, 51
Bardossy, Lázslo, 75
Bartov, Omer, 28, 32
Batizfalvy, Nándor, 279, 336, 364
Bauer, Margareta, 213, 365
Bauer, Yehuda, 82
Becher, Kurt, 78–9, 172, 277, 278–9, 302, 308–9
Bédarida, F., 30, 32–3
Békásmegyer assembly camp, 178
Benedicks (German Jew), 59
Berg, Lars, 213, 229–30, 250, 277, 302, 325, 365, 370
Bernadotte, Count Folke, 137, 150, 217
Bierman, J., 2, 19, 27, 59–60, 63, 308
Billitz, Vilmós, 309
Billitzer, Dezsö, 300
Birkenau, dismantling of gas chambers, 297; *see also* Auschwitz-Birkenau
Björkman, Erik, 107
Black, Peter, 97
Bloxham, D., 20
Boheman, Erik, 139–40, 142, 143, 147, 149
Böhm, Vilmos, 106–7, 140, 170
Born, Frederic, 88, 212, 310, 311, 348
Braham, Randolph, 218, 252, 364; and Holocaust in Hungary, 73, 79, 88–9; and Swedish diplomacy, Budapest, 126–7; and Wallenberg, 293–4
Brand, Joel and Hansi, 83
bribery, 185–7, 353; by Schindler, 4
Brown, Gordon, 4
Browning, C., 203
Brulin, Berit, 213
Brunner, Alois, 78
Buchinger, Elizabeth, 238
Buda, capture of Red Army (1945), 372
Budapest, 10, 78, 136, 292; background to international diplomacy in, 81–5; genocide in, 318–24; ghettoization process, 77, 201–5; 'Indian Summer', 250–3; international diplomacy in prior to R.W.'s arrival, 85–9; neutral diplomats in, 310–12; occupation of, 75, 76–7, 105–9; Swedish diplomacy in, prior to R.W. arrival, 101–27; *see also* Budapest, R.W. in; Hungary
Budapest, R.W. in, 164–87; arrival, 80, 170–2; business, 271–6, 310; context of

Budapest, 166–70; funding issues, 185–7, 253–62; historical sources, 38; initial activities, 180–5; initial reports, 176, 181–2; international diplomacy prior to arrival, 85–9; mandate to 'save Hungarian Jewry', 164–6; motives of R.W., examining, 58–65; organization of activities, 175–80; reasons for, 66–7; two-month period, 172–4; unanswered questions, 157–9; *see also* Budapest
'bureaucratic resistance', 90–7, 110, 139
bystander, role, 203

C

Cape Town, R.W. in, 40, 41, 44, 45; travelogue on, 47–8
Carlsson, Göte, 213, 302
celebrity status of R.W., 3, 5, 7
'central ghetto', Pest, 11, 204, 205, 336; whether saved by R.W., 26, 365–8; *see also* 'international' ghetto
Central Intelligence Agency (CIA), and OSS, 134, 159n
Cesarani, David, 168
Chamberlain, Richard, 308
Churchill, Winston, 73, 135
Clarke, T., 2
Cohen, Asher, 85, 113, 169, 281, 325, 332
Cole, Tim, 202, 203, 204, 345
collective memory, 16, 21
coup (Arrow Cross), 123, 140, 274, 318; reaction of R.W. to, 302–8; Swedish Legation prior to, 298–302
criticism of heroes, 11–15
Crown Council (Horthy), 113, 115
cultural identity, 21
cumulative radicalization process, 96

D

Dagens Nyheter (Swedish newspaper), 57
Dahlberg, Gunnar, 107
Danielsson, Carl Van, 245, 264–5, 321, 322, 328–31, 333, 338, 346, 348, 355; battle with Stockholm, 349–52; and Langlet, 223, 224, 227, 230, 231, 327; on occupation of Hungary, 76–7; replacement of Undén, 75; as Spanish Civil War veteran, 228; and Swedish cooperation, 139; and Swedish diplomacy, Budapest, 102, 104, 105, 108–13, 116, 118, 136; and Swedish Foreign Ministry (UD), 229; as 'unknown hero', 213; as veteran diplomat, 75, 228–32; and Wallenberg, 142–3, 147, 150, 154, 164, 165, 170, 178, 187n, 228, 299, 305, 335
Danish Jewry, salvation (1943), 56, 238
Dannecker, Theodor, 78
D-Day landings, 166, 205

de Sousa Mendes, Aristides, 91
death camps, 77, 78, 80, 119; *see also* Auschwitz-Birkenau
deportations, 56, 73; halting of, 79–81, 89, 126–7, 167, 191–2; height of, 109–13; and Hungary's refusal to deport, 73, 74; *see also* Auschwitz-Birkenau
'desk-top' killers/rescuers, 158
detention of R.W. by Soviet Red Army, 16, 22, 132; Swedish response to, 372–4; Working Group on, 159n
diary of R.W., 171–2, 335
diplomats, Swedish, 176
documents, protective power of, 123–6, 324–32
Dohany Synagogue, 11
Don River, Ukraine, 75

E

Ehrenpreis, Marcus (Rabbi), 137, 139, 145, 173, 257, 262, 299, 327
Eichmann, Adolf, 114, 168, 194, 298; and deportations to death camps, 77, 78, 80; meeting with R.W., alleged, 26, 27–8, 188n, 276–80; as threat to R.W., 361–4
Eichmannkommando, 362, 363
Eidem, Erling, 198–9, 200, 201
Eisman, Alice, 103–5
Eisman, Eva, 103–5
Eisman, Josef, 103, 104
Ekmark, Yngve, 213, 328
Eliasson, Jan, 34n
Eliasson Commission, 373
Ember, Maria, 171
Endre, László, 80, 89
Engzell, Gösta, 191, 194–6, 301; and Danielsson, 230–1; and Langlet, 223, 224; and Swedish diplomacy, Budapest, 102–8, 116, 117, 119–20, 136, 265, 266, 268; as 'unknown hero', 213; and Wallenberg, 179
Erdmanndorff (Prussian civil servant), 363
eugenics movement, 128n

F

Favez, Jean-Claude, 73, 348
Feller, Harald, 310
Ferenczy, László, 172, 279, 335, 336, 364
Filse, Tove, 256
Final Solution: and ghettoization, 202; in Hungary, 72, 73; in Norway, 92; *see also* Holocaust
Fischer-Tóth, Annie, 220
Fleischmann, Max, 369
Fogelman, Eva, 63
Foley, Frank, 91
Forgács, Gábor, 179
Forgacs, Vilhelm, 369

Freund (Dutch Jew), 44, 49
Friedländer, Saul, 76
Fry, Varian, 91
funding issues, 185–7, 253–62, 353

G

gas chambers, 78
genocide: Anger, confronting, 192–7; in
   Budapest, 318–24; memory of, 13; 'politics
   of', 234
ghettoization process, Budapest, 77, 178,
   201–5, 336, 364
Gorbachev, Mikhail, 171
GOW see Wallenberg, Gustaf Oscar (R.W.'s
   grandfather)
Grafström, Sven, 123, 141, 142, 173,
   198–201, 329; telegram sent by, 153–4
Grede, Kjell, 69n
Grell, Theodor, 111, 193, 266, 284
'grey zone', 13, 31
Günther, Christian, 107, 112, 116, 135, 146
Gur, David, 325
Gustav V, Swedish King, 87, 114, 115, 197,
   222, 304, 321

H

hagiographic publications, 37, 46, 48, 54,
   64; and Swedish diplomacy, Budapest,
   101, 121
Haifa, R.W. in, 41, 44, 45, 46–7, 48, 50, 64
Handler, Andrew, 251, 303
Hansson, Per Albin, 102, 120, 167
Heggedys, Paul, 369
Hellstedt, Svante, 208, 221, 260
Hennyey, Gusztáv, 263
heroes: criticism of, 11–15; making hero
   more human, 15–16; R.W. as misunderstood hero, 16; unknown, 212–14
Herzog, Rabbi Isaac, 198
Hilberg, Raul, 1, 93, 169
Himmler, Heinrich, 78, 82, 121, 270, 277,
   297, 309
historian: goals/social role of, 19; role in
   society, 29–33; social responsibilities,
   21–2, 31
historic memory, 21
history: and myth, 7–10, 26–9, 308–10; and
   Wallenberg, 1–7; see also myth; mythical
   status of R.W.
Hitler, Adolf, 251, 295, 296; and Holocaust
   in Hungary, 73, 75, 76; officials, on
   Swedish diplomacy, 120–3; Rhineland,
   retaking, 48–9
Högstedt, C.F., 221
Holocaust: and bureaucratic resistance, 90–7;
   defeat of Germany as cause for defeat of,
   14; 'good' and 'evil', contemporary
   conceptions, 13, 14; in Hungary, 72–97;

and myth, 19–22; survivors see survivor
   testimony; Swedish diplomacy during,
   101–3; see also Auschwitz-Birkenau;
   deportations; Final Solution
Holocaust history, 20, 28, 167; 'town' and
   'gown' gap in, 13, 20, 30
Holocaust studies, and public memory,
   12–13, 19, 20–1, 22
Horodenka, massacre of Hungarian Jews in,
   74
Horthy, Admiral Miklós, 156, 192, 251,
   290; anti-Semitism of, 167; and Báky,
   167–8; halting of deportations, 79–81,
   89, 126–7, 167, 191–2; and Holocaust in
   Hungary, 74, 79–80, 81, 87; and mythical
   status of R.W., 26, 27; new government
   appointed by, 262; and Swedish diplomacy,
   Budapest, 113, 114, 115, 118
Hotel Ritz, 335
Hotell Géllert, 170
Hungarian Jewry: destruction of before July
   1944, 73–9; halting of deportations to
   Auschwitz-Birkenau, 79–81, 89, 126–7,
   167, 191–2; refusal to deport, 73, 74, 76;
   Swedish assistance, in Budapest, 234
Hungary: Allies on, 85; Final Solution in,
   72, 73; German-Hungarian relations,
   73–4, 75, 166, 192; Holocaust in, 72–97;
   KEOKH (National Central Authority for
   Control of Foreigners), 84, 85, 196; Red
   Cross, 88; refusal to deport Jews, 73, 74,
   76; US war on, 85–6; see also Budapest;
   Budapest, R.W. in

I

ICRC (International Committee of the Red
   Cross), 88, 89, 145
Ignotus, Paul, 197
individual choices, importance, 36
International Committee of the Red Cross
   (ICRC), 88, 89, 145
international diplomacy, Budapest: background to, 81–5; prior to R.W.'s arrival,
   85–9
'international ghetto', 10, 26, 88, 336,
   344–9, 364; see also 'central' ghetto,
   Pest
Italy, yellow star, refusal to implement, 75–6

J

Jansson, K.E., 106
'Jewish Council', Budapest, 197, 260, 280,
   281; and Holocaust in Hungary, 78, 88
Jewish leadership, 280
Johnson, Herschel, 234, 313, 351, 361; and
   Langlet, 217, 218; and Wallenberg, 60,
   61, 139–41, 146–9

Kádár, G., 79, 278, 279, 367
Kállay, Miklós, 74, 76, 84
Kallner (Captain), 51
Kamenets-Podolsk, massacre of Hungarian
    Jews in, 74
Karsai, L., 84, 98n, 295, 297
Kassa, deportation site, 178
Kasztner, Reszö, 83, 280
Katz, Fred, 93
Kelemen, Lajos, 172
Kemény (Foreign Minister), 304, 305, 308,
    311, 332, 350
KEOKH (National Central Authority for
    Control of Foreigners), Hungary, 84, 85,
    196, 279
Kertész (Hungarian Jew), 111
Kinberg, Professor, 220
Koblik, Steven, 9, 137, 138, 201
Kokum, Erik, 269
Komoly, Ottó, 83, 88, 281
Krauss, Miklós (Moshe), 83, 170
Krumey, Hermann, 78
Kubissy (Police Commissioner), 368
Kushner, T., 20
Kwiet, Konrad, 31–2

L

labour brigades, 74
Lagergren, Nina (née Wallenberg, sister of
    R.W.), 54, 55, 57, 59, 61, 160n
Lajos, Attila, 9, 84–5
Lakatos, General Géza, 251, 299
Landsorganisationen (LO), 106
Langer, Lawrence, 10, 14
Langfelder, Vilmos, 370
Langlet, Nina, 214, 216–17, 226
Langlet, Valdemar, 267, 312; and Anger,
    137, 215, 218, 223, 227, 327; and Arrow
    Cross coup, 305; and Danielsson, 223,
    224, 227, 230, 231, 327; as eccentric
    diplomat, 214–17; efforts, 217–28; human-
    itarian work, 161n; manner/methods, 220;
    and Swedish diplomacy, Budapest, 113;
    and Swedish Red Cross (SRK), 208, 215,
    216, 218, 223; as 'unknown hero', 212,
    213–14, 245; and Wallenberg, 136, 137,
    216
Lauer, Koloman: correspondence with R.W.,
    185–6, 250, 258, 273, 275–6, 301, 340,
    341, 343–4; and Langlet, 218; and money
    issues, 255, 256–7; and recruitment and
    mission of R.W., 137–8, 140–1, 143,
    145–6, 155; and Swedish diplomacy,
    Budapest, 107; and Wallenberg prior to
    Budapest, 38, 55, 56, 66; and Wallenberg
    in Budapest, 183, 184–5, 273–4, 275–6
Lester, E., 2
Lévai, Jenö, 1, 2, 138, 282, 365, 368, 369
Levi, Primo, 13, 31

Levine, P.A., 160n
Levy, Alan, 19
Lindfors, Vivica, 63
Löcsey, István, 365
London, 'Religious Emergency Council',
    119
Lubyanka prison (Moscow), detention of
    R.W. in, 16, 22; Swedish response to,
    372–4
Lundborg, Östen, 200
Lutheran Church, Sweden, 197
Lutz, Karl, 84–5, 90, 124, 170, 194, 212,
    310, 311, 324

M

Maier, Charles, 169
Malinovsky, Marshal, 318, 369
Mallet, Victor, 135, 234
Maltet, Professor, 217–18
A Man for All Connections (Handler), 303
Mantello, Georges, 310
Marton, K., 2, 60, 62
Masur, Norbert, 137, 139, 157, 170
Mellaneuropeiska Handels AB (import-export
    firm), 138
memory, collective, 16, 21
memory of Holocaust, 12–13; sanctity
    around, 31; and social responsibility of
    historian, 20–1, 22; and 'unknown
    heroes', 213
military service obligations of R.W., 51,
    160n
Minkus, Eva, 180
Molnár, Judith, 77
Mommsen, Hans, 96
money matters *see* funding issues
Montagu-Pollock, W., 235
Morgenthau, Henry (Hans), 133, 145, 235
Morley, John, 86, 87, 347
Mundy, Simon, 21
Mussolini, Benito, 44, 333
myth: and history, 308–10; and Holocaust,
    19–22; importance of versus history,
    7–10; numbers of Jews saved, 10–11;
    separating from fact, 132–4; *see also*
    mythical status of R.W.
mythical status of R.W., 2, 3, 8; background,
    22–3; challenging with history, 26–9;
    common myths, 23–6, 297; 'Jewish
    blood' ('one-sixteenth'), alleged, 58, 59,
    60, 61, 64; meeting with Eichmann,
    alleged, 26, 27–8, 276–80; revision of
    accepted picture, attitudes to, 30, 31;
    see also Wallenberg, Raoul

N

Nákó, Elisabeth, 171
National Archive, Sweden, 10

neutral diplomatic papers, 124–5
neutral diplomats, 176–7, 310–12
Nice, R.W. in, 45
Nilsson, Asta, 213, 226, 227
Norway, Final Solution in, 92
Norwegian Jews, Sweden's reception of (1942), 56
Novak, Franz, 78
Novi Sad, massacre of Hungarian Jews in, 74
numbers of Jews saved, accuracy concerns, 3, 10–11, 26, 101, 320–4
numerus clausus (1922), 74
Nuremburg Laws (1935), 54
Nyilas (Arrow Cross): achievement of power, 81, 290–2; coup by (15 October 1944), 123, 140, 274, 298–308, 318; destruction of documents by, 10; violence of, 291, 297, 320, 351–2
Nylander, L., 122, 123

O

Obuda (community), 282
occupation of Budapest, 75, 76–7; response to, 105–9
Office of Strategic Services (OSS), 25, 34n, 133, 134, 159n
Olsen, Iver: and Anger, 236–7; as 'unknown hero', 236–9; and Wallenberg, 133, 134, 139, 140–1, 143, 145, 175, 254, 259, 283, 329
Operation Barbarossa, 74
Operation Market-Garden, 320
OSS (Office of Strategic Services), 25, 34n, 133, 134, 159n
Oswiecim gas chambers, 119

P

Palestine (Haifa), R.W. in, 41, 44, 45, 46–7, 48, 50, 64
Palosuo, Laura, 282
Parádi, István, 366
passports, 91, 92; emergency, 104;   *see also* *Schutzpass* (protective passport)
Pehle, John, 86, 150, 313, 351, 361; and Wallenberg, 141, 143, 144–5, 149, 150, 318; and War Refugee Board, 133, 235
Perlasca, Giorgio, 212, 310, 332, 348–9
Pesti Posta (Budapest newspaper), 252
Petö, Ernö, 171, 197
Petö, László, 369
Pius XII, Pope, 86, 87, 88, 114
Praeger, Joshua, 159n
Przybyszewski-Westrup, Z., 108, 128n

R

race question, South Africa, 47–8

Rädda barnen (Save the Children), 108–9, 137, 226, 328
Raoul Wallenberg Case, 373
Raoul Wallenberg Project, Uppsala University, 17n
Red Cross, 110, 112; Hungarian, 217, 218; International Committee, 88, 89, 145; Swedish *see* SRK (Swedish Red Cross)
Reichskristallnacht, 54, 92
Reichssicherheitshauptamt (RSHA), 72, 97n
Reichwald, Bruno, 221
'Religious Emergency Council', London, 119
repatriation train, 193, 227
Reuki, Naomi, 250, 282
Richert, Arvid, 116–17, 229, 301–2, 363
'Righteous Gentile', R.W. as, 2, 4
Roboz, Otto, 129n, 281
Romania: capitulation to Red Army, 232; yellow star, refusal to implement, 75–6
Roosevelt, F.D., 25, 86, 87, 114, 133, 162n, 188n
Rosenfeld, H., 2, 59, 60
Rotta, Nuncio Angelo, 86–7, 212, 305, 310, 311, 333, 346, 347–8
Rozett, Robert, 159n, 311
Runberg, Björn, 214, 216

S

Sakharov, Andrei, 3, 17n
Salamon, Otto, 241
Salén, Sven, 56, 146
Sanz-Briz, Angel, 212, 349
Schellenberg, Walter, 363
Schindler, Oskar, 1, 4, 11; 'Schindler's List', 179
Schmidhuber, General, 367
Schutzpass (protective passport), 90, 123, 124, 125, 218, 227, 259, 324; and mythical status of R.W., 25
selection process, 78
Sereni, Agnes, 19
Sheehan, James, 91
skyddsbrev (protective letter), 120, 125, 218
social responsibilities, of historian, 21–2, 31
Sohlman, Rolf, 235
South Africa (Cape Town), R.W. in, 40, 41, 44, 45; travelogue on, 47–8
Soviet Union, former: armistice with, 290; detention of R.W. by Soviet Red Army, 16, 22, 132, 372–4; dissolution of, 159n, 373; success in battle, 75
spaciality, 203, 204
special situation reports, 146
Specialkommando Eichmann, 362
spy, notion of R.W. as, 374
SRK (Swedish Red Cross): expansion of activities, 227; and Langlet, 208, 215, 216, 218, 223; leadership, 306; and

Nyilas violation of locations, 327; and Swedish diplomacy, Budapest, 108; and Wallenberg, 136, 137, 150, 153, 165

Stalin, Joseph, encounter with army of, 368–70

Stanislau, massacre of Hungarian Jews in, 74

Stark, Tamás, 76

Stern, Fritz, 36

Stern, Samu, 171, 172, 197

Stockholm, US Legation in, 134, 145

The Stones Cry Out: Sweden's Response to the Persecution of the Jews (Koblik), 9

Storch, Hillel, 266

Sugihara, Chiune, 91

summer of 1944, 191–208, 232; and Wallenberg, 239–45

survivor testimony, 9, 10, 31; on armistice with Soviet Union, 294; belief as to best sources, 23; false, 32; importance of, 339; misleading by, 287n

Svenska Dagbladet (Swedish newspaper), 200

Swedish clergy, failure to understand, 197–201

Swedish diplomacy, Budapest, 262–71; commencement of, 103–5; deportations, height of, 109–13; Hitler's officials on, 120–3; during Holocaust, 101–3; occupation, response to, 105–9; prior to R.W.'s arrival, 101–27

Swedish Foreign Ministry *see* UD (Utrikesdepartementet, Swedish Foreign Ministry)

Swedish Legation, 10, 148–9, 298–302

Swedish Red Cross *see* SRK (Swedish Red Cross)

Swedish-German trade relations, 53

Szálasi, Ferenc, 81, 233, 290, 295, 297, 311, 319, 329, 332, 333, 346, 351

Szigrol, Anton, 151

Szita, Szabolcs, 83, 278, 279, 366

Sztójay, D. (Prime Minister), 170, 191, 228, 251

T

territoriality, 203

testimony, survivor *see* survivor testimony

Thompson, Dorothy, 91

'town' and 'gown', gap in Holocaust history between, 13, 20, 30

Tre Kronor (Three Crowns), 124

U

UD (Utrikesdepartementet, Swedish Foreign Ministry), 8, 58, 90, 137, 138; Anger on, 352; and Danielsson, 229; and Langlet, 221; leadership, pledges to, 273; and sum-

mer 1944, 207–8; and Swedish diplomacy, Budapest, 106, 107; and Wallenberg, 146, 150, 152, 182, 374; and WRB, 134–5

Undén, Torsten, 75, 97–8n, 229

Ungváry, Krisztián, 292, 345–6, 368

United States: R.W. in, 39, 40, 46, 148; war on Hungary (1942), 85

Unváry, K., 348–9

Uppsala University: National Institute for Racial Biology, 107, 128n; Raoul Wallenberg Project, 17n

V

Va'ada (Zionist) group, 83, 280

Vági, Z., 79, 278, 279, 367

Vajna (Interior Minister), 304, 305, 332, 368

Valdemar Langlet, Rescuer in Danger (Runberg), 214

Vasarhelyi, Jenő, 152

Vatican, 86, 87, 159n

Veesenmayer, Edmund, 81, 89, 121, 122, 168, 192, 193, 205, 207, 251, 266, 333

Verés, Thomas, 290, 337

Verolino, Gernaro, 212, 310

visas, exit and entry, 91, 92

von Bayer, Sixten, 300

von Ribbentrop, Joachim, 121, 193, 205, 334

von Thadden, Eberhard, 122, 123, 196, 302, 326

W

Wallenberg, André Oscar (R.W.'s great-grandfather), 68n

Wallenberg, Gustaf Oscar (R.W.'s grandfather), 35, 38–58, 68n, 144; correspondence with R.W, as historical source, 37–8, 39–43, 45, 64, 270

Wallenberg, Jacob (cousin to R.W.), 38, 52–3, 54, 55, 56, 144, 272, 274, 342, 374

Wallenberg, Maj (née Wisling), mother of R.W., 38, 50–1, 60, 290

Wallenberg, Marcus Jr (cousin to R.W.), 38, 52, 53, 54, 55, 144, 145, 342, 374

Wallenberg, Raoul: attitudes towards Jews, 47, 62, 65; biography, 35–7; in Budapest *see* Budapest, R.W. in; correspondence with grandfather, as historical source, 37–8, 39–43, 45, 64; defining motives and mission, 154–7; detention of *see* detention of R.W. by Soviet Red Army; early life, 38–9; encounter with Stalin's army, 368–70; meeting with Eichmann, alleged, 188n; memorandum drafted by, 155–6; in mid-summer 1944, 239–45; as misunderstood hero, 16; mythology

surrounding *see* mythical status of R.W.;
personality, 36; recognition of, 1, 2, 3;
recruitment of, 136–46; 'Scarlet
Pimpernel' period, 291; Schindler
compared, 4; tasks and mission, defining,
146–54; threats to, 361–4
Wallenberg, Raoul Sr (father of R.W.), 38
Wannsee Conference (1942), 78
War Refugee Board (WRB), 25, 34n, 235,
239; establishment, 86; nature of opera-
tions, 149; in Stockholm, 235; and
Wallenberg, 133, 134, 142, 149
Weiss-Manfred (industrial concern), forced
sale to Germans, 178, 309, 340
Werbell, F., 2
Westring, Claes, 139
Weyermann, Hans, 348
Wilhelm, Karl, 197
Wisliceny, Dieter, 78
Wohl, Hugo, 179, 369
World Jewish Congress, 266
WRB *see* War Refugee Board (WRB)

Y

yellow star: ordering of adoption, upon
occupation of Hungary, 76–7; refusal to
implement, 75–6
Yeltsin, Boris, 373
Yerushalmi, Yosef H., 9
Yishuv (pre-state Jewish community), 64

Z

Zionism/Zionist groups, 47, 65, 83, 280,
325